THE CANADIAN YEARBOOK OF INTERNATIONAL LAW

2000

ANNUAIRE CANADIEN DE DROIT INTERNATIONAL

The Canadian Yearbook of International Law

VOLUME XXXVIII   2000   TOME XXXVIII

Annuaire canadien de Droit international

Published under the auspices of

THE CANADIAN BRANCH, INTERNATIONAL LAW ASSOCIATION

AND

THE CANADIAN COUNCIL ON INTERNATIONAL LAW

Publié sous les auspices de

LA SECTION CANADIENNE DE L'ASSOCIATION DE DROIT INTERNATIONAL

ET

LE CONSEIL CANADIEN DE DROIT INTERNATIONAL

UBC Press

VANCOUVER/TORONTO

Printed in Canada on acid-free paper ∞

ISBN 0-7748-0866-7
ISSN 0069-0058

National Library of Canada Cataloguing in Publication Data

The National Library of Canada has catalogued this publication as follows:

The Canadian yearbook of international law — Annuaire canadien de droit international

    Annual.
    Text in English and French.
    "Published under the auspices of the Canadian Branch, International Law Association and the Canadian Council on International Law."
    ISSN 0069-0058

    1. International Law — Periodicals. I. International Law Association. Canadian Branch. II. Title: Annuaire canadien de droit international.
JC 21.C3   341'.05   C75-34558-6E

Données de catalogage avant publication (Bibliothèque nationale du Canada)

La Bibliothèque nationale du Canada a catalogué cette publication comme suit:

The Canadian yearbook of international law — Annuaire canadien de droit international

    Annuel.
    Textes en anglais et en français.
    "Publié sous les auspices de la Branche canadienne de l'Association de droit international et le Conseil canadien de droit international."
    ISSN 0069-0058

    1. Droit international — Périodiques. I. Association de droit international. Section canadienne. II. Conseil canadien de droit international. III. Titre: The Canadian yearbook of international law.
JC 21.C3   341'.05   C75-34558-6F

UBC Press
University of British Columbia
2029 West Mall
Vancouver, BC V6T 1Z2
(604) 822-5959
www.ubcpress.ubc.ca

Contents / Matière

Cases / La Jurisprudence

Book Reviews / Recensions de Livres

THE CANADIAN YEARBOOK OF INTERNATIONAL LAW

2000

ANNUAIRE CANADIEN DE DROIT INTERNATIONAL

Using Treaties in Canadian Courts

GIBRAN VAN ERT

T he Supreme Court of Canada's decision in *Baker* v. *Canada (Minister of Citizenship and Immigration)*[1] has sparked new interest in the question of what use domestic courts and litigants may make of Canada's international treaty obligations. The matter is complicated because treaties vary greatly in their content, significance, and status in domestic law. Elusive, yet important, distinctions exist between ratified and unratified treaties, implemented and unimplemented treaties, treaties requiring provincial implementation and treaties that are subject to implementation by Parliament, and (in my contention) human rights treaties and other treaties. The object of this article is to give a complete account of how Canadian courts may (and may not) make use of international treaties in domestic adjudication. I attempt to set out the various rules according to which treaties take effect in domestic Canadian law. Some of these rules arise from the unwritten constitution. Others have their source in the demands of federalism. Still others are rules of statutory interpretation. Beyond simply explaining the rules, I attempt to demonstrate the origin of these rules in two fundamental, yet competing, principles of Canadian reception law: self-government and respect for international law. It is with these principles that the discussion must begin.

Gibran van Ert, BA (McGill), BA (Cantab.), LL.M. (Toronto). The author is indebted to Patrick Macklem, Sujit Choudhry, Mike Taggart, David Dyzenhaus, and Murray Hunt. This work was funded by fellowships from the Law Foundation of British Columbia and the University of Toronto.

[1] *Baker, infra* note 133.

PRINCIPLES OF THE CANADIAN RECEPTION SYSTEM

A reception system, for the purposes of this article, is a scheme for determining how rules of public international law are applied, considered, or set aside — in a word, received — into domestic law. Although a reception system may be dictated by constitutional or statutory law, in Canada, it is founded on English common law, with adjustments for the federalism and rights-protection provisions of our written constitution. There are two basic reception models described in the literature. According to the "monist" model, international law takes effect in the domestic (or "municipal") jurisdiction immediately and directly without any legislative or executive action. The theory behind this model is that international law and the domestic law of the state in question are one (hence monism, from the Greek word "*monos*," meaning single). Where a conflict between the two orders of law arises, monist theory would have international law prevail by means of a process of "incorporation," whereby the international norm is incorporated ("formed into one body") with the domestic law.[2] The second reception model described in the literature is "dualism," according to which international law and domestic law are distinct legal systems whose discrepancies can only be cured by positive acts of the legislative and/or executive organs of the state. This process is referred to as "transformation" or (especially in the case of treaty-made international laws requiring legislative enactment) "implementation." One of the many unsatisfying things about the monism/dualism literature is that it fails to depict the actual operation of the Anglo-Canadian reception system. For Canada's reception system is neither monist nor dualist. Rather, it is a hybrid of these two models: it allows for the incorporation of customary international law[3]

---

[2] Some writers describe the application of international law in monist jurisdictions as proceeding by "adoption," meaning that the international norm is adopted automatically by domestic law. I dislike this term, for to adopt something suggests a positive act of acceptance by someone, whereas the whole point of the monist/adoptionist model is that no such act is needed. I prefer the term "incorporation," which is more common in modern English writing on the subject. Confusingly, incorporation is sometimes used to mean its opposite, namely, the implementation of treaty law by statute. See, for instance, Murray Hunt, *Using Human Rights Law in English Courts* (Oxford: Hart, 1998), 12 n. 43, where the author lucidly explains the difference between the "incorporation" of customary international law and the "transformation" of international treaty law, only to proceed immediately (at 15) to speak of "unincorporated conventions"!

[3] For a lengthy treatment of the incorporation of customary international law in Canada, see Gibran van Ert, *International Law in Canada: Principles, Customs, Treaties and Rights* (LL.M. thesis: University of Toronto, 2000) at chapter 3.

but demands the implementation of conventional international law.

A lengthy consideration of the distinction between customary and conventional international law is unnecessary, but it is helpful to recall the basic features of each. International law, much like Canadian law, may be divided into two broad categories: customary law (somewhat analogous to common law) and conventional, or treaty-made, law (which is broadly analogous to statute law). Customary international law, formerly known as the law of nations, arises when consistent state practice is joined with the belief that such practice is required by law (*opinio juris*).[4] The force of custom lies not in any posited instrument but in the sense of obligation that motivates its practice. Conventional international law arises where two or more states conclude an agreement with each other at international law with the intent to create legal relations.[5] This agreement need not take written form,[6] but, in practice, it almost always does. The force of conventional international law lies both in the consensual nature of the undertaking on the part of the states parties and on the founding principle of the international legal system *pacta sunt servanda* (agreements must be kept).

For constitutional reasons explained later in this article, the Canadian reception system takes a monist approach to customary international law but a more dualist approach to treaties. This

---

[4] On international custom generally, see Sir Robert Jennings and Sir Arthur Watts, eds., *Oppenheim's International Law*, 9th ed., vol. 1 (Harlow: Longman, 1992), section 10, and Claude Emanuelli, *Droit international public: contribution à l'étude du droit international selon une perspective canadienne* (Montreal: Wilson and Lafleur, 1998) at 41-61.

[5] At common law, the definition of an international convention (or treaty) is apparently the same as that recognized in international law, thus eliminating the unattractive argument that states: "While this agreement may be a treaty at international law, it is not one for the purposes of our law." By contrast, American constitutional law distinguishes between treaties, which are part of "the supreme Law of the Land" under Article 6 of the constitution, and executive agreements, which are not necessarily self-executing. See Jennings and Watts, *supra* note 4 at 74-7. If, as is doubtful, there was a distinct common law definition of "treaty," it has been swept aside by the 1969 Convention on the Law of Treaties, Can. T.S. 1980 No. 37 [hereinafter Vienna Convention], to which Canada is a party and which, in any event, is at least partly declaratory of customary international law: Malcolm N. Shaw, *International Law*, 4th ed. (Cambridge: Cambridge University Press, 1997) at 633, citing *Advisory Opinion on the Legal Consequences for States of the Continued Presence of South Africa in Namibia (South West Africa) notwithstanding Security Council Resolution 276*, [1971] I.C.J. Rep. 16, 47, and the *Fisheries Jurisdiction Case (United Kingdom v. Iceland) (Jurisdiction)*, [1973] I.C.J. Rep., 3, 18.

[6] Vienna Convention, *supra* note 5 at art. 3.

hybridity makes for a rather complex reception system. Indeed, some commentators complain that it is not a system at all, but only a haphazard collection of ancient rules overlaid with an equally haphazard modern jurisprudence. Elsewhere I have challenged this view.[7] It is my contention that there is indeed a Canadian reception system and that it is comprehensible as an expression of, and a compromise between, two underlying principles. These two principles do not sit easily together. Given free reign, either one would consume the other and, in doing so, utterly transform the reception system. Such a transformation would not be objectionable were it not that both principles are compelling descriptions of who we are and who we should be. Thus, the rules of reception are not only instantiations of the underlying principles but also the means of balancing these principles to assure the survival of both. The principles may be termed "respect for international law" and "self-government."

The principle of respect for international law requires that the international laws that regulate the relations of states with each other, and increasingly with their own citizens, be observed and applied in domestic law. There is perhaps no single reason why international law merits such respect. For William Blackstone, international law is a system of rules "deducible by natural reason" and resulting from "principles of natural justice." As such, international law was established by, and has enjoyed, "universal consent among the civilized inhabitants of the world." Thus the authority of international law is backed not only by reason and justice but also by common consent.[8] Respect for international law may also be justified on the more prosaic ground that violations may lead to international responsibility and breaches of international comity. (Indeed, the principle of *pacta sunt servanda* may be as much a prudential as a normative claim.) Ultimately, the question of why we should respect international law leads us to jurisprudential questions about the nature of law's obligatoriness. While this is not the subject of the present article, simply raising the question reveals something important about the principle that we are considering: respect for international law requires us to treat international law as just that — law — as deserving of the name as any domestic statute or judgment of the court. The principle requires that international laws that have domestic application be applied and that

---

[7] See generally van Ert, *supra* note 3, especially at chapter 1.

[8] Sir William Blackstone, *Commentaries on the Laws of England*, vol. 4 (Chicago: University of Chicago Press, 1979) at 66-7.

international laws without domestic application not be violated or frustrated by inconsistent interpretations of domestic law. In short, respect for international law requires that international law be treated as actually or potentially, mediately or immediately, part of Canadian law.

To say that international law should be respected because it is law, and that it is therefore obligatory for the same reason (whatever that may be) that other forms of law are obligatory, is not as trite as it may seem given the all-too-common attitude that international law is not "real" law. However, there is a further reason why the principle of respect for international law is compelling. This reason concerns our identity. The principle depicts those who observe it as members of an international community. Blackstone explains that if we do not respect international law we "must cease to be a part of the civilized world."[9] The language of civilization is tainted with eurocentrism and has come to be replaced with the language of international community. Thus the Canadian Charter of Rights and Freedoms's single reference to international law speaks of "the general principles of law recognized by the community of nations."[10] While the language has changed, the opprobrium associated with violations of international law remains. We may now hesitate to use words such as barbarous and uncivilized to describe countries that routinely violate international law, but the words we do use — totalitarian, oppressive, and renegade — bring the same obloquy. The principle of respect for international law depicts those countries in which it thrives in glowing terms: civilized, democratic, western (so much for avoiding eurocentrism), the leading members of the international community. The force of the principle derives in part from our desire to be so identified and to see ourselves in this light.

I am calling the second principle of the Canadian reception system self-government. By self-government, I mean a community's power and practice of determining its beliefs, status, and future for itself. The opposite of self-government is coercion by any external force. An external force — be it an institution, a people, a legal order, or an idea — is any force that does not enjoy the consent of whomever it seeks to control. Submission is not consent. Consent is satisfied only by deliberative, representative, and participatory decision-making processes, which are the best means of assuring

---

[9] *Ibid.*

[10] Canadian Charter of Rights and Freedoms, s. 11 (g), Part I of the Constitution Act 1982, being Schedule B to the Canada Act 1982 (U.K.), 1982, c. 11.

that what purports to be consent is not merely acquiescence or indifference. Westminster-model constitutions such as Canada's are informed by a commitment to self-government at several points. Examples of this commitment include the doctrine that the Crown cannot make law outside Parliament, the requirement that legislative initiatives be approved by a majority vote, and, in the Canadian federation, the inability of one legislature to make law in another's jurisdiction.

The principle of self-government looks on international law, in its current state of development, as a coercive external force in the sense given above. It views the methods of international law-making as unconsensual in comparison to the deliberative, representative, and participatory decision-making model that is the parliamentary process. We may look on this depiction of the parliamentary process with some suspicion, given the degree to which our parliamentary institutions have deteriorated and the increasingly active role of citizens and non-governmental organizations on the international scene. However, rightly or wrongly, the reception system does not share this cynicism about the parliamentary system. Instead, it looks suspiciously on the treaty-making process. Treaty-making in Canada and in similarly constituted states remains a prerogative of the Crown. Treaty negotiation frequently takes place behind closed doors (especially in the case of bilateral agreements) and the results of such negotiations are only occasionally brought before Parliament or the provincial Legislatures. Even when a treaty is presented to our legislatures, it comes in the form of a "take it or leave it" proposition: approve or disapprove the treaty (or its implementing legislation) but do not seek to amend it. Self-government's suspicion of the democratic credentials of conventional international law-making may lessen, particularly if the international law-making process takes on the qualities of deliberation, representation, and participation, which are the hallmarks of consensual self-government. In the meantime, this principle seeks to reserve for Canadians, through their legislatures, the power to override international law in the name of self-government.

The Anglo-Canadian reception system is based on, and committed to, both of the principles described here. Each common law and interpretive rule for the application of international law in Canada emanates from, or embodies, one of the principles. Yet the two principles are ultimately at odds with each other. Left to its own devices, respect for international law would remove all legal obstacles between the international legal system and domestic law, thereby harmonizing the two legal systems. Since the principle treats international law as law, it characterizes dissent from international norms as unlawful or lawless and therefore to be suppressed. Thus, the principle of self-government is under constant threat from the principle of respect for international law. However, the inverse is also true. Carried to its logical conclusion, the power to violate international law in the name of self-government would circumscribe the place of international law in Canada's domestic law so narrowly as to threaten the existence of the principle of respect for international law. For the parliamentary process (which, as I have explained, is self-government's standard of consensual law-making) is an impossible ideal for an international legal system predicated on the sovereignty of states. Thus, each of the founding principles of the reception system has in it the seed of the other's destruction. Yet the two principles co-exist in Canadian law. They do so by a careful balance that is at once the foundation and the sustenance of the reception system.

This balance is in the form of a series of compromises running throughout the system. The standard form of the compromise is as follows. Respect for international law is granted the default position in the reception system. It is assumed from the outset and serves as the starting point of every discussion. Yet the system recognizes in our domestic laws an ultimate power, as required by self-government, to dissent from and violate international law. Thus, self-government operates as the exception to the rule of respect for international law. The reception system balances the demands of both principles by granting respect for international law the wider application while granting self-government an ultimate veto. This careful balancing of the principles throughout the reception system is what prevents either from consuming the other, thus ensuring the survival of both. Judicial decisions that threaten this balance jeopardize the entire system, turning a functioning whole into a muddled assortment of scattered parts. Observance of both principles and due regard for their balance within the system are therefore the best criteria — perhaps the only criteria — for judging the soundness of decisions in this area of the law.

TREATY-MAKING IN OUTLINE

The rules governing judicial use of treaties in domestic litigation, and the principles that underlie those rules, are profoundly informed by the facts of the treaty-making process. Therefore, it is helpful to recall, if only in outline, how Canada enters into treaty obligations.[11]

Every state possesses the capacity to conclude treaties.[12] Treaties are consensual: no state may be bound by a treaty at international law without its consent. This consent may be expressed by various means.[13] The two most usual means of expressing consent are signature and ratification. Where a treaty is to be concluded by signature, the act of signing the treaty represents the state's expression of its consent to be bound by the treaty at international law. Where a treaty is to be concluded by ratification, the process is more formal. The state's consent to be bound is expressed more elaborately, whether through the exchange of instruments of ratification (in the case of a bilateral treaty) or through the deposition of an instrument of ratification with some specified depository (in the case of a multilateral treaty). Where treaty-making proceeds by means of ratification, a state's representative may sign the treaty, but that signature will not express the state's consent to be bound. Such a signature is at best a legally unenforceable, if politically significant, expression by the signatory state of its intent to bind itself at some later date (for instance, after enacting implementing legislation).

Who is empowered to express Canada's consent to a treaty? In Canada, as in other Westminster-model states, the power to conclude treaties is vested in the executive. Treaty-making is viewed in Anglo-Canadian constitutional law as an aspect of the royal prerogative over foreign affairs.[14] Prerogative powers were described by A.V. Dicey as "nothing else than the residue of discretionary or arbitrary authority, which at any given time is legally left in the

---

[11] For more on treaty-making, see Peter Hogg, *Constitutional Law of Canada*, loose-leaf ed. (Scarborough: Carswell, 1997) at chapter 11; Maurice Copithorne, "Canadian Treaty Law and Practice" (1996) 54 The Advocate 35. A dated, but still useful, work is A.E. Gotlieb, *Canadian Treaty-Making* (Toronto: Butterworths, 1968). For a description of Canadian treaty-making practice by the Legal Bureau of the Department of External Affairs, see (1986) 24 C.Y.I.L. 397.

[12] Vienna Convention, *supra* note 5 at art. 6.

[13] See *ibid.* at art. 11.

[14] In *Thomson* v. *Thomson,*, [1994] 3 S.C.R. 551 at 610, L'Heureux-Dubé J., in a concurring opinion, held that the federal treaty-making power is found in Section 132 of the Constitution Act 1867. That finding is, with respect, wrong. Section 132 grants the "Parliament and Government of Canada ... all Powers necessary or proper for performing the Obligations of Canada or of any Province thereof, as Part of the British Empire, towards Foreign Countries, arising under Treaties between the Empire and such Foreign Countries." This section only grants power to perform treaty obligations; it grants no power to incur such obligations.

hands of the Crown."[15] Prerogative acts are those that governments can lawfully do without the authority of the legislatures to which they are responsible. Some prerogatives remain personal powers of the sovereign or her representatives, but most prerogative acts are now done on the advice of ministers. Thus, the foreign affairs prerogative is exercised in practice by ministers and the government departments that they head (chiefly the federal minister of foreign affairs and his department). This means that the power to negotiate, conclude, and ratify treaties on behalf of Canada is vested wholly in the executive.[16] As a matter of law, no involvement by Parliament or the provincial Legislatures is required to bind Canada to international obligations.[17] The executive's power to

---

Canada lacked such power for much of its early history. Furthermore, Section 132 only grants power respecting Empire treaties. Such treaties no longer exist, and Section 132 is now spent. In a letter of February 1, 1985 to the Council of Europe explaining Canadian treaty practice (reprinted in (1986) 24 C.Y.I.L. 397), the Legal Bureau of the Department of External Affairs stated: "The Canadian Constitution contains no provisions regarding treaty-making apart from Section 132 of the Constitution Act, 1867 which has fallen into disuse ... Treaty-making in Canada is part of the Royal Prerogative, the residue of authority left in the Crown, and in practice exercised by the Governor General in Council, *i.e.* the Governor General of Canada acting on the advice of Privy Councillors who are Ministers of the Government."

[15] A.V. Dicey, *Introduction to the Study of the Law of the Constitution*, 10th ed. (London: Macmillan, 1964) at 424.

[16] Whether this power is vested wholly in the federal executive or divided between the federal and provincial executives is not entirely clear as a matter of domestic law. However, in practice, it is the government of Canada and not the provincial governments that binds Canada internationally. See Gibran van Ert, "The Legal Character of Provincial Agreements with Foreign Governments" (2001) 42 Les Cahiers de droit (forthcoming), and Emanuelli, *supra* note 4 at 72-3.

[17] The *Canadian Abridgment* gets this simple point of Canadian constitutional law wrong, confusing the meanings of "ratify" and "implement." The *Abridgment*'s case digests on international law describe cases as concerning "Treaties — Effect of failure of Parliament to ratify." This description is mistaken, for the Crown ratifies treaties without the participation of Parliament. Where the *Abridgment* says "failure to ratify" it means "failure to implement." See the *Canadian Abridgment*, 2nd ed. (Scarborough: Carswell, 1998) at 716. Our courts occasionally make the same mistake. In *Re Canada Labour Code*, [1992] 2 S.C.R. 50 at 90, La Forest J. said, "I would note that SOFA [the *North Atlantic Treaty Status of Forces Agreement*, [1953] Can. T.S. No. 13] has no legal effect in Canada, as it has not been ratified by domestic legislation." In *R.* v. *Rumbaut* (1998), 127 C.C.C. (3d) 138 (N.B.Q.B.) at 140, Deschênes J. said: "Neither the Geneva Convention on the High Seas, 1958 ... nor the United Nations Convention on Law of the Sea, 1982 ... have been ratified by the Canadian Parliament and are not, as such, part of Canadian domestic law."

conclude treaties without the participation of our legislatures has great consequences for the reception system, which will become more clear when we consider the constitutional objection to self-executing treaties.

A duly ratified treaty binds the Canadian state at international law. It does not, however, bind Parliament or the provincial Legislatures to legislate consistently with it. Our legislatures are not sovereign in the classical sense of the word, for they are constrained by the entrenched provisions of our written constitution, yet they retain a residual sovereignty to violate international law. This sovereignty has been repeatedly affirmed in case law, both implicitly[18] and explicitly.[19] Canadian legislatures may fail to live up to Canadian international obligations either intentionally, by explicitly legislating contrary to international law or by omitting to pass legislation that would implement Canada's treaty obligations, or unintentionally, by negligently enacting laws that are inconsistent with our treaty commitments. The fact that our legislatures can violate international law in these ways reveals the nature of Canada's international obligations, namely that they are international rather than domestic: Canada's international obligation to live up to its promises or conform to certain norms does not produce domestic obligations that prevail over inconsistent legislation in Canadian courts. Yet the radical implications of our legislatures' competence

---

[18] Implicit recognition comes in the form of statements affirming that the legislative competence of the federal and provincial legislatures is, subject to the federalism provisions of the Constitution Act 1867 (and now the entrenching Section 52 of the Constitution Act 1982), as great as that possessed by the imperial Parliament. Thus, English authorities to the effect that the Parliament at Westminster may legislate contrary to international law apply also to Canadian legislatures. See *Hodge* v. *The Queen* (1883), 9 A.C. 117 (P.C.); *Arrow River & Tributaries Slide & Boom Co. Ltd.* v. *Pigeon Timber Co. Ltd.*, [1932] S.C.R. 495 at 509-10 [hereinafter *Arrow River*], per Lamont J.; *Croft* v. *Dunphy*, [1933] A.C. 156 (P.C.) at 164; and *British Columbia Electric Railway Co. Ltd.* v. *The King*,, [1946] A.C. 527 at 541 (quoting Rand J.) [hereinafter *British Columbia Electric Railway*].

[19] The leading cases are *Capital Cities Communications* v. *C.R.T.C.* [1978] 2 S.C.R. 141 at 173, per Laskin C.J. [hereinafter *Capital Cities*]; *Daniels* v. *White and the Queen*, [1968] S.C.R. 517 at 539, per Hall J. (dissenting, but not on this point, and with the concurrence of Ritchie and Spence JJ.); and *Gordon* v. *The Queen in Right of Canada*, [1980] 5 W.W.R. 668 at 670-1 (B.C.S.C.), per Meredith J. See also *Re Foreign Legations*, [1943] S.C.R. 208 at 231; *Arrow River, supra* note 18 at 510; *Swait* v. *Board of Trustees of Maritime Transportation Unions*, [1967] B.R. 315 (Que. Q.B.) at 319; *British Columbia Electric Railway, supra* note 18 at 542; and *R.* v. *Meikleham* (1906), 11 O.L.R. 366 (Ont. Div. Ct.) at 373. For a discussion of the residual sovereignty of Canadian legislatures to violate international law, see van Ert, *supra* note 3 at chapter 2.

to violate international law are curbed by an important practical qualification of parliamentary sovereignty. This is the rule of statutory interpretation that domestic law should be read, where possible, so as not to violate international law. I call this rule the presumption of international legality or, in the case of conventional international laws, the treaty presumption. It is discussed at length later in this article.

THE CONSTITUTIONAL OBJECTION TO SELF-EXECUTING TREATIES

There is no *prima facie* reason for a country's constitutional law to require that international obligations assumed by the state be without legal effect unless made law by legislative act. Indeed, some written constitutions explicitly grant the force of law to treaties without legislation.[20] However, in Canada and similarly constituted states, treaties are said not to be "self-executing," meaning that they are not stand-alone sources of law.[21] Rather, they must be introduced into Canadian law by statute. The principle of respect for international law is, to this extent, set aside by our reception system in favour of self-government. What renders self-executing treaties antithetical to self-government is the fact that treaty-making is a prerogative of the Crown. For Canadian law to treat international conventions as binding domestic law without intervention by legislatures would confer upon the Crown a power to make law. That

---

[20] Article 55 of the French constitution of October 4, 1958 provides that "Les traités ou accords régulièrement ratifiés ou approuvés ont, dès leur publication, une autorité supérieure à celle des lois, sous réserve, pour chaque accord ou traité, de son application par l'autre partie." Article 25 of the German Basic Law of May 23, 1949, provides that "the general rules of public international law constitute an integral part of federal law. They take precedence over statutes and directly create rights and duties for the inhabitants of the federal territory." Article VI of the US constitution provides that "all Treaties made, or which shall be made, under the Authority of the United States, shall be the supreme Law of the Land." However, subsequent US constitutional law has narrowed this provision by drawing a distinction between treaties and executive agreements (both of which constitute treaties for the purposes of international law).

[21] A treaty may be declaratory of, or come to represent, customary international law. In that case, a Canadian court may look to the treaty, though unimplemented or even unratified, to discern customary international law. When a court does so, it is not applying the treaty but rather the customary law that the treaty represents. An example is the use of the 1958 Convention on Fishing and Conservation of the Living Resources of the High Seas and the 1982 United Nations Convention on the Law of the Sea by Deschênes J. in *R.* v. *Rumbaut* (1998), 127 C.C.C. (3d) 138 (N.B.Q.B.).

power was removed from the Crown several hundred years ago and has not been restored to it since that time.

The rule that the executive lacks the power to legislate outside Parliament finds no explicit expression in Canada's written constitutional texts. It is, in the main, an unwritten law of the constitution.[22] The rule is implicit, however, in the preamble to the Constitution Act 1867, which endowed Canada with a constitution "similar in Principle to that of the United Kingdom."[23] Many centuries ago, the sovereign did have a power to legislate, but that power has long since passed to Parliament. In the *Proclamations* case of 1611, Coke C.J. held that "the king by his proclamation cannot create any offence which was not an offence before, for then he may alter the law of the land by his proclamation" and "the law of England is divided into three parts, common law, statute law, and custom; but the King's proclamation is none of them."[24] At about the same time, it was held in *Archbishop of York and Sedgwick*'s case that "the King could not by His grant alter the law of the land."[25] Some eighty years and two revolutions later, a statute confirmed the common law position enunciated in these judgments. Article 1 of the Bill of Rights 1689 declares that "the pretended Power of suspending of Laws, or the Execution of Laws, by regal authority, without Consent of Parliament, is illegal."[26] All of these texts refer to the

---

[22] It is unwritten in the sense that it is not entrenched in the constitution of Canada as described in Section 52(2) of the Constitution Act 1982, being Schedule B to the Canada Act 1982 (U.K.), 1982, c. 11 [hereinafter Constitution Act 1982]. Yet the rule that the Crown cannot unilaterally make law finds written expression in case law and in the Bill of Rights 1689, an act of the UK Parliament that passed into Canadian law by reception. This act continues in force in all Canadian jurisdictions. As Henri Brun and Guy Tremblay observe, "on peut toujours plaider l'application au Canada de certains anciens statuts anglais qui constituent l'armature de base du droit constitutionnel britannique, tels la *Magna Carta* de 1215, la *Petition of Right* de 1627, le *Bill of Rights* de 1689 ou l'*Act of Settlement* de 1700." Henri Brun and Guy Tremblay, *Droit constitutionnel*, 2nd ed. (Cowansville, PQ: Les éditions Yvon Blais, 1990), 19.

[23] Constitution Act 1867 (U.K.), 30 & 31 Vict., c. 3, preamble, reprinted in R.S.C. 1985, App. II, No. 5. On the role of the preamble in importing unwritten constitutional rules, see *Reference Re Remuneration of Judges of the Provincial Court of Prince Edward Island; Reference re Independence and Impartiality of Judges of the Provincial Court of Prince Edward Island*, [1997] 3 S.C.R. 3 at 68-74, per Lamer C.J. The rule that the executive lacks legislative power is also implied by the definitions of the federal and provincial legislatures in the Constitution Act 1867.

[24] *Proclamations* case, (1611) 12 Co. Rep. 75 at 76; 77 E.R. 1352 at 1354.

[25] *Archbishop of York and Sedgwick*, (1612) Godbolt 201 at 201; 78 E.R. 122 at 122.

[26] Bill of Rights, 1689 (U.K.), 1 William & Mary, sess. 1, c. 6.

sovereign personally, but the prohibition on regal law-making had been transformed, by the time of the Constitution Act 1867 (indeed, long before), into a broader prohibition on legislation by the executive, meaning not just the sovereign but also the Cabinet and the executive branch generally.[27]

This broadening of the prohibition in order to cover not only the sovereign but all those who govern in his or her name tells us something about the nature of the objection to regal law-making. It was not simply an objection to legislation by a single, hereditary ruler. It was also, and perhaps principally, an objection to legislation by remote, exclusive, and non-participatory means — whether these means were invoked by the king himself or by ministers and officials acting in his name. The prohibition on executive law-making bars both unconstitutional monarchy and Cabinet-based oligarchy from our system of government. In their place is posited a parliamentary procedure founded upon the values of representation, deliberation, and consent that inform the principle of self-government. The prohibition on executive legislation reveals a subtlety in the self-government principle: that the executive is drawn from ourselves and responsible to us for its conduct does not suffice to satisfy the principle. What is lacking in executive, as opposed to parliamentary, law-making is a deliberative, representative, and participatory decision-making process. Likewise, the reception system looks on international law as a coercive external force not simply because international law is external to the Canadian legal order—for the executive is clearly internal to that order yet is treated as objectionably remote nonetheless. It is not externality, but the absence of a deliberative, representative, and participatory legislative process, that founds self-government's objection to the direct application of conventional international law in Canada.

While the Crown's legislative prerogative was abolished long ago, other prerogatives have remained. Chief among these is the federal government's power over foreign affairs and, in particular, its power to conclude treaties with foreign states.[28] The majority of

---

[27] Of course, the executive may exercise law-making power where that power is delegated to it by the legislature. Secondary legislation is not a violation of the rule that the Crown is not a source of law because the ultimate source of secondary legislative power is not the Crown but the legislature.

[28] The Canadian executive has not always enjoyed a foreign affairs prerogative. Until the Statute of Westminster, the prerogative continued to be formally vested in the Imperial Crown (though Canada began to represent itself internationally to a limited extent soon after the close of the First World War).

treaties entered into by Canada each year are not intended to change Canada's domestic law.[29] Occasionally, however, and with growing frequency, states conclude treaties that purport to regulate their domestic affairs. The federal government's continuing power to conclude such treaties without Parliament, combined with the rule that the Crown has no power unilaterally to make or unmake any law (what I call the bar on executive legislation), necessitates the implementation by legislative enactment of treaties that require the alteration of domestic law. The inability of the Crown to alter the law simply by concluding treaties was declared in the famous English case *The Parlement Belge*. The defendant argued that the plaintiff's right to bring a claim against the owner of the ship was excluded by a treaty between the United Kingdom and Belgium. Rejecting this argument, Sir Robert Phillimore said:

> If the Crown had power without the authority of parliament by this treaty to order that the *Parlement Belge* should be entitled to all the privileges of a ship of war, then the warrant, which is prayed for against the wrong-doer on account of the collision, cannot issue, and the right of the subject, but for this order unquestionable, to recover damages for the injuries done to him by her is extinguished. This is a use of the treaty-making prerogative of the Crown which I believe to be without precedent, and in principle contrary to the laws of the constitution.[30]

The Implementation Requirement

English and Canadian authorities are in agreement on the rule that treaties must be implemented by statute in order to alter domestic law. This agreement in the two countries' case law is unsurprising given that our constitutional structures are, in this respect, identical. The similarities of English and Canadian law in this area are nicely demonstrated by the fact that the most authoritative description of the implementation requirement in both jurisdictions is that of Lord Atkin in *Attorney General for Canada* v. *Attorney General for Ontario* (*Labour Conventions*), an appeal to the Privy Council from the Supreme Court of Canada. His Lordship explained that

> Within the British Empire there is a well-established rule that the making of a treaty is an executive act, while the performance of its obligations,

---

[29] As examples of such treaties, Hogg gives those "relating to defence, foreign aid, the high seas, the air, research, weather stations, diplomatic relations and many other matters." Hogg, *supra* note 11 at section 11.4.

[30] *The Parlement Belge*, [1878-9] 4 P.D. 129 at 154.

if they entail alteration of the existing domestic law, requires legislative action. Unlike some other countries, the stipulations of a treaty duly ratified do not within the Empire, by virtue of the treaty alone, have the force of law. If the national executive, the government of the day, decide to incur the obligations of a treaty which involve alteration of law they have to run the risk of obtaining the assent of Parliament to the necessary statute or statutes.[31]

A recent enunciation of the implementation requirement in Canada came from L'Heureux-Dubé J. in *Baker,* who stated that "[i]nternational treaties and conventions are not part of Canadian law unless they have been implemented by statute."[32] As authority for this proposition, L'Heureux-Dubé J. cited *Francis* v. *The Queen* and *Capital Cities Communications Inc.* v. *Canadian Radio-Television Commission.* In *Francis,* Kerwin C.J. held that "in Canada such rights and privileges as are here advanced of subjects of a contracting party to a treaty are enforceable by the Courts only where the treaty has been implemented or sanctioned by legislation."[33] In *Capital Cities,* Laskin C.J. held that an international convention could have "no domestic, internal consequences unless they arose from implementing legislation."[34] Many more Canadian authorities may be cited.[35]

---

[31] *Attorney General for Canada* v. *Attorney General for Ontario* (*Labour Conventions*), [1937] A.C. 326 (P.C.) at 347, per Lord Atkin [hereinafter *Labour Conventions*]. In *Operation Dismantle* v. *The Queen,* [1985] 1 S.C.R. 441 at para. 89 [hereinafter *Operation Dismantle*], Wilson J. quoted this passage and described it as having "definitively established" the "law in relation to treaty-making power ... for Canada and the rest of the Commonwealth." Her Ladyship went on to observe (at para. 90) that it is not every treaty which requires implementation: "Legislation is only required if some alteration in the domestic law is needed for its implementation."

[32] *Baker, infra* note 133 at 861.

[33] *Francis, infra* note 76 at 621, per Kerwin C.J.

[34] *Capital Cities, supra* note 19 at 173. This statement is too sweeping. See the discussion in the section entitled "Unimplemented Treaties and the Treaty Presumption" later in this article.

[35] For instance, "les dispositions de l'ALENA ne font pas partie du droit interne applicable au Canada et, plus particulièrement, au Québec, par les tribunaux nationaux et ... les dispositions mêmes de l'ALENA ne donnent pas ouverture au recours direct devant les tribunaux nationaux en cas, par hypothèse, de contravention de certaines dispositions de l'ALENA": *Les Entreprises de rebuts Sanipan* v. *Procureur général du Québec,* [1995] R.J.Q. 821 at 844. "According to well-established case law the rights created or conferred by an international treaty belong exclusively to the sovereign countries which are the contracting parties to it ... it results from this principle that the provisions of an international treaty

The implementation requirement applies equally where the treaty at issue purports to confer or deprive legal rights. Sir Elihu Lauterpacht has argued that courts should treat rights-advancing treaties and rights-limiting treaties differently. He suggests that where an obligation entered into by the executive is to the benefit of the public and imposes a burden on itself, courts should hold the executive to that commitment.[36] Whatever the merits of this suggestion, it clearly does not represent English law as it now stands. In *J.H. Rayner Ltd* v. *Department of Trade and Industry*, Lord Oliver observed that

as a matter of the constitutional law of the United Kingdom, the royal prerogative, whilst it embraces the making of treaties, does not extend to altering the law or conferring rights on individuals or depriving individuals of rights which they enjoy in domestic law without the intervention of Parliament. Treaties, as it is sometimes expressed, are not self-executing. Quite simply, a treaty is not part of English law unless and until it has been incorporated into the law by legislation.[37]

---

confer no right on an individual unless the treaty is implemented by legislation": *R.* v. *Vincent* (1993), 12 O.R. (3d) 427 (Ont. C.A.) at 437-8. "A treaty ... may be in full force and effect internationally without any legislative implementation and, absent such legislative implementation, it does not form part of the domestic law of Canada": *Operation Dismantle, supra* note 31 at 484. "Treaties ... only become part of municipal law if they are expressly implemented by statute": *Re R. and Palacios* (1984), 45 O.R. (2d) 269 at 276 (Ont. C.A.). "[N]o Canadian legislation has been passed which expressly implements the Covenant. Such enabling legislation is required in order to make the Covenant part of the domestic law of Canada": *Re Mitchell and The Queen* (1983), 42 O.R. (2d) 481 (Ont. H.C.) at 492, per Linden J. "In the absence of some ... legislative act the making of a treaty does not change the domestic law of Canada": *Mastini* v. *Bell Telephone of Canada* (1971), 18 D.L.R. (3d) 215 (Ex. Ct.) at 217 [hereinafter *Mastini*]. "It has been settled law that a treaty binding the Government does not *ipso facto*, become part of our law and enforceable in the Courts": *R.* v. *Canada Labour Relations Board ex p. Federal Electric Corporation* (1964), 44 D.L.R. (2d) 440 (Man. Q.B.) at 454. "[I]t has never, so far as I have been able to ascertain, been decided or admitted that the Crown could by its own act in agreeing to the terms of a treaty alter the law of the land or affect the private rights of individuals": *Bitter* v. *Secretary of State of Canada*, [1944] Ex. C.R. 61 at 76-7, per Thorson J. "[T]he Crown cannot alter the existing law by entering into a contract with a foreign power": *Arrow River, supra* note 18 at 510, per Lamont J. See also the knowledgeable discussion, too long to quote here, of Roberts J. in *R.* v. *Rehmann* (1995), 122 Nfld. & P.E.I.R. 111 (Newf. S.C.T.D.) at 121-6.

36 Murray Hunt, *Using Human Rights Law in English Courts* (Oxford: Hart, 1998) at 34, citing an unpublished lecture by E. Lauterpacht, "International Law and Her Majesty's Judges," F.A. Mann Memorial Lecture, 1993; see also Hunt at 258-9.

37 *J.H. Rayner Ltd* v. *Department of Trade and Industry*, [1990] 2 A.C. 418 (H.L.) at 500, per Lord Oliver.

Similarly, Sir Hersch Lauterpacht, writing in 1939, observed that treaties require implementation to affect private rights "favourably or adversely." He explained, "it is ... clearly established that in the absence of express municipal legislation to that effect, subjects cannot, as against the Crown, derive benefits directly under a treaty on the ground that the Crown acts as agent or trustee for the subject."[38] In Canadian law, the point has not been clearly made. However, given the great similarity between English and Canadian law in this area, the Canadian position is likely to be the same.

The implementation requirement means that a complaint that Canada or any other state has breached its obligations under an unimplemented treaty is not justiciable in domestic courts. The meaning of the doctrine of non-justiciability in regard to unimplemented treaties was considered in the English Court of Appeal.[39] Kerr L.J. identified two general principles upon which the doctrine rests. First, unincorporated treaties do not form part of domestic law, and, therefore, no private rights or obligations can be derived from them. Second, treaties are not contracts that can be enforced by domestic courts. "But that is as far as the doctrine goes," said Kerr L.J. "It does not preclude the decision of justiciable issues which arise against the background of an unincorporated treaty in a way which renders it necessary or convenient to refer to, and consider, the contents of the treaty."[40]

Kerr L.J.'s second principle — that treaties are not contracts enforceable in domestic courts — means that the remedy for breach of treaty obligations lies not in Canadian courts but in other forums. International tribunals are one such forum. Resort may also be had to diplomatic and political activity. Such activity is not a "remedy" in the domestic legal sense of the word. But it may be effective nonetheless. As Muldoon J. observed in *Aerlinte Eireann Teoranta* v. *Canada*, "[if] the executive do not seek legislative incorporation of treaties bearing on the legislative jurisdiction of Parliament under the Constitution, Canada could be seen to acquire

---

[38] H. Lauterpacht, "Is International Law a Part of the Law of England?" (1939) Transactions of the Grotius Society 51 at 75. Lauterpacht cites three authorities: *Civilian War Claimants' Association* v. *The King,* [1932] A.C. 14; *Rustomjee* v. *The Queen* (1876), 1 Q.B.D. 487; 2 Q.B.D. 69; and *Baron de Bode* v. *The Queen* (1848), 1 Q.B. 383, "where," says Lauterpacht, "the question seems, in a sense, to have been left open."

[39] *J.H. Rayner* v. *Department of Trade,* [1989], Ch. 72.

[40] *Ibid.* at 163-4.

a poor reputation among nations."[41] A good illustration of the consequences, or lack thereof, of breaching an unimplemented treaty is *R. v. Bonadie*.[42] A consul for St. Vincent and the Grenadines was charged with attempting to obstruct justice. He pleaded immunity under the terms of the 1963 Vienna Convention on Consular Relations,[43] a treaty partially implemented in Canadian law by the Foreign Missions and International Organizations Act.[44] The Ontario Court (Provincial Division) held that the effect of the merely partial implementation was that while the consul's act may be a breach of the convention, it was not a breach of Canadian law. The remedy, therefore, was a political one and not the loss of immunity.

Implementation is required to give domestic legal effect to treaties. It remains to consider what implementation consists in. Jurisdiction to implement treaties is determined according to the division of powers described in Sections 91 and 92 of the Constitution Act 1867. This was decided in the *Labour Conventions* case, which we will consider in detail later in this article. The implementing instrument must be legislation[45] since merely tabling a treaty in the House of Commons does not constitute implementation[46] nor will a resolution of the House of Commons approving ratification of the treaty suffice.[47] These rules have been enunciated with respect to the federal Parliament, but they undoubtedly apply equally in the provincial Legislatures. The procedure for enacting implementing legislation is no different than that of any other bill. It may be introduced by any member, from a government

---

[41] *Aerlinte Eireann Teoranta* v. *Canada* (1987), 9 F.T.R. 29 at 43.

[42] *R.* v. *Bonadie* (1996), 109 C.C.C. (3d) 356.

[43] Vienna Convention on Consular Relations, Can. T.S. 1974 No. 25.

[44] Foreign Missions and International Organizations Act, S.C. 1991, c. 41.

[45] In the term legislation, I include subordinate legislation, such as regulations promulgated by statutory authority. Where the legislature confers its law-making power upon a delegate, that power may be exercised to implement treaties (provided that such an exercise of the power is not *ultra vires* the grant). An example is *Pan American World Airways* v. *The Queen*, [1981] 2 S.C.R. 565, in which the appellants argued, *inter alia*, that the relevant treaty had been implemented in Canada by Section 6 of the Aeronautics Act, R.S.C. 1970, c. A-3 and the Air Regulations promulgated thereunder. See also *Schavernoch*, *infra* note 99, and the English case *Benin* v. *Whimster*, [1976] 1 Q.B. 297 at 308-9.

[46] *R.* v. *Canadian Labour Relations Board* (1964), 44 D.L.R. (2d) 440 (Man. Q.B.) at 455, per Smith J.

[47] *Mastini, supra* note 35 at 217.

minister to an opposition backbencher.[48] In the federal Parliament (Canada's only bicameral legislature), implementing legislation may be introduced by members of the Senate or the House of Commons. The usual practice is for implementing legislation to be drafted by a government department and brought to the floor of the House by that department's minister. However, opposition members of parliament will sometimes bring private member's legislation to implement treaties. An important example, in the light of the Supreme Court of Canada's decision in *Baker*,[49] is a bill that was introduced in the Commons in 1995 by Chris Axworthy, who was at the time a member for the opposition New Democratic party. The bill sought to implement the 1989 Convention on the Rights of the Child[50] by amending the Interpretation Act to require that federal legislation be read in conformity with Canada's obligations under that treaty. The parliamentary secretary to the prime minister, Jean Augustine, spoke for the government against the bill, and it died on the Order Paper.[51]

The novel form of implementation proposed by this bill suggests the variety of ways in which legislation can implement treaties. Legislatures, being sovereign in the residual sense described earlier, are not bound by any particular form of implementation. The only formal requirement to speak of is not legal but common sense — that the legislature must make its intent to implement sufficiently clear so that the courts treat the statute as an implementing act. The primacy of intent over form is illustrated by an old British Columbian case, *In re Nakane and Okazake*.[52] Two Japanese subjects, detained under an act of the British Columbia Legislature, challenged the act as invalid because it was inconsistent, they argued, with a federal act implementing a treaty between the United Kingdom and Japan. This treaty assured Japanese subjects full liberty to enter, travel, or reside in any part of Canada. The attorney-general of British Columbia contended that the federal act was ineffective to implement the treaty for it merely declared the treaty to be "hereby sanctioned" and reproduced it in a schedule to

---

48 This is subject to the rule, in the federal Parliament, that money bills can only be introduced upon recommendation by the governor general, that is, by ministers. Constitution Act 1867, *supra* note 22 at s. 54.

49 *Baker, infra* note 133.

50 Convention on the Rights of the Child, Can. T.S. 1992 No. 3.

51 *House of Commons Debates* (April 25, 1995) at 11794-800. The bill was C-254.

52 *In Re Nakane and Okazake* (1908), 13 B.C.R. 370 (Full Ct.).

the act. Hunter C.J. held that the act implemented the treaty and thereby invalidated the inconsistent provincial law. Neither the use of the unorthodox term "sanction" nor the placement of the treaty in a schedule to the act detracted from Parliament's intent, which was to make the provisions of the treaty a part of the law of Canada. The chief justice was upheld on appeal to the Full Court. This intent-based approach to implementation has much to recommend it. Courts should avoid interpretations of laws that unnecessarily frustrate a legislature's intent (however badly phrased) to implement a treaty. International law should not founder for poor drafting.

It is easy enough to say that intent should prevail over form. The difficulty, of course, is in determining intent where the form is equivocal. A recent consideration of this problem is the Supreme Court of Canada's judgment in *British Columbia (Attorney General)* v. *Canada (Attorney General)* (*Re Vancouver Island Railway*).[53] The agreement at issue was not an international treaty but rather the "Dunsmuir agreement" between the governments of British Columbia and Canada. That agreement was scheduled to an act of Parliament that declared the agreement "approved and ratified." Iacobucci J., speaking for eight justices, held that these words were insufficient to give the agreement force of law. Relying on a 1945 Supreme Court judgment,[54] his Lordship found that "statutory ratification and confirmation of a scheduled agreement, standing alone, is generally insufficient reason to conclude that such an agreement constitutes a part of the statute itself."[55] He added, "simple "ratification" or "confirmation" of a scheduled agreement, without more, is equivocal in terms of the required legislative intention."[56]

Happily, most implementing statutes are reasonably clear.[57] Some acts simply declare that a treaty is to be applied as law. An example is Section 3(1) of the Foreign Missions and International Organizations Act, which provides that

Articles 1, 22 to 24 and 27 to 40 of the Vienna Convention on Diplomatic Relations, and Articles 1, 5, 15, 17, 31 to 33, 35, 39 and 40, paragraphs 1

---

[53] *British Columbia (Attorney General)* v. *Canada (Attorney General)* (*Re Vancouver Island Railway*), [1994] 2 S.C.R. 41 [hereinafter *Re Vancouver Island Railway*].

[54] *Ottawa Electric Railway Co.* v. *Corporation of the City of Ottawa*, [1945] S.C.R. 105.

[55] *Re Vancouver Island Railway, supra* note 53 at 109.

[56] *Ibid.* at 110. For a consideration of Iacobucci J.'s argument, see *Pfizer Inc.* v. *Canada (T.D.)*, [1999] 4 F.C. 441.

[57] I am relying in part on examples provided in Emanuelli, *supra* note 4 at 88-9.

and 2 of Article 41, Articles 43 to 45 and 48 to 54, paragraphs 2 and 3 of Article 55, paragraph 2 of Article 57, paragraphs 1 to 3 of Article 58, Articles 59 to 62, 64, 66 and 67, paragraphs 1, 2 and 4 of Article 70 and Article 71 of the Vienna Convention on Consular Relations, have the force of law in Canada in respect of all foreign states, regardless of whether those states are parties to those Conventions.[58]

Other statutes use wording that, while somewhat less direct, is nonetheless effective. Section 3 of the old Extradition Act stated in part that "this Part shall be read and construed as to provide for the execution of the [extradition] arrangement." This section went further and provided that inconsistencies between the act and an extradition treaty were to be resolved in favour of the treaty.[59] Still, other implementing statutes do not rely directly on the text of the treaty but simply effect legal changes that, in the estimation of the legislature, suffice to meet Canada's treaty commitments. An example is the Québec Loi sur les aspects civils de l'enlèvement international et interprovincial d'enfants,[60] which implements the 1980 Hague Convention on the Civil Aspects of International Child Abduction (Hague Convention)[61] but does not, in the words of L'Heureux-Dubé J. in *W. (V.) v. S. (D.)*, "adopt the integral wording thereof."[62] The Québec act nonetheless made its intention to implement the treaty sufficiently clear by referring to it in the preamble[63] and declaring Québec's adherence to its principles. Yet even this declaration is not necessary. An implementing statute need make no mention at all of the treaty it implements.[64] An example is the

---

58 Foreign Missions and International Organizations Act, *supra* note 44.

59 Extradition Act, R.S.C. 1985, c. E-23, now repealed and replaced by the Extradition Act, S.C. 1999, c. 18.

60 Loi sur les aspects civils de l'enlèvement international et interprovincial d'enfants, R.S.Q., c. A-23.01.

61 Hague Convention on the Civil Aspects of International Child Abduction, Can. T.S. 1983 No. 35.

62 *W. (V.) v. S. (D.)*, [1996] 2 S.C.R. 108 at 133.

63 Schabas suggests that reference to a treaty in the preamble of a statute may be sufficient to implement the treaty. I disagree. The established rules of statutory construction accord preambles too little weight to accomplish the task of implementing a treaty in domestic law. See William A. Schabas, *International Human Rights Law and the Canadian Charter*, 2nd ed. (Scarborough, ON: Carswell, 1996), 22-3 (but see also 25-6).

64 The Legal Bureau of the Department of External Affairs affirmed, in a 1985 letter to the Council of Europe, that implementation may occur "by enacting the required legislation without express reference to the treaty"; reprinted in (1986) 24 C.Y.I.L. 397 at 401. Yet see the discussion of *MacDonald, infra* note 229, later in this article.

Ocean Dumping Control Act,[65] which was at issue in *Crown Zeller-bach*.[66] The task of determining whether an act seeks to implement a treaty is no different than that of discerning the legislature's intent more generally. Counsel and courts may determine intent to implement using such accepted methods as legislative history and Hansard.

A nice illustration of the difficulties to which implementation can give rise is *Thomson* v. *Thomson*.[67] This was the first Supreme Court decision on the 1980 Hague Convention. Since it concerned matters of child custody, it fell to be implemented by the provinces. In his reasons, La Forest J. described the various ways in which the provinces implemented it:

The preliminary draft Convention that had been completed by the Hague Conference Special Commission in November 1979 was submitted to the Uniform Law Conference of Canada in August 1980 by its Committee on International Conventions on Private International Law ... The Uniform Law Conference agreed upon the text of a "Uniform Act" to implement the Hague Convention. Four provinces (New Brunswick, Nova Scotia, Saskatchewan and Alberta) enacted legislation that paralleled the Uniform Act, including its provision that, in the event of a conflict between the Convention and any other enactment, the Convention prevailed: *International Child Abduction Act*, S.N.B. 1982, c. I-12.1; *Child Abduction Act*, S.N.S. 1982, c. 4; *The International Child Abduction Act*, S.S. 1986, c. I-10.1; and *International Child Abduction Act*, S.A. 1986, c. I-6.5.

Quebec chose not to enact the Convention at all, but to legislate equivalent provisions: *An Act respecting the civil aspects of international and interprovincial child abduction*, S.Q. 1984, c. 12. The five remaining provinces (Manitoba, Ontario, British Columbia, Prince Edward Island and Newfoundland) adopted the Convention in a more general statute dealing with the civil aspects of child abduction: *The Child Custody Enforcement Act*, S.M. 1982, c. 27 (now R.S.M. 1987, c. C360); *Children's Law Reform Amendment Act, 1982*, S.O. 1982, c. 20; *Family Relations Amendment Act, 1982*, S.B.C. 1982, c. 8, as am. by S.B.C. 1985, c. 72, s. 20; *Custody Jurisdiction and Enforcement Act*, S.P.E.I. 1984, c. 17; and *The Children's Law Act*, S.N. 1988, c. 61. Of these five, Ontario, Prince Edward Island and Newfoundland's enactments all contain the provision that, in the event of a conflict between the Convention and any other legislative scheme, the Convention prevails. Only the British Columbia and Manitoba Acts do not contain such supremacy provisions.[68]

It was the Manitoba implementation scheme that was before the Court in *Thomson*. As noted in the preceding quotation, Manitoba's

---

[65] Ocean Dumping Control Act, S.C. 1974-75-76, c. 55.

[66] *Crown Zellerbach, infra* note 235.

[67] *Thomson* v. *Thomson*, [1994] 3 S.C.R. 551 [hereinafter *Thomson*].

[68] *Ibid.* at 601-2.

Child Custody Enforcement Act (CCEA) included both a general scheme for the enforcement of custody orders and an implementing provision (Section 17(2)), which read: "On, from and after December 1, 1983, the convention is in force in Manitoba and the provisions thereof are law in Manitoba." La Forest J., writing for the majority, considered that the CCEA created two child enforcement schemes in Manitoba: the convention scheme, which was adopted in Section 17(2), and the general scheme, which was established by the rest of the act. L'Heureux-Dubé and McLachlin JJ. dissented on this point. They preferred to read the entire CCEA as implementing the convention and to resolve conflicts between the two schemes according to the principle that legislatures, while possessing sovereign power to violate international law, are presumed not to intend to do so.[69]

SUPPOSED EXCEPTIONS TO THE IMPLEMENTATION REQUIREMENT

There are suggestions in the English[70] and Canadian[71] literature that treaties of peace (sometimes called treaties of war or treaties affecting belligerent rights) and treaties of cession are exempt from the implementation requirement. Such treaties, it is contended, have force of law without legislation. The case law in the area is obscure. For instance, in *Walker* v. *Baird*,[72] an appeal to the Privy Council from the Supreme Court of Newfoundland, the Board explicitly left open the question of whether the Crown had the power to compel subjects to obey an unimplemented treaty either for the purpose of ending a war or preserving peace. What is clear is that if an exception to the implementation rule exists, it grants the executive certain legislative powers that, in any other context, would be unconstitutional.

The rule that treaties of peace do not require implementation was approved in *obiter* by Duff J. (as he then was) in the Supreme Court of Canada in *Secretary of State of Canada* v. *Alien Property*

---

[69] *Ibid.* at 617-18.

[70] See Jennings and Watts, *supra* note 4 at section 19 n. 23, and Ian Brownlie, *Principles of Public International Law*, 5th ed. (Oxford: Clarendon Press, 1998) at 47.

[71] See Anne F. Bayefsky, *International Human Rights Law: Use in Canadian Charter of Rights and Freedoms Litigation* (Toronto: Butterworths, 1992) at 25; R. St. J. Macdonald, "International Treaty Law and the Domestic Law of Canada" (1975) 2 Dalhousie L.J. 307 at 308-10, 313-14; J.E. Read, "International Agreements" (1948) 26 Can. Bar. Rev. 520 at 528.

[72] *Walker* v. *Baird*, [1892] A.C. 491 (P.C.).

Custodian for the United States.[73] This dictum was cited approvingly by Angers J. in *Ritcher* v. *The King.*[74] Yet in *Bitter* v. *Secretary of State for Canada,* Thorson J. rejected Duff J.'s argument:

What legal effect should be given to the terms of a Treaty of Peace is an interesting question. In *Secretary of State of Canada* v. *Alien Property Custodian for the United States* ... Duff J made the following striking statement: "The treaty it is to be observed, being a Treaty of Peace, had the effect of law quite independently of legislation." With the utmost respect, I venture the opinion that there is no authority for this statement and that it cannot be accepted without important qualifications. While a Treaty of Peace can be made only by the Crown, it still remains an Act of the Crown. While it is binding upon the subjects of the Crown without legislation in the sense that it terminates the war, it has never, so far as I have been able to ascertain, been decided or admitted that the Crown could by its own act in agreeing to the terms of a treaty alter the law of the land or affect the private rights of individuals.[75]

This strong statement was ignored by Kerwin C.J. in *Francis* v. *The Queen,* who remarked that the treaty in question in that case could not exempt an Aboriginal man from customs duties without implementing legislation because it was not a peace treaty.[76] Also in that case, Rand J. (Cartwright J. concurring) held that implementation was required of all treaties "which purport to change existing law or restrict the future action of the legislation" save those concerning "diplomatic status and certain immunities and to belligerent rights."[77] This is a broad and ill-defined category — one that Rand J. seemed to think might extend to peace treaties having fiscal effects upon domestic law.[78] Rand J.'s discussion is unhelpful. Indeed, it illustrates just how unsatisfying the supposed peace treaty exception is. It is unsurprising, then, that in *Mastini*

---

[73] *Secretary of State of Canada* v. *Alien Property Custodian for the United States,* [1931] S.C.R. 169 at 198.

[74] *Ritcher* v. *The King,* [1943] Ex. C.R. 64 at 69.

[75] *Bitter* v. *Secretary of State for Canada,* [1944] Ex. C.R. 61 at 76-7.

[76] *Francis* v. *The Queen,* [1956] S.C.R. 618 at 621 [hereinafter *Francis*]. The remaining justices reached the same conclusion on other grounds.

[77] *Ibid.* at 626. See also Rand J.'s similar observation in *Attorney General for Ontario* v. *Scott,* [1956] S.C.R. 137 at 142: "A treaty is an agreement between states, political in nature, even though it may contain provisions of a legislative character which may, *by themselves* or their subsequent enactment pass into law." "By themselves" apparently refers to peace treaties.

[78] "To the enactment of fiscal provisions, certainly in the case of a treaty not a peace treaty, the prerogative does not extend." *Francis, supra* note 76 at 626, per Rand J.

v. *Bell Telephone*,[79] Jackett P. largely ignored *Francis* and held that the 1947 Treaty of Peace with Italy[80] was not law without implementation. The law as stated by Thorson J. in *Bitter*, and applied by Jackett P. in *Mastini*, is more consistent with the bar on executive legislation, and the self-government principle that informs it, than the opposing dicta in the cases reviewed here. This is not only my view but also that of J.E. Read,[81] J.E.S. Fawcett,[82] and R. St. J. Macdonald.[83] The supposed peace treaty exception to the rule that the Crown is not a source of law discloses no foundation in reason or principle. *Bitter* and *Mastini* are to be preferred over *Francis*, *Ritcher*, and *Alien Property Custodian* on this point.[84]

In addition, no special rule should apply to treaties of cession.[85] The distinction between treaties of peace and treaties of cession is a false one. Where a cession occurs in peacetime, it is inconceivable that it be done on the authority of the executive alone. As Fawcett puts it, "[i]f the Crown cannot, without authority of Parliament, modify private rights within the framework of existing law, it cannot *a fortiori* remove the protection of that law altogether."[86] In the case of a cession provided for by a peace treaty, the same rule

---

[79] *Mastini, supra* note 35.

[80] Treaty of Peace with Italy, Can. T.S. 1947 No. 4.

[81] Read, *supra* note 71 at 528.

[82] J.E.S. Fawcett, *The British Commonwealth in International Law* (London: Stevens and Sons, 1963) at 58. See also the report of July 13, 1870 by the British Crown Law Officers to the Colonial Office in A.D. McNair, *The Law of Treaties: British Practice and Opinions* (New York: Columbia University Press, 1938) at 27-8, who advised the colonial secretary that territory could not be ceded in peacetime by prerogative alone.

[83] R. St J. Macdonald, "The Relationship between Domestic Law and International Law in Canada," in R. St J. Macdonald et al., eds., *Canadian Perspectives on International Law and Organization* (Toronto: University of Toronto Press, 1974), 88 at 120.

[84] In *R. v. Rebmann* (1995), 122 Nfld. & P.E.I.R. 111 (Newf. S.C.T.D.) at 121-2, Roberts J. rejected the accused's argument that a fishing treaty between Canada and France constituted a "prerogative treaty" analogous to a treaty of peace and therefore not requiring implementation. The learned judge did not deny the existence of such a category of treaty (though he quoted Read, *supra* note 71 at 528, that such a category is "doubtful"); rather, he held that the treaty purported to affect the rights and duties of Canadians and therefore required implementation.

[85] Kerwin C.J. noted Indian and New Zealand authorities requiring implementation of treaties of cession in *Francis, supra* note 76 at 621.

[86] Fawcett, *supra* note 82 at 59. This proposition is strengthened in Canadian law, I suggest, by the decision of the Supreme Court of Canada in the *Re Secession of Quebec*, [1998] 2 S.C.R. 217 [hereinafter *Re Secession of Quebec*].

should apply, but tempered (though only *in extremis*) by the principle that the safety of the people is the highest law.[87] Happily, the prospect of Canada being forced to cede territory to make peace with an enemy is remote. However, the cession of territory in peacetime is no mere theoretical issue as long as powerful separatist movements prosper in this country.

Unimplemented Treaties and the Treaty Presumption

A rigorous application of the implementation requirement might seem to require that the courts wholly ignore unimplemented treaties. Such an approach has been taken at times by Canadian, English, and other common law courts. But it is a mistake to derive from the rule that treaties are not self-executing the further rule that treaties are legally irrelevant. As Scarman L.J. (as he then was) stated in *Ahmad* v. *ILEA*,

> it is no longer possible to argue that because the international treaty obligations of the United Kingdom do not become law unless enacted by Parliament our courts pay no regard to our international obligations. They pay very serious regard to them: in particular, they will interpret statutory language and apply common law principles, wherever possible, so as to reach a conclusion consistent with our international obligations.[88]

This statement is an enunciation of what I call the presumption of international legality: the interpretive rule that statutes should be construed consistent with the presumption that the legislature does not intend to violate international law. To this point, this discussion of the interaction between treaties and domestic law has been dominated by self-government concerns: the Crown's prerogative to conclude treaties without Parliament, the ensuing unenforceability of treaties without implementation, and the sovereignty of Canadian legislatures to violate international law. Now, as I turn to consider the presumption of international legality, the principle of respect for international law becomes the theme. The presumption of international legality is the means by which the principle of respect for international law is vindicated in the treaty-law rules of the reception system.

The application of this presumption in cases concerning unimplemented treaties brings special difficulties that do not arise in cases concerning customary international law. It is helpful, then, to

---

[87]   *Salus populi est suprema lex.*

[88]   *Ahmad* v. *ILEA*, [1978] 1 Q.B. 36 (Eng. C.A.) at 48D-E.

distinguish a treaty-specific version of the presumption of international legality from the more general rule. I call this the treaty presumption. The treaty presumption is rebuttable, for, as we have seen, our legislatures possess a residual sovereignty to violate international law. However, for a court to find that the presumption is rebutted is to ascribe to the legislature an intention to act unlawfully or at least a failure to act in accordance with international law. This is an undesirable finding, which our courts are right to avoid.

An example of a court applying the treaty presumption is *Aerlinte Eireann Teoranta* v. *Canada.*[89] The plaintiff airlines sought to challenge regulations promulgated by the minister of transport under a statutory discretion enjoyed under Section 5 of the Aeronautics Act.[90] The plaintiffs argued, *inter alia,* that the minister's regulations were *ultra vires* because they were unlawfully discriminatory. They relied in part on the 1944 Chicago Convention on International Civil Aviation, which Canada had ratified but which it had not implemented in domestic law.[91] The plaintiffs conceded that unimplemented treaties have no domestic legal effect, but they argued that the impugned regulations should be interpreted so as to comply with the treaty and with the declarations of the Council of the International Civil Aviation Organization. Far from rejecting the unimplemented treaty as irrelevant, Muldoon J. reviewed the convention and relevant statements of the council, from which he concluded that the impugned regulations neither violated the convention nor "disgraced Canada's membership in ICAO."[92]

This example illustrates how the treaty presumption mitigates the Canadian constitution's dualism. Ultimately, Canada remains dualist with respect to international treaties, for the treaty presumption is rebuttable. Yet the presumption operates as a significant qualification of the dualist stance. While unimplemented treaties are not formal sources of law, it is nonsense to treat them as

[89] *Aerlinte Eireann Teoranta* v. *Canada* (1987), 9 F.T.R. 29 (F.C.T.R.) [hereinafter *Aerlinte Eireann Teoranta*].

[90] Aeronautics Act, R.S.C 1970, c. A-3.

[91] Chicago Convention on International Civil Aviation, Can. T.S. 1944 No. 36.

[92] *Aerlinte Eireann Teoranta, supra* note 89 at 43. It is interesting to observe, in the light of the dissent in *Baker, infra* note 133, that no objection was raised by Muldoon J. to the plaintiffs' attempt to use an unimplemented treaty to structure a statutory discretion. Counsel for the Crown included Ian Binnie Q.C., who later, as Binnie J., sided with the majority in *Baker.* The Crown's solicitor of record, Frank Iacobucci Q.C. (as he then was), dissented in *Baker* on this point alone.

having no legal consequence. As we will see, the related maxims that the Crown is not a source of law and that treaties are not self-executing are essentially accurate but also oversimplifications. English and Canadian courts, striving to remain faithful to the dualist position and the constitutional rules that inform it, have revealed uncertainties in the application of the presumption. Four areas of controversy arise from the case law. They are the so-called ambiguity requirement; the nature of the legislation to be construed; the relevance of chronology; and the application of the treaty presumption to statutory grants of discretion.

AMBIGUITY

For part of the twentieth century, English and Canadian courts observed a rule that no regard could be given to treaties in interpreting legislation unless that legislation was somehow ambiguous. The "ambiguity requirement" became a trigger for the application of the treaty presumption. Without such ambiguity, the treaty could not be consulted and the presumption could not be applied. This is out of step with earlier authorities, such as *Bloxam* v. *Favre*,[93] which appeared to favour a broad application of the treaty presumption. The questions of whether an ambiguity requirement exists or should exist, and what it consists in, have troubled courts and commentators for some time. The ambiguity requirement, as it has been formulated in the leading English cases, results in a weak adherence to the principle of respect for international law without any concomitant strengthening of self-government. Thus, the requirement is impossible to justify on the reception system's own terms. For this reason, I reject the ambiguity requirement as it has been formulated in past cases and attempt to give an account of the proper role of ambiguity in internationally informed statutory interpretation.[94]

F.A.R. Bennion describes the interpreter's duty as "to determine and apply the legal meaning of the enactment, that is the meaning that correctly conveys the legislative intention."[95] The legal meaning

---

[93] *Bloxam* v. *Favre* (1883), 8 P.D. 101 at 107 (Eng. C.A.) [hereinafter *Bloxam*].

[94] I am using the term "statutory" for simplicity's sake. The presumption of international legality applies equally to secondary legislation (*Schavernoch, infra* note 99) and instruments made under the royal prerogative (*Post Office* v. *Estuary Radio,* [1968] 2 Q.B. 740 (Eng. C.A.) at 757).

[95] F.A.R. Bennion, *Statutory Interpretation: A Code,* 3rd ed. (London: Butterworths, 1997) at section 150; see also section 2.

is, in easy cases, the same as the grammatical meaning. Where this is not so, the legal meaning is arrived at by informing one's interpretation of the grammatical meaning with other indications of the legislative intent. Ambiguity arises when the enactment has two or more grammatical meanings. It can also arise when the grammatical meaning is at odds with legislative intent as indicated by sources other than the grammatical meaning. One such indication of the legislative intent is the existence of a treaty obligation, for the treaty presumption dictates that the legislature be presumed not to intend to violate international law. Thus, in order to determine the legal meaning of an enactment and, in particular, to determine whether it is ambiguous, it will sometimes be necessary to refer to a treaty.

This account of when a court may refer to a treaty represents a break with certain English authorities that require grammatical ambiguity before referring to a treaty. In *Salomon* v. *Customs and Excise Commissioners,*[96] Diplock L.J. (as he then was) held that no regard could be had to treaty obligations without first demonstrating ambiguity in the text of the statute. Lord Diplock seems to have abandoned this grammatical ambiguity requirement in *Garland* v. *British Rail Engineering,*[97] although the House of Lords held otherwise in *R.* v. *Secretary of State for the Home Department, ex p. Brind.*[98] The grammatical ambiguity requirement was seemingly approved by the Supreme Court of Canada in *Schavernoch* v. *Foreign Claims Commission,* when Estey J. explained that,

[i]f one could assert an ambiguity, either patent or latent, in the Regulations it might be that a court could find support for making reference to matters external to the Regulations in order to interpret its terms. Because, however, there is in my view no ambiguity arising from the above-quoted excerpt from these Regulations, there is no authority and none was drawn to our attention in argument entitling a court to take recourse . . . to an underlying international agreement.[99]

---

[96] *Salomon* v. *Customs and Excise Commissioners,* [1967] 2 Q.B. 116 (Eng. C.A.).

[97] *Garland* v. *British Rail Engineering,* [1983] 2 A.C. 751 (H.L.). This case was in European law, but the same principles arguably apply to international law. See Hunt, *supra* note 36 at 17-21.

[98] *R.* v. *Secretary of State for the Home Department, ex p. Brind,,* [1991] 1 A.C. 696 (H.L.) [hereinafter *Brind*]. Nevertheless, Brownlie considers English courts to have accepted the need to refer to relevant treaties even in the absence of ambiguity: Brownlie, *supra* note 70 at 48.

[99] *Schavernoch* v. *Foreign Claims Commission,* [1982] 1 S.C.R. 1092 at 1098 [hereinafter *Schavernoch*].

This passage has since been interpreted to remove grammatical ambiguity as a precondition for judicial consideration of treaties. In the Supreme Court decision in *National Corn Growers* v. *Canadian Import Tribunal*,[100] Gonthier J. considered Estey J.'s remarks in *Schavernoch* and observed:

> Though the language used by Estey J is perhaps not explicit, I do not understand his remarks to mean that consultation of the treaty is proper only where it appears that the text to be interpreted is ambiguous on its face ... The suggestion that recourse can be had to an underlying international agreement where a latent ambiguity can be asserted implies that there is no need to find a patent ambiguity *before* consultation of the agreement is possible. As a latent ambiguity must arise out of matters external to the text to be interpreted, such an international agreement may be used, as I have just suggested, at the preliminary stage of determining if an ambiguity exists.[101]

In this passage, Gonthier J. denies any need to find grammatical ambiguity in the enactment to be construed before consulting the relevant treaty.[102] He also affirms that ambiguity in an enactment can arise when the grammatical meaning is inconsistent with the apparent legislative intent, as evidenced by the existence of a treaty that the legislature is presumed not to intend to violate.[103] This is the correct approach. To use ambiguity as a trigger for judicial consideration of treaties, as suggested in the English cases, is to ask the courts to construe legislation without regard to the context in which it was enacted. That approach is detrimental to the principle of respect for international law, without advancing in any important way the principle of self-government. The Canadian approach, by contrast, shows greater respect for international law without at all prejudicing self-government.

If, having considered the enactment in the light of the relevant treaty, the interpreter finds that the enactment appears to violate a

---

100 *National Corn Growers* v. *Canadian Import Tribunal*, [1990] 2 S.C.R. 1324 [hereinafter *National Corn Growers*].

101 *Ibid.* at 1372-3 [original emphasis].

102 See Ruth Sullivan, *Driedger on the Construction of Statutes*, 3rd ed. (Toronto: Butterworth, 1994) at 462-3.

103 An example of this approach is *Minister of National Revenue* v. *Seaboard Lumber* (1994), 74 F.T.R. 231 (F.C.T.D.), in which Dubé J. held (at 239) that Section 2(3) of the Softwood Lumber Products Export Charge Act, R.S.C. 1985, c. 12 (3rd Supp.), which explicitly permitted judicial recourse to a 1986 memorandum between Canada and the United States for the purpose of "interpreting the schedule" of the act, did not preclude the application of the treaty presumption to the rest of the act.

Canadian treaty obligation, what should she do? Here again, the question of ambiguity arises. In the leading Canadian case on the treaty presumption, *Daniels* v. *White and the Queen*,[104] Hall J. described the role of ambiguity in the following way:

> It is argued that this is a case for the application of the rule of construction that Parliament is not presumed to legislate in breach of a treaty or in any manner inconsistent with the comity of nations and the established rules of international law. The rule does not, of course, come into operation if a statute is unambiguous for in that event its provisions must be followed even if they are contrary to the established rules of international law.[105]

Hall J. proceeded to cite similar language from Viscount Simonds in *Collco Dealings* v. *Inland Revenue Commissioners*:[106] "My Lords, the language that I have used is taken from a passage at p. 148 of the 10th edition of 'Maxwell on the Interpretation of Statutes' which ends with the sentence: 'But if the statute is unambiguous, its provisions must be followed even if they are contrary to international law.'"[107] These dicta are properly understood as affirmations of the sovereignty of our legislatures to violate international law. They hinge on the finding of unambiguous statutes. Thus, only when the statute is found to be unambiguous will the treaty presumption be rebutted and an internationally unlawful meaning be accorded to the provision. We have seen that ambiguity can arise from the grammatical meaning of a provision or from inconsistency with the grammatical meaning and the apparent legislative intent. Therefore, to rebut the presumption of international legality a provision must be both grammatically unambiguous and supported by proof of the legislature's intent to violate international law. The two go hand in hand, for the legislature must signal its intent to violate international law through unambiguous language. *Daniels* and *Collco* permit legislative assertion of self-government to the detriment of respect for international law, but only upon finding unmistakable intent and clear words.

The enactment's grammatical meaning may be clear, yet its intent to violate international law is either unclear or plainly lacking. Bad drafting can produce legislation that breaches Canadian treaty obligations by mistake. Bad politics can produce legislation that breaches Canadian treaty obligations by negligence. Evidence

---

[104] *Daniels* v. *White and the Queen*, [1968] S.C.R. 517 [hereinafter *Daniels*].

[105] *Ibid.* at 539.

[106] *Collco Dealings* v. *Inland Revenue Commissioner*, [1962] A.C. 1 (P.C.) at 19.

[107] *Ibid.*

of the legislature's lack of intent or equivocal intent to violate international law, in spite of its clear words, can be found in several places, including statements in Hansard indicating that a breach of international law was not contemplated by the legislature, a repugnance between the words of the enactment and other laws, and an error in the text (such as an omitted word) that plainly falsifies the legislature's intent. Where it is an error in the text, and not legislative intent to violate international law, that has produced the grammatically unambiguous meaning, courts should apply the treaty presumption to the enactment even though to do so would produce what Bennion calls a strained construction, meaning a construction that is different from the grammatical meaning.[108] For it is contrary to the principle of respect for international law, and bad policy besides, for a court to hold the legislature to the effects of drafting errors and, in doing so, place Canada in default of its international obligations. (However, for the sake of clarity, the legislature should amend the erroneous text even after its strained reading by an indulgent court.) The more difficult case is where the grammatical meaning is clearly in violation of international law, but where the legislature's intent, as evidenced by the consultation of Hansard and other statutes instead of by the wording of the enactment, is unclear. To apply the treaty presumption in this case and to produce a strained construction consistent with international law is arguably to usurp the legislative function contrary to the principle of self-government. Courts should do all they can to promote respect for international law, but there is only so much that they can do. Where an enactment's grammatical meaning is in clear violation of international law, but the legislature's intent as deduced from other sources is equivocal, self-government demands that courts take the grammatical meaning as a true expression of the legislature's intent. As useful as Hansard and other sources may be, the enactment itself is the pre-eminent statement of the legislature's intent and must be respected. If that statement is mistaken, the legislature can correct the mistake by amendment.

The reverse situation is when the legislature's intent to violate international law is demonstrable by other means, but the enactment by which it intended to do so is grammatically ambiguous. How should a court proceed? Should it read the enactment as it was intended despite the grammatical ambiguity or should it apply the treaty presumption? The underlying question is: What does it take

---

[108] See Bennion, *supra* note 95 at sections 157-8.

to rebut the presumption of international legality? I submit that unlawful intent should not suffice. The court should assert the principle of respect for international law by applying the presumption of international legality in order to favour the internationally lawful interpretation of the enactment. The legislature is undoubtedly sovereign to violate international law, yet it must do so in unmistakable language. It cannot leave the court to do its dirty work. It must give the court no other option. Finally, where there is no ambiguity in either the enactment's grammatical meaning or the legislature's intent as deduced by other means, parliamentary sovereignty demands that the court defer to the legislature. The presumption of international legality is rebutted by the legislature's assertion of the principle of self-government.

In summary, there is an ambiguity requirement attached to the treaty presumption in Canadian law, but it is not the one that was formulated in *Salomon, Brind,* and similar cases. There is no need to demonstrate grammatical ambiguity in a Canadian statute before resorting to a treaty to interpret it. There is, however, ambiguity needed before applying the treaty presumption. It may consist of grammatical ambiguity, ambiguous legislative intent, or both. To describe ambiguity as a condition precedent to the application of the treaty presumption is strictly accurate but misleading. A better description of this part of the reception system depicts consistency with international treaty obligations and respect for international law as the habitual interpretive policy of our courts. Legislation in violation of international law should therefore be subject to a "no ambiguity requirement," whereby the courts will decline to interpret a statute as contrary to international law unless it is unambiguously so.

NATURE OF THE LEGISLATION

A second question about the limits of the treaty presumption concerns the type of legislation to be interpreted. Can the treaty presumption be applied to any legislation or must it only be applied to legislation that is meant to implement a treaty? Murray Hunt argues that the true position of English law was expressed by A.V. Dicey, who maintained that all acts of Parliament are subject to the treaty presumption whether they are implementing acts or not.[109] This position was adopted in the nineteenth-century English case

---

[109] Hunt, *supra* note 36 at 23, citing A.V. Dicey, *supra* note 15 at 62-3.

of *Bloxam* v. *Favre*,[110] in which the court approved the statement in Maxwell's *Interpretation of Statutes* that "*every* statute is to be interpreted and applied, as far as its language admits, as not to be inconsistent with the comity of nations or with the established rules of international law."[111] The scope of the treaty presumption has not, it seems, been the subject of authoritative decision in Canada.[112] There are two possibilities: a strict application of the presumption (which would allow its application only to legislation that is meant to implement international treaty law in domestic law) and a liberal application of the presumption (which would permit its application to any statute).

Some support for a strict application of the presumption is suggested in Laskin C.J.'s judgment in *Capital Cities*. Faced with the submission that the Broadcasting Act should be interpreted in the light of the 1937 Inter-American Radio Communications Convention, the chief justice remarked that "the Convention ... is, in any event, nowhere mentioned in the *Broadcasting Act*."[113] This suggests that the treaty presumption is applicable only where statutes expressly implement treaty obligations. Similarly, the following comments by Gonthier J. in *National Corn Growers* v. *Canadian Import Tribunal* may also suggest a strict approach:

I note that it was not disputed in either of the courts below that the Canadian legislation was designed to implement Canada's *GATT* obligations. Since I am prepared to accept that such is the case, the only issue that

---

[110] *Bloxam, supra* note 93.

[111] *Bloxam* is cited approvingly in Sullivan, *supra* note 102 at 330 [emphasis added].

[112] *Re Canada Labour Code*, [1992] 2 S.C.R. 50, is cited in Sullivan, *supra* note 102 at 464, as an authority that holds that courts may rely on international instruments to interpret non-implementing legislation. While the case suggests a liberal approach, it does so in a roundabout way only. Sullivan's short discussion of this matter is the only one I am able to find by a Canadian author. No mention of the scope of the treaty presumption is made in the discussion of treaties in Hugh M. Kindred et at., *International Law Chiefly as Interpreted and Applied in Canada*, 5th ed. (Toronto: Emond Montgomery, 1993) at 168-95. Hogg's chapter on treaties considers the treaty presumption only briefly, without discussing its scope. See Hogg, *supra* note 11 at 294, n. 21 (section 11.4(a)). Emanuelli's discussion implies, but does not say expressly, that the treaty presumption applies only to incorporating legislation. See Emanuelli, *supra* note 4 at 95-6. An earlier article by Emanuelli treats the treaty presumption in passing but does not consider its scope. Claude Emanuelli and Stanislas Slosar, "L'application et l'interprétation des traités internationaux par le juge canadien" (1978) 13 R.J.T. 69.

[113] *Capital Cities, supra* note 19 at 173; Inter-American Radio Communications Convention, Can. T.S. 1938 No. 18; Broadcasting Act, R.S.C. 1970, c. B-11.

really needs to be discussed concerns the exact use which may be made of the *GATT* in interpreting s. 42 [of the Special Import Measures Act].[114]

However, a liberal approach to the treaty presumption also enjoys support from Canadian authorities. *Driedger* cites *Re Canada Labour Code,* in which La Forest J. seems to allow that an unimplemented treaty might influence the interpretation of the State Immunity Act, were it not for an article in a Canada-United States treaty to the effect that Canadian law should not derogate from American authority at a US military base located in Canada.[115] In *Re Mitchell and the Queen,* Linden J. held that the 1966 International Covenant on Civil and Political Rights "may ... be used to assist a court to interpret ambiguous provisions of a domestic statute, notwithstanding the fact that the Covenant has not been formally incorporated into the law of Canada, provided that the domestic statute does not contain express provisions contrary to or inconsistent with the Covenant."[116] Earlier authority to the same effect comes from the Court of Appeal for Ontario in *Arrow River.* In interpreting legislation that seemed to contravene the 1842 Ashburton Treaty, Riddell J.A., writing for the court, held that the treaty is "binding in honour upon her Majesty's successor, his present Majesty" and that

[c]onsequently, the Sovereign will not be considered as enacting anything that will conflict with his plain duty, unless the language employed in the statute is perfectly clear and explicit, admitting of no other interpretation ... The King cannot be thought of as violating his agreement with the other contracting Power; and, if the legislation can fairly be read in such a way as to reject any imputation of breaking faith, it must be so read.[117]

This honour-bound approach was noted, and appears to have been approved, by Lamont J. in the Supreme Court of Canada's consideration of the same case.[118] It is a somewhat old-fashioned, but nonetheless compelling, endorsement of an application of the treaty presumption to all statutes enacted by the Crown-in-Parliament.[119]

---

[114] *National Corn Growers, supra* note 100 at 1371.

[115] *Re Canada Labour Code,* [1992] 2 S.C.R. 50 at 90.

[116] *Re Mitchell and the Queen* (1983), 42 O.R. (2d) 481 (Ont. H.C.) at 493.

[117] *Arrow River & Tributaries Slide & Boom Company* v. *Pigeon Timber Company,* (1930-1) 66 O.L.R. 577 at 579.

[118] *Arrow River, supra* note 18 at 509.

[119] I find a similarity between the rhetoric of honour in this case and the language of the New Zealand Court of Appeal in *Tavita* v. *Minister of Immigration,*

Surely this liberal approach is the correct one. There is no reason
not to consider Canada's international obligations when interpreting domestic law, so long as the consideration is properly conducted.
A properly conducted consideration is one that recalls that the treaty
presumption is just that — a presumption, rebuttable by the legislature's clear and unmistakable intent. So long as the presumption is
not made unrebuttable, applying it to non-implementing legislation advances the principle of respect for international law without
in any way prejudicing the principle of self-government.

THE RELEVANCE OF CHRONOLOGY

A more difficult question is the application of the treaty presumption in cases where the legislation to be interpreted was
enacted prior to the assumption of the treaty obligation. This question leads us to a deeper question about the nature of the rule. Is
it, as I have described thus far and as it is generally depicted in the
case law, a presumption about legislative intent? Or is it rather a
free-standing rule of judicial interpretation and, therefore, not
reliant on legislative intent? If the treaty presumption is a presumption about the intent of the legislature, namely that it does not
intend to violate international law, then it is nonsensical to apply it
to a statute enacted before the Crown assumed the relevant treaty
obligation. This argument is especially true where the treaty in
question did not exist at the time of enactment. However, if the
treaty presumption operates independent of legislative intent
(except, of course, where that intent is clearly to violate international law), then the presumption applies to all legislation, regardless of its enactment date. This difficult issue is neglected in
Driedger[120] and in Bennion's admirable work,[121] but it has been considered, if only briefly, in the case law.

   The most fully reasoned — but perhaps also least satisfying —
discussion of the matter is *In re Californian Fig Syrup Company's
Trade-Mark*.[122] In March 1883, the 1883 International Convention

---

[1994] 2 N.Z.L.R. 257. Cooke P., as he then was, expressed his dissatisfaction
with an argument that the minister was entitled to ignore New Zealand's treaty
commitments, saying (at 266): "That is an unattractive argument, apparently
implying that New Zealand's adherence to the international instruments has
been at least party window-dressing."

120   Sullivan, *supra* note 102 at 298-9.

121   Bennion, *supra* note 95 at section 270.

122   *In Re Californian Fig Syrup Company's Trade-Mark* (1888), 40 Ch. D. 620.

for the Protection of Industrial Property was signed by several European states, excluding Great Britain. In August 1883, the United Kingdom enacted a statute, seemingly along lines similar to the convention, whereby foreigners could apply for the protection of their trademarks in Great Britain subject to certain administrative requirements. Then, in March 1884, the UK government acceded to the convention. The Californian Fig Syrup Company registered a trademark in the United States in 1885. In February 1888, the company applied to register their trademark in the United Kingdom under the provisions of the UK act and the convention. The comptroller-general denied registration on the ground that the act required that such applications be made within four months of registration in their home state — a requirement not found in the convention. The company argued that the act should be read "in such a way as to make it harmonize with the provisions of the Convention."[123] Stirling J. rejected the argument. He said:

Certainly, according to my construction of the Act, the Act does not afford the means of carrying out the article, and it will be for her Majesty's Government to consider, and seeing the Attorney-General here, I have no doubt that they will consider, what legislative steps ought to be taken to give effect to that article, if necessary. But with that I have nothing to do. I have simply to consider this question; dealing as I am with, and being bound by, a statute of this realm, whether I can give it a different interpretation from that which I should otherwise give it, simply because at the date of the passing of the Act, the Convention had been entered into between certain foreign states, and it was within the bounds of possibility that her Majesty might afterwards accede to it, and several years afterward, in point of fact, her Majesty did accede to it. I am of opinion that I cannot do so.[124]

This case is difficult. At one extreme, there is the unsatisfying result of denying the company registration of its trademark and forcing the legislature to amend an act that, it would seem, was brought forward in contemplation of recent international activity on the subject. Stirling J. exaggerates in saying that it was merely "within the bounds of possibility that her Majesty might afterwards accede to [the Convention], and several years afterward, in point of fact, her Majesty did accede to it," for the United Kingdom acceded only nine months after passing the act. At the other extreme, however, is the proposition that the treaty presumption

---

[123] *Ibid.* at 624.

[124] *Ibid.* at 627-8.

can in effect disapply a statutory requirement that applications be brought within four months of registration in the applicant's home country. This would be a strained construction (indeed, a very strained construction) of the statute, as described earlier. Adding to the difficulty is the chronology of events. While it is arguable that the treaty presumption should not apply to statutes enacted prior to binding treaty action by the Crown, on the facts of this case it seems entirely possible that Parliament had the recently established convention in its contemplation. Yet if that is so, why did it enact a four-month limitation that is not found in the treaty?

The remaining cases on the chronological limits of the treaty presumption consider the problem more briefly. In *Ahmad* v. *ILEA*, Scarman L.J. (as he then was) held, in dissent, that Section 30 of the Education Act 1944 was to be interpreted in light of the international human rights obligations subsequently assumed by the United Kingdom: "[W]e have to construe and apply section 30 not against the background of the law and society of 1944 but in a multi-racial society which has accepted international obligations and enacted statutes designed to eliminate discrimination on grounds of race, religion, colour or sex."[125] This approach was implicitly rejected by Lord Lowry in *R.* v. *Brown*, who, in discussing the applicability of Article 8 of the European Convention on Human Rights, observed that the convention had not been implemented and that there was no "post-Convention" legislation to be construed according to the treaty presumption.[126] Finally, the only Canadian case that I am aware of on this point is the Supreme Court's recent decision in *Baker*.[127] In this case, which is discussed at length later in this article, the court effectively applied the treaty presumption to Section 114(2) of the Immigration Act. The treaty in question was this 1989 Convention on the Rights of the Child, which was ratified by Canada in 1992. The act, by contrast, was enacted in 1977.[128] L'Heureux-Dubé J., writing for the majority, did not acknowledge the chronological problem explicitly. Yet she may have done so implicitly by relying in her reasons on a non-binding,

---

125 *Ahmad* v. *ILEA*, [1978] Q.B. 36 (Eng. C.A.) at 48D.

126 *R.* v. *Brown*, [1994] 1 A.C. 212 (H.L.) at 256.

127 *Baker*, *infra* note 133.

128 Immigration Act, R.S.C. 1985, c. I-2. Section 1 gives the short title of the act as "Immigration Act, 1976-7."

but much earlier, text, namely the preamble to the 1959 United Nations Declaration of the Rights of the Child.[129]

No clear rule about chronology and the treaty presumption arises from these cases. The judges in *California Fig* and *Brown* proceeded from the notion that the treaty presumption is to be understood strictly as a presumption about the legislature's historical intent. The conception of the judicial role suggested by this approach is the traditional one in Westminster-model constitutions, namely that it is the duty of the court to carry out the legislature's intent. In contrast, the approaches of Scarman L.J. and L'Heureux-Dubé J. in *Ahmed* and *Baker* respectively suggest that the treaty presumption is a rule of judicial interpretation that holds, in the language of *Bloxam* v. *Favre*, that "*every* statute is to be interpreted and applied, as far as its language admits, as not to be inconsistent with the comity of nations or the established rules of international law."[130] This approach sets legislative intent partially aside. It does not go so far as to ignore clear legislative intent to violate international law, for legislatures remain sovereign, but it does set aside the absence of legislative intent where that intent was lacking only because the treaty in question was not yet in force. The conception of the judicial role suggested by this approach moves somewhat away from that of carrying out Parliament's intent and towards the conception described by Lord Denning M.R. in *Corocraft* v. *Pan American Airways*: "[I]t is the duty of these courts to construe our legislation so as to be in conformity with international law and not in conflict with it."[131]

What, then, is the nature of the treaty presumption? I suggest that the treaty presumption, and the presumption of international legality in general, is more than simply a means of giving effect to legislative intent. The presumption is a characterization of that intent: that it is respectful of international law, that it strives to assure and maintain the place of the state in the international community, and, ultimately, that it is lawful in the sense of being consistent with

---

[129] Declaration of the Rights of the Child, 20 November 1959, G.A. Res. 1386(XIV). The status of the declaration as a non-binding, but morally forceful, resolution — as contrasted with the legally binding 1989 convention — is discussed in Geraldine Van Bueren, *The International Law on the Rights of the Child* (Dordrecht: Martinus Nijhoff, 1995) at 12.

[130] *Bloxam, supra* note 93 at 107 [emphasis added].

[131] *Corocraft* v. *Pan American Airways*, [1968] 3 W.L.R. 1273 (Eng. C.A.) at 1281.

international law. The presumption of international legality is a claim about what legislation should be. There is, however, a parallel and sometimes conflicting claim that our courts must heed. This claim is not about what legislation should be but rather about what people should be — that they should be self-governing.

A proper balancing of these two principles gives the following answer to the chronology question. Courts should apply the treaty presumption without regard to chronology in every case where they can do so without harm to the principle of self-government. That principle imposes this limit on the application of the presumption: it must not be applied so as to liberate the executive from the implementation requirement. Legislation that predates newly acquired treaty obligations may be read as being consistent with those obligations so long as such an interpretation does not remove the need for the government to seek implementation of those aspects of the obligation that require significant changes to Canadian law. The implementation requirement may be the most important assertion of the principle of self-government in the reception system. So long as treaty-making remains a prerogative of the Crown, treaties cannot be self-executing in Canadian law consistently with self-government. For, as we have seen, the Crown is not a fitting source of law. It lacks the features of representation, deliberation, and consent that are the criteria of a self-governing law-maker. To eliminate the implementation requirement, even if only with respect to treaties touching matters that are already the subject of existing legislation, would serve further to bolster the already considerable powers of the federal executive[132] at the expense of democratically elected legislatures. In particular, the federal principle might suffer under too rigorous an application of the treaty presumption to provincial statutes, given that treaties are concluded at the federal level (albeit with varying levels of provincial participation). So long as the treaty presumption is applied in a manner that does not harm the principle of self-government, there should be no objection to applying it irrespective of chronology.

UNIMPLEMENTED TREATIES AND STATUTORY DISCRETIONS

A final consideration is the applicability of the treaty presumption to statutes that vest ministers, tribunals, or other administrative

---

[132] On the concentration of executive power in the Canadian system, see Donald J. Savoie, *Governing from the Centre: The Concentration of Power in Canadian Politics* (Toronto: University of Toronto Press, 1999).

decision-makers with discretionary powers. It is uncontentious that statutory discretions are interpreted and controlled by courts applying the Charter and the rules of natural justice and procedural fairness expressed in administrative law. What is at issue is how ratified but unimplemented treaties interact with statutory discretions: do such treaties take their place beside recognized constitutional and administrative law limitations on the exercise of discretionary power or is such use of unimplemented treaties a violation of the implementation requirement and thus unconstitutional? This question is the heart of the issue, but it also oversimplifies a complex problem. A more subtle inquiry is needed to determine the proper place of the treaty presumption in construing administrative discretions.

The Crown Is a Source of Law

Throughout this article, and particularly in the discussion of chronology immediately above, we have relied upon the rule, founded on the principle of self-government, that the Crown is not a source of law. This rule is what necessitates the implementation of treaties: were the Crown an unobjectionable lawmaker, there would be no implementation requirement and, therefore, no treaty presumption. However, since the executive is considered an objectionable legislator in our parliamentary form of government, the treaty presumption must not be applied in those cases where to do so, would give legal effect to unimplemented treaties and thus render the Crown a source of law. This, at least, is the orthodoxy. It is arguable, however, that to apply the treaty presumption to a statute *always* gives legal effect to unimplemented treaties and, therefore, always violates the implementation requirement and the bar on executive legislation.

Consider the application of the treaty presumption in the case of a statute enacted after the federal government's ratification of a treaty. A court, confronted with two possible interpretations of the statute, one of which is inconsistent with the treaty, rules out the inconsistent interpretation by applying the treaty presumption. The portrayal of legislative intent here may be entirely accurate, for the legislature may have had the treaty in its actual contemplation and may truly have sought to legislate consistently with it. It is also possible that the legislature did not have the treaty in its actual contemplation but that it nonetheless had no intent to violate the treaty. In this case, the portrayal of legislative intent demanded by the treaty presumption is slightly further removed from reality: the legislature did not actually intend to legislate consistently with Canada's international obligations, but then neither did it actually intend to violate them. It simply did not consider the matter. We can agree that to apply the treaty presumption in both of these cases is entirely appropriate. Yet it would be disingenuous to say that the presumption's application in these cases does not in some sense change the law, for it rules out otherwise viable constructions of the law on the ground that they are inconsistent with an un-implemented treaty. Therefore, the Crown's act of ratifying the treaty is given a certain legal consequence by the application of the treaty presumption. To this extent, minor though it is, the treaty presumption may be said to set aside the implementation require-ment and violate the constitutional rule that the Crown is not a source of law.

Now consider the application of the treaty presumption to a statute enacted before the ratification of a treaty. Once again, a court confronted with various possible interpretations of the act rules out those that are inconsistent with the supervening treaty. In this case, the portrayal of legislative intent demanded by the treaty presumption is wholly fictitious: the legislature did not have the treaty in its contemplation because Canada was not bound by it at the time of enactment. The application of the treaty presumption in this case is not based on historical legislative intent but rather on a policy of the court to interpret Canadian law consistently, where possible, with international law. Here, the argument that the treaty presumption is a violation of the bar on executive legislation and a flouting of the implementation requirement is very strong, for the legal effect of the statute in question is being determined by the court's reference to the Crown's subsequent act of treaty ratifica-tion. To apply the treaty presumption in this case is to confer upon the executive some power unilaterally to make or amend law.

This analysis reveals a conceptual weakness in the statements — found not only in English and Canadian case law but also through-out this article — that treaties are not self-executing and the Crown is not a source of law. These statements are revealed as simplifica-tions of the effect of unimplemented treaties in domestic law. For most purposes, these simplifications are useful and accurate depic-tions of the law. Yet the close examination of the treaty presump-tion that I now propose requires a more subtle vocabulary.

Courts and commentators justify the treaty presumption as con-sistent with the bar on executive legislation by saying that it involves no application of treaty law in domestic law but rather serves only as a guide to legislative intent. On those occasions where courts have refused to apply the treaty presumption, insisting that the treaty at issue must be implemented by legislation before it can have the effect that is pleaded for, they declare that the Crown is not a source of law, that treaties are not self-executing, and that the treaty presumption involves no importation of international law into the domestic field. Yet the critique given above has revealed that every application of the treaty presumption involves some breach, however small, of the bar on executive legislation. How then are we to make sense of refusals by the courts to apply the treaty presumption in some cases?

The answer, I suggest, is that cases in which courts consent to the treaty presumption and cases in which they refuse it are not different in nature but only in degree. There is a sense in which all applications of the treaty presumption amount to recognition of a certain power in the Crown to legislate without Parliament in violation of the implementation requirement. However, these violations of the bar on executive legislation are so minor that we do not complain of them. Courts and commentators have not decried the treaty presumption as executive legislation, even though it amounts to that, because the legislative effect of applying the presumption is usually minimal. It is only when the application of the presumption would serve to grant significant legal consequence to the Crown's act of ratification that courts and commentators resort to the constitutional injunction against executive legislation. Yet what constitutes a significant legal consequence? How do courts know when to insist upon implementation and when to apply the treaty presumption? The test is not as simple as "Does this application of the treaty presumption set aside the implementation requirement?" for, as the earlier analysis shows, the treaty presumption always does that to some extent. Instead, the test is provided by the principle of self-government: Does this application of the treaty presumption, in support of the principle of respect for international law, offend the principle of self-government? Where the treaty presumption furthers respect for international law without detriment to self-government, as is most often the case, the courts apply it and do not characterize its application as a breach of the bar on executive legislation. Where, however, the treaty presumption furthers respect for international law at the expense of self-government, the courts insist upon self-government by refusing to apply the presumption and requiring legislative implementation of the treaty.

The case in which the truth of these claims is most clearly revealed
is the landmark decision of the Supreme Court of Canada in *Baker
v. Canada (Minister of Citizenship and Immigration)*.[133]

The Revelations of Baker

Mavis Baker was a Jamaican citizen who arrived in Canada in
1981 and overstayed her visitor's visa by eleven years. Having been
ordered to be deported, she sought to apply for permanent residence in Canada. Normally these applications must be made from
outside the country, but Section 114(2) of the Immigration Act[134]
grants the minister of immigration a discretion, on "humanitarian
and compassionate" grounds, to allow applications from within
Canada. The minister refused to exercise her discretion in Baker's
favour. Baker sought judicial review, arguing, *inter alia,* that the
decision unreasonably failed to give sufficient weight to the interests of her Canadian-born children as required by the 1989 Convention on the Rights of the Child.[135] Canada is a party to that
treaty, but neither Parliament nor the provincial Legislatures have
implemented it. (Indeed, as was noted earlier, Parliament declined
to implement it when given the opportunity by Mr. Axworthy's bill.)

Baker was unsuccessful both in the Trial Division of the Federal
Court and in the Federal Court of Appeal. However, the majority
of the Supreme Court of Canada allowed the appeal. They found
that notes made by the decision-maker (an immigration officer
under the minister) gave rise to a reasonable apprehension of bias.
Furthermore, they held that the decision unreasonably neglected
international law and was thus an unlawful exercise of the minister's discretion. The path to this conclusion is clear but winding.
First, L'Heureux-Dubé J., for the majority, declared, in a passage
that is bound to be of lasting significance for Canadian administrative law, that "though discretionary decisions will generally be given
considerable respect, that discretion must be exercised in accordance with the boundaries imposed in the statute, the principles of
the rule of law, the principles of administrative law, the fundamental values of Canadian society, and the principles of the *Charter*."[136]
Second, having determined the appropriate standard of review to

---

[133] *Baker v. Canada (Minister of Citizenship and Immigration),* [1999] 2 S.C.R. 817
[hereinafter *Baker*].

[134] Immigration Act, *supra* note 128.

[135] Convention on the Rights of the Child, *supra* note 50.

[136] *Baker, supra* note 133 at 820.

be reasonableness *simpliciter*, the learned judge held that the decision of the immigration officer was faulty for being "inconsistent with the values underlying the grant of the discretion."[137] In order to determine what those values are, the decision-maker was not to look solely to Section 114(2), which Strayer J.A. in the Federal Court of Appeal characterized as conferring upon the minister "a virtually unfettered discretion."[138] Rather, in the third step of her reasoning, L'Heureux-Dubé J. held that "[c]hildren's rights, and attention to their interests, are central humanitarian and compassionate values in Canadian society,"[139] and that this fact was revealed by the following "indications" of the importance of children's rights and interests in Canadian society: the objectives of the act (as set out in Section 3), the minister's guidelines, and international law (particularly the 1989 Convention on the Rights of the Child).

The majority's use of an unimplemented treaty as an element in defining the extent of the discretion granted by the statute amounts to an application of the treaty presumption: the discretion conferred by the statute is presumed to be consistent with the requirements of international law. L'Heureux-Dubé J. did not describe her invocation of the Convention on the Rights of the Child as an application of this canon of construction.[140] Yet, there is no reason to distinguish *Baker's* use of unimplemented treaties from the ordinary presumption of international legality. Indeed, in the recent decisions of *R* v. *Sharpe*[141] and *Spraytech* v. *Hudson*,[142] L'Heureux-Dubé J. cited *Baker* as an example of the application of the treaty presumption.

---

[137] *Ibid.* at 859.

[138] *Baker* v. *Canada (Minister of Citizenship and Immigration)*, [1997] 2 F.C. 127 (F.C.A.) at 141 [hereinafter *Baker* F.C.].

[139] *Baker, supra* note 133 at 860.

[140] Why she did not do so is an interesting question. One reason may be that the applicability of the treaty presumption to statutory grants of discretion has been a matter of controversy in other Commonwealth jurisdictions. By not invoking the presumption explicitly, L'Heureux-Dubé J. may have hoped (in vain) to sidestep the debate. Another possible reason is the chronology problem: the act in question preceded the Convention on the Rights of the Child by over a decade.

[141] *R.* v. *Sharpe*, [2001] S.C.C. 2 at para. 175, per L'Heureux-Dubé, Gonthier, and Bastarache JJ., citing Sullivan, *supra* note 102 at 330.

[142] *114957 Canada Ltée (Spraytech, Société d'arrosage)* v. *Hudson (Town)* [2001] S.C.C. 40 [hereinafter *Spraytech*] at para. 30 per L'Heureux-Dubé, Gonthier, Bastarache, and Arbour JJ., again citing Sullivan, *supra* note 102 at 330.

In arriving at their result, the majority in *Baker* disavowed any intention of upsetting the established rule that treaties are not part of Canadian law unless implemented by statute.[143] As was noted earlier in this article, L'Heureux-Dubé J. affirmed the implementation requirement, citing *Francis* v. *The Queen* and *Capital Cities*. In the majority's view, the use of an unimplemented treaty in this context did not violate or circumvent the implementation requirement. This is not to say, however, that the majority's use of the Convention on the Rights of the Child did not grant it some legal consequence. While the majority denied that they had set aside the implementation requirement, they did not deny having recognized domestic legal consequences arising from the unimplemented treaty. Nor could they plausibly do so once they had held that the treaty was an indicator of the fundamental values of Canadian society underlying and, therefore, controlling the grant of discretion. Herein lie the revelations of *Baker*. The majority in *Baker* must be understood as holding that the implementation requirement and the self-government principle that it expresses are not necessarily inconsistent with the recognition of some degree of legal effect in unimplemented treaties. Rather than insist upon the simplistic orthodoxy that unimplemented treaties are of no legal consequence, a court should determine the interpretive significance of an unimplemented treaty on a case-by-case basis. The test to apply in determining whether to invoke the treaty presumption in a given case is not, "Is this a violation of the implementation requirement?" for *Baker* makes clear that the answer is "not necessarily." Rather, there is a further test that I have expressed as, "Does the use of the unimplemented treaty here violate the principle of self-government?" These revelations bring Canadian law into line with the unorthodox, but seemingly correct, proposition stated earlier, that the Crown is, in fact, a source of law, if only to a degree that is consistent with the principle of self-government.

To say that *Baker* reveals the true nature of the treaty presumption is not necessarily to say that the case itself was rightly decided. Michael Taggart has observed that there are "several good constitutional and policy reasons which underpin" the implementation requirement, "including separation of powers and (in federations, like Australia and Canada) distribution of legislative competence."[144] Whether *Baker* was for some reason an inappropriate case

---

[143] *Baker, supra* note 133 at 861.

[144] Michael Taggart, "Legitimate Expectation and Treaties in the High Court of Australia" (1996) 112 L.Q.R. 50 at 53.

for the application of the treaty presumption must be determined by testing its results against the principle of self-government. This is the purpose of the next two subsections. The question in both is whether the results produced by applying the treaty presumption to a grant of statutory discretion violate the principle of self-government and therefore demand the rebuttal of the treaty presumption. There are, as Taggart notes, two issues: the separation of powers and the distribution of powers.

Baker *and the Separation of Powers*

I have suggested that the test for determining whether the treaty presumption is rebutted in a particular case is the consistency of its application in the case at bar with the principle of self-government. That this is so can be seen in the dissenting reasons of Iacobucci J. in *Baker*. His Lordship, with the concurrence of Cory J., wrote:

> In my view, one should proceed with caution in deciding matters of this nature, lest we adversely affect the balance maintained by our Parliamentary tradition, or inadvertently grant the executive the power to bind citizens without the necessity of involving the legislative branch. I do not share my colleague's confidence that the Court's precedent in *Capital Cities . . .* survives intact following the adoption of a principle of law which permits reference to an unincorporated convention during the process of statutory interpretation. Instead, the result will be that the appellant is able to achieve indirectly what cannot be achieved directly, namely, to give force and effect within the domestic legal system to international obligations undertaken by the executive alone that have yet to be subject to the democratic will of Parliament.[145]

This passage is redolent with the language of self-government. His Lordship affirms, in his reference to *Capital Cities*, that the Crown is not a source of law. He goes further and characterizes the executive as an inappropriate and ill-suited law-maker in contrast to democratic legislatures. In reasserting the legislature's monopoly on law-making, Iacobucci J. gives voice to self-government's creed that laws are properly made by a parliamentary process. While his Lordship's wording is somewhat strong, he must not be understood as rejecting the application of the treaty presumption altogether. Rather, he objects to its application in this instance. His reasoning can be understood as follows: he applies the self-government test to this proposed application of the treaty presumption, finds that it fails the test and, therefore, declines to use the treaty to construe

---

[145] *Baker, supra* note 133 at 865-6.

the statute.[146] By contrast, the majority found this application of the presumption to be consistent with self-government and therefore did not hesitate to apply it in the ordinary way.

Iacobucci J. is not the first judge to express self-government-based concerns about the application of the treaty presumption to statutory grants of discretion. In *Ashby* v. *Minister of Immigration*,[147] the New Zealand Court of Appeal was asked to declare invalid a decision by the minister of immigration to issue temporary entry permits to apartheid South Africa's Springbok rugby team. The minister's power was a discretionary one under Section 14 of the Immigration Act 1964. The appellants argued alternatively that the minister's discretion could only be lawfully exercised in conformity with the 1965 International Convention on the Elimination of All Forms of Racial Discrimination or that the minister was bound to take the convention into account and had failed to do so. The convention was implemented in New Zealand by the Race Relations Act 1971 but not by any amendment of the Immigration Act. The court unanimously dismissed the appeal in separate judgments. The decision of Richardson J. most resembles that of the dissent in *Baker*, for he held that to limit the minister's discretion by resorting to the treaty "would amount to legislating rather than interpreting"[148] and was therefore impermissible. He gave three reasons. First, he noted that the Immigration Act provided categories of persons to whom the minister may not issue temporary permits but that the rugby team did not fall into any of them. Second, he pointed to a chronology problem. The section in issue was adopted prior to New Zealand's ratification of the treaty. (As we have seen,

---

[146] This is not to say that a judge, considering Ms. Baker's claim that the decision-maker must treat the best interests of her children as a primary consideration, must refuse that argument merely because it has been the subject matter of an unimplemented treaty. The claim is simply that a judge must not arrive at this conclusion by giving such a degree of legal effect to the unimplemented treaty. She might arrive at this conclusion in other ways. She could, for instance, determine that the common law requires decision-makers to treat the best interests of the child as a primary consideration. In *Minister for Immigration and Ethnic Affairs* v. *Teoh*, (1995), 69 A.L.J.R. 423, three of five justices of the High Court of Australia (Mason C.J., Deane and Gaudron JJ.) advanced this proposition in *obiter dicta*. (A judge arriving at this conclusion must go on to conclude that this common law principle has not been displaced by the statute in question.)

[147] *Ashby* v. *Minister of Immigration*, [1981] 1 N.Z.L.R. 222 (N.Z.C.A) [hereinafter *Ashby*].

[148] *Ibid.* at 229.

this fact alone should not be dispositive but may support a finding that the treaty presumption is rebutted.) Finally, his Lordship observed that when Parliament enacted legislation to implement the convention it did not amend the Immigration Act.

Another example of the self-government test in action is the English case of *Brind*.[149] The case concerned a statutory discretion to prohibit the broadcast of certain matters. The UK home secretary issued directives, pursuant to a discretion that he enjoyed under the Broadcasting Act 1981 and the British Broadcasting Corporation's licence, prohibiting the broadcast of statements by representatives of proscribed organizations in Northern Ireland (notably the Irish Republican Army and loyalist paramilitaries). Journalists argued that this was a breach of the right to freedom of expression recognized by the 1950 European Convention on Human Rights — a treaty to which the United Kingdom is a party but which, at the time, had not been implemented into UK law. The journalists admitted that the convention did not apply directly in the United Kingdom. Yet they argued that courts interpreting the discretion must presume that Parliament intended that it be exercised within the limits of the convention. The appeal was unanimously dismissed. Lord Bridge of Harwich declared that

[w]hen confronted with a simple choice between two possible interpretations of some specific statutory provision, the presumption whereby the courts prefer that which avoids conflict between our domestic legislation and our international treaty obligations is a mere canon of construction which involves no importation of international law into the domestic field ... When Parliament has been content for so long to leave those who complain that their Convention rights have been infringed to seek their remedy in Strasbourg, it would be surprising suddenly to find that the judiciary had, without Parliament's aid, the means to incorporate the Convention into such an important area of domestic law and I cannot escape the conclusion that this would be a judicial usurpation of the legislative function.[150]

Here, as in Iacobucci J.'s dissent in *Baker,* the application of the treaty presumption is rejected in terms evocative of the principle of self-government. Lord Bridge describes the treaty presumption as a mere canon of construction, although, as we have seen, it must be more than that. He affirms Parliament's role in implementing legislation and strives to defend its legislative function from usurpation. The usurpation he describes is judicial not executive,

[149] *Brind, supra* note 98.

[150] *Ibid.* at 748.

but it amounts to the same thing (for the plaintiffs sought to rely not merely on human rights in the abstract but also on human rights obligations undertaken by the Crown).

The methodology in *Ashby, Brind,* and the dissent in *Baker* can be understood in the following way. In each case, the judge began with the treaty presumption's rule that statutes should be read as presumptively consistent with the state's international obligations. Each judgment appears to accept the existence of the presumption and agree with it in principle. Yet, in each case, the judges declined to apply the presumption for fear of violating the principle of self-government, expressed in these cases as respect for the separation of powers: the Crown concludes treaties, Parliament implements them, and the judiciary looks to the legislature, rather than to the executive, to know what the law is. These judgments, like that of L'Heureux-Dubé J. for the majority in *Baker,* reveal that the treaty presumption is rebutted where its application in the case at bar is inconsistent with the principle of self-government.

Knowing that the presumption is rebuttable on the ground of self-government is helpful but hardly dispositive. As we have seen, the majority and dissent in *Baker* divided on the proper result of the self-government test. The majority found no violation of the separation of powers doctrine, or at least no sufficiently important violation to rebut the application of the presumption. By contrast, the dissent viewed this application of the treaty presumption as a threat to the balance of executive and legislative power in Canada's parliamentary tradition. Both sides of the debate agreed upon the importance of the separation of powers and, by extension, of the self-government concerns that inform it. The difference of opinion turned not on the significance of the self-government principle but on the degree of zeal with which courts should vindicate it. In my view, courts should take the following factors into consideration.

First, a court should consider the extent to which applying the treaty presumption to the case at bar will relieve the executive of the need to seek implementation of the treaty by Parliament or the provincial Legislatures. At the heart of the separation of powers doctrine is the conviction that the only proper way to subject self-governing peoples to law is through the representative, deliberative, participatory, consensual, and public law-making procedures of the parliamentary process. The implementation requirement vindicates our commitment to this oldest of constitutional ideals. Yet, as we have seen, there is a sense in which the treaty presumption sets aside the implementation requirement, if only to a minor extent. A court faced with a contentious application of the treaty presumption must balance due awareness of the constitutional importance of the implementation requirement with a realistic assessment of the extent to which the presumption's application in the case at bar would set the requirement aside. A workable rule of thumb may be that a court should decline to apply the treaty presumption only in those cases where to apply it would wholly or significantly remove the necessity of implementing legislation.

A second consideration should be the content of the treaty obligation under consideration. Treaty provisions of a purposive, interpretive, or general nature will often be more susceptible to judicial application by means of the treaty presumption than specific, particular, or detailed commitments, which will usually require implementing legislation to be given domestic legal effect. The same reasoning suggests that international human rights guarantees, which are frequently drafted as broad statements of principle rather than as specific requirements, will generally be more amenable to application through the treaty presumption than more narrowly drawn international commitments.[151] This second point is really an elaboration of the first point, namely that courts should refrain from applying the treaty presumption in cases where to do so would make implementation of the treaty significantly unnecessary.

Finally, courts should be cognizant of the respective roles of legislatures and the judiciary in the Canadian reception system. The system assigns the task of vindicating the principle of self-government to Parliament and the provincial Legislatures in exercise of their sovereignty to legislate in violation of international law and their discretion as to whether, and to what extent, to implement treaty obligations incurred by the executive. In contrast, the role of asserting the principle of respect for international law is confided in the judiciary. It is the judiciary that assures the incorporation of customary international law by the common law. And it is the judiciary that applies the treaty presumption to legislative acts. We have seen that the reception system works by balancing the twin imperatives of self-government and respect for international law. Courts risk upsetting that balance when they take it upon themselves to vindicate

---

[151] I offer this reasoning as a generalization only. It is clear that a human rights instrument may contain specific provisions requiring explicit legislative implementation. Likewise, other international instruments may contain broadly phrased commitments, such as the national treatment obligations found in many investment treaties.

self-government rather than leave that responsibility to the legislature. This is not to say that the treaty presumption is unrebuttable. Rather, it is to say that courts should depart from the principle of respect for international law that founds the treaty presumption only where to do otherwise would jeopardize the self-governing character of our parliamentary and constitutional arrangements.

Applying these considerations to *Baker* suggests, in my view, that the case was rightly decided on the separation of powers matter. The dissent was right to notice the separation of powers problems arising from applying the treaty presumption to a grant of statutory discretion. Yet the dissent gave these problems too much weight in this instance. The treaty presumption clearly gave real legal significance to the unimplemented 1989 Convention on the Rights of the Child, by requiring the minister to exercise her discretion consistently with the values it discloses, yet it cannot be said that this holding wholly or significantly removed the necessity of implementing legislation. At most, the legal effect of the majority's judgment was to render the best interests of the child a primary, but not necessarily a determinative, consideration for decision-makers who are acting on humanitarian and compassionate grounds under the Immigration Act. The convention's many other substantive and procedural guarantees, some of which are remarkably far-reaching, are untouched by *Baker.* The majority relied only on the convention's broad statements of principle and not on its more specific requirements. The limited degree of quasi-implementation effected by the majority in *Baker* demonstrates due respect for Canada's international obligations under the convention without threatening or violating our self-government.

To say that *Baker* was rightly decided on the separation of powers issue is not, in my opinion, to say as a general principle that unimplemented treaty obligations may be used to control the exercise of statutory discretions. What *Baker* reveals about this larger question is that it cannot be answered so sweepingly but must be determined in each case by applying the self-government test described in this article. Thus, while *Baker* is highly revealing methodologically, its precedential value on this point may be more limited.

Baker *and the Division of Powers*

Federalism is not a necessary condition of self-government. Many self-governing peoples live in unitary regimes. In Canada, however, federalism has been considered a precondition of our union from the very outset. Though federalism is not a necessary condition of self-government in general, it may very well be a necessary condition of self-government for us. It is the defining feature of our written constitutional arrangements. The Supreme Court of Canada has described federalism as "the lodestar by which the courts have been guided" in interpreting the constitution.[152] The Supreme Court in *Baker* gave no consideration to the implications of the majority's judgment for federalism.[153] Yet these implications are worth thinking about.

The power to conclude treaties rests with the federal executive.[154] Agreements concluded by the federal government bind not only itself but also Canada as a whole, for it is a rule of international law that a state may not plead its constitutional arrangements to evade its international obligations.[155] Similarly, the treaty presumption applies to all Canadian statutes be they federal or provincial in origin. Moreover, it is presumed that all Canadian legislatures intend not to violate international law. Applying the presumption to provincial statutes does not violate the federal principle, even though the treaty in question was concluded at the federal level, so long as the presumption involves no significant incursion of the federal power into the provincial sphere. The question is what constitutes a significant incursion.

In my view, the test for a possible violation of the division of powers ought to be self-government, just as it is when considering a possible violation of the separation of powers. The ultimate concern in both cases is the same, namely that only a properly constituted body should have the power to make our laws. In the context of the separation of powers, that body is the legislature rather than the executive. In the context of the division of powers, that body is whichever legislature enjoys jurisdiction under the Constitution Act 1867. The object of the self-government test is to prevent the treaty presumption from being applied to circumvent the division of powers. Unlike the separation of powers, which remains largely a feature of the unwritten constitution, the division of powers is entrenched constitutional law. Entrenchment may leave the courts somewhat less flexibility in applying the self-government test. The

---

[152] *Re Secession of Quebec, supra* note 86 at 251.

[153] However, Strayer J.A. in the Federal Court of Appeal raised federalism concerns. See *Baker* F.C., *supra* note 138 at 141.

[154] Subject to the observations made in note 16 in this article.

[155] See Jennings and Watts, *supra* note 4 at 84-5.

court should find the treaty presumption to be rebutted in those cases where to apply it would permit a federally concluded treaty, the subject matter of which falls within an area of provincial jurisdiction, to be used to oblige delegates of provincial statutory discretions (from ministers to tribunals) to act consistently with that federally made treaty or be found *ultra vires.*

As in separation of powers cases, the self-government test will not always give the same result. Rather, it must be worked out case by case. It is too sweeping to draw from *Baker* the conclusion that all unimplemented treaties express values underlying a provincial Legislature's grants of discretion. This claim is improbable as a matter of politics. The federal government and the provinces often have divergent views, and the one level of government may act without awareness of, or interest in, the other's perspective. Politics aside, it would be exceedingly difficult to reconcile our constitution's federalism with a federal capacity to determine, in every instance, the limits of a provincial decision-maker's discretion by exercising the treaty power. On the other hand, it is equally sweeping to declare that an unimplemented treaty can never be used to control the exercise of a provincial decision-maker's discretion. Provinces, though not major players on the international scene, do not entirely disregard international affairs.[156] A provincial Legislature might enact a grant of statutory discretion and, while not explicitly providing that its ambit is curtailed by Canada's international obligations, nevertheless intend that to be the case. Furthermore, the historic human rights guarantees that figure in some of the twentieth century's leading international instruments do not lend themselves to a division between the federal and provincial orders of government. Such an instrument as the 1966 International Covenant on Civil and Political Rights[157] should not be made off-limits to courts construing provincial statutory discretions simply

---

[156] See generally "Numéro spécial: les politiques extérieures des états non souverains: convergences et divergences" (1994) 25(3) Études internationales; A. Jacomy-Millette, Françoise Coulombe, and James Lee, "Canadian Provinces and Foreign Relations," background paper BP-97E of the Library of Parliament Research Branch, revised December 1990; Tom Keating and Don Munton, eds., *The Provinces and Canadian Foreign Policy: Proceedings of a Conference,* University of Alberta, Edmonton, Alberta, March 28-30, 1985 (Toronto: Canadian Institute of International Affairs, 1985); A. Jacomy-Millette, "Le rôle des provinces dans les relations internationales" (1979) 10(2) Études internationales 285; P.R. Johannson, "Provincial International Activities" (1978) International Journal 357.

[157] International Covenant on Civil and Political Rights, *infra* note 244.

because the government of Canada, rather than a provincial government, was its signatory. There may be other treaties, too, whose application, via the treaty presumption, does not give rise to federalism concerns. Courts faced with a contentious application of the treaty presumption to a provincial grant of statutory discretion should weigh the three factors given in the earlier separation of powers discussion, but with the proviso that the third factor (the court's role in the reception system of furthering respect for international law) may be constrained by its prior function of enforcing the written constitution's division of powers.

On the facts of *Baker,* of course, there can be no violation of the division of powers, for the decision-maker was a federal minister acting under valid federal law. The question is whether *Baker* gives rise to a doctrine that may imperil the division of powers in later cases. In my view, this scenario need not be so, provided that we are guided by the considerations stated earlier.

Baker *and the Content of Treaties*

I conclude this discussion of *Baker* with some thoughts on the significance of a treaty's content to the application or rebuttal of the treaty presumption. The majority's decision in *Baker* may be summarized as follows: "Grants of statutory discretion may be presumed not to breach Canada's obligations under unimplemented treaties. That presumption is rebuttable." The question is, does the treaty presumption control statutory grants of discretion no matter what the unimplemented treaty in question is about, or does the application or rebuttal of the presumption turn on the treaty at issue?

Nothing we have considered so far has suggested that the treaty presumption applies only to certain types of treaty. To the contrary, the presumption has always been expressed as including treaties of any sort. There are at least two reasons why this is so. The first is that the founding rule of international law expressed by the treaty presumption, *pacta sunt servanda,* makes no distinction between *pacta* — in other words, no valid agreement is any less worthy of being kept than any other.[158] By showing no preference between treaties, our courts have followed the international position. A second reason is that historically in Anglo-Canadian law the Crown's foreign affairs prerogative has not been reviewable in Her

---

[158] The exception is for invalid agreements, that is, those agreements that violate norms of *jus cogens.*

Majesty's own courts.[159] For a court to sit in judgment of which treaties are presumptively respected by our legislatures and which are not would come harrowingly close to reviewing executive treaty acts. Why, then, might a treaty's content matter when applying the treaty presumption to grants of statutory discretion? There are two related points.

The first point arises from L'Heureux-Dubé J.'s choice of words in *Baker*. We have seen that her Ladyship did not invoke the treaty presumption in its usual terms, though she has since characterized it that way.[160] Instead, L'Heureux-Dubé J. explained that the un-implemented treaty was relevant because it served to reveal that "[c]hildren's rights, and attention to their interests, are central humanitarian and compassionate values in Canadian society."[161] This language suggests that the treaty presumption applied to the statute not simply because Canada was bound by international law to observe the treaty but also because of the content of the treaty itself. If so, one cannot help but wonder whether other treaties — just as binding on Canada internationally but less revealing of Canadian values — might not be subject to the treaty presumption, either as applied to statutory grants of discretion or to ordinary legislative provisions. Does the rule enunciated in *Baker* require that an unimplemented treaty be declaratory of Canadian values, as determined by the court, before the treaty presumption is applied? I think not. L'Heureux-Dubé J. should not be taken as enunciating any new, content-reliant approach to the treaty presumption. Rather, L'Heureux-Dubé J. considered the content of the treaty (particularly its rights-advancing provisions) only for the purpose of determining whether self-government required the rebuttal of the presumption in this instance. This content analysis is not ordinarily a feature of the application of the treaty presumption. In the case of a statutory grant of discretion, however, the separation of powers problem raised by the application of the presumption rendered the content of the treaty relevant as a factor to be considered in applying the self-government test.[162]

---

[159] *Blackburn* v. *Attorney-General*, [1971] 1 W.L.R. 1037 (C.A.); *Rustomjee* v. *The Queen* (1876) 2 Q.B.D. 69. For the most recent Canadian discussion, see *Black* v. *Chrétien*, [2001] O.J. No. 1853.

[160] See the text accompanying notes 141-2 in this article.

[161] *Baker, supra* note 133 at 860.

[162] Any suggestion that the rule in *Baker* applies only in respect of human rights treaties like the 1989 Convention on the Rights of the Child, and not in the case of international law more generally, has seemingly now been laid to rest by the

The second point concerns the application of the treaty presumption to statutory discretions in the case of unimplemented treaties that might be described as rights-limiting rather than as rights-advancing. In *Baker,* the application of the treaty presumption gave Ms. Baker and her children additional procedural protections. However, not all treaties grant people rights. The treaty at issue in *The Parlement Belge*[163] purported to limit, not expand, the rights of individuals. Would a court, following *Baker,* use an unimplemented rights-limiting treaty to control statutory discretion? This question is related to the first point, for both turn on the relevance of the treaty's contents. The difference is that the question here is not whether the treaty can be said to be declaratory of Canadian values, but whether courts must control discretionary decision-makers who grant individuals rights and benefits contrary to Canada's international obligations. The choice is between upholding an administrative decision that puts Canada in breach of its international obligations and invalidating a right- or benefit-conferring exercise of statutory discretion.

This dilemma was faced by the Supreme Court of Canada in *Capital Cities Communications* v. *C.R.T.C.*[164] At issue was a decision of the Canadian Radio-Television Commission (CRTC) to alter the licence of Rogers Cable to permit them to delete advertisements from US television channels, broadcast by Rogers on its cable service, and replace them with public service announcements. This decision was informed by the pro-Canadian broadcasting policy enshrined in Section 3 of the Broadcasting Act[165] and a non-statutory policy statement published by the CRTC, which explicitly permitted "the removal . . . of the commercial value" contained in US television signals.[166] The treaty in issue was Article 11 of the 1937 Inter-American Radiocommunications Convention,[167] which contained guarantees against interference in the services of

---

Supreme Court of Canada's ruling in *Spraytech, supra* note 142. There, L'Heureux-Dubé J. for the majority invoked the precautionary principle (which she controversially identified as a rule of customary international law) as an example of a principle of international law to which the Court may resort in construing statutes in the internationally consistent manner advocated in *Baker.*

[163] See the text accompanying note 30 in this article.

[164] *Capital Cities, supra* note 19.

[165] Broadcasting Act, S.C. 1967-68, c. 25.

[166] *Capital Cities, supra* note 19 at 148.

[167] Inter-American Radiocommunications Convention, Can. T.S. 1938 No. 18.

another country, and Article 21, which sought to prevent unauthorized retransmissions. The status of the convention in Canadian law was a matter of dispute. Section 7(1)(d) of the Radio Act provided that the minister may make regulations to carry out such international agreements,[168] and one such regulation required licensees, such as Rogers, to observe the provisions of telecommunication agreements in force.[169] However, Rogers was a licensee under the later Broadcasting Act, which, in the majority's opinion, did not implement the convention.[170]

The court's dilemma was whether to rely on the seemingly unimplemented treaty to deny Rogers the benefit, accorded them by the CRTC decision, to replace US advertisements, or whether to uphold the CRTC decision and Rogers' benefit in the face of Canada's treaty obligations. The majority opted for the latter approach. Laskin C.J. went so far as to hold that the CRTC was not bound by the convention:

I am unable to appreciate how it can be said that the Commission [CRTC] is an agent or arm of the Canadian Government and as such bound by the Convention provisions in the same way as the Government. There is nothing in the *Broadcasting Act,* nor was our attention directed to any other legislation which would give the Commission any other status than that of a federal regulatory agency established with defined statutory powers. There is nothing to show that it derives any authority from the Convention or that the Convention, *per se,* qualifies the regulatory authority conferred upon the Commission by the *Broadcasting Act.*[171]

This finding, that an administrative decision-maker operating under statutory authority is free to make determinations without considering Canada's treaty obligations, because such obligations do not bind it, is in direct conflict with the majority's judgment in *Baker.* It is an unmeritorious proposition in its own right, for it is clear that Canada could not be heard at international law to plead, in defence of its treaty violation, that the CRTC was not part of the government. Treaties concluded by the Crown bind Canada as a whole and not just the Canadian government narrowly defined. The dissenting judgment of Pigeon J. (for himself and Beetz and Grandpré JJ.) held that the CRTC could not properly issue decisions in violation of Canada's treaty obligations. Pigeon J. explained

---

[168] Radio Act, R.S.C. 1970, c. R-1.

[169] General Radio Regulations, SOR/63/297, s. 11.

[170] *Capital Cities, supra* note 19 at 173.

[171] *Ibid.* at 172-3.

that the CRTC's "duty is to implement the policy established by Parliament," and he continued: "While this policy makes no reference to Canada's treaty obligations, it is an integral part of the national structure that external affairs are the responsibility of the Federal Government. It is an oversimplification to say that treaties are of no legal effect unless implemented by legislation."[172]

In my view, the dissenting judgment is to be preferred. Only that judgment is consonant with the proper role of the judiciary in the reception system, namely to advance respect for international law. While it may be unsatisfying in particular instances to contemplate statutory decision-makers being required to deny rights and benefits to claimants on the ground of the provisions of an unimplemented treaty, it is nonetheless the duty of administrative decision-makers and the courts that review them to see that Canada's international obligations be respected and, where at all possible, not violated by exercises of administrative discretion. An unimplemented treaty cannot affect the rights of Canadians without implementation (*The Parlement Belge*). Yet grants of statutory discretion are presumptively consistent with Canadian treaty obligations and must be so exercised unless the presumption is rebutted (*Baker*). Where these two propositions conflict, the judiciary's proper role is not to vindicate our legislatures' undoubted power to violate international law (for *ex hypothesi* no clear intent to breach international law exists) but rather to assert the treaty presumption and the principle of respect for international law that underlies it.

UNIMPLEMENTED TREATIES AND LEGITIMATE EXPECTATIONS

In *Minister for Immigration and Ethnic Affairs* v. *Teoh*,[173] the High Court of Australia held that ratification by Australia of the 1989 Convention on the Rights of the Child[174] gave rise to a legitimate expectation that the minister exercising his discretion would act in conformity with the treaty by treating the best interests of the applicant's child as a primary consideration in determining whether to grant him a permanent entry permit. It was not necessary that the applicant be aware of the convention or that he or she personally entertain the expectation. All that was needed was that

---

[172] *Ibid.* at 188.

[173] *Minister for Immigration and Ethnic Affairs* v. *Teoh* (1994-5), 183 C.L.R. 273 (H.C.A.).

[174] Convention on the Rights of the Child, *supra* note 50.

the expectation be a reasonable one. *Teoh* represents a different approach to the legal effect of unimplemented treaties. To allow unimplemented treaties to found legitimate expectations of procedural (and perhaps substantive?) rights is to accord such treaties palpable legal weight while arguably side-stepping the separation of powers problem. In England, *Teoh* has been accepted by a strong Court of Appeal (Lord Woolf M.R., Hobhouse and Thorpe L.JJ.) in *R. v. Secretary of State for the Home Department, Ex parte Ahmed*[175] and by the Queen's Bench Division in *R. v. Uxbridge Magistrates' Court, Ex parte Adimi,* in which the Australian decision was described as a "seminal judgment."[176] *Teoh* was also accepted by the Privy Council in *Thomas v. Baptiste.*[177]

Given this support for *Teoh* in Australian and English jurisprudence, it is surprising that the legitimate expectation argument has received such scant attention in Canadian law. Most remarkably, the case went uncited by both the majority and the dissent in the Supreme Court's judgment in *Baker.* L'Heureux-Dubé J., for the majority, recognized legitimate expectations as being a factor affecting the content of the duty of fairness[178] yet held that, on the facts, the Convention on the Rights of the Child did not give rise to a legitimate expectation, on the part of Ms. Baker, to specific procedural rights or to the application of particular criteria.[179] No supporting reasons were given for this conclusion nor was there any discussion of whether Ms. Baker was aware of the treaty or whether she needed to be.

L'Heureux-Dubé J. left the question open slightly, however, when she declared it "unnecessary to decide whether an international instrument ratified by Canada could, in other circumstances, give rise to a legitimate expectation."[180] Advocates of the *Teoh* approach may take some comfort in that, but they will take little comfort in the judgment of the court below. Strayer J.A. for the Federal Court of Appeal observed that, in Canada, the doctrine of legitimate expectations cannot create substantive rights and that what Ms. Baker sought was a substantive, not a procedural, matter. His Lordship

---

[175] *R. v. Secretary of State for the Home Department, Ex parte Ahmed,* [1999] Imm. L.R. 22 (Eng. C.A.) at 36.

[176] *R. v. Uxbridge Magistrates' Court, Ex parte Adimi,* [2000] W.L.R. 434 (Q.B.) at 456.

[177] *Thomas v. Baptiste,* [1999] 3 W.L.R. 249 (P.C.).

[178] *Baker, supra* note 133 at 839-40.

[179] *Ibid.* at 841.

[180] *Ibid.*

went on to reject explicitly the reasoning of the majority in *Teoh* and to adopt the dissent of McHugh J.[181] Strayer J.A. did purport to leave open "the interesting question of whether the ratification of multilateral conventions can in any realistic sense be regarded as a meaningful representation to all Canadians that public affairs will thereafter be conducted in accordance with those conventions."[182] Nonetheless, this rejection of *Teoh,* combined with the Supreme Court's tacit approval of this approach, strongly suggests that the doctrine of legitimate expectation will make as little inroad into the reception system as it has in the rest of Canadian law.

FEDERALISM AND IMPLEMENTATION: THE RULE IN *LABOUR CONVENTIONS*[183]

Federalism has posed no great difficulty for the incorporation of customary international law in Canada, for the common law has never been an obstacle to federalism and the doctrine of incorporation makes customary international law and the common law one. The implementation of treaty law is another matter, however. The foundation of Canadian federalism is the Constitution Act 1867, also known as the British North America (BNA) Act. The only provision concerning the implementation of treaties in this statute is Section 132, which reads: "The Parliament and Government of Canada shall have all Powers necessary or proper for performing the Obligations of Canada or of any Province thereof, as Part of the British Empire, towards Foreign Countries, arising under Treaties between the Empire and such Foreign Countries."[184] "With the adoption of the Statute of Westminster," remarked the prime minister, Mr. Bennett, in 1931, "the political Empire disappears." Disappearing along with it, *de facto* if not *de jure,* was Section 132 for there was no longer such a thing as an Empire treaty. With no legislative provision made to fill the gap, it was left to the courts to determine how treaties would be implemented in Canada in the future.

The matter was decided — for now, if not forever — by the Privy Council in the *Labour Conventions* case. Their Lordships' judgment

---

[181] *Baker* F.C., *supra* note 138 at 147-51.

[182] *Ibid.* at 146.

[183] *Labour Conventions, supra* note 31.

[184] Bennett's statement was only true for the original dominions, of course. Quoted in John S. Ewart, *The Independence Papers,* vol. 2 (Ottawa: n.p., 1932), 601.

can be seen as a vindication of the principle of self-government as embodied in Canada by our federal system. Lord Atkin, for the Board, interpreted Canadian federalism in the light of the common law reception system and found that an incursion by the federal government into provincial jurisdiction by means of the treaty power was as much an affront to the self-government principle as is executive legislation or the direct application of international law.

Before *Labour Conventions* came down, however, a pair of 1932 Privy Council decisions suggested quite a different result. In *In Re the Regulation and Control of Aeronautics in Canada*,[185] the Privy Council considered questions that had been referred to the Supreme Court of Canada by the governor in council concerning federal authority to perform the obligations of Canada, or of any province thereof, under the 1919 Convention Relating to the Regulation of Aerial Navigation.[186] Lord Sankey L.C. found that legislative authority to implement the treaty rested with the Dominion Parliament, principally on the ground that the treaty was an Empire treaty of the sort contemplated by Section 132 of the BNA Act but also in light of federal legislative powers under Subsections 91 (2), (5), and (7) and, if that was not sufficient, under the residual peace, order, and good government power. This finding suggested that, were the treaty not the sort described by Section 132, their Lordships would have found for the federal power anyway. In *In Re the Regulation and Control of Radio Communication in Canada*,[187] the treaty at issue, the 1927 International Radiotelegraph Convention,[188] was not an Empire treaty since Canada and Great Britain entered it separately. A differently constituted board than that which decided *Re Aeronautics* appeared nevertheless to come to a similar result. Treaty-implementing legislation, since it was not mentioned explicitly in either Sections 91 or 92 of the BNA Act, fell within Parliament's residual power to legislate for the peace, order, and good government of Canada. Viscount Dunedin stated:

[185] *In Re the Regulation and Control of Aeronautics in Canada*, [1932] A.C. 54 (P.C.) [hereinafter *Re Aeronautics*]. The attorney-general for Canada was represented by two King's Counsel and a junior by the name of A.T. Denning.

[186] Convention Relating to the Regulation of Aerial Navigation, U.K.T.S. 1922 No. 2, Cmd. 1609.

[187] *In Re the Regulation and Control of Radio Communication in Canada*, [1932] A.C. 304 (P.C.) [hereinafter *Re Radio*].

[188] International Radiotelegraph Convention, 1928-9, 84 L.N.T.S. No. 1905.

[T]he argument of the Province [of Quebec] comes to this: Go through all the stipulations of the convention and each one you can pick out which fairly falls within one of the enumerated heads of s. 91, that can be held to be appropriate for Dominion legislation; but the residue belongs to the Province under the head either of head 13 of s. 92 — property and civil rights, or head 16 — matters of a merely local or private nature in the Province. Their Lordships cannot agree that the matter should be so dealt with.[189]

Lord Dunedin went on to emphasize the absurdity of a regime whereby radio transmitters would fall under federal authority and radio receivers under provincial jurisdiction. These comments must have appeared to be *obiter* in light of the reasoning quoted above. However, Lord Atkin would rely on them effectively to distinguish and effectively reverse the result of *Re Radio* five years later.

In *Labour Conventions,* as in *Re Radio,* the question was whether the federal Parliament was competent to implement treaty obligations incurred on Canada's behalf by the federal government. Unlike *Re Radio,* however, it was common ground in *Labour Conventions* that the subject matter of the treaty at issue fell within the legislative jurisdiction of the provinces. The acts at issue sought to implement significant labour reforms proposed by conventions adopted by the International Labour Organization in accordance with the Labour Part of the 1919 Treaty of Versailles.[190] The Supreme Court of Canada, sitting as a six-person bench, divided evenly.[191] On appeal, counsel for the attorney-general of Canada (including the future prime minister, Louis St. Laurent) contended that the Dominion had jurisdiction under Section 132 or, in the alternative, under the federal residual power. The attorneys-general of Ontario, New Brunswick, and British Columbia all contended that implementing legislation was subject to the division of powers described in Sections 91 and 92.

In his reasons, Lord Atkin favoured the provinces in terms that depicted federalism as an aspect of the Canadian conception of self-government. His Lordship rejected the Section 132 argument (and therefore any reliance on *Re Aeronautics*) for it was plain that the treaties in question were not Empire treaties but rather treaties made independently by Canada. He drew a distinction between the formation of treaty obligations, which is an executive act, and the

---

[189] *Re Radio, supra* note 187 at 311-2.

[190] Treaty of Versailles, Can. T.S. 1919 No. 4.

[191] *Attorney-General for Canada* v. *Attorney-General for Ontario,* [1936] S.C.R. 461.

performance of such obligations, which, insofar as it may require alteration of the law, is a legislative act.[192] He famously explained that "there is no such thing as treaty legislation as such. The distribution [of legislative powers] is based on classes of subjects; and as a treaty deals with a particular class of subjects so will the legislative power of performing it be ascertained."[193] Lord Atkin seemed to acknowledge that these rules were born in a unitary state and that their application to federal states such as Canada was "complex."[194] Yet he was undeterred. The result contended for by the federal government would, in his view, upset the foundation of the Canadian constitution, namely the distribution of powers under Sections 91 and 92. Lord Atkin observed: "No one can doubt that this distribution is one of the most essential conditions, probably the most essential condition, in the inter-provincial compact to which the British North America Act gives effect."[195] His Lordship continued:

> If the position of Lower Canada, now Quebec, alone were considered, the existence of her separate jurisprudence as to both property and civil rights might be said to depend upon loyal adherence to her constitutional right to the exclusive competence of her own Legislature in these matters. Nor is it of less importance for the other Provinces, though their law may be based on English jurisprudence, to preserve their own right to legislate for themselves in respect of local conditions which may vary by as great a distance as separates the Atlantic from the Pacific.[196]

The theme of this passage, and, indeed, of Lord Atkin's entire judgment, is provincial self-government. His Lordship argued that the provinces' inherent differences demanded a federal arrangement in 1867 and the preservation of that arrangement in 1937. He treated the federal government, armed with the treaty power, as a threat to provincial self-government in much the same way that he depicted international law as a coercive external force inimical to self-government (until incorporated by the common law) in *Chung Chi Cheung* v. *The King*.[197] Lord Atkin's judgment was an application

---

[192] *Labour Conventions, supra* note 31 at 347-8.

[193] *Ibid.* at 351.

[194] *Ibid.* at 348.

[195] *Ibid.* at 351.

[196] *Ibid.* at 351-2.

[197] In *Chung Chi Cheung* v. *The King,*, [1939] A.C. 160 (P.C.) at 167-8, Lord Atkin famously declared: "It must always be remembered that, so far, at any rate, as the Courts of this country are concerned, international law has no validity save in so far as its principles are accepted and adopted by our own domestic law. There is

of the reception system's principle of self-government to Canadian federalism.

As for the decision in *Re Radio* and the suggestions of federal jurisdiction independent of Section 132 in *Re Aeronautics*, his Lordship set these cases aside with little fuss. He dismissed the comments in *Re Aeronautics* as *obiter* (which they were, technically, but rather influential *obiter*, one might have thought). As for *Re Radio*, he characterized "the true ground of the decision" as an application of the gap theory of the peace, order, and good government power, whereby subject matters, such as radio, which were contemplated neither by Sections 91 nor 92, fell to Parliament under its residual power to legislate for the peace, order, and good government of Canada.[198] In closing, Lord Atkin emphasized that, in the totality of its legislative powers, Canada was fully equipped to implement any treaty obligation it might assume. "But the legislative powers remain distributed," and the solution to the problems that this might pose was not legal but political, namely, "co-operation between the Dominion and the Provinces."[199]

ACADEMIC CRITICISM OF THE DECISION

Labour Conventions was received very badly by prominent Anglo-Canadian commentators. Perhaps the most outrageous comments were those of W.P.M. Kennedy, who decried the "bastard loyalty" that gave the BNA Act "the doubtful devotion of primitive ancestor worship," and intoned biblically that "this is the law, and it killeth."[200] Other commentators did not write so vividly yet expressed their disapproval clearly enough.[201] Since that time, Anglo-Canadian criticism of the decision has been constant. R.J. Matas, writing in 1945, referred to the result of the case as "this unhappy state of affairs" and bemoaned the Privy Council's overly literal interpretation of

---

no external power that imposes its rules upon our own code of substantive law or procedure." For an explanation of this somewhat deceptive statement, see van Ert, *supra* note 3 at ch. 3.

[198] *Labour Conventions, supra* note 31 at 351.

[199] *Ibid.* at 354.

[200] W.P.M. Kennedy, "The British North America Act: Past and Future" (1937) 15 Can. B.R. 393 at 399.

[201] An entire issue of the *Canadian Bar Review* was dedicated to the topic, with contributions from F.R. Scott, Vincent MacDonald, Ivor Jennings, and others. See (1937) 15 Can. B.R. 393-508.

Section 132.[202] G.J. Szablowski, writing in 1956, candidly admitted his bias against the decision in the opening line of his article on the subject, saying: "The treatment of the topic of this article is based on the assumption that a modern state, unitary or federal, cannot effectively function in the international forum without possessing full capacity, in law and in fact, to create and to perform binding obligations."[203] Edward McWhinney, who favoured the result in *Labour Conventions*, nonetheless wrote in 1969 that it "has been perhaps the most bitterly assailed and certainly the most often ridiculed judicial opinion in Canadian constitutional history."[204] Gerard La Forest (as he then was) observed in 1974 that it has "long been fashionable to predict" that the case would be overruled.[205] Tortsten Strom and Peter Finkle, writing in 1993, trotted out all the standard objections to *Labour Conventions* but added a castration theme to their analysis. They themselves concluded that the "effect of the judgment was to emasculate the federal power."[206] In support, they quoted F.R. Scott's conclusion that "so long as Canada clung to the Imperial apron strings, her Parliament was all powerful ... once she became a nation in her own right, impotence descended."[207] Finally, they quoted Rand J.'s view that *Labour Conventions* "besides sterilizing national action would invert the underlying scheme of Dominion and provincial relations."[208] Perhaps the most thorough contemporary critique of *Labour Conventions* is by Peter Hogg. He questions almost every aspect of Lord Atkin's "poorly reasoned decision," in particular, his conclusion that Section 132 could not have been "strained" to cover Canada's achievement of full statehood and his statement that "there is no such thing as treaty legislation as such." Yet Hogg acknowledges that the case may be good policy even if it is bad law and accepts that the rule in *Labour Conventions* may be "one of the prices of federalism."[209]

[202] R.J. Matas, "Treaty Making in Canada" (1947) 25 Can. B.R. 458 at 462, 470.

[203] G.J. Szablowski, "Creation and Implementation of Treaties in Canada" (1956) 34 Can. B.R. 28.

[204] Edward McWhinney, "Canadian Federalism and the Foreign Affairs and Treaty Power. The Impact of Quebec's 'Quiet Revolution'" (1969) 7 C.Y.I.L. 3 at 4.

[205] Gerard V. La Forest, "The Labour Conventions Case Revisited" (1974) 12 C.Y.I.L. 137 at 147.

[206] Torsten H. Strom and Peter Finkle, "Treaty Implementation: The Canadian Game Needs Australian Rules" (1993) 25 Ottawa L.R. 39 at 47.

[207] F.R. Scott, quoted in Strom and Finkle, *supra* note 206 at 57.

[208] Rand J., quoted in Strom and Finkle, *supra* note 206 at 57.

[209] Hogg, *supra* note 11 at section 11.5(c).

A constant refrain from the critics of *Labour Conventions* has been that it hampers Canada's ability to conduct foreign affairs. Vincent MacDonald, writing in 1937, called the decision "suicidal in point of governmental efficiency."[210] Other early critics agreed, though without illustrating the point with evidence. This lack of evidence led later writers to argue that the efficiency critique was unwarranted. Gotlieb (1968) pointed out that most treaties do not even require implementation, that many of those that do can be implemented under the federal power, and that consultation with the provinces was standard practice even prior to the decision in *Labour Conventions*.[211] McWhinney (1969) went further, saying that "no single example has ever been cited, in the years since 1937 when that decision was first handed down, where its *rationale* has presented any practical difficulties, or even mild inconvenience, in the conduct of Canada's foreign relations."[212] If that statement was true at the time, it was not true for long, for Bernier's 1973 monograph *International Legal Aspects of Federalism* included a lengthy illustration of the problems Canada had faced due to the rule in *Labour Conventions*.[213] Nevertheless, La Forest (1974) dismissed such concerns as difficult to take seriously in the light of Canada's major role in international relations.[214] Ziegel (1988) considered McWhinney's statement to have gone too far, but conceded that Canada's record of ratifying conventions, compared to other federal states, is not bad.[215] More recently, Howse (1990) has argued that justifications of the status quo are becoming "less and less satisfactory"[216] while Rafuse (1995) has shorn up the efficiency

---

[210] Vincent MacDonald, 'The Canadian Constitution Seventy Years After' (1937) 15 Can. B.R. 401 at 419.

[211] A.E. Gotlieb, *Canadian Treaty-Making* (Toronto: Butterworths, 1968), 76-7; see also 83.

[212] McWhinney, *supra* note 204 at 5.

[213] Ivan Bernier, *International Legal Aspects of Federalism* (London: Longman, 1973), 152-8.

[214] La Forest, *supra* note 205 at 148.

[215] Jacob S. Ziegel, "Treaty Making and Implementing Powers in Canada: the Continuing Dilemma" in Bin Cheng and E.D. Brown, eds., *Contemporary Problems of International Law: Essays in Honour of Georg Schwarzenberger on his 80th Birthday* (London: Stevens and Sons, 1988), 339-40, 342.

[216] Robert Howse, "The *Labour Conventions* Doctrine in an Era of Global Interdependence: Rethinking the Constitutional Dimensions of Canada's External Economic Relations" (1990) 16 Can. Bus. L.J. 160 at 171.

critique somewhat.[217] Hogg is persuaded by it.[218] Yet the thesis that *Labour Conventions* hinders Canada's ability to conduct foreign affairs, and the further argument that this hindrance outweighs the benefits of the *Labour Conventions* rule, remain unproven. A comprehensive study of this question has yet to be written.

Throughout this discussion I have depicted the critics of *Labour Conventions* as Anglo-Canadian. With very few exceptions,[219] English Canadian commentators have derided the decision and

---

[217] Rosemary Rayfuse, "Treaty Practice: The Canadian Perspective" in Philip Alston and Madelaine Chiam, eds., *Treaty-Making and Australia: Globalisation versus Sovereignty?* (Sidney: Federation Press, 1995), 253 at 257-9.

[218] Hogg, *supra* note 11 at s. 11.5(c).

[219] Edward McWhinney defended the decision in several articles published in the 1960s. In particular, he drew Canadian attention to the fact that the Federal Constitutional Court of West Germany, faced with a problem identical to that in the Canadian case, explicitly preferred Lord Atkin's judgment to the approach taken in American law. See Edward McWhinney, "Federal Constitutional Law and the Treaty-making Power — German-Vatican Concordat of 1933 — Decision of West German Federal Constitutional Court" (1957) 35 Can. B.R. 842; Edward McWhinney, "The Constitutional Competence within Federal Systems as to International Agreements" (1966) 3 Can. Legal Stud. 145 at 146; Edward McWhinney, *supra* note 204 at 5. The German decision is the *Reichskonkordat* case, Decision of the Federal Constitutional Court (Second Senate), March 26, 1957, (1957) 6 B. Verf. G.E. 309

W.R. Lederman, while not uncritical of the rule in *Labour Conventions*, sympathized with the federalism concerns that supported it and proposed a compromise whereby Parliament would enjoy concurrent but paramount power to implement treaties of national importance. See W.R. Lederman, "Legislative Power to Implement Treaty Obligations in Canada," in J.H. Aitchison, ed., *The Political Process in Canada: Essays in Honour of R. MacGregor Dawson* (Toronto: University of Toronto Press, 1963) at 171.

Robert Howse's contributions to the *Labour Conventions* debate are notable for their general acceptance of the decision, subject to judicial recognition of federal jurisdiction under the peace, order, and good government and trade and commerce powers of the Constitution Act 1867. This argument is similar to the argument that I advance later in this article. In his 1990 article, Howse criticizes the "watertight compartments" approach to federalism espoused by Lord Atkin, yet demonstrates that critics of the judgment have failed to address his Lordship's concern to maintain "the federal balance." See Howse, *supra* note 216, especially at 163-71. In a later article, Howse argues that the 1992 North American Free Trade Agreement can be fully implemented by the federal Parliament. This article does not challenge *Labour Conventions* at all, though its subtitle suggests otherwise. See Robert Howse, "NAFTA and the Constitution: Does *Labour Conventions* Really Matter Any More?" (1994) 5 Const. Forum 54.

Another supportive, or at least less critical, Anglo-Canadian commentator is J.P. Meekison, "Provinces and Foreign Affairs. Provincial Activity Adds New Dimension to Federalism. A Western View" (1977) 2 International Perspectives 8.

Québec commentators have favoured it. As La Forest observed in 1974, "French Canadians overwhelmingly support the decision."[220] This stark division between francophone and anglophone commentators on the case is one of its most notable aspects. Also notable is the tacit acceptance of *Labour Conventions* by the federal government, which has never overtly challenged the decision before the courts. Ziegel, writing in 1988, referred to *Labour Conventions* as "a constitutional doctrine that the federal government itself has respected for the past 50 years."[221] Nor has the matter been seriously proposed in recent debates about constitutional reform. As Wallace Struthers reminds us, for all its wide-ranging proposals, the Charlottetown Accord expressly left the matter of treaty implementation off the agenda.[222]

JUDICIAL CONSIDERATION OF THE DECISION

Criticism of *Labour Conventions* has not been limited to academic writings but has also come from the bench. Lord Simon, speaking for the Privy Council in *Attorney-General for Ontario v. Canada Temperance Foundation,* suggested that where the subject matter of implementing legislation "goes beyond local or provincial concern or interests and must from its inherent nature be the concern of the Dominion as a whole (as, for example, in the *Aeronautics* case and the *Radio* case), then it will fall within the competence of the Dominion Parliament as a matter affecting the peace, order and good government of Canada, though it may in another aspect touch on matters specially reserved to the provincial legislatures."[223] Lord Simon's comments were seen as significant. Even more significant were the extra-judicial reflections of Lord Wright in a posthumous tribute to Duff C.J. in the 1955 *Canadian Bar Review.* His Lordship,

---

[220] La Forest, *supra* note 205 at 137. La Forest, cited Jacques-Yvan Morin "La conclusion d'accords internationaux par les provinces canadiennes à la lumière du droit comparé" (1965) 3 C.Y.I.L. 127 at 137; A.M. Jacomy-Millette, *L'Introduction et l'Application des Traités Internationaux au Canada* (Paris: LGDJ, 1971) 75 *et seq.*; André Dufour, "Fédéralisme canadien et droit international," in R. St. J. Macdonald et al., eds., *Canadian Perspectives on International Law and Organization* (Toronto: University of Toronto Press, 1974) at 72.

[221] Ziegel, *supra* note 215.

[222] *Final Text of the Consensus Report on the Constitution* (Charlottetown, 26 August 1992), quoted in Wallace W. Struthers, "'Treaty Implementation ... Australian Rules': a Rejoinder" (1994) 26 Ottawa L.R. 305 at 308.

[223] *Attorney-General for Ontario v. Canada Temperance Foundation,* [1946] A.C. 193 (P.C.) at 205 [hereinafter *Canada Temperance*].

who was himself a member of the board that decided *Labour Conventions,* criticized Lord Atkin's judgment and indicated his preference for *Re Aeronautics, Re Radio,* and *Canada Temperance.*[224] These comments inspired a correspondent to the *Canadian Bar Review* to speculate that the decision in "one of the most important cases in Canadian constitutional law was determined by the vote of Sir Sidney Rowlatt, a 'taxation judge,' who, I am told, sat throughout the 1937 hearings in his overcoat making neither note nor comment."[225] Emboldened perhaps by the prevailing irreverence, Kerwin C.J. indicated one year later, in *Francis* v. *The Queen,* that "it may be necessary ... to consider in the future the judgment of the Judicial Committee."[226] More indication that *Labour Conventions* was for the chop came with the unsigned judgment of the Supreme Court in *Reference Re Ownership of Offshore Mineral Rights,*[227] which was read as implicitly breaching the rule in *Labour Conventions* by granting Parliament legislative jurisdiction to implement the 1958 Geneva Convention on the Continental Shelf.[228]

By far the most significant judicial doubting of *Labour Conventions* is that of Laskin C.J. in *MacDonald* v. *Vapor Canada.*[229] The chief justice began his consideration of *Labour Conventions* by describing the case as "too well-known to require either quotation or statement of its holding." Thus, without quoting from Lord Atkin's judgment, the chief justice proceeded immediately to consider its critics, starting with the dictum of Kerwin C.J. in *Francis* and Lord Wright's extra-judicial comments in the *Canadian Bar Review.* The chief justice then cited *Re Aeronautics* and quoted at length from *Re Radio.* Following this passage is a citation of another extra-judicial critique, this one from Rand J.[230] Having thus discredited the rule in *Labour Conventions,* Laskin C.J. declined to overrule it, finding instead that the implementing legislation in question was within federal legislative jurisdiction. Yet the chief justice went on to

---

[224] Lord Wright of Durley, "Rt. Hon. Sir Lyman Poore Duff, G.C.M.G." (1955) 33 Can. B.R. 1123 at 1125-8.

[225] B.J. MacKinnon, letter to the editor, (1956) 34 Can. B.R. 115 at 117.

[226] *Francis, supra* note 76 at 621.

[227] *Reference Re Ownership of Offshore Mineral Rights,* [1967] S.C.R. 792.

[228] Geneva Convention on the Continental Shelf, Can T.S. 1970 No. 4.

[229] *MacDonald* v. *Vapor Canada,* [1977] 2 S.C.R. 134 at 168-9 [hereinafter *MacDonald*].

[230] Ivan Rand, "Some Aspects of Canadian Constitutionalism" (1960) 38 Can. B.R. 135 at 142.

suggest, if only in *obiter*, a rule by which Parliament could possibly gain jurisdiction to implement treaties whose subject matter fell otherwise within provincial competence:

> In my opinion, assuming Parliament has power to pass legislation implementing a treaty or convention in relation to matters covered by the treaty or convention which would otherwise be for provincial legislation alone, the exercise of that power must be manifested in the implementing legislation and not be left to inference. The Courts should be able to say, on the basis of the expression of the legislation, that it is implementing legislation. Of course, even so, a question may arise whether the legislation does or does not go beyond the obligations of the treaty or convention.[231]

This is a stark denial of Lord Atkin's holding that there is no such thing as treaty legislation as such. What the chief justice is suggesting, it seems, is that courts may allow treaties to be implemented by Parliament alone where Parliament has explicitly signalled to the courts its 'implementative' intent.[232] To do so, of course, the government (who, in the normal case, would sponsor the implementing bill) must also signal to the opposition, the rest of Parliament, the provinces, and Canadians at large its intent to intrude upon the provincial sphere. The merit of the signal requirement is that it forces a government seeking to breach the established division of powers to pay the political price.[233]

Laskin C.J.'s comments in *MacDonald* were *obiter*. Yet they are a curious sort of *obiter*, for they were seemingly applied as a rule by Dickson C.J. (speaking for himself and seven other justices) in *Schneider* v. *The Queen*. The chief justice questioned the appellant's submissions concerning Parliament's jurisdiction to implement treaties in the face of Lord Atkin's famous judgment, from which he quoted. Yet Dickson C.J. went on to describe Laskin C.J.'s comments in *MacDonald* as a holding of the court and applied them to the case at bar, finding that there was nothing in the act to indicate Parliament's intent to implement Canadian treaty obligations. The chief justice concluded: "The *Heroin Treatment Act* is not legislation

---

[231] *MacDonald, supra* note 229 at 171.

[232] This "signal requirement" bears a striking resemblance to the dissenting opinion of Beetz J. concerning the emergency doctrine of the peace, order, and good government power in *Re Anti-Inflation*, [1976] 2 S.C.R. 373.

[233] This approach to our constitution, namely that legislatures should be allowed to breach it so long as they are willing to pay the political price, is quite out of step with our post-Charter constitutional settlement, in which certain constitutional values are recognized as politically off-limits (subject, in certain cases, to the override provided in Section 33 of the Constitution Act 1982).

falling within the scope of any federal power to legislate for the implementation of international treaties."[234]

Another judgment that has been viewed (wrongly, in my view) as detracting from the authority of *Labour Conventions* is the decision of the Supreme Court of Canada in *R. v. Crown Zellerbach.*[235] Section 4(1) of the federal Ocean Dumping Control Act prohibits the dumping of substances at sea, including provincial maritime waters. Large parts of the act appear to implement Canada's obligations under the 1972 Convention on the Prevention of Marine Pollution by Dumping of Wastes and Other Matter (London Convention),[236] although the act does not say so explicitly. In the Provincial Court of British Columbia, Judge Schmidt heard the argument that Parliament had legislative jurisdiction to enact Section 4(1) of the Ocean Dumping Control Act under its power to implement treaties. The judge rejected this argument, applying the dicta in *MacDonald* to the effect that there was an insufficiently clear indication in the act that it was enacted in implementation of a treaty. This argument was adopted by the BC Court of Appeal in upholding the lower court's decision.[237]

Before the Supreme Court, the attorney-general of Canada abandoned the *MacDonald* argument. Instead, he relied exclusively upon Parliament's jurisdiction under its residual power to make laws for the peace, order, and good government of Canada (so-called POGG power).[238] Le Dain J., speaking for the majority, admitted that the act's definition of the sea to include provincial waters was not supported by any of the grounds of federal jurisdiction enumerated in Section 91 of the Constitution Act 1867. Yet he accepted the attorney-general's submission that the act was a valid exercise of Parliament's jurisdiction under the national concern branch of the POGG power. Le Dain J. relied on the treatment of marine dumping in the convention in finding that the subject

---

[234] *Schneider* v. *The Queen*, [1982] 2 S.C.R. 112 at 134-5. For trenchant criticism of this case, see A.L.C. de Mestral's case note in (1983) 61 Can. B.R. 856.

[235] *R. v. Crown Zellerbach*, [1988] 1 S.C.R. 401 [hereinafter *Crown Zellerbach*].

[236] Convention on the Prevention of Marine Pollution by Dumping of Wastes and Other Matter, Can. T.S. 1979 No. 36.

[237] See *Crown Zellerbach, supra* note 235 at 416.

[238] Section 91 of the Constitution Act 1867 reads in part: "It shall be lawful for the Queen, by and with the Advice and Consent of the Senate and House of Commons, to make Laws for the Peace, Order, and Good Government of Canada, in relation to all Matters not coming within the Classes of Subjects by this Act assigned exclusively to the Legislatures of the Provinces."

matter of the legislation met the "singleness, distinctiveness and indivisibility" requirements of the national concern doctrine.[239]

Anne Bayefsky has argued that the decision in *Crown Zellerbach* "clearly contradicted the rule in *Labour Conventions* that Canada's international obligations were irrelevant to determining constitutional validity."[240] With respect, I disagree. There is no contradiction between a finding of jurisdiction under the national concern doctrine of the POGG power and the rule in *Labour Conventions*. This was Lord Simon's point in *Canada Temperance*. Lord Atkin's judgment in *Labour Conventions* was that treaty implementation occurs according to the established jurisdictions of the federal and provincial legislatures rather than according to some overriding federal power to implement treaties regardless of their subject matter. Federal legislative jurisdiction clearly includes jurisdiction under the two branches of the POGG power, namely national concern and emergency. If it can be shown that legislation in implementation of a treaty amounts to a matter of national concern, federal jurisdiction is established. Lord Atkin's famous phrase, that there is no such thing as treaty legislation as such, cuts both ways: the label "treaty legislation" can no more be used to attack an act as being *ultra vires* than it can be used to defend an act as *intra vires*. The fact that legislation takes its inspiration from an intention to carry out Canada's international obligations is wholly irrelevant in the determination of its validity. The argument of the attorney-general of Canada in *Crown Zellerbach* is correct. It is enough to show that the implementing legislation is within Parliament's jurisdiction to legislate in matters of national concern. The argument is neither strengthened nor weakened by proving it to be in implementation of a treaty.

If *Crown Zellerbach* was wrongly decided, it was not on this point but on the separate question of whether the legislation in question was truly a matter of national concern. Bayefsky bases her claim that the case violates the rule in *Labour Conventions* on Le Dain J.'s use of the 1972 London Convention in determining whether the act satisfied the national concern test. Bayefsky considers that *Labour Conventions* precluded the court from considering the existence of the treaty in determining whether the legislation is truly a matter of national concern. I agree with Bayefsky in part: the mere fact that an act seeks to implement a treaty cannot improve

---

[239] *Crown Zellerbach*, *supra* note 235 at 436, per Le Dain J.

[240] Bayefsky, *supra* note 71 at 30.

an argument for its validity under the national concern doctrine. The legislation must be of national concern in and of itself. The rule in *Labour Conventions* precludes the argument that runs: "This legislation is of national concern because Canada as a nation is committed internationally to implementing it." I cannot see that *Labour Conventions* prevents a court from considering the substance of a treaty, as Le Dain J. did in determining whether the act that incorporates it is, in substance, a matter of national concern. However, if Le Dain J.'s finding that the legislation was a matter of national concern was influenced by the fact that it was in implementation of a treaty, that finding is wrong.

In dissent, La Forest J. (Beetz and Lamer JJ. concurring) held that the convention could not justify the act's prohibition of dumping in provincial maritime waters, for the convention addressed itself only to marine waters other than those internal to the state, whereas the act included internal waters. "I do not understand," said La Forest J., "how the fact that Parliament has chosen to adopt a similar regime in internal waters not covered by the Convention can be of any assistance in determining whether it has authority to prohibit dumping in internal waters within the province."[241] If by this La Forest J. means simply that he does not consider Section 4(1) to be a matter of national concern, with or without the convention, then this point says little more than that he disagrees with Le Dain J.'s analysis. If, however, La Forest J. means that the London Convention establishes Parliament's jurisdiction and that Section 4(1) is *ultra vires* because it goes further than the convention does, he is, with respect, wrong. The source of Parliament's legislative power is not the treaty. It is the national concern branch of the peace, order, and good government power of Section 91 of the Constitution Act 1867.

THE CURRENT POSITION OF THE LAW

As recently as 1994, L'Heureux-Dubé J. in the Supreme Court of Canada affirmed that the rule in *Labour Conventions* is the law, without any mention of *MacDonald*.[242] That case cannot properly be viewed as anything more than an influential dictum, despite the court's use of it in *Schneider*. As the law now stands, no power inheres in Parliament to legislate in matters of provincial jurisdiction

---

[241] *MacDonald, supra* note 229 at 443, per La Forest J.

[242] L'Heureux-Dubé J. in *Thomson, supra* note 67 at 611.

simply on the ground that the legislation in question seeks to implement treaty obligations incurred by the federal government.[243] The validity of treaty-implementing legislation is determined in exactly the same way as the validity of any other enactment: by applying Sections 91 and 92 of the Constitution Act 1867. In the normal case, the division of powers described in these sections will require provincial implementation of certain types of treaty obligation. However, if it can be shown that a treaty-implementing enactment is within Parliament's jurisdiction to legislate for the peace, order, and good government of Canada, this enactment will be valid to implement the treaty within what is otherwise the provincial sphere. The fact that such an enactment seeks to implement a treaty is irrelevant to the consideration of validity, for there is no such thing as treaty legislation as such. The federal argument in favour of validity is not strengthened by the claim of implementation nor is the provincial argument against validity improved by the fact that the legislation is pursuant to a treaty obligation. In particular, the fact that an act of Parliament seeks to implement a treaty is of no assistance in determining whether that act is of national concern, as that phrase is used in Canadian constitutional discourse.

IN DEFENCE OF *LABOUR CONVENTIONS*

The rule in *Labour Conventions* is an application of the implementation requirement to Canadian federalism. Lord Atkin's concern that federalism in Canada would be dangerously undermined by a rule that the federal Parliament can legislate in provincial jurisdiction when implementing treaties was valid in 1937 and is unanswerable today, for the subject matters of contemporary treaties fall increasingly within provincial jurisdiction. As impractical as some

---

[243] As this article went to press, a decision of McKeown J. of the Federal Court (Trial Division) again cast doubt on *Labour Conventions*. In *Chua* v. *Minister of National Revenue*, [2001] 1 F.C. 608 (F.C.T.D.), the applicant sought judicial review of the minister's decision to collect tax debts owing by the applicant to the United States government. The applicant argued, *inter alia*, that the law implementing the Third Protocol of the Canada-US Tax Convention 1980 was *ultra vires* Parliament as a matter of property and civil rights per section 92(13) of the Constitution Act 1867. In considering this argument, McKeown J. quoted both from Lord Atkin in *Labour Conventions* and Laskin C.J. in *MacDonald*. This discussion was clearly *obiter*, however, for McKeown J. decided the matter by holding that the legislation in question "deals with taxation and therefore falls within the competence of the federal Parliament under section 91, class 3 as legislation in respect of taxation" (at para. 36).

critics say *Labour Conventions* is, the proposed rule in *MacDonald* has its own problems. Under this rule, Parliament's jurisdiction would be determined not by Section 91 but by the executive in exercise of its treaty power. Where Parliament purported to implement a treaty falling in whole or in part within provincial jurisdiction, that legislation could be challenged by the provinces as being overbroad, meaning that the legislation invades the provincial jurisdiction more than the treaty requires (or more accurately, allows). Furthermore, the provinces might seek review of the Crown's exercise of the treaty power on the ground of colourability. The provinces might argue that the federal government entered the treaty for no good reason but only to gain provincial jurisdiction in a manner not contemplated by the Constitution Act 1867. Both of these challenges would involve courts in highly complicated legal and political questions. The rule in *Labour Conventions* has the virtue of sparing courts these difficulties.

Practicalities aside, I suggest that the rule in *Labour Conventions,* as nuanced by *Canada Temperance* and *Crown Zellerbach,* is the best means of balancing the reception system's principles of self-government and respect for international law. The principle of respect for international law is admittedly hindered by the rule in *Labour Conventions,* for that rule requires that some treaties be implemented by ten or eleven legislatures instead of one, thus significantly increasing the likelihood that such treaties will not become law in some part of the country. The rule may also force the federal government to delay or even decline ratification of certain treaties for fear of not being able to ensure their implementation in provincial law. Nevertheless, a rule that Parliament can legislate in the provincial jurisdiction to implement treaties would be a greater blow to the reception system. As we saw earlier, self-government is a community's power and practice of determining its beliefs, status, and future for itself. Our federal state combines a federal, pan-Canadian community with ten provincial communities — a point that Lord Atkin made explicitly in his observations on Québec and "local conditions." For one level of government to violate another's jurisdiction amounts to an unconsensual imposition of law by one community upon another, thus denying the imposed community its self-government. One might answer that all Canadians elect the federal Parliament, that it meets the criteria of deliberative, representative, and participatory decision-making demanded by self-government, and, therefore, that Parliament cannot be an unconsensual law-maker. That answer ignores the most basic principle of federalism, namely that in matters of provincial jurisdiction the proper instruments of our self-government are the provincial Legislatures (and likewise in matters of federal jurisdiction Parliament is the proper site for our exercise of self-government). Although the federal Parliament is undoubtedly elected, it is not elected to make law in the provincial jurisdiction.

It remains only to add that the principle of respect for international law is by no means wholly rejected in *Labour Conventions*. We have seen that over sixty years of Canadian treaty-making suggests that Canada remains capable of assuming and living up to international obligations in spite of its onerous implementation requirement. Furthermore, a hitherto unexploited means of balancing the principles of self-government and respect for international law can be seen in *Crown Zellerbach*. Consistent with Lord Simon's observations in *Canada Temperance, Crown Zellerbach* demonstrates that the rule in *Labour Conventions* allows some scope — narrow and extraordinary though it is — for the federal implementation of treaties within provincial jurisdiction, where the content of the treaty at issue constitutes a matter of national concern. To allow Parliament to legislate within what would otherwise be the provincial jurisdiction in matters of national concern is not a violation of provincial self-government, for Parliament's jurisdiction to legislate for the peace, order, and good government of Canada is set out in the Constitution Act 1867 and established in Canadian case law. *Canada Temperance* and *Crown Zellerbach* add an important nuance to the rule in *Labour Conventions*. This nuance increases the reception system's respect for international law in the area of treaty implementation while preserving the concern for self-government that federalism and the reception system both demand.

HUMAN RIGHTS TREATIES: SOME SPECIAL CONSIDERATIONS

So far in this article, treaties have been considered independent of their subject-matters. I have approached the issue this way because the implementation requirement, the treaty presumption, and the demands of federalism apply to all treaties, regardless of their content. Anglo-Canadian reception law applies the same rules to all treaties for the simple reason that international law requires all treaties to be kept. The notion of a hierarchy of treaties, with some being more binding than others, is as anathema to international law as the proposition, in domestic law, that some statutes are more binding than others. With treaties as with statutes, the degree of censure arising from breach will vary from treaty to treaty, but the fact of censure is constant.

Human rights treaties, however, are increasingly seen as occupying a class by themselves. They resemble other treaties in form, but the substance of their provisions is unlike that of any other international instrument in one essential respect. While other treaty provisions derive their bindingness from the simple fact of concluding the treaty, the bindingness of human rights guarantees lies beyond this legalism and is founded upon the notion that such rights and obligations "derive," in the words of the 1966 International Covenants on Civil and Political Rights and on Economic, Social and Cultural Rights, "from the inherent dignity of the human person."[244] There is a sense in which human rights treaties do not establish new obligations but merely declare the "inherent," "self-evident,"[245] or "universal"[246] rights of humanity. This doctrine of the universality of human rights is not simply one philosophical viewpoint or one competing political theory among others. Whatever one may think of it as an ontological proposition, the doctrine of universality is unquestionably a rule of international law, enshrined in conventional international law by the 1966 covenants and perhaps also in customary international law as suggested by, *inter alia,* the 1948 Universal Declaration of Human Rights. [247]

The universality of human rights imports special considerations for Canadian courts and counsel working with international human rights treaties.[248] Universality means that the relevance of human rights treaties as aids to the interpretation of constitutional provisions, ordinary statutes, or the common law should not rise

---

[244] Common preamble to the 1966 International Covenant on Civil and Political Rights, Can. T.S. 1976 No. 47 and the 1966 International Covenant on Economic, Social and Cultural Rights, Can. T.S. 1976 No. 46.

[245] The US 1776 Declaration of Independence described it as "self-evident" that "all men are created equal" and endowed with "certain unalienable rights."

[246] See, for instance, the 1789 French Déclaration des Droits de l'homme et du citoyen, which described the rights of man as "naturels, inaliénables et sacrés," and the 1948 Universal Declaration of Human Rights, G.A. Res. 217 A (III), U.N. Doc. A/810, which declares in Article 1 that "[a]ll human beings are born free and equal in dignity and rights" and in Article 2 that "[e]veryone is entitled to all the rights and freedoms set forth in this Declaration, without distinction of any kind."

[247] 1948 Universal Declaration of Human Rights, *ibid.*

[248] For a longer discussion of the interaction of international human rights instruments and domestic human rights provisions (particularly the Charter), see van Ert, *supra* note 3 at chapter 5.

and fall on their status of being ratified or unratified by Canada. Human rights instruments are properly of interest to Canadian courts, independent of their bindingness upon the Canadian state at international law, as attempts to express a conception of personhood to which Canada has committed itself domestically, primarily through the Charter but also through statutory rights instruments and even, beyond these posited laws, through implicit commitments to lawfulness and justice "without which it must cease to be a part of the civilized world."[249] Canadian courts should not hesitate to apply the treaty presumption to non-binding human rights instruments (that is, those instruments to which Canada is not a party), for though such instruments may not express Canadian obligations to other states at international law, they are nonetheless expressions of a conception of personhood that has been established as universal in international law and reflected in our own domestic human rights laws.[250]

Likewise, in construing the Charter, unentrenched domestic human rights legislation,[251] and other laws, Canadian courts should

---

[249] Blackstone, *supra* note 8 at 67.

[250] That Canadian courts are free to consult unratified human rights instruments in construing the Charter is suggested by Dickson C.J.'s observation in *Re Public Service Employee Relations Act,* [1987] 1 S.C.R. 313 [hereinafter *Re PSERA*] at 349-50, that international human rights laws "provide a relevant and persuasive source for interpretation of the provisions of the *Charter,* especially when they arise out of Canada's international obligations under human rights conventions." By "especially," the chief justice appears to mean especially but not exclusively. In the same judgment, however, Dickson C.J. explains that "the Charter should generally be presumed to provide protection at least as great as that afforded by similar provisions in international human rights which Canada has *ratified*" (at 349) [emphasis added]. The Supreme Court appears to have followed the former dictum, as Schabas demonstrates in his helpful collection of Supreme Court references to such unratified treaties as the 1969 American Convention on Human Rights, 1979, 1144 U.N.T.S 123, the 1950 European Convention on Human Rights, 1955, 213 U.N.T.S. 2889, the 1981 African Charter on Human and Peoples' Rights, O.A.U. Document CAB/LEG/67/3, rev. 5, and certain International Law Organization conventions. See William A. Schabas, *International Human Rights Law and the Canadian Charter,* 2nd ed. (Scarborough: Carswell, 1996) at 284-7.

[251] The leading federal human rights statutes are the Canadian Bill of Rights, S.C. 1960, c. 44, reprinted in R.S.C. 1985, App. III, and the Canada Human Rights Act, R.S.C. 1985, c. H-6. The major provincial rights-protecting instruments (excluding amendments) are as follows: Human Rights, Citizenship and Multiculturalism Act, R.S.A. 1980, c. H-11.7 (Alberta); Individual's Rights Protection Act, R.S.A. 1980, c. I-2 (Alberta); Civil Rights Protection Act, R.S.B.C. 1996, c. 49 (British Columbia); Human Rights Code, R.S.B.C. 1996, c. 210

forcefully apply the treaty presumption to ratified, but unimplemented, treaties. This contention is supported by the fact that Canadian practice is not to implement human rights treaties because, as Irit Weiser points out, "most human rights treaties are ratified by Canada on the basis that existing domestic laws and programs already conform with a treaty's obligations and no new legislation is required."[252] Furthermore, the treaty presumption should be applied in the same fashion to all domestic rights provisions, be they constitutional or statutory in origin. The approaches to Charter interpretation described by Dickson C.J. in *Re Public Service Employee Relations Act*[253] and *Slaight Communications* v. *Davidson*[254] have been phrased as applying to the Charter only, as though there were some reason for resorting to international human rights law differently when interpreting the Charter than when interpreting statutory human rights codes or other domestic rights legislation. There is no such reason: all these rights are human rights, and international human rights law is relevant to them all.

Another consideration for courts and counsel using human rights treaties is the Bangalore declarations of 1988 and 1998. In these two documents,[255] some of the leading judges in the common law world declared their determination to give international human rights norms a special pre-eminence. The first Bangalore

---

(British Columbia); Human Rights Code, S.M. 1987-8, c. 45 (Manitoba); Human Rights Code, R.S.N.B. 1973, c. H-11 (New Brunswick); Human Rights Code, R.S.N. 1990, c. H-14 (Newfoundland); Human Rights Act, R.S.N.S. 1989, c. 214 (Nova Scotia); Human Rights Code, R.S.O. 1990, c. H.19 (Ontario); Human Rights Act, R.S.P.E.I. 1988, c. H-12 (Prince Edward Island); Charter of Human Rights and Freedoms, R.S.Q. c. C-12 (Québec); Saskatchewan Human Rights Code, S.S. 1979, c. S-24.1 (Saskatchewan). Also of note is the Human Rights Act, R.S.Y. 1986 (Supp.), c. 11 (Yukon Territory).

[252] Irit Weiser, "Effect in Domestic Law of International Human Rights Treaties Ratified without Implementing Legislation," in Canadian Council on International Law, *The Impact of International Law on the Practice of Law in Canada: Proceedings of the 27th Annual Conference of the Canadian Council on International Law*, Ottawa October 15-17, 1998 (The Hague: Kluwer Law International, 1999), 132 at 132.

[253] *Re PSERA, supra* note 250.

[254] *Slaight Communications* v. *Davidson*, [1989] 1 S.C.R. 1038 at 1056-7.

[255] The Bangalore judicial colloquium of 1988 was the first of a series of annual meetings of leading Commonwealth and American judges. There are human rights statements similar to the Bangalore Principles arising from each annual meeting. See Lord Lester, "The Challenge of Bangalore: Making Human Rights a Practical Reality" (1999) Eur. H.R.L.R. 273.

declaration[256] begins by affirming the universality of human rights with the words: "Fundamental human rights and freedoms are inherent in all humankind and find expression in constitutions and legal systems throughout the world and in the international human rights instruments." It continues:

These international human rights instruments provide important guidance in cases concerning fundamental human rights and freedoms ...

7. It is within the proper nature of the judicial process and well-established judicial functions for national courts to have regard to international obligations which a country undertakes — whether or not they have been incorporated into domestic law — for the purpose of removing ambiguity or uncertainty from national constitutions, legislation or common law.

The 1998 Bangalore Declaration[257] much strengthened the judges' commitment to using international human rights law domestically. It reads in part:

Fundamental human rights and freedoms are universal ...

2. The universality of human rights derives from the moral principle of each individual's personal and equal autonomy and human dignity. That principle transcends national political systems and is in the keeping of the judiciary.

3. It is the vital duty of an independent, well-trained legal profession, to interpret and apply national constitutions and ordinary legislation in harmony with international human rights codes and customary international law, and to develop the common law in the light of the values and principles enshrined in international human rights law ...

5. ... even where human rights treaties have not been ratified or incorporated into domestic law, they provide important guidance to law-makers, public officials and the courts.

It is difficult to say what weight can properly be given to extra-judicial declarations such as these. Obviously they are not sources of law. Some courts may even hesitate to take judicial notice of them. I suggest, however, that the Bangalore declarations lend support to the existence and ardent application of the treaty presumption (and indeed the presumption of international legality generally). Furthermore, the declarations lend credence to my

---

[256] 1988 Bangalore Principles, reproduced in Hunt, *supra* note 36 at 385-6.

[257] Reproduced in Lord Lester, *supra* note 255 at 287-91.

earlier suggestion[258] that the rule is not simply a presumption of legislative intent but also an interpretive policy of Commonwealth judges.

Finally, there is support in the case law for the proposition that international human rights instruments can be looked to by courts as evidence of Canadian public policy. The leading case is the once-forgotten but now resuscitated judgment of Mackay J. in *Re Drummond Wren*.[259] A covenant in a deed of land required that it not be "sold to Jews or persons of objectionable nationality." A motion was brought to declare the covenant invalid as being contrary to public policy. In granting the motion, Mackay J. looked to the recently signed Charter of the United Nations[260] and the Atlantic Charter as indications of Canada's public policy against racial discrimination. He explained that the fact

that the restrictive covenant in this case is directed in the first place against Jews lends poignancy to the matter when one considers that anti-semitism has been a weapon in the hands of our recently-defeated enemies, and the scourge of the world. But this feature of the case does not require innovation in legal principle to strike down the covenant; it merely makes it more appropriate to apply existing principles.[261]

Re Drummond Wren was cast in doubt only three years after it was decided. In *Re Noble and Wolf*,[262] a covenant against selling, renting, or otherwise assigning land to "any person of the Jewish, Hebrew, Semitic, Negro or coloured race or blood" was upheld by Schroeder J. in spite of the fact that both the vendor and the purchaser attacked the covenant's validity. "It is the province of the statesman," explained the judge, "and not the lawyer, to discuss, and of the Legislature to determine, what is best for the public good."[263] This case went on to the Supreme Court, where it was disposed of without comment on the public policy argument.[264] In *Bhadauria v. Seneca College*,[265] Wilson J.A. (as she then was) relied

---

[258] See the discussion in this article under the heading "The Relevance of Chronology."

[259] *Re Drummond Wren,* [1945] O.R. 778 [hereinafter *Re Drummond Wren*].

[260] Charter of the United Nations, Can. T.S. 1945 No. 7.

[261] *Re Drummond Wren, supra* note 259 at 783.

[262] *Re Noble and Wolf,* [1948] O.R. 579.

[263] *Ibid.* at 594.

[264] *Noble and Wolf v. Alley,* [1951] S.C.R. 64.

[265] *Bhadauria v. Seneca College* (1980), 27 O.R. (2d) 142.

on *Re Drummond Wren* without mentioning the contrary authority.[266] On appeal to the Supreme Court of Canada, Laskin C.J. declared: "I do not myself quarrel with the approach taken in *Re Drummond Wren*," yet he went on to observe that there was authority against it.[267]

The solution to the difficulty, I suggest, lies in the universality of human rights. The general proposition that treaties concluded by Canada may be relied upon as statements of Canadian public policy cannot be sound as long as treaty-making remains an executive, rather than a legislative, function. Courts should not, as a rule, look to the executive's prerogative acts as indicators of the values held by Canadian society, for prerogatives have much weaker representative and democratic credentials than legislative acts and are therefore less likely to reflect Canadian public policy or social values. There is surely an exception to this rule, however, for human rights treaties. These treaties not only reflect Canadian public policy, as evidenced by our constitutional and statutory human rights provisions, but they are also attempts to depict the universal legal significance of being human. To suggest that Canadian public policy does not incorporate conceptions of humanity that are recognized as universal in international law comes close to saying that Canada is a pariah among nations.

CONCLUSION

The use of treaties, and, indeed, of international law as a whole, in Canadian courts is bound to become more frequent in the coming years. The complaint so often voiced about international law, namely that it lacks enforcement, has always been overstated and is now shown to be simply wrong. Domestic courts in Canada and other Commonwealth countries are embracing international law more than ever. To do so, they have not needed to adopt new practices but instead have looked to the principles and precedents of the common law, which has always regarded international law as an aspect of itself. In this article and elsewhere, I have suggested that the rules according to which public international law takes effect in Anglo-Canadian law are not, as they might at first seem, a jumble of unrelated common law, statutory, interpretive, and constitutional requirements. Rather, these rules are internally consistent

---

[266] *Ibid.* at 147-9.

[267] *Seneca College* v. *Bhadauria*, [1981] 2 S.C.R. 181 at 192.

propositions following from the principles of self-government and respect for international law, and the necessity of balancing these principles to secure their survival and the integrity of the reception system as a whole. As has ever been the case with the common-law constitution, the reception system is in the care of the courts. When using treaties in their judgments, courts should strive, as the reception system itself does, to preserve the balance between self-government and respect for international law. For by advancing either principle too much to the detriment of the other, we may transform the system entirely, rendering it unrecognizable, if not unintelligible.

Sommaire

Le recours aux traités internationaux par les tribunaux canadiens

De plus en plus, les parties à un contentieux cherchent la résolution de leurs différends en ayant recours avant tout aux traités internationaux. Les difficultés auxquelles elles font face sont nombreuses. Le droit international public est un domaine inconnu pour une grande majorité de juristes canadiens, aussi bien des avocats que des juges. Au surplus, les règles selon lesquelles les traités internationaux s'appliquent au droit interne canadien portent sur une diversité de sources de droit, comprenant l'ancienne jurisprudence de la common law, les règles constitutionnelles non écrites, le fédéralisme, les dispositions de la Charte et d'autres instruments canadiens des droits de la personne. L'objet de cet article consiste à décrire comment les traités internationaux devraient être utilisés par les tribunaux canadiens. Les normes disparates et en apparence sans rapport les unes avec les autres, renseignent sur le droit anglo-canadien de l'adoption (reception) des traités, notamment l'obligation de mise en œuvre, la présomption de traité, la règle dans l'affaire Labour Conventions *et l'importante décision dans l'affaire* Baker *c.* Canada, *sont ici décrits comme des manifestations des deux principes devant servir de guide à l'application du droit international dans le système juridique canadien, à savoir autonomie gouvernementale et respect du droit international.*

Summary

Using Treaties in Canadian Courts

Increasingly, litigants are seeking to rely on international treaties before domestic courts. The difficulties they face, together with the judges hearing these cases, are great. Public international law is unknown territory for the vast majority of Canadian lawyers, both at the bar and on the bench. Moreover, the rules according to which international treaties take effect in Canadian domestic law engage a wide variety of legal sources, including ancient common law jurisprudence, unwritten constitutional rules, federalism, and the provisions of the Canadian Charter of Rights and Freedoms *and other Canadian human rights instruments. The object of this article is to describe in a comprehensive manner how international treaties may be used in Canadian courts. The disparate and seemingly unrelated norms informing the Anglo-Canadian law of treaty reception, including the implementation requirement, the treaty presumption, the rule in* Labour Conventions, *and the landmark decision in* Baker v. Canada, *are depicted as internally-consistent manifestations of the guiding principles of the Canadian reception system: self-government and respect for international law.*

Regulatory Expropriation
and State Intent

KATHARINA A. BYRNE

The only purpose for which power can be rightfully exercised over any member of a civilized community, against his will, is to prevent harm to others.

John Stuart Mill, *On Liberty* (1859)

INTRODUCTION

This article addresses the following question: When should state regulatory action be regarded as expropriatory of private property interests. The debate is longstanding,[1] but its importance has been enhanced by the inclusion of provisions in recent multilateral investment treaties, in particular, the North American Free Trade Agreement (NAFTA), the Energy Charter Treaty, and the draft Multilateral Agreement on Investment, which provide a private investor with a direct right of recourse against a foreign state if the investor has suffered loss as a result of measures taken by the state that are "tantamount" to expropriation. This right of recourse has implications for national sovereignty in general as well as raising more specific concerns regarding the extent to which private business interests are able to take precedence over such matters as environmental protection, workers' rights, and public health. Furthermore, the over-emphasis in current legal debate on the consequences of a regulatory measure *vis-à-vis* private individuals is, one may suppose, one reason for the vehement opposition to multilateral investment agreements containing investor-state provisions.

Katharina Byrne, of the Bar of British Columbia, is a solicitor (non-practising) in England and Wales as well as Hong Kong. The author wishes to acknowledge the assistance of John Ames and the law firm of Thomas and Partners in Vancouver.

[1] For example, see A. Fachiri, "Expropriation and International Law" (1925) 6 B.Y. I.L. 159; B. Wortley, *Expropriation in Public International Law* (New York: Arno Press, 1977); G. Christie, "What Constitutes a Taking of Property under International Law?" 38 (1962) B.Y.I.L. 307; Burns Weston, "'Constructive Takings' under International Law: A Modest Foray into the Problem of 'Creeping Expropriation,'" 16 (1975) Va. J. Int'l Law 102.

Recent studies of the issue of regulatory taking, particularly those studies concerning claims under Chapter 11 of NAFTA, have tended to approach the problem from the angle of a cost-benefit analysis, whereby business interests are balanced against social welfare interests.[2] Alternatively, one can pose the question of whether the regulation seeks to further a public purpose, and, if so, is it unchallengeable.[3] Other theories require the application of a number of criteria to the regulation in order to establish whether it constitutes an expropriation.[4] The recent debate over indirect takings appears to have been especially influenced by the United States, not only in terms of its jurisprudence concerning the Fifth Amendment to the Constitution[5] but also by its stance on investment protection as evidenced in the *Restatement of the Law Third: The Foreign Relations Law of the United States*[6] and in its bilateral investment treaties.

This article, however, proposes an alternative approach: whether the regulator's intent should be the determining factor. In doing so, it is recognized that the issue of intent has been generally regarded by both writers[7] and judicial bodies[8] as being irrelevant or at least not determinative of the matter. It may also be argued that the investigation of intent is contrary to the principle of objective

---

[2] Julie A. Soloway, "Environmental Regulation as Expropriation: The Case of NAFTA's Chapter 11" (2000) 33 Can. Bus. L.J. 92.

[3] Samrat Ganguly, "The Investor-State Dispute Mechanism (ISDM) and a Sovereign's Power to Protect Public Health" (1999) 38 Colum. J. Transnat'l L. 113.

[4] For example, Thomas Waelde and Abba Kolo, in "Multilateral Investment Treaties and Environmental Expropriation of Foreign Investment," state: "It is therefore unlikely that an environmental regulation which is legitimate, non-discriminatory, and which did not render the investment economically unviable, could be found by an international tribunal as tantamount to expropriation." CEPMLP Internet Journal, vol. 5-2, accessible at <http://www.dundee.ac.uk/cepmlp/journal/html/article5-2.html>.

[5] See for example, D. Schneiderman, "NAFTA's Takings Rule: American Constitutionalism Comes to Canada" (1996) 46 U.T.L.J. 499.

[6] *Restatement of the Law Third: The Foreign Relations Law of the United States* (St. Paul, MN: American Law Institute, 1987).

[7] "The object pursued by the State in carrying out expropriations is of no concern to third parties, whether these be private individuals or foreign States, any more than are the motives for such measures." S. Friedman, *Expropriation in International Law* (London: Stevens, 1953), 142-3.

[8] For example, the Iran-United States Claims Tribunal, discussed in the first section of this article.

responsibility of states.[9] However, as will be demonstrated, insofar as this intention can be ascertained objectively, the two concepts are not irreconcilable.

The article will first examine the respective approaches of the Iran-United States Claims Tribunal and the United States to regulatory expropriation, and will demonstrate why they are unsatisfactory. This discussion will then be briefly contrasted with the unique jurisprudence of the European Court of Justice and the European Court of Human Rights. Finally, the role of intent under municipal law will be addressed, and a case will be made as to why this approach should not apply by analogy in international law.

THE IRAN-UNITED STATES CLAIMS TRIBUNAL AND THE ISSUE OF REGULATORY EXPROPRIATION

The Iran-United States Claims Tribunal is one of the most significant international arbitral fora of recent times. Its jurisprudence with respect to expropriation, in particular, has received a great deal of international attention.[10] However, in regard to the specific issue of intent and *de facto* expropriation, the tribunal's approach is, at the very least, inconsistent. In two early and almost simultaneous awards,[11] the tribunal expressed two quite different views concerning the question of intent.

In *Sea-Land Service, Inc.* v. *Iran,* for example, Sea-Land Service claimed that it had been deprived of the right to continued use of a containerized cargo facility constructed and operated by it at the

---

[9] "It is not by their intentions but by their acts that States incur responsibility." Friedman, *supra* note 7 at 142. See also I. Brownlie, *Principles of Public International Law,* 5th ed. (Oxford: Oxford University Press, 1998), 440 *et seq.*

[10] For example, G. Aldrich, *The Jurisprudence of the Iran-United States Claims Tribunal* (New York: Oxford University Press, 1996); A.B. Avanessian, *The Iran-United States Claims Tribunal in Action* (London: Graham and Trotman, 1993); Rahmatullah Khan, *The Iran-United States Claims Tribunal: Controversies, Cases and Contributions* (Boston: Kluwer Academic Publishers, 1990); Allahyar Mouri, *The International Law of Expropriation as Reflected in the Work of the Iran-US Claims Tribunal* (Dordrecht: Kluwer Academic Publishers, 1994); Wayne Mapp, *The Iran-United States Claims Tribunal: The First Ten Years 1981-1991* (New York: St. Martin's Press, 1993); C.N. Brower and J.D. Brueschke, *The Iran-US Claims Tribunal* (Boston: Kluwer Academic Publishers, 1998).

[11] *Sea-Land Service, Inc.* v. *Iran,* Award No. 135-33-1 (June 22, 1984), reprinted in 6 Iran-U.S. C.T.R. 149 [hereinafter *Sea-Land Service*]; *Tippetts, Abbett, McCarthy, Stratton* v. *TAMS-AFFA,* Award No. 141-7-2 (June 29, 1984), reprinted in 6 Iran-U.S. C.T.R. 219 [hereinafter *Tippetts*].

port of Bandar Abbas. The Iranian government agency chiefly responsible for the alleged deprivation was the Ports and Shipping Organization (PSO), which was responsible for the administration and control of Iranian ports. Sea-Land advanced a number of alternative arguments in support of its claim, including one of expropriation as a result of interference in its operations on the part of governmental agencies. In the tribunal's opinion, the chaotic situation at the port was simply a result of the general social upheaval that was taking place in Iran during the period leading up to the success of the Islamic Revolution. There was no evidence "that PSO had embarked upon a policy of deliberate disruption or non-cooperation directed at Sea-Land in particular."[12] In the tribunal's view, proof of intent was fundamental to a finding of expropriation:

> A finding of expropriation would require, at the very least, that the Tribunal be satisfied that there was *deliberate governmental interference* with the conduct of Sea-Land's operation, the effect of which was to deprive Sea-Land of the use and benefit of its investment. Nothing has been demonstrated here which might have amounted to an intentional course of conduct directed against Sea-Land. A claim founded substantially on omissions and inaction in a situation where the evidence suggest a widespread and indiscriminate deterioration in management, disrupting the functioning of the port of Bandar Abbas, can hardly justify a finding of expropriation.[13]

In complete contrast to the majority decision, however, Judge Holtzmann dissented strongly with respect to the issues of both law and fact.[14] In particular, he disagreed with the majority concerning the elements constituting expropriation, specifically the need to show an intention on the part of the government to interfere with Sea-Land's business.[15] In support of his conclusion, Judge Holtzmann cited three other tribunal awards: *Tippetts, Abbett, McCarthy, Stratton* v. *TAMS-AFFA; ITT Industries, Inc.* v. *Iran;*[16] and

---

[12] *Sea-Land Service, supra* note 11 at 165.

[13] *Ibid.* at 166 [emphasis added].

[14] "I believe that it ignores the facts, misapplies the law, and is blind to realities." Separate Opinion of Judge Holtzmann, *ibid.* at 175.

[15] Judge Holtzmann states: "I believe that the pattern of acts and omissions by Respondents did in fact represent a deliberate effort to drive Sea-Land from Iran. More fundamentally, I believe that the critical question is the objective effect of a government's acts, not its subjective intentions. Acts by a government which have the effect of depriving an alien of his property are considered expropriatory in international law, whatever the government's intentions." *Ibid.* at 207.

[16] *ITT Industries, Inc.* v. *Iran,* Award No. 47-156-2 (26 May 1983), reprinted in 2 Iran-U.S. C.T.R. 348 [hereinafter *ITT Industries*].

Starrett Housing Corp. v. *Iran.*[17] His only other source of authority was the well-known article by G. Christie, "What Constitutes a Taking of Property under International Law?"[18]

It is questionable, however, whether these authorities are sufficient to dismiss the relevance of government intention in expropriation claims in general. First, as discussed below, the uniqueness of the circumstances surrounding the establishment and operation of the Iran-United States Claims Tribunal make it doubtful that its case law can be of general application. Second, there is a great deal of cross-referencing within the cases cited. For example, in his reference to *Starrett,*[19] Judge Holtzmann is relying on his *own* concurring opinion, whereas, in *Tippetts* and *ITT Industries,* he is referring to cases in which Judge Aldrich acted as the United States-appointed judge. It is to be expected that both Judge Holtzmann and Judge Aldrich would maintain a consistent approach throughout their time of office. In fact, the wording in *Tippetts* and *ITT Industries* on the issue of governmental intent is identical.[20] However, reliance on tribunal cases is of little significance other than promoting internal consistency, unless the reasoning in those cases can be regarded as correct in the first place. Third, in his article, G. Christie does *not* reject the role of intention as such. He merely makes the point that an express disclaimer on the part of a state of the intent to expropriate is not decisive. It should also be noted that in the two cases to which Christie was specifically referring in his discussion on this issue, the *Norway* v. *The United States*[21] and *German Interests in Polish Upper Silesia (Germany* v. *Poland),*[22] a key issue was whether contractual and other intangible rights that were ancillary to tangible property, which had been the subject of express

---

[17] *Starrett Housing Corp.* v. *Iran,* Award No. ITL 32-24-1, reprinted in 4 Iran-U.S. C.T.R. 122 [hereinafter *Starrett*].

[18] G. Christie, "What Constitutes a Taking of Property under International Law?" 38 (1962) B.Y.I.L. 307 at 311.

[19] In *Starrett,* Judge Holtzman refers to, *inter alia,* Judge Aldrich' s opinion in *ITT Industries* (*Starrett, supra* note 17 at 163-4).

[20] In both *Tippetts* and *ITT Industries,* Aldrich J. states: "The intent of the government is less important than the effects of the measures on the owner, and the form of the measures of control or interference is less important than the reality of their impact" (*Tippetts, supra* note 11 at 225-6; *ITT Industries, supra* note 16 at 352).

[21] *Norwegian Shipowners' Claims case (Norway* v. *United States),* (1922), 1 U.N.R.I.A.A. 307 [hereinafter *Norwegian Shipowners*].

[22] *German Interests in Polish Upper Silesia (Germany* v. *Poland),* P.C.I.J. Series A, No. 7 (25 May 1926) (Merits).

expropriation, had also been expropriated. Fourth, Judge Holtz-mann cites no authority for his view that expropriation is to be determined solely on the basis of the effect of state acts. Further-more, his view that intent is merely a subjective notion and on that basis is unreliable is open to challenge. As will be demonstrated later, state intent can be the subject of an objective enquiry.

In *Tippetts*, the claimants, who were known as TAMS, were a US engineering and architectural consulting partnership with a 50 per cent ownership share in TAMS-AFFA, an Iranian entity created for the sole purpose of performing engineering and architectural services on the Tehran International Airport. The articles of part-nership required that any decision of the partnership required the consent of at least one representative of each partner. Documents creating obligations for the partnership had to be signed by two persons, one appointed by each partner. One of the claims pre-sented to the tribunal was for the alleged expropriation of the part-nership interest by the government of Iran. This claim arose chiefly out of the acts and omissions of a government-appointed manager.

The tribunal concluded that the government of Iran had been responsible for depriving TAMS-AFFA of its property interests since at least March 1, 1980, as a result of "measures affecting prop-erty rights."[23] On the issue of intent, the tribunal held: "The intent of the government is less important than the effects of the measures on the owner, and the form of the measures of control or interfer-ence is less important than the reality of their impact."[24] This state-ment is inconsistent with Judge Holtzmann's categorical view in *Sea-Land*, noted earlier, that the "critical question" in cases of alleged *de facto* expropriation is the effect of government acts, not intention. In this case, the tribunal did not rule out the possible rel-evance of intent but, instead, merely subordinated it to the form and effect of a particular measure. The tribunal did not provide any authority for its view, although it should be noted that the word-ing is identical to that used by one of the tribunal members, Judge Aldrich, in his concurring opinion in *ITT Industries*,[25] which was issued just three days earlier. Moreover, a comparison of the cir-cumstances surrounding the awards in *ITT Industries* and *Tippetts* raises doubts as to their value in ascertaining the view of the tri-bunal on *de facto* expropriation. In *ITT Industries*, Judge Aldrich was

[23] *Tippets, supra* note 11 at 225.

[24] *Ibid*, at 225-6.

[25] *ITT Industries, supra* note 16.

expressing his position in a separate opinion in connection with an award on agreed terms, whereas the statement in *Tippetts* was made in the context of a deprivation arising out of "other measures affecting rights."[26] Finally, it should be noted that the decision in *Tippetts* makes no reference to the decision in *Sea-Land,* which was signed only two days earlier.

Another case that was in line with these decisions was *Phillips Petroleum Co. Iran* v. *Iran, et al.,*[27] which was one of three cases concerning the *de facto* nationalization of the petroleum industry in Iran. Phillips Petroleum brought two claims, one of which was for the alleged taking of its rights under a joint structure agreement with the National Iranian Oil Company for the exploration and exploitation of the petroleum resources of a certain area offshore in the Persian Gulf (JSA). The tribunal found that Phillips Petroleum's rights under the JSA had been taken as a result of "a series of concrete actions"[28] and, in doing so, it rejected Iran's defences of *force majeure* and changed circumstances. On the issue of governmental intent, the tribunal merely referred to the findings in *Tippetts*[29] on the subject and concluded "[t]herefore, the Tribunal need not determine the intent of the Government of Iran."[30] The tribunal then continued: "[H]owever, where the effects of actions are consistent with a policy to nationalize a whole industry and to that end expropriate particular alien property interests, and are not merely the incidental consequences of an action or policy designed for an unrelated purpose, the conclusion that a taking has occurred is all the more evident."[31] Although this statement is useful insofar as it appears that the tribunal recognized the need to examine all the circumstances surrounding an alleged taking before determining whether an expropriation had actually taken place, it is flawed in its conclusion concerning government intent because, in fact, there was no need to consider the issue of intent at all.

---

[26] Mouri, *supra* note 10 at 260.

[27] *Phillips Petroleum Co. Iran* v. *Iran, et al,* Award 425-39-2 (29 June 1989), reprinted in 21 Iran-U.S. C.T.R. 79 [hereinafter *Phillips Petroleum*].

[28] *Ibid.* at 116, para.100.

[29] *Ibid.* at 115. It should be noted that Judge Aldrich was a member of the bench in both *Tippetts* and *Phillips Petroleum*.

[30] *Ibid.* at 115.

[31] *Ibid.* at 115.

A policy of nationalization, whether *de jure* or *de facto,* is an objective manifestation of government intent to assume ownership and control over certain property within its jurisdiction. In the case of a *de jure* nationalization, there is express intent to expropriate; in the case of a *de facto* nationalization, the intent is latent, yet can be determined from an examination of all the circumstances, in particular, the result of government measures. In *Phillips Petroleum,* although there was no formal decree of nationalization, there was no doubt, based on the facts, that the Iranian government was carrying out the nationalization of the oil industry and that the termination of the JSA was part of that process. In fact, the tribunal noted that this had been "an important objective of the Revolutionary movement — and a first order of business of the Government."[32] It is odd that the tribunal should have been reluctant to find explicitly that Phillips Petroleum's loss of its interests under the JSA was the direct and *intended* result of a general nationalization policy of the Iranian government.

It is perhaps important to note that *Phillips* was one of three petroleum cases,[33] which were among the largest claims presented to the tribunal. They were also considered more important politically than many of the other claims.[34] For this reason alone, *Phillips Petroleum* should not be regarded as having much authoritative value with respect to the issue of state intent and expropriation.

In regard to the general applicability of the tribunal's jurisprudence, it must be emphasized that the tribunal is a creature of unique circumstances, and, therefore, the precedential value of its decisions is doubtful:

[T]he world beyond the Tribunal should expect to gain little from its deliberations, either in the elaboration of substantive law or in the development of a model structure for international arbitration. The Tribunal is a very complex creature: part public and part private; part international

---

[32] *Ibid.* at 117, para. 101. Moreover, in his statement entitled "Statement by Judge Khalilian as to Why It Would Have Been Premature to Sign the Award," which was annexed to the award, Judge Khalilian, the arbitrator appointed by Iran, described Iran's actions as "a lawful nationalisation in the oil industry" (*ibid.* at 197, para.9).

[33] The other cases were *Mobil Oil Iran Inc.* v. *Iran,* Partial Award No. 3131-74/76/81/150-3 (July 14, 1987), reprinted in 16 Iran-U.S. C.T.R. 3 and *Amoco International Finance Corp.* v. *Iran,* Partial Award No. 310-56-3 (14 July 1987), reprinted in 15 Iran-U.S. C.T.R. 189.

[34] Aldrich, *supra* note 10 at 196.

and part transnational; part legal and part political. This complexity alone should cause one to be wary in searching for general principles.[35]

For the purposes of the present discussion, two particularly notable features of the tribunal are its jurisdiction and the scope of the law applicable to its decisions. With respect to the former feature, Article II of the Declaration of the Government of the Democratic and Popular Republic of Algeria concerning the Settlement of Claims by the Government of the United States of America and the Government of the Islamic Republic of Iran (Algiers Declaration)[36] gave the tribunal jurisdiction over claims arising out of "debts, contracts including transactions which are the subject of letters of credit or bank guarantees), expropriations or other measures affecting property rights." The scope of this clause with respect to both "expropriations" and "other measures affecting property rights" suggests that "neither the terminology nor the intent of actions attributable to either Government would affect the Tribunal's jurisdiction to award compensation if the actions had adversely affected a claimant's property rights."[37] Consequently, in *Eastman Kodak Co.* v. *Iran*,[38] *Seismograph Service Corp.* v. *NIOC*,[39] and *United Painting C. Inc.* v. *Iran*,[40] the tribunal awarded compensation for measures affecting property rights while refusing to make a finding of expropriation.

In so far as the applicable law was concerned, Article V of the Algiers Declaration stated that "[t]he Tribunal shall decide all cases on the basis of respect for law, applying such choice of law rules and principles of commercial and international law as the Tribunal determines to be applicable, taking into account relevant

---

[35] S. Toope, *Mixed International Arbitration* (Cambridge: Grotius, 1990), 381. For a thorough analysis of the tribunal's relevance as a model for international claims adjudication, see generally chapters 8 and 9 of Toope's work.

[36] Declaration of the Government of the Democratic and Popular Republic of Algeria Concerning the Settlement of Claims by the Government of the United States of America and the Government of the Islamic Republic of Iran, 19 January 1981 (1981), 20 I.L.M. 223, reprinted in 1 Iran-U.S. C.T.R. 9 [hereinafter Algiers Declaration].

[37] Aldrich, *supra* note 10 at 173.

[38] *Eastman Kodak Co.* v. *Iran*, Award No. 329-227/12384-3 (November 11, 1987), reprinted in 17 Iran-U.S. C.T.R. 153.

[39] *Seismograph Service Corp.* v. *NIOC*, Award No. 420-443-3 (March 31, 1989), reprinted in 22 Iran-U.S. C.T.R. 3.

[40] *United Painting C. Inc.* v. *Iran*, Award No 458-11286-3 (December 20, 1989), reprinted in 23 Iran-U.S. C.T.R. 351.

usages of the trade, contract provisions and changed circumstances."[41] The tribunal, therefore, was not limited to deciding
claims under international law but could rely upon *any* law that it
found applicable. As a result, although expropriation was alleged
in a number of cases, the tribunal based its decision on other
grounds, such as contractual or commercial law.[42] One such example was *Sedco, Inc.* v. *Iran Marine Industrial Co.*,[43] where the tribunal
awarded the claimant amounts owed to it in promissory notes
issued by its Iranian subsidiary and held that it need not decide the
claim of expropriation of that subsidiary for the reason that, "given
the validity of the promissory note debts, as held *supra*, IMICO [the
subsidiary] could not have had a positive net worth on the date any
such deprivation may have occurred."[44]

The flexibility that was afforded the tribunal in its choice and
application of law has not gone without criticism: "In resolving
disputes on the basis of 'respect for law,' the tribunal is forced to
display enormous flexibility; it must be willing to compromise. This
has led to an essentially idiosyncratic approach to choice of law
and even to the application of substantive legal principles."[45] Other
factors that may be said to militate against the use of the tribunal's
decisions as generally applicable precedents include:

- the likely ideological empathy between the third-country arbitrators, as nationals of Western states, and the United States;[46]
- the highly politicized environment in which the tribunal
  operated;
- the possible self-interest on the part of the third-country arbitrators in not appearing strongly opposed to Western economic
  interests where the individual concerned wished to continue
  working as an international arbitrator;[47]

---

[41] *Algiers Declaration, supra* note 36.

[42] Aldrich, *supra* note 10 at 172.

[43] *Sedco, Inc.* v. *Iran Marine Industrial Co.*, Award No. 419-128/129-2 (March 30,
1989), reprinted in 21 Iran-U.S. C.T.R. 31 [hereinafter *Sedco*].

[44] *Ibid.* at 56. In relation to the issue of internal consistency discussed earlier in the
article, it should also be noted that Judge Aldrich was a member of the tribunal
in *Sedco* and that the award (at 70) refers to both *Tippetts, supra* note 11 and *Starrett, supra* note 17.

[45] Toope, *supra* note 35 at 383.

[46] *Ibid.* at 346.

[47] *Ibid.*

- a tendency of the party-appointed arbitrators of both the United States and Iran to favour their own side. It was said that they acted as "the leading counsel for the party in question ... even if they don't admit it."[48] It has also been observed that "on the few occasions when American claimants do lose, the American arbitrator is almost invariably to be found dissenting";[49]
- the fact that unanimous decisions were "extremely rare";[50]
- the existence of the security account for the purpose of enforcing awards;[51]
- the fact that the reasoning in awards has tended to be short and vague;[52] and
- the heavy case load of the tribunal,[53] which would necessarily affect the quality of the decisions.

With respect to the specific issue of regulatory expropriation, the decisions are not particularly helpful given the fact that the tribunal has awarded compensation in some cases even if a deprivation "resulted from measures that arguably were legitimate regulatory actions."[54] The apparent basis for such decisions was that the tribunal "was doubtless influenced by its perception that the deprivations were likely to be permanent, even when termed 'provisional,' and by the fact that the provisional managers were accountable

[48] Judge Nils Mangård, transcript of interview (September 14, 1984), referred to by S. Toope, *ibid.* at 351.

[49] *Ibid.* at 350.

[50] *Ibid.*

[51] "Typically, the American and Iranian arbitrator will not agree on the legal reasoning applicable in any given case. The burden then falls upon the Chairman to conduct Chamber business and to author awards, order, etc. in such a manner that some equilibrium and some rational communication can be maintained. To do so, it will often be necessary to compromise, to play down differences of opinion and to render decisions that are intentionally vague and obfuscatory. The Security Account makes such an approach more attractive because its existence precludes the need for separate enforcement proceedings." *Ibid.* at 369.

[52] As Professor Carbonneau has observed: "The awards rendered by the Tribunal have been essentially devoid of substantive legal content and, as a result, [are] incapable of having much precedential value." ("The Elaboration of Substantive Legal Norms and Arbitral Adjudication: The Case of the Iran-United States Claims Tribunal," in R. Lillich, ed., *The Iran-United States Claims Tribunal 1981-1983* (Charlottesville: University Press of Virginia, 1984), 104 at 126.

[53] By January 19, 1981, the deadline for the filing of claims, approximately 950 claims for more than US $250,000 each, and nearly 2,800 small claims had been filed with the tribunal. Aldrich, *supra* note 10 at 13-14.

[54] *Ibid.* at 181.

only to the Government, not to the owners of the companies, for whatever happened during their period of management, even if control were ultimately returned to the owners."[55]

"REGULATORY" EXPROPRIATION: THE APPROACH OF THE UNITED STATES

Although a full treatment of this topic is beyond the scope of this article, a brief discussion will assist in demonstrating that the US approach to regulatory takings is not necessarily the correct or desirable one.[56] The US approach to the issue of expropriation is based on case law arising out of the Fifth Amendment of the United States Constitution, which provides that "[n]o person shall be ... deprived of life, liberty, or property, without due process of law; nor shall private property be taken for public use, without just compensation." Protection under the Fifth Amendment was originally limited to governmental seizures of real property or tangible assets.[57] Governmental action that caused economic loss, however substantial, was not compensable, provided that it fell within the scope of the state's "police power."[58]

At the turn of the century, however, following the case of *Lochner* v. *New York*,[59] the Supreme Court used a combination of the Fourteenth Amendment and the Fifth Amendment to invalidate legislative actions relating to income tax, minimum wage laws, and labour laws.[60] It was a time when governmental regulation in several areas was expanding. The approach used by the Supreme Court was one of balancing public need and private loss, and, hence, the right to compensation depended largely on the magnitude of the loss.[61]

---

[55] *Ibid.*

[56] For more detailed discussions on this topic, see, for example, *The Property Rights Issue*, produced for the U.S. Congressional Research Service by Robert Meltz, Legislative Attorney, American Law Division, January 20, 1995, available at <http://www.cnie.org/nle/econ-11.html>; and Raymond R. Coletta, "The Measuring Stick of Regulatory Takings: A Biological and Cultural Analysis," 1 (1998) U. Pa. J. Const. L. 20, also available at http://www.law.upenn.edu/conlaw/issues/vol 1>.

[57] Edward M. Graham, "National Treatment of Foreign Investment: Exceptions and Conditions" (1998) 31 Cornell Int'l L.J. 599.

[58] In general, the police power of a state encompasses matters of public safety, health, and welfare.

[59] *Lochner* v. *New York*, 198 U.S. 45 (1905).

[60] Graham, *supra* note 57.

[61] Joseph L. Sax, "Takings and the Police Power" (1964-5) 74 Yale L.J. 36 at 37.

Following the New Deal era of the 1930s, the Supreme Court upheld most economic regulation even if compensation for regulatory taking was not provided. This reversal was apparently due to new appointments to the Supreme Court.[62] Since the 1980s, there has been a re-emergence of the *Lochner* approach to regulatory takings, at least in regard to land.[63]

The "magnitude of loss" test appears to govern the issue of whether compensation is payable for loss through regulation. According to this test, the court must determine whether the regulation in question "goes too far" in reducing the value of the affected property. Unfortunately, US law has not established a clear test for determining at which point on the spectrum a compensable taking can be distinguished from a non-compensable one. As Joseph Sax has argued,

[n]evertheless, the predominant characteristic of this area of law is a welter of confusing and apparently incompatible results. The principle upon which the cases can be rationalized is yet to be discovered by the bench: what commentators have called the "crazy-quilt pattern of Supreme Court doctrine" has effectively been acknowledged by the court itself, which has developed the habit of introducing its uniformly unsatisfactory opinions in this area with the understatement that "no rigid rules" or "set formula" are available to determine where regulation ends and taking begins.[64]

Even in more recent years, the approach of US courts to regulatory takings has not been consistent. One of the leading cases on the subject, *Penn Central Transportation Co.* v. *City of New York*,[65] attempted to outline a three-pronged balancing test for determining whether a regulatory taking had occurred. The factors to be considered in making such a determination were:

- the character of the government action: "[a] 'taking' may more readily be found when the interference with property can be characterised as a physical invasion by government than when interference arises from some public program adjusting the benefits and burdens of economic life to promote the common good";
- interference with "reasonable investment-backed expectations"; and
- the extent of the diminution of value: in this case, the plaintiff

---

[62] Graham, *supra* note 57.

[63] *Ibid.*

[64] Sax, *supra* note 61 at 37 [footnotes omitted].

[65] *Penn Central Transportation Co.* v. *City of New York*, 438 U.S. 104; 57 L. Ed. 2d 631.

could still make a "reasonable return" on its investment by continuing to use the facility as a rail terminal with office rentals and concessions; moreover, the city specifically permitted owners of landmark sites to transfer to other sites the right to develop those sites beyond the otherwise permissible zoning restrictions.[66]

However, the *Penn* decision has been roundly criticized by some writers for having done very little, despite appearances, to assist in resolving the "regulatory taking" problem. For example, it has been said of the criteria that they are "vague and have been applied so inconsistently as to be of little use for lawyers to advise clients."[67] Furthermore, the court did not give any indication of the weight that each criterion is to be given.[68]

The issue of regulatory expropriation is closely linked to the problem of the nature and scope of the police power under US law. In particular, it is not altogether clear whether the "regulatory taking" debate arises out of a broadening of the concept of expropriation or out of the restriction of the scope of the police power.[69]

Certain political and historical factors have also had a significant influence on the development of police power. Landowning in the colonies was based more on the allodial model than on the tenurial one. Thus, the rights of the landowners in their use of, and management of, land could be made to yield to the needs of

---

[66] *Ibid.* at 648.

[67] William A. Fischel, *Regulatory Takings: Law, Economics, and Politics* (Cambridge, MA: Harvard University Press, 1995), 51. Fischel continues: "To paraphrase a less sympathetic critic, Gideon Kanner, the Court has always been suspected of basing regulatory takings decisions on ad hoc factors, and *Penn Central* was a signed confession that the justices do not care to do better."

[68] It is worth noting that in several Commonwealth jurisdictions, where land is expropriated, there is statutory provision for compensation for the "injurious affection" done to the adjacent land that is not subject to expropriation proceedings. This approach recognizes that economic loss may arise out of a regulatory measure that indirectly affects property, without characterizing it as expropriation.

[69] "Since individual rights must be left a breathing space in which government does not intrude, the limits of the police power must be ascertained with some precision. Alas, this task has proved too daunting. The Supreme Court has never repudiated the admonition of Justice William O. Douglas "that [a comprehensive] attempt to define [the police power's] reach or trace its outer limits is fruitless" (footnotes omitted). Steven J. Eagle, *Regulatory Takings* (Charlottesville: Michie Law Publishers, 1996), 14.

the community only through the general law rather than through any restrictions on title.[70] Moreover, the protection of property rights has always been a fundamental aspect of the Republican tradition.[71] Another important influence has been the fact that the Supreme Court is appointed by the Executive — an influence that is demonstrated by the dramatic shifts in the court's attitude towards the scope of takings, as mentioned earlier in this article.

In considering the status of property rights in the United States, therefore, there is little justification for attempting to apply the US approach in international fora, particularly because of the uncertain state of US law concerning the issue of regulatory expropriation as well as the fact that the case law is largely confined to real property.

THE EUROPEAN APPROACH TO REGULATORY EXPROPRIATION

An examination of the jurisprudence of the European Court of Justice (ECJ) and the European Court of Human Rights (ECHR) to property rights would also merit an extensive article in its own right. The main aim in making reference to it in this article, however, is to demonstrate that both of these fora have developed their own unique principles in balancing the public need behind a particular piece of legislation and private property rights. Moreover, although *de facto* expropriation is not infrequently invoked by applicants before either Court, it has very rarely been found to be applicable to the claim in question.

THE EUROPEAN COURT OF JUSTICE (ECJ)

To begin, it is important to note that the ECJ's jurisdiction is restricted to measures of member states that are intended to implement Community law. Therefore, a matter that falls within the purview of a member state cannot be challenged before the ECJ.[72] It should also be noted that the ECJ has held that there are no

---

[70] *Ibid.* at 15.

[71] James Madison, the "father of the constitution" asserted that the rights of persons and the rights of property were "cardinal objects of government."

[72] *Daniele Annibaldi v. Sindaco del Commune di Guidonia and Presidente Regione Lazio,* Judgment of December 18, 1997 (Case C-309/96) [hereinafter *Annibaldi*], which held that measures relating to the common organization of the agricultural markets had no effect on systems of agricultural property ownership. In *Annibaldi,* the applicant had challenged a law that restricted activities within a regional park.

specific Community rules on expropriation.[73] Second, in contrast to the US position, under Community law, personal rights and freedoms generally do not constitute an "unfettered prerogative."[74] Instead, their scope depends on the "social function" of the right or freedom. Restrictions on the right are therefore permissible, but they must satisfy the principle of proportionality — that is, a restriction must "correspond to objectives of general interest pursued by the Community" and "not constitute a disproportionate and intolerable interference which would adversely affect the very substance of the right so guaranteed."[75] There does not appear to be an exhaustive list of "objectives of general interest," however, case law indicates that these objectives include environmental protection,[76] public health,[77] the completion of the internal market,[78] and so on.

It is significant that recent case law of the ECJ indicates a reluctance on the part of the court to uphold an allegation of *de facto* expropriation. In many cases, the court makes no reference to the allegation other than in the recitation of relevant facts. Even where the ECJ has applied the principle of proportionality and made a finding of "undue interference" with property rights, it has not drawn any analogies with expropriation or taking. Although the

---

[73] *Ibid.*

[74] *Boehringher Ingelheim Vetmedica GmbH and C.H. Boehringer Sohn* v. *Council,* Judgment of December 1, 1999 (in joined cases T-125/96).

[75] *Ibid.* The European Court of Justice [hereinafter ECJ] has set out the following three-part test of proportionality in *R.* v. *Min. of Agriculture, Fisheries and Food and Another ex p. National Farmers' Union and Others,* [1998] E.C.R. I-2211, para. 60: "[T]he principle of proportionality ... requires that measures adopted by Community institutions do not exceed the limits of what is appropriate and necessary in order to attain the objectives legitimately pursued by the legislation in question; when there is a choice between several appropriate measures recourse must be had to the least onerous, and the disadvantages caused must not be disproportionate to the aims pursued." See also "The Principle of Proportionality: Review of Community Measures," in T. Tridimas, ed., *The General Principles of EC Law* (Oxford: Oxford University Press, 1999).

[76] *Standley and Others* v. *UK,* Judgment of April 29, 1999 (Case C-293/97), available at <http://europa.eu.int/eur-lex>.

[77] *Imperial Tobacco and Others,* June 15, 2000 (Opinion). On October 5, 2000, the ECJ announced that it would not make a final ruling in this case because of the judgment handed down in Case C-376/98, *Germany* v *Parliament and Council,* also dated October 5, 2000. All three documents are available at <http://europa. eu.int/eur-lex>.

[78] *Edouard Dubois et Fils,* Judgment of January 29, 1998 (Case T-113/96), available at <http://europa.eu.int/eur-lex>.

ECJ has not addressed the issue of intent in cases of alleged *de facto* expropriation, this does not necessarily mean that the ECJ regards intent as being irrelevant. Rather, the inference of the court is simply that the facts of the case did not indicate that the impugned legislation had a latent expropriatory intent.

EUROPEAN COURT OF HUMAN RIGHTS (ECHR)

The jurisdiction of the ECHR is set out in the Convention for the Protection of Human Rights and Fundamental Freedoms.[79] The protection of property rights is provided for in Article 1 of the First Protocol:

Every natural or legal person is entitled to the peaceful enjoyment of his possessions. No one shall be deprived of his possessions except in the public interest and subject to the conditions provided for by law and by the general principles of international law.

The preceding provisions shall not however, in any way impair the right of a State to enforce such laws as it deems necessary to control the use of property in accordance with the general interest or to secure the payment of taxes or other contributions or penalties.

This provision has been interpreted as comprising three distinct rules. However, the rules are connected in the sense that the second and third rules, which are enunciated in the second sentence of the first paragraph and in the second paragraph, are concerned with particular instances of interference with the right to peaceful enjoyment of property and should therefore be construed in the light of the general principle set out in the first sentence of the first paragraph.

Many of the cases brought before the ECHR involve allegations of *de facto* expropriation. However, there appear to be only two cases where such an allegation was upheld. In *Papamichalopoulos and Others* v. *Greece,*[80] the Greek Navy had taken over land owned by the applicants without the latters' permission and had built on it a naval base and holiday resort for officers and their families. Although the expropriation was never confirmed by any formal legislative action, the ECHR nevertheless held that an expropriation had taken place on the grounds that the property had become

---

[79] Convention for the Protection of Human Rights and Fundamental Freedoms, signed in Rome under the auspices of the Council of Europe, November 4, 1950, 213 U.N.T.S. 221 (1950).

[80] *Papamichalopoulos and Others* v. *Greece,* Judgment of June 24, 1993 (Case 18/1992/363/437).

wholly unusable. In addition, all attempts by the owners to remedy the situation within the Greek judicial system had failed. The consequences were sufficiently serious to amount to a *de facto* expropriation within the meaning of Article 1 of the First Protocol. In *Loizidou* v. *Turkey,*[81] the applicant, a Greek Cypriot, had been physically prevented from gaining access to her property in the Turkish-occupied zone in northern Cyprus since 1974. The ECHR held that, in the circumstances, the actions of the Turkish authorities constituted both a "purported expropriation without compensation" and a "complete negation of the applicant's property rights."[82] Of significance to the main proposal of this article, namely the relevance of state intent to a finding of expropriation, is that in both *Papamichalopoulos* and *Loizidou,* an objective assessment of the facts leads one to the unavoidable conclusion that the authorities intended to deprive the applicants of their property rights. The deprivations were not simply incidental to the exercise of a legitimate government power.

Where the ECHR has found a breach of Article 1 of the First Protocol, proportionality has often been a guiding principle in order to determine whether there is a "fair balance" between the demands of the general interest of the community and the requirements of the protection of the individual's fundamental rights. The leading case on this issue is *Sporrong and Lönnroth* v. *Sweden,*[83] in which the impugned measures consisted of expropriation permits and prohibitions on construction. In other cases, the ECHR has analyzed the interference with property rights as a "control of use" rather than as a "deprivation of possessions."[84]

INTENT AS THE BASIS FOR DISTINGUISHING
VARIOUS FORMS OF "TAKING"

Having considered the current approaches of certain international and municipal fora to the issue of intent, this section of the

---

[81] *Loizidou* v. *Turkey,* Judgment (Merits and Just Satisfaction) of December 18, 1996 (Case 40/1993/435/514), available at <http://hudoc.echr.coe.int/hudoc/>.

[82] *Ibid.* at para. 64.

[83] *Sporrong and Lönnroth* v. *Sweden,* Judgment (Merits) of 23 September, 1982 (Series A, no. 52).

[84] For example, see *Tre Traktörer AB* v. *Sweden,* Judgment of July 7, 1989 (Series A, no. 159), which concerned the loss of a restaurant business consequent on withdrawal of a drinks licence. See also *Pinnacle Meat Processors Company and 8 Others* v. *United Kingdom* (determination as to admissibility) October 21, 1998 and *Ian*

article will examine some commonly recognized measures that affect property rights in order to demonstrate that the intent of the state in implementing the measure, as a matter of objective enquiry, is central to its characterization. This discussion then raises the question of whether intent can also be the differentiating factor in cases of alleged "regulatory expropriation."

EXPROPRIATION

Expropriation in its classic sense is essentially "the deprivation by state organs of a right of property either as such, or by permanent transfer of the power of management and control."[85] It is usually effected by means of specific legislation in furthering a specific "public purpose," such as town planning and environmental protection. As such, there is the explicit coincidence of legislative purpose and result. The legislation usually also provides for compensation to be paid to the persons whose property has been expropriated.

In order to be lawful as a matter of international law, the manner in which an expropriation of foreign-owned property is carried out must conform to international standards. In exercising its right of expropriation, a state normally enjoys a wide discretion with respect to the determination of the nature, extent and duration, and method that it uses to achieve its aim. However, such discretionary power must be exercised in good faith, which means that it must be exercised "reasonably, honestly, in conformity with the spirit of the law, and with due regard to the interest of others."[86]

NATIONALIZATION

According to some jurists, the difference between nationalization and expropriation is merely one of degree. In other words, they are identical in terms of result, both entailing private persons

---

Edgar (Liverpool) Ltd. v. *UK* (determination as to admissibility), January 25, 2000, where the impugned legislation imposed a total ban on the respective businesses of the applicants and enforced such a ban by means of criminal sanctions. *Tre Traktörer, Pinnacle Meat Processors,* and *Ian Edgar* are all available at <http://hudoc.echr.coe.int/hudoc/>.

[85] Brownlie, *supra* note 9 at 534.

[86] B. Cheng, *General Principles of Law* (Oxford: Oxford University Press, 1953), 133-4.

being deprived of private property rights.[87] Unlike expropriation, however, which often targets specific property and may even consist of an isolated incident, nationalizations are usually of a general and impersonal nature, carried out in "pursuance of some national political programme intended to create out of existing enterprises, or to strengthen, a nationally controlled industry."[88]

Another difference is that nationalization entails reservation to the state of a particular legal competence (the ownership of a particular type of property), whereas expropriation is merely a deprivation of specific benefits arising from such competence, but not the competence itself:

[L]a nationalisation est la suppression totale et définitive d'une compétence juridique au profit de l'Etat. L'expropriation au contraire, n'est autre chose que la privation particulière des bénéfices que l'individu a pu retirer à un moment donné d'une compétence déterminée. La nationalisation, à la différence de l'expropriation supprime définitivement pour l'avenir toute utilisation quelconque de la compétence nationalisée. La nationalisation touche le droit dans son essence, l'expropriation dans son objet.[89]

In other words, the intent behind a nationalization measure is radically different from that of an act of expropriation. Nationalization involves a change in the underlying concept of property, while expropriation is carried out for a specific public purpose, such as the construction of a road, which will benefit the whole community, but does not prevent the expropriated individual from acquiring property that is identical, or almost identical, to that of

---

[87] For example, the report of A. de La Pradelle, *Yearbook of the International Law Institute*, vol. XLIV-II, cited by G. Fouilloux, *La Nationalisation et le Droit International Public* (Paris: Librarie générale de droit et de jurisprudence, 1962), 143 *et seq.*; Brownlie, *supra* note 9 at 534-5.

[88] Wortley, *supra* note 1 at 36.

[89] ["[N]ationalization is the total and definitive suppression of a legal competence for the benefit of the State. Expropriation on the other hand, is nothing more than a particular act of deprivation of the benefits which an individual has been able, at a given moment, to draw from a specific competence. In contrast to expropriation, nationalization suppresses for good any and all use of the competence that has been nationalised. Whereas nationalization affects the essence of a right, expropriation concerns the object of a right."] Fouilloux, *supra* note 87 at 146, n.24, citing G. Scelle, *Yearbook of the International Law Institute*, vol. XLIV-II (Bâle: Éditions juridiques et sociologiques S.A.), 267. Friedman makes a further distinction between socialization, which is "incompatible with the capitalist system" and nationalization "from which the participation of private capital is excluded": Friedman, *supra* note 7 at 12.

which he has been deprived: "L'expropriation ne met pas en cause l'appropriation privée ni le droit qui permet au citoyen de devenir propriétaire de tel bien et exige qu'il sacrifie son intérêt particulier à l'intérêt public."[90] Nationalization can therefore be viewed as an integral part of a state's overall political philosophy. Expropriations, on the other hand, are carried out by governments no matter where they lie on the political spectrum. Accordingly, if intent is central to distinguishing between nationalization and expropriation, it should be also be the key element in distinguishing expropriatory from non-expropriatory measures.

The furtherance of the public good is often cited as a key criterion in the case of both expropriation and nationalization.[91] However, what constitutes the public good in each case is often different. In the case of nationalization, the notion of the public good lies in the change in the notion of property ownership that nationalization represents. Expropriations, on the other hand, take place because of a pre-existing public need that has nothing to do with the nature or character of the affected property.[92] As with expropriation, the manner in which nationalization is carried out must conform to international standards. The state should provide for the payment of adequate compensation; the means that it employs to effect the nationalization should be "reasonable"; and those individuals whose property is to be nationalized should be allowed sufficient time to reorganize their affairs in order to minimize financial loss as far as possible.[93]

---

[90] Fouilloux, *supra* note 87 at 148.

[91] "[L]a nationalisation recouvre l'expropriation pour cause d'utilité publique." [There is an overlap between nationalization and expropriation by reason of [the notion of] public utility]. *Ibid.* at 144.

[92] "[L]e bien exproprié n'a aucun rapport par sa nature et ses qualités intrinsèques avec l'usage auquel le destinent les exigences de l'intérêt public. Autrement dit l'intérêt public, s'il n'est pas toujours détachable de l'objet du droit de propriété, préexiste toujours à l'objet qu'il désigne." [There is no relationship between the nature and intrinsic qualities of the expropriated property and the use for which the demands of the public interest intend it. In other words, the public interest, if it cannot always be separated from the object of the property right, nonetheless it is always a prerequisite to its designated object.] *Ibid.* at 152.

[93] For a discussion of the concept of "reasonableness," see Jean J.A. Salmon, *Le Concept de Raisonnable en Droit International Public,* "Mélanges Offerts à Paul Reuter: le droit international : unité et diversité" (Paris: Éd. A. Pedone, 1981), 447. See also the extract from the decision of "Claim of the British Ship, *I'm Alone,*" *infra* note 97 and accompanying text.

CONFISCATION

The term confiscation is often applied to situations in which a state is in breach of its obligation to make reparation for the taking of property and thus has moral connotations. However, the term is only appropriate where the *purpose* of the confiscatory act is to sanction the conduct of the individual whose property has been taken.[94] Although the result of a confiscation may be that the property is transferred to the state, this is incidental to its disciplinary function.[95] It is thus a distinct type of measure affecting property rights. To apply the term to every measure affecting property where no, or rather inadequate, compensation has been paid only gives rise to confusion since it fails to distinguish between claims based on a legal right to compensation and those where no such right is recognized.[96]

As with expropriation and nationalization, the manner in which the confiscation is carried out may also constitute grounds for a claim against the state. If force is used to effect the confiscation, it must be reasonable, otherwise the state may incur liability for any ensuing losses.[97] Authorities may also carry out a confiscation of property in consequence of the non-observance of sanitary regulations or to protect public safety.[98]

---

[94] By way of example, Fouilloux cites the confiscations of property belonging to collaborators undertaken by European governments following the end of the Second World War, one notable example being the seizure by the French government of the shares in the Renault car manufacturer: Fouilloux, *supra* note 87 at 166-8. Confiscation, for what were often political "offences," was also a major means of redistributing land in Eastern Europe following the end of the Second World War. Friedman, *supra* note 7 at 29 *et seq.*

[95] Friedman, *supra* note 7 at 1; Wortley, *supra* note 1 at 39.

[96] Fouilloux, *supra* note 87 at 165.

[97] "On the assumptions stated in the question [i.e., the right of hot pursuit existed in the circumstances], the United States might, consistently with the Convention, use necessary and reasonable force for the purpose of effecting the objects of boarding, searching, seizing and bringing into port the suspected vessel; and if sinking should occur incidentally, as a result of the exercise of necessary and reasonable force for such purpose, the pursuing vessel might be entirely blameless." "Claim of the British Ship *I'm Alone*" (1935), 3 U.N.R.I.A.A., 1609. *In casu*, the admittedly intentional sinking of the Canadian schooner by the United States was considered unjustified.

[98] For example, see Friedman, *supra* note 7 at 8.

MONOPOLIES

Although a monopoly may also be brought about by means of a taking measure, it does not, in and of itself, constitute expropriation but is instead a particular mode of exploiting property.[99] The purpose of establishing a monopoly may include a desire to achieve greater efficiency in the delivery of public services. Alternatively, it may provide a new source of state revenue.[100] The creation of a monopoly may be said to have the characteristics of an indirect expropriation since it involves giving a sole party the right to engage in a particular activity and thereby denies others the freedom to engage in the same activity.[101] Moreover, the economic value of the private property that is utilized in the activity is affected, particularly since any disposition of the property will, in future, have to take place under unfavourable economic conditions. However, the fact that the owner retains the power to dispose of his property necessarily precludes expropriation. Furthermore, the difficulties of disposing of property following the establishment of a monopoly are not unique to the latter but arise instead whenever there is an imbalance in the supply and demand for goods or services. Nevertheless, as with other measures that affect property rights, the creation of a monopoly may entail international responsibility because of the manner in which the monopoly is established or because there exists an element of unlawful discrimination.[102]

One notable example involving a monopoly is the *Italian Insurance Monopoly* case.[103] In 1911, the Italian government placed a bill before the Italian Parliament providing for the creation of a national institute to which the entire life insurance business of the country was to be entrusted. The bill also provided that insurance companies established in Italy, whose business would be brought to an end by the monopoly, were to have no rights to any

---

[99] Fouilloux, *supra* note 87 at 163.

[100] Friedman, *supra* note 7 at 52.

[101] *Ibid.*

[102] "Il en résulte que les mesures d'exécution qui peuvent porter atteinte à la propriété privée, quelle que soit leur nature juridique, sont indépendantes de la décision instituant le monopole." [Consequently, the means of execution that may affect private property, whatever their legal nature, are independent of the decision to create the monopoly."] Fouilloux, *supra* note 87 at 163.

[103] Discussed by Friedman, *supra* note 7 at 53, citing Clunet, *Consultation pour les Sociétés d'Assurance sur la vie établies en Italie* (1912) See also Fouilloux, *supra* note 87 at 162, n. 69.

compensation or indemnity whatsoever in respect of the consequences, direct or indirect, of the establishment of the monopoly.
Several governments quickly lodged formal protests, forcing the
Italian government to amend the bill. For instance, foreign insurance companies were henceforth permitted to carry on business
for a period of ten years, subject to certain conditions. The companies were also entitled to demand that the national institute assume
their insurance contracts in return for a share of the premiums
paid on the policies. In terms of intent, the Italian government, in
establishing the monopoly, did not intend to expropriate the foreign insurance companies. However, prior to the amendment of
the legislation, the proposed measure was open to challenge under
international law, particularly because of the short notice that was
apparently afforded to the foreign insurance companies for reorga-
nizing their business affairs.

REQUISITION

Requisition is a measure affecting property, which a state usually
resorts to only in time of war or under threat of the same. The purpose of such a measure, therefore, is national defence. It may
involve the temporary or permanent cession of property, but it
always gives rise to the right of indemnity if restitution is not possible.[104] The intent behind the requisition, the existence of an emergency situation, and the fact that a requisition does not always
entail the transfer of property is what distinguishes it from other
"taking" measures. The celebrated case of *Norway* v. *United States*
(the *Norwegian Shipowners' Claims*),[105] although usually discussed in
the context of expropriation, is, in actual fact, an act of wartime
requisition by the US authorities. In this case, compensation
became payable because of the failure to make restitution of the
ships once the emergency had ceased.

In concluding this section, therefore, it is apparent, if one
accepts the above characterizations of measures that effect a deprivation of private property, that the common feature that clearly distinguishes one measure from another is the purpose, or intent, of
the state in enacting the measure. In these cases, intent can usually

---

[104] "In cases when the requisitioned property is not restored the respondent government is liable for the payment of damages in an amount to make good the
loss sustained." M. Whiteman, *Damages in International Law*, vol. II (Millwood,
NY: Kraus Reprint, 1976), 902.

[105] *Norwegian Shipowners, supra* note 93.

be ascertained not only from the terms of the legislative or administrative diktat authorizing the particular measure but also from the means by which the measure was carried out as well as from the result of the measure. Hence, if intent can be a criterion in differentiating between municipal law measures that are explicitly intended to affect property rights, it would not be unreasonable to use this same approach in the international sphere in differentiating between genuinely regulatory acts of government and those that are ostensibly regulatory in nature but are, in fact, intended to realise an expropriation of property rights.

VIRES AND STATE INTENT

In addition to being the basis for classifying various "taking" measures, intent is also key to establishing whether a particular legislative measure is within or without the *vires* of a governmental body. The determination of *vires* is necessarily preceded by a characterization process in which the determination of the intent or purpose of the measure is critical. Discussed below are a number of Commonwealth cases involving "takings" of property. In all of them, the intent of the legislature played a decisive role in determining whether the legislative measure in question was an act of "mere regulation" or was in fact designed to effect an unauthorized taking.

GALLAGHER V. LYNN [106]

This case concerned, *inter alia,* the constitutional validity of the 1934 Milk and Milk Products Act of Northern Ireland. The appellant, a farmer in Southern Ireland, had been convicted for selling milk in the city of Londonderry in Northern Ireland, in contravention of the act. Prior to the act coming into force, he and other farmers close to the border with Northern Ireland had sold their milk over the border in Londonderry, which appeared to have been their "natural market." The imposition of criminal sanctions under the act, however, meant that the appellant lost a substantial amount of his business. The appellant argued that the act was in contravention of the 1920 Government of Ireland Act, which prohibited the Parliament of Northern Ireland from legislating in respect of trade, subject to certain exceptions. However, for the purposes of the present discussion, the case can also be viewed in terms of regulatory

[106] *Gallagher*v. *Lynn,* [1937] 3 All E.R. 598.

expropriation. The House of Lords upheld the validity of the act on the grounds that its object was not to interfere with trade but rather was "a law for the peace, order, and good government of Northern Ireland 'in respect of' precautions taken to secure the health of the inhabitants of Northern Ireland, by protecting them from the dangers of an unregulated supply of milk."[107] Accordingly, the fact that the act incidentally affected trade between Northern and Southern Ireland was irrelevant.

In coming to its conclusion that the act was *intra vires,* the House of Lords, citing *Russell* v. *R.,*[108] looked at the "true nature and character of the legislation ... the pith and substance of the legislation."[109] This investigation involved an assessment of the act as a whole since it was also implicit in the reasoning that the legislative purpose as gleaned from the act was critical to the process of characterization.

ULSTER TRANSPORT AUTHORITY V. *JAMES BROWN & SONS, LTD*[110]

Section 5(1) of the 1920 Government of Ireland Act prohibited the Parliament of Northern Ireland from making a law so as either directly or indirectly to take any property without compensation. Section 18(1) of the 1948 Transport Act of Northern Ireland prohibited the use by any person other than the Ulster Transport Authority of a motor vehicle on a public highway to carry for reward any passengers or luggage or merchandise except with the consent of the authority and the approval of the Ministry of Commerce. Section 19(1) excepted from the restrictions imposed by Section 18(1) the use by furniture removers of motor vehicles "to move furniture or effects, not being part of the stock in trade of the owner thereof, from or to premises occupied by such owner to or from other premises occupied by such owner or to or from a store." The respondents, James Brown and Sons, had been convicted and fined for carrying furniture that had been purchased as stock in trade by a dealer at an auction mart from the auction mart to the purchaser's premises. The issue that is relevant to the present discussion is whether Section 18(1) of the Transport Act was a

107 *Ibid.* at 601, judgment of Lord Atkins.
108 *Russell* v. *R.,* (1882), 7 App. Cas. 829.
109 *Gallagher* v. *Lynn,* [1937] 3 All E.R. 598 at 601.
110 *Ulster Transport Authority* v. *James Brown & Sons, Ltd.,* [1953] N.I. 79 [hereinafter *Ulster Transport*].

taking of property without compensation contrary to Section 5(1) of the Government of Ireland Act.

It was held by the Northern Ireland Court of Appeal that the intention of the Transport Act was "to offer the appellants a ready and practical means of acquiring the respondents' goodwill without paying for it"; Accordingly, Section 18(1) of the Transport Act was *ultra vires* in so far as it purported to prohibit the use of a motor vehicle for the collection or delivery of furniture by a person in connection with his business as a remover or storer of furniture. The court's statements on the relevance of the legislature's intention and the manner in which this intention could be ascertained are worthy of note. In his judgment, Lord Chief Justice MacDermott first examined the legislative history of the impugned section. He noted that an earlier act, the 1935 Road and Railway Transport Act of Northern Ireland, had effected a general acquisition of road motor undertakings *on payment of compensation* for both intangible and tangible assets. The Road and Railway Transport Act did not cover furniture removal businesses. In fact, there was a specific exemption for the use of a motor vehicle for the collection of merchandise by a person "where the merchandise consists of furniture collected or delivered by such person in connection with his business as a remover or storer of furniture."

The Transport Act, in contrast, prohibited the respondents from carrying on a substantial part of their trade *without making any provision for compensation*. The court held that the divergence between the 1935 Road and Railway Transport Act and the 1948 Transport Act was "unmistakably deliberate and intentional," and continued:

But what was the intention? Parliament must be presumed to intend the necessary effect of its enactments, and the answer to this question cannot overlook the fact that in this specialized field ... the natural consequence of the enforcement of the relevant prohibition would be to divert to the appellants the business, or at least the substantial part of the business, which their erstwhile competitors were no longer allowed to transact ... Nor could the appellants [Ulster Transport Authority] well stand aloof from such business, if there was no one else to do it, having regard to the nature of their duty to provide for the needs of the public as imposed by section 5 of the Act of 1948. I can find no other intention which offers a more likely explanation of the provisions in view which would fit the circumstances as well or better were unable to advance an alternative.[111]

Clearly, in Lord MacDermott's view, intent was the crucial factor in characterizing the Transport Act as an attempt to nationalize

---

[111] *Ibid.* at 112-13, judgment of Lord MacDermott L.C.J.

private property without compensation. Moreover, intent could be ascertained through an objective enquiry.[112] Another significant conclusion is that the result of a particular measure is relevant to the enquiry into intent; it is not determinative *per se* to characterize the measure as expropriatory.

GOVERNMENT OF MALAYSIA AND ANOTHER V. SELANGOR PILOT ASSOCIATION (A FIRM)[113]

Article 13 of the constitution of Malaysia provided that "(1) [n]o person shall be deprived of property save in accordance with law; (2) [n]o law shall provide for the compulsory acquisition or use of property without adequate compensation." In 1969, six licensed pilots formed a partnership (hereinafter the association) to provide pilotage services in Port Swettenham (now called Port Kelang), the principal port in Malaysia. The association had physical assets and employed other licensed pilots. Its income was the pilotage dues earned by the pilots. In 1972, the 1963 Port Authorities Act was amended in order to impose a duty on a port authority to provide pilotage services. Prior to the amendment, the duties of the port authority had been couched in general terms, with no specific reference to pilotage services. Under the terms of the act as amended, however, pilot licences could only be issued to pilots who were employed by the port authority. Moreover, a licence would become invalid upon the termination of a pilot's employment with the authority. The amended act also made it a criminal offence under Section 35A for (1) any person who was not an authority pilot to engage in pilotage acts or to attempt to obtain employment as a pilot of a vessel entering or being within any pilotage district, and (2) any master or owner of a ship entering or being within a pilotage district to knowingly employ as a pilot any person who was not an authority pilot. Prior to the amendments coming into force, the port authority offered employment to all licensed pilots, and all but a few of the pilots employed by the respondents had accepted the offer. The respondents also voluntarily sold their pilot launches and equipment to the port authority.

---

[112] "I see no reason to speculate upon the motives of the Legislature in enacting this particular piece of legislation. Whatever in fact those motives may have been, the intention of the legislature, as gleaned from its terms, is what must guide the court in this instance." *Per* Lord MacDermott L.C.J., *ibid.* at 114.

[113] *Government of Malaysia and Another* v. *Selangor Pilot Association (A Firm)*, [1978] A.C. 337.

The respondents' action against the port authority and the government of Malaysia was dismissed at first instance, but, on appeal to the Federal Court, the respondents were granted a declaration that they were entitled to compensation for loss of goodwill. A majority of the Privy Council, however, allowed the appeal of the government of Malaysia and the port authority. The majority, in a decision based on very narrow reasoning, acknowledged that the respondents could no longer carry on business as a result of Section 35A. However, "unless [the association] was deprived of property otherwise than in accordance with law or its property was compulsorily acquired or used by the port authority, there was no breach of article 13." What is of relevance to the present discussion is the fact that there was an indication in the judgment that had the respondents addressed the issue of "in accordance with law," the result may well have been different.

The majority referred to a number of cases upon which the respondents had relied before the Malaysian Federal Court, including *Ulster Transport* and acknowledged the principle set out in that case that where "the prohibition imposed by the legislature is a colourable device to secure property without paying compensation, the prohibition may properly be held to be ultra vires."[114] Unfortunately, the respondents did not advance this particular argument before the Judicial Committee,[115] submitting instead that the relevant legislation was in its "pith and substance" confiscatory.[116] Lord Salmon, dissenting, was the only one of their Lordships to focus on the issue of intent. He clearly considered that the intention of the Malaysian legislature in passing the impugned legislation was to effect a nationalization without compensation.[117] Lord Salmon used an objective approach in assessing the purpose of Section 35A. He considered a number of factors, including the circumstances surrounding the legislation amending the Port Authority Act as well as its effect on the respondents' business. In doing so, he found that the circumstances of the instant case were very similar to those of *Ulster Transport* in that the inevitable result of the enforcement of Section 35A would be to divert all pilotage

---

[114] *Per* Viscount Dilhorne, *ibid.* at 346.

[115] Noted by Lord Salmon, *ibid.* at 356.

[116] *Ibid.* at 341.

[117] "In my opinion, this appeal raises constitutional issues of vital importance. I fear that it will encourage and facilitate nationalisation without compensation throughout the Commonwealth." *Per* Lord Salmon, *ibid.* at 355.

business to the port authority.[118] Furthermore, the inevitability that the respondents' business would be taken over by the port authority was brought about by the fact that Section 35A made it a criminal offence for pilots to be employed by anyone other than the port authority.

Admittedly, Lord Salmon was in the minority. His reasoning, however, is to be preferred. One possible explanation for the majority view in this case could be a desire on the part of the British establishment not to be seen as too interventionist in the affairs of a former colonial possession that had only recently achieved independence.[119] Although technically sustainable, it ignores very obvious signs that the underlying intent of the legislature was to nationalize pilotage businesses at no cost to the government.

The preceding discussion has attempted to show that the key role that intent plays in characterizing a governmental measure where the scope of legislative competence is at issue with respect to the characterization of a governmental measure that effects a deprivation of private property. If such an approach is feasible in the municipal sphere, then why not in the international one?

CONCLUSION

Given the current importance of the issue, it is critical that the definition of regulatory expropriation be a matter of international consensus. Consequently, it should not be assumed that the principles developed by any particular municipal or regional legal systems, for example, the United States and the European Union, can be automatically applied on a global basis.

An alternative approach, as proposed by this article, is to categorize a regulatory measure according to the legislative intent of the state. As G. Fouilloux persuasively demonstrates, distinguishing between measures that affect private property rights can be

---

[118] "In the present case it is impossible to see where the respondents' business could have gone other than to the port authority and, although just as in the Northern Ireland case [*Ulster Transport*], nothing was spelt out in the relevant Act about the acquisition of the respondents' business, it is quite obvious that the appellants intended that that is where that business should go as a result of the amending Act of 1972 — and that is where it went." *Per* Lord Salmon, *ibid.* at 356.

[119] Malaya (what is now Peninsular Malaysia) was formed on August 31, 1957. The federation of Malaysia, consisting of Malaya, Sabah, Sarawak, and Singapore was established on July 9, 1963. Singapore subsequently left the federation on August 9, 1965.

achieved by ascertaining the intent of the state in undertaking that measure.[120] Expropriation, confiscation, and nationalization may all *result* in a deprivation of property rights, yet the rights and obligations of the state and private party that are concomitant with a particular measure differ depending on the categorization of that measure. It is submitted that the same approach may be used to distinguish between measures that further a legitimate public purpose and those that are designed to effect a taking of property without compensation. Clear examples of the latter are the cases of *Ulster Transport* and *Government of Malaysia*, which are discussed above, where there was no other conceivable purpose to the contested regulation other than to nationalize the private party's business without compensating that party for its loss. A test based on objective intent also obviates the need for international arbitrators to become embroiled in making social policy decisions. As this test is problematic enough in the municipal sphere, it is difficult to see how it would be acceptable at an international level.

The critical role of intent will necessarily reduce the scope of expropriation claims that private investors may bring under investment treaties since the consequences of a measure will only play a subordinate role. However, existing principles of international law should ensure that investors with a genuine grievance are not left without a remedy. This necessity has already been alluded to in the discussion of recognized forms of taking. For instance, possible grounds for challenging a regulatory measure that results in a loss of property rights include denial of justice, abuse of rights, and unlawful discrimination. An additional method of attack under European Community law is lack of proportionality.

Finally, intent as the primary criterion for evaluating the international lawfulness of a measure that causes loss of private property rights permits variation among nations in the manner in which they carry out social and economic policies. This point is important, given the political and cultural differences that often exist between the host state and the state of the investor. Furthermore, it permits the state to balance the obligations that it owes to its own citizens and those that it has assumed towards foreign investment on its territory. As Ian Brownlie has so cogently stated, "it is not possible to postulate an international minimum standard [for the treatment of aliens] which in effect supports a particular philosophy of economic life at the expense of the host state."[121]

---

[120] Fouilloux, *supra* note 87.

[121] Brownlie, *supra* note 9 at 530.

Sommaire

L'expropriation par réglementation et l'intention de l'État

La caractérisation d'un règlement comme un acte d'expropriation, dépend-elle de l'intention objective de l'État en édictant la mesure? Telle est la question soulevée dans cet article. Le problème de l'expropriation par réglementation est d'importance particulière, puisque plusieurs traités d'investissement multilatéraux récemment conclus, y compris l'ALÉNA, accordent aux investisseurs le droit d'intenter un procès directement contre un État étranger pour récupérer les pertes qui résultent des mesures qu'on estime comme "équivalent" à l'expropriation.

Cet article commence par examiner les façons respectives du Tribunal Iran-États-Unis et des États-Unis d'aborder le problème de l'expropriation par réglementation. Ensuite, on les contraste brièvement avec la jurisprudence unique de la Cour de justice des Communautés européennes et de la Cour européenne des Droits de l'Homme. Puis, on évalue le rôle de l'intention dans le droit municipal comme moyen de catégorisation et on soutient que ce rôle est aussi viable au niveau international. Pour conclure, on fournit des raisons pour lesquelles une analyse fondée sur l'intention est préférable aux autres théories.

Summary

Regulatory Expropriation and State Intent

This article examines whether the characterization of a regulatory measure as expropriatory depends upon the objective intent of the state in enacting that measure. The issue of regulatory expropriation is of particular importance, given the fact that a number of recent multilateral investment treaties, including the North American Free Trade Agreement, grant investors a right of direct action against a foreign state for losses arising out of measures that are "tantamount" to expropriation.

This article will first consider the respective approaches of the Iran-United States Claims Tribunal and the United States to regulatory expropriation. These approaches will be then briefly contrasted with the unique jurisprudence of the European Court of Justice and the European Court of Human Rights. Next, the role of intent in municipal law as a means of categorization will be addressed and a case made as to why this approach is equally viable on the international plane. In conclusion, reasons will be given as to why a test based on intent is to be preferred over other theories.

Peut-on justifier l'intervention de l'OTAN au Kosovo sur le plan humanitaire? Analyse de la politique occidentale et ses conséquences en Macédoine

Michael Barutciski

Introduction

L'opération aérienne de l'OTAN déclenchée contre la Yougoslavie le 24 mars 1999 a suscité plusieurs débats importants sur l'avenir des relations internationales. Nombreux commentateurs se sont montrés critiques par rapport à certains aspects de l'intervention tels que l'utilisation de munitions contenant de l'uranium appauvri[1] et le bombardement de cibles qui ne sont pas clairement militaires.[2] Cependant, il est intéressant de noter que presque tous les analystes occidentaux qui ont émis des réserves semblent partager la même conviction: une opération militaire était moralement

Michael Barutciski est Avocat (Barreau du Québec). Nous remercions la Queen Elizabeth House de l'Université d'Oxford où nous avons enseigné de 1996 à 2000. Une partie de la recherche pour cet article a été possible grâce à une subvention accordée par le gouvernement britannique (Department for International Development) en 1998-1999. Nous tenons à remercier nos assistants de recherche: James Milner, Yongmi Schibel et Dasantila Dajti. Nous étions également membre de l'équipe commandée par le Haut Commissariat des Nations Unies pour les réfugiés à mener une évaluation indépendante de la réaction internationale à la crise des réfugiés du Kosovo. Les opinions exprimées dans cet article sont uniquement les nôtres.

[1] Il est possible que ces munitions continuent de nuire à l'environnement et aux populations de la région. Voir Robert James Parsons, "Loi du silence sur l'uranium appauvri," *Le Monde diplomatique*, février 2001, p. 22; Laurent Zecchini, "Balkans: les morts d'après la guerre," *Le Monde*, 4 janvier 2001; Marlise Simons, "1999 U.S. Document Warned of Depleted Uranium in Kosovo," *New York Times*, 9 janvier 2001.

[2] Associated Press, *La radio et télévision serbe sont des "cibles légitimes," selon l'OTAN*, 9 avril 1999; Assemblée parlementaire de l'OTAN (Commission des affaires civiles), *Kosovo and International Humanitarian Law*, rédigé par le rapporteur général Volker Kröning, 15 octobre 1999, Doc. AS 245 CC (99) 11.

nécessaire pour faire cesser l'oppression d'une minorité par un régime responsable d'agissements inacceptables.[3] En effet, nombreux observateurs semblent d'accords que l'intervention était illégale mais légitime.[4]

Cette position répandue peut paraître étrange: comment peut-on soutenir qu'une action illégale demeure néanmoins légitime? Il est souhaitable de s'entendre sur les faits avant d'engager un débat sur la relation compliquée entre la légitimité et la légalité. La mise à l'écart du droit positif[5] ou l'émergence d'une nouvelle norme en droit international[6] serait plus convaincante si la situation sur le terrain pouvait clairement être qualifiée d'exceptionnellement grave.[7]

Mais peut-on vraiment affirmer que la situation au milieu de mars 1999 était telle que seule une intervention militaire pouvait sauver la population albanaise du Kosovo d'une catastrophe humanitaire? L'examen de la situation sur le terrain est l'objet de cet article. L'analyse qui suit ne découle pas d'une hostilité de principe aux actions militaires, mais plutôt d'un esprit critique face aux "idées reçues" qui font partie de la pensée conventionnelle de la plupart des commentateurs occcidentaux de la crise.

---

[3] Voir, par exemple, Hubert Thierry, "L'ingérence humanitaire: vers un nouveau droit international?" *Défense nationale,* mars 2000, p. 36.

[4] International Independent Commission on Kosovo, *The Kosovo Report,* Oxford, Oxford University Press, 2000, p. 4; Antonio Cassese, "Ex iniuria jus oritur: Are we moving towards international legitimation of forcible countermeasures in the world community?" (1999) 10 Eur. J. Int'l L. 155; House of Commons Select Committee on Foreign Affairs, *Fourth Report — Kosovo,* Londres, 23 mai 2000, par. 128.

[5] "The United States, the most assertive proponent of military action (although the State Department's enthusiasm was not shared by the Pentagon), quite simply set the legal argument aside. When questioned at a press conference in London on 8 October [1998], Secretary of State Madeleine Albright replied that she did not think she had to answer international legal questions in detail." Cité dans Assemblée parlementaire de l'OTAN (Commission des affaires civiles), *Kosovo as a Precedent: Towards a Reform of the Security Council?* rédigé par le rapporteur général Arthur Paecht, 16 septembre 1999, Doc. AS244CC-E, par. 14.

[6] Antonio Cassese, "Ex iniuria jus oritur: Are we moving towards international legitimation of forcible countermeasures in the world community?" (1999) 10 Eur. J. Int'l L. 155.

[7] Selon certains juristes qui militent en faveur du droit d'ingérence humanitaire, l'intervention de l'OTAN était légitime car elle a été menée "contre une épuration ethnique particulièrement grave." Mario Bettati, "Théorie et réalité du droit d'ingérence humanitaire," *Géopolitique,* n° 68, janvier 2000, p. 26.

Il est possible d'être en faveur d'un changement de gouvernement à Belgrade tout en soulevant des doutes quant à la justification du recours à la force présentée par les capitales occidentales. Il
est aussi possible d'être en faveur d'un Kosovo bénéficiant d'une
grande autonomie tout en reconnaissant que les excès nationalistes
albanais ont rendu difficile la situation de cette province depuis
le début des années 1980. La question est plutôt de savoir si une
interprétation équilibrée et réaliste du conflit opposant Albanais[8]
et Serbes au Kosovo a été présentée aux populations occidentales.
La réponse à cette question qui concerne les faits affecte de façon
fondamentale un problème d'ordre juridique et moral qui est
apparu depuis la fin du processus de Rambouillet: est-ce que les
puissances occidentales ont véritablement épuisé tous les moyens
diplomatiques avant d'avoir recours à la force? Les États ont intérêt
à réglementer l'usage de la force et le droit demeure une source
de légitimité qui ne devrait pas être écartée facilement en faveur
d'arguments humanitaires incertains.

LE CONTEXTE DIPLOMATIQUE ET LA SITUATION HUMANITAIRE AVANT LES BOMBARDEMENTS DE L'OTAN

Les hostilités entre la guérilla séparatiste albanaise et les forces
répressives du gouvernement yougoslave se sont intensifiées au
début de 1998. L'intervention des troupes serbes contre une
famille d'insurgés notoires dans la région de Drenica a particulièrement attiré l'attention des médias occidentaux. En assiégeant
les résidences semi-fortifiées du clan Jasheri dans cette région his-
toriquement rebelle,[9] les troupes serbes ont tué une quarantaine

---

[8] Avant les bombardements de l'OTAN, le Kosovo était habité par plusieurs
groupes ethniques qui avaient le statut de "nation constitutive" ou "minorité"
dans l'État yougoslave établi à la suite de la Seconde Guerre mondiale. Cet article
évite l'utilisation du terme "Kosovar" qui n'a pas été reconnu officiellement
parce qu'il pourrait suggérer qu'un des groupes est plus autochtone que les
autres. L'article utilise les identités officielles reconnues par toutes les parties qui
ont participé à l'arrangement constitutionnel de l'ancienne Yougoslavie. Pour
une objection similaire concernant l'utilisation du terme "Bosniaque" par nombreux commentateurs occidentaux lors du conflit en Bosnie-Herzégovine, voir
Michael Barutciski, "Politics Overrides Legal Principles: Tragic Consequences of
the Diplomatic Intervention in Bosnia-Herzegovina (1991-1992)," (1996) 11
Am. Univ. J. Int'l L. and Policy 769.

[9] Région native d'Azem Bejta, un "kaçak" (partisan albanais) célèbre de la Première Guerre mondiale et des années 1920. Voir, par exemple, Ivo Banac, *The
National Question in Yugoslavia*, Ithaca, Cornell University Press, 1984, pp. 302-3.

de membres de la famille qui étaient parmi les combattants.[10] Des reportages sur ce massacre ont été diffusés largement par les médias qui ont fait pression pour que les gouvernements occidentaux interviennent avec plus de force contre Belgrade.[11]

Les journaux albanais modérés et extrémistes vendus dans les rues de Pristina ont publié des photographies explicites de la tuerie ainsi que des commentaires de plus en plus radicaux.[12] À partir de ce moment, la description suivante par un ambassadeur italien explique bien la dynamique politico-humanitaire relativement subtile qui a caractérisé l'intervention internationale:

L'Occident prêche le respect des droits humanitaires; les dirigeants de la minorité opprimée, traduisant 'droits humanitaires' par 'indépendance,' cherchent à dramatiser leur situation, quitte à provoquer la riposte de la majorité; l'État central réagit, exacerbant les sentiments nationalistes de sa propre opinion publique: la minorité opprimée réagit à son tour en donnant cours à un nationalisme tout aussi radical. Il suffisait, dès lors, à ce stade, d'une étincelle pour mettre le feu aux poudres. Paradoxalement, la campagne en faveur des droits humanitaires a généré le nationalisme, rendant la perspective d'un ordre international plus lointaine encore.[13]

Pendant que les diplomates occidentaux exigeaient que Belgrade rétablisse l'autonomie considérable dont le Kosovo bénéficiait durant les années 1980, les forces de sécurité yougoslaves ont procédé à des opérations militaires contre les guérilleros et leurs sympathisants tout au long de l'été 1998. L'OTAN commençait à menacer la Yougoslavie afin d'obtenir le retrait des forces gouvernementales et de promouvoir une solution politique.

La diplomatie occidentale avait obtenu des résultats positifs jusqu'à la fin de février 1999. Le gouvernement de Belgrade avait fait plusieurs concessions sous pression des occidentaux. Contrairement aux résultats d'un référendum et d'un vote au parlement fédéral en avril 1998, le gouvernement yougoslave a accepté une médiation internationale.[14] Il est difficile d'imaginer des États

---

[10] CNN Interactive, *Clashes in Kosovo leave at least 22 dead,* 5 mars 1998; Amnesty International, *Violence in Drenica,* 30 juin 1998; Zoran Kusovac, "The KLA: braced to defend and control," *Jane's Intelligence Review,* 1er avril 1999.

[11] CNN Interactive, *World leaders condemn Kosovo violence,* 7 mars 1998.

[12] Voir, par exemple, les photographies publiées dans le quotidien *Koha Ditore* qui sont affichées sur le site www.kohaditore.com/ARTA/drenica.htm.

[13] Sergio Romano, "Droits de l'homme et nationalismes," *Géopolitique,* n° 68, janvier 2000, p. 62.

[14] BBC Online News, *Serb 'no' to foreign mediation in Kosovo,* 24 avril 1998.

indépendants permettant une ingérence étrangère dans de tels problèmes internes. En effet, l'accord Milosevic-Holbrooke d'octobre 1998 a permis le déploiement de plus de 1 400 moniteurs de la Mission de Vérification du Kosovo (MVK).[15] Ces moniteurs se trouvaient sous l'autorité de l'Organisation pour la sécurité et la coopération en Europe et ils étaient composés principalement de militaires occidentaux habillés en civils.[16] Ils patrouillaient à travers le Kosovo dans des véhicules 4×4 et rapportaient les circonstances des abus commis par les deux parties au conflit. Cette mission s'ajoutait au personnel diplomatique déjà présent sur le terrain. L'accord permettait également à l'OTAN de mener des missions de surveillance aérienne au-dessus du Kosovo.[17] Le personnel du Haut Commissariat des Nations Unies pour les réfugiés a été autorisé de distribuer l'aide d'urgence et des vivres directement aux familles rurales des guérilleros.[18] Pour un gouvernement qui s'inquiète que la souveraineté sur son territoire lui échappe, il s'agit de concessions sans précédent.[19]

De plus, le gouvernement de Belgrade avait accepté de façon générale l'aspect politique du plan de Rambouillet: une autonomie élargie pour la province du Kosovo.[20] Durant la décennie précédente, Belgrade se justifiait de limiter l'autonomie locale et de gouverner la province directement en invoquant la menace

---

[15] *Agreement between the Organization for Security and Cooperation in Europe and the Federal Republic of Yugoslavia on the Kosovo Verification Mission,* 16 octobre 1998.

[16] Ces informations sont basées sur nos discussions avec des membres de la MVK durant 1998-1999. Voir aussi Jeffrey Smith, "US Swells Kosovo Observer Unit," *Washington Post,* 8 novembre 1998, p. A32.

[17] *Kosovo Verification Mission Agreement between the North Atlantic Treaty Organization and the Federal Republic of Yugoslavia,* 15 octobre 1998. Pour un des rares commentaires sur cette mission, voir Agence France Presse, *Pendant la crise, la mission "Eagle Eye" se poursuit,* 5 mars 1999.

[18] Nous avons accompagné plusieurs de ces convois.

[19] Laura Silber et David Buchan, "A diplomatic missile," *Financial Times,* 18 octobre 1998, p. 7: "These are considerable concessions from the man [président Milosevic] who had insisted until then that what happened in Kosovo was an internal matter."

[20] CNN Interactive, *Kosovo talks yield partial accord on autonomy,* 23 février 1999: "International mediators in Rambouillet said the two sides agreed in principle to granting autonomy to Kosovo"; BBC Online News, *Kosovo deadline extended,* 20 février 1999: "A Serbian source said Serbian President Milan Milutinovic and Yugoslav Deputy Prime Minister Nikola Sainovic had told Contact Group foreign ministers that Belgrade could agree to the political part of the proposed accord, subject to some minor changes."

sécessionniste. À partir de l'hiver 1999, les politiciens yougoslaves avaient accepté publiquement que les Albanais du Kosovo pourraient se gouverner eux-mêmes avec une ingérence minimale de la part de Belgrade. La pression occidentale avait réussi ces avancées bien que les politiciens albanais n'avaient pas renoncé à leur revendication d'indépendance. En fait, ces derniers n'avaient pas fait de véritables concessions et il est possible que l'intervention occidentale les ait encouragé dans leurs aspirations plus extrêmes.

Cependant, ce sont les dispositions militaires qui ont assuré le rejet du plan de Rambouillet. Le gouvernement américain insistait pour que le contrôle du Kosovo soit assumé par une force imposante menée par l'OTAN. Si la protection des droits fondamentaux des Albanais du Kosovo était l'objectif prioritaire des efforts diplomatiques, les membres de l'OTAN n'ont pas expliqué la raison pour laquelle il s'agissait de la seule forme de présence internationale qu'ils pouvaient accepter. Il faut souligner que la dimension politique du plan de Rambouillet comprenait une autonomie pour le Kosovo sur toutes questions internes, y compris les questions de sécurité. Autrement dit, les forces serbes devaient se retirer et les membres des diverses factions rebelles pouvaient se transformer en policiers.[21] Il est clair que le retrait des forces serbes allait réduire de façon dramatique la menace contre les populations albanaises.

Les puissances occidentales n'ont pas exploré publiquement d'autres formes de présence internationale bien que le président Milutinovic de la Serbie avait indiqué que son gouvernement était prêt à discuter d'une expansion de la présence déjà sur le terrain. Si l'objectif était de sauver les populations albanaises d'un "génocide," pourquoi les efforts diplomatiques occidentaux ne se sont pas concentrés sur l'expansion de la MVK et le déploiement additionnel de troupes légères sanctionnées par le Conseil de sécurité qui pourraient surveiller le retrait serbe? Les gouvernements

---

[21] *Understanding the Rambouillet Accords,* Fact sheet released by the Bureau of European Affairs, US Department of State, Washington, 1er mars 1999: "Serb security forces will withdraw completely except for limited number of border police and, for a transitional period, a limited number of civil police officers who will serve at the direction of the international Implementation Mission until local police are trained to replace them." Voir aussi Tim Judah, "The KLA: Out from the shadows," *BBC Online News,* 4 février 1999: "Under the proposed agreement ethnic Albanian police would take over security functions in majority Albanian areas. Since most of the province is majority ethnic Albanian this would suit the KLA as, inevitably, it would provide the backbone for the force. With few Serbs remaining in Kosovo as it is, many of the rest would then leave."

occidentaux auraient pu même avoir recours aux sanctions ou à l'usage de la force si le retrait n'était pas respecté rigoureusement par Belgrade.

Un des aspects controversés de la dimension militaire du plan de Rambouillet concerne l'accès quasiment sans limites au reste de la Yougoslavie qui devait être accordé à l'OTAN.[22] Les dispositions relatives à cet accès avaient peu attiré l'attention des observateurs. Si les puissances occidentales avaient véritablement épuisé tous les moyens diplomatiques avant d'avoir recours à la force, pourquoi est-ce que l'accès à la Serbie entière n'avait pas été obtenu dans l'entente signée avec les autorités yougoslaves pour mettre fin aux bombardements le 9 juin 1999?[23] Le gouvernement américain avait déjà décidé que des frappes aériennes seraient lancées si la Yougoslavie refusait d'accorder à l'OTAN le contrôle du Kosovo et l'accès au reste de la Serbie, bien que ces conditions n'étaient pas nécessaires pour une protection effective des populations albanaises. La plupart des États occidentaux se sont laissés dominer par une approche américaine qui avait pris le contrôle de la conférence de Rambouillet[24] et qui était problématique: soit elle reflétait un manque de connaissance du sentiment profond d'attachement qu'éprouvent les Serbes envers cette partie historique de leur territoire,[25] soit le rejet anticipé était une manœuvre cynique pour justifier une action militaire.[26] En tout cas, les téléspectateurs

---

[22] Voir *Appendice B: Statut de la Force armée multinationale de mise en œuvre*, par. 7-22.

[23] *Military-technical agreement between the international security force (KFOR) and the Governments of the Federal Republic of Yugoslavia and the Republic of Serbia*, 9 juin 1999.

[24] Le processus de paix de Rambouillet était une initiative franco-britannique: "This is Dayton transferred to France, but without American muscle. At Dayton, Secretary of State Warren Christopher turned the key, but Madelaine Albright has no plans to attend Rambouillet." Hugo Young, "The British people should be told what they're getting into in Kosovo," *The Guardian*, 4 février 1999.

[25] Bien que le Kosovo soit plus prêt au cœur des Serbes que le destin des communautés serbes en Bosnie-Herzégovine ou en Krajina, l'ancien ambassadeur américain à Belgrade prétend ce qui suit: "A reasonable Serbian leader could probably, with some show of reluctance, have accepted the Rambouillet proposal. But Milosevic rejected the plan, objecting mainly to the NATO force, although he had accepted a similar force in Bosnia against the will of the Bosnian Serbs." Warren Zimmermann, "Milosevic's Final Solution," *New York Review of Books*, 10 juin 1999.

[26] "Si, en revanche, l'intention des puissances coalisées était de faire avorter la négociation diplomatique pour ne laisser place qu'à l'option militaire, elles n'auraient pas agi autrement." Éric Rouleau, "Errements de la diplomatie française

occidentaux demeuraient persuadés que les autorités yougoslaves continuaient leur entêtement en refusant le plan occidental.

Pour justifier cette position de l'OTAN, un rapport du parlement britannique déclare que la présence d'une telle force était nécessaire compte tenu de la tuerie autour du village de Racak en janvier 1999.[27] En effet, la frustration des membres de l'OTAN est illustrée par ce massacre présumé qui avait incité la convocation de la conférence de Rambouillet. Selon *The Washington Post,* cet incident représente l'événement clé qui a transformé la politique occidentale.[28] Pourtant, quelques témoignages de cet incident bien médiatisé auraient dû provoquer une réaction plus prudente. Plusieurs journalistes avaient rapporté des faits qui soulevaient la possibilité de manipulation de la part des belligérants et qui suggéraient que le chef américain de la MVK avait accusé les Serbes avec un empressement mal à propos.[29]

Les résultats peu concluants du rapport médico-légal d'une équipe internationale[30] ont été rendus publics discrètement quelques jours avant les bombardements de l'OTAN. L'attitude générale dans les pays occidentaux est bien reflétée dans la déclaration d'un des membres de la "commission indépendante sur le Kosovo"

---

au Kosovo," *Le Monde diplomatique,* décembre 1999, p. 8. Bien que le commentaire suivant vienne d'un auteur qui était en faveur des bombardements contre la Yougoslavie, il offre une interprétation qui corrobore la citation précédente et qui souligne involontairement l'abus des moyens diplomatiques: "other officials maintain that the real point of Rambouillet was to persuade the Europeans, and especially the Italians, who tended to think of the Albanians as terrorists and drug trafickers, that the Albanians were actually "the good guys" — if nothing else, Rambouillet served to get the Europeans to "stop blaming the victims" and to build NATO's resolve to use force." Michael Ignatieff, "Annals of Diplomacy: Balkan Physics," *New Yorker,* 10 mai 1999, p. 76.

[27] "It is clear why the presence of a NATO force—the point which was most difficult for Milosevic to accept—was non-negotiable for the co-chairs, in the light of the Racak massacre which had occurred despite the presence of unarmed OSCE monitors." House of Commons Select Committee on Foreign Affairs, *Fourth Report — Kosovo,* Londres, 23 mai 2000, par. 57.

[28] Barton Gellman, "The Path to Crisis: how the United States and its Allies went to war," *Washingtom Post,* 18 avril 1999, p. A1: "[Racak] transformed the West's Balkan policy as singular events seldom do."

[29] Christophe Châtelot, "Kosovo: l'Europe face à la barbarie," *Le Monde,* 19 janvier 1999, et Renaud Girard, "Kosovo: massacre," *Le Figaro,* 20 janvier 1999. Voir également *Preliminary Forensic Report on 40 Racak Dead,* 30 janvier 1999.

[30] Kurt Schork (Reuters), "Autopsy report inconclusive on Kosovo massacre," 17 mars 1999, et Jovana Gec (Associated Press), "Autopsy report inconclusive on Kosovo massacre," 17 mars 1999.

qui prétend que la poursuite des moyens diplomatiques après l'incident de Racak risquait de ressembler à l'apaisement.[31] Toutefois, quand le texte du rapport a été rendu public, il indiquait que toutes les parties (y compris le chef de la MVK et le gouvernement américain) avaient fait des déclarations fausses ou non corroborées[32] sur un incident qui ne correspondait pas au "massacre" présenté aux téléspectateurs occidentaux.[33] Néanmoins, les dés avaient déjà été jetés.[34]

Le processus de Rambouillet avait aussi renforcé les pires éléments de la scène politique au Kosovo. Le chef plus modéré des Albanais, Ibrahim Rugova, a été ouvertement marginalisé par un gouvernement américain qui appuyait dorénavant les leaders extrémistes de la guérilla.[35] Ce changement d'alignement a été

---

[31] "By then, moral disgust at Racak would have made further diplomacy look like appeasement." Michael Ignatieff, "Annals of Diplomacy: Balkan Physics," *New Yorker,* 10 mai 1999, p. 78.

[32] La presse américaine a été particulièrement flagrante en publiant des récits qui ont été par la suite refutés par les expertises médico-légales. Voir R. Jeffrey Smith, "Kosovo killings called a massacre: some victims shot while on their knees," *Washington Post,* 17 mars 1999, p. A1: "An independent forensic report into the killings of 40 ethnic Albanians in the Kosovo village of Racak in January has found that the victims were unarmed civilians executed in an organized massacre, some of them forced to kneel before being sprayed with bullets, according to Western sources familiar with the report." Pour la réplique à cet article, voir Associated Press, "40 Kosovo dead said to be civilians," publiée dans *The Guardian,* 17 mars 1999: "Helena Ranta, head of the [médecins légistes] team, denied a report in The Washington Post today that described the team's findings as proof of an organized massacre and said some of the victims were forced to kneel before they were shot. "If we want to speculate about what happened, we would be speculating for days," she told a news conference ... she noted they could not say definitively that the victims had never used firearms." Pour un autre exemple de déclaration non corroborée, voir Jane Perlez, "Uncertainty about delegates clouds Kosovo talks," *New York Times,* 10 février 1999.

[33] *Report of the EU forensic expert team on the Racak incident,* 17 mars 1999.

[34] Karin Kneissl, "Ob es ein Massaker war, will keiner mehr wissen," *Die Welt,* 8 mars 1999.

[35] "Une autre question se pose, celle des relations entre Ibrahim Rugova et les Occidentaux. S'il a conservé de bonnes relations avec plusieurs pays européens, l'action du leader modéré ne semblait plus entrer dans la stratégie des États-Unis dans les Balkans. Le département d'État américain avait fait le pari, depuis les négociations de paix entre Serbes et Albanais à Rambouillet (France) en février 1999, de soutenir, voire même de chouchouter le jeune et bouillant Hashim Thaci. Un choix qui se révèle aujourd'hui fort peu judicieux." Agence France Presse, *Rugova après Kostunica: deux modérés pour un dialogue très incertain,* 30 octobre 2000. "The Kosovar delegates [dirigé par Thaci] have now said that

effectué bien que le Département d'État avait jusqu'alors qualifié les guérilleros de "terroristes" et que nombreux commentateurs occidentaux connaissaient leurs liens avec des réseaux mondiaux du crime organisé.[36] Les chefs des autres minorités du Kosovo étaient simplement ignorés car ils avaient tendance à préférer des liens avec la fédération yougoslave plutôt que la domination par des nationalistes albanais. La composition multinationale de la délégation yougoslave à Rambouillet a été écartée d'emblée comme une manipulation publique bien qu'elle reflète une tendance historique concernant les relations interethniques au Kosovo. La composition mono-ethnique de la délégation albanaise et son programme d'émancipation national effrayait les autres groupes ethniques, tandis que la plupart des médias occidentaux semblaient ignorer cette dimension identitaire du conflit.

Durant la période février 1998 – février 1999, les statistiques du HCR suggèrent que peut-être entre 200 000 et 300 000 personnes ont été déplacées au Kosovo.[37] Ce mouvement représentait essentiellement un déplacement rural temporaire qui résultait des opérations gouvernementales contre des villages soupçonnés de sympathiser avec la guérilla. Les chiffres sont cumulatifs dans le sens que beaucoup des personnes déplacées sont retournées dans leur maison parfois endommagée. Les sources occidentales suggèrent que les victimes liées au conflit s'élèvent peut-être jusqu'à 1 000 ou 2 000 morts durant cette année de conflit armé.[38] Bien que les journalistes étrangers ont eu raison de mettre l'accent sur la détresse et les souffrances des populations albanaises, ces statistiques comprennent également des victimes serbes tombées

---

they will sign in two weeks, and it's normal for them to proceed with consultations at home because they're starting to play by democratic rules of the type that don't exist for the Serbs." Said the State Department spokesman, James Rubin." Joseph Fitchett, "Kosovar Team Accepts Conditional Agreement," *International Herald Tribune,* 24 février 1999, p. 1. "In the bush of Kosovo, Hashim Thaci is known as 'the snake'." Jane Perlez, "Uncertainty about delegates clouds Kosovo talks," *New York Times,* 10 février 1999.

[36] Voir, par exemple, Jerry Seper, "KLA finances war with heroin sales," *Washington Times,* 3 mai 1999.

[37] Les statistiques officielles peuvent être plus élevées, bien que nous avons observé la méthodologie peu fiable utilisée pour la collecte des données dans les régions rurales du Kosovo. Le personnel du HCR nous a admis que des statistiques élevées ont permis une plus grande donation de vivres.

[38] Voir, par exemple, *Statement in the United Nations Security Council by Sir Jeremy Greenstock KCMG,* Représentant permanent du Royaume Uni, 24 mars 1999.

dans les embuscades tendues par les guérilleros ou qui étaient les cibles de vendettas locales. Il est intéressant de noter que des ONG suggèrent qu'un nombre similaire de personnes ont été tuées en Albanie durant l'anarchie interne de 1997.[39]

Si ces statistiques sont comparées à celles concernant d'autres conflits sécessionnistes à travers le monde, il est apparent qu'elles sont relativement faibles. Bien qu'impliquant des durées et niveaux d'intensité variés, les conflits dans la région habitée par les Tamouls au Sri Lanka, la région habitée par les Kurdes en Turquie et la région du Kashmir sur le continent indien ont chacun produit des dizaines de milliers de morts et plus d'un million de personnes déplacées.[40] Les souffrances réelles au Kosovo méritaient un engagement international, mais il était important de placer la situation dans son contexte pour déterminer une réponse appropriée qui ne serait pas dominée par des réactions émotionnelles.

Les commentateurs occidentaux ont généralement ignoré que l'Albanie était impliquée dans le conflit de son voisin yougoslave. Ceci se reflétait dans les déclarations du gouvernement de Tirana relatives à la solidarité de toutes les populations albanaises dans les Balkans: "Si les massacres au Kosovo se poursuivent et si une solution n'est pas trouvée, alors les Albanais ... en Albanie, en Macédoine, au Kosovo et au Monténégro ont le devoir d'organiser une défense collective' a déclaré M. Majko [premier ministre de l'Albanie]."[41] Le gouvernement albanais avait longtemps appuyé la lutte indépendantiste au Kosovo[42] et il permettait à diverses

---

[39] Human Rights Watch, *Annual Report 1998:* "1997 was a tumultuous and tragic year for Albania, in which approximately 2,000 people lost their lives during a popular revolt, the government's violent response, and the chaos that ensued." Voir aussi Lawyers Committee for Human Rights, *Protection of Kosovar Refugees in Albania: Report on the Mission to Tirana and Kukes,* juin 1999, par. 1.3.1.

[40] Voir statistiques dans Stockholm International Peace Research Institute, SIPRI Yearbook 1998, Oxford, Oxford University Press, pp. 24-30.

[41] Associated Press, *Tirana évoque la défense collective des Albanais des Balkans,* 9 février 1999.

[42] Selon un ancien ambassadeur albanais à l'ONU: "Prior to the democratic victory [en 1992], the chances of achieving national unification looked good. German reunification offered a valuable precedent. The major task facing the Albanian state was to institutionalise the Kosova question and to have the Kosova Republic recognized by all international institutions and organizations ... [M]embership in the [Organisation de la Conférence islamique] would allow Albania to gain Islamic backing for a settlement of the national question in the framework of a Greater Albania where Islam would be the common element." Agim Nesho, "Political Developments after 22 March 1992 and the Albanian

factions de la guérilla d'établir leur base dans le nord de l'Albanie.[43] Les escarmouches frontalières avec des soldats yougoslaves étaient fréquentes dans les mois qui ont précédé les bombardements de l'OTAN. En fait, l'effondrement du gouvernement de Tirana en 1997 a contribué à l'escalade du conflit au Kosovo dans la mesure où les armes sont devenues de plus en plus disponibles à travers les régions frontalières anarchiques de l'Albanie et du Kosovo.[44]

Pendant que les menaces occidentales s'intensifiaient vers la fin des pourparlers à Rambouillet, les contingents de l'OTAN se regroupaient à la frontière macédonienne.[45] Cette situation frontalière tendue et l'intensification de l'insurrection ont mené à une augmentation de la présence de l'armée yougoslave au Kosovo. Les forces yougoslaves ont renforcé leur présence le long de la frontière à cause de la menace d'une invasion terrestre. Cette présence et les escarmouches avec les guérilleros ont poussé un nombre important d'habitants de cette zone à fuir en Macédoine.[46]

La décision unilatérale de la MVK de se retirer du Kosovo le 20 mars indiquait que les moyens diplomatiques avaient été abandonnés par les puissances occidentales. Il est intéressant de noter que le rapport final de l'OSCE qui décrit la situation jusqu'au déclenchement des frappes aériennes de l'OTAN a été rendu public neuf mois plus tard.[47] Son contenu présente une interprétation

---

National Question," dans Thanos Veremis et Evangelos Kofos (dir.), *Kosovo: Avoiding Another Balkan War,* Athènes, Hellenic Foundation for European and Foreign Policy, 1998, pp. 311 et 313.

[43] Voir "Recent Background to Current Crisis in Kosovo," *Jane's Sentinel,* 1er mars 1999, et BBC World News Service, *Albania Admits Training KLA,* 3 mai 1999.

[44] Tim Judah, "The KLA: Out from the shadows," *BBC Online News,* 4 février 1999: "An opportunity to begin planning a real uprising came unexpectedly in the spring of 1997. Albania, which borders Kosovo, collapsed into anarchy. The looting of military arsenals meant that hundreds of thousands of cheap Kalashnikovs were now on the market and within easy smuggling distance of Kosovo."

[45] Nous avons observé le deploiement de chars d'assaut allemands et britanniques en Macédoine dans les semaines précédant les frappes aériennes de l'OTAN. Une capacité offensive limitée a été confirmée par le personnel militaire allemand. Voir aussi Agence France Presse, *Chars allemands à l'étranger: une première depuis la Deuxième guerre mondiale,* 10 mars 1999, et Agence France Presse, *L'OTAN en Macédoine: 10 000 soldats d'élite déployés à la fin de la semaine,* 8 mars 1999.

[46] Le nom "Macédoine" est utilisé pour désigner l'État reconnu par l'ONU sous le nom de "l'Ancienne République yougoslave de Macédoine."

[47] OSCE, *Kosovo/Kosova As Seen, As Told,* 6 décembre 1999.

généralement nuancée d'une situation sur le terrain qui implique des abus et excès de toutes les parties. C'est la situation qui est généralement décrite dans le dernier rapport mensuel de la MVK juste avant son départ.[48]

La situation sur le terrain était telle que la plupart des employés internationaux et albanais des organisation humanitaires qui ont été évacués au même moment croyaient qu'ils allaient retourner au Kosovo dans les plus brefs délais et que l'évacuation (la troisième en six mois) leur donnerait une chance de prendre quelques jours de vacances en Macédoine.[49] Peu avant les bombardements de l'OTAN, les États occidentaux qui financent les opérations du HCR faisaient pression pour que celui-ci se prépare à rapatrier le nombre relativement restreint de réfugiés en Albanie et en Macédoine.[50] Il n'y avait aucune planification sérieuse pour un nouveau flux massif de réfugiés.[51]

La situation humanitaire après le déclenchement des bombardements de l'OTAN

Les frappes aériennes de l'OTAN qui ont commencé le 24 mars 1999 avaient pour but de faire cesser la violence serbe au Kosovo et

---

[48] Voir *Lettre datée du 23 mars 1999, addressée au Président du Conseil de sécurité par le Secrétaire général* qui inclut le *Rapport mensuel sur la situation au Kosovo, établi en application des résolutions 1160 (1998) et 1203 (1998) du Conseil de sécurité, 15 février – 20 mars 1999*, 23 mars 1999, UN Doc. S/1999/315. Les deux premiers paragraphes commencent avec les phrases suivantes: "Au Kosovo, la situation sur le terrain est demeurée grave. Des accrochages localisés entre l'ALK et les forces de sécurité serbes se sont poursuivis. Les attaques non provoquées de l'ALK contre la police ont continué et le nombre des victimes parmi les forces de sécurité a augmenté…Par suite de la détérioration de la situation sur le plan de la sécurité, le Président en exercice de l'OSCE, le Ministre norvégien des affaires étrangères, M. Knut Vollebaek, a décidé le repli temporaire de la Mission sur le territoire de l'ex-République yougoslave de Macédoine."

[49] Ces informations sont basées sur nos entrevues avec plus d'une douzaine d'organisations humanitaires.

[50] Nicholas Morris, "Genèse d'une crise," *Réfugiés*, vol. 3, n° 116, 1999, p. 19.

[51] Ceci n'était pas dû à un manquement de préparation ou d'ignorance comme suggéré dans International Independent Commission on Kosovo, *Kosovo Report*, Oxford, Oxford University Press, 2000, pp. 86 et 201. Les gouvernements occidentaux n'ont pas renseigné le HCR sur un projet d'expulsions organisées parce qu'il s'agissait probablement d'une allégation destinée aux médias et au public. Voir prochains paragraphes. Pour un reportage sur la preuve concernant l'existence d'une opération de nettoyage nommée "Potkova," voir John Goetz et Tom Walker, "Serbian ethnic cleansing scare was a fake, says general," *Sunday Times*, 2 avril 2000.

d'obliger les autorités yougoslaves à accepter le plan de Rambouillet. Les dirigeants de l'OTAN croyaient que ces objectifs pouvaient
être atteints rapidement. Ceci représentait un mauvais calcul.[52] Les
bombardements ont été accompagnés par une escalade de la violence sur le terrain et un flux massif de réfugiés qui comprenait
quelques expulsions organisées. Les frappes aériennes ont néanmoins été présentées par les politiciens occidentaux comme étant
nécessaires pour prévenir un «nettoyage ethnique» planifié contre
les Albanais du Kosovo.[53] Si les services de renseignements occidentaux avaient vraiment connaissance avant le 24 mars d'un tel
programme impliquant des expulsions, ils n'ont pas informé les
organisations humanitaires.[54] Ces dernières ne s'attendaient pas à
un déplacement soudain et massif de populations civiles. Comme
les autres acteurs internationaux sur le terrain, elles étaient prises
au dépourvu.

La décision de l'OTAN paraît mal conçue du point de vue de la
protection des populations civiles. Il n'est pas étonnant qu'il y ait
eu une augmentation de violence durant les bombardements. Un
nombre beaucoup plus élevé de gens a été déplacé pendant que les
forces serbes se sont déchaînées à travers la province et la guérilla
albanaise a tenté d'exploiter tactiquement les frappes aériennes
contre des positions ennemies. Il est probable que plus de la moitié
des deux millions d'habitants a été déplacée pendant les onzes
semaines de l'opération aérienne de l'OTAN.

Il est possible d'identifier au moins quatre types de déplacement.
Premièrement, les villageois ont fui l'intensification des opérations
gouvernementales contre les fiefs des guérilleros. Ce déplacement
rural temporaire a sans doute été particulièrement désespéré à
cause de l'escalade du conflit et la difficulté de trouver un refuge
dans les villages voisins. Deuxièmement, certains habitants liés aux
activités insurgées se sont repliés à cause de l'incapacité des guérilleros de tenir des sites stratégiques. Troisièmement, les bombardements concentrés sur le Kosovo ont provoqué le départ de nombreux civils qui cherchaient des endroits plus sûrs de la même
manière que les résidents à travers la Yougoslavie ont quitté des

---

[52] "NATO officials acknowledge the campaign was started in the belief that
Milosevic would quickly sue for peace ... The campaign thus began on the basis
of mistaken political judgment about Mr Milosevic." Alexander Nicoll, "The lin-
gering question," *Financial Times*, 1ᵉʳ juillet 1999, p. 25.

[53] CNN Interactive, *NATO, British leaders allege "genocide" in Kosovo*, 29 mars 1999.

[54] UNHCR, *The Kosovo refugee crisis: An independent evaluation of UNHCR's emergency
preparedness and response*, UN Doc. EPAU/2000/001, février 2000, par. 89.

zones qui pourraient être potentiellement ciblées par l'OTAN. Quatrièment, les forces serbes ont procédé à des expulsions de certaines populations perçues comme ennemies. Il est vraisemblable que les troupes serbes étaient motivées par une vengeance furieuse contre les Albanais qui étaient contents de voir l'OTAN bombarder plusieurs villes à travers la Yougoslavie. Les images d'Albanais de Pristina expulsés par train au début de la crise ont eu une grande influence sur les téléspectateurs occidentaux durant les fêtes de Pâques du début d'avril. Bien que ces expulsions n'étaient pas représentatives des déplacements, elles ont été décisives dans la mobilisation de l'opinion publique occidentale contre la Yougoslavie.[55] Les flux organisés de réfugiés déferlant sur les frontières macédonienne et albanaise étaient probablement destinés à créer une crise humanitaire dans les États d'accueil en première ligne et à encombrer les accès routiers qui pouvaient être utilisés par des troupes de l'OTAN pour une invasion. La violence serbe ne peut pas être justifiée, mais il faut noter que beaucoup d'Albanais avaient de la difficulté à quitter le Kosovo parce que des policiers leur interdisaient de fuir.[56]

Nombreux commentateurs et politiciens occidentaux ont fait référence aux crimes commis par les Nazis durant la Seconde Guerre mondiale pour décrire le drame humanitaire des Albanais du Kosovo.[57] La description et analyse ci-dessus suggèrent que ces

[55] Ces informations sont basées sur nos discussions durant l'automne 1999 avec des hauts gradés de l'ambassade américaine à Skopje et des douzaines d'Albanais de diverses régions du Kosovo qui ont été déplacés durant les bombardements. Aucun des anciens réfugiés interviewés n'avait été expulsé, bien que plusieurs avaient entendu parler des cas d'expulsion.

[56] Ces informations nous ont été communiquées par des anciens réfugiés.

[57] Agence France Presse, *Hillary Clinton likens Kosovars' plight to Holocaust*, 14 mai 1999: "US First Lady Hillary Clinton toured a refugee camp here Friday, where she likened the plight of Kosovo's ethnic Albanians to the agony of the Jews under the Third Reich. Clinton said the suffering of the Kosovars reminded her of 'Schindler's List' and 'Sophie's Choice' — movies portraying the fate of Jews systematically murdered or persecuted by the Nazis." Nous avons évalué les conditions dans les camps en Macédoine et il faut noter que le camp visité par Hillary Clinton était connu pour ses conditions "de luxe" qui ne sont pas comparables aux camps en Afrique ou en Asie. Sur l'abondance d'assistance humanitaire, voir Raymond Apthorpe, *Kosovo Humanitarian Programme Evaluations: Towards Synthesis, Meta-analysis and Sixteen Propositions for Discussion*, Londres, Overseas Development Institute, 28 septembre 2000, p. 6: "As is usual elsewhere the relief response was donor driven, but, unusually, not by a paucity of aid but by its abundance." Pour un autre exemple où le président américain fait un lien avec les crimes du régime nazi, voir Kevin Galvin (Associated Press), *Clinton Compares Holocaust, Kosovo*, 13 mai 1999.

analogies ne sont pas justifiées et ne contribuent pas à une compréhension plus nuancée du conflit au Kosovo.[58]

Contrairement à la suggestion avancée par la "commission indépendante sur le Kosovo" parrainée par le gouvernement suédois, l'évaluation commandée par le HCR sur la crise du Kosovo ne permet pas de conclure que le gouvernement de Belgrade préparait le nettoyage ethnique des Albanais ou que ceux-ci ont généralement été expulsés par les forces serbes.[59] Au contraire, les interviews réalisées dans le cadre de cette évaluation suggèrent qu'un nombre limité d'Albanais a été expulsé à la suite des premiers bombardements et que la grande majorité des réfugiés ont fui la violence généralisée et ont cherché à éviter les représailles potentielles. Les déclarations des capitales occidentales concernant la nature des flux de réfugiés et son utilisation pour justifier une intervention militaire relèvent en partie du domaine de la propagande.[60]

Après que des organisations internationales (ONU, OTAN, OSCE) aient assumé la responsabilité pour le Kosovo, les chefs albanais locaux ont pris le contrôle *de facto* pendant que des vagues de violences[61] ont mené à l'exode de la plupart des Serbes.[62] Les

[58] Le directeur du centre de recherche sur l'anti-sémitisme à Berlin a suggéré que de telles comparaisons inexactes risquent de relativiser l'holocauste. Voir Reporters sans frontières, *Yougoslavie: les "bavures" médiatiques de l'OTAN,* juin 1999.

[59] International Independent Commission on Kosovo, *Kosovo Report,* Oxford, Oxford University Press, 2000, pp. 3, 88-90.

[60] Stephen R. Graubard, "Une nouvelle approche des droits de l'homme," *Géopolitique,* n°68, janvier 2000, p. 59: "Milosevic, un tyran, a été diabolisé, le peuple serbe représenté comme autant de victimes impuissantes, contraintes à être les esclaves d'un leader impitoyable et dément. Quelle que soit la part de vérité dans ces présentations, la propagande, comme lors du premier et du second conflit mondial, a fait de la désinformation, décrivant une situation indéniablement tragique, mais dans des termes, en général, grossis et amplifiés. Faire accepter l'intervention militaire aux électeurs des démocraties, notamment lorsque celle-ci n'a pas produit les résultats immédiats escomptés, exige des gouvernements un grand déploiement d'inventivité dans les relations publiques."

[61] Voir, par exemple, Tim Butcher, "Serbs take refuge as revenge killings grow," *Daily Telegraph,* 25 juin 1999; Susan Milligan, "A reversal in roles: Serbs become targets," *Boston Globe,* 9 juillet 1999; BBC World News Online, *Kosovo reprisals horrify UN,* 17 juillet 1999; Tom Walker, "Vengeful KLA turns on nuns and Gypsies," *The Times,* 21 juillet 1999; Agence France Presse, *Zorica, 20 ans, a identifié son mari parmi les cadavres du site d'Ugljare,* 29 août 1999.

[62] Agence France Presse, *L'ONU appelle les Serbes à rester — sans garantie,* 30 juin 1999: "La communauté internationale a appelé mercredi les Serbes à prendre le risque de rester au Kosovo, tout en admettant n'avoir pas les moyens de les

Serbes ne sont pas les seules victimes de la vengeance albanaise au Kosovo, comme en témoigne la fuite des autres minorités.[63] Le personnel de l'OTAN s'attendait à de telles réactions violentes avant d'investir la province.[64] Même avant l'arrivée de l'OTAN sur son territoire, le Kosovo était en train de devenir une des entités les plus homogènes dans les Balkans car les non-Albanais se sentaient obligés de quitter[65] et le taux de natalité albanais excédait de loin les standards de la région.[66]

Ce dernier exemple de "nettoyage ethnique" dans les Balkans se compare aux pires exemples des guerres yougoslaves des années 1990 et va probablement représenter un changement démographique à long terme qui accompagnera la transformation *de facto* du Kosovo en État national albanais. Malgré les ressources considérables des puissances occidentales, il est possible de conclure que l'intervention n'a pas mis un terme aux violations des droits de l'homme et qu'elle a simplement permis un changement dans le rôle de persécuteur.[67] Il faut souligner que des sources

---

protéger contre les violences des Albanais." Voir aussi Agence France Presse, *Les civils serbes font leurs valises,* 15 juin 1999, et Agence France Presse, *Le Kosovo d'après-guerre reste une terre de déplacements forcés de populations,* 30 août 1999.

[63] Agence France Presse, *Les Tziganes reprochent à l'ONU et l'OTAN de ne pas les protéger au Kosovo,* 6 septembre 1999; Agence France Presse, *La minorité turque du Kosovo priée de "s'albaniser,"* 23 août 1999.

[64] Ces informations sont basées sur notre correspondance électronique.

[65] Agence France Presse, *De nombreux Serbes du Kosovo ont déja voté avec leurs pieds,* 21 février 1999: "'C'est la guerre, les Serbes pensent que leur avenir et celui de leurs enfants n'est pas ici,' assure un autre agent immobilier à Pristina. 'Si j'étais serbe, je ferais sans doute pareil'."

[66] Selon les recensements officiels, les Albanais représentaient 67,1 % de la population du Kosovo en 1961 et 77,5 % en 1981. La plupart des sources occidentales considèrent qu'ils représentaient au-delà de 90 % vers la fin des années 1990. Voir Bogoljub Kocovic, *Etnicki i demografski razvoj u Jugoslaviji od 1921 do 1991 godine,* Paris, Bibliothèque Dialogue, 1998, p. 324. L'auteur de cette étude démographique considère que les statistiques officielles doivent être modifiées pour tenir compte des douzaines de milliers de Turcs et Tziganes Roms qui se sont déclarés "Albanais": il croit que les Albanais représentaient *de facto* 60,4 % en 1961 et 74,4 % en 1981. *Id.,* p. 346.

[67] Veton Surroi, "Victims of the Victims," *New York Review of Books,* 7 octobre 1999: "I cannot stop myself from stating my concern that our moral code, according to which women, children, and the elderly should be left unharmed, has been violated ... We are dealing with a most vicious, organized system of violence against Serbs. And we are also dealing with a conviction that lurks behind such violence, that every Serb should be condemned for what happened in Kosova ... This system, based on such a conviction, is called fascism ... And those who think these

occidentales suggéraient dès l'automne 1999 que la violence avant et après les bombardements de l'OTAN était comparable.[68] Le résultat actuel sur le terrain et la continuation des violations des droits de l'homme malgré la présence imposante d'organisations internationales[69] témoignent de la politique malavisée adoptée par les puissances occidentales.

Au lieu d'encourager un discours prudent sur le Kosovo qui tiendrait compte des droits fondamentaux des Albanais et des craintes légitimes des Serbes, le langage humanitaire a exacerbé les problèmes délicats de coexistence dans cette région des Balkans. Usurpé par les puissance occidentales,[70] le langage de l'humanitarisme a permis de transformer un conflit à faible intensité en crise humanitaire régionale qui a presque déstabilisé la Macédoine voisine. Cette dernière servait de tremplin pour les troupes de l'OTAN et le gouvernement américain a dû initier un programme d'évacuation[71] pour une centaine de milliers de réfugiés parce

---

actions will end once the last Serbs have left Kosova will be wrong. It will be the Albanians' turn once more, only this time at the hands of other Albanians. We fought for this?"

[68] Voir Daut Dauti, "The Killings in Kosovo Continue: levels of violence in Kosovo are the same as before the war," *Balkan Crisis Reports (Institute for War and Peace Reporting)*, n° 91, 9 novembre 1999.

[69] *Situation des droits de l'homme en Bosnie-Herzégovine, dans la République de Croatie et dans la République fédérale de Yougoslavie (Serbie et Monténégro)*, UN Doc. S/1999/1000/Add.1, A/54/396/Add.1, 3 novembre 1999, par. 34; Reuters, *Dernier appel de Kouchner à l'arrêt des violences au Kosovo*, 12 janvier 2001; BBC News Online, *UN "failed" Kosovo Serbs*, 12 janvier 2001.

[70] "Toutes ces critiques concernant le danger de récupération de l'humanitaire par les États sous la bannière de l'ingérence sont aggravées par la situation au Kosovo mais elles ne sont pas réellement nouvelles ... Critiquer le droit d'ingérence, ce n'est pas mettre en doute la sincérité et la générosité de ses créateurs. Ce n'est pas non plus brandir sa carte d'admirateur de la dictature, ce n'est pas enfin scier notre branche humanitaire qui ploie sous les fruits du prix Nobel. Il est seulement nécessaire de rappeler que les bons sentiments de quelques-uns ne permettent pas de faire l'économie du cynisme de tous les autres ... Enfin, c'est vouloir la survie de l'action caritative — et non sa mort — que de lui recommander de ne pas monter aujourd'hui dans la barque kosovare. Si elle vient à chavirer (nous ne le souhaitons pas), c'est tout l'humanitaire qui prendra l'eau. Or, bien des tâches l'attendent de par le monde, dans des endroits où l'Otan n'enverra jamais d'avion." Jean-Christophe Rufin, "Le droit d'ingérence ou la tragédie des bons sentiments," *Géopolitique*, n° 68, janvier 2000, pp. 31-32.

[71] Lettre du Secrétaire d'État au Haut Commissaire pour les réfugiés, datée du 17 avril 1999: "The United States is working with Macedonia to keep borders

que les autorités macédoniennes menaçaient d'exiger le retrait de l'OTAN.[72] Malgré l'autosatisfaction de certains rapports occidentaux sur l'intevention au Kosovo,[73] il ne faut pas oublier que cette aventure militaire avait provoqué des moments cauchemardesques pour les dirigeants occidentaux et que l'avenir de l'OTAN était mis en péril.[74]

Étant donné que les droits de l'homme ont joué un rôle primordial dans la justification de l'intervention de l'OTAN, il est utile d'examiner le rôle des acteurs humanitaires sous cet angle. Le HCR mérite une attention particulière parce qu'il est la plus grande organisation humanitaire qui ait assisté les civils au Kosovo et dans le reste de l'ancienne Yougoslavie depuis une décennie. Dans les mois qui ont précédé les bombardements de l'OTAN, le HCR souhaitait publiquement une ingérence plus musclée de la part de la communauté internationale.[75] Cette position soulevait des doutes quant à l'impartialité de l'organisation.[76] Aussitôt que les flux de réfugiés ont suivi les bombardements de l'OTAN, le HCR s'est empressé de déclarer qu'il s'agissait d'expulsions orchestrées

---

open and with NATO to expand current camps and to build new ones, but these efforts will only go so far. I know that UNHCR and others prefer a regional solution to this refugee crisis, as do we. The reality is, however, that the absorptive capacity of Albania and Macedonia has been stretched to the limit, the stability of the region as a whole is threatened, and refugees are suffering. We must therefore move ahead with plans to temporarily relocate refugees in third countries, and I have urged many countries to activate their pledges to host refugees as soon as possible."

[72] Voir UNHCR, *The Kosovo refugee crisis: An independent evaluation of UNHCR's emergency preparedness and response,* UN Doc. EPAU/2000/001, février 2000, par. 55.

[73] Voir, par exemple, International Independent Commission on Kosovo, *The Kosovo Report,* Oxford, Oxford University Press, 2000, et Ivo H. Daalder et Michael O'Hanlon, *Winning Ugly: NATO's War to Save Kosovo,* Washington, Brookings Institution Press, 2000.

[74] "When the reason for continuing a war shifts from its original goals and toward maintaining credibility, the policy is in trouble. In a subtle way, that is what is happening to NATO. The organization should not reject a chance to end the war just because the organization needs to save face. With each escalation there are new and often unforeseen consequences." Éditorial, "A self-defeating war," *Boston Globe,* 22 avril 1999, p. A24.

[75] Voir, par exemple, Communiqué de presse du HCR, Genève, 11 mars 1999: "Ogata says situation deteriorating in Kosovo, urges action to avert disaster."

[76] Voir UNHCR, *The Kosovo refugee crisis: An independent evaluation of UNHCR's emergency preparedness and response,* UN Doc. EPAU/2000/001, février 2000, par. 70-73.

par le régime serbe.[77] Bien que l'agence onusienne n'était pas en mesure de corroborer ces déclarations,[78] elles ont sans doute été appréciées par l'OTAN qui cherchait à justifier son recours à la force. De même, le HCR déclarait durant les bombardements qu'il fallait une présence militaire importante pour permettre le rapatriement des réfugiés.[79] Cette déclaration était conforme aux exigences de l'OTAN, alors même que plusieurs autres propositions en provenance d'autres acteurs circulaient à ce stade. Ces prises de position du HCR convenaient aux puissances occidentales qui financent la quasi-totalité de son budget.[80]

Dans un numéro spécial sur le Kosovo de son magazine *Réfugiés,* le HCR estime qu'au moins 11 000 Albanais ont été "massacrés" dans les semaines qui ont suivi le déclenchement des bombardements de l'OTAN. L'épisode est décrit comme "l'une des plus effroyables tragédies de l'histoire."[81] Bien que le HCR insiste officiellement sur le maintien de son impartialité et hésite en ce qui concerne le rôle assumé par l'OTAN dans le soutien logistique des humanitaires, il appuie son estimation des victimes du conflit

---

[77] Agence France Presse, *Le HCR dénonce une action "forcée, planifiée et orchestré" au Kosovo,* 6 avril 1999: "La vague de réfugiés quittant le Kosovo est de nature 'forcée, planifiée et orchestrée,' a déclaré le Haut commissaire des Nations Unies pour les réfugiés, Sadako Ogata, mardi à Genève lors d'une réunion sur la situation dans cette province et ses répercussions dans les pays voisins. La responsable du HCR a estimé que les dramatiques événements au Kosovo étaient une tentative pour 'détruire son identité collective'"; Agence France Presse, *Le HCR chargé de la coordination de l'aide humanitaire au Kosovo,* 6 avril 1999: "Ce mouvement de population a été 'forcé, planifié et orchestré,' a estimé Mme Ogata. Depuis le début de cette migration, le HCR a recueilli de nombreux témoignages allant dans le sens de déplacements forcés de l'ensemble de la population, à l'exception de nombreux hommes dont certains sont exécutés. Les milices paramilitaires du chef de guerre serbe Arkan sont régulièrement désignées par les réfugiés comme étant les auteurs de ces exactions, selon le porte-parole du HCR à Genève, Kris Janowski. 'Les hommes sont manquants et les réfugiés racontent tous qu'ils ont été tués et torturés devant leur familles,' a-t-il expliqué."

[78] "Precisely when Belgrade decided on the tactics it employed in Kosovo after the bombing began, and indeed just what it decided ... are questions that cannot be seriously addressed without access to such records as the Milosevic regime may have kept." Michael Mandelbaum, "A Perfect Failure: NATO's War Against Yugoslavia," *Foreign Affairs,* vol. 78, n° 5, septembre-octobre 1999, p. 3.

[79] Associated Press, *Mme Ogata (HCR) pour une "force militaire internationale assez importante" au Kosovo,* 23 avril 1999.

[80] HCR, *Appel Global 2000,* Genève, 2000.

[81] Fernando del Mundo et Ray Wilkinson, "Une course contre la montre," *Réfugiés,* vol. 3, n° 116, 1999, pp. 6 et 11.

sur un rapport du gouvernement britannique. Autrement dit, il cite sans réserve des statistiques controversées diffusées par un des membres de l'OTAN qui a été particulièrement critiqué pour ses efforts de désinformation.[82]

Le Comité international de la Croix-Rouge estime pour sa part que 5 313 personnes ont disparu au Kosovo entre janvier 1998 et avril 2001. Ces statistiques comportent des personnes disparues appartenant à toutes les communautés ethniques et concernent les périodes avant et après les bombardements de l'OTAN. Sur les 1 788 personnes disparues qui ont été effectivement tracées par le CICR, 1 298 sont toujours vivantes ou leur cas n'est pas lié au conflit.[83] À la suite de son programme d'exhumations au Kosovo, le Procureur du Tribunal Pénal International pour l'ex-Yougoslavie a déclaré que les médecins légistes avaient examiné 3 685 cadavres retrouvés au Kosovo dans la période 1999–2000.[84] Les détails concernant les cadavres (cause et moment de décès, appartenance ethnique) n'ont pas été communiqués par le Procureur.

C'est particulièrement à cause des conflits de l'ancienne Yougoslavie que le budget annuel du HCR a augmenté considérablement au cours des années 1990.[85] Pour un organisme onusien qui est censé représenter les divers membres de l'Assemblée générale et qui se voit explicitement interdire par son mandat de s'impliquer dans des questions politiques,[86] certaines des prises de position du HCR sont contestables et peuvent paraître biaisées. Par exemple, le

---

[82] Reporters sans frontières, *Yougoslavie: les "bavures" médiatiques de l'OTAN,* juin 1999.

[83] Comité international de la Croix-Rouge, *Communiqué de presse: Le CICR publie une deuxième édition du Book of Missing Persons in Kosovo,* 10 avril 2001. Associated Press, *Kosovo: 3 525 personnes portées disparues, selon la Croix-Rouge,* 10 avril 2001.

[84] "As a result we have finished our exhumation programme and can now build up a complete picture of the extent and pattern of crimes … Of course it will never be possible to provide an accurate figure for the number of people killed, because of deliberate attempts to burn the bodies or to conceal them in other ways." Tribunal Pénal International pour l'ex-Yougoslavie (Bureau du Procureur), Communiqué de presse: *Address to the Security Council by Carla del Ponte, Prosecutor of the International Criminal Tribunals for the former Yugoslavia and Rwanda, to the UN Security Council,* Doc. JL/P.I.S./542-e, 24 novembre 2000.

[85] Voir Michael Barutciski, "The Reinforcement of Non-Admission Policies and the Subversion of UNHCR: Displacement and Internal Assistance in Bosnia-Herzegovina (1992-1994)" (1996) 8 Int'l J. Refugee L. 49.

[86] Statut du Haut Commissariat des Nations Unies pour les réfugiés, annexe de la résolution 428(V) de l'Assemblée générale, 14 décembre 1950, par. 2: "L'activité du Haut Commissaire ne comporte aucun caractère politique."

numéro spécial du magazine *Réfugiés* contient un article introductif sur le contexte des tensions au Kosovo, dans lequel le HCR
remet en question ouvertement la légitimité des frontières balka-
niques établies avant la Première Guerre mondiale et néglige de
mentionner les excès nationalistes albanais qui ont précédé l'arrivée au pouvoir du président Milosevic à la fin des années 1980.[87]
Les affirmations du HCR concernant les "45 Albanais ... massacrés
dans le village de Racak"[88] et "le nettoyage ethnique systématique
de la province par les autorités serbes"[89] sont d'autres exemples de
déclarations publiques non fiables.[90]

Le HCR proteste dorénavant publiquement de sa dépendance
sur les fonds des donateurs et il critique les deux poids/deux
mesures qui résultent du fait que "les États les plus puissants au
monde, qui sont les principaux donateurs, engageront toujours

---

[87] Fernando del Mundo et Ray Wilkinson, "Une course contre la montre," *Réfugiés,*
vol. 3, n° 116, 1999, pp. 7-10.

[88] Fernando del Mundo, "Un sentiment de déjà vu," *Réfugiés,* vol. 3, n° 116, 1999,
p. 25.

[89] Fernando del Mundo et Ray Wilkinson, "Une course contre la montre," *Réfugiés,*
vol. 3, n° 116, 1999, p. 10.

[90] Voir particulièrement Audrey Gillan, "The Propaganda War," *London Review of
Books,* vol. 21, n° 11, 27 mai 1999:

Earlier that day, Ron Redmond, the baseball-capped spokesman for the
United Nations High Commissioner for Refugees, stood at the Blace border
crossing from Kosovo into Macedonia and said there were new reports of mass
rapes and killings from three villages in the Lipljan area: Sllovi, Hallac Evogel
and Ribari Evogel. He spoke to the press of bodies being desecrated, eyes
being shot out. The way he talked it sounded as if there had been at least a hundred murders and dozens of rapes. When I pressed him on the rapes, asking
him to be more precise, he reduced it a bit and said he had heard that five or
six teenage girls had been raped and murdered. He had not spoken to any
witnesses. 'We have no way of verifying these reports of rape,' he conceded.
'These are among the first that we have heard of at this border.' Other
UNHCR officials later told stories of women being tied to the walls of their
houses and burned, 24 bodies buried in Kosovo Polje. Another report, again
from Sllovi, put the dead at a hundred. Mr and Mrs Nimari were adamant that
it was 16. Truth can be scarce at the Blace border and in the camps dotted
around Macedonia, but you are not allowed to say that during a war like this,
where it may be that bad things are being done on both sides, just as you are
not allowed to doubt atrocity. It's as if NATO and its entourage were trying to
make up for the witlessness of the past: trying to show that whatever we do, we
won't be turning a blind eye. But the simple-minded reporter in me wants to
ask a question: is there any real evidence for what is being said? In Macedonia,
listening to the stories and the UNHCR accounts, you would find it hard to
tell what was hearsay and what was fact.

plus de fonds et de ressources humaines dans des crises suscep-
tibles d'affecter leurs propres intérêts nationaux."[91] Pourtant il
semble avoir bien compris que son avenir dépend en partie de sa
capacité de maîtriser "l'information et l'opinion" dans un contexte
de "guerre médiatique"[92] et que l'ancienne Yougoslavie a joué un
rôle clé à cet égard. En effet, une évaluation interne de ses opérations en Bosnie-Herzégovine reconnaît que ses liens avec les
médias occidentaux ont contribué à son expansion[93] et un rapport
confidentiel rédigé pendant la crise du Kosovo souligne l'intérêt
à exploiter ces liens pour dénoncer le régime de Belgrade.[94] On est
loin de la tradition humanitaire et de la prudence, à la manière
du Comité international de la Croix-Rouge. Il est possible de se
demander si le renforcement des capacités de communication du
HCR reflète un désir d'améliorer la qualité de l'information ou
s'il constitue un maniement opportuniste des médias. De toute
manière, il n'est pas possible d'excuser les déclarations non corroborées des journalistes[95] et des employés du HCR qui semblent

---

[91] Éditorial, "L'aide humanitaire est-elle distribuée de manière équitable?" *Réfugiés,* vol. 3, n° 116, 1999, p. 2.

[92] Dennis McNamara, "Interview: Il est difficile d'être optimiste," *Réfugiés,* vol. 3, n° 116, 1999, p. 22.

[93] "By demonstrating its expertise in launching such a large-scale relief programme, the organization has gained a greatly enhanced public reputation and
boosted its credibility with donor states ... For UNHCR, the operation has had
particularly important implications for the future. The organization has clearly
moved into new areas, somewhat away from its more traditional role as a refugee
protection agency ... UNHCR's experience in former Yugoslavia has demonstrated the benefits that can be gained when media relations are treated as an
important and integral part of the organization's operational activities. With
the expertise and reputation UNHCR has acquired, the organization is now
well placed to make better use of the international media." UNHCR, *Working
in a War Zone: A review of UNHCR's Operations in former Yugoslavia,* UN Doc.
EVAL/YUG/14, avril 1994, par. 32, 52, 99.

[94] Mémorandum de l'Envoyé spécial du HCR, *The Crisis in Kosovo,* 22 septembre
1998, p. 3.

[95] Audrey Gillan, "The Propaganda War," *London Review of Books,* vol. 21, n° 11, 27
mai 1999:

> But what we have is a situation where Western journalists accept details
> without question. Almost every day, the world's media, jostling for stories in
> Macedonia, strain to find figures that may well not exist. In the absence of any
> testimony, many just report what some agency or other has told them. I stood
> by as a reporter from BBC World reeled off what Ron Redmond had said,
> using the words "hundreds," "rape" and "murder" in the same breath. By way
> of qualification (a fairly meaningless one in the circumstances), he added

ignorer les processus psychologiques et motivations variés qui
mènent à des témoignages exagérés en temps de conflit.[96]

La prolifération récente des ONG a créé un marché intense
où les humanitaires doivent se concurrencer pour attirer des dons
limités des secteurs public et privé dans un contexte influencé
par la capacité de jouer au sensationnalisme des médias. Après
tout, un représentant d'une ONG qui arrive sur la scène d'un massacre présumé et qui fait un compte-rendu prudent ne sera pas
nécessairement attrayant pour les équipes de télévision internationales. L'opportunité ratée pour cette ONG de se faire de la

---

that the stories had yet to be substantiated. Why, then, had he reported them
so keenly in the first place? When I went to see Benedicte Giaever, the coordinator for OSCE's field office in Skopje, I saw that she was angered by the
behaviour of the media. I squirmed when she said she had heard of a female
journalist getting onto a bus to question some refugees. She said almost every
journalist who came to see her asked one thing: could she give them a rape victim to interview. I know of several tabloid reporters who were despatched to
Macedonia and Albania with the sole purpose of finding a rape victim. Talking to each other in the bar of Skopje's Hotel Continental we rehearsed the
question which has now become notorious: "Is there anyone here who's been
raped and speaks English?" We were aware of the implications of some of our
more despicable behaviour. We knew that one woman, raped by Serbian soldiers then forced to leave her country, was traumatised all over again by a journalist looking for a good story. The things you come to know as a journalist do
not march in single file. Facts are often renegade.

[96] Audrey Gillan, "The Propaganda War," *London Review of Books,* vol. 21, n° 11, 27
mai 1999:

Unlike the media and the UNHCR, the OSCE works in a slow, methodical way,
waiting a few days till the refugees have settled in before they begin to ask
questions. "These people have just arrived and I would say they are still under
a lot of stress and tension," Giaever says. "In that situation, 5 people can easily
turn into 75. It's not that they want to lie but often they are confused. It's not
to say it didn't happen. But a story could have moved around from village to
village and everyone from that village tells it as if it happened to them."
Another senior OSCE source spoke even more clearly than any of us were
inclined to do. He told me he suspected that the Kosovo Liberation Army had
been persuading people to talk in bigger numbers, to crank up the horror so
that NATO might be persuaded to send ground troops in faster. Robin Cook's
rape camp was the same thing, he said: an attempt to get the British public
behind the bombing. And wasn't all this a lesson in how propaganda works in
modern war? Watching the television images and listening to the newscasters
thunder about further reports of Serb massacres and of genocide, I feel
uneasy about saying that they have very little to go on. Yet almost every news-
paper journalist I spoke to privately in Macedonia felt the same way. The story
being seen at home is different from the one that appeared to be happening
on the ground.

publicité pourrait bien être ressentie lors des appels aux dons.[97] Cette dynamique explique partiellement certains des témoignages simplistes concernant la crise du Kosovo. La critique suivante d'une organisation qui travaille discrètement sur le plan humanitaire et diplomatique est appropriée: "Beaucoup, à Sant'Egidio, se méfient aussi de certaines ONG... équipées pour capter les crédits internationaux. Et qui servent de plus en plus de caution au désengagement des pays riches, tentés par 'l'approche de l'ambulance': on fait beaucoup de bruit, on sauve des vies, on repart."[98]

Il est aussi difficile d'ignorer que l'intervention de l'OTAN reflète une application efficace des tactiques insurgées et qu'elle a permis aux Albanais du Kosovo de se rapprocher à leur objectif politique séparatiste. Les mouvements sécessionistes à travers le monde ont dorénavant un bel exemple d'une façon efficace de provoquer une escalade d'un conflit pour atteindre des fins politiques.[99] Comme la diaspora tamoule et son rôle dans le conflit au Sri Lanka, les émigrés albanais dans le reste de l'Europe et en Amérique ont fortement influencé les évènements dans les Balkans.[100]

Il importe de mentionner que le drapeau de l'Albanie se trouve

---

[97] Cette analyse se base sur des communications privées du chercheur principal d'une des plus grandes ONG qui travaillent pour la protection des droits de l'homme au Kosovo. Elles concernent un massacre présumé qui a été fortement médiatisé en septembre 1998 grâce à l'intervention hâtive d'une ONG rivale. Pour une critique générale de la société civile internationale, voir Hubert Védrine, "Refonder la politique étrangère française," *Le Monde diplomatique,* décembre 2000, p. 3, et "Sins of the secular missionaries," *The Economist,* 29 janvier 2000, p. 25.

[98] Philippe Leymarie, "Les bâtisseurs de paix de Sant'Egidio," *Le Monde diplomatique,* septembre 2000, p. 16.

[99] Pour un exemple de l'application de cette stragégie en Macédoine, voir la lettre du Président des États-Unis citée dans BBC News Online, *Clashes break Macedonia truce,* 19 mai 2001: "'The extremists want nothing more than to provoke the indiscriminate shelling of villages and killing of civilians, in order to swell their ranks and bolster their illegitimate claim to represent the ethnic Albanian community,' Mr Bush wrote." Voir aussi l'analyse de Dejan Anastasijevic dans "In Macedonia, a Day of Reckoning Looms Large," *Time,* 16 mai 2001: "The NLA [armée de libération nationale] in Macedonia, whose recently elected leader had been a senior officer of the Kosovo Protection Force under NATO's auspices, had calculated that if they could repeat the Kosovo Liberation Army's strategy of provoking a clumsy and brutal response from the authorities, they too could get NATO to come in and bomb their enemies. They certainly didn't believe NATO would move against them."

[100] Sur les évènements récents en Macédoine, voir Nicholas Wood, "Albanian exiles threaten to escalate war," *The Guardian,* 21 mai 2001.

désormais dans tout le Kosovo et dans plusieurs régions de la Macédoine. L'importance de ce symbôle devrait nous rappeler que les interventions en faveur des populations en détresse ont des implications sur l'ordre régional et international qui au bout du compte sous-tendent la sécurité des États et le respect des droits de l'homme. Alors que la souveraineté yougoslave diminue dans les Balkans et la souveraineté des populations albanaises augmente sur plusieurs territoires, il sera difficile de maintenir des principes cohérents la prochaine fois que la communauté internationale sera confrontée à une lutte sécessioniste similaire avec un rôle ambigu assumé par une mère patrie voisine.[101]

Depuis les bombardements de l'OTAN, toutes les élections en Macédoine ont été accompagnées d'irrégularités et de violences dans les circonscriptions albanaises. Pourquoi est-ce que les Albanais qui sont concentrés dans l'ouest de la Macédoine et qui forment environ le quart de la population totale[102] devraient accepter un statut inférieur aux Albanais de la province du Kosovo qui forment 15 % de la population yougoslave? Pendant que le Kosovo se détache graduellement du reste de la Yougoslavie, il faut noter que Skopje, sous la crainte d'une submersion démographique à terme,[103] a toujours été plus sévère que Belgrade en ce qui

---

[101] Voir, par exemple, Llazar Semini, "Greater Albania Gaffe: The Tirana government attempts to limit damage caused by a minister's shock support for a Greater Albania," *Balkan Crisis Reports (Institute for War & Peace Reporting)*, n° 239, 20 avril 2001.

[102] La Macédoine comporte une minorité albanaise qui compte presque 23 % de la population totale selon le recensement de 1994 financé et approuvé par la communauté internationale. La méfiance entre les groupes ethniques du pays est illustrée par le fait que les politiciens albanais ont appelé la population à boycotter ce recensement et que certains militants albanais prétendent que le vrai pourcentage de la population d'origine albanaise s'élève jusqu'à 40 %. Voir U.S. Department of State, *Macedonia Country Report on Human Rights Practices for 1996*: "Representatives of the ethnic Albanian community, by far the largest minority group with 22.9 percent of the population, are the most vocal in charging discrimination. Expressing concern about government manipulation of the data, the Albanian community boycotted a 1990 census. An internationally monitored census held during the summer of 1994 to correct the situation was marred by some boycott threats. Experts from the Council of Europe monitored the conduct of the census and were generally satisfied that it was carried out fairly and accurately and that virtually the entire ethnic Albanian community took part."

[103] Isabelle Lasserre, "En Macédoine la démographie est une arme," *Le Figaro*, 14 avril, p. 4.

concerne l'octroi d'un statut constitutionnel particulier pour les Albanais ou leur langue.

Le mouvement d'émancipation nationale des Albanais dans l'ancienne Yougoslavie n'a jamais été limité au territoire du Kosovo.[104] Tout au long des années 1990, des opérations policières ont eu lieu contre des individus soupçonnés d'organiser des milices albanaises en Macédoine. Par exemple, des membres importants d'un parti politique albanais représenté au parlement macédonien ont été arrêtés lors d'une de ces opérations en 1993 pendant qu'ils occupaient des postes gouvernementaux de haut rang.[105] Les nombreux reportages sur les activités de groupes armés albanais au milieu des années 1990 concernaient aussi bien la Macédoine que le Kosovo. L'extension en Macédoine de la lutte armée albanaise implique indirectement les puissances occidentales étant donné leur défense des Albanais au Kosovo et leur engagement de démilitariser la guérilla qui a lutté contre le gouvernement yougoslave.[106] Pourtant, les guérilleros albanais ont depuis poursuivi leurs opérations en dehors du Kosovo dans le sud de la Serbie et le nord de la Macédoine.

Deux ans après les bombardements de l'OTAN, les mêmes passages montagneux utilisés par les réfugiés pour fuir le Kosovo sont utilisés par des maquisards pour leurs opérations de déstabilisation en Macédoine. Les guérilleros connaissent bien les villages albanais du nord-ouest de la Macédoine car ils recrutaient activement parmi les réfugiés et la population locale pendant le conflit

---

[104] Voir, par exemple, Renaud Girard, "L'OTAN piégée par les irrédentistes albanais," *Le Figaro,* 5 mars 2001, p. 6: "En juin 1998, M. Jakup Krasniqi, porte-parole officiel de l'UCK, avait déclaré que la lutte de libération nationale des Albanais ne s'arrêtaient pas au Kosovo, citant le sud du Monténégro et le Nord-Ouest de la Macédoine comme exemples de territoires supplémentaires à 'libérer'."

[105] Human Rights Watch, *A Threat to "Stability": Human Rights Violations in Macedonia,* juin 1996. Ce rapport soutien que de nombreuses violations des règles de droit ont eu lieu lors des opérations policières et procédures judiciaires. Voir aussi US Department of State, *Macedonia Country Report on Human Rights Practices for 1994:* "The Albanian Paramilitary case, which was tried in Skopje in May and June, was at least in part politically motivated. The prosecution presented substantial evidence that most, if not all, of the 10 defendants had committed firearms and hard currency trading offenses. However, there was some indication that the arrests and prosecution of a Deputy Minister of Defense and a former secretary general of the National Democratic Party (PDP), a party representing ethnic Albanians, may have taken place as a result of political intrigue involving the Government and the PDP, apparently maneuvering over jobs."

[106] Résolution 1244 du Conseil de sécurité, 10 juin 1999, par. 9(b) et 15.

avec les Serbes et les bombardements de l'OTAN. Il faut donc voir les combats récents sur la périphérie de la ville de Tetovo et dans les villages au nord de la capitale Skopje comme la continuation d'un processus qui a commencé il y a plusieurs années. Ce processus a été particulièrement influencé par la crise humanitaire qui a suivi les bombardements de l'OTAN et qui a aggravé les divisions entre les communautés locales.

CONCLUSION

Les préoccupations de l'OTAN concernant la protection des Albanais du Kosovo étaient compréhensibles compte tenu des politiques abusives appuyées par Belgrade lors du conflit en Bosnie-Herzégovine.[107] D'autant plus que le Conseil de sécurité avait condamné la réaction yougoslave excessive face à la menace terroriste au Kosovo.[108] La tendance internationale à placer des limites à l'exercice d'une souveraineté absolue en matière des droits de l'homme représente généralement un développement positif en termes de sécurité de la personne humaine. Cette entreprise importante mérite toutefois un traitement médiatique plus nuancé que celui offert par le sensationalisme télévisuel durant la crise du Kosovo.

La situation au Kosovo a largement été compliquée par les interventions de politiciens et commentateurs occidentaux qui ont simplifié le conflit au point de la déformation. Les complexités des tensions serbo-albanaises ont été réduites à une campagne de haine raciale déclenchée par le "dictateur" Milosevic de la Yougoslavie.[109]

---

[107] Michael Barutciski, "Brutalité, manipulation et humanitarisme aveugle en Bosnie-Herzégovine (1992-1995)," *Dialogue: Revue Internationale d'Arts et de Sciences,* vol. 4, n° 16, décembre 1995, p. 11.

[108] Résolution 1160 du 31 mars 1998.

[109] Pour un usage de terminologie plus exacte, voir Timothy Garton Ash, "Cry, the Dismembered Country," *New York Review of Books,* 14 janvier 1999, pp. 31-32: "Milosevic's regime is an extreme post-communist example of what Latin Americans call demokratura: formally democratic, substantially authoritarian. Post-communist demokraturas maintain their power through state television, the secret police, and the misappropriation of large parts of the formerly state-owned economy. Such regimes may be overthrown peacefully, but this requires a grand coalition of virtually all the forces opposed to them. I come to Belgrade from Slovakia, where the demokratura of Vladimir Meciar has recently been overthrown, at the ballot box." Pour une interprétation plus nuancée de la nature du régime de Belgrade, voir Michael Mandelbaum, "A Perfect Failure: NATO's War Against Yugoslavia," *Foreign Affairs,* vol. 78, n° 5, septembre-octobre

Selon ce point de vue, ce chef totalitaire[110] des Balkans a essayé d'exécuter un plan fasciste qui aurait éliminé tous les Albanais du Kosovo. L'action de l'OTAN était censée empêcher cette "solution finale."[111]

Une analyse objective de la situation sur le terrain aurait dû suggérer une situation plus complexe. Il faut souligner que les statistiques fiables en temps de conflit sont difficiles à établir. Cependant, il est probable que le nombre de personnes tuées au Kosovo avant les bombardements de l'OTAN était comparable aux victimes des conflits en Colombie, en Turquie, en Algérie ou au Sri Lanka durant la même période.[112] Il faut ajouter que les conflits mentionnés ci-dessus impliquent des formes de violence similaires (activités de guérilla, ripostes gouvernementales, vengeances locales, etc.) et des complexités politiques comparables à la situation au Kosovo. Contrairement à ces autres conflits qui n'ont pas suscité de réactions musclées de la part des acteurs internationaux, le public occidental a généralement été amené à croire une interprétation simpliste et manichéenne des tensions au Kosovo. L'ingérence dans un tel contexte risque de compliquer la situation sur le terrain.

La décision occidentale sur le recours à la force aurait dû être inspirée par des interprétations prudentes du conflit au lieu d'une

---

1999, p. 4: "He was not popular with Serbs (the subsequent NATO assault temporarily increased his popularity), he did not exercise anything resembling totalitarian control over Serbia, and prolonged demonstrations in 1996–97 had almost toppled him."

[110] Voir, par exemple, Warren Zimmermann, "Milosevic's Final Solution," *The New York Review of Books,* 10 juin 1999: "In … totalitarian control of Serbia — its government, politics, business, and media — he had shown that he would tolerate no challenge to his authority. A dictator is authoritarian by definition; but Milosevic is also uncommonly ruthless."

[111] C'est le point de vue présenté par l'ancien ambassadeur américain à Belgrade: "Slobodan Milosevic's decision to expel the entire Albanian population of Kosovo was so audacious and so ruthless that it caught the West by surprise … If he had failed to repopulate Kosovo with Serbs, he could depopulate it of Albanians. So he determined to get rid of the entire Albanian population of Kosovo. The primary method would be forcible expulsion … The scope of Milosevic's design would cause most dictators to quail. There is evidence that it was too ambitious for some officers in his army and secret police, organizations infamous for their expertise in ethnic cleansing. Milosevic purged them both at high levels in the autumn of 1998." *Ibid.*

[112] Voir statistiques dans Stockholm International Peace Research Institute, *SIPRI Yearbook 1998* (Oxford: Oxford University Press), pp. 24-30.

démagogie moralisatrice.[113] Contrairement aux certitudes concernant la justification présentées par les dirigeants occidentaux,[114] l'action de l'OTAN reposait sur une interprétation non équilibrée du conflit au Kosovo qui correspondait fidèlement à la propagande d'une des parties impliquées dans cette guerre civile.

Il est probable que la déstabilisation régionale qui a suivi les frappes aériennes de l'OTAN aurait pu être évitée si les puissances occidentales avaient respecté le droit international en épuisant tous les moyens diplomatiques avant d'avoir recours à la force. La suggestion que le Conseil de sécurité n'était pas en mesure d'aborder le problème humanitaire n'est pas correcte. Tous les membres permanents ont démontré qu'ils pouvaient ne pas appliquer leur véto sur des opérations militaires onusiennes contre les forces serbes en Bosnie-Herzégovine.[115] À la suite de débats sérieux et prolongés sur la crise du Kosovo, le Conseil de sécurité a adopté une résolution qui déclarait de façon claire que la situation représentait une menace à la sécurité et à la paix internationales.[116] Bien qu'il s'agissait d'une indication que plusieurs mesures coercitives pouvaient être envisagées par l'ONU, quelques membres

---

[113] Voir, par exemple, Barnaby Mason, "Tony Blair: Kosovo Crusader," *BBC World News*, 22 avril 1999:

> In speeches that seem to come from the heart, Mr Blair has taken the moral high ground and sounded a call to arms against barbarism — personified in the demonisation of Slobodan Milosevic ... Mr Blair's public idealism is backed up by an intensely professional information or propaganda machine — the choice of label depends on your point of view. It is run by the man who is much more than his spokesman, Alastair Campbell. After the damage to Nato's credibility caused by the mistaken bombing of refugee vehicles in Kosovo, Mr Campbell devoted some of his energy and talent trying to remedy the defects of the Nato media operation in Brussels. The scrutiny of 24-hour television news has made the concentration on presentation, the rise of the spin doctors, inevitable. Tony Blair is using the media machine to put across a moral message.

[114] Agence France Presse, *Texte intégral de l'allocution du président Jacques Chirac*, 12 avril 1999: "Aucune femme de cœur, aucun homme de cœur ne peut contester le bien-fondé de la réaction de la communauté internationale. Il fallait mettre un terme à une barbarie qui s'exerce depuis trop longtemps." Voir aussi Anthony Blair, *Doctrine of International Community*, discours prononcé par le premier ministre britannique, Economic Club of Chicago, 22 avril 1999: "No-one in the West who has seen what is happening in Kosovo can doubt that NATO's military action is justified ... This is a just war, based not on any territorial ambitions but on values."

[115] Résolution 836 du 4 juin 1993, par. 5 et 9.

[116] Résolution 1129 du 23 septembre 1998.

ne croyaient pas que le moment était opportun pour une action militaire contre un État souverain. L'OTAN s'est engagée dans une opération militaire sans l'autorisation du Conseil de sécurité précisément parce que ses chefs savaient que l'action était controversée et ne pouvait pas bénéficier d'un appui international répandu.[117] La marginalisation du système onusien aura des conséquences néfastes sur le plan des relations internationales dans les années à venir.[118]

La prochaine fois qu'une puissance régionale agit en violation de la Charte des Nations Unies et invoque une justification morale pour son intervention dans le territoire d'un voisin souverain, il sera plus difficile pour la communauté internationale de répondre avec crédibilité à cause de ses actions au Kosovo. Les préoccupations morales[119] ou les tentatives d'innovation exprimées par de nombreux juristes qui appuyaient l'action de l'OTAN perdent leur force de persuasion aussitôt que la situation sur le terrain est perçue de manière nuancée et équilibrée. Un scénario clair d'abus à sens unique aurait provoqué un débat différent au sein du Conseil de sécurité: dans un système multilatéral authentique, il appartient aux partisans de l'intervention à persuader les membres réticents de ne pas appliquer un véto "honteux." L'exemple de cette intervention confirme l'importance et la pertinence des règles actuelles sur l'usage de la force car elles permettent de meilleures chances aux actions guidées par la raison au lieu de la pression médiatique ou d'une opinion publique mal informée.

L'exemple du Kosovo illustre la tendance à l'arrogance qui motive l'ingérence occidentale dans certains conflits. Il s'agissait en l'occurrence d'une occasion pour de nombreux moralistes de démontrer une fois de plus qu'il ne fallait pas reconduire l'erreur historique de Neville Chamberlain vis-à-vis du régime criminel de

---

[117] *Communiqué publié par le Groupe de Rio,* 25 mars 1999, UN Doc. A/53/884-S/1999/347 et *Déclaration sur la situation au Kosovo publiée le 9 avril 1999 par le Mouvement des pays non alignés,* UN Doc. S/1999/451.

[118] Dimitri Trenin et Yekaterina Stepanova (dir.), *Kosovo: medjunarodnie aspekti krizisa,* Moscou, Moskovski Centr Karnegi, 1999; Youri Roubinski, "Quelques leçons de la crise des Balkans," *Géopolitique,* n° 68, janvier 2000, p. 66.

[119] "My answer is that from an ethical viewpoint resort to armed force was justified. Nevertheless, as a legal scholar I cannot avoid observing in the same breath that this moral action is contrary to current international law." Antonio Cassese, "Ex iniuria jus oritur: Are we moving towards international legitimation of forcible countermeasures in the world community?" (1999) 10 Eur. J. Int'l L. 155.

l'Allemagne nazie en 1938.[120] Naturellement, ils se trompaient de conflit. Le cas du Kosovo donne également un exemple des problèmes qui résultent quand une intervention prétend sortir du politique pour s'inscrire exclusivement en fonction de l'humanitaire.[121] Le langage humanitaire ou la propagande ne peut pas cacher le problème fondamental qui existe au Kosovo depuis plus d'une décennie: quelle réponse politique les gouvernements et les organisations concernés par la protection internationale des droits de l'homme devraient formuler face au mouvement sécessionniste albanais et la réaction serbe? Même avec une présence internationale imposante au Kosovo qualifiée par certains de "protectorat," la question demeure toujours pertinente.

Malheureusement, l'extension en Macédoine de la lutte d'émancipation albanaise[122] complique la tâche pour les occidentaux.[123] À moins que les partis politiques albanais de la Macédoine cessent de profiter des actes de violence pour faire avancer leur propositions constitutionnelles,[124] une nouvelle guerre civile risque d'éclater dans les Balkans. La différence cette fois serait que les pays voisins auront beaucoup de difficulté de rester en dehors du conflit, étant donné leurs attachements historiques avec les populations et le territoire de ce pays fragile.

[120] "When the Italian and French ministers proposed a softening in the language they would use to threaten the Serbs, Albright's close aide Jamie Rubin whispered to her that she could probably accept it. She snapped back, 'Where do you think we are, Munich?'" Walter Isaacson, "Madelaine's War," *Time Magazine*, vol. 153, n° 19.

[121] Pierre Manent, "La tentation humanitaire," *Géopolitique*, n° 68, janvier 2000, p. 8: "Le grand danger de l'humanitarisme contemporain est d'habituer les peuples à mépriser la réflexion politique."

[122] Pour un point de vue macédonien sur la manipulation du langage humanitaire, voir Sasho Cholakovski, "Se vodi borba za teritorija, a ne za 'chovekovi prava'!," *Utrinski Dnevnik*, 22 mars 2001, p. 6.

[123] "L'OTAN se trouve dans une position très inconfortable, pour avoir gravement sous-estimé la force de l'irrédentisme albanais dans les Balkans," Renaud Girard, "L'erreur de l'OTAN," *Le Figaro*, 7 mars 2001, p. 6.

[124] "Arben Xhaferi, Macedonia's pivotal Albanian," *The Economist*, 31 mars 2001, p. 50: "If and when Macedonia's towns and villages become polarised, then everybody will simply reach for the nearest gun, including the DPA's [Parti démocratique des Albanais, membre de la coalition au pouvoir] activists, who are no strangers to hidden arms caches and have connections with the smuggling underworld." Timothy Garton Ash, "Cry, the Dismembered Country," *New York Review of Books*, 14 janvier 1999, p. 31:

I talk to ... Arben Xhaferi [chef nationaliste albanais en Macédoine], a brooding, steely, black-bearded man, in a small, dark room in a headquarters

Summary

Can NATO's intervention in Kosovo be justified on humanitarian grounds? An analysis of Western policy and its consequences in Macedonia.

It is generally accepted that NATO's military intervention against Yugoslavia did not conform to recognized rules of legal positivism. For most western observers, the justification relies on its legitimacy rather than its legality. This moral argument is based on the belief that the humanitarian plight of the Albanian populations in Kosovo was exceptionally grave. While the situation on the ground prior to NATO's bombing campaign warranted western involvement, the article shows that it was not exceptional in relation to other armed conflicts around the world. Western diplomacy in this Balkan crisis reflects an element of selectivity concerning respect for public international law that will have negative consequences on the future of international relations. The result in the immediate region is a change in the balance of power accompanied by general destabilization. Despite the large international military and civilian presence, Kosovo has been transformed into an almost homogeneous Albanian territory and neighbouring Macedonia is threatened by an extension of the Albanian insurrection. This international intervention confirms the relevance of established legal norms on the use of force because they allow better chances for action guided by reason rather than one-sided media pressure.

---

festooned with the black double-headed Albanian eagle on a red background. He says people chant 'UCK' at his rallies, not the name of his party. His own support for the Kosovo armed struggle is passionate. This is not surprising since he spent most of his adult life as a journalist in Pristina ... There was ... a coordinating body of Albanian political parties in former Yugoslavia which, after playing with much more radical variants, decided in 1992 that the Albanians in Kosovo should go for independence, the Albanians in Macedonia should aim for equal rights as a state-creating nation in the new state, while the Albanians in Montenegro and Serbia would have to settle for plain citizenship rights. One step at a time ... Indeed, the Albanians here may never need to reach for a gun. All they need to do is what they do anyway: have many, many children. Albanians are now at least one quarter of the Macedonian population. On current birth rates, they will be a majority in about 2025. And doesn't democracy mean rule by the majority?

Voir aussi la dépêche de la Macedonian Information Agency, "Arben Xaferi: Makedonija ke opstane ako go smeni ustavot," 26 mai 2001, où le leader du plus important parti albanais déclare que la "Macédoine va exister si la constitution est modifiée" (notre traduction).

Sommaire

Peut-on justifier l'intervention de l'OTAN au Kosovo sur le plan humanitaire? Analyse de la politique occidentale et ses conséquences en Macédoine

Il est généralement admis que l'intervention militaire de l'OTAN contre la Yougoslavie n'était pas conforme aux règles reconnues du droit positif. Pour la plupart des observateurs occidentaux, la justification repose sur la légitimité plutôt que la légalité. Cet argument d'ordre moral s'appuie sur l'affirmation du caractère exceptionnellement grave de la situation humanitaire concernant les populations albanaises au Kosovo. Bien que la situation sur le terrain avant les bombardements de l'OTAN méritait l'attention des puissances occidentales, l'article montre qu'elle n'était pas exceptionnelle par rapport aux autres conflits armés à travers le monde. La diplomatie occidentale dans cette crise balkanique reflète un élément de sélectivité face au respect du droit international public qui aura des conséquences néfastes sur le plan des relations internationales. Le résultat dans la région immédiate est un changement dans les rapports de force accompagné par une déstabilisation généralisée. Malgré la présence imposante d'acteurs militaires et civils de la communauté internationale, le Kosovo s'est transformé en territoire albanais presque homogène et la Macédoine voisine se trouve menacée par l'extension de l'insurrection albanaise sur son territoire. Cette intervention internationale confirme la pertinence des règles juridiques actuelles sur l'usage de la force car elles permettent de meilleures chances aux actions guidées par la raison au lieu d'une pression médiatique partisane.

Parallel Proceedings — Converging Views: The *Westec* Appeal

JANET WALKER

INTRODUCTION

In the jungles of transnational litigation,[1] there is probably nothing quite as savage as parallel litigation. It is savage because the commencement of a second proceeding on the same matter in a different forum almost inevitably represents some form of abuse. It is either an abusive tactic to avoid an orderly determination by the first forum of whether it is an appropriate forum or it is an act of despair at the opportunistic choice by the opposing party of a court that is either unwilling or incapable of making a principled determination of whether it is an appropriate forum. Parallel litigation is savage also because it can seem to pit courts against one another by requiring them to make determinations that threaten to impinge on each court's most basic entitlement — its inherent jurisdiction to control its own process and to determine its own jurisdiction.

It might be thought that the situation would be less egregiously bad when parallel proceedings are commenced in two courts

Janet Walker is an Assistant Professor at Osgoode Hall Law School. This article was developed from a paper entitled "Parallel Proceedings: A Bird's-Eye View of the Jungle," which was written for the panel presentation entitled "International Comity and the *Westec* Case," given in Ottawa on May 3, 2001 at the Canadian Bar Association's International Section Conference entitled *The Practice of International Law in the Twenty-First Century: It's Everybody's Business* [hereinafter CBAO Conference Proceedings]. The author is grateful to Professors Vaughan Black and John Claydon for their helpful comments on a draft of this article.

[1] In *Airbus Industrie GIE v. Patel*, [1998] 2 W.L.R. 686, [1988] 2 All E.R. 257 (HL), at para. 12 [hereinafter *Airbus*], Lord Goff described the common law world as "a jungle of separate, broadly based, jurisdictions" in which "potential excesses ... are generally curtailed by the adoption of the principle of *forum non conveniens* ... [which] cannot, and does not aim to, avoid all clashes of jurisdiction."

that take similar, even-handed approaches to the determination of appropriate forum. Under such circumstances, the effects of the abuse would be less obvious because the matter would not be left to be determined in an *inappropriate* forum. However, the problem would remain a serious one because, in fact, it might be more difficult to resolve. If one forum was clearly inappropriate, a stay or an injunction might be available to resolve the multiplicity on the traditional grounds of *forum non conveniens* alone. However, where neither forum was clearly inappropriate and the multiplicity could not be resolved in that way, the parallel litigation will foster a race to judgment and the potential for one court to have its proceeding abruptly terminated by the tender of a judgment from the other court. The defendant in each forum would have a strong incentive to frustrate the resolution of the matter in that forum and little incentive to participate in good faith.

Abuse is almost inevitably present in situations of parallel proceedings, but the vexing question can be "which is the abusive party?"[2] Is it the party that has made the pre-emptive strike by being the first to commence an action or is it the party that has not sought to resolve the forum dispute in the first forum? Neither the way in which an action is framed, such as in the case of declaratory relief, nor the sequence in which the proceedings are commenced is determinative. It could be entirely appropriate to respond to the threat of litigation in an inappropriate forum by commencing an action in an appropriate forum for a declaration that the applicant is not liable. A pre-emptive strike could be warranted to prevent an imminent abuse. Similarly, where a principled determination of appropriate forum is not available in an inappropriate forum (or even where the defendant is simply incapable of travelling to the plaintiff's chosen forum for a determination of appropriate forum), it is hardly abusive to respond by commencing a proceeding in an appropriate forum instead of making the hopeless or heroic effort to seek a stay in the first forum. While it may

---

[2] It should be clarified at the outset that the situations of "parallel proceedings" considered in this article are not those in which a plaintiff commences claims against a defendant in the same matter in more than one forum or those in which more than one claimant seeks the same relief in a matter from one or more defendants (on which, see, for example, E Sherman "Antisuit Injunction and Notice of Intervention and Preclusion: Compementary Devices to Prevent Duplicative Litigation" (1995) Brigham Young U. L. Rev. 925). Furthermore, the question of what constitutes the same matter so as to establish the existence of parallel proceedings is also not addressed.

be hard to know which party has acted opportunistically, the elements of abuse and the threat to the efficient administration of justice are almost inevitably present. While both parties may have contributed to an abuse in that they have produced a situation that breaches the edict that "[a]s far as possible, a multiplicity of legal proceedings should be avoided,"[3] it is also extremely unlikely that neither has done so. In short, with parallel proceedings, it's a jungle out there.

And so it was with considerable interest that many individuals looked on as the hearing of the appeal in *Westec Aerospace Inc.* v. *Raytheon Aircraft Co.*[4] approached in the Supreme Court of Canada. It was the first opportunity for the Court to consider directly the relevance of parallel proceedings in determinations of appropriate forum. Unfortunately, hopes for an authoritative pronouncement from the Court were disappointed when the appeal was dismissed without reasons. As the record shows, Raytheon had obtained summary judgment in its Kansas declaratory action and there was, therefore, no longer a situation of parallel proceedings on which to base the appeal. The challenges presented by parallel proceedings are likely to become more prevalent as litigants take advantage of the increased flexibility in jurisdiction selection that is made possible under the current Canadian law relating to jurisdiction and judgments. For this reason, despite the lack of an authoritative pronouncement by the Supreme Court on the issues, they are ripe for comment.

This article takes a bird's eye view of the emergence of parallel proceedings as an issue in transnational litigation, and it considers the various approaches that have been taken, including the rules that have emerged to deal with them. It seeks to link these approaches with the views of comity that are held in particular legal systems and the particular conditions in which such situations arise in an effort to conceive of an approach that would be suitable for Canadian courts. While there is reason to be confident that Canadian courts will make sound decisions in individual cases, an awareness of the range of situations in which parallel proceedings may be commenced and of the implications of the various responses that have been established elsewhere to parallel proceedings could

---

[3] Section 138 of the Courts of Justice Act, RSO 1990, c.34.

[4] *Westec Aerospace Inc.* v. *Raytheon Aircraft Co.* (1999), 84 A.C.W.S. (3d) 479, leave to appeal granted, 86 A.C.W.S. (3d) 697, reversed (1999), 173 D.L.R. (4th) 498 (CA), appeal dismissed without reasons, 2001, S.C.C. 26 [hereinafter *Westec*].

assist in developing an approach that will reduce the opportunities for abuse without compromising fairness.

The Emerging Challenge of Parallel Proceedings

Given the seriousness of the problems that parallel proceedings represent, one might wonder why the issues that they raise have not yet been canvassed at length and why effective means for dealing with them have not yet been devised. Surprisingly, they are a relatively new phenomenon, which is the by-product of technological advances in communication and increased mobility.[5] In the past, the logistics of commencing two proceedings in different fora in order to gain strategic advantages have militated against such proceedings.

Parallel proceedings are a relatively new phenomenon also because, until the advent of a liberal regime for the mutual recognition and enforcement of judgments, defendants with assets in countries applying the traditional Anglo-American enforcement rules generally had considerable *de facto* control over a plaintiff's choice of forum — indeed, in many cases, a virtual veto over many of the fora that a plaintiff might choose. Under the rules for the enforcement of judgments, a plaintiff was generally limited in pursuing an action that would yield an internationally enforceable judgment either to the defendant's home forum or to one to which the defendant has consented.[6] It would seem relatively unusual for defendants to object to litigating in their home forum and to prefer to travel elsewhere to commence an action, and relatively unusual for them to object to litigating in a forum to which they had consented and to claim to be entitled to travel elsewhere to commence an action. If a plaintiff chose a third forum, the judgment would be enforceable only within it and a defendant would be free to wait until the plaintiff commenced another proceeding in one of the other two fora mentioned above, thus obviating the need for the

---

[5] On the emergence of these issues in Canada, see H.P. Glenn, "The Supreme Court, Judicial Comity and Anti-suit Injunctions" (1994) 28 U. British Columbia L. Rev. 193.

[6] That is, a forum to which the defendant either *implicitly* consented, as when the action was a counterclaim to an action begun by the defendant in that forum, or *explicitly* consented, as when the defendant had entered into an agreement to resolve disputes in that forum.

defendant to commence a parallel proceeding to pre-empt the result.

Defendant control over the scope of choice of fora available to the plaintiff in transnational litigation was standard in the law of most countries until fairly recently. It continues to be the norm in cases in which the judgments are enforced outside Canada or outside the federal or regional judgments regime in which they are obtained. However, there have been three notable exceptions.

First, when the United States was founded, the framers of the constitution felt that it was necessary to provide more favourable terms for the recognition and enforcement of judgments between states and so they included in Article IV.1 the requirement that the states give "full faith and credit" to the judicial proceedings of other states.[7] In time, this requirement gave rise to the "minimum contacts" doctrine, which permitted plaintiffs to obtain an enforceable judgment in fora other than those in which the defendant could be served or to which the defendant had consented.[8] Second, when the European Economic Community was established, it was provided in Article 220 that member states would simplify the formalities governing the reciprocal recognition and enforcement of judgments.[9] In time, the 1968 Brussels Convention on Jurisdiction and Enforcement of Judgments in Civil and Commercial Matters (Brussels Convention) and the 1988 Lugano Convention on Jurisdiction and the Enforcement of Judgments in Civil and

---

[7] Article IV.1 of the United States constitution provides in part that "[f]ull faith and Credit shall be given in each State to the public Acts, Records, and Judicial Proceedings of every other State." US Constitution, Art. IV, para. 1. A similar requirement to give full faith and credit is found in section 118 of the Commonwealth of Australian Constitution Act (Imp.), 1900, 63 and 64 Vict., c. 2, which provides, "[f]ull faith and credit shall be given, throughout the Commonwealth, to the laws, the public Acts and records, and the judicial proceedings of every State."

[8] It must be acknowledged that these rules have also been applied to foreign judgments in many American states under the Uniform Foreign Money-Judgments Recognition Act, 13 U.L.A. 263 (1962).

[9] Article 220 of the 1957 Treaty Establishing the European Economic Community states, in part, that "Member States shall, so far as is necessary, enter into negotiations with each other with a view to securing for the benefit of their nationals ... the simplification of formalities governing the reciprocal recognition and enforcement of judgments of courts or tribunals and of arbitration awards." Treaty Establishing the European Economic Community, Mar. 25, 1957, 298 U.N.T.S. 11 1973, Gr. Brit. T. S. No. 1 (Cmd. 5179 — II), art. 220.

Commercial Matters were established[10] in order to permit bases of jurisdiction for reciprocally enforceable judgments other than the defendant's domicile or the defendant's consent. Third, following the Supreme Court of Canada's decision in *Morguard Investments Ltd* v. *De Savoye*[11] in which Canadian courts were required to recognize the jurisdiction of other courts issuing judgments not only where jurisdiction had been exercised on one of the traditional bases mentioned above (that is, the presence or consent of the defendant) but also where jurisdiction had been exercised on the basis of a real and substantial connection between the matter and the forum.

These departures from the traditional model of recognition and enforcement of judgments altered the conditions under which fora are chosen and thereby facilitated the prospect of parallel proceedings. By increasing the range of plaintiff choice in forum selection, they increased the opportunities for plaintiffs to manipulate the outcome of dispute resolution through the choices they made and they increased the range of opportunities for defendants to respond by choosing a different forum and commencing a parallel action. This increase resulted whether the choice was itself manipulative or a response to a manipulative choice by the plaintiff. Each of these departures from the traditional model has emerged in a slightly different federal or regional context, and each has given rise to a slightly different mechanism for dealing with parallel proceedings. A brief review of various mechanisms within the context of the schemes for the recognition and enforcement of judgments in which they have been developed will help to identify some of the considerations relevant to the development of a suitable mechanism for Canada.

Before embarking on this review, a clarification is in order. Each of these departures has occurred as part of a federal or regional

---

[10] Brussels Convention on Jurisdiction and Enforcement of Judgments in Civil and Commercial Matters, Official Journal of the European Communities, O.J.N.L. 304, October 30, 1978 and Cmnd. 7395 [hereinafter Brussels Convention], modified in 1995 to incorporate a reference to the 1988 Lugano Convention on Jurisdiction and the Enforcement of Judgments in Civil and Commercial Matters (1989), 28 I.L.M. 620 [hereinafter Lugano Convention], which is now EC Regulation No. 44/2001 of December 22, 2000 on Jurisdiction and the Recognition and Enforcement of Judgments in Civil and Commercial Matters, Official Journal L 12, 16/01/2001 p. 1 [hereinafter EC Regulation No. 44/2001].

[11] *Morguard Investments Ltd.* v. *De Savoye*, [1990] 3 S.C.R. 1077 [hereinafter *Morguard*].

regime and has thereby been a departure from the norm for the international recognition and enforcement of judgments for the purposes of facilitating that regime. While one approach to international parallel proceedings has been proposed by a committee of the International Law Association (ILA)[12] and another approach is contained in the Preliminary Draft Convention on Jurisdiction and Foreign Judgments in Civil and Commercial Matters,[13] there is no established approach to international parallel proceedings yet in place. Indeed, it would not be expected that there would be one in the absence of a multilateral arrangement for the recognition and enforcement of judgments because it would be the arrangement itself that would foster parallel proceedings and necessitate such a response.

Nevertheless, the *Westec*[14] appeal did involve international parallel litigation.[15] To the extent that parallel proceedings are facilitated by special arrangements for the mutual recognition and enforcement of judgments, such as those found in federal and regional systems, it might be thought that the rules appropriate for international and inter-provincial parallel litigation would differ. Yet, the BC Court of Appeal made no distinction between them, possibly because the Canadian rules that were developed for inter-provincial recognition and enforcement of judgments have since been applied to international cases. Still, a distinction between inter-provincial and international parallel litigation might be a relevant consideration, and, despite the fact that the issues came before the Supreme Court of Canada in an international case, it could be helpful to begin by developing an approach based on parallel litigation in Canadian courts and then to consider the extent to which the

---

[12] International Law Association [hereinafter ILA], Committee on International Civil and Commercial Litigation, *Third Interim Report: Declining and Referring Jurisdiction in International Litigation*, which includes the Leuven-London Principles and which is available online at <http://www.ila-hq.org>.

[13] Which was prepared as part of the negotiations under the auspices of the Hague Conference for a Multilateral Judgments Convention, entitled Preliminary Draft Convention on Jurisdiction and Foreign Judgments in Civil and Commercial Matters, adopted by the Special Commission, October 30, 1999, available online at <www.hcch.net/e/conventions/ draft36e.html>.

[14] *Westec, supra* note 4.

[15] Although the precedent on which the British Columbia Court of Appeal relied — which was laid down in *472900 BC Ltd.* v. *Thrifty Canada* (1998), 168 D.L.R. (4th) 602 (BCCA) [hereinafter *Thrifty*] — involved *inter-provincial* parallel litigation.

approach could apply to situations in which the other proceeding was underway in a foreign court. This is the process by which the Canadian approach to jurisdiction and judgments developed, and it focuses the analysis most effectively on the particular view of comity taken by the Canadian courts.

THE AMERICAN DIVIDE: THE COMITY AND VEXATIOUSNESS STANDARDS

The review begins with the American approach to parallel proceedings.[16] The United States is the oldest common law federal system and it, therefore, represents the first approach to parallel proceedings that was developed. When the founders of the United States established the requirement that courts in the United States give full faith and credit to judicial decisions emanating from other states in the union, they also established, albeit unwittingly, the conditions that fostered parallel proceedings.[17] The minimum contacts doctrine, which defines a generous scope for judicial jurisdiction, provides ample opportunity for the commencement of parallel proceedings, and the due process guarantees, which underlie the minimum contacts doctrine, have not been regarded as requiring restraints on parallel litigation.

Although Canadians might regard the wastefulness and the risk of inconsistent results in parallel litigation as fundamental concerns warranting action, there has been a marked ambivalence about the need to prevent parallel proceedings from going forward in the United States. This ambivalence seems to be a result of the nature of American legal tradition, in which there exists a tension

[16] See generally, L. Teitz, "Parallel Proceedings and the Guiding Hand of Comity" (2000) 34 Int'l Lawyer 545.

[17] Early on in the history of the law of jurisdiction in the United States, the United States Supreme Court determined that full faith and credit could be a source of unfairness to defendants if there were not some restrictions placed on the choice of forum available to plaintiffs: *Pennoyer* v. *Neff*, 95 U.S. 714 (1877). In time, these restrictions came to be associated with the due process clauses of the Fifth and Fourteenth Amendments of the US Constitution, which prohibited the deprivation of property without due process of law. Eventually, the due process requirements gave rise to the minimum contacts doctrine by which courts were constitutionally required to confine their exercise of jurisdiction in *in personam* claims to matters with "sufficient contacts or ties with the state of the forum to make it reasonable and just according to our traditional notions of fair play and substantial justice to permit the state" to assume jurisdiction over the defendant. *International Shoe Co.* v. *State of Washington*, 326 U.S. 310, 320 66 S. Ct. 154 (1945).

between the desire to avoid a multiplicity of proceedings and the obligation of courts to give effect to the policies of the forum in the course of adjudicating private party disputes. This tension has resulted in carefully circumscribed limits on the capacity of the courts to take steps to resolve situations of parallel proceedings. In considering whether to grant a stay to resolve a competition between fora, the United States Supreme Court has held that in cases in which the parallel proceedings are in federal and state courts in the United States, "federal courts have the power to dismiss or remand cases based on abstention principles *only where the relief being sought is equitable or otherwise discretionary.*"[18] Where the relief being sought is mandated by statute, the court must not abstain from hearing the case. There is some doubt about whether this should prevent a court in the United States from granting a stay in favour of a *foreign* proceeding that is already underway in international situations.[19] Still, in deciding whether they should grant stays, American courts have rarely distinguished situations of parallel litigation from situations in which stays are sought on the basis of *forum non conveniens.*[20] The concerns raised for American courts by parallel litigation seem limited to the threat that it poses to judicial efficiency. While this limitation might seem to support a rule requiring deference to the forum in which the proceedings were first commenced, courts have tended to engage in a case-specific review, whereby they do not defer to a foreign proceeding that has been commenced first if the local proceeding has progressed further by the time the stay is sought.[21]

In considering whether to grant injunctions, courts in some parts of the United States have been more troubled by parallel litigation than courts in other parts. Two approaches have emerged: one that is based on "comity" and one that is based on "vexatiousness." In the comity-based approach, courts have avoided interfering whenever possible in proceedings before other courts, and

---

[18] *Quackenbush* v. *Allstate Ins. Co.,* 517 U.S. 706, 730-31 (1996) [emphasis added].

[19] *Posner* v. *Essex Ins Co.,* 178 F 3d 1209, 1223 (11th Cir 1999); *Goldhammer* v. *Dunkin' Donuts,* 59 F Supp 2d 248, 252 (D. Mass. 1999); *Evergreen Marine Corp.* v. *Welgrow Int'l Inc.,* 954 F Supp 101, 104 n. 1 (S.D.N.Y. 1997); *EFCO Corp.* v. *Aluma Sys USA Inc.,* 983 F Supp 816, 824 (S.D. Iowa 1997); *Abdullah Sayid Rajab Al-Rifai & Sons* v. *McDonnell Douglas Foreign Sales Corp,* 988 F Supp 1285, 1291 (ED Mo. 1997).

[20] See *American Cyanimid Co.* v. *Picaso-Anstalt,* 741 F Supp 1150, 1154 (D. NJ 1990).

[21] *Ibid.*

they have refrained from issuing anti-suit injunctions unless it is necessary to do so in order to protect the jurisdiction of the United States forum or to prevent the evasion of important public policies.[22] Under the comity-based approach, the emphasis on non-interference in foreign proceedings has meant that parallel proceedings are often tolerated and are not regarded as a sufficient basis on which to issue anti-suit injunctions.[23] The version of comity that provides the rationale for this approach is one that requires deference to another court's obligation to discharge the policies of the forum with respect to the claim made by the plaintiff before it.

In the approach based on vexatiousness or oppressiveness, the courts are prepared to enjoin proceedings in other courts where those proceedings would frustrate local polices, where they are vexatious or oppressive, where they threaten the local forum's jurisdiction, or where they could produce delay, inconvenience, expense, inconsistency, or a race to judgment.[24] Under the vexatiousness-based approach, the duplicative nature of foreign proceedings and the potential for "unwarranted inconvenience, expense and vexation" are relevant considerations,[25] as is the potential for inconsistent results[26] in determining whether or not to grant an injunction, apart from the general considerations relating to appropriate

---

[22] See, for example, *Laker Airways* v. *Sabena, Belgian World Airlines*, 731 F 2d 909, 926-27 (DC Cir. 1984) [hereinafter *Laker*]. This is the standard not only in the DC Circuit, as indicated in the *Laker* decision, but also in the Second, Third, and Sixth Circuits as indicated in *China Trade and Dev. Corp.* v. *Ssangyong Shipping Co.*, 837 F 2d 33, 35, 37 (2d Cir. 1987) [hereinafter *China Trade*]; *Compagnie Des Bauxites de Guinea* v. *Ins. Co. of N. America*, 651 F 2d 877 (3d Cir. 1981) cert. denied, 457 U.S. 1105 (1982); and *Gau Shan, Ltd.* v. *Bankers Trust Co.*, 956 F 2d 1349 (6th Cir. 1992).

[23] *China Trade, supra* note 22.

[24] See, for example, *Kaepa, Inc.* v. *Achilles Corp.*, 76 F 3d 624 (5th Cir. 1996) [hereinafter *Kaepa*]. This case is the standard not only in the Fifth Circuit as indicated by the *Kaepa* decision but also in the Seventh, Eighth, and Ninth Circuits, as indicated in the *Allendale Mutual* case, *infra* note 25, and in the decisions in *Cargill, Inc.* v. *Hartford Acc. and Indem. Co.*, 531 F Supp 710 (D. Minn. 1982) [hereinafter *Cargill*] and *Seattle Totems Hockey Club* v. *The National Hockey League*, 652 F 2d 852 (9th Cir. 1982), cert. denied, 457 US 1105 (1982) [hereinafter *Seattle Totems*].

[25] *Kaepa, supra* note 24. See also *Allendale Mutual Ins. Co.* v. *Bull Data Sys.*, 10 F 3d 425, 431 (7th Cir. 1993) [hereinafter *Allendale Mutual*], which indicates that the difference between the two standards was the desire to have evidence of an impairment to comity arising from an anti-suit injunction before refusing an injunction on that basis.

[26] See *Seattle Totems, supra* note 24; and *Cargill, supra* note 24.

forum. It is not clear whether this approach is less concerned with comity *per se* or whether it is based on a different version of comity — one that is more like that which is found in the English jurisprudence discussed later in this article.

The approaches taken in the United States to parallel proceedings would appear to be very similar to those that are likely to be endorsed in Canada under the traditional rules, yet in many ways they are quite different. The approaches taken in the United States demonstrate confidence in the courts' ability to determine which is the more appropriate forum and to act, either by way of stay or injunction, to resolve a competition between proceedings as warranted. However, there is a perceived obligation of non-interference that is derived from the deep-seated commitment to forum independence and the recognition of the duty of the courts to assert local policies of the forum.[27] This seems to be far less compelling to Canadian courts, which are therefore less apt to tolerate parallel litigation. Indeed, the use of the term "comity" in the United States to describe a form of respect shown through non-interference seems different from the mutual support and cooperation that is normally associated with the term in Canada as it is used to describe, for example, the currently expanded scope with which to recognize and enforce judgments.[28] Therefore, it would seem likely that the higher level of interest in Canadian courts in resolving a

---

[27] An interesting analogue to this exists in the "public interest factors," which have been endorsed by the US Supreme Court as being relevant in deciding whether to grant a stay based on the doctrine of *forum non conveniens*. *Gulf Oil Corp.* v. *Gilbert*, 330 U.S. 501, 508-09 (1947). These factors included the need to manage court congestion, to prevent undue burden on the public for jury duty, to facilitate the local interest in having localized controversies decided at home, and to resolve a matter in a forum that will be in a position to apply its own law. The Canadian jurisprudence on the granting of stays based on the doctrine of *forum non conveniens* suggests that public interest factors such as this are unlikely to be considered, let alone to outweigh factors that relate primarily to the relative convenience to the parties and the relative logistical and administrative efficiency of resolving the matter in the alternative fora.

[28] See *Morguard, supra* note 11. See also *United States of America* v. *Ivey,* (1996) 26 O.R. (3d) 533 (Gen. Div.), *aff'd.* (1996) 30 O.R. (3d) (CA), leave to appeal to S.C.C. refused S.C.C. Bulletin, 1997, p. 1043. in which the court observed that the principle of comity should inform the development of the law in the area of the foreign public law exception to the enforcement of judgments and that "[i]n an area of law dealing with such obvious and significant transborder issues, it is particularly appropriate for the forum court to give full faith and credit to the laws and judgments of neighbouring states." This is a view of comity that emphasizes active support and cooperation more than restraint and deference.

multiplicity of actions and avoiding the risk of inconsistent results would prompt Canadian courts to search out a more orderly and certain means of resolving them. For a more orderly means, they might consider the European approach.

THE EUROPEAN "FIRST-SEISED" RULE

Once the drafters of the Brussels Convention, which is now the Brussels I Regulation,[29] decided to pursue a convention that provided both for the obligation to enforce the judgments of other members states and for the jurisdictional standards of member state's courts, it was clear that the resulting potential for parallel proceedings would need to be addressed. Numerous provisions in the regulation prohibit the exercise of forms of exorbitant jurisdiction that are available under the national laws of member states, but the remaining scope for jurisdiction continues to be broad. In the absence of a mechanism for declining jurisdiction on a discretionary basis, the obligation to give effect to the judgments of member states "without any special procedure being required" eliminates many of the ways in which courts might otherwise have prevented the inconsistent results of parallel litigation that is facilitated by the regulation. In order to address the concerns of multiplicity and inconsistent results, the Europeans established a simple rule for situations of parallel proceedings or "*lis pendens.*" This rule requires all courts, other than the court first seized, to stay proceedings on the same matter before them of their own motion until the court first seized has decided the matter or has determined that it cannot decide the matter.[30]

---

[29] EC Regulation No. 44/2001, *supra* note 10.

[30] Special accommodations are made for situations in which a forum other than the forum first seised has exclusive jurisdiction. The provisions for parallel litigation found in Articles 21-23 of the Brussels and Lugano Conventions, *supra* note 10, are now found in Articles 27-30 of the EC Regulation No. 44/2001, *supra* note 10:

Section 9 — *Lis pendens* — Related actions

Article 27

1. Where proceedings involving the same cause of action and between the same parties are brought in the courts of different Member States, any court other than the court first seised shall of its own motion stay its proceedings until such time as the jurisdiction of the court first seised is established.

2. Where the jurisdiction of the court first seised is established, any court other than the court first seised shall decline jurisdiction in favour of that court.

The "first-seised" rule is an effective means of eliminating both the potential for inconsistent results and the tactical manoeuvring that is associated with the race to judgment. In fact, the sequence in which courts are seized has been considered by Canadian courts to be a factor supporting the outcome in at least two cases involving parallel proceedings, but it has only been a supporting factor and not the decisive factor.[31] The European experience with a prescribed rule, which requires automatic deference to the court first seized, is instructive. Without any principled means of assuring that cases are heard in the most appropriate fora, the "first-seised" rule has been criticized as replacing the unseemly race to judgment with an equally unseemly "race to the courthouse." It has not prevented the underlying abuse that is associated with parallel proceedings in that it has encouraged pre-emptive strikes by litigants wishing to engage in forum shopping. As a result, the "first-seised" rule has

---

Article 28

1. Where related actions are pending in the courts of different Member States, any court other than the court first seised may stay its proceedings.

2. Where these actions are pending at first instance, any court other than the court first seised may also, on the application of one of the parties, decline jurisdiction if the court first seised has jurisdiction over the actions in question and its law permits the consolidation thereof.

3. For the purposes of this Article, actions are deemed to be related where they are so closely connected that it is expedient to hear and determine them together to avoid the risk of irreconcilable judgments resulting from separate proceedings.

Article 29

Where actions come within the exclusive jurisdiction of several courts, any court other than the court first seised shall decline jurisdiction in favour of that court.

Article 30

For the purposes of this Section, a court shall be deemed to be seised:

1. at the time when the document instituting the proceedings or an equivalent document is lodged with the court, provided that the plaintiff has not subsequently failed to take the steps he was required to take to have service effected on the defendant, or

2. if the document has to be served before being lodged with the court, at the time when it is received by the authority responsible for service, provided that the plaintiff has not subsequently failed to take the steps he was required to take to have the document lodged with the court.

[31] See, for example, *Canadian National Railway Co.* v. *Sydney Steel Corp.* (1998), 167 N.S.R. (2d) 28 (S.C.), aff'd (1998), 164 D.L.R. (4th) 747 (NS CA) [hereinafter *Canadian National Railway*]; and *Thrifty, supra* note 15.

also been criticized for curtailing pre-litigation efforts to seek a negotiated result by diverting energy from such negotiations to the "race to file." In sum, the benefits of order and certainty that would be gained by embracing a simple, mechanical rule such as the "first-seised" rule of the Brussels I Regulation could come at a considerable price in terms of the interests that Canadian courts have in discouraging opportunistic forum selection and ensuring that matters are determined in appropriate fora. It has been observed that the "first-seised" rule "achieves its purpose, but at a price. The price is rigidity, and rigidity can be productive of injustice."[32] There is at least one Canadian case in which a court was not persuaded to defer to the court first seized. This fact raises the question of whether it is possible to benefit from the assurances that are provided by the "first-seised" rule without its drawbacks.

THE ILA AND THE HAGUE CONFERENCE PROPOSALS: COMBINING THE "FIRST-SEISED" RULE AND *FORUM NON CONVENIENS*

Last year, the Committee on International Civil and Commercial Litigation of the ILA[33] presented a report proposing the "Leuven-London Principles." The Leuven-London principles contain an approach to parallel proceedings that combines the orderliness of the European "first-seised" rule with the case-specific sensitivity of appropriate forum analysis, which is undertaken by common law courts under the doctrine of *forum non conveniens*. The principles require courts in different jurisdictions that are seized with the same matter to give the court first seized exclusive carriage of the matter, but only for the purposes of determining appropriate forum[34] — a determination that would be undertaken in the way

---

[32] *Airbus, supra* note 1.

[33] The ILA is an international non-governmental organization established for the "study, elucidation and advancement of international law, public and private, the study of comparative law, the making of proposals for the solution of conflicts of law and for the unification of law, and the furthering of international understanding and goodwill." Its work is carried on primarily through international committees that present reports at biennial conferences for discussion and endorsement. This report was presented at the sixty-ninth biennial conference in London in July 2000. Information about the ILA is available online at <http://www.ila-hq.org>.

[34] Pursuant to Article 4.1, "[w]here proceedings involving the same parties and the same subject-matter are brought in the courts of more than one state, any court other than the court first seised shall suspend its proceedings until such time as the jurisdiction of the court first seised is established, and not declined under this

that *forum non conveniens* determinations are made in common law courts. A similar proposal for resolving situations of parallel proceedings, though more elaborate and detailed, was included in the Preliminary Draft Convention on Jurisdiction and Foreign Judgments in Civil and Commercial Matters, which was published in 1999 by the Special Commission of the Hague Conference on Private International Law as part of the process of negotiating a multilateral convention on the recognition and enforcement of judgments. The Special Commission's proposal also involved a combination of the "first-seised" rule and the case-specific determination of appropriate forum, based on factors ordinarily found in the common law determinations of *forum non conveniens*.[35]

Principle, and thereafter it shall terminate its proceedings. The court first seised shall apply Principle 4.3 [appropriate forum analysis]. Should that court refer the matter to a court subsequently seised in accordance with Principle 4.3, the latter court will not be obliged to terminate its proceedings." The commentary explained that "the Committee gave anxious consideration to whether it ought to preserve a formal *lis pendens* rule, or whether it should simply include the existence of parallel litigation as one of factors to be considered by the court as a ground for referral of jurisdiction. In the end, it concluded that the special complexities of parallel litigation, which carry with it the problems of conflicts between courts, justify a separate rule. But the Committee desired to avoid some of the rigidity, and the potential for forum shopping, which could be the result of the strict operation of a 'first past the post' rule ... But it departs in the result radically from the automatic priority on the merits vouchsafed to the court first seised under the Brussels Convention ... [because what] it does is to give priority to the court first seised in the determination of the appropriate court for the determination of the merits of the matter. In this way, the Committee considered that the potential for the abuse of a *lis pendens* system by a race to the courthouse could be curbed, whilst a specific regime for the determination of priorities between competing actions was still preserved." ILA, *supra* note 12.

[35] Article 21 — *Lis pendens*

1. When the same parties are engaged in proceedings in courts of different Contracting States and when such proceedings are based on the same causes of action, irrespective of the relief sought, the court second seised shall suspend the proceedings if the court first seised has jurisdiction and is expected to render a judgment capable of being recognised under the Convention in the State of the court second seised, unless the latter has exclusive jurisdiction under Article 4 or 12.

2. The court second seised shall decline jurisdiction as soon as it is presented with a judgment rendered by the court first seised that complies with the requirements for recognition or enforcement under the Convention.

3. Upon application of a party, the court second seised may proceed with the case if the plaintiff in the court first seised has failed to take the necessary steps to bring the proceedings to a decision on the merits or if that court has not rendered such a decision within a reasonable time.

Adopting these proposed methods would go a long way towards resolving the difficulties that have been encountered when using the mechanisms for resolving parallel proceedings that are used in the American and European systems. On the one hand, these proposed methods would supply the orderliness lacking in the common law system — an orderliness that would prevent the race to judgment in most situations. On the other hand, these methods would entail a principled determination of appropriate forum that is lacking in the European system — a determination that in most situations would operate to discourage the race to file. If this approach was to be adopted in a reciprocal international regime, whether bilateral or multilateral, it might afford the best results that could presently be obtained in situations of international parallel litigation. Indeed, such a mechanism would seem to be a necessary adjunct to any international regime of enhanced recognition and the enforcement of judgments. As explained earlier, such a regime would increase the scope of forum selection used by litigants and thereby increase the potential for problems associated with parallel litigation. Moreover, as the commentary on these

---

4. The provisions of the preceding paragraphs apply to the court second seised even in a case where the jurisdiction of that court is based on the national law of that State in accordance with Article 17.

5. For the purpose of this Article, a court shall be deemed to be seised:

   a) when the document instituting the proceedings or an equivalent document is lodged with the court, or

   b) if such document has to be served before being lodged with the court, when it is received by the authority responsible for service or served on the defendant [as appropriate, universal time is applicable].

6. If in the action before the court first seised the plaintiff seeks a determination that it has no obligation to the defendant, and if an action seeking substantive relief is brought in the court second seised:

   a) the provisions of paragraphs 1 to 5 above shall not apply to the court second seised, and

   b) the court first seised shall suspend the proceedings at the request of a party if the court second seised is expected to render a decision capable of being recognised under the Convention.

7. This Article shall not apply if the court first seised, on application by a party, determines that the court second seised is clearly more appropriate to resolve the dispute, under the conditions specified in Article 22.

See Preliminary Draft Convention on Jurisdiction and Foreign Judgments in Civil and Commercial Matters, *supra* note 13, which has since been revised to accommodate other developments in the negotiations.

proposed methods suggests, they would virtually eliminate the friction caused by the more aggressive remedy — namely, the anti-suit injunction — by eliminating the need for one court to take unilateral steps to prevent multiplicity by enjoining the plaintiff from proceeding in the other forum.[36]

Still, there is a sizeable and increasing minority of situations in which the mechanisms described in these proposals might not succeed in eliminating the underlying unfairness and abuse. For instance, in one situation, unfairness might arise because although both courts have ostensibly applied a principled approach to the determination of appropriate forum, their standards for granting stays of proceedings differ enough, either in stringency or in the nature of the factors considered, for one court not be content to be bound by the determination of the other. While a less generous approach to the granting of stays might be suitable in one legal system, it could still be frustrating to a court faced with a parallel proceeding in another legal system that would grant a stay if presented with the situation faced by the first court. For example, although a stay may be granted pursuant to Article 3135 of the Québec Civil Code[37] on a discretionary basis on considerations resembling those that apply in motions for stays based on the doctrine of *forum non conveniens,* the standard for doing so is more stringent than that which applies in common law jurisdictions. Accordingly, a situation could arise in which a Québec court would refuse a stay in circumstances in which another court in Canada would regard a stay of a Québec proceeding to be warranted. Under circumstances in which the other Canadian court regarded itself to be a clearly more appropriate forum, should that court decline to exercise jurisdiction merely because the Québec court had refused to grant a stay?[38]

---

[36] See ILA, *supra* note 12.

[37] Article 3135 of Book 10 of the Québec Civil Code, which deals with the International Jurisdiction of Québec Authorities, provides that "[e]ven though a Québec authority has jurisdiction to hear a dispute, it may exceptionally and on an application by a party, decline jurisdiction if it considers that the authorities of another country are in a better position to decide."

[38] Courts in Ontario and in Nova Scotia on at least two occasions have not been willing to grant stays solely on the basis that Québec courts have refused to grant stays in parallel proceedings. See *Guarantee, infra* note 63; and *Canadian National Railway, supra* note 31. However, it should be noted that the Québec proceedings in *Guarantee,* were subsequently stayed by the Québec Court of Appeal and the dispute in *Canadian National Railway* was ultimately settled by the parties. See C. Richter, "Living with Multi-Jurisdictional Litigation," in CBAO Conference Proceedings, see first unnumbered note.

In another example, although the courts of both the United States and the United Kingdom apply the doctrine of *forum non conveniens*, their views of what constitutes an appropriate forum and which factors are relevant for determining which forum is appropriate differ in ways that have sometimes given rise to rather heated trans-Atlantic debates.[39] As mentioned earlier in this article, the obligation to serve the interests of the forum might prevent the granting of a stay in a court in the United States under circumstances in which a stay would be thought to be warranted by an English court.

In another situation, unfairness might arise because the defendant cannot travel to the jurisdiction in which the matter has been commenced in order to seek a stay in that forum. Concerns about the hardships of litigating in distant fora have usually been raised in cases involving plaintiffs who find it difficult to travel to commence a claim. But the hardships of responding to a notice of a distant proceeding and of retaining and instructing local counsel to defend against a claim in a distant forum are also capable of producing unfairness in the determination of appropriate forum. Moreover, being aware of the difficulty that an opposing party might have in responding to a notice of a distant proceeding could encourage an opponent to seek an unfair advantage. Even among the common law provinces of Canada, where the harmonizing effect of the Supreme Court of Canada tends to ensure that the doctrine of *forum non conveniens* is applied in a fairly uniform manner, there could still be a risk that the difficulty of responding to a claim commenced in a court thousands of miles away could be used to secure a default judgment in an unmeritorious claim simply because the defendant is not able to challenge the choice of an inappropriate forum from such a distance.

How should the potential for such situations of unfairness be addressed? The experience of the English courts could assist since they are the only common law courts within a regional system otherwise comprised of civil law jurisdictions that entails a multilateral judgments regime. The English courts have needed to develop ways to respond to parallel litigation involving other courts that take a different approach to the issue of appropriate forum. The English courts have also needed to develop responses to parallel litigation in a multi-jurisdictional regime in which the logistics of travelling to challenge an exercise of jurisdiction could affect a defendant's

---

[39] See *British Airways Board* v. *Laker Airways Ltd.*, [1985] A.C. 53 and *Laker, supra* note 22.

ability to ensure that a proceeding does not go forward in a forum
that should decline jurisdiction.

THE ENGLISH EXPERIENCE WITH PARALLEL PROCEEDINGS IN EUROPEAN COURTS

The general approach to parallel proceedings that is taken by the
English courts is fairly standard for common law courts. In motions
for stays of local proceedings in situations of parallel litigation,
English courts, like the courts of the United States, Australia, and,
at one time, Canada, have treated the existence of foreign proceedings as merely one more factor in the analysis of appropriate
forum.[40] They have acknowledged that the commencement of parallel proceedings in another country could constitute a form of
interference in local proceedings that could warrant the granting
of an injunction.[41] However, the analysis in cases of parallel proceedings remains focused, as it does in the United States, on the
determination of appropriate forum, and the existence of parallel
proceedings operates simply as another factor to be considered.
Where the foreign proceedings are well advanced,[42] the existence
of parallel proceedings could warrant a stay, but where the parties
have agreed in their contract to resolve disputes in the local
forum[43] or where important issues of local public policy are likely to
be resolved appropriately only in the local forum,[44] a stay will not
be granted. What is notably different from the approach under the
Brussels and Lugano regimes, however, is that while it is recognized
that foreign parallel proceedings might be instituted as an abusive
tactic, one that would warrant an injunction, they are not otherwise

---

[40] See L. Collins, ed, *Dicey and Morris on the Conflict of Laws*, 13th ed. (London: Sweet and Maxwell, 2000) at 400; *The Abidin Daver*, [1984] A.C. 398 at 411-12; and P. North and J.J. Fawcett eds, *Cheshire and North's Private International Law*, 13th ed. (London: Butterworths, 1999) at 347-50. Although, there seems to be some recognition that in matters such as those involving divorce decrees the potential for inconsistent results presents a greater concern. *de Dampierre* v. *de Dampierre*, [1988] A.C. 92 (HL) and *Henry* v. *Henry* (1995), 185 C.L.R. 571 (Aus. HC).

[41] *South Carolina Insurance Co.* v. *Assurantie Maatschappij "De Zeven Provincien,"* [1987] A.C. 24, 40-41. And see *CSR* v. *Cigna Insurance Australia Ltd.* (1997), 189 C.L.R. 345 (HC).

[42] See *Cleveland Museum of Art* v. *Capricorn Art International SA*, [1990] Lloyd's Rep. 166.

[43] See *Akai Pty Ltd* v. *People's Insurance Co. Ltd*, [1998] 1 Lloyd's Rep. 90.

[44] See in *E I Du Pont de Nemours & Co.* v. *Agnew and Kerr*, [1987] 2 Lloyd's Rep. 585 (Eng. CA).

considered sufficiently problematic *per se* to warrant steps to eliminate them. Accordingly, in situations of parallel litigation when
another court has refused a stay, it does not necessarily follow that
the multiplicity should be resolved by an injunction.

However, the experience of the English courts in addressing
situations of parallel proceedings within the Brussels and Lugano
regimes — which involves other courts within a regional regime
that take a different approach to the question of appropriate forum
— is more instructive. As discussed earlier, the Brussels regime contains its own mechanism for eliminating parallel proceedings, but,
in rare cases, where litigants demonstrate the potential to evade the
effects of this mechanism, the existence of the enhanced regime
for the recognition and enforcement of judgments will tend to
exacerbate the effects of the abuse underlying the parallel proceedings. As the decision of the English Court of Appeal in *Turner*
v. *Grovit*[45] demonstrates, the response that can be evoked by such
abuse reflects a version of comity quite different from the deferent
version contemplated by the American jurisprudence.[46]

In *Turner*, the Court of Appeal granted an injunction to prevent
the continuation of proceedings that were commenced in Spain
by Turner's employer after Turner had made a claim for relief for
constructive dismissal before the Industrial Tribunal in London.
Ordinarily, under the "first-seised" rule, the Spanish court would
have been required to defer to the English tribunal, but the
employer had argued that the Industrial Tribunal was not a court,
that the two sets of proceedings differed from one another and so
were not duplicative, and that, in any event, the English court did
not have authority under the Brussels Convention to issue an anti-
suit injunction to restrain the pursuit of proceedings in the courts
of another member state. On upholding the injunction, the English
court rejected these propositions and observed that where proceedings are "launched in another Brussels Convention jurisdiction for no purpose other than to harass and oppress a party who
is already a litigant here," the court has the power to enjoin the
plaintiff in the foreign proceeding from continuing the abuse, and
the granting of an injunction "entails not the slightest disrespect to
the Spanish court" because it "would underpin and support the
proper application of the Brussels Convention."[47]

[45] *Turner* v. *Grovit*, [2000] 1 Q.B. 345 (CA) [hereinafter *Turner*].

[46] See discussion under the heading "The American Divide: The Comity and Vexatiousness Standards" earlier in this article.

[47] *Turner, supra* note 45 at paras. 29 and 43.

In the *Turner* case, the English court was faced with an abuse that drew on both of the concerns about unfairness mentioned earlier in this article. In the view of the English court, the Spanish court was obliged to stay its proceeding (pursuant to the Brussels Convention) and so there was no reason to wait to find out whether the Spanish court would do so. As a result, it was unfair to put Turner to the trouble of going to Spain to seek this result. The result in the *Turner* case illustrates a view of comity in the granting of injunctions that reflects a different alignment of the underlying relationships between litigants and courts. In this view of comity, the granting of an injunction is not a matter of choosing between the local court's obligation to grant a hearing to the plaintiff that is before it over the foreign court's obligation to do the same for the plaintiff that is before it. Rather, the injunction is granted on the strength of the courts' common interest in preventing an abuse — one that could affect proceedings before either court and one that should be resolved either by a stay or an injunction — once it is determined which proceedings are abusive — by whichever court is better placed to do so.

The lesson for Canadian courts as they develop an approach to parallel proceedings is an interesting one. Where courts operate within a regime of enhanced recognition and enforcement of judgments — one in which they take the same approach to the determination of appropriate forum — their shared interest in cooperating to eliminate parallel proceedings could reduce their concern to determine appropriate forum independently. Thus, Canadian courts might be more willing to defer to determinations by other Canadian courts of appropriate forum and they might even be prepared to regard litigants as bound by such determinations. For example, where another Canadian court has already denied a stay, that determination might be regarded as sufficient to warrant a stay of the local proceeding.[48] Similarly, one Canadian court might be less likely to take affront to the granting of an injunction by another Canadian court to restrain a parallel proceeding. Historically, Canadian courts have demonstrated considerable reluctance about taking such pre-emptive steps in matters that they feel should be decided by other courts,[49] but this could

---

[48] As was the case in *Thrifty, supra* note 15. However, see *Canadian National Railway, supra* note 31.

[49] See *Hunt* v. *T & N plc*, [1993] 4 S.C.R. 289 [hereinafter *Hunt*], in which the British Columbia courts hesitated to pronounce on the constitutionality of a

change should such a step seem warranted[50] to prevent an abuse — for instance, situations in which the approach to comity taken in *Turner* v. *Grovit* would seem applicable.

The lessons for Canadian courts that can be found in the experience of the English courts could extend beyond refining the approach to injunctions. Developing appropriate responses to parallel proceedings might also help in refining the approach to determining which proceeding should be eliminated. For example, it was once thought that an action for a declaration that the plaintiff was not liable to the defendant (a "negative declaration") was likely to be commenced only as a pre-emptive strike on forum selection, that is, as a means to secure a trial in a forum other than the one likely to be chosen by the party to the dispute who would seek substantive relief (the "natural plaintiff").[51] Clearly, negative declarations could be particularly effective as a tactic of this sort in a regime such as exists in Europe, where the court first seized has carriage of the matter. But they could also be effective in situations where the "natural plaintiff" was not in a position to travel to challenge the choice of forum by the applicant for the declaration. In either situation, it would constitute an abuse. Accordingly, negative declarations were once treated with considerable suspicion. However, as the recent English experience demonstrates,[52] it might be appropriate to seek a negative declaration in a situation in which the opposing party was about to commence a proceeding in a forum that was less appropriate but that might not relinquish jurisdiction in a forum that was less appropriate but that would be

---

Québec blocking statute that impeded litigation before them. On appeal to the Supreme Court of Canada, the court found that the British Columbia courts had jurisdiction to make such a determination and that the statute was constitutionally inapplicable to litigation in Canadian courts.

[50] It is arguable that the act of certifying a multi-province plaintiff case in a class action — an act that has gained the approval of a number of courts — has virtually the same preclusive effect (subject of course to the plaintiff class members' entitlement to exclude themselves from the class). See *Harrington* v. *Dow Corning* (1997), 29 B.C.L.R. (3d) 88, aff'd (2000), 193 D.L.R. (4th) 67 (BCCA) leave to appeal to S.C.C. refused, S.C.C. Bulletin 2001 at 1540; *Wilson* v. *Servier Canada Ltd* (2000), 50 O.R. (4th) 219, leave to appeal to Div. Court, refused 52 O.R. (4th) 20, leave to appeal to S.C.C. refused, S.C.C. Bulletin 2001 at 1539.

[51] See *The Volvox Hollandia*, [1988] 2 Lloyd's Rep. 361 at 371 (CA).

[52] On negative declarations, see *Messier Dowty* v. *Sabena*, [2000] 1 Lloyd's L.R. 428 (CA). See also L. Collins, *Essays in International Litigation and the Conflict of Laws* (Oxford: Clarendon Press, 1994).

logistically difficult for the defendant to challenge. In other words, in developing a mechanism to respond to parallel proceedings, it might be necessary to review the assumption that it is abusive to attempt to secure access to a particular forum by seeking a negative declaration.[53] There might be nothing abusive about commencing an action for a declaration in an appropriate forum where there is a genuine risk that a claim might otherwise be commenced in a less appropriate forum from which the proceeding could not be dislodged. In addition, there might be nothing abusive about a party who has been repeatedly threatened with proceedings (whether or not in an inappropriate forum) taking the step of commencing an action for a declaration in order to resolve outstanding issues of liability.

In time, Canadian courts will develop sophisticated responses to the various strategies that emerge from the greater flexibility in forum selection that is available under the current enhanced rules for the recognition and enforcement of judgments. These responses will include a means of identifying which of the proceedings should go forward and a means for terminating the proceedings that should not go forward. Still, as they refine their approach, Canadian courts are likely to come to regard the traditional mechanisms of independent fora — stays, injunctions, and negative declarations — as being, in the final analysis, fairly crude tools for addressing the increased complexity of the issues of jurisdiction and forum that give rise to parallel litigation. This perception could provide fresh impetus to develop a mechanism for transfers of proceedings, such as that which operates in the Australian cross-vesting scheme, as a more effective means of addressing many of the concerns that give rise to parallel proceedings and make them difficult to resolve.

TRANSFERS OF PROCEEDINGS — THE AUSTRALIAN
CROSS-VESTING LEGISLATION

Initially developed to address the jurisdictional complexities of the Australian federal judicial system, the cross-vesting scheme emerged from the proposals formulated for the Australian Constitutional Conventions in the 1970s and early 1980s, and taken up by

---

[53] Or one seeking a declaration that a judgment in a particular proceeding would not be enforceable.

the Solicitors-General who prepared the legislation.[54] The scheme is composed of concurrent enactments of the states, territories, and the Commonwealth and is entitled the Jurisdiction of Courts (Cross-Vesting) Act 1987, which vest every other Australian court to the largest extent possible with the jurisdiction of the enacting jurisdiction's courts.[55] In achieving the maximum flexibility in choice of jurisdiction, it became necessary to develop a mechanism to ensure that this flexibility was not abused and that matters were disposed of in appropriate fora. This was achieved by providing for the transfer of matters to more appropriate fora either upon the application of a party or by the court itself.[56]

The cross-vesting scheme mandates the transfer of a proceeding in situations involving related proceedings in different courts, situations in which the receiving court would have had jurisdiction without the cross-vesting scheme, situations involving the interpretation of another jurisdiction's law, and when it was otherwise in

---

[54] Jurisdiction of Courts (Cross-Vesting) Act 1987, (Cth). The cross-vesting initiative was all the more effective for having been undertaken by the solicitors-general of the Australian states led by the Solicitor-General of Australia, Dr. Gavan Griffith, Q.C., because, as the senior counsel for the governments in Australia, they had the procedural expertise and experience necessary to craft a scheme that would work well within the Australian judicial system.

[55] Unfortunately, the seamless efficiency of the operation of the cross-vesting scheme was impaired by a 1999 High Court determination in *Re Wakim; Ex parte McNally* (1999), 163 A.L.R. 270 that the state courts were constitutionally incapable of vesting their jurisdiction in the Federal Court. Still, the vesting of jurisdiction between state courts, which is the feature of the model of primary relevance for the Canadian federation, remains intact.

[56] The operative provision in the cross-vesting legislation reads as follows:
5(1) Where-
(a) proceeding (in this sub-section referred to as the "relevant proceeding") is pending in the Supreme Court of a State or Territory (in this sub-section referred to as the "first court"); and
(b) it appears to the first court that-
i) the relevant proceeding arises out of, or is related to, another proceeding pending in ... [another Australian court] and it is more appropriate that the relevant proceeding be determined by ... [the other Australian court];
ii) having regard to-
    ...
(c) the interests of justice-
it is more appropriate that the relevant proceeding be determined by ... [the other Australian court], as the case may be; or
iii) it is otherwise in the interests of justice that the relevant proceeding be determined by ... [the other Australian court],-
the first court shall transfer the relevant proceeding to ... [the other Australian court], as the case may be.
See Jurisdiction of Courts (Cross-Vesting) Act, *supra* note 54.

the interests of justice. There is no onus on the application for a transfer, the principles of *forum non conveniens* do not apply, and no appeal is available following a decision to transfer,[57] as this was not intended to be the kind of cumbersome deliberative exercise properly reserved for judicial determinations of the merits, but rather an administrative decision — "a 'nuts and bolts' management decision."[58]

The Australian cross-vesting scheme is not the only example of a mechanism for transfers of proceedings that has been proposed or developed. A similar scheme operates in the American federal system. The diversity jurisdiction of the Federal Courts was created to enable those courts to act as neutral fora for disputes between persons of different states, and the transfer mechanism in section 1404 of the United States Code permits changes of venue between districts or divisions in the Federal Court system.[59] In addition, in Canada, the Uniform Law Conference of Canada proposed a transfer mechanism in Part 3 of the Uniform Court Jurisdiction and Proceedings Transfer Act.[60] This proposal was, in some ways, even more ambitious than the cross-vesting scheme. Not only would it permit courts to send or to receive a transfer of the whole of a matter or a part of a matter, it would also permit international transfers between participating courts. However, the act is not yet been proclaimed in force in any of the Canadian provinces. Finally, the Leuven-London Principles, which were discussed earlier in this article, also contain a mechanism for transfer, which is described as "referral" for dealing with matters commenced in the wrong forum.[61]

---

[57] See A. Mason and J. Crawford, "The Cross-Vesting Scheme" (1988) 62 Admin. L.J. 328; G. Griffith, D. Rose, and S. Gageler, "Further Aspects of the Cross-Vesting Scheme" (1988) 62 Admin. L.J. 1016. While there was no appeal, it would seem that an error could be corrected by sending the matter back from whence it came, which could occur either on motion of a party or on the receiving court's own motion.

[58] *Bankinvest AG* v. *Seabrook* (1988), 14 N.S.W.L.R. 711 at 714.

[59] 28 U.S.C.A. para. 1404.

[60] Uniform Law Conference of Canada, "Uniform Court Jurisdiction and Proceedings Transfer Act" in Proceedings (ULCC, 1994), which can be found online at <http://www.ulcc.ca>.

[61] Principle 5 provides

5.1 On the hearing of an application under Principle 4.3 [for *forum non conveniens*-like relief], and subject to any terms of referral under Principle 5.3, the applicant shall satisfy the originating court that the alternative court that the alternative court

(a) has and will exercise jurisdiction over the matter; and

(b) is likely to render its judgment on the merits within a reasonable time.

There is a great deal to recommend the establishment of a transfer mechanism within Canada for proceedings that could more suitably be determined in fora other than those in which they have been commenced. Such a mechanism would be an effective means of preventing or resolving instances of parallel proceedings. Perhaps, in time, Part 3 of the Uniform Court Jurisdiction and Proceedings Transfer Act, which deals with transfers of proceedings, will be considered for adoption even if Part 2, which codifies court jurisdiction is not.

EMERGING ELEMENTS OF A CANADIAN APPROACH: A "SECOND-SEIZED" RULE?

The foregoing survey of the experiences of federal and regional systems with mechanisms for parallel litigation has identified some of the concerns that might apply to Canadian courts and some of the features of the models to which Canadian courts might refer in developing an approach tailored to their needs. When these concerns and features are considered in the context of the growing jurisprudence on parallel proceedings in Canada, the significance of certain elements begins to emerge.

5.2 The originating court may communicate directly with the alternative court on any application for referral in order to obtain information relevant to its determination under Principle 4, where such communication is permitted by the respective states. States are encouraged to permit their courts to make, and respond to, such communications. Any such communication shall be either on the application of one of the parties or on its own motion. Where the court acts on its own motion it shall give reasonable notice to the parties of its intention to do so, and hear the parties on the information to be sought. The originating court shall either communicate in writing or otherwise on the record. It shall communicate in a language acceptable to the alternative court.

5.3 The parties and the originating court are encouraged to consider appropriate terms of referral. These may deal in particular with:

   (a) the applicant's submission to the jurisdiction of the alternative court;

   (b) the terms on which the applicant may assert a defence of limitation or prescription of action in the alternative court.

5.4 Save where the international convention provides otherwise, the originating court, if satisfied of the matters in paragraph 5.1, shall on an order to decline jurisdiction either suspend further proceedings at least until the jurisdiction of the alternative court has been established, or, where national law provides, terminate its proceedings.

ILA, *supra* note 12.

In the Canadian common law jurisprudence on parallel proceedings, five decisions stand out: two involving parallel proceedings in a common law province and in Québec, a third involving parallel proceedings in Ontario and Japan, and two other decisions involving the courts of British Columbia and Ontario. Taken in chronological order, they seem to follow the same pattern similar to that indicated by the various issues and concerns outlined earlier in this article.

In 1994, in *Guarantee Co. of North America* v. *Gordon Capital Corp.*,[62] which involved a dispute over a claim on an insurance bond, the Ontario courts refused to stay a proceeding that was commenced two weeks after a proceeding on the same matter had been commenced in Québec. The court held that the prior commencement of proceedings in Québec was not a reason *per se* to grant a stay and that a stay should be refused because it had not been shown that Québec was clearly the more appropriate forum. The court saw no reason why both proceedings could not continue. Significantly, there was no suggestion that the granting of an injunction restraining the Québec proceedings necessarily followed from the refusal of a stay of the Ontario proceedings. This decision appears to reflect the traditional approach taken in common law courts and, in particular, the "comity"-based approach that is followed by some of the United States courts in which parallel proceedings are generally tolerated. Interestingly, the Québec Superior Court had refused a stay sought on the grounds of *forum non conveniens* in November 1993, because the Civil Code provision in Article 3135 for the granting of discretionary stays on this basis had not yet come into force, but in 1995 the Québec Court of Appeal relied upon the authority in this article to stay the matter.[63] Also worth noting is the fact that the Québec Civil Code contains a provision in Article 3137 specifically recognizing the independent significance of parallel proceedings.[64] Unlike the provision in the Brussels I

---

[62] *Guarantee Co. of North America* v. *Gordon Capital Corp.* (1994), 18 O.R. (3d) 9 (Gen. Div.), leave to appeal to Div. Ct refused, leave to appeal to S.C.C. refused, [1994] S.C.C.A. No. 304 [hereinafter *Guarantee*].

[63] *Gordon Capital Corp.* c. *Garantie, Cie d'assurance de l'Amérique du Nord*, C.S.M. 500-05-009714-930, [1995] R.D.J. 537 (C.A.).

[64] Article 3137 provides: "On the application of a party, a Québec authority may stay its ruling on an action brought before it if another action between the same parties, based on the same facts and having the same object is pending before a

Regulation, Article 3137 permits a Québec court to stay its proceeding but does not require it to do so.

In 1997, in *Hudon v. Geos Language Corporation*,[65] the Ontario Divisional Court upheld the granting of an anti-suit injunction to restrain proceedings commenced in Japan by Geos Language Corporation for a declaration that it was not liable to Hudon. Hudon had commenced an action in Ontario, and Geos had sought a stay of the proceeding. The Divisional Court was not prepared to hold that the determination by the Ontario court that Ontario was an appropriate forum was a decisive factor in determining whether an anti-suit injunction should be issued, but it did hold that it was not necessary for Hudon to seek a stay of the Japanese proceeding in order to qualify for an order restraining Geos from continuing it. Thus, the possibility of treating one court's determination of appropriate forum as binding on the litigants in both proceedings was raised. Further, the court seemed moved by considerations that were similar to those in the *Turner* case[66] in that it regarded the subsequent Japanese proceedings as an effort to take advantage of a forum that was either unlikely to be persuaded to relinquish jurisdiction or that would be a difficult forum for the plaintiff to reach to seek a stay.

In 1998, in *Canadian National Railway Co. v. Sydney Steel Corp.*,[67] which involved a dispute over the supply of steel rails, the Nova Scotia Court of Appeal upheld a decision of the Chambers judge refusing to stay a local proceeding in favour of a proceeding commenced subsequently in Québec. The Court of Appeal made this decision despite the fact that the Québec courts had refused a stay and they had decided that they should determine which forum was the appropriate forum because they had determined that Québec law should apply.[68] The Nova Scotia Court of Appeal was not persuaded that estoppel applied to the determination of appropriate forum by the Québec courts (which was interlocutory under Québec law) or that comity required the Nova Scotia courts to defer

---

foreign authority, provided that the latter action can result in a decision which may be recognized in Québec, or if such a decision has already been rendered by a foreign authority."

[65] *Hudon v. Geos Language Corporation* (1997), 34 O.R. (3d) 14 (Div. Ct) [hereinafter *Hudon*].

[66] *Turner, supra* note 45.

[67] *Canadian National Railway, supra* note 31 at para. 22.

[68] *Sydney Steel Corp. c. Canadian National Railway* (Sept 8, 1997) 500-05-026912-962 (C.S.), appeal dismissed (March 13, 1998) 500-09-005566-971 (C.A.).

to that determination. Instead, the Court of Appeal observed: "[I]f any deference is to be shown, it would be to the jurisdiction in which proceedings were first commenced." While the Court of Appeal permitted the multiplicity to continue, it demonstrated sensitivity to the kinds of concerns that could ultimately lead to the development of a mechanism for resolving parallel proceedings. Implicit in its reasoning was the recognition of the importance of resolving a multiplicity of proceedings as well as the importance of establishing a common standard for determining appropriate forum so that it would be suitable for one court to defer to the decision of another.

The real breakthrough for the common law courts in Canada, however, came in the 1998 decision of the British Columbia Court of Appeal in *472900 BC Ltd* v. *Thrifty Canada,*[69] when it overruled a leading precedent[70] that had emphasized the traditional approach of forum independence. In the *Thrifty* case, a dispute had arisen over the franchise agreement between 472900, a British Columbia company, and Thrifty, an Ontario company. Thrifty sued 472900 in Ontario, and, five days later, 472900 sued Thrifty in British Columbia. 472900 asked the Ontario court to stay its proceeding in favour of the British Columbia proceeding but this request was refused because there was a clause in the parties' agreement attorning to the Ontario courts and the case could be tried in either forum "without great difficulty for either side." An application for leave to appeal the Ontario decision was denied. Thrifty then sought a stay of the British Columbia proceeding and, on appeal to the British Columbia Court of Appeal, the stay was granted as a matter of comity between the provinces of Canada, with the explicit acknowledgment that the matter of appropriate forum had already been considered by the Ontario courts and that this point was a relevant factor in the determination. Although the decision in *Thrifty* focused primarily on providing reasons for the result that the court had reached rather than on the method that might be adopted by courts in the future for resolving situations of parallel proceedings, the result would appear to advocate a process resembling that which was proposed in the Leuven-London principles.[71]

---

[69] *Thrifty, supra* note 15.

[70] Which was set in *Avenue Properties Ltd* v. *First City Development Corp.* (1986), 32 D.L.R. (4th) 40 (BC CA).

[71] See the discussion under the heading "The ILA and The Hague Conference Proposals: Combining the 'First-Seised' Rule and *Forum Non Conveniens*" earlier in this article.

The *Thrifty* decision is a particularly compelling precedent because it was established in a situation in which a court was *ceding* jurisdiction to another court explicitly for the purposes of resolving a multiplicity and not a situation in which a court was *claiming* jurisdiction for itself.

Finally, in *Westec Aerospace Inc.* v. *Raytheon Aircraft Co.*,[72] which involved a commercial dispute between Westec, a British Columbia company, and Raytheon, a Kansas company, over a contract to supply computer software and hardware. While Westec's offer to settle was still outstanding, Raytheon commenced an action in Kansas for a declaration that it had not breached its contract with Westec and that Westec had not suffered any damage caused by Raytheon. Westec then commenced an action in British Columbia against Raytheon for breach of contract. Raytheon sought a stay of the British Columbia proceedings, which was refused by the Chambers judge but granted by the Court of Appeal. Citing the decision in *Thrifty,* the Court of Appeal endorsed the following test:

Where parallel proceedings are alleged, as they are in the case at bar, Thrifty Canada invites the following analysis:

1. Are there parallel proceedings underway in another jurisdiction?
2. If so, is the other jurisdiction an appropriate forum for the resolution of the dispute?
3. Assuming there are parallel proceedings in another appropriate forum, has the plaintiff established objectively by cogent evidence that there is some personal or juridical advantage that would be available to him only in the British Columbia action that is of such importance that it would cause injustice to him to deprive him of it?[73]

Like the *Thrifty* decision, the decision of the British Columbia Court of Appeal is a compelling one in that it invokes comity not merely to encourage tolerance of multiplicity but to resolve it. The decision in *Westec* goes even further than the decision in *Thrifty* in two respects. First, the court was prepared to cede jurisdiction to a *foreign* court and not just to another Canadian court and, second, the court deferred to a proceeding in which the applicant was not seeking substantive relief but rather a negative declaration. The court explicitly rejected arguments concerning "unstated and unsavoury assumptions about the quality of American justice," which it would not accept "without cogent proof that Westec could not get fair treatment" in the Kansas court. The court also explicitly rejected arguments that the Kansas proceedings were to be regarded

[72] *Westec, supra* note 4.

[73] *Ibid.* at 507.

as abusive simply because they were commenced while an offer was outstanding and because they sought only declaratory relief. The court found the allegations regarding the deleterious effect of this approach on the settlement process overstated, and it observed that both of these arguments were answered by the fact that Kansas was an appropriate forum.

Despite the fact that the *Westec* appeal was dismissed without reasons by the Supreme Court of Canada,[74] it would seem that certain fundamental principles are emerging from the jurisprudence, which, when compared with other federal and regional systems, seem likely to form the foundation for a *Canadian* approach to parallel litigation. First, the common law courts in Canada seem to be converging on a view that, rejects the traditional tolerance for parallel litigation and that regards multiplicity as inherently at odds with the principles of order and fairness that underlie the constitutional imperatives for the law of jurisdiction and judgments in Canada.[75] Given such a view, multiplicity would not be just another factor in the analysis of appropriate forum but one that could provide an independent basis for granting a stay or an injunction. To be sure, this view would also imply a recognition of the necessity of a rapprochement of standards between the common law provinces and Québec. Further, it would imply a reconsideration of some of the *dicta* in the 1993 decision of the Supreme Court of Canada in *Amchem Products Inc.* v. *British Columbia (Workers' Compensation Board)*,[76] which suggested that the consequences of the commencement of parallel litigation "would not be disastrous"[77] and should be tolerated where both fora are appropriate.

Second, the view of inter-provincial comity that seems to be emerging in Canada is one that calls for collegiality and cooperation among courts rather than deference in the form of non-interference.[78] It is one in which it should not matter which court decides the issue of appropriate forum, provided that both courts apply the same test for determining appropriate forum. Under these circumstances, it might be possible to develop a unique

---

[74] See the description of the appeal process in this case in the text surrounding note 3.

[75] See *Morguard, supra* note 11.

[76] *Amchem Products Inc.* v. *British Columbia (Workers' Compensation Board)*, [1993] 1 S.C.R. 897.

[77] *Ibid.* at 914.

[78] See, generally, *Hunt, supra* note 49.

approach to resolving situations of parallel litigation — one that relied on the court *second* seized to determine whether it, or the court first seized, was the more appropriate forum. This approach would be in contrast to the European approach and the methods proposed by the Committee of the ILA and the Special Commission of the Hague Conference, which required the court first seized to make this determination. While a "second-seized" rule would obviate the concerns about the "race to file" that were raised in the *Westec* case, it would need to be couched in specific terms that would reduce the potential for abuse. For example, deference to the court second seized in making the determination of appropriate forum might be accompanied by requiring the plaintiff in the second proceeding to show that he or she could not, or should not, have to defend in the first forum. Permitting a challenge to a plaintiff's choice of forum to proceed in this way could accommodate concerns raised by the fact that some defendants cannot travel to request a stay from the first forum.[79] Indeed, it might make the commencement of a second proceeding function simply as a preferable means of dealing with those situations rather than an application for an injunction. It would be preferable because it would operate in a context in which the courts had acknowledged the importance of cooperating to resolve the dispute over forum (and so would not risk raising sensitive issues of comity), and it would involve the commencement of a proceeding that thereby demonstrated the availability of the proposed alternative forum.

Finally, further procedural requirements might need to be introduced to protect against abuse. They could include, for example, the requirement that a plaintiff commencing a parallel proceeding seek a determination of the issue of appropriate forum as a prerequisite to making the claim and that the plaintiff notify the first court of the second proceeding to apprise the first court of the determination ongoing in the second court. To be sure, the mechanism would benefit from refinement as courts became more experienced with it. In addition, it could be improved by enhanced mechanisms for direct communication and cooperation between courts such as have been suggested by the Uniform Law Conference's proposed transfer process,[80] which would, for example, permit the trial of an issue in an alternative forum, thereby securing trial in the most

---

[79] Which would raise issues of access to justice that were simply the obverse of those canvassed in *Oakley* v. *Barry* (1998), 158 D.L.R. (4th) 679 (N.S.C.A.).

[80] See the discussion under the heading "Transfers of Proceedings under Australian Cross-Vesting Legislation" earlier in this article.

appropriate forum even in situations where it might vary within a single case, for example, in respect of liability and of damages.

CHALLENGES AHEAD: ADAPTING A CANADIAN APPROACH TO INTERNATIONAL CASES

As noted in the introduction, Canadian courts have tended to apply the approaches to jurisdiction and judgments that they developed in inter-provincial cases to international cases. To what extent will that be likely to occur in the Canadian approach to parallel proceedings? It seems likely that Canadian courts will carry over to international cases the principle that multiplicity is not just a factor in the analysis but also an independent basis for a judicial response.[81] However, they are unlikely to regard it as being necessary to avoid multiplicity at all costs, for instance, forcing a local plaintiff to resolve the matter in an inappropriate foreign forum. Canadian courts have shown that they are prepared to consider the issuance of an injunction as a logical corollary to the refusal of a stay,[82] but it is not clear whether this result would occur in every case or only in cases where the court determined for other reasons that the commencement of the foreign proceeding was an abuse.

In addition, it seems likely that Canadian courts will often be prepared to respect a foreign court's determination of which proceeding should go forward, as they did in *Westec* when the denial of the stay in Kansas was cited as being a reason for granting a stay in British Columbia. In this regard, it is possible that the rule of sequence that might develop in Canada in international parallel litigation between common law courts will not relate to the order in which the courts are seized but will relate instead to the order in which they are asked to determine which is the more appropriate forum. However, in the absence of a multilateral judgments regime that establishes harmonized standards for jurisdiction, there will probably always be a residual category of international cases in which the approach of the foreign court to jurisdiction is sufficiently at odds with the Canadian approach, that it will not be suitable to forego more primitive mechanisms, such as those involving the refusal to enforce foreign judgments, the issuance of anti-suit injunctions, and even the tolerance of parallel proceedings. There is hope, though, that, in time, instances of parallel litigation entailing real savagery will become relatively rare.

[81] As seemed evident in *Westec, supra* note 4.

[82] In *Hudon, supra* note 67.

Sommaire

Procédures parallèles — des vues convergentes? L'appel Westec

La flexibilité offerte par les nouvelles règles canadiennes sur la compétence et les jugements crée des opportunités pour les parties adverses à former des recours parallèles l'une contre l'autre. Dans la mesure où les parties à un litige commencent à recourir à ces opportunités, les tribunaux canadiens font face à des problèmes spéciaux relatifs aux procédures parallèles et à l'éventualité d'obtenir des résultats contradictoires. Plusieurs mécanismes ont été développés dans d'autres systèmes juridiques pour résoudre ces questions, mais certains de ces mécanismes n'empêchent pas la course au jugement ou la course au dossier. Une revue des expériences résultant de ces mécanismes, et des décisions canadiennes rendues jusqu'à maintenant, peuvent aider à formuler des règles correspondant à l'appréciation canadienne de la règle de courtoisie et cherchant à prévenir les abus sans compromettre la justice.

Summary

Parallel Proceedings — Converging Views? The *Westec* Appeal

The flexibility afforded by the new rules in Canada for jurisdiction and judgments creates opportunities for opposing parties to commence parallel proceedings against one another in different jurisdictions. As litigants begin to take advantage of these opportunities, Canadian courts are faced with the special concerns associated with parallel proceedings and the potential for inconsistent results. Various mechanisms have been developed in other legal systems for addressing these concerns but some of these mechanisms do not prevent the "race to judgment" or the "race to file." A review of the experiences with these mechanisms, and of the Canadian decisions to date, can help in formulating rules that accord with the Canadian appreciation of comity and that seek to prevent abuse without compromising fairness.

Notes and Comments /
Notes et commentaires

The Nova Scotia-Newfoundland Dispute over the Limits of Their Respective Offshore Areas

INTRODUCTION

It has been ten years since one of Canada's maritime boundaries has been the subject of arbitration before an ad hoc arbitral tribunal. This time, however, the dispute is not between Canada and another state. It is between the province of Nova Scotia and the province of Newfoundland and Labrador. The disputed area is thought to contain valuable mineral resources and, therefore, the resolution of the dispute is important not only for Newfoundland and Labrador and Nova Scotia, but also for the numerous oil and gas companies that are keen to know which province has jurisdiction and to authorize exploration and exploitation in the area.

On May 17, 2001, a tribunal, which was established by the federal minister of natural resources, issued its decision in Phase I of the *Arbitration between Newfoundland and Labrador and Nova Scotia Concerning Portions of the Limits of Their Offshore Areas as Defined in the Canada-Nova Scotia Offshore Petroleum Resources Accord Implementation Act and the Canada-Newfoundland Atlantic Accord Implementation Act.* For the first phase, the tribunal was requested to "determine whether the line dividing the respective offshore areas of the Province of Newfoundland and Labrador and the Province of Nova Scotia has been resolved by agreement."[1] Nova Scotia argued that it had been so resolved, while Newfoundland and Labrador argued that it had not. The tribunal determined that the line had not been

---

[1] Terms of Reference, Article 3.2(i), which can be accessed at <www.nrcan.gc. ca:8o/css/imb/hqlib/200040eb.htm> and <www.gov.nf.ca/mines&en/dispute/ references.htm> [hereinafter Terms of Reference].

resolved by agreement. This decision meant that it was necessary to proceed with Phase II of the arbitration, in which the tribunal is to "determine how in the absence of any agreement the respective offshore areas of the Province of Newfoundland and Labrador and the Province of Nova Scotia shall be determined."[2] A decision in Phase II is expected to be made in 2002. This note explains the dispute settlement mechanism, reviews the parties' arguments, and summarizes the tribunal's decision in Phase I.

THE DISPUTE SETTLEMENT MECHANISM AND THE UNDERLYING LEGISLATION

The dispute settlement mechanism for the Nova Scotia-Newfoundland[3] dispute has its origins in the federal and provincial legislation that implements the Canada-Nova Scotia Offshore Petroleum Resources Accord (Canada-Nova Scotia Accord)[4] and the Memorandum of Agreement between the Government of Canada and the Government of the Province of Newfoundland on Offshore Petroleum Resource Management and Revenue Sharing (Canada-Newfoundland Accord).[5] These bilateral accords, which were signed in 1985 (Canada-Newfoundland) and 1986 (Canada-Nova Scotia), establish administrative management and revenue-sharing regimes between the federal government and the provinces for oil and gas exploration in the offshore regions. The dispute settlement provision in the legislation that implements these accords authorizes the federal minister of natural resources to refer disputes between provinces relating to the limits of their respective offshore areas to an arbitral tribunal. The legislation also provides that the federal minister shall determine the membership of the arbitral tribunal and the dispute settlement procedures following consultation with the provinces concerned in the dispute. In addition, the legislation stipulates that the arbitrator shall apply the principles of the international law governing maritime

---

[2] *Ibid.* at Article 3.2 (ii).

[3] For the remainder of this note, the province of Newfoundland and Labrador will be referred to either as the "province of Newfoundland" or "Newfoundland."

[4] Canada-Nova Scotia Offshore Petroleum Resources Accord," dated August 26, 1986, Nova Scotia Annex 2 [hereinafter Canada-Nova Scotia Accord].

[5] Memorandum of Agreement between the Government of Canada and the Government of the Province of Newfoundland on Offshore Petroleum Resource Management and Revenue Sharing," dated February 11, 1985, Nova Scotia Annex 1 [hereinafter Canada-Newfoundland Accord].

boundary delimitation with such modifications as the circumstances require.[6]

The dispute in question relates only to resources of the seabed and subsoil and does not involve jurisdiction over fisheries resources.

TERMS OF REFERENCE

The precise origin of the inter-provincial dispute is subject to debate between the disputing provinces. What can be confirmed, however, is the fact that Ralph Goodale, the minister of natural resources, wrote to the premiers of Nova Scotia and Newfoundland and Labrador on January 7, 1998, requesting that negotiations begin with a view to resolving the issue of the offshore boundary. Three years later, with the dispute still unresolved, the minister wrote to the premiers indicating that he had decided to establish an arbitration process in order to resolve the dispute. Attached to the letter were the Terms of Reference for the arbitration process.

The tribunal is composed of the Honourable Gérard La Forest,[7] who serves as chairman, Leonard Legault, Q.C.,[8] and James

---

[6] For the Canada-Nova Scotia Accord, the dispute settlement provision is found in section 48 of the federal implementing legislation (Canada-Nova Scotia Offshore Petroleum Resources Accord Implementation Act, S.C.1988, c. 28) and in section 49 in the provincial implementing legislation (Canada-Nova Scotia Offshore Petroleum Resources Accord Implementation (Nova Scotia) Act, S.N.S.1987, c. 3). The provisions are almost identical, save for the reference in the provincial legislation to the condition that both the federal and provincial governments are unable to bring about a resolution of the dispute within a reasonable time prior to its referral to arbitration, while the federal legislation refers only to the federal government's failure to bring about a resolution.

For the Canada-Newfoundland Accord, the dispute settlement provision is found in section 6 of the federal implementing legislation (Canada-Newfoundland Atlantic Accord Implementation Act, S.C. 1987, c. 3) and in section 6 of the provincial implementing legislation (Canada-Newfoundland Atlantic Accord Implementation Newfoundland Act, R.S.N. 1990, c. C-2). Both provisions are virtually identical.

[7] Justice Gérard La Forest served on the Supreme Court of Canada from 1985 to 1997.

[8] Leonard Legault is a leading expert in maritime boundary delimitation. He served as agent and counsel for Canada in the *Case Concerning Delimitation of the Maritime Boundary in the Gulf of Maine Area*, [1984] I.C.J. Rep. 246 [hereinafter *Gulf of Maine*], before the International Court of Justice in The Hague. He also served as counsel in the *Canada-France Maritime Boundary Delimitation* case [hereinafter *Canada-France Maritime Boundary* case], before an ad hoc arbitral tribunal.

Crawford.[9] The mandate of the tribunal is set out in Article 3 of the Terms of Reference, which provide as follows:

Applying the principles of international law governing maritime boundary delimitation with such modifications as the circumstances require, the tribunal shall determine the line dividing the respective offshore areas of the Province of Newfoundland and Labrador and the Province of Nova Scotia, as if the parties were states subject to the same rights and obligations as the Government of Canada at all relevant times.

The mandate requires the tribunal to determine the line dividing the respective offshore areas in two phases. In the first phase, the tribunal must determine "whether the line dividing the respective offshore areas of the Province of Newfoundland and Labrador and the Province of Nova Scotia has been resolved by agreement."[10] In the second phase, the tribunal shall determine "how in the absence of any agreement the line dividing the respective offshore areas of the Province of Newfoundland and Labrador and the Province of Nova Scotia shall be determined."[11] The government of Nova Scotia appointed L. Yves Fortier[12] as its agent for the arbitration. The government of Newfoundland and Labrador appointed Donald M. McRae[13] as its agent for the arbitration.

The Terms of Reference set out the procedure for Phase I, calling for the simultaneous exchange of memorials, followed by a simultaneous exchange of counter-memorials and an oral hearing.[14] Memorials were exchanged on December 1, 2000. Counter-memorials were exchanged on February 15, 2001. The oral hearing took place in Fredericton, New Brunswick, on March 12-20, 2001.

[9] James Crawford is Whewell Professor of International Law at Cambridge University.

[10] Terms of Reference, *supra* note 1 at Article 3.2(i).

[11] *Ibid.* at Article 3.2(ii).

[12] L. Yves Fortier is chairman of the law firm Ogilvy Renault. He has served as counsel for Canada in the *Gulf of Maine* case and the *Canada-France Maritime Boundary* case, and as judge ad hoc on the International Court of Justice in *Case Concerning Maritime Boundary Delimitation and Territorial Questions between Qatar and Bahrain*, March 16, 2001, I.C.J. General List No. 87, see <www.cij-icj.org>.

[13] Donald M. McRae is a professor of international law at the University of Ottawa. He has served as counsel for Canada in the *Gulf of Maine* case and the *Canada-France Maritime Boundary* case, and was deputy agent for Canada in the *Dispute Concerning Filleting within the Gulf of St. Lawrence by the French Trawlers Referred to in Article 4(b) of the Fisheries Agreement between Canada and France of March 27, 1972.*

[14] Terms of Reference, *supra* note 1 at Article 4.

The decisions of the tribunal are final and binding on the disputing parties and on the government of Canada.[15]

THE ARGUMENTS OF THE PARTIES

THE APPLICABLE LAW

Nova Scotia's Position

A preliminary issue arose concerning the applicable law for Phase I. Nova Scotia was of the view that the tribunal was required to apply international law, while Newfoundland argued that the question that was raised in Phase I (whether the line had been resolved by agreement) had to be answered through the application of domestic Canadian law.

Nova Scotia posited that the Terms of Reference required the tribunal to answer the question that was raised in Phase I and, if necessary, the question raised in Phase II (in the absence of an agreed line, how the line should be determined) by applying the "principles of international law governing maritime boundary delimitation."[16] Nova Scotia relied on what it claimed were the plain words of the Terms of Reference, which state in Article 3.1 that "[t]he Tribunal shall, in accordance with Article 3.1 above, determine the line dividing the respective offshore areas of the Province of Newfoundland and Labrador and the Province of Nova Scotia in two phases." Article 3.1 stipulates the following edict:

> Applying the principles of international law governing maritime boundary delimitation with such modifications as the circumstances require, the Tribunal shall determine the line dividing the respective offshore areas of the Province of Newfoundland and Labrador and the Province of Nova Scotia, as if the parties were states subject to the same rights and obligations as the Government of Canada at all relevant times.

Nova Scotia argued that the principles of international law governing maritime boundary delimitation, beginning with the Truman Proclamation and confirmed by the 1958 Convention on the Continental Shelf and subsequent case law,[17] called for

---

[15] *Ibid.* at Article 14.

[16] Nova Scotia Memorial, p. I-13, para. 29.

[17] Truman Proclamation No. 2667, Policy of the United States with Respect to the Natural Resources of the Subsoil and Sea Bed of the Continental Shelf, September 28, 1945, 10 Federal Register 12303 (October 2, 1945); Convention on the Continental Shelf, April 29, 1958, 499 U.N.T.S. 312; *North Sea* Cases, [1969] I.C.J. Rep. 3; *Case Concerning Maritime Delimitation in the Area between Greenland*

delimitation by agreement, followed by arbitration in the event that negotiations to reach an agreement were to fail. According to Nova Scotia, therefore, the international law governing the conclusion and interpretation of international agreements is part and parcel of the principles of international law governing maritime boundary delimitation.

In other words, Nova Scotia was of the view that in Phase I the tribunal had to consider whether, on the facts of the case, two sovereign states would be found to have concluded a binding agreement at international law regarding the boundary dividing their offshore areas. If Phase II were necessary, the tribunal would also be required to apply the principles of international law governing maritime boundary delimitation in order to determine the boundary line.

Newfoundland's Position

Newfoundland considered that the Terms of Reference provided no specific guidance on the applicable law for the question in Phase I. In Newfoundland's view, since any agreement resolving the boundary must be an agreement that is binding between two provinces, the applicable law must be the law that governs whether or not the provinces have entered into a legally binding agreement. Since there are no rules of international law for determining whether the provinces have resolved an issue by agreement, the applicable law for Phase I was domestic Canadian law.

Newfoundland drew attention to the words "with such modifications as the circumstances require" in Article 3.1 of the Terms of Reference in order to support its theory that the terms required only qualified application of the "principles of international law governing maritime boundary delimitation." It protested that the retroactive application of a system of law that could not possibly have been in the minds of the parties at the time that the alleged agreement was concluded would be absurd and unjust. Newfoundland also argued that it was incorrect to assume, as Nova Scotia had done, that by requiring the application of "principles of international law governing maritime boundary delimitation," the Terms of Reference automatically intended an incorporation of a separate body of law governing the conclusion of treaties.

With respect to the question in Phase II, which concerned the

---

and Jan Mayen, [1993] I.C.J. Rep. 38; and *Guinea — Guinea Bissau Maritime Delimitation,* 77 I.L.R. 636, Award of February 15, 1985.

delimitation of the respective offshore areas, Newfoundland indicated that it had to be resolved with reference to the international law of maritime boundaries because Canadian domestic law contains no rules on the delimitation of maritime boundaries.

A BINDING AGREEMENT OR A CONDITIONAL PROPOSAL?

Nova Scotia's Position

Nova Scotia argued that the line dividing the offshore areas of Nova Scotia and Newfoundland was resolved by agreement in 1964 and that the line had been relied upon by the disputing provinces (and others) since that time. According to Nova Scotia, on September 30, 1964, while at a conference of provincial premiers, the premiers of Nova Scotia, Newfoundland, New Brunswick, and Prince Edward Island agreed on inter-provincial boundaries that divided their respective offshore areas, adjacent to their coasts, for the entire continental shelf. Shortly thereafter, the province of Québec joined in the agreement. Nova Scotia claimed that this agreement of the four Atlantic provinces was recorded in numerous documents, including a communiqué that was released at the conclusion of the premiers' conference. The communiqué referred to a document (entitled *Notes re: Boundaries*[18] that described the agreed boundaries by metes and bounds as well as to an attached map that depicted the agreed boundaries. Québec's adherence was evidenced in an exchange of letters between the premiers.

The *Notes re: Boundaries* describes the Nova Scotia-Newfoundland section of the boundary as follows:

> From this mutual corner [the three-way boundary between Quebec, Nova Scotia and Newfoundland] the boundary with Newfoundland runs southeasterly to the midpoint between St. Paul Island (Nova Scotia) and Cape Ray (Newfoundland); thence to a point midway between Flint Island (Nova Scotia) and Grand Bruit (Newfoundland); then southeasterly to International waters.

Newfoundland's boundary with Nova Scotia is described by the case as follows:

> From the above common point [the tri-junction point with Nova Scotia and Quebec], southeasterly to the midpoint between St. Paul Island and Cape Ray; thence southeasterly to the midpoint between Flint Island and Grand Bruit; thence S.E. to International waters.[19]

---

[18] *Notes re: Boundaries,* Nova Scotia Annex 31, p. 21.

[19] *Ibid.* at 25.

The map illustrates the inter-provincial boundaries in the Gulf of St. Lawrence (a line following mid-points between opposing coastal features) and in the offshore beyond the gulf to an undefined point in the Laurentian Channel.

Nova Scotia argued that what it called the 1964 Agreement followed several years of inter-provincial discussions relating to provincial claims to ownership of the offshore. The Atlantic provinces believed that the provinces owned the submarine lands under the continental shelf that stretched from the shore to a distance of about 200 miles.[20] According to Nova Scotia, the provinces determined that they should first of all agree among themselves as to their respective offshore boundaries, after which they would seek recognition from the federal agreement that the submarine mineral resources belonged to them. The boundary was, according to Nova Scotia, established for any and all purposes. In other words, it would bind the provinces together among themselves, regardless of the eventual form of jurisdictional settlement that they secured with the federal government.

The provinces presented their agreement to the government of Canada at a federal-provincial conference on October 14-15, 1964. Premier Stanfield of Nova Scotia, speaking on behalf of the Atlantic provinces in the presence of the other premiers, declared that the provinces were entitled to ownership and control of the submarine minerals on legal and equitable grounds and confirmed the agreement on boundaries as described in the *Notes re: Boundaries* and as depicted on the aforementioned map. The *Notes re: Boundaries* and the map were appended to the Atlantic provinces' joint submission (see Figure 1). Furthermore, as Nova Scotia maintained, the provinces demonstrated their intent to be bound by the boundary agreement in requesting the federal government to give effect to the boundaries that were thus agreed by legislation pursuant to section 3 of the 1871 British North America Act.[21]

---

[20] The provinces relied on a legal opinion prepared by Gérard La Forest, who was then a law professor at the University of New Brunswick. It was not until 1967, in the *Reference re: Offshore Mineral Rights of British Columbia*, [1967] S.C.R. 792, and subsequently in *Reference re: the Seabed and Subsoil of the Continental Shelf Offshore Newfoundland*, [1984] 1 S.C.R. 86, that the Supreme Court of Canada determined that jurisdiction over the continental shelf rests with the federal government.

[21] Section 3 states that "[t]he Parliament of Canada may, with the consent of the Legislature of any Province . . . increase, diminish, or otherwise alter the limits of such Province, upon such terms and conditions as may be agreed to by the said Legislature." British North American Act, 34-35 Vict. c. 28 (U.K.).

In 1968, the East Coast provinces formed the Joint Mineral Resources Committee (JMRC) to facilitate continuing cooperation in mineral resource management both in the offshore and within provincial land boundaries. Provincial Cabinet ministers represented their respective provinces on the committee. The JMRC in turn formed a technical committee to fix the precise technical coordinates of the offshore boundaries by plotting the latitude and longitude of the turning points along the line. It was necessary to fix the precise coordinates in order to facilitate the granting and precise location of offshore exploration permits. Nova Scotia explained that it was typical of the two-stage process in boundary delimitation, whereby the technical plotting of coordinates follows the initial determination that sets out the principles according to which the boundary is to be demarcated.

The technical committee prepared the list of coordinates, referring to the *Notes re: Boundaries* and the joint submission of October 1964 and prepared a map depicting the boundary line joined by the turning points. Each of the Atlantic provinces verified that the coordinates conformed to the verbal description of the boundary agreed in 1964. The technical committee submitted the results of its work to the JMRC in January 1969.

The last turning point, number 2017, was located at the last midpoint named in the *Notes re: Boundaries,* namely the midpoint between Flint Island (Nova Scotia) and Grand Bruit (Newfoundland). Hence, the technical committee's line did not extend as far seaward as the line depicted on the 1964 map, which extended some eighty-five nautical miles farther seaward. Nova Scotia explained that this discrepancy was in keeping with the 1964 agreement boundary and the mandate of the committee, which was solely to plot the turning points of the 1964 agreed boundary. The *Notes re: Boundaries* described the last segment of the line as continuing beyond the last midpoint "to International waters."[22] According to Nova Scotia, these words indicated that there were no turning points to be precisely located after Point 2017.

Nova Scotia cited various documents (provincial, which included Newfoundland, as well as federal sources) in support of its position that the coordinates plotted for the turning points of the 1964 boundary and the map depicting them were approved by the East Coast premiers at a Conference of First Ministers of

---

[22] *Notes re: Boundaries, supra* note 18 at 21 and 25.

the Atlantic Provinces and Québec in June 1972 and that were in turn confirmed by the prime minister. In addition, according to Nova Scotia, Newfoundland's agreement was stated clearly by its premier at the time, Frank Moores, in a speech to the Newfoundland House of Assembly the day following the premiers' conference.

Nova Scotia argued that it had consistently acted in good faith by relying on, respecting, and applying the boundary that had been established in the 1964 agreement, be it in its subsequent negotiations and agreements with the federal government, in its own legislation defining the limits of its offshore, and in the issuance of exploration permits to oil companies from 1965 to the present day, which conformed precisely to the Nova Scotia-Newfoundland boundary line. Several permit maps were filed with the tribunal and illustrated the boundary line in the pleadings in support of these claims. In addition, Nova Scotia referred to the similar conduct of Prince Edward Island, New Brunswick, and Québec, which it claimed confirmed the fact that the boundary had been agreed definitively by the East Coast provinces. Nova Scotia filed official provincial maps, exploration permits, and legislation for the three other provinces that reflected the 1964 boundary.

Nova Scotia also sought to demonstrate Newfoundland's adherence to, and respect for, the 1964 boundary in its permit practice with illustrations of permits issued by Newfoundland that Nova Scotia claimed conformed to the 1964 boundary in the Gulf of Saint Lawrence and in the offshore area between the two disputing provinces. Attention was also drawn to Newfoundland's 1977 petroleum regulations that, according to Nova Scotia, recognized the applicability of offshore boundaries with the other provinces. Nova Scotia also argued that Newfoundland had never disavowed the 1964 agreement, not even during the negotiations of the Canada-Newfoundland Accord, until the commencement of the current dispute.

As a matter of law, Nova Scotia argued that international law does not require any particular form for the conclusion of a binding agreement. Such an agreement may be made orally or in writing and may be signed or unsigned.[23] Nova Scotia claimed that the form of the 1964 agreement was irrelevant and that the contemporaneous

---

[23] Nova Scotia cited the *Legal Status of Eastern Greenland* (1933), P.C.I.J. (Ser. A/B) No. 53; *Nuclear Tests Cases (Australia v. France, New Zealand v. France)*, [1974] I.C.J. Rep. 253; *Aegean Sea Continental Shelf Case*, [1978] I.C.J. Rep. 3; and *Case Concerning the Temple of Preah Vihear (Preliminary Objections)*, [1961] I.C.J. Rep. 17 [hereinafter *Temple of Preah Vihear*].

evidence of it in various documents was considerable, demonstrating conclusively that such an agreement was concluded.

Nova Scotia asserted that the fundamental requirement for concluding a binding agreement at international law is intent to be bound, and the parties' intent to be bound was evidenced in the various documents it filed with the tribunal, including the joint submission to the federal-provincial conference of first ministers when the provinces demonstrated their firm resolve by requesting the federal government to confirm the provinces' agreed boundary through legislation pursuant to Section 3 of the 1871 British North American Act. Furthermore, the object and purpose of the boundary agreement, namely to provide the East Coast provinces with the certainty they desired for negotiations with the federal government regarding jurisdiction and for granting exploration rights to industry, demonstrated the provinces' intent to create mutually binding obligations regarding their boundaries.

Nova Scotia also relied on the provinces' subsequent conduct in order to reinforce its conclusion that the parties intended to be bound by the 1964 agreement, arguing that international law recognizes that subsequent conduct provides highly reliable evidence as to the intention of the parties at an earlier time.[24] Nova Scotia claimed that its conduct subsequent to the 1964 agreement in federal provincial negotiations, legislation as well as in its oil and gas regime demonstrated a consistent application of, and reliance on, the boundary established in that agreement.

In addition, Nova Scotia claimed that Newfoundland's conduct, both active and passive, was evidence of Newfoundland's intention to be bound by the 1964 boundary. The active conduct included the province's participation in the lead up and conclusion of the agreement in September 1964, the joint submission to the federal government in October 1964, the work of the JMRC and the technical committee in 1968-69, the approval of the technical coordinates in 1972, the issuance of exploration permits that respected the 1964 boundary in the 1960s and 1970s, and the promulgation of regulations recognizing the applicability of the offshore boundaries with the other provinces. Nova Scotia also relied on what it termed Newfoundland's passive conduct, claiming that Newfoundland failed to object to the boundary on the many occasions when

---

[24] Nova Scotia relied, *inter alia*, on *Case Concerning Kasikili/Sedudu Island (Botswana v. Namibia)*, [1999] I.C.J. General List No. 98; *Case Concerning the Temple of Preah Vihear (Merits)*, [1962] I.C.J. Rep. 6; *International Status of Southwest Africa*, [1950] I.C.J. Rep. 128.

it was declared, and it never objected to the use of the boundary by the other provinces in federal-provincial negotiations, legislation, and permit issuance.

Nova Scotia applied the principles of international law in order to confirm that the 1964 boundary extended well beyond the Gulf of St. Lawrence in a southeasterly direction and on an azimuth of 135 degrees to the outer limits of the continental shelf. It argued that the ordinary meaning of the language used in the various documents evidencing the 1964 agreement, including the communiqué, the joint submission, and subsequent federal and provincial documents, referred to areas comprising the entire continental shelf. Nova Scotia also reasoned that, given the object and purpose of the boundary agreement (which was to provide the East Coast provinces with the certainty they desired for negotiations with the federal government regarding offshore jurisdiction and for granting exploration rights to industry), the provinces would have divided among themselves the entire continental shelf under claim by Canada at the time, which they knew extended some 300 nautical miles from the shores of Newfoundland. Moreover, the subsequent conduct of the parties to the agreement, which included issuing exploration permits that conformed with the 1964 line and that extended as far as 300 miles from shore, confirmed that the boundary extended to the limits of the continental shelf jurisdiction.

Finally, Nova Scotia claimed that the principles of acquiescence and estoppel constituted alternative grounds for finding that the boundary between Nova Scotia and Newfoundland had been resolved by agreement. Nova Scotia sought to demonstrate that Newfoundland made numerous representations at the highest level of government in words and deeds regarding its acceptance of the 1964 boundary. Moreover, according to Nova Scotia, Newfoundland raised no objection to the boundary that was established in 1964, to the technical delineation of the agreed boundary in 1968-69, to the approval of the technical delineation by the premiers in 1972, to the consistent use by Nova Scotia and the other provinces of the 1964 boundary in issuing oil and gas permits, or to the use of the Newfoundland-Nova Scotia boundary in federal-provincial agreements and in legislation implementing these agreements.

Nova Scotia claimed that Newfoundland was estopped from denying the existence of the 1964 agreed boundary. Nova Scotia claimed to have relied on Newfoundland's representations, undertaking legal obligations with private companies in the issuance of oil and gas permits, and in limiting its offshore claims in negotiations with the federal government to the area delimited by the agreed boundary.[25]

Nova Scotia submitted that the tribunal should declare:

- that the line dividing the respective offshore areas of the province of Newfoundland and Labrador and the province of Nova Scotia had been resolved by agreement;
- that this finding determined the line dividing the respective offshore areas of the province of Newfoundland and Labrador and the province of Nova Scotia in accordance with Article 3 of the Terms of Reference;
- that the delineation of that line was correctly set out in the Canada-Nova Scotia Offshore Petroleum Resources Implementation Act as it relates to the limits of the offshore area of Nova Scotia along the boundary with Newfoundland as follows:
  - from a point at latitude 47°25'28" and longitude 60°24'17", being approximately the midpoint between Cape Anguille (Newfoundland) and Point de l'Est (Québec);
  - thence southeasterly in a straight line to a point at latitude 47°25'28" and longitude 59°43'33", being approximately the midpoint between St. Paul Island (Nova Scotia) and Cape Ray (Newfoundland);
  - thence southeasterly in a straight line to a point at latitude 46°54'50" and longitude 59°00'30", being approximately the midpoint between Flint Island (Nova Scotia) and Grand Bruit (Newfoundland);
  - thence southeasterly in a straight line and on an azimuth of 135°00'00" to the outer edge of the continental margin.
- that the federal minister of natural resources should have recommended that the governor-in-council, by regulation made pursuant to sections 5(1), 6(5), and 7 of the Canada-Newfoundland Atlantic Accord Implementation Act, prescribe the line dividing the parties' respective offshore areas for the purpose of paragraph (a) of the definition of "offshore area" in section 2 of the Canada-Newfoundland Atlantic Accord Implementation Act, in accordance with the delineation set out in the relevant parts of Schedule I to the Canada-Nova Scotia Offshore Petroleum Resources Implementation Act.

---

[25] Nova Scotia relied, *inter alia*, on *Temple of Preah Vihear, supra* note 23, and *Case Concerning the Continental Shelf (Libyan Arab Jamahiriya* v. *Chad)*, [1994] I.C.J. Rep. 6.

Newfoundland's Position

Newfoundland denied that the line dividing the respective off-shore areas of the province of Newfoundland and Labrador and the province of Nova Scotia had been resolved by agreement. Newfoundland argued that no inter-provincial agreement was ever drawn up or executed and that Nova Scotia had not produced any evidence to support its theory that a boundary had been agreed in 1964 or at any other time.

Newfoundland's appreciation of the historical record was profoundly different from Nova Scotia's, even though both parties relied on many of the same documents. In Newfoundland's view, the September 30, 1964 meeting of Atlantic premiers produced nothing more than a political consensus on tentative boundaries that was inextricably linked to provincial ownership of offshore mineral resources. Provincial agreement on the boundary was predicated on federal acceptance and recognition of provincial offshore jurisdiction and, hence, the boundary agreement could not survive federal rejection of the ownership proposal.

The provinces presented their proposal to the federal government at the federal-provincial conference in October 1964 and requested the federal government to give effect to the tentative boundaries through the adoption of federal legislation pursuant to Section 3 of the 1871 British North America Act. Newfoundland argued that the proposal for provincial ownership of the offshore was rejected, that no legislation was prepared, and that the negotiating proposal, including the 1964 boundary lines, came to nothing.

Newfoundland pointed to numerous documents (federal and provincial) in order to support its contention that the "1964 initiative" was nothing more than a negotiating proposal and that no inter-provincial agreement on boundaries was ever achieved. Newfoundland explained that the work of the technical committee of the JMRC, which had resulted in the list of coordinates for the turning points described in the *Notes re: Boundaries* as well as a map depicting those turning points, had not resulted in an agreement because it was never incorporated as intended in an inter-provincial agreement for approval by the provincial ministers. According to Newfoundland, it would have been inconceivable for the provincial premiers to commit their provinces on a matter of such fundamental importance as maritime boundaries without reference to the legislature. For Newfoundland, the subsequent approval of the turning points at the East Coast premiers conference in 1972 constituted a renewed proposal on provincial boundaries that was made in connection with the objective of provincial jurisdiction over the offshore. However, it was not a binding agreement, and it was again rejected by the federal government.

Newfoundland considered that Nova Scotia's contention regarding the extent of the line to the outer edge of the continental margin and the direction of the line on an azimuth of 135 degrees was without any foundation in the historical record. If anything, the 1964 and 1972 proposals focused on the Gulf of St. Lawrence, without any precision on the direction or extent of the line in the outer area beyond Cabot Strait.

Although maintaining that international law did not govern the inquiry in Phase I, Newfoundland agreed with Nova Scotia that no particular formalities are required at international law for the conclusion of an international agreement. Both parties also stressed that intent is fundamental to the conclusion of a legally binding agreement at international law. In Newfoundland's submission, there was no evidence of such intent, hence no legally binding agreement. Newfoundland posited that intent is a question of fact and, therefore, any examination of the conclusion of an agreement between Newfoundland and Nova Scotia would have to be considered in the light of the Canadian constitutional framework that governed the parties at the time. Newfoundland reasoned that the parties could not possibly have intended legal consequences that could not have resulted from their conduct within the legal framework in which they were operating. According to Newfoundland, legally binding inter-governmental agreements were always subject to supervening implementing legislation[26] and other requirements, such as a degree of formality. Since expectations and perspectives at the time were necessarily based upon this framework, it could not be established on the facts that there was the necessary intent on the part of Newfoundland or Nova Scotia to enter into a legally binding agreement on the basis of vague, conditional undertakings that had been made through speeches or communiqués by politicians, which were never implemented through legislation. Newfoundland pointed out that there was no precedent for an inter-governmental agreement constituted without formal

---

[26] Newfoundland relied, *inter alia*, on *Reference re Canada Assistance Plan*, [1991] 2 S.C.R. 525; *South Australia v. The Commonwealth* (1962), 108 C.L.R. 130 (H.C. of A.); and *A.G. Can. v. Higbie*, [1945] S.C.R. 385.

documentation of any kind, especially one designed to create significant legal obligations of an enduring character.

Newfoundland argued that Nova Scotia confused the rules regarding the formation of agreements that focused on the intention of the parties with rules governing the interpretation of agreements that addressed the issues of the ordinary meaning of words used in the agreement, the object and purpose of the agreement, and the subsequent practice of the parties. Newfoundland suggested that such arguments begged the question for they presupposed the existence of an agreement. In any event, in Newfoundland's view, the plain words of the documents that were relied upon by Nova Scotia revealed the tentative nature of the inter-provincial agreement rather than proving Nova Scotia's theory of an agreed line. In addition, Newfoundland regarded the object and purpose of the agreement as an element of a proposal inextricably linked to the provincial objective of securing federal recognition of provincial ownership of the offshore rather than as providing the certainty desired for federal-provincial negotiations or as a necessity in the issuance of exploration permits. Finally, in regard to subsequent practice, Newfoundland denied that practice alone could constitute a legally binding agreement, and, in any event, it felt that the practice did not demonstrate any adherence to a particular offshore boundary.

With respect to the permit practice, Newfoundland dismissed the Nova Scotia practice as being irrelevant and as revealing nothing more than Nova Scotia's desire for authority that it did not have. It also disagreed with Nova Scotia's interpretation of Newfoundland's permit practice, claiming that it did not respect any alleged agreed boundary, and, in support, it filed permit maps of its allegations. In sum, the permit practice did not demonstrate any common intention of the parties to respect a particular line. Newfoundland also dismissed as irrelevant the legislation and permit practice of the other provinces upon which Nova Scotia sought to rely, since those provinces had no role in the arbitration and no interest in the Nova Scotia-Newfoundland offshore boundary.

Newfoundland pointed out that the Canada-Nova Scotia Accord and the Canada-Newfoundland Accord dealt with resource management and revenue sharing — matters that were significantly different from the original objective of securing federal recognition of provincial ownership and jurisdiction over the offshore. Thus, the 1964 initiative was incongruous with the arrangements contemplated in the offshore accords.

Finally, Newfoundland disputed Nova Scotia's arguments founded on the doctrines of acquiescence and estoppel. Newfoundland stated that an agreement is conceptually distinct from acquiescence, the former contemplating an affirmative act and a meeting of the minds, while the latter is founded on passive conduct that does not involve a meeting of the minds or an intention to create an agreement.[27] Newfoundland suggested that a party's practice would be relevant only in determining where a boundary should be and not whether an agreement on a boundary had been concluded. Regarding estoppel, Newfoundland did not consider that the requisite elements, including detrimental reliance, were present. Yet it argued in any event that estoppel, which is founded on good faith and equity, has nothing to do with the existence of an agreed boundary line.[28] According to Newfoundland, territorial rights in Canadian law are fixed by the constitution and can only be altered by legislation. Conduct has no relevance in such matters. Newfoundland submitted that the tribunal should determine that the line dividing the respective offshore areas of Newfoundland and Labrador and Nova Scotia had not been resolved by agreement.

THE AWARD OF THE TRIBUNAL

On May 17, 2001, the tribunal issued a unanimous award finding that the line dividing the respective offshore areas of Newfoundland and Labrador and Nova Scotia had not been resolved by agreement. In the tribunal's view, the parties had at no stage reached a definitive agreement resolving their offshore boundary. The tribunal considered that the boundary agreement was linked to the ownership proposal made to the federal government, which was ultimately rejected, and that it was subject to a process of confirmation or ratification that had never taken place. Moreover, the tribunal did not consider that any agreement that was sufficiently

---

[27] Newfoundland relied, *inter alia*, on *Case Concerning the Rights of United States Nationals in Morocco*, [1952] I.C.J. Rep. 176; *Temple of Preah Vihear, supra* note 23, *North Sea Continental Shelf Cases*, [1969] I.C.J. Rep. 3; and *International Status of South-West Africa*, [1950] I.C.J. Rep. 128.

[28] Newfoundland relied, *inter alia*, on the *Fisheries Case* [1951] I.C.J. Rep. 116; *Delimitation of the Maritime Boundary in the Gulf of Maine Area*, [1984] I.C.J. Rep.246; *Land, Island and Maritime Frontier Dispute (El Salvador v. Honduras) (Judgment, Application to Intervene)*, [1990] I.C. J. Rep. 118; *Case Concerning the Land and Maritime Boundary (Cameroon v. Nigeria) (Preliminary Objection)*, June 11, 1998, I.C.J. General List No. 94.

clear had been concluded so as to permit the determination of the boundary by a process of legal interpretation of the agreement.

THE APPLICABLE LAW IS INTERNATIONAL LAW

The tribunal held that the Terms of Reference clearly required the application of international law in determining the questions before it in both phases of the arbitration.[29] Although the tribunal admitted that there were difficulties in applying the international law of maritime boundary delimitation to the question of whether the provincial premiers had entered into a binding agreement, it rejected Newfoundland's contention that there was something inherently fallacious in applying international law to such circumstances. The tribunal pointed out that the accord legislation — federal and provincial — stipulates the application of international law for resolving boundary issues, and it noted that the rules of international law on maritime boundary delimitation refer, and always have referred, to agreement as the primary mode of delimitation.[30]

The tribunal determined that the governing provision (*"prima facie* at least"[31]), having regard for the requirement that it treat the parties as "states subject at all relevant times to the rights and obligations of Canada"[32] and for the fact that Canada had ratified the 1958 Convention on the Continental Shelf but not the 1982 United Nations Convention on the Law of the Sea,[33] is Article 6 of the 1958 convention. Article 6 stipulates that the boundary of the continental shelf shall be determined in the first place by agreement between the states, and only in the absence of agreement is the boundary to be determined by the principle of equidistance, unless another boundary line is justified by special circumstances.[34] The tribunal explained that agreement as contemplated in Article 6 refers to an agreement that is binding on the parties as a matter of

---

[29] *Arbitration between Newfoundland and Labrador and Nova Scotia Concerning Portions of the Limits of Their Offshore Areas as Defined in the Canada-Nova Scotia Offshore Petroleum Resources Accord Implementation Act and the Canada-Newfoundland Atlantic Accord Implementation Act*, para. 3.24 [hereinafter Award].

[30] *Ibid.* at para. 3.24.

[31] *Ibid.* at para. 3.11.

[32] Terms of Reference, *supra* note 1 at Article 3.1.

[33] United Nations Convention on the Law of the Sea, December 10, 1982, U.N. Doc. A/CONF.62/122.

[34] Award, *supra* note 29 at para. 3.11.

international law. Thus, the fact that two states might be *ad idem* on a boundary would not be sufficient to establish a boundary agreement if the agreement were subject to ratification and that step had not yet been completed.[35]

The tribunal explained that the Terms of Reference did not require it to attribute to the premiers in 1964 or 1972 an intention that they could not have had at the time, namely to enter into a treaty binding at international law. Rather, they called for the application of international law by analogy to the conduct of provincial governments within Canada claiming ownership of, and jurisdiction over, mineral resources of the continental shelf.[36] In any event, the tribunal considered that the essential question was whether the premiers intended to enter into an immediate commitment as to the delimitation of their respective maritime areas and whether these areas already existed in accordance with the provincial claims or would subsequently be conceded under some eventual offshore settlement. This was essentially a question of fact and would arise whether the applicable law was Canadian or international law.[37]

Finally, the tribunal considered that the circumstances required two modifications that were contemplated by the Terms of Reference in order that the principles of international law governing maritime boundary delimitation could be applied to the provinces as envisaged in the accord legislation and the Terms of Reference. First, the tribunal did not consider that it had to look for a provincial intent to be bound under international law. All that was required to conclude a binding agreement was that those individuals authorized to act on behalf of the provinces intended to make an immediate good faith commitment as to their respective boundaries. Second, to the extent that any such commitment was considered conditional upon subsequent confirmation by some other authority, an analogy should be drawn to the situation of a treaty becoming effective only upon ratification.[38]

The tribunal established the following test for making its determination in Phase I:

The Tribunal regards it as sufficient to establish an agreement which resolves the boundary if it can be shown that the premiers definitively

---

[35] *Ibid.* at para. 3.13.

[36] *Ibid.* at para. 3.26.

[37] *Ibid.* at para. 3.28.

[38] *Ibid.* at para. 3.29.

agreed on a boundary separating their respective offshore areas. To establish a definitive agreement, it is necessary to show that the premiers agreed on the boundary:

- for all purposes, and not only for the purpose of presenting to the Federal Government a proposal which was ultimately rejected;
- by an agreement which was not subject to any subsequent process of confirmation or ratification or any analogous process in order to be considered binding; and
- which was sufficiently clear, so as to allow the boundary to be determined by a process of legal interpretation of the agreement.

Only if these conditions were met could it be said that the boundary was "resolved by agreement" for the purposes of the Terms of Reference.[39]

THE LINE HAS NOT BEEN RESOLVED BY AGREEMENT

The tribunal held that the documentary record when considered as a whole did not disclose a definitive agreement resolving the offshore boundaries between Nova Scotia and Newfoundland. The tribunal was of the view that the 1964 joint statement revealed a "clear appreciation that the provincial claims required some form of recognition or acceptance from the federal government" and that it was "predicated on the (eventually unfulfilled) hope of federal recognition of the provincial claim for ownership."[40] The *Notes re: Boundaries* and the accompanying map provided no clear indication that the boundaries described therein "were agreed to conclusively or for any purpose other than that of the provincial claim to ownership."[41] The tribunal held that an ownership claim required further action by the federal and provincial governments in order to give the boundaries legal effect, such action being in the nature of ratification. Moreover, the boundaries suffered from a "lack of precision and attention to detail that were hardly consistent with an intent to enter into a final and binding agreement,"[42] especially in regard to the line to the southeast of Cabot Strait, suggesting that further refinement would be undertaken at a later time.

The tribunal did not find that the 1972 agreement was definitive either because it too was linked to the provincial claim to ownership that was rejected by the federal government.[43] The tribunal

[39] *Ibid.* at para. 3.30.

[40] *Ibid.* at para. 7.2.

[41] *Ibid.* at para. 7.2.

[42] *Ibid.* at para. 7.2.

[43] *Ibid.* at para. 7.5.

confirmed that questions of form are not decisive in concluding binding agreements at international law. However, it considered that such matters are not without relevance. The tribunal opined that

> the absence of a signed document, especially on a matter of importance such as the determination of an international boundary; the use of language which is vague or which does not appear to embody any immediate commitment; a shared understanding between the parties to negotiations that their in principle agreement is to be embodied in some later formal document or is to be subject to some subsequent process of implementation in order to become binding — such factors may together or separately lead to the conclusion that a statement does not constitute a binding agreement under international law.[44]

With respect to the question concerning the relevance of subsequent conduct, the tribunal indicated that evidence subsequent to the adoption of a document may help to establish its status as an agreement at international law. It recalled cases where the International Court of Justice had taken subsequent conduct into account in determining whether the parties considered a particular instrument to be binding or not. However, the tribunal was of the view that generally such evidence has limited probative value. The tribunal explained:

> It is not enough to show that the parties acted consistently with a document claimed by one of them to have the status of a binding agreement, since that may be explicable on other grounds. It would be necessary to show that the conduct was referable to the treaty and was adopted because of the obligations contained in it.[45]

The tribunal did not consider that the subsequent practice of the parties, be it in the context of federal-provincial negotiations after 1972 or in their permit practice, supported the view that the line dividing the offshore had been resolved by agreement. And it made no finding regarding the conduct of the other East Coast provinces, which it considered irrelevant to the question posed in Phase I. The tribunal considered it "a striking feature of the negotiating history"[46] that none of the parties sought to rely on the agreements nor did they make departures from them in order to evoke any protests. However, the tribunal pointed out that the conduct of the parties, in seeking to arrive at a common position on a boundary,

[44] *Ibid.* at para. 3.18.

[45] *Ibid.* at para. 66.

[46] *Ibid.* at para. 7.6.

would be relevant for Phase II of the arbitration, when the question would be one of delimitation rather than whether a binding agreement at international law had been concluded.[47]

In regard to the line southeasterly of Point 2017 (the last point defined by the JMRC technical committee), the tribunal indicated that it was not necessary, under the circumstances, for it to say anything about that part of the line. The tribunal nevertheless commented that even if the joint submission or the 1972 communiqué had amounted to a binding agreement, this agreement would not have resolved the issue of that line given the lack of any rationale or precision as to its direction. Hence, even if the line had been resolved up to Point 2017, it would still have been necessary to proceed to the delimitation phase for that portion of the line.[48]

CONCLUSION

The Terms of Reference provide that all decisions of the tribunal shall be final and binding on the parties and on the government of Canada. Having determined that the line dividing the respective offshore areas of Newfoundland and Labrador and Nova Scotia has not been resolved by agreement, the tribunal has launched Phase II of the arbitration, where it must decide how that line will be determined. The process for the second phase will be similar to the process followed in Phase I, namely a simultaneous exchange of memorials and counter-memorials, followed by an oral hearing. The hearing is scheduled for mid-November 2001. The decision of the tribunal is to be rendered within four months after the hearing, which means sometime in March 2002.

VALERIE HUGHES
Ogilvy Renault, Ottawa

---

[47] *Ibid.* at para. 7.8.
[48] *Ibid.* at para. 7.10.

Sommaire

Le différend entre la Nouvelle-Écosse et Terre Neuve relatif à leurs zones maritimes

Le 17 mai 2001, un tribunal d'arbitrage, établi par le Ministre des ressources naturelles du Canada, a rendu sa décision dans la phase I du différend entre les provinces de la Nouvelle Écosse et de Terre-Neuve et Labrador portant sur la frontière délimitant leurs zones maritimes respectives. Il est demandé au tribunal dans la Phase I de déterminer, selon les principes de droit international régissant la délimitation des frontières maritimes, si la frontière qui divise les zones extra-côtières avait été résolue par accord entre les deux provinces. Cet essai traite du mécanisme de règlement du différend établi en vue de régler le contentieux, présente les arguments des parties devant le tribunal, et résume la décision du tribunal.

Summary

The Nova Scotia-Newfoundland Dispute over the Limits of Their Respective Offshore Areas

On May 17, 2001, an arbitral tribunal established by the minister for natural resources of the government of Canada issued its decision in Phase I of the dispute between the provinces of Nova Scotia and Newfoundland and Labrador over the boundary dividing their respective offshore areas. The tribunal was required to determine in Phase I, in accordance with the principles of international law governing maritime boundary delimitation, whether the line dividing the offshore areas of the two provinces had been resolved by agreement. This note discusses the dispute settlement mechanism set up to deal with this issue and the arguments made by the parties before the tribunal, and it summarizes the decision of the tribunal.

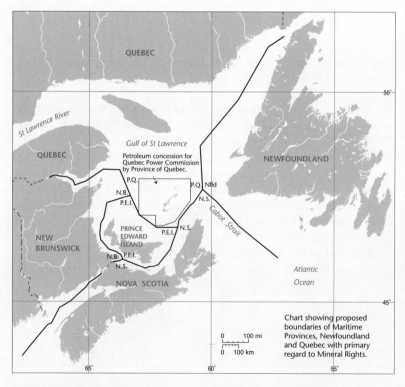

Figure 1. Map attached to joint submission to the federal-
provincial conference of October 14-15, 1964.

L'affaire "*CE — Amiante*" et la nouvelle jurisprudence de l'Organe d'appel de l'OMC concernant les risques à la santé

Introduction

L e 20 mars 2001, l'Organe d'Appel de l'Organisation mondiale du commerce (OMC) rendait sa décision dans l'affaire *Communautés européennes — Mesures affectant l'amiante et les produits en contenant.*[1] Dans ce rapport, l'Organe d'appel clarifie l'état du droit concernant l'obligation de traitement national de l'article III:4 du GATT, les conditions d'application de l'exception pour la protection de la santé prévue à l'article XX, et le rôle que peut jouer le risque à la santé dans l'appréciation de ces deux dispositions fondamentales de l'architecture des règles de l'OMC.

Mettant de côté la littérature et l'approche traditionnelle qui mettaient en opposition les soucis des environnementalistes (et défenseurs de la protection de la santé) et les réalités des marchés, l'Organe d'appel va statuer que les risques à la santé peuvent affecter la détermination de "similarité" entre marchandises (celles à risque et celles sans risque à la santé) qui repose essentiellement sur la relation de concurrence entre ces marchandises nationales ou importées. De ce fait l'Organe d'appel conclura que les risques à la santé peuvent affecter les propriétés physiques des marchandises, de même que les goûts et perceptions de consommateurs concernant ces marchandises, deux des quatre critères qui tous doivent nécessairement faire l'objet d'analyse dans la détermination de

---

Les opinions exprimées dans cette note le sont à titre strictement personnel et ne lient aucunement le Secrétariat de l'OMC ni les Membres de l'OMC.

[1] Voir le Rapport de l'Organe d'appel *Communautés européennes — Mesures affectant l'amiante ou les produits en contenant,* WT/DS135/AB/R, adopté le 5 avril 2001 (*CE — Amiante*).

similarité entre marchandises importées et marchandises d'origine nationale. Les risques à la santé que représentent certaines marchandises peuvent affecter leur situation de concurrence dans un marché spécifique.

Pour la première fois l'Organe d'appel offrira une analyse plus globale de la relation entre l'obligation de traitement national et la possibilité d'invoquer des exceptions, une analyse qu'elle avait débuté dans l'affaire *Corée — Mesures affectant les importations de viande de bœuf fraîche, réfrigérée et congelée*[2] où l'on retrouve la première analyse de l'Organe d'appel du test de "nécessité" de l'article XX du GATT.

LE RAPPORT DE L'ORGANE D'APPEL DANS L'AFFAIRE *CE — AMIANTE*

LES PRINCIPAUX FAITS DE CETTE AFFAIRE

Le Décret français n° 96-1133 relatif à l'interdiction de l'amiante, pris en application du code du travail et du code de la consommation, entré en vigueur le 1er janvier 1997, interdit généralement l'usage en France de l'amiante et des produits contenant des fibres d'amiante mais certaines exceptions sont prévues. Le 25 novembre 1998, le Canada a demandé l'établissement d'un groupe spécial alléguant que le décret violait l'article III:4 du GATT de 1994 et l'article 2 de l'Accord sur les obstacles techniques (l'accord OTC).[3]

LA DISCUSSION DE L'ORGANE D'APPEL

Article III:4 du GATT de 1994 — obligation du traitement national pour les règlements domestiques autres que fiscaux

La partie pertinente de l'article III:4 du GATT de 1994 se lit comme suit:

Les produits du territoire de tout Membre importés sur le territoire de tout autre Membre ne seront pas *soumis à un traitement moins favorable* que le traitement accordé aux *produits similaires* d'origine nationale en ce qui concerne toutes lois, tous règlements ou toutes prescriptions affectant la vente, la mise en vente, l'achat, le transport, la distribution et l'utilisation de ces produits sur le marché intérieur.

[2] Voir le Rapport de l'Organe d'appel *Corée — Mesures affectant les importations de viande de bœuf fraîche, réfrigérée et congelée*, WT/DS161, 169/AB/R, adopté le 10 janvier 2001 (*Corée — Mesures affectant le boeuf*).

[3] Voir le document WT/DS135/4.

Pour faire la preuve d'une violation de l'article III:4, un Membre doit donc prouver que (1) des produits importés *similaires* aux produits nationaux (2) sont traités de façon moins favorable que ces produits nationaux.

Sens de l'expression "produits similaires" au sens de l'article III:4 du GATT de 1994

L'Organe d'appel va d'abord rappeler que l'objectif fondamental de l'article III est d interdire le protectionnisme. "Plus précisément, l'objet de l'article III est de veiller à ce que les mesures intérieures ne soient pas appliquées aux produits importés ou nationaux de manière à protéger la production nationale."[4] Le "principe général" énoncé à l'article III vise à éviter que les Membres n'appliquent des taxes et des réglementations intérieures d'une façon qui fausse le rapport de concurrence, sur le marché, entre les produits nationaux et les produits importés considérés, "de manière à protéger la production nationale."[5] Pour ce faire, il oblige les Membres de l'OMC à garantir l'égalité des conditions de concurrence entre les produits importés et les produits nationaux.

[L']article III ne vise pas à protéger les anticipations concernant un volume d'échanges donné, mais plutôt les anticipations relatives à l'égalité du rapport compétitif entre les produits importés et les produits nationaux...[6]

Ceci amènera l'Organe d'appel à conclure:

Ainsi, une détermination relative au concept de "similarité" énoncé à l'article III:4 est essentiellement une détermination sur la nature et l'importance d'un rapport de concurrence entre et parmi les produits.[7]

Ce test de similarité fondé essentiellement sur la *concurrence* entre marchandises importées et nationales sera toutefois mis en doute par l'opinion particulière d'un membre de l'Organe d'appel.[8] Plus loin l'Organe d'appel ajoutera "S'il *n'*y a *pas* - ou *ne* peut *pas* y

---

[4] Rapport de l'Organe d'appel dans l'affaire *CE — Amiante* au par. 98.

[5] *Idem.*

[6] *Idem,* au par. 97.

[7] *Idem,* au par. 99.

[8] *Idem,* au par. 154: "Ma seconde observation est que la nécessité ou le bien-fondé d'une interprétation "fondamentalement" économique de la "similarité" de produits au titre de l'article III:4 ne me paraît pas exempt d'un doute important. En

avoir - de rapport de concurrence entre les produits, un Membre ne peut intervenir, au moyen d'impositions ou d'une réglementation intérieures, pour protéger la production nationale."[9]

L'Organe d'appel va noter que l'expression "produits similaires" est mentionnée aux paragraphes 2 et 4 de l'article III sur l'obligation du traitement national. L'obligation de traitement national en regard des règlements fiscaux interdit toute taxation supérieure des produits importés par rapport aux produits similaires nationaux et avait fait l'objet d'analyses détaillées dans les affaires *Japon — Boissons alcooliques, Corée — Boissons alcooliques* et *Chili — Boissons alcooliques.*[10] L'article III:2 contient toutefois une deuxième interdiction *vis-à-vis* les marchandises importées *qui sont en concurrence directe* avec les marchandises nationales (même si non similaires aux produits nationaux): elles ne peuvent faire l'objet d'une taxation supérieure si celle-ci a pour objet la protection de la production nationale. L'Organe d'appel va conclure:

Nous reconnaissons toutefois que le lien entre ces deux dispositions est important, parce que la distinction n'est pas nette entre la réglementation fiscale visée par l'article III:2 et la réglementation non fiscale visée par l'article III:4. *Ces deux types de réglementation peuvent souvent être utilisés pour parvenir au même résultat.* Il serait incongru que, à cause d'une différence importante entre les produits visés par ces deux dispositions, les Membres ne puissent pas recourir à une forme de réglementation — par exemple la réglementation fiscale — pour protéger la production nationale de certains produits, mais soient en mesure d'utiliser une autre forme de réglementation — comme la réglementation non fiscale — pour parvenir

---

outre, dans des contextes concrets futurs, la limite entre une conception "fondamentalement" et une conception "exclusivement" économique des "produits similaires" au titre de l'article III:4 pourrait bien se révéler très difficile à déterminer dans la pratique. Il me semble donc plus judicieux de réserver son opinion sur une question aussi importante et même philosophique, qui peut avoir des conséquences imprévisibles, et de le laisser pour un autre appel et un autre jour, voire pour d'autres appels et d'autres jours. Je réserve donc mon opinion à sur ce sujet.

[9] *Idem,* au par. 117.

[10] Rapport de l'Organe d'appel dans l'affaire *Japon — Taxes sur les boissons alcooliques* ("*Japon — Boissons alcooliques*"), WT/DS8, 19, 11/AB/R, adopté le 1er novembre 1996; Rapport de l'Organe d'appel dans l'affaire *Corée — Taxes sur les boissons alcooliques* ("*Corée — Boissons alcooliques*"), WT/DS75, 84/AB/R, adopté le 17 février 1999; rapport de l'Organe d'appel dans l'affaire *Chili — Taxes sur les boissons alcooliques,* ("*Chili — Boissons alcooliques*") WT/DS87, 110/AB/R, adopté le 12 janvier 2000.

au même résultat. Cela irait à l'encontre d'une application cohérente du "principe général" énoncé à l'article III:1 ... [n]ous concluons que le champ des produits visés par l'article III:4, tout en étant plus vaste que le champ couvert par la *première* phrase de l'article III:2, n'est certainement *pas* plus vaste que le champ *combiné* des produits visés par les *deux* phrases de l'article III:2 du GATT de 1994 [par. 99].[11]

Faisant référence à sa théorie de l'accordéon, et conscient du fait que les règlements fiscaux et autres peuvent avoir le même effet protectionniste sur la concurrence entre produits importés et produits nationaux,[12] l'Organe d'appel va conclure que le sens de l'expression "produits similaires" telle qu'utilisé au paragraphe 4 est certes plus large que le sens à être donné aux mêmes termes dans la première phrase de l'article III:2.

Compte tenu de cette différence de libellé, et bien que nous ne devions pas statuer, et que nous ne statuions pas, sur le champ précis des produits visés par l'article III:4, nous concluons que le champ des produits visés par l'article III:4, tout en étant plus vaste que le champ couvert par la *première* phrase de l'article III:2, n'est certainement *pas* plus vaste que le champ *combiné* des produits visés par les *deux* phrases de l'article III:2 du GATT de 1994.[13]

Nous reconnaissons que, en interprétant de cette façon l'expression "produits similaires" telle qu'elle figure à l'article III:4, nous attribuons à cette disposition un champ des produits visés relativement vaste — mais pas plus vaste que celui de l'article III:2.[14]

Sens de l'expression "traitement moins favorable" distincte du traitement différencié

Comme il l'avait déjà clairement établi dans l'affaire *Corée —*

---

[11] Rapport de l'Organe d'appel dans l'affaire *CE — Amiante* au par. 99.

[12] Voir le Rapport de l'Organe d'appel dans l'affaire *CE — Amiante:* "99.... Nous reconnaissons toutefois que le lien entre ces deux dispositions est important, parce que la distinction n'est pas nette entre la réglementation fiscale visée par l'article III:2 et la réglementation non fiscale visée par l'article III:4. Ces deux types de réglementation peuvent souvent être utilisés pour parvenir au même résultat. Il serait incongru que, à cause d'une différence importante entre les produits visés par ces deux dispositions, les Membres ne puissent pas recourir à une forme de réglementation — par exemple la réglementation fiscale — pour protéger la production nationale de certains produits, mais soient en mesure d'utiliser une autre forme de réglementation — comme la réglementation non fiscale — pour parvenir au même résultat."

[13] Rapport de l'Organe d'appel dans l'affaire *CE — Amiante*, au par 99.

[14] *Idem*, au par. 100.

Mesures affectant le Boeuf,[15] l'Organe d'appel rappelle que "Un Membre peut toutefois établir des distinctions entre des produits qui ont été jugés "similaires," sans accorder, pour cela, au groupe des produits *importés* "similaires" un "traitement moins favorable" que celui qui est accordé au groupe des produits *nationaux* "similaires.""[16] C'est donc dire qu'une partie plaignante aux termes de l'article III:4 doit prouver d'abord la similarité entre marchandises importées; marchandises origine nationale; deuxièmement, que les marchandises sont soumises à des traitements différents mais *également*; troisièmement, que ces distinctions imposées sont en fait moins favorables aux marchandises importées qu'aux marchandises nationales. La simple distinction de traitement basée sur l'origine du produit importé n'est en soi pas suffisante pour créer une violation de l'obligation de traitement national.

Détermination de similarité aux termes de l'article III:4

Critères d'analyse de cette similarité

Pour déterminer cette similarité entre marchandises importées et marchandises nationales, l'Organe d'appel rappelle la nécessité de procéder à l'analyse des quatre critères généraux mentionnés dans le Groupe de travail sur les Ajustements fiscaux à la frontière:[17] (i) propriétés, nature et qualité des produits; (ii) utilisations finales des produits; (iii) goûts et habitudes des consommateurs; et (iv) classement tarifaire des produits.[18] Plus tard, l'Organe d'appel

---

[15] Par. 135 du Rapport de l'Organe d'appel dans l'affaire *Corée — Mesures affectant le Boeuf*: "Une différence formelle de traitement entre les produits importés et les produits nationaux similaires n'est donc ni nécessaire, ni suffisante pour démontrer qu'il y a violation de l'article III:4. La question de savoir si les produits importés sont soumis ou non à un traitement "moins favorable" que les produits nationaux similaires devrait plutôt être appréciée en se demandant si une mesure modifie les *conditions de concurrence* au détriment des produits importés sur le marché en question."

[16] Rapport de l'Organe d'appel dans l'affaire *CE — Amiante* au par. 100.

[17] Rapport du Groupe de travail Ajustements fiscaux à la frontière, adopté le 2 décembre 1970, IBDD, S18/105.

[18] Pour l'Organe d'appel ces quatre critères recouvrent quatre catégories de "caractéristiques" qui peuvent être communes aux produits visés: (i) les propriétés physiques des produits; (ii) la mesure dans laquelle les produits peuvent avoir les mêmes utilisations finales ou des utilisations finales semblables; (iii) la mesure dans laquelle les consommateurs perçoivent et considèrent les produits comme d'autres moyens de remplir des fonctions particulières pour satisfaire à un désir

dira que les éléments de preuve relatifs aux deuxième et troisième critères "revêtent une importance particulière au titre de l'article III du GATT de 1994, précisément parce que cette disposition concerne les rapports de concurrence sur le marché."[19]

Pour l'Organe d'appel, ces quatre critères servent de cadre à l'analyse de la "similarité" de produits particuliers au cas par cas et ne sont que des *"outils"* permettant de répertorier et d'examiner les éléments de preuve pertinents. Il ne s'agit pas d'une liste de critères énoncée dans un accord ni d'une liste définitive qui déterminera la qualification juridique des produits. Surtout, l'adoption d'un cadre particulier pour faciliter l'examen des éléments de preuve n'élimine pas le devoir ni la nécessité d'examiner, dans chaque cas, tous les éléments de preuve pertinents.

En outre, même si chaque critère se rapporte en principe à un aspect différent des produits considérés, qui *devrait être examiné séparément,* les différents critères sont interdépendants. Par exemple, les propriétés physiques des produits conditionnent et limitent les utilisations finales que ces produits peuvent avoir. Les perceptions des consommateurs peuvent de même influencer — modifier ou même rendre obsolètes — les utilisations traditionnelles des produits. Le classement tarifaire correspond clairement aux propriétés physiques d'un produit.[20]

Le "Risque à la santé" n'est pas un critère en soi

Dans la présente affaire cette similarité devait être établie entre fibres d'amiante chrysotile (importés) et produits nationaux de substitution d'AVC — fibres d'APV, de cellulose et de verre — et entre produits à base de ciment contenant des fibres chrysotiles (importés) et ceux d'AVC (nationaux). La Communauté européenne contestait la décision du groupe spécial à l'effet que les risques à la santé que peuvent représenter les fibres d'amiante et produits contenant de l'amiante ne sont pas pertinents dans la détermination de la similarité entre fibres d'amiante chrysotile (importés) et produits nationaux d'AVC et entre produits à base de ciment contenant des fibres chrysotiles (importés) et ceux d'AVC (nationaux). L'Organe d'appel va immédiatement déclarer:

---

ou à une demande spécifique; et (iv) la classification internationale des produits à des fins tarifaires. Voir le par.100 du Rapport de l'Organe d'appel dans l'affaire *CE — Amiante.*

[19] Rapport de l'Organe d'appel dans l'affaire *CE — Amiante* au par. 117.

[20] *Idem,* au par.102.

Nous sommes très nettement d'avis que les éléments de preuve relatifs aux risques qu'un produit présente pour la santé peuvent être pertinents dans un examen de la "similarité" au titre de l'article III:4 du GATT de 1994. Nous ne considérons cependant pas que les éléments de preuve relatifs aux risques que les fibres d'amiante chrysotile présentent pour la santé doivent être examinés au titre d'un critère séparé, car nous estimons que cet élément de preuve peut être évalué au titre des critères existants relatifs aux propriétés physiques [premier critère] et aux goûts et habitudes des consommateurs [troisième critère] que nous aborderons ci-après.[21]

Quant à l'argument du Canada à l'effet que l'analyse des risques à la santé dans le contexte de l'article III:4 dénuderait l'article XXb) de son effet (puisque l'article XX autorise les Membres, par exception, à imposer des restrictions commerciales pour des raisons de protection de la santé), l'Organe d'appel semble suggérer une distinction claire entre les situations où le risque à la santé affecte les relations de concurrence entre marchandises importées et domestiques — au terme de l'article III:4 — et les situations où la politique ("policies") d'un Membre peut justifier une mesure par ailleurs incompatible avec les règles du GATT/OMC — au terme de l'article XX.

On peut imaginer l'explication suivante. L'article XX autorise un Membre, pour protéger la santé des personnes, animaux et plantes, à déroger aux règles du GATT même si le risque à la santé ou le problème de santé en question n'affecte pas (n'a pas encore affecté) les consommateurs ou lorsque la discrimination mise en oeuvre par la réglementation contestée (par exemple 10 % de taxe pour les boissons contenant moins de 5 % d'alcool et 25 % de taxe pour les boissons contenant plus de 5 %) ne peut trouver justification dans les distinctions physiques des produits concernés ou dans la concurrence générale entre produits importés et produits nationaux. On peut également concevoir des situations où l'existence du risque n'affecte pas du tout les propriétés physiques des marchandises, ou encore une situation où les consommateurs ne sont pas encore informés de l'existence du risque donc ne réagissent pas aux différents risques. Dans pareil cas, le risque à la santé n'affecterait pas la concurrence et les produits seraient donc similaires au titre de l'article III. La réglementation défavorable aux marchandises importées similaires serait incompatible avec l'article III du GATT. Toutefois, un gouvernement Membre (nouvellement informé d'un risque ou prudent) pourrait décider de protéger la santé de sa population et s'il en respecte les paramètres,

---

[21] *Idem,* au par. 113.

le Membre pourrait invoquer l'article XX pour déroger des règles du GATT.

Il faut également noter que, dans l'affaire sous étude, le risque à la santé était occasionné par la "toxicité" de l'amiante et des fibres d'amiante. De toute évidence, la toxicité est une caractéristique physique des marchandises concernées. Mais le terme "risque à la santé" est beaucoup plus large et couvre des situations où la santé peut être affectée sans être mise en danger, ou du moins à court terme. Dans cette situation, ce critère (le fait qu'il affecte un peu la santé) a peut-être moins d'impact sur la relation de concurrence entre les marchandises importées et nationales.

Tous les critères quoique interdépendants doivent être analysés à chaque fois

À cause de la nature même de l'obligation de l'article III:4, l'Organe d'appel insistera sur le fait "qu'il est important au titre de l'article III:4 de prendre en compte les éléments de preuve qui indiquent s'il y a — ou pourrait y avoir — un rapport de concurrence sur le marché entre les produits considérés, et dans quelle mesure."[22] À plusieurs reprises, l'Organe d'appel va réitérer que *chacun* de ces quatre critères doit être examiné séparément — et tous doivent l'être — pour déterminer la similarité entre marchandises importées et domestiques.[23] L'opinion particulière d'un membre de l'Organe d'appel mettra toutefois en doute la nécessité de toujours procéder à une analyse de chacun de ces critères.[24]

---

[22] *Idem*, au par. 103.

[23] *Idem*, aux par. 109, 111, 113, 120, 121 et 145.

[24] *Idem*, aux par. 152 et 153: "152 … J'estime en outre que cette qualification définitive peut et devrait être établie même en l'absence d'éléments de preuve relatifs aux deux autres critères (catégories de "caractéristiques potentiellement communes") des utilisations finales et des goûts et habitudes des consommateurs, appliqués dans l'affaire *Ajustements fiscaux à la frontière*. Il m'est difficile d'imaginer quels éléments de preuve relatifs aux rapports de concurrence économique tels qu'ils ressortent des utilisations finales et des goûts et habitudes des consommateurs pourraient l'emporter sur le caractère incontestablement mortel des fibres d'amiante chrysotile comparées aux fibres d'ACV lorsqu'elles sont inhalées par des êtres humains, et réduire à néant ce caractère, obligeant de ce fait à qualifier de "similaires" les fibres d'amiante chrysotile et les fibres d'ACV" (153).

Je ne suggère pas par là que *tout* type ou degré de risque pour la santé que présente un produit donné contredirait *a priori* une constatation établissant la "similarité" entre ce produit et un autre au titre de l'article III:4 du GATT de 1994. La suggestion est très étroite et se limite seulement aux circonstances

Propriétés physiques

Puis l'Organe d'appel va vérifier l'examen fait par le groupe spécial de la relation de concurrence entre marchandises importées et marchandises nationales eu égard à chacun des quatre critères identifiés. Il aborde d'abord le critère des caractéristiques physiques. Il conclura que le caractère cancérogène de l'amiante est crucial pour établir que les propriété physiques des fibres d'amiante chrysotile (importées) sont très différentes de celles des produits nationaux d'AVC (et que les propriétés physiques des produits à base de ciment contenant des fibres chrysotile (importés) sont très différentes de celles d'AVC (nationaux).[25] Pour l'Organe d'appel, ces différences importantes des propriété physiques des marchandises pertinentes sont telles qu'il devient douteux que les dites marchandises importées et nationales soient véritablement en concurrence.[26] L'Organe d'appel écrit alors:

Nous considérons qu'il en est particulièrement ainsi dans les cas où les éléments de preuve relatifs aux propriétés établissent que les produits en cause sont très différents du point de vue physique. *En pareil cas, pour surmonter cette indication selon laquelle les produits ne sont pas "similaires," les Membres plaignants ont la charge plus lourde d'établir que, malgré des différences physiques marquées, il y a entre les produits un rapport de concurrence tel que tous les éléments de preuve, pris ensemble, démontrent que les produits sont "similaires" au sens de l'article III:4 du GATT de 1994.* En l'espèce, puisqu'il est clair que les fibres ont des propriétés très différentes, du fait notamment que le chrysotile a un caractère cancérogène avéré, le Canada a la charge très lourde de montrer, au titre des deuxième et troisième critères, que les fibres d'amiante chrysotile et les fibres d'ACV entretiennent un tel rapport de concurrence.[27][Emphase ajoutée.]

L'Organe d'appel réitère de façon spécifique que "dans un cas comme celui-ci, où les fibres sont physiquement très différentes, un groupe spécial *ne peut* conclure qu'il s'agit de "produits similaires"

---

propres à la présente affaire, et elle se cantonne aux fibres d'amiante chrysotile comparées aux fibres d'ACV. Estimer que ces fibres ne sont pas "similaires" en raison du caractère incontestablement carcinogène des fibres d'amiante chrysotile n'est à mes yeux qu'un petit pas modeste de plus ... Ce petit pas, les autres membres de la section ne se sentent toutefois pas en mesure de le franchir en raison de leur conception du rôle "fondamental," peut-être déterminant, des rapports de concurrence économique dans la détermination de la "similarité" de produits au titre de l'article III:4.

[25] Rapport de l'Organe d'appel dans l'affaire *CE — Amiante* au par. 114.

[26] *Idem*, aux par. 117-18.

[27] *Idem*, au par. 118.

s'il *n'examine pas* les éléments de preuve relatifs aux goûts et habitudes des consommateurs."[28] L'Organe d'appel ajoute que:

Dans une telle situation, s'il *n'y a pas* d'enquête sur cet aspect de la nature et de l'étendue du rapport de concurrence entre les produits, il n'y a pas de fondement permettant de surmonter la déduction selon laquelle les produits ne sont pas "similaires," tirée du fait qu'ils ont des propriétés physiques différentes.[29]

L'Organe d'appel sera d'opinion qu'en l'absence de preuve fondée notamment sur le critère des goûts et habitudes des consommateurs (3e critère), le Canada ne s'est pas déchargé de la charge qui lui incombait de *prouver* que malgré leurs caractéristiques physiques très différentes les produits en questions sont néanmoins en concurrence.[30] La majorité de l'Organe d'appel conclura que, ne s'étant pas déchargé de la preuve qui lui incombait, le Canada n'a pas réussi à prouver la violation de l'article III:4. La majorité de l'Organe d'appel ne conclura toutefois pas de façon définitive que les marchandises importées et nationales ne sont pas similaires, mais se limitera à conclure que la preuve soumise par le Canada était insuffisante.

Un membre de l'Organe d'appel fut toutefois d'opinion que même en l'absence de preuve relative aux goûts des consommateurs (et autres critères déterminant la similarité entre marchandises nationales et marchandises importées), l'Organe d'appel aurait dû conclure que les produits sous examen n'étaient définitivement pas similaires:

[J]'estime qu'il y a d'amples raisons de qualifier définitivement, une fois complétée l'analyse juridique, ces fibres de *non* "similaires" aux fibres d'ACV ... Il m'est difficile d'imaginer quels éléments de preuve relatifs aux rapports de concurrence économique tels qu'ils ressortent des utilisations finales et des goûts et habitudes des consommateurs pourraient l'emporter sur le caractère incontestablement mortel des fibres d'amiante chrysotile comparées aux fibres d'ACV lorsqu'elles sont inhalées par des êtres humains, et réduire à néant ce caractère, obligeant de ce fait à qualifier de "similaires" les fibres d'amiante chrysotile et les fibres d'ACV.[31]

Sans trop d'explications et peut-être pour s'assurer que le Canada ne tente d'initier de nouvelles procédures dans lesquelles il entendrait effectuer cette démonstration de similarité initialement mal

---

[28] *Idem,* aux par. 121-39.

[29] *Idem,* au par.121. L'Organe d'appel va répéter le même message aux par. 136 et 139.

[30] *Idem,* aux par. 141, 147 et 148.

[31] *Idem,* au par. 152.

complétée, l'Organe d'appel abordera l'analyse de la défense des Communautés européennes fondée sur l'article XX. Cette approche n'est pas sans reproche d'illogisme juridique: s'il n'est pas ultimement prouvé que les marchandises sont similaires, il n'existe pas de concurrence entre elles, donc l'article III:4 n'a pas pu être violé et nul recours aux exceptions n'est nécessaire.

ANALYSE DE LA DÉFENSE DES CE FONDÉE SUR L'ARTICLE XX(B)

Après avoir réitéré l'importance du pouvoir discrétionnaire des groupes spéciaux dans l'appréciation des faits — tels ceux relatifs aux risques à la santé — l'Organe d'appel va réitérer ce qu'il avait dit dans l'affaire *CE — Hormones* sur la nature de l'exercice d'évaluation des risques prévu à l'article 5 de l'Accord SPS "comme l'*Accord SPS,* l'article XXb) du GATT de 1994 ne prescrit la *quantification* en tant que telle du risque pour la santé et la vie des personnes. *Un risque peut être évalué d'un point de vue quantitatif ou qualitatif.*"[Emphase ajouté.][32]

L'Organe d'appel rappelle également que les Membres de l'OMC ont "*le droit de fixer le niveau de protection de la santé qu'ils jugent approprié dans une situation donnée*" et qu'il est "parfaitement légitime qu'un Membre cherche à arrêter la propagation d'un produit à haut risque tout en permettant d'utiliser à sa place un produit présentant un risque moindre,"[33] rejetant ainsi l'argument du Canada que les produits dont l'utilisation était autorisée représentaient également un certain risque pour la santé.

L'Organe d'appel va d'abord rappeler certains passages de l'affaire *Corée — Mesures affectant le boeuf* quant à l'interprétation du terme "nécessaire" contenu à l'article XX(b) qui autorise les Membres de l'OMC à prendre les mesures "nécessaires pour la protection de la santé et de la vie des personnes, animaux et plantes" pour autant que ces mesures soient appliquées de bonne foi (sans discrimination injustifiée ni comme restriction déguisée au commerce).

Nous avons indiqué dans l'affaire *Corée — Viande de bœuf* qu'un aspect du "processus de soupesage et de mise en balance ... compris dans la détermination de la question de savoir si une mesure de rechange compatible avec l'Accord sur l'OMC" est raisonnablement disponible est la mesure dans laquelle la mesure de rechange "favorise la réalisation de l'objectif poursuivi." De plus, dans cette affaire, nous avons fait observer ce qui suit: "[p]lus [l']intérêt commun ou [l]es valeurs communes [poursuivis] sont

---

[32] *Idem,* au par. 167.

[33] *Idem.*

vitaux ou importants," plus il sera facile d'admettre la "nécessité" de mesures conçues pour atteindre ces objectifs. *En l'espèce, l'objectif poursuivi par la mesure est la protection de la vie et de la santé des personnes au moyen de la suppression ou de la réduction des risques pour la santé bien connus et extrêmement graves que présentent les fibres d'amiante. La valeur poursuivie est à la fois vitale et importante au plus haut point.* Il ne reste donc plus qu'à savoir *s'il existe une autre mesure* qui permettrait d'atteindre le même objectif et qui a moins d'effets de restriction des échanges qu'une interdiction.[34]

L'Organe d'appel sera d'opinion qu'"on ne pouvait pas raisonnablement s'attendre à ce que la France emploie une autre mesure *quelle qu'elle* soit, si cette mesure supposait la continuation du risque même que le Décret cherchait à "arrêter." Une telle mesure empêcherait, en fait, la France d'atteindre le niveau voulu de protection de la santé."[35] La mesure alternative suggérée par le Canada qui avait la charge de prouver l'existence d'une telle alternative[36] — l'utilisation contrôlée — ne pouvait garantir ce niveau de protection.

En effet, dans l'affaire *Corée — Mesures affectant le boeuf,* l'Organe d'appel avait discuté pour la première fois la maniere dout devait être interprété le test de nécessité de l'article XX. L'affaire *Corée — Mesures affectant le Boeuf* concernait de multiples plaintes à l'encontre de diverses mesures afférentes à l'importation, la distribution et la vente de boeuf étranger en Corée. La Corée invoquait l'article XXd) pour justifier le maintien d'un système de vente au détail de produits bovins importés parallèle au système de distribution du boeuf d'origine nationale. L'article XXd) autorise des mesures "nécessaires pour assurer le respect des lois et règlements internes compatible avec les règles du GATT." Dans ce contexte, l'Organe d'appel procéda à une discussion détaillée du concept de "nécessité" de l'article XX.

Dans cette affaire *Corée — Mesures affectant le boeuf,* l'Organe d'appel va écrire que pour déterminer si une mesure est "nécessaire" malgré le fait qu'elle ne soit pas "indispensable" (définition du dictionnaire pour le terme "nécessaire"),[37] au moins trois facteurs doivent être soupesés: (1) l'efficacité de la mesure, (2) l'importance des valeurs défendues par la mesure et (3) l'impact de la

---

[34] *Idem,* au par. 171.

[35] *Idem,* au par. 174.

[36] *Idem,* au par. 175.

[37] Rapport de l'Organe d'appel dans l'affaire *Corée — Mesures affectant le boeuf* au par. 161.

mesure sur les importations ou exportations (son caractère restrictif). De façon plus particulière, l'Organe d'appel établit que

Nous estimons que tel qu'il est employé dans le contexte de l'article XXd), la portée du mot "nécessaire" n'est pas limitée à ce qui est "indispensable," "d'une nécessité absolue" ou "inévitable." Les mesures qui sont soit indispensables, soit d'une nécessité absolue ou inévitables pour assurer le respect d'une loi remplissent assurément les conditions posées par l'article XXd). *Mais d'autres mesures peuvent elles aussi ressortir à cette exception.* Tel qu'il est employé à l'article XXd), le terme "nécessaire" désigne, à notre avis, des nécessités d'ordre différent. *À une extrémité du champ sémantique, on trouve "nécessaire" dans le sens d'"indispensable"; à l'autre extrémité, on trouve "nécessaire" pris dans le sens de "favoriser." Dans ce champ sémantique, nous estimons qu'une mesure "nécessaire" se situe beaucoup plus près du pôle "indispensable" que du pôle opposé: "favoriser" simplement.*[38]

Puis l'Organe d'appel va se référer au *caractère vital ou non des valeurs ou intérêts* que protège la mesure attaquée, comme l'un des critères d'appréciation du caractère "nécessaire" d'une telle mesure.

Il nous semble que l'interprète d'un traité qui apprécie une mesure dont on prétend qu'elle est nécessaire pour assurer le respect d'une loi ou d'un règlement compatible avec l'Accord sur l'OMC *peut,* s'il y a lieu, *tenir compte de l'importance relative de l'intérêt commun ou des valeurs communes* que la loi ou le règlement que l'on veut faire respecter est censé protéger. *Plus cet intérêt commun ou ces valeurs communes sont vitaux ou importants, plus il sera facile d'admettre la "nécessité" d'une mesure conçue comme un instrument d'application.*[39]

Pour l'Organe d'appel, différents aspects de la mesure d'application doivent être examinés afin de déterminer si celle-ci est "nécessaire," telle l'efficacité de la mesure choisie eu égard aux objectifs poursuivis ou encore l'effet restrictif de cette mesure sur le commerce international. L'un de ces aspects est la mesure suivant laquelle elle favorise la réalisation de l'objectif poursuivi: garantir le respect de la loi ou du règlement en question. Plus cet apport est grand, plus il sera facile de considérer que la mesure peut être "nécessaire." Un autre aspect est la mesure suivant laquelle la mesure d'application a des effets restrictifs sur le commerce international, c'est-à-dire pour ce qui est d'une mesure incompatible avec l'article III:4, des effets restrictifs *sur les produits importés*. Une mesure qui a une incidence relativement faible sur les produits importés pourra plus facilement être considérée comme "nécessaire" qu'une mesure qui a des effets restrictifs profonds

---

[38] *Idem,* au par. 161.

[39] *Idem,* au par. 162.

ou plus larges.[40] On constate que le test traditionnel qui voulait qu'une mesure ne soit nécessaire que s'il n'existait pas d'alternatives moins restrictives sur le commerce a été changé de façon importante.

Reconnaissant peut-être comment un certain principe de précaution pourrait être introduit dans le contexte de l'article XX du GATT, l'Organe d'appel précisera:

> Pour justifier une mesure au regard de l'article XXb) du GATT de 1994, un Membre peut également se fonder, de bonne foi, sur des sources scientifiques qui, à ce moment-là, peuvent constituer une opinion divergente mais qui provient de sources compétentes et respectées. Un Membre n'est pas tenu, dans l'élaboration d'une politique de santé, de suivre automatiquement ce qui, à un moment donné, peut constituer une opinion scientifique majoritaire. Par conséquent, un groupe spécial ne doit pas forcément parvenir à une décision au titre de l'article XXb) du GATT de 1994 sur la base du poids "prépondérant" de la preuve.[41]

En effet, la même conclusion avait été rendue dans l'affaire *CE — Hormones,* que "des gouvernements ... responsables et représentatifs peuvent agir de bonne foi sur la base de ce qui peut être, à un moment donné, une opinion divergente provenant de sources compétentes et respectées."[42]

Nous connaissons maintenant mieux comment doit s'effectuer l'analyse des défenses basées sur l'Article XX:

> En somme, pour déterminer si une mesure qui n'est pas "indispensable" peut néanmoins être "nécessaire" au sens de l'article XXd), il faut dans chaque cas soupeser et mettre en balance une série de facteurs parmi lesquels figurent au premier plan le rôle joué par la mesure d'application dans le respect de la loi ou du règlement en question, l'importance de l'intérêt commun ou des valeurs communes qui sont protégés par cette loi ou ce règlement et l'incidence concomitante de la loi ou du règlement sur les importations ou les exportations.[43]

Toutefois, cet exercice de soupesage et de balance, en vue de l'appréciation de l'applicabilité de l'article XXb), n'est pas sans difficulté. Non seulement l'Organe d'appel demeure notamment l'ultime juge du caractère vital ou non des valeurs ou intérêts

---

[40] *Idem,* au par. 163.

[41] *Idem,* au par. 178.

[42] Rapport de l'Organe d'appel dans l'affaire *Communautés européennes — Mesures communautaires concernant les viandes et les produits carnés (Hormones)* ("*CE — Hormones*"), WT/DS26, 48/AB/R, adopté le 13 février 1998 au par. 194.

[43] Rapport de l'Organe d'appel dans l'affaire ~~CE — Amiante~~ au par. 164.

communs visés par la mesure contestée, mais l'Organe d'appel avait déjà prescrit un autre exercice de balance ou d'équilibre dans l'appréciation du chapeau (paragraphe introductif) de l'article XX du GATT. Dans l'affaire *E.-U. — Crevettes,* continuant son analyse débuté dans l'affaire *E.-U. — Essence,*[44] l'Organe d'appel écrivait:

> S'agissant du texte introductif de l'article XX, nous considérons que les Membres de l'OMC y reconnaissent la nécessité de maintenir l'équilibre des droits et des obligations entre le droit qu'a un Membre d'invoquer l'une ou l'autre des exceptions spécifiées aux paragraphes a) à j) de l'article XX, d'une part, et les droits fondamentaux que les autres Membres tiennent du GATT de 1994, d'autre part.[45]

Tant les pays Membres qui invoqueront l'article XX du GATT que les membres des groupes spéciaux et ceux de l'Organe d'appel devront faire preuve de beaucoup d'équilibre pour suivre tous les maux de cœur qui résulteront de cette balançoire!

L'APPLICATION DE L'ACCORD OTC DANS L'AFFAIRE *CE — AMIANTE*

Un autre aspect de ce rapport mérite notre examen. Il n'existait, avant l'affaire *CE — Amiante,* aucun rapport GATT ou OMC discutant l'Accord OTC. Dans l'affaire *CE — Amiante,* le Canada était d'opinion que la mesure européenne violait les dispositions de l'article 2 de l'Accord OTC.[46] La première question était donc de

---

[44] Rapport de l'Organe d'appel dans l'affaire *États-Unis — Normes concernant l'essence nouvelle et ancienne formules* ("*E.-U. — Essence*"), WT/DS2/AB/R, adopté le 20 mai 1996 aux pp. 22-23.

[45] Rapport de l'Organe d'appel dans l'affaire *États-Unis — Prohibition à l'importation de certaines crevettes et de certains produits à base de crevettes* ("*E.-U. — Crevettes*"), WT/DS58/AB/R, adopté le 6 novembre 1998 au par. 156.

[46] L'article 2 de l'Accord OTC se lit comme suit:

> 2.1 Les Membres feront en sorte, pour ce qui concerne les règlements techniques, qu'il soit accordé aux produits importés en provenance du territoire de tout Membre un traitement non moins favorable que celui qui est accordé aux produits similaires d'origine nationale et aux produits similaires originaires de tout autre pays.

> 2.2 Les Membres feront en sorte que l'élaboration, l'adoption ou l'application des règlements techniques n'aient ni pour objet ni pour effet de créer des obstacles non nécessaires au commerce international. À cette fin, les règlements techniques ne seront pas plus restrictifs pour le commerce qu'il n'est nécessaire pour réaliser un objectif légitime, compte tenu des risques que la non-réalisation entraînerait. Ces objectifs légitimes sont, entre autres, la sécurité nationale, la prévention de pratiques de nature à induire en erreur, la

savoir si le règlement contesté constituait un "règlement technique" qui appellerait l'application de l'Accord OTC.

Après avoir déclaré qu'"il n'est pas possible de déterminer le caractère juridique correct de la mesure en cause sans examiner la mesure dans son ensemble,"[47] l'Organe d'appel établit que (1) "l'élément essentiel de la définition d'un 'règlement technique' est qu'un 'document' doit 'énoncer' — à savoir, exposer, stipuler ou prévoir — les *caractéristiques* d'un produit;" (2) les "'caractéristiques d'un produit' incluent non seulement les particularités et qualités intrinsèques du produit lui-même, mais aussi des caractéristiques connexes, telles que les moyens d'identification, la présentation et l'apparence d'un produit,"[48] (3) que "les 'caractéristiques d'un produit' peuvent … être prescrites ou imposées, en ce qui concerne les produits, sous une forme soit positive, soit négative;"[49] et (4) qu'un "'règlement technique' doit, bien entendu, être applicable à un produit, ou groupe de produits, *identifiable*… [mais] rien dans le texte de cet accord ne donne à entendre que ces produits doivent être nommés ou bien *expressément* identifiés dans un "règlement technique."[50]

Puis l'Organe d'appel va établir qu'un règlement qui imposerait une "simple interdiction" pourrait ne pas constituer un "règlement technique:" "En conséquence, si cette mesure consistait *seulement* en une interdiction des *fibres* d'amiante, il se peut qu'elle ne constitue pas un "règlement technique."[51] Mais, pour l'Organe d'appel, puisque le règlement sous examen contient des exceptions qui précisent les situations où les produits peuvent contenir des

---

protection de la santé ou de la sécurité des personnes, de la vie ou de la santé des animaux, la préservation des végétaux ou la protection de l'environnement. Pour évaluer ces risques, les éléments pertinents à prendre en considération sont, entre autres, les données scientifiques et techniques disponibles, les techniques de transformation connexes ou les utilisations finales prévues pour les produits.

2.3 Les règlements techniques ne seront pas maintenus si les circonstances ou les objectifs qui ont conduit à leur adoption ont cessé d'exister ou ont changé de telle sorte qu'il est possible d'y répondre d'une manière moins restrictive pour le commerce.

[47] Rapport de l'Organe d'appel dans l'affaire *CE — Amiante* au par. 64.

[48] *Idem*, au par. 67.

[49] *Idem*, au par. 68.

[50] *Idem*, au par. 70.

[51] *Idem*, au par. 71.

fibres d'amiante, le décret français n'est pas une simple restriction et s'avère donc un "règlement technique."

Pour l'Organe d'appel, la mesure énonce des "caractéristiques" pour tous les produits qui peuvent contenir de l'amiante; elle énonce également les "dispositions administratives qui ... [s']appliquent" à certains produits contenant des fibres d'amiante chrysotile qui sont exclus des interdictions prévues par la mesure. En conséquence, la mesure est un "document" qui "énonce les caractéristiques d'un produit ... y compris les dispositions administratives qui s'y appliquent, dont le respect est obligatoire," donc un "règlement technique" au sens de l'Accord OTC.[52]

Après avoir reconnu que l'Accord OTC est applicable, l'Organe d'appel va toutefois refuser d'examiner les plaintes de violation de l'Accord OTC alléguant que le sujet est nouveau, que le groupe spécial n'a pas traité ces allégations, et qu'une analyse factuelle plus détaillée préalable aurait été nécessaire.[53]

Ces brèves conclusions sur l'Accord OTC peuvent avoir des conséquences importantes. Si l'articulation de la relation entre l'article XX et l'Accord TBT reste à être précisée, il est maintenant établi que ces deux dispositions peuvent trouver application en même temps sur la même mesure. De plus, puisqu'une interdiction totale ne semblerait pas constituer un règlement technique, on peut comprendre qu'un "règlement technique" serait plus souvent de la nature d'un règlement intérieur (article III du GATT)[54] plutôt qu'une mesure de restriction à la frontière (article XI du GATT), et ce contrairement aux mesures sanitaires et phytosanitaires qui peuvent prendre l'une ou l'autre forme.

En effet dans le langage du GATT, le terme "règlement" a toujours visé les règlements intérieurs et non les mesures à la frontière. De plus les termes de l'Accord OTC semblent viser des critères relatifs au contenu des produits, leur description, etc., éléments qui sont généralement l'objet de réglementation et non de simples restrictions en nombre ou en volume. Toutefois la couverture de l'article XI du GATT est beaucoup plus large que de "simples interdictions" et vise toutes formes de restrictions quantitatives alors

---

[52] *Idem,* au par. 75.

[53] *Idem,* aux par. 78-82.

[54] *Idem,* au par. 77: "Nous relevons toutefois — et nous soulignons — que cela ne veut pas dire que *toutes* les mesures internes visées par l'article III:4 du GATT de 1994 'affectant la vente, la mise en vente, l'achat, le transport, la distribution et l'utilisation' d'un produit sont, forcément, des 'règlements techniques' au sens de l'*Accord OTC.*"

que l'Accord OTC ne couvre pas les simple interdictions mais couvre les interdictions conditionnelles. Existerait-il des mesures qui seraient couvertes et par l'Accord OTC (restrictions partielles et conditionnelles) et par l'article XI du GATT de 1994?

LA POSSIBILITÉ DE RECOURS EN NON-VIOLATION À L'ENCONTRE DES EXCEPTIONS DE L'ARTICLE XX DU GATT.

Devant le groupe spécial, le Canada a allégué, au titre de l'article XXIII:1b) du GATT de 1994, que l'application de la mesure en cause annulait ou compromettait des avantages lui revenant. Les Communautés européennes ont soulevé des exceptions préliminaires, faisant valoir pour deux motifs que la mesure n'entrait pas dans le champ d'application de l'article XXIII:1b). Premièrement, les Communautés européennes ont soutenu que l'article XXIII:1b) ne s'appliquait qu'aux mesures qui ne relevaient pas autrement d'autres dispositions du GATT de 1994. Deuxièmement, les Communautés européennes ont fait valoir que, s'il pouvait y avoir une "attente légitime" en ce qui concernait une mesure purement "commerciale" (un des critères d'application du recours en non-violation aux termes de l'article XXIII:1b)),[55] il ne pouvait y avoir "d'attente légitime" pour ce qui était d'une mesure prise afin de protéger la santé et la vie des personnes et qui pouvait être justifiée au regard de l'article XXb) du GATT de 1994. Le panel rejeta ces deux exceptions préliminaires. Les Communautés européennes ont interjeté appel de ces exceptions préliminaires soulevées devant le groupe spécial.

À deux reprises déjà, mais très indirectement, l'Organe d'appel s'était prononcé sur le concept "d'attentes légitimes" et des

---

[55] "L'article XXIII:1a) prévoit un motif d'action pour une allégation selon laquelle un Membre ne remplit pas une ou plusieurs des obligations qu'il a contractées aux termes du GATT de 1994. Par conséquent, il y a allégation au titre de l'article XXIII:1a) lorsqu'il est allégué qu'un Membre a agi d'une manière incompatible avec une disposition du GATT de 1994. L'article XXIII:1b) indique un motif d'action distinct pour une allégation selon laquelle, en appliquant une mesure, un Membre a "annulé ou compromis" des "avantages" revenant à un autre Membre, que cette mesure soit "contraire ou non aux dispositions" du GATT de 1994. Ainsi, il n'est pas nécessaire, au regard de l'article XXIII:1b), d'établir que la mesure considérée est incompatible avec une disposition du GATT de 1994 ou constitue une violation de cette disposition. C'est pour cette raison que des affaires relevant de l'article XXIII:1b) sont parfois qualifiées d'affaires "en situation de non-violation;" nous observons, cependant, que le terme "non-violation" ne figure pas dans cette disposition." Rapport de l'Organe d'appel dans l'affaire *CE — Amiante* au par. 185.

recours en non-violation.[56] Comme il l'avait fait dans ces deux affaires, l'Organe d'appel insista sur le caractère exceptionnel de ce recours:

Comme le Groupe spécial chargé d'examiner l'affaire *Japon — Mesures affectant les pellicules et papiers photographiques destinés aux consommateurs* ("*Japon — Pellicules*"), nous considérons que le recours prévu à l'article XXIII:1b) "devrait être envisagé avec prudence et demeurer exceptionnel."[57]

Puis il écrit "qu'une mesure peut être, *à un seul et même moment,* incompatible avec une disposition du GATT de 1994 ou contraire à celle-ci *et,* néanmoins, constituer un motif d'action au titre de l'article XXIII:1b). Bien entendu, si une mesure est 'contraire' à une disposition du GATT de 1994, elle doit réellement entrer dans le champ d'application de cette disposition du GATT de 1994."[58] L'Organe d'appel rejeta donc le premier motif d'appel des Communautés européennes à l'effet que XXIII:1b) ne s'appliquait qu'aux mesures qui ne relevaient pas autrement d'autres dispositions du GATT de 1994.

L'Organe d'appel rejeta également le deuxième appel des Communautés européennes au motif que le texte de l'article XXIII:1b) ne fait pas de distinction entre certains types de mesures ni ne les exclut. "À l'évidence, le texte de l'article XXIII:1b) contredit donc l'argument des Communautés européennes selon lequel certains types de mesures, à savoir celles qui poursuivent des objectifs de santé, sont exclus du champ d'application de l'article XXIII:1b)."[59]

---

[56] Voir les Rapports de l'Organe d'appel dans les affaires *CE — Matériels informatiques,* WT/DS62, 67, 68/AB/R, adopté le 22 juin 1998 au par. 80, et *Inde — Protection conférée par un brevet,* WT/DS50/AB/R, adopté le 16 janvier 1998, en particulier ce passage du par. 41: "Les plaintes 'en situation de non-violation' tirent leur origine du fait que le GATT a été conçu comme un accord destiné à protéger les concessions tarifaires réciproques négociées par les parties contractantes au titre de l'article II. En l'absence de règles juridiques de fond dans de nombreux domaines touchant le commerce international, la disposition de l'article XXIII:1b) relative aux actions 'en situation de non-violation' visait à empêcher les parties contractantes de recourir à des obstacles non tarifaires ou à d'autres mesures de politique générale pour neutraliser les avantages des concessions tarifaires négociées."

[57] Rapport de l'Organe d'appel dans l'affaire *CE — Amiante* au par. 186, citant le rapport du Groupe spécial *Japon — Film,* adopté le 22 avril 1998, WT/DS44/R, par. 10.37.

[58] Rapport de l'Organe d'appel dans l'affaire *CE — Amiante* au par. 187.

[59] *Idem,* au par. 188.

En appel un aspect important de l'argument des Communautés européennes était qu'un Membre ne peut pas raisonnablement s'attendre à un accès au marché continu pour des produits dont il est démontré qu'ils présentent un risque sérieux pour la santé et la vie des personnes. La détermination des attentes raisonnable dans les situations de mesures relatives à la santé est une question toujours ouverte puisque, comme la souligé l'Organe d'appel, "les Communautés européennes *ne* font *pas* appel des constatations du Groupe spécial concernant 'l'annulation ou la réduction' d'un 'avantage' à cause des attentes raisonnables déçues du fait de l'application de la mesure en cause."[60]

Il est donc maintenant établi que les situations d'exception de l'article XX (et donc de l'article XXI du GATT) peuvent, du moins en théorie, donner lieu à des recours en compensation pour demande de non-violation. Le respect des conditions du recours en non-violation, dont la démonstration effective des attentes "légitimes" déçues par l'adoption de la mesure par ailleurs compatible avec les règles de l'OMC demeurera toujours difficile, en faisant un recours bien exceptionnel.

CONCLUSIONS

Encore une fois l'Organe d'appel dans l'affaire *CE — Amiante* nous impressionne favorablement . Après l'affaire *E.-U. — Essence* et l'affaire *E.-U. — Crevettes* où la jurisprudence traditionnelle du GATT concernant aux exceptions relatives à l'environnement avait été mise de côté, l'Organe d'appel nous dit que les risques à la santé sont des critères qui affectent la concurrence entre les marchandises; ils ne doivent donc pas être considérés uniquement dans le cadre de l'article XX mais également dans le cadre de l'appréciation des obligations de base de non-discrimination dont celle du traitement national de l'article III. Ce nouveau droit nous forcera-t-il à reconsidérer l'approche traditionnelle du GATT dans son traitement des distinctions réglementaires basées sur les modes de productions et autres politiques n'ayant pas d'effet sur les caractéristiques physiques des marchandises (la question des fameux "PPMs")?

C'était également la première fois qu'un membre de l'Organe d'appel imposait une opinion particulière(notons que le terme "opinion dissidente" n'a pas été utilisé). En effet, si les opinions

---

[60] *Idem,* au par. 190.

des membres de l'Organe d'appel doivent demeurer anonymes,[61] les opinions particulières ou dissidentes ne sont pas formellement interdites. Ces opinions particulières peuvent toutefois rendre la mise en oeuvre des recommandations de l'ORD plus délicate et le travail des groupes spéciaux chargés d'examiner la compatibilité avec les règles de l'OMC, aux termes de l'article 21.5 du Mémorandum d'accord, beaucoup plus ardu.

GABRIELLE MARCEAU
Division des affaires juridiques de l'OMC, Génève

Summary

The *EC — Asbestos* Dispute and the New Jurisprudence of the Appellate Body Concerning Health Risks

For the first time, the Appellate Body in EC — Asbestos *offers a more global analysis of the relationship between the obligation of national treatment (Article III of GATT) and the possibility of invoking exceptions (Article XX of GATT). The Appellate Body sets aside the traditional view, which seems to have opposed the interests of environmentalists and those of the markets. It concludes that health risks may affect the determination of likeness between imported and domestic products (those containing health risks and those without any), which is a prerequisite for the application of the national treatment obligation. The Appellate Body concludes that risks to health may affect the determination of the physical characteristics of the concerned merchandise as well as the tastes and habits of consumers, two of the four criteria that must be used to determine whether imported and domestic products are like for the purpose of Article III:4 of GATT — a determination based essentially on the nature and extent of the competitive relationship between and among products. In pursuing its crusade to define the scope of Article XX of GATT, the Appellate Body reiterates the new parameters of the necessity test of Article XX, which calls for an evaluation of the common values and interests defended by the challenged legislation, its effectiveness, and its impact on trade. In doing so, it seems to set aside the traditional test based essentially, if not exclusively, on the availability of less trade restrictive alternatives.*

---

[61] Article 17.11 du Mémorandum d'accord.

Sommaire

L'affaire "*CE — Amiante*" et la nouvelle jurisprudence de l'Organe d'appel de l'OMC concernant les risques à la santé

Pour la première fois, l'Organe d'appel, dans l'affaire CE — Amiante*, offre une analyse plus globale de la relation entre l'obligation de traitement national (article III du GATT) et la possibilité d'invoquer des exceptions (article XX du GATT). Mettant de côté la littérature et l'approche traditionnelle qui semblaient mettre en opposition les soucis des environnementalistes (et défenseurs de la protection de la santé) et les réalités des marchés, l'Organe d'appel statue que les risques à la santé peuvent affecter la détermination de "similarité" entre marchandises (celles à risque et celles sans risque à la santé). De ce fait, l'Organe d'appel conclut que les risques à la santé peuvent affecter les propriété physiques des marchandises, de même que les goûts et perceptions de consommateurs concernant ces marchandises, deux des quatre critères qui doivent nécessairement faire l'objet d'analyse dans la détermination de similarité entre marchandises importées et marchandises domestiques — une détermination reposant essentiellement sur la relation de concurrence entre ces marchandises nationales ou importées. Continuant sa croisade sur le sens et la portée de l'Article XX du GATT, l'Organe d'appel réitère les nouveaux paramètres du test de "nécessité" de l'article XX — dont l'importance relative de l'intérêt commun ou des valeurs communes que la loi ou le règlement que l'on veut faire respecter est censé protéger, l'efficacité de la mesure et son impact sur le commerce — et mettra ainsi de coté le test traditionnel basé essentiellement sinon exclusivement sur l'existence d'alternatives moins restrictives sur le commerce.*

Talisman Energy, Sudan, and Corporate Social Responsibility

INTRODUCTION

Sudan is a big country. It covers some 2.5 million square kilometres — the size of Ontario and Québec combined. It is ethni-
cally rich but developmentally poor: in 2001 it stood 138th in the
UN Development Program's Human Development Index, a broad
measure of attainments in life expectancy, education, and real
income.

For all but twelve years since its independence in 1956, Sudan
has been marked by a low-intensity civil war between the largely
Arab and Muslim northern half of the country and the largely
Black and Christian/animist south. The conflict involves an array
of ethnic groups and has roots going back several centuries.[1] In
recent times, the conflict has had devastating repercussions on the
civilian population. The United Nations estimates that two million
people have died in the fighting since 1983 and at least four million
more are internally displaced.[2] There have been reports of serious
human rights violations by all sides, including abduction, slavery,
forced displacement, starvation, and murder. In 1999, the UN
rapporteur on human rights in Sudan termed the plight of civilians

---

The author would like to thank Amy Jacob for her assistance in locating tabular
information for this comment.

[1] For a background to the conflict, see generally P.M. Holt and M.W. Daly, *A History
of the Sudan: From the Coming of Islam to the Present Day*, 5th ed. (Harlow, UK: Longman, 2000); P. Woodward, *Sudan, 1898-1989: The Unstable State* (London: L.
Crook Academic Publishers, 1990).

[2] UN Economic and Social Council, *The Situation of Human Rights in the Sudan*,
E/CN.4/1999/38/Add.1, para. 42 (1999).

caught in the conflict "one of the most important human rights concerns facing the international community."[3]

The civil war entered a new and particularly vicious phase in the late 1990s with the discovery of commercially viable quantities of oil in the south. The Sudanese government granted concessions to foreign oil companies and sponsored the construction of a 1,540-kilometre pipeline from the southern oil fields to Port Sudan, a site on the Red Sea, in order to get the oil to market. The Chinese-built pipeline was one of the largest civil works projects in Sudanese history and represented a considerable achievement when oil began flowing through it in mid-1999. Sudan, which had previously spent foreign exchange to import oil, suddenly attained a degree of energy self-sufficiency and started to make money from oil exports. From 1998 to 2000, inflows of oil money went from being negligible to contributing 28.4 per cent to the government's revenue.[4] The money represented an opportunity to increase development spending, but at least some of it has gone towards military purchases.[5] Consequently, this has given a new edge to the government forces. In January 2001, the UN rapporteur indicated that "[o]il exploitation has resulted in the exacerbation of the war."[6]

The Khartoum government's principal opponent in the war is the Sudan People's Liberation Army (SPLA), which sees oil exploitation as enhancing the government's ability to fight.[7] In 1994, the government and southern opposition groups concluded a Declaration of Principles,[8] the cornerstone of which was the official

---

[3] *Ibid.* at para. 159.

[4] International Monetary Fund [hereinafter IMF], *Sudan: Staff Report for the 2000 Article IV Consultation and Fourth Review of the First Annual Program under the Medium-Term Staff-Monitored Program,* IMF Country Report No. 00/70 (June 2000) at p. 21.

[5] IMF staff observe that military expenditures increased by 35 per cent in the 2000 program compared with 1999 and have "encouraged the authorities to keep it below budgeted levels" but note that "pressures for increased expenditures in this area are not likely to abate in the near future." *Ibid.* at 24 and 35.

[6] UN Economic and Social Council, *The Situation of Human Rights in the Sudan: Note by the Secretariat,* E/CN.4/2001/48, para. 21 (January 25, 2001).

[7] Amnesty International, *Sudan: The Human Price of Oil,* May 2000, AFR 54/01/2000, at p. 2.

[8] The Declaration of Principles was concluded under the auspices of the East African Intergovernmental Agency for Development. It can be accessed at <www.web.net/~iccaf/humanrights/sudaninfo/cdnpolicysudanbkgd.htm>.

recognition of the right of self-determination for the people of southern Sudan. The declaration specifically provided that "rights of self-determination of the people of South Sudan to determine their future status through a referendum must be affirmed." In 1995, however, the government chose to pursue a strategy of "peace from within," and, in April 1997, it signed the Khartoum Peace Agreement[9] with six splinter rebel groups in which it emphasized that the general principles of the declaration would guide future talks. The SPLA refused to sign the agreement because the government declared that it did not consider the declaration to be binding but saw it merely as a basis for future discussions. As a result, hostilities continue.

Plans for an oil pipeline from the south were first made by Chevron, an American oil company, which began exploration in 1975. In 1984, the company halted its Sudan operation in response to the abduction and killing of three expatriate Chevron workers by the SPLA. Chevron eventually pulled out of Sudan altogether and sold its Sudanese assets to a small Canadian oil company that was acquired by Talisman Energy Incorporated of Calgary in October 1998. As a part of the purchase, Talisman took over a 49,200-square-kilometre concession 700 kilometres south of Khartoum. Talisman decided to operate the concession with the help of Chinese, Malaysian, and Sudanese partners through a Mauritius-registered joint venture, the Greater Nile Petroleum Operating Company (GNPOC), in which it retains a 25 per cent interest.[10] In 2000, Talisman provided the government of Sudan with Cdn $306 million worth in royalties from its share in GNPOC and reported Cdn $126.2 million in results from Sudan operations.[11]

---

[9] Khartoum Peace Agreement, signed on April 21, 1997 in Khartoum, see <http://www.sudmer.com/StatsP/New_Folder/agreement.htm>.

[10] Other partners in the GNPOC consortium are a wholly owned subsidiary of the China National Petroleum Corporation (40 per cent), a wholly owned subsidiary of the national oil company of Malaysia, Petronas (30 per cent), and the national petroleum company of Sudan, Sudapet (5 per cent). Key management positions are occupied by representatives of each member of the consortium. Decisions made by committees within the GNPOC require an affirmative vote of two members of the board representing at least 60 per cent interest.

[11] See *Talisman Corporate Social Responsibility Report, 2000*, available at <http://www.talisman-energy.com/responsibility/CorpResp.pdf> at p. 28 [hereinafter *CSR Report*]; and *Talisman Energy Annual Report 2000*, at p. 59, which can be accessed at <www.talisman-energy.com/financial/2000annual.html>.

The GNPOC concession sits in the heart of disputed territory. Southern rebel groups have threatened that those individuals
working with the consortium will be regarded as "northern" accom-
plices.[12] Talisman has therefore requested that the Sudanese government ensure law and order in the concession.[13] In order to meet
this request, the government has employed the military and gov-
ernment-armed militias. There is, however, considerable evidence
that the government has been using concession facilities in order to
launch offensive operations within the concession as well as further
south.[14]

Talisman's investment in Sudan therefore raises profound concerns about corporate operations in countries where there are serious and frequent human rights violations. The company's presence
has been interpreted by many individuals as providing essential
support to a repressive regime and as condoning the government's
policies towards the south. What are Talisman and Canada's obligations at this particular juncture — a point of fertile development
in the field of international corporate social responsibility? This
comment examines this question in light of recent events.

TALISMAN ENERGY AND *HUMAN SECURITY IN SUDAN:* *THE REPORT OF A CANADIAN ASSESSMENT MISSION (HARKER REPORT)*

Talisman has been the subject of scrutiny and criticism from
church groups and other non-governmental organizations (NGOs)
since the outset of its involvement in Sudan. These groups allege
that GNPOC operations are aiding and abetting aggression against
the civilian population. The principal criticisms made against Talisman can be grouped into three categories. The first concerns discriminatory hiring and the forcible displacement of the population

---

[12] In its *CSR Report, supra* note 11, Talisman notes that "periodic threats are made
by rebel forces and clearly indicate that both [GNPOC] personnel and property
are considered legitimate targets in the war against the Government of Sudan."

[13] Amnesty International, *Sudan: The Human Price of Oil,* May 2000, AFR
54/01/2000, at p. 8.

[14] In its *CSR Report, supra* note 11, Talisman notes that "[d]espite the Company's
stated position regarding the use of the Heglig airstrip and advocacy efforts in
this regard, we believe that there were at least four instances of non-defensive
usage of the Heglig airstrip in 2000. On these occasions, helicopters or planes
landed on the airstrip for reasons that we could not determine were related to
oilfield security and their presence was considered non-defensive by Talisman."
See *CSR Report, supra* note 11 at 16. See also J. Sallot, "Ottawa Covering Up for
Talisman in Sudan, MP Says," *Globe and Mail* (May 5, 2001) A5.

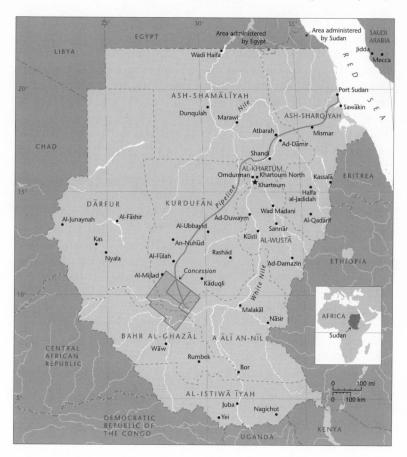

Figure 1. Greater Nile Petroleum Operating Company concession and the route of the oil pipeline in Sudan.

in the concession area and along the pipeline route. The second involves the utilization of GNPOC-built facilities by Sudanese government forces for offensive military purposes. The third centres on the use of GNPOC-generated oil revenue by the Sudanese government for prosecution of the war.

In October 1999, growing criticism led the Canadian government to announce that it would send an envoy, former ILO representative John Harker, to Sudan to conduct an assessment of

Talisman's operations. The inquiry was premised on the idea that
there was a link between oil exploitation and human rights abuses,
particularly slavery and slave-like practices, and that Canada was, in
some sense, internationally responsible for the acts of its corporate
"citizen," Talisman Energy. Harker's report concluded that
GNPOC installations had been used to commit human rights violations, "that Sudan is a place of extraordinary suffering ... and
[that] the oil operations in which a Canadian company is involved
add more suffering."[15]

The Canadian government did not respond in any legal way
to Harker's conclusions.[16] Instead, it requested that Talisman abide
by the International Code of Ethics for Canadian Business, a voluntary code of corporate conduct, which was designed to be
monitored by neutral third parties.[17] The Canadian government
also instituted a policy of engagement with the Sudanese regime,
opening a consular office in Khartoum and holding talks with
Sudanese officials on the human rights situation in the country.
Talisman adopted the code in December 1999. Despite this action,
the company continues to be dodged by criticism and threats
of shareholder divestment. In February 2000, the United States
announced sanctions against the GNPOC. Later, in May 2000, a
group of shareholders asked Talisman's Board of Directors to
prepare an independently verified report on the company's compliance with the code within 180 days. Talisman subsequently
released its first corporate social responsibility report under the
code in April 2001.[18]

---

[15] J. Harker, *Human Security in Sudan: The Report of a Canadian Assessment Mission*
(January 2000), which can be accessed at <www.dfait-maeci.gc.ca/africa/sudan-
e.asp> at 15 [hereinafter *Harker Report*].

[16] The *Harker Report* suggested that the Canadian government adopt a step-by-step
approach to the situation, with a public statement expressing grave concern by
the Minister of Foreign Affairs, followed by an announcement that certain
exports to Sudan would be subjected to scrutiny under the Export and Import
Permits Act, R.S.C. 1985, ch. E-19, followed, if necessary, by placement of Sudan
on the Area Control List. Harker also identified application of the Special Economic Measures Act, S.C. 1992, c. 17 as a possibility. *Ibid.*

[17] The text of the International Code of Ethics for Canadian Business is available at
<www.uottawa.ca/hrrec/busethics/codeint.html> [hereinafter Code of Ethics].
For background information, see S. Chase, "Talisman Bows to Ottawa, Adopts
Business Code of Ethics," *Globe and Mail* (December 11, 1999) A1.

[18] *CSR Report, supra* note 11.

CORPORATE SOCIAL RESPONSIBILITY IN DOMESTIC AND INTERNATIONAL LAW

A corporation is a legal entity distinct from its shareholders with separate liability and the capacity of continuous succession.[19] Although it is not unknown in international law, the corporation is principally a creation of domestic law and is generally organized according to the laws of one jurisdiction.[20] The typical corporation's business and affairs are managed by the board of directors who owe a duty to the corporation's collective ownership, the shareholders. Traditionally, this duty was thought of as being to protect the corporation's capital and to produce profits.

In the twentieth century, duties owed by directors in law began to expand to employees, consumers, and the general public. Recent literature on corporate governance refers to the "stakeholder" concept of the corporation or, rather, the idea that the conduct of the corporation's business affects not only shareholders but also other sectors of the public. There is the increasingly current view that these other interests should be accounted for in some way.

Apart from specific statutory obligations, however, courts in Canada and elsewhere have generally been reluctant to accept the idea that corporate directors owe a duty to the general public.[21] Instead, changes taking place in corporate governance are being

---

[19] *Dictionary of Canadian Law* (2nd ed.) (Scarborough, ON: Carswell: 1995) at 260. For a discussion on the international context, see *Barcelona Traction, Light and Power Co. (Belgium v. Spain)*, [1970] I.C.J. Rep. 3.

[20] Ian Brownlie refers to the situation of intergovernmental corporations of private law whereby "states may by treaty create legal persons the status of which is regulated by the national law of one or more of the parties" and gives the example Eurofima, a company set up by 14 European countries under Swiss law in 1955 to jointly manage railway rolling stock. Even in this instance, however, there was reference to a governing system of domestic law. See I. Brownlie, *Principles of Public International Law* (5th ed.) (Oxford: Oxford University Press, 1998) at 67.

[21] "The firmly established rule at common law was that directors owe a fiduciary obligation to the corporation, but not to individual shareholders. The current view would appear to be that, while special circumstances may give rise to a fiduciary relationship between a director and shareholders, no general fiduciary obligation exists." McCarthy Tétrault, *Directors' and Officers' Duties and Liabilities in Canada* (Toronto: Butterworths, 1997) at 42-3; see *Bell v. Source Data Control Ltd.* (1988), 66 O.R. (2d) 78 (C.A.); *Brant Investments Ltd. v. KeepRite Inc.* (1987), 60 O.R. (2d) 737 (H.C.), aff'd (1991), 3 O.R. (3d) 289 (C.A.). In the United Kingdom, see *Howard Smith Ltd. v. Ampol Petroleum*, [1974] A.C. 821 (P.C.); in the United States, see *Revlon Inc. v. MacAndrews & Forbes Holdings, Inc.*, 506 A. 2d 173 (Del. 1986).

self- or statutorily imposed. For instance, many mutual funds already keep a close watch on how firms deal with a variety of controversies. This growing interest is also reflected in amendments to legislation in countries such as Britain, where new rules require pension funds to disclose how they deal with outside issues.[22]

International law does not yet have much to say formally about corporate social responsibility. The language of the Universal Declaration of Human Rights[23] speaks of "every individual and every organ of society" as having a duty to strive for the promotion of human rights, and is, for this reason, sometimes referred to as evidence that corporations, as legal persons, have such a duty. Certain instruments, such as the ILO Tripartite Declaration of Principles Concerning Multinational Enterprises and Social Policy (Tripartite Declaration of Principles),[24] the OECD Guidelines for Multinational Enterprises,[25] and the UN Draft International Code of Conduct on Transnational Corporations,[26] could be considered a framework for international corporate behaviour, but none has been consistently endorsed in terms of adherence or practice by a clear majority of the international community. There remains, in addition, the question of how to regulate private entities in a system of public law. Moreover, most instruments have been drafted by existing states, and, in deference to sensitivities of sovereignty, they have focused more on individual human rights than on group rights to self-determination, which are now at the heart of the conflict in Sudan. For instance, the Tripartite Declaration of Principles provides that

[a]ll parties concerned by this Declaration should respect the sovereign rights of States, obey the national laws and regulations, give due consideration to local practices and respect relevant international standards. They should respect the Universal Declaration of Human Rights and the

---

[22] In July 2000, the British government introduced a socially responsible investment regulation under section 35 of the Pensions Act 1995 (c. 26), which requires pension funds to disclose the extent to which they consider social, environmental, or other ethical criteria in investment decisions and policies directing the exercise of rights attached to their investments.

[23] Universal Declaration of Human Rights, G.A. Res. 217 A (III), U.N. Doc. A/810 at 71 (1948).

[24] Tripartite Declaration of Principles Concerning Multinational Enterprises and Social Policy, 17 I.L.M. 422 (1978) [hereinafter Tripartite Declaration of Principles].

[25] OECD Guidelines for Multinational Enterprises, 15 I.L.M. 969 (1976).

[26] International Code of Conduct on Transnational Corporations, 23 I.L.M. 626 (1984).

corresponding International Covenants adopted by the General Assembly of the United Nations as well as the Constitution of the International Labour Organisation and its principles ... They should also honour commitments which they have freely entered into, in conformity with the national law and accepted international obligations.[27]

These human rights are important, but on their own they are not a useful measure of Talisman's activities in the current context. Some accounting of Talisman's activities in relation to group rights is necessary.

Recently, the position of international law regarding corporate social responsibility has begun to change. This shift is happening for two reasons. First, there has been a tremendous development of soft law codes of conduct, a development that was prompted in part by the lack of anything similar at an official level. Initiatives such as the Amnesty International Guidelines for Companies,[28] Social Accountability 8000,[29] the UN Global Compact,[30] the Taskforce on the Churches and Corporate Responsibility Benchmarks for Measuring Business Performance,[31] and the Global Sullivan Principles[32]

---

[27] Tripartite Declaration of Principles, *supra* note 24 at 424.

[28] Amnesty International Guidelines for Companies, available at <www.amnesty.org.uk/business/pubs>.

[29] Social Accountability 8000 is a standards association established in 1997 to verify international labour conditions in a transparent manner. It is modeled on the International Standards Organization (ISO) 9000 standard that is used by companies for quality control purposes. See <www.cepaa.org/introduction.htm>.

[30] UN Secretary-General Kofi Annan first proposed the UN Global Compact in an address to the World Economic Forum in January 1999. He challenged world business leaders to help build the social and environmental pillars required to sustain the new global economy. The compact encompasses nine principles drawn from the Universal Declaration of Human Rights, *supra* note 23, the ILO's Fundamental Principles and Rights at Work, 88th Session, Geneva, June 1998, and the Rio Principles on Environment and Development, U.N. Doc.A/CONF.151/5/Rev. 1; 31 I.L.M. No. 874. The compact promotes good practices by corporations. It does not endorse companies. See <www.unglobalcompact.org>.

[31] The Taskforce on the Churches and Corporate Responsibility (TCCR) is an ecumenical coalition of major churches in Canada. It assists member organizations in promoting and implementing policies adopted by the TCCR on the social and environmental responsibility of Canadian-based corporations and financial institutions. See <www.web.net/~tccr/>.

[32] The Global Sullivan Principles [hereinafter GSP) derive from the original Sullivan Principles, a code of conduct for companies operating in South Africa that was devised by a Philadelphia cleric, the Reverend Leon Sullivan, in 1977. In 1997, they were updated and renamed the GSP. See <globalsullivanprinciples.org>.

have proliferated. These non-governmental and self-regulating initiatives seem to appeal to the free-market tenor of the times. Second, the foregoing private initiatives, together with renewed concern about international corporate power and business ethics, are promoting something of a renaissance in multilateral efforts to define corporate social responsibility. Thus, new voluntary instruments have either been adopted or are under consideration by the UN,[33] the OECD,[34] and the European Union (EU).[35]

One multilateral initiative meriting particular attention is the United Nations Draft Human Rights Guidelines for Companies (Human Rights Guidelines).[36] Work on the Human Rights Guidelines was begun in 1999 in response to concern about the unwieldy proliferation of soft law. Simply put, the fear was that the multiplicity of mechanisms was allowing companies to pick and choose or to claim that the range of choices inhibited them from acting. The guidelines therefore seek to interpret comprehensively the Universal Declaration of Human Rights in a form that can be implemented by private entities. The Human Rights Guidelines are more precise and nuanced than the Universal Declaration of Human Rights and therefore better at covering the variety of circumstances in which human rights need protection. For example, Draft Article 16 states that "Companies shall have the responsibility to ensure that their business operations do not contribute directly or indirectly to human rights abuses and actively to speak out or otherwise use their influence in order to help promote and ensure respect for human rights." The reference regarding indirect corporate contribution to human rights abuses is particularly noteworthy.

[33] The UN Commission on Human Rights Sub-Commission on the Promotion and Protection of Human Rights is currently working on a set of draft Universal Human Rights Guidelines for Companies. See UN Doc. E/CN.4/Sub.2/2001/ WG.2/WP.1/Add.1 (2001).

[34] Guidelines for Multinational Enterprises, 40 I.L.M. 237 (2001). The guidelines are recommendations made by OECD member governments to multinational enterprises that address a range of corporate activities that have become of pressing concern since the last set of general OECD guidelines, which were issued in 1976.

[35] In January 1999, the European Parliament adopted a set of proposals on the accountability of European-based multinationals. The proposals, derived from a report entitled *Towards a European Code of Conduct*, A4-0508/98, aim to establish a European monitoring platform concerning multinational accountability on a broad range of social issues.

[36] UN Draft Human Rights Guidelines for Companies, UN Commission on Human Rights, E/CN.4/Sub.2/2000/WG.2/WP.1/Add.1 (May 25, 2000).

Likewise, Draft Article 18 states that "Companies shall respect the rights of indigenous communities and minorities to own, develop, control, protect, and use their lands and cultural and intellectual property; indigenous communities and minorities may not be deprived of their own means of subsistence." This last provision presents something of an advance over the statist position of previous documents. Properly implemented, it could sanction the kind of activity that Talisman now finds itself undertaking in southern Sudan. However the Human Rights Guidelines remain both a "draft" and "guidelines," with all the limited normative significance that those terms entail.

In the meantime, it is possible to conclude that Talisman, in continuing to operate in Sudan with clear evidence that oil revenues are financing the civil war, is indirectly contributing to serious human rights abuses. In this respect, it is in breach of the Human Rights Guidelines and, by extension, the Universal Declaration of Human Rights. A second conclusion is that Talisman is operating in the south with permission of the government. Given the state of civil war in the country, however, that permission cannot be said to reflect the will of southerners. As a minority, they are entitled to a degree of control over resources emanating from their lands. This view is confirmed by a number of new instruments.[37] It is also rapidly becoming a norm of state practice. Talisman is therefore in breach of the Human Rights Guidelines and of an emerging norm of international law by appropriating resources without consent.

INTERNATIONAL CODE OF ETHICS FOR CANADIAN BUSINESS (CODE OF ETHICS)

A Canadian attempt to deal with issues of corporate social responsibility occurred in 1997 when a roundtable of corporate, NGO, and academic representatives created the Code of Ethics. It followed a public outcry over Canadian corporate activity in the Nigerian petroleum industry under the Abacha dictatorship. The Code of Ethics is a collection of beliefs, values, and principles guided by an overall vision of Canadian business abroad as being both profitable and socially responsible. Thirteen companies

---

[37] See Convention Concerning Indigenous and Tribal Peoples in Independent Countries, ILO Convention No. 169, 28 I.L.M. 1382 (1989); Convention on Biological Diversity, 31 I.L.M. 818 (1992); Draft Universal Declaration on Indigenous Rights, 34 I.L.M. 541 (1995).

adopted the Code of Ethics at the time of its creation. The most recent information available indicates that only two Canadian companies, including Talisman, have signed on since. The code is voluntary and non-binding, and, in this sense, it does not add much to the instruments already reviewed. However, since Talisman's efforts in corporate responsibility are measured according to it, the Code of Ethics should be examined.

The code reflects five generations of corporate conduct, with the first (conflict of interest) bearing primarily on direct corporate interest while the remaining four (commercial conduct, employee and other third party concerns, community and environmental concerns, and accountability and social justice) refer to external interests and values. The Code of Ethics expresses the belief that "businesses should take a leadership role through establishment of ethical business principles" and that while "confrontation should be tempered by diplomacy" and "national governments have the prerogative to conduct their own government and legal affairs in accordance with their sovereign rights," "all governments should comply with international treaties and other agreements that they have committed to."[38] In addition, the code enshrines principles that hold that companies will "support and promote the protection of international human rights within our sphere of influence" and "not be complicit in human rights abuses."[39] Similarly, it dictates that companies will "comply with all applicable laws" and will "strive for social justice and promote freedom of expression in the workplace."[40]

The Code of Ethics is to be implemented in individual firms through the development of operational codes and practices. There is no guide as to how this translation is to be effected, except that the result must be "consistent" with the code's provisions. Verification is to be effected by outside parties that have been hired by signatories to the code for that purpose.

TALISMAN ENERGY'S *Corporate Social Responsibility Report, 2000 (CSR Report)*

Talisman's *CSR Report* was released in April 2001 in an effort to comply with the Code of Ethics. The forty-two-page report was

---

[38] Code of Ethics, *supra* note 17.

[39] *Ibid.*

[40] *Ibid.*

verified by PricewaterhouseCoopers (PwC), a worldwide consulting firm, and provides a snapshot of Talisman and its operations in Sudan. Unlike audited accounting reports, the *CSR Report* is self-admittedly not "a broad overall assessment of our presence in Sudan. Rather, it describes how we have interpreted the Code through the Principles which we have adopted."[41] Talisman notes that there are no generally accepted standards against which its activities can be measured. Consequently, it plans to spend the period between 2001 and 2003 developing performance indicators. Using these indicators, Talisman will presumably be in a better position to be assessed. The *CSR Report* observes that "we intend to expand the reporting process in future years."[42]

The prototypical nature of the *CSR Report* is underlined in PwC's verification statement, which observes that "[t]here are currently no statutory requirements or generally accepted international standards for the preparation, public reporting and attestation or corporate social responsibility reports." For this reason, PwC's verification approach "reflects emerging best practice and is in accordance with the International Standard on Assurance Engagements."[43] The verification statement also notes significant limitations on PwC's work. Certain visits had to be cleared with GNPOC and national security, who have a record of antipathy towards southerners and who might make access to southern representatives difficult. Likewise, the verification statement indicates that PwC auditors "did not visit any sites in the south of Sudan outside the concession area but we did speak to Southern Sudanese in Khartoum and to international non-governmental organisations in Nairobi."[44] Thus, it is not entirely clear how, or in what parts of Sudan, PwC consulted with independent southern sources.

The *CSR Report* goes on to define corporate social responsibility as "conducting activities in an economically, socially and environmentally responsible manner."[45] Responsibility is, in turn, conceived of according to the Code of Ethics as well as a translation of the code for GNPOC purposes (the Sudan Operating Principles) and key stakeholder concerns. From these are derived concrete aims in the form of Talisman objectives ("those which are under

[41] *CSR Report, supra* note 11 at 9.

[42] *Ibid.* at 41.

[43] *Ibid.* at 11.

[44] *Ibid.*

[45] *Ibid.* at 4.

our direct control and responsibility"), GNPOC objectives ("those objectives whose achievement depends on the agreement or support of our GNPOC business partners"), and advocacy objectives ("those over which we have minimal control but for which we believe we have a responsibility to advocate within governments or international organizations").

The *CSR Report* is divided into several sections. Its objectives are considered in chapters on human rights, community participation, employee rights, ethical business conduct, health safety and the environment, and stakeholder engagement. For instance, the Code of Ethics' principle of support for human rights is translated into a commitment to uphold the Universal Declaration of Human Rights under the Sudan Operating Principles, followed by an account of key stakeholder concerns, and several specific objectives. An overview of this translation is provided in Figure 2.

The translation of principles and concerns into objectives is generally worthwhile. Where problems arise, they usually concern the appropriateness of the objectives in context. For instance, Talisman has translated the Code of Ethics' principle that it will "support and promote the protection of international human rights within our sphere of influence" into "we are committed to upholding the Universal Declaration of Human Rights." This formulation is questionable inasmuch as the declaration itself is generally regarded as aspirational and refined in the International Covenant on Civil and Political Rights and the International Covenant on Economic, Social and Cultural Rights, both of which Sudan has ratified.[46] These later instruments, together with such documents as the International Convention on the Elimination of All Forms of Racial Discrimination,[47] the ILO Convention on Discrimination (Employment and Occupation),[48] the 1994 Declaration of Principles, and the 1997 Khartoum Peace Agreement[49] — which have been approved by the Sudanese government — would constitute a more specific and effective basis for Talisman's advocacy. Talisman

---

[46] International Covenant on Civil and Political Rights, 993 U.N.T.S. 3 (1976); International Covenant on Economic, Social and Cultural Rights, 999 U.N.T.S. 171 (1976).

[47] International Convention on the Elimination of All Forms of Racial Discrimination, 660 U.N.T.S. 195 (1966).

[48] ILO Convention on Discrimination (Employment and Occupation), 362 U.N.T.S. 31 (1958).

[49] Declaration of Principles, *supra* note 8; and Khartoum Peace Agreement, *supra* note 9.

counters that it can only be expected to advocate within its "sphere of influence," but this sphere should be broadly conceived by the company given its major role in the Sudanese economy and its record of influence with the Khartoum government. There is, moreover, no requirement that Talisman limit itself to lobbying on the basis of documents that apply to it. The company should recall the Code of Ethics principle that "all governments should comply with international treaties and other agreements that they have committed to."[50]

A second concern detailed in the *CSR Report* is the failure of Talisman to account for, and seek the return of, civilians forcibly displaced from their homes in the concession area and along the pipeline route. The relevant international standard in this respect, the UN Guiding Principles on Internal Displacement, mandates that "[d]isplacement shall last no longer than required by the circumstances."[51] The *CSR Report* takes a more restricted view of the appropriate GNPOC objective and instructs the company to "promote the principle that people adversely impacted by GNPOC operations receive fair and just compensation." The report details the events that took place during the planning and construction of the pipeline and explains that the government formed a Pipeline Compensation Committee and "through this process thousands of compensation cases have been paid." However, Talisman admits that "the process of identifying people affected by such activity and the provision of fair compensation has not been well documented."[52] It seems necessary for Talisman to press the GNPOC to conduct some accounting of the massive human displacement related to its oil exploration, as detailed in the *Harker Report* and elsewhere, and to seek the return of those people that have been displaced. Instead, the *CSR Report* speaks merely in terms of compensation and, in this respect, suggests sums that could not possibly compensate for the dislocation and hardship that have taken place.

The dissonance between Talisman and these independent sources is repeated elsewhere. The *CSR Report* notes, for instance, that Talisman has developed "a detailed human rights monitoring and investigation program manual to address concerns arising from

---

[50] Code of Ethics, *supra* note 17.

[51] UN Guiding Principles on Internal Displacement, contained as an annex to the *Report of the Representative of the Secretary-General*, Francis M. Deng, UN Doc. E/CN.4/1998/53/Add.2 (February 1998). See Principle 6(3).

[52] *CSR Report, supra* note 11 at 17.

Figure 2. Talisman's formulation of corporate responsibility objectives in the field of human rights.

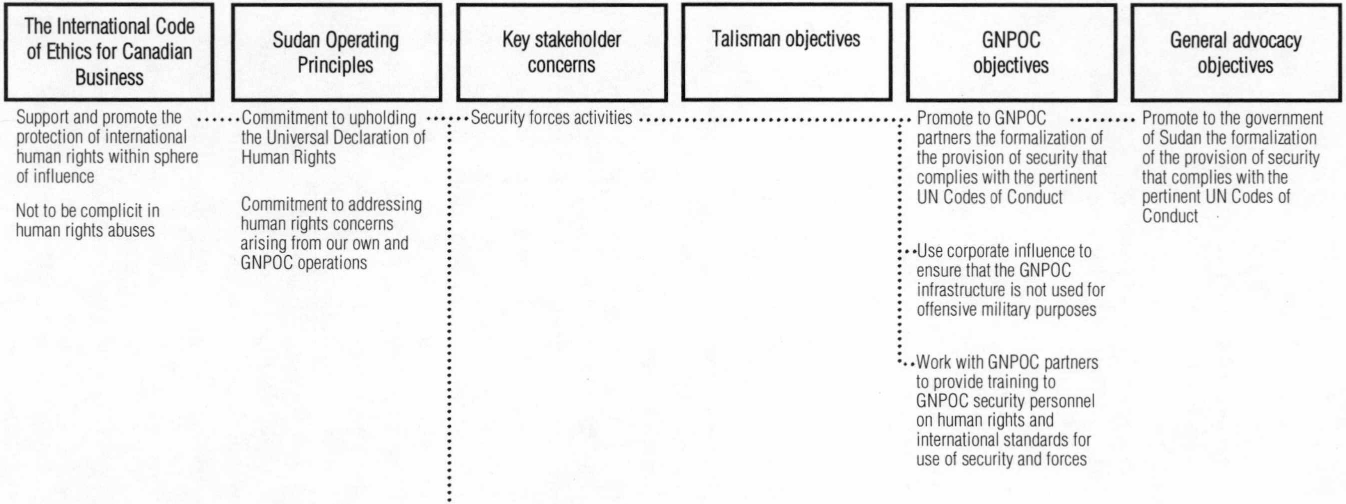

The International Code of Ethics for Canadian Business	Sudan Operating Principles	Key stakeholder concerns	Talisman objectives	GNPOC objectives	General advocacy objectives

Support and promote the protection of international human rights within sphere of influence

Not to be complicit in human rights abuses

Commitment to upholding the Universal Declaration of Human Rights

Commitment to addressing human rights concerns arising from our own and GNPOC operations

Security forces activities

Promote to GNPOC partners the formalization of the provision of security that complies with the pertinent UN Codes of Conduct

Use corporate influence to ensure that the GNPOC infrastructure is not used for offensive military purposes

Work with GNPOC partners to provide training to GNPOC security personnel on human rights and international standards for use of security and forces

Promote to the government of Sudan the formalization of the provision of security that complies with the pertinent UN Codes of Conduct

Use of oilfield infrastructure

- Promote to GNPOC partners the development of guidelines on the acceptable uses of oilfield infrastructure and promote the implementation of this program to our GNPOC partners
  - Promote to the government of Sudan the development of guidelines on the acceptable uses of oilfield infrastructure

Human rights

- Develop a human rights training and awareness program for all managers and employees working in Sudan
- Develop and implement a program to monitor and investigate human rights concerns arising from our own and GNPOC operations
- Develop a framework for a program of independent monitoring of human rights concerns arising from Talisman and GNPOC operations
  - Encourage GNPOC partners to adopt a code of ethics that addresses the protection of human rights
    - Meet with officials from the government of Sudan to advocate support for the Universal Declaration of Human Rights
  - Promote the principle that people adversely impacted by GNPOC operations receive fair and just compensation
  - Promote a program of independent monitoring of human rights to GNPOC partners
    - Promote a program of independent monitoring of human rights to the government of Sudan

GNPOC operations." However, the small number of complaints with which this manual deals does not match the reports by third parties of the numerous atrocities and abuses that have taken place, suggesting that there is some other explanation for the company's results. For instance Talisman refers to the situation in Paryang, a community on the eastern edge of the concession, as follows:

Our records show that a further 10 cases were opened in November 2000 to keep files of initial interviews with people who have been displaced. These cases include six individuals who have come to Paryang during 2000 from surrounding villages to escape from famine, disease or conflict; and two people who left Paryang, seven and 20 years ago respectively, and have now returned.[53]

Contrast this description with the testimony of a refugee — which is far from unique — about the conditions in Paryang. It was given to the Harker mission in 1999, a year before Talisman's report, but it is hard to reconcile with the few complaints received by the company:

About 200 people came to Biem from Paryang. I came from Paryang in May. My family was repatriated to Paryang from Khartoum by the Government of Sudan and the Government would not let us leave Paryang town. The Government of Sudan forces mistreated us. We were not given any services, we had to find our own food and make our own living. When the women would go to gather wood and cut grass to build shelters, the Arab militia followed us to take what we had and rape us. I tried to escape with three others from the town. The Government of Sudan [forces] shot at us. The others were killed. I was hit in the leg but managed to escape.[54]

A similar discrepancy exists in Talisman's version of the military use of the Talisman-built Heglig airstrip, which the company describes as involving "at least four instances of non-defensive usage of the Heglig airstrip in 2000." The *Harker Report,* on the other hand, notes:

We also learned, and have reported, that flights clearly linked to the oil war have been a regular feature of life at the Heglig airstrip, which is adjacent to the oil workers' compound. It is operated by the consortium, and Canadian chartered helicopters and fixed wing aircraft which use the strip have shared the facilities with helicopter gunships and Antonov bombers of the Government of Sudan. These have armed and re-fuelled at Heglig and from there attacked civilians.[55]

---

[53] *Ibid.* at 18.

[54] *Harker Report, supra* note 15 at 84.

[55] *Ibid.* at 15.

Given such details in the *Harker Report* and similar incidents raised by the UN rapporteur and NGOs, one could have reasonably expected Talisman's auditors to make some effort to deal with them, yet there is nothing of the sort in the *CSR Report*. For example, the murder of eight Nuer tribesmen who had gone seeking jobs with the GNPOC in August 1999 and were put to death for it, which was recorded in the *Harker Report*, is no where addressed.[56] In general, there is an empty, dream-like quality to the *CSR Report*'s descriptions and numbers, which vary so considerably from reliable outside reports that they must be taken to greatly understate the magnitude of the situation. Simply put, the effort made by Talisman does not meet its obligation under the Code of Ethics in an emerging field of international law to "take a leadership role" in investigating and correcting human rights abuses caused by its activities.

Perhaps the most profound weakness of the *CSR Report* is its failure to address explicitly the question of the company's continuing presence in Sudan. This is an issue that looms large over Talisman's operation and consequently concerns any reader of the report. However, it receives almost no attention. Instead, the company side-steps the question, adopting a sort of earnest "gee shucks — we're learning" tone, and justifies its operation in the narrowest and most formal of terms, as the following passage demonstrates:

There is a legitimate debate regarding the role of development in areas of civil unrest. We believe that our involvement in Sudan is a positive one and that our actions are in compliance with the International Code of Ethics for Canadian Business. We also believe that we can help the people of Sudan by providing employment and skills training, enhancing local infrastructure, supporting further economic development, and by doing what we can to support peace and stability in the region. We recognize that others have differing opinions.[57]

Talisman's implicit position appears to be that "it's better for us to be doing this than someone else who might not be as committed to human rights as we are." The point is, however, that misery remains, and pumping oil *by anyone* exacerbates it. One might, of course, ask the question that was posed by a Sudanese academic

---

[56] With respect to this particular incident, John Harker went so far as to express in the report his hope that the government of Canada "will call for an investigation of [this] serious allegation" and added that "[w]e hope Talisman will join us in calling for, and facilitating, the investigation we seek." *Ibid.* at 14.

[57] *CSR Report, supra* note 11 at 42.

and is headlined in the report: "If Talisman were to leave, would the oil stop flowing?" but this question undermines the principle of the universality of human rights and has to be dismissed. Human rights are rights as well as obligations, and they are Talisman's to uphold regardless of what other companies might do in its place. At the very least, the company could have expressed a more considered rationale for its presence in Sudan. Without one, Talisman's commitment to corporate social responsibility in this context appears questionable.

There are some positive developments outlined in the *CSR Report*. Talisman indicates that it will use its influence to ensure that GNPOC job candidates are treated equally and not discriminated against, which is a problem identified in the *Harker Report*.[58] More generally, the company is trying to instill a community of respect for human rights among its employees by sending Talisman employees to courses at the Pearson Peacekeeping Centre in Clementsport, Nova Scotia. Assistance of a material nature is also being provided through Talisman philanthropy. The *CSR Report* refers to Talisman-supplied medical services, waterworks, education, and emergency relief, totalling almost $1 million in 2000. More money will be given in the future. The *CSR Report* includes a profile of the GNPOC's national employee complex in Khartoum, although systemic bias in GNPOC hiring means few southerners are likely to benefit from the complex. It also highlights Talisman's assistance to a vocational school, again in Khartoum, which provides trades training to 1,000 boys. The *CSR Report* does not say, however, what Talisman is doing to improve vocational prospects for Sudanese women.

Talisman's efforts are noteworthy. At the same time, however, they must be understood in the context of what the GNPOC is doing. Oil development is the indirect cause of serious human rights abuses in Sudan. Talisman and its partners appear to be trying to do something about these abuses, but they have completely neglected the group rights that are at the root of these acts and have failed to undertake a honest examination of their own contribution

---

[58] "Certainly, there seem to be few, if any, Nuer or Dinka at work at Heglig, which seems to fit a widely held view in Western Upper Nile that the [government of Sudan], thus GNPOC, views all non-Arabs as potential threats to security ... If Talisman was serious about being a good corporate citizen, it would win *the support of its GNPOC partners to have an audit of hiring and employment practices carried out by the International Labour Organization.*" *Harker Report, supra* note 15 at 14 [emphasis in original].

to the conflict. Many critical questions have been raised by others, and these questions should have been addressed in the report. In most respects, they were not. Consequently, the *CSR Report* comes across as a superficial document at best, and it falls well short of evoking the robust spirit in which the Code of Ethics was conceived.

Conclusion

Talisman Energy's *CSR Report* presents a mixed, but ultimately disappointing, picture of its activities in southern Sudan. On the one hand, the company has committed itself to a leadership role in corporate social responsibility and has done some things to alleviate some individual human rights abuses. On the other hand, the company's actions to date appear insufficient. It has failed to adequately examine the most profound question, which is whether it should pull out of the country entirely. There can be nothing but a sense of dissatisfaction at Talisman's failure to assess its Sudan operation critically.

What can be done? The situation is complicated by the way in which Talisman operates in Sudan. The GNPOC is Mauritius registered and Khartoum based. It has a part-owner, who is Canadian. Could Canada be held responsible for the Talisman/GNPOC acts? International law does not provide a general rule on the attribution of responsibility for corporate activity. Some reference to broad principle is necessary.

The general rule of international law is to authorize the national state of a company to exercise a right of diplomatic protection on its behalf. At the same time, several regimes and authorities of international law require a genuine link or connection between a company and a protecting state based on the nature and quality of the contacts in question.[59] If a right of diplomatic protection is enjoyed, there is presumptively no reason why a duty of diplomatic responsibility should not arise. It makes sense that this duty should be proportional to the foreseeability and degree of corporate involvement, to the capacity to act, and to the nature and gravity of the wrong.

In this instance, it is clear that Mauritius has no real connection with the situation and that the national governments of Talisman's major co-partners, China and Malaysia, will not pursue the matter. Canada is left to deal with the abuses, which are serious and not

---

[59] C.F. Amerasinghe, "Jurisdiction Ratione Personae under the Convention on the Settlement of Investment Disputes between States and Nationals of Other States" (1974-5) 47 Brit. Y.B. Int'l L. 227 at 267.

entirely unforeseen.[60] The government has asked Talisman to adhere to the Code of Ethics and has undertaken a process of dialogue with the Sudanese government. In light of the Code of Ethic's modest impact on Talisman's corporate conduct, however, what else can be done? The *Harker Report* referred to several options, including the placement of certain Sudanese goods on the Import Control List, the placement of Sudan itself on the Area Control List, or, in the case of multilateral sanctions against Sudan, the invocation of the Special Economic Measures Act. The difficulty with all of these options is that Canada-Sudan trade is negligible and that there is no enthusiasm for multilateral sanctions against Sudan.[61] This situation leaves the government's current strategy of constructive engagement as the only practical prospect.

Another consideration is the United States. Sudan may be distant, but it has not gone unnoticed in Washington. In November 1997, the Clinton administration imposed import and export sanctions on Sudan. The fact that Canadian and other foreign oil companies are profiting from Sudanese ventures has increased American oil companies' interest in joining them, but at present they are unable to do so. Recent American diplomacy has indicated a desire to find a solution to the conflict and there are signs that Sudanese political figures have been receptive to this pressure.[62]

---

[60] "Canada has in the past expressed grave reservations concerning private sector involvement that may heighten tensions or otherwise fuel ongoing conflicts. Canada has consistently discouraged companies from doing business in Sudan and in 1992 suspended all support, including export finance and trade development programs. It has also issued warnings regarding the risks of working in the Sudanese oilfields due to security concerns and the potential danger to employees." *Harker Report, supra* note 15 at 25.

[61] Article 4 of the Special Economic Measures Act, S.C. 1992, c. 17, provides that the government may only invoke the Act "for the purpose of implementing a decision, resolution or recommendation of an international organization of states or association of states, of which Canada is a member, that calls on its members to take economic measures against a foreign state." Alternatively, measures may be taken where the government "is of the opinion that a grave breach of international peace and security has occurred that has resulted or is likely to result in a serious international crisis." The phrase "grave breach of international peace and security" is generally taken to mean Security Council action under Chapter VII of the UN Charter, June 26, 1945, Can. T.S. 1945 No. 7.

[62] See M. Lacey, "Sudan War in Agenda for Powell in Africa Visit," *New York Times* (May 23, 2001); J. Perlez, "Suddenly in Sudan, a Moment to Care," *New York Times* (June 17, 2001); J. Harker, "A Small Start on Peace," *Globe and Mail* (June 1, 2001) (referring to the commencement of negotiations between the Khartoum government and southern forces in Nairobi).

Could Canadian corporate behaviour be a catalyst for change abroad? This hope is clearly held by Talisman and the government of Canada. Those who observe events in Sudan with history in mind will recall the "intermediate" period of Canadian corporate participation in South Africa in the 1970s after the Canadian government's prohibition on new investment but before the push for divestment. At that time, similar arguments were made about continuing the corporate presence of enlightened foreign employers under apartheid. It is hard, however, to make any such analogy in the case at hand. The prevailing political constellation, the specificity of the actors involved, the rights at issue, and the magnitude of abuse call for a serious re-evaluation of Canadian corporate activity in Sudan. In this respect, it should also be recalled that the intermediate period in apartheid-era South Africa was followed by widespread divestment.

CHI CARMODY
Faculty of Law, University of Western Ontario

Sommaire

Talisman Energy, Soudan, et responsabilité sociale corporative

En 1998, une compagnie pétrolière canadienne, la Talisman Energy Incorporated de Calgary a acquit des parts dans une concession pétrolière dans le sud du Soudan. En 1999, elle commença l'exportation du pétrole à partir de cette région et paya des royalties au gouvernement soudanais, argent dont une partie a servi au financement des forces gouvernementales engagées dans une guerre civile contre les forces séparatistes du sud. La guerre a causé de nombreux abus aux droits de la personne. Les investissements de Talisman au Soudan ont par conséquent soulevé plus d'inquiétudes concernant les opérations commerciales dans les pays où de graves et fréquentes violations aux droits de la personne sont perpétrées. Quelles sont, en pareille situation, les obligations de la compagnie Talisman et du Canada dans cette conjoncture favorable où se pose la question de la responsabilité sociale des compagnies commerciales? Le présent commentaire analyse la question à la lumière d'événements récents.

Summary

Talisman Energy, Sudan, and Corporate Social Responsibility

In 1998, a Canadian oil company, Talisman Energy Incorporated of Calgary, acquired part interest in an oil concession in southern Sudan. In 1999, it began exporting oil from the region and paying royalties to the Sudanese government, some of which have been used to fund government forces engaged in a civil war against separatists in the south. The war has caused numerous human rights abuses. Talisman's investment in Sudan therefore raises concerns about corporate operations in countries where there are serious and frequent human rights violations. What are Talisman and Canada's obligations at this particular juncture — a point of fertile development in the field of international corporate social responsibility? This comment examines this question in light of recent events.

Reporting to the Human Rights Committee: The Canadian Experience

On December 16, 1966, the United Nations General Assembly adopted the International Covenant on Civil and Political Rights (ICCPR)[1] and the Optional Protocol to the International Covenant on Civil and Political Rights.[2] A decade later, the ICCPR internationally entered into force.[3] Once Canada acceded to the ICCPR, it became bound to follow its terms.[4] Pursuant to Article 2(1) of the ICCPR, Canada, as a contracting party, undertook to respect the human rights recognized in the ICCPR[5] and to ensure

[1] International Covenant on Civil and Political Rights, GA Res. 2200/A (XXI), 999 U.N.T.S. 171 [hereinafter ICCPR].

[2] Optional Protocol to the International Covenant on Civil and Political Rights, GA Res. 2200/A (XXI), 999 U.N.T.S. 302.

[3] The ICCPR entered into force after the deposit of thirty-five instruments of ratification (Article 49) on March 23, 1976.

[4] The Canadian government, after obtaining the support of the provinces, acceded to the ICCPR in May 1976 (see Privy Council Decision no. 1976-1156). The ICCPR formally entered into force in August 1976.

[5] In general terms, the rights and freedoms set out in Parts 1 and 3 of the ICCPR, *supra* note 1, cover the right of all people to self-determination (Article 1); the right to life (Article 6); the prohibition of torture and cruel, inhuman, or degrading treatment or punishment (Article 7); the prohibition of slavery, servitude, and forced or compulsory labour (Article 8); the liberty and security of the person (Article 9); the humane treatment of persons deprived of their liberty (Article 10); non-imprisonment for failure to fulfil a contractual obligation (Article 11); freedom of movement and residence (Article 12); the non-expulsion of aliens lawfully in the territory of a state party (Article 13); the right to a fair trial (Article 14); the prohibition of the retroactive application of criminal law (Article 15); equal recognition of persons before the law (Article 16); the right to privacy (Article 17); freedom of thought, conscience, and religion (freedom 18); freedom of opinion and expression (Article 19); the prohibition of propaganda for war or advocacy of national, racial, or religious hatred (Article 20); the right

their application without discrimination to all individuals within its territory and subject to its jurisdiction.[6] It also undertook, "where not already provided for by existing legislative or other measures," "to take the necessary steps, in accordance with its constitutional processes and with the provisions of the ... Covenant, to adopt such legislative or other measures as may be necessary to give effect to the rights recognised" in the ICCPR.[7] Under Article 2(3), Canada further committed itself to ensure that any individual whose ICCPR rights had been violated would receive an effective remedy in national law.[8]

With the ratification of the ICCPR, Canada also undertook the obligation to make regular reports to the Human Rights Committee (the independent body of experts established under the

---

to peaceful assembly (Article 21); the right to freedom of association (Article 22); rights relating to the protection of the family and children (Articles 23 and 24); certain political rights of citizens (Article 25); equality before the law and equal protection of the law (Article 26); and rights of ethnic, religious, and linguistic minorities (Article 27).

[6] Article 50 of the ICCPR stipulates that the provisions of the ICCPR apply to all parts of federal states.

[7] ICCPR, *supra* note 1 at Article 2(2). Article 2(2) does not require that a party incorporate the ICCPR into its law. See Human Rights Committee [hereinafter HRC], *General Comment 3*, HRI/Gen/1/Rev.3 (1997), para. 1 as well as the committee decision in *A. and S.N.* v. *Norway,* Comm. No. 224/1987, para. 6.2. See also D. Harris, "The International Covenant on Civil and Political Rights and the United Kingdom: An Introduction," in D. Harris and S. Joseph, eds., *The International Covenant on Civil and Political Rights and United Kingdom Law* (Oxford, 1995), 1 at 5.

[8] Article 2(3) of the ICCPR provides:

Each State Party to the Covenant undertakes:

(a) To ensure that any person whose rights and freedoms as herein recognized are violated shall have an effective remedy, notwithstanding that the violation has been committed by persons acting in an official capacity;

(b) To ensure that any person claiming such a remedy shall have his right thereto determined by competent judicial, administrative or legislative authorities, or by any other competent authority provided for by the legal system of the State, and to develop the possibilities of judicial remedy;

(c) To ensure that the competent authorities shall enforce such remedies when granted.

For further discussion of Article 2(3), see W.M. Walker, "The Remedies of Law of the ICCPR: Current Trends and a Conceptual Framework for the Future" (1988) 20 N.Y.U.J. Int'l L. & P. 525.

ICCPR)[9] in regard to its protection of human rights and to its progress in implementing the new treaty.[10] In the next few pages, the reports submitted by Canada, as well as the comments issued by committee members in the course of analysis of these reports, will be examined in order to get a better sense of whether Canada is fulfilling its ICCPR commitments.

HUMAN RIGHTS COMMITTEE AND THE SUBMISSION OF REPORTS

The Human Rights Committee monitors compliance with the provisions of the ICCPR through the examination of national reports.[11] All states must prepare a report within one year of ratification and, "thereafter, whenever the Committee so requests."[12] In

[9] Article 28 provides for the establishment of the HRC. For discussion of the composition and role of the HRC, see D. McGoldrick, *The Human Rights Committee: Its Role in the Development of the International Covenant on Civil and Political Rights* (Oxford, 1996), 44-55. The committee's two main functions are to consider reports from, and complaints against, state parties. While the former is obligatory for all states parties, the latter is optional and exists in two forms: interstate communications under the ICCPR (Article 41) and individual communications under the Optional Protocol. On October 29, 1979, Canada made a declaration pursuant to Article 41 of the ICCPR accepting the committee's jurisdiction over interstate complaints. Canada's declaration is subject to a condition of reciprocity. Thus, Canada will only accept petitions directed against it if the petitioning state has made a similar declaration at least twelve months earlier. See (1979) 1147 U.N.T.S. 316.

[10] For discussion of federal and provincial governmental participation in the reporting procedure as set out in Article 40 of the ICCPR, see D. Turp, "La preparation des rapports periodiques du Canada en application des traites relatifs aux droits et libertes" (1986) 23 C.Y.I.L. 161.

[11] For a general overview of the reporting obligation, see T. Opsahl, "The Human Rights Committee," in P. Alston, ed., *The United Nations and Human Rights* (Oxford, 1992), 369 at 397-419; McGoldrick, *supra* note 9 at 62-104; and M. Nowak, *United Nations Covenant on Civil and Political Rights: CCPR Commentary* (Kehl, 1993) at 546-76.

[12] ICCPR, *supra* note 1 at Article 40. Subsequent periodic reports are usually requested every five years. The five-year periodicity is a matter of practice that can be changed. See HRC, Decision on Periodicity, Doc. A/36/40, Ax. V., amended by Decision on Periodicity, Doc. A/3740, Ax.IV, CCPR/C/19/Rev. 1 (July 22, 1981), as amended on July 28, 1982, August 26, 1982. For subsequent periodic reports, the committee has adopted a practice of stating, at the end of its concluding observations, a date by which the following periodic report should be submitted. See *Consolidated Guidelines for State Reports under the International Covenant on Civil and Political Rights*, CCPR/C/66/GUI/Rev. 2, at para B.2 (the consolidated guidelines replace all earlier versions of the reports issued by the committee, which are effective after December 31, 1999) [hereinafter *Consolidated*

these reports, state parties must indicate "the measures they have adopted" to give effect to the rights recognized in the ICCPR and "the progress made in the enjoyment of those rights."[13] The reports must also indicate the "factors and difficulties" affecting the implementation of the ICCPR.[14]

In its reporting guidelines, the committee has articulated the fact that initial reports should "establish the constitutional and legal framework for the implementation of Covenant rights," "explain the legal and practical measures adopted to give effect to Covenant rights," and "demonstrate the progress made in ensuring enjoyment of Covenant rights by the people within the State party and subject to its jurisdiction."[15] Every article found in Parts 1, 2, and 3 of the ICCPR must be dealt with by state parties. While legal norms must be described, their description alone is not sufficient. The factual situation, the practical availability, and the effect and implementation of remedies for violation of ICCPR rights have to be explained and exemplified.[16] Article D.2.2 of the guidelines also stipulates that reports should explain:

- [h]ow article 2 of the Covenant is applied, setting out the principal legal measures which the State party has taken to give effect to Covenant rights; and the range of remedies available to persons whose rights may have been violated;
- [w]hether the Covenant is incorporated into domestic law in such a manner as to be directly applicable;
- [i]f not, whether its provisions can be invoked before and given effect to by courts, tribunals and administrative authorities;

Guidelines]. A procedure also exists for special reports in cases of emergency. See *Report of the Human Rights Committee to the General Assembly*, A/49/40, vol. 1, paras. 45-7 as well as p. 111 [hereinafter *Report of the HRC*]; and Rule 66 of the *Rules of Procedure of the Human Rights Committee*, CCPR/C/3/Rev.5, 13-14 [hereinafter *Rules of Procedure*].

13 ICCPR, *supra* note 1 at Article 40(1).

14 *Ibid.* at Article 40(2). See also Rule 66(1) of the *Rules of Procedure*, *supra* note 12, and Article C.4 of the *Consolidated Guidelines*, *supra* note 12, elaborating that reports "should explain the nature and extent of, and reasons for every such factor and difficulty, if any such exist; and should give details of the steps taken to overcome these."

15 *Consolidated Guidelines*, *supra* note 12 at Article D.1

16 *Ibid.* at Article D.2.1.

- [w]hether the Covenant rights must be enacted or reflected in domestic law by legislation so as to be enforceable.[17]

Information regarding which national authorities possess jurisdiction to secure ICCPR rights must be included in initial reports.[18] Furthermore, reports should contain data pertaining to any institution or machinery that has a role to play in implementing Covenant rights or in responding to complaints of violations of such rights.[19]

The content and form of periodic reports is also determined by committee guidelines. Essentially, in these reports, state parties are asked to bring to the committee's attention any development that has occurred with respect to the implementation of the ICCPR since they submitted their last report.[20] The introduction of new legal or administrative measures must be touched upon,[21] and an article-by-article report may be required if fundamental changes in a state party's political and legal approach affecting Covenant rights have occurred.[22]

Since the committee's aim in considering reports is to engage in "constructive" dialogue with state parties so as to "improve the situation pertaining to Covenant rights in the State,"[23] governmental delegates are invited to present their national reports to the committee and to answer questions at oral hearings.[24] Rule 68 of the committee's rules of procedures provides that

[t]he Committee shall, through the Secretary-General, notify the States parties as early as possible of the opening date, duration and place of the session at which their respective reports will be examined. Representatives

---

[17] *Ibid.* at Article D.2.2.

[18] *Ibid.* at Article D.2.3.

[19] *Ibid.* at Article D.2.4.

[20] *Ibid.* at Article E.1. From a structural point of view, the reports should follow the articles of the ICCPR. See *ibid.* at Article E.2.

[21] *Ibid.* at Article E.4.

[22] *Ibid.*

[23] *Ibid.* at Article G.1.

[24] State parties are supplied in advance with a list of issues that will be addressed by the HRC during the consideration of their report (*ibid.* at Article G.2). The committee guidelines suggest that a state party's delegation should be composed of persons who possess the required knowledge and competence to adequately respond to the HRC's questions and comments (*Ibid.* at Article G.3).

of the States parties may be present at the meetings of the Committee when their reports are examined. The Committee may also inform a State party from which it decides to seek further information that it may authorize its representative to be present at a specified meeting. Such a representative should be able to answer questions which may be put to that representative by the Committee and make statements on reports already submitted by the State party concerned, and may also submit additional information from that State party.[25]

Once the Human Rights Committee has examined a national report, it transmits "such general comments as it may consider appropriate" to the state party.[26] Since 1992, the committee has completed its consideration of national reports by adopting concluding observations specific to the state concerned.[27] These observations reflect the views of the committee as a whole and are later used as one of the starting points for the state party's subsequent periodic reports.[28]

CANADIAN REPORTS

Since Canada ratified the ICCPR in 1976, it has presented four reports to the Human Rights Committee. It submitted its initial report in 1979[29] and a supplementary report in 1983 in which it outlined the general nature and contents of the Canadian Charter

---

[25] *Rules of Procedure, supra* note 12 at 14.

[26] ICCPR, *supra* note 1 at Article 40(4). See also Rule 70(3) of the *Rules of Procedure, supra* note 12 at 15, and of the *Consolidated Guidelines, supra* note 12 at Article G.4.

[27] The observations of the HRC are additional to the comments made by individual members. The committee's concluding observations are included in the HRC's reports to the General Assembly. The committee's concluding observations provide a general evaluation of a state party's report. The observations make note of positive developments that may have occurred during the period under review, factors and difficulties affecting the implementation of the ICCPR, and specific issues of concern relating to the application of the provisions of the ICCPR. They also include suggestions and recommendations to the state party concerned. See *Consolidated Guidelines, supra* note 12 at Article G.4.

[28] See *ibid.* at Article E.1.

[29] *Consideration of Reports Submitted by States Parties under Article 40 of the Covenant, Initial Reports of States Parties Due in 1977 — Canada*, CCPR/C/1/Add. 43 [hereinafter *First Report*]. The report was examined March 25, 26, and 28, 1979. *Summary Records of the Human Rights Committee*, CCPR/C/SR 205-8 and 211 [hereinafter *First Examination*].

of Rights and Freedoms.[30] Canada's second[31] and third[32] reports were submitted in 1989 and 1990,[33] and its fourth report was proffered in 1997.[34] All of Canada's reports contain information on measures adopted by the federal government and each of the provincial and territorial governments.

CANADA'S INITIAL REPORT[35]

Canada's first report was divided into two parts. The first part placed the ICCPR in the context of the Canadian constitutional system, while the second part examined Canadian law at the national, territorial, and provincial levels in order to determine to what degree it was consistent with the ICCPR. In its introduction, the federal government informed the committee that, in Canada, international treaty law was not automatically a part of the law of the land. Hence, the provisions of a treaty could be incorporated into domestic law either by enacting legislation giving force of law to a

---

[30] *Consideration of Reports Submitted by States Parties under Article 40 of the Covenant, Initial Reports of States Parties Due in 1977 — Canada,* CCPR/C/1/Add. 62 [hereinafter *Supplementary Report*]. The report was examined October 31 and November 1 and 2, 1984. *Summary Record of the Human Rights Committee,* CCPR/C/SR 558-60 and 562 [hereinafter *Supplementary Examination*]. Canadian Charter of Rights and Freedoms, Part 1 of the Constitution Act, 1982, being Schedule B to the Canada Act 1982 (U.K.), 1982, c. 11 [hereinafter Charter].

[31] *Consideration of Reports Submitted by States Parties under Article 40 of the Covenant, Second Periodic Reports of States Parties Due in 1988 — Canada,* CCPR/C/51/Add.1 [hereinafter *Second Report*].

[32] *Consideration of Reports Submitted by States Parties under Article 40 of the Covenant, Third Periodic Reports of States Parties Due in 1990 — Canada,* CCPR/C/64/Add.1 [hereinafter *Third Report*]. The *Third Report* was submitted, at the request of the United Nations Secretariat, as an update of the second report.

[33] Canada's second and third reports were examined together on October 23 and 24, 1990. *Summary Record of the Human Rights Committee,* CCPR/C/SR 1010-13 [hereinafter *Second and Third Examinations*].

[34] *Consideration of Reports Submitted by States Parties under Article 40 of the Covenant, Fourth Periodic Reports of States Parties Due in 1995 — Canada,* CCPR/C/103/Add.5 [hereinafter *Fourth Report*]. The *Fourth Report* was examined on March 26, 1999. *Summary Record of the Human Rights Committee,* CCPR/SR.1737-8 [hereinafter *Fourth Examination*]. The HRC's concluding observations were adopted on April 6, 1999. *Concluding Observations of the Human Rights Committee: Canada,* CCPR/C/79/Add. 105 [hereinafter *Concluding Observations*].

[35] For a summary of the HRC's consideration of Canada's first report, see *Report of the Human Rights Committee to the General Assembly,* A/35/40, paras. 154-96.

treaty or, if necessary, by amending domestic law to make it accord with a treaty.[36] It explained that, since "the Canadian constitution does not authorize Parliament to legislate in fields under provincial jurisdiction to give effect to obligations assumed under a treaty," the "implementation of a treaty whose provisions come under one or the other, or both levels of government requires action by the Parliament of Canada, the provincial legislatures and, unless, Parliament decided otherwise, the territorial legislative councils for those portions of the treaty that fall under their respective jurisdictions."[37]

The Canadian government informed the committee that since "Parliament did not have jurisdiction to give effect to all the obligations which Canada assumed toward the international community by acceding to the Covenant," it had engaged in a consulting process with the provinces before accession.[38] During these consultations, the provincial governments had undertaken to ensure compliance with those provisions of the ICCPR that fell within their jurisdiction.[39] Although all governments in Canada undertook to give effect to the provisions of the ICCPR, no government has, as yet, decided to incorporate into its domestic legislation the provisions of the ICCPR that fell within the scope of its jurisdiction."[40] Since the Covenant was not incorporated into domestic law and, therefore, did not have force of law at the federal, provincial and territorial levels, an individual could not base a recourse on the ICCPR itself if there has occurred within Canada a breach of a right or freedom therein recognized. An individual could, however, resort to the remedies provided in Canadian law to have his or her rights respected.[41]

---

[36] *First Report, supra* note 29 at 3.

[37] *Ibid.* In responding to questions raised by HRC members, the Canadian delegate clarified that "[u]nder the Canadian Constitution, international agreements were concluded by the federal Government" (the Governor General acting on the advice of the Prime Minister and his Cabinet) "but international agreements did not alter domestic law. If the federal law had to be amended in order to comply with an international obligation, it lay with Parliament to legislate for that purpose. If the subject of the law to be changed was within provincial jurisdiction, only the provincial legislatures had the power to make the amendments required" (*First Examination, supra* note 29 at 211, para.3).

[38] *First Report, supra* note 29 at 5. See also *Supplementary Report, supra* note 30 at question 2.

[39] *First Report, supra* note 29.

[40] *Ibid.* at 6.

[41] *Ibid.*

After examining the Canadian report, most members of the committee expressed their satisfaction not only with its comprehensiveness but also with the frank manner in which it was drafted.[42] Some members, however, regretted the fact that the report had not provided more information on the way in which Canada discharged its obligations in practice.[43] In addition, several committee members made comments regarding compliance with Article 1 of the ICCPR.[44] Particular concern was expressed over the fact that the right to self-determination was not expressly guaranteed in any of the Canadian provinces and that it was not even mentioned in the laws of some provinces.[45] In order to gain a better understanding of the situation in Canada, the committee requested that it be furnished with more information on any specific guarantees that existed within the country to ensure respect for the right of self-determination. It also asked that the federal government elucidate its position in regard to the right of secession.[46]

[42] See, for example, *First Examination, supra* note 29 at 205, paras. 17, 33, and 47; at 206, paras. 4, 13, 25, and 43; at 207, paras. 1, 19, 29, and 33; and at 208, para. 1.

[43] See *ibid.* at 205, para. 21; and at 208, para. 1.

[44] ICCPR, *supra* note 1 at Article 1 states that

1. All peoples have the right to self-determination. By virtue of that right they freely determine their political status and freely pursue their economic, social and cultural development.

2. All peoples may, for their own ends, freely dispose of their natural wealth and resources without prejudice to any obligations arising out of economic co-operation, based upon the principle of mutual benefit, and international law. In no case may a people be deprived of its own subsidence.

3. The State Parties to the present Covenant ... shall promote the realization of the right to self-determination, and shall respect that right, in conformity with the provisions of the Charter of the United Nations.

[45] See *First Examination, supra* note 29 at 205, para. 23; and at 206, para. 26.

[46] See *ibid.* at 205, paras. 23 and 35; at 206, para. 3; at 207, para. 21; and at 208, para. 3. For the response of the Canadian delegation, see *First Examination, supra* note 29 at 211, para. 10. The supplementary report submitted by Canada did not address the question of Canadian compliance with Article 1 of the ICCPR (see *Supplementary Report, supra* note 30). During discussions of this report, M. Al Douri maintained that it was regrettable that "the Canadian Government had not seen fit to devote more attention either in the initial or the supplementary report to Article 1 of the Covenant" (*Supplementary Examination, supra* note 30 at 559, para. 40). In responding to this criticism, the Canadian representative maintained that the "Canadian attitude to Article 1 of the Covenant had been fully covered in the initial report" (*Supplementary Examination, supra* note 30 at 559, para. 44).

Canadian compliance with Articles 2, 4, 9, 14, 15, 20, and 26 of the ICCPR did not escape criticism. Committee members pointed out that the prohibited grounds for discrimination set forth in various Canadian laws did not correspond to those specified in Articles 2 and 26 of the ICCPR[47] and that, contrary to the requirements of Article 14 of the ICCPR,[48] there did not exist within Canada a system of compensation for persons wrongly convicted.[49] Statements were made to the effect that some of the provisions of the War Measures Act[50] were contrary to Section 4 of the ICCPR[51] and that Canadian law, which permitted a person arrested under a warrant to be arrested without informing him or her of the contents of the warrant, fell short of the requirements of Article 9(2)

---

[47] Articles 2 and 26 of the ICCPR prohibit discrimination "on any ground such as race, colour, sex, language, religion, political or other opinion, national or social origin, birth or other status." For HRC criticism, see *First Examination, supra* note 29 at 206, paras. 2, 15, 27, and 28; at 207, para. 6; and at 208, para. 2. Concern was particularly shown over the fact that political opinions were not among the prohibited grounds of discrimination in Canada. See *First Examination, supra* note 29 at 205, para. 24; at 206, paras.10, 17, and 36; and at 207, para. 6. For the Canadian response, see *First Examination, supra* note 29 at 211, para. 9; and *Supplementary Report, supra* note 30 at 62. See also *Yearbook of the Human Rights Committee 1985-6*, CCPR/5/Add.1, at 41-2 and 63; and *Supplementary Examination, supra* note 30 at 562, para. 32.

[48] ICCPR, *supra* note 1 at Article 14(6), provides that

when a person has by a final decision been convicted of a criminal offence and when subsequently his convictions have been reversed or he has been pardoned on the ground that a newly discovered fact shows conclusively that there has been a miscarriage of justice, the person who has suffered punishment as a result of such conviction shall be compensated according to law, unless it is proved that the non-disclosure of the unknown fact in time is wholly or partly attributable to him.

[49] Questions of non-compliance with Article 14(7) of the ICCPR were also raised as it appeared possible that, in Canada, if Parliament so chose, a person could be convicted twice for the same offence. Article 14(7) of the ICCPR states that "no one shall be liable to be tried or punished again for an offence for which he has already been finally convicted or acquitted in accordance with the law and penal procedure of each country." For HRC inquiries, see *First Examination, supra* note 29 at 205, paras. 30, 55, and 59; at 206, paras. 23, 30, and 50; and at 207, para. 13. For the Canadian response, see *Supplementary Report, supra* note 30 at 62, para. 61; *Supplementary Examination, supra* note 30 at 562, para. 25.

[50] War Measures Act, S.C. 1914, Sess. 2, c. 2.

[51] Article 4 of the ICCPR deals with permissible derogations to ICCPR obligations in times of public emergencies. For HRC discussions, see *First Examination, supra* note 29 at 205, para. 25; and at 208, para. 4.

of the ICCPR.[52] Negative comments were also made over the fact that, in Canada, no statutory provisions expressly prohibited propaganda for war[53] or expressly prohibited Parliament from enacting retroactive laws.[54]

Another issue that drew the committee's attention was the handling of minorities within Canada.[55] In focusing on the treatment of indigenous peoples,[56] many members observed that, unfortunately, instances of distinctions between Indians and Canadian citizens seemed to exist within Canadian society.[57]

CANADA'S SUPPLEMENTARY REPORT[58]

This report was prepared in order to supplement the information contained in Canada's initial report. Part 1 of the report contained information on the new provisions of Canada's constitution as well as information on matters falling under federal

---

[52] Article 9(2) of the ICCPR posits that "anyone who is arrested shall be informed, at the time of arrest, of the reasons for his arrest and shall be promptly informed of any charges against him." For the HRC's inquiries, see *First Examination, supra* note 29 at 205, paras. 27 and 40; at 206, para. 48; and at 207, paras. 10 and 32. See also *Supplementary Examination, supra* note 30 at 562, para. 31. For the Canadian position, see *First Examination, supra* note 29 at 211, para. 46; *Supplementary Report, supra* note 30 at 62, para. 52.

[53] Article 20(1) of the ICCPR sets out that "any propaganda for war shall be prohibited by law." For HRC comments, see *First Examination, supra* note 29 at 205, para. 62; at 206, paras. 7, 32, and 39; and at 207, paras. 3 and 27. For the Canadian position, see *Supplementary Report, supra* note 30 at 62, para. 65; *Supplementary Examination, supra* note 30 at 562, para. 45.

[54] Article 15 of the ICCPR expressly prohibits retroactive criminal laws. For the HRC's comments see *First Examination, supra* note 29 at 205, paras. 43 and 60; and at 207, para. 25. For the Canadian response, see *Supplementary Report, supra* note 30 at 62, paras. 61-2.

[55] See *First Examination, supra* note 29 at 206, paras. 15, and 26; at 207, para. 28. See also *Supplementary Examination, supra* note 30 at 560, paras. 23 and 37. For Canadian explanations, see *Supplementary Report, supra* note 30 at 62, paras. 69-70.

[56] See *First Examination, supra* note 29 at 206, paras. 12, 51; at 207, paras. 28, 31. See also *Supplementary Examination, supra* note 30 at 560, para. 24. For the Canadian response, see *First Examination, supra* note 29 at 211, paras. 11-24; *Supplementary Report, supra* note 30 at 62, paras. 70-3; *Supplementary Examination, supra* note 30 at 562, paras. 24, 41-4.

[57] See *First Examination, supra* note 29 at 205, para. 35; at 207, paras. 4, 37.

[58] For an account of the issues raised during the HRC's examination of Canada's supplementary report, see *Report of the Human Rights Committee to the General Assembly*, A/40/40, at paras. 176-250.

jurisdiction.[59] Essentially, the Canadian government sought to bring to the attention of the Human Rights Committee's its adoption of the Canadian Charter of Rights and Freedoms and its efforts to protect the rights of Aboriginal peoples in its constitution. Part 2 of the report contained an analytical summary of the replies provided by provincial and territorial governments to the questions raised by members of the committee during consideration of the initial report.

In introducing Canada's supplementary report to the committee, the Canadian delegation expounded on which sections of the *Charter* corresponded to the respective sections of the ICCPR.[60] A Canadian representative affirmed that although "it was true that the Charter and the Covenant were not identical in every respect, there was a high degree of similarity and complementarity between them."[61] Not only had the Charter given effect to many of Canada's obligations under the ICCPR,[62] it had also been the source for many of the changes in the original draft of the Charter — as had

[59] See *Supplementary Report, supra* note 30.

[60] See *Supplementary Examination, supra* note 30 at 558, paras. 5-7. Section 2 of the Charter (recognition of fundamental freedoms) corresponds generally to the provisions of Articles 18, 19, 21, and 22 of the ICCPR. Sections 3 to 5 of the Charter (guarantee of democratic rights) correspond to Article 25 of the ICCPR. Section 6 of the Charter (guarantee of freedom of movement and residence) has its counterpart in Article 12 of the ICCPR. Sections 7 to 14 of the Charter (guarantee of legal rights) are comparable to Articles 6, 7, 8, 9, 14, and 15 of the ICCPR. Section 15 of the Charter (recognition of the right to equality) is the counterpart of Article 26 of the ICCPR. As for Articles 16 to 22 (status and use of French and English languages) and 23 (educational rights), they contribute to the implementation of Articles 26 and 27 of the ICCPR.

[61] *Supplementary Examination, supra* note 30 at 558, para.12.

[62] In its supplementary report, the federal government addressed the question of what would be the international and domestic implications if Canada did not carry out the obligations it had assumed in acceding to the treaty (See *Supplementary Report, supra* note 30 at 62, para. 40, question 5). It set out that, from a domestic point of view, if Canada did not give effect to the provisions of the treaty, individuals who had suffered as a result could submit written communications to the HRC. However, if Canada ignored its international obligations, notwithstanding its accession to the ICCPR and the Optional Protocol, the only remedy available would be of a "political" nature. Pressure could be put on the federal and provincial governments to comply with their respective undertakings. In international law, failure by Canada to comply with the undertakings given by it in acceding to the ICCPR would imply that a communication could be submitted against Canada by an individual (under the protocol) or by a state (pursuant to Article 41 of the ICCPR). It would also be possible for a state

the comments made by members of the committee during the review of Canada's initial report.[63]

After examining and discussing the applicability and scope of the Charter, several members of the committee expressed regret that it did not seem to afford protection from violation of individual rights committed by non-governmental or private entities.[64] While questions were raised in regard to the compatibility of Sections 1[65] and 24[66] of the Charter with the provisions of the ICCPR, most reservations were directed towards Section 33 of the Charter.[67] Several members voiced their apprehension about the fact that the application of Section 33 could lead to derogations from rights guaranteed under the ICCPR.[68] In particular, it was noted that the Charter did not make reference to all the non-derogable rights mentioned in Article 4 of the ICCPR[69] and that

---

member of the United Nations to bring the question of Canada's failure to comply with its obligations under the ICCPR to the attention of the General Assembly. Possibly, Canada's non-compliance with its obligations under the ICCPR could also confer on other states that were parties to the treaty, the right to seek compensation from Canada for damages resulting from such non-compliance.

[63] See *Supplementary Examination*, supra note 30.

[64] See *Supplementary Examination*, *supra* note 30 at 558, paras. 43, 44, and 49; at 559, paras. 3, 8. For the Canadian position, see *Supplementary Examination*, *supra* note 30 at 559, paras. 34-5.

[65] See *ibid.* at 558, paras. 35 and 43. For the Canadian response, see *ibid.* at 559, paras. 25-6.

[66] See *ibid.* at 558, paras. 46, 49; *ibid.* at 561, para. 37.

[67] Section 33 of the Charter states that "Parliament or the legislature of a province may expressly declare in an Act of Parliament or of the legislature, as the case may be, that the Act or a provision thereof shall operate notwithstanding a provision included in section 2 or sections 7 to 15 of this Charter."

[68] See *Supplementary Examination*, *supra* note 30 at 558, paras. 48, 50; at 559, paras. 9, 11. For the Canadian justification for inclusion of section 33, see *Supplementary Examination*, *supra* note 30 at 559, paras. 27-9. The Canadian representative sought to appease the worries of the HRC by affirming that

In the view of the Federal Government, any resort to section 33 would have to be compatible with Canada's international obligations, which would be invoked if there were any real derogation from the rights and freedoms set out in the Canadian Charter. Canada was obliged to report to the Human Rights Committee and was a party to the Optional Protocol so that anyone seeking to assert a right would be able to have recourse to the Committee if deprived of a remedy under section 33 (para. 27).

[69] The state parties to the ICCPR have the right, in certain circumstances, to take measures derogating from the obligations they assumed by adhering to the treaty. Article 4 of the ICCPR states that

Section 33 did not mention, as Article 4 did, that derogations could only occur in times of public emergency and that they had to be non-discriminatory.[70]

CANADA'S SECOND AND THIRD REPORTS[71]

Canada's second and third reports focused on Charter jurisprudence, more specifically on the changes brought about to the

---

1. In time of public emergency which threatens the life of the nation and the existence of which is officially proclaimed, the States Parties to the present Convention may take measures derogating from their obligations under the present Covenant to the extent strictly required by the exigencies of the situation, provided that such measures are not inconsistent with their obligations under international law and do not involve discrimination solely on the ground of race, colour, sex, language, religion or social origin.

2. No derogation from Articles 6, 7, 8 (paragraphs 1 and 2), 11, 15, 16 and 18 may be made under this provision.

For a discussion on Article 4, see J. Fitzpatrick, *Human Rights in Crisis: The International System for Protecting Rights during States of Emergency* (Philadelphia, 1994) at 88-105.

70 See also HRC, *General Comment 5*, HRI/GEN/1/Rev.3 (1997), where the HRC stated that

1. Article 4 of the Covenant has posed a number of problems for the Committee when considering reports from States parties. When a public emergency which threatens the life of a nation arises and it is officially proclaimed, a State party may derogate from a number of rights to the extent strictly required by the situation. The State party, however, may not derogate from certain specific rights and may not take discriminatory measures on a number of grounds. The State party is also under an obligation to inform the other States parties immediately, through the Secretary-General, of the derogations it has made including the reasons therefore and the date on which the derogations are terminated ...

3. The Committee holds the view that measures taken under Article 4 are of an exceptional and temporary nature and may only last as long as the life of the nation concerned is threatened and that, in times of emergency, the protection of human rights becomes all the more important, particularly those rights from which no derogations can be made. The Committee also considers that it is equally important for States parties, in times of public emergency, to inform the other States parties of the nature and extent of the derogations they have made and of the reasons therefore and, further, to fulfil their reporting obligations under Article 40 of the Covenant by indicating the nature and extent of each right derogated from together with the relevant documentation.

71 For a summary of the issues raised during a review of Canada's second and third reports, see *Report of the Human Rights Committee to the General Assembly*, A/46/40, paras. 45-101 [hereinafter *Report of the HRC*].

Canadian legal system as a result of judicial decisions. Aboriginal issues also occupied an important part of both reports as the committee was informed, *inter alia,* that the process of discussions on Aboriginal constitutional issues, which were mandated by Part 4 of the Constitution Act, 1982, had come to an end;[72] that steps were being taken towards the achievement of self-government for Aboriginal groups;[73] that the federal government had revised its policy on land claims;[74] and that a Royal Commission of Inquiry had been appointed to investigate the wrongful conviction of Donald Marshall.[75] References were also made to the 1987 Constitutional Accord[76] and to the tabling of the Canadian Multiculturalism Act.[77]

In its dialogue with the Canadian government delegation presenting the reports, the Human Rights Committee zoomed in on the treatment reserved to minorities within Canada, especially indigenous peoples.[78] The committee urged the federal government to engage in constitutional reforms in order to facilitate indigenous peoples' movement towards autonomy[79] and to rapidly settle the problems encountered by indigenous peoples "in a spirit of equity and respect for the rights enshrined in the ICCPR, in

---

[72] *Third Report, supra* note 32 at 1, para. 10.

[73] *Ibid.* at para. 144.

[74] *Ibid.* at para. 145.

[75] *Ibid.* at para. 327.

[76] *Ibid.* at para. 11.

[77] *Ibid.* at para. 149 and *Second and Third Examinations, supra* note 33 at 1010, para. 68. Canadian Multiculturalism Act, S.C. 1988, c. 31.

[78] See, for example, *Second and Third Examinations, supra* note 33 at 1010, paras. 61, 62, 69; and at 1013, paras. 13, 17, 30, and 31.

[79] See *Second and Third Examinations, supra* note 33 at 1013, para. 21. After reading both reports, the HRC distributed a series of questions to the Canadian representatives. These questions were to be answered during oral discussions. Two inquiries targeted the issue of self-governance. The committee, referring to paragraph 10 of the second report, wanted to know if there had been progress in the effort to reach agreement on providing a constitutional basis for self-government by aboriginal people. With reference to paragraph 63 of the third report, the committee also wanted explanations on the content of the self-government proposals being negotiated with Indian communities as well as an estimation of the prospects for a successful outcome of those negotiations. See *Second Report, supra* note 31 at 1; and *Third Report, supra* note 32 at 1. For Canada's response to these questions, see *Second and Third Examinations, supra* note 33 at 1010, para. 32; at 1012, paras. 24-5; at 1013, paras. 5-7.

particular in its articles 2, 26 and 27."[80] It also demanded that in future the question of the right to self-determination must be dealt with in a more complete fashion.[81]

Canada's policy regarding asylum seekers also played a prominent part in the committee's examination of the Canadian reports. Uneasiness was expressed not only towards the accumulation of applications for asylum but also towards the system adopted by the Canadian government to accelerate the processing of these applications.[82] Other areas for which the committee articulated concerns included respect for trade union rights and the right to collective bargaining[83] as well as respect for Article 14 of the ICCPR.[84]

As with Canada's previous report, the committee's main area of apprehension centred on the scope and applicability of Section 33 of the Charter. While some committee members worried that Section 33 could be used to depart from obligations in the ICCPR from which no derogations were permitted,[85] others were concerned with the fact that the section was itself incompatible with Article 4 of the ICCPR.[86] Despite some scattering comments made

[80] See *Report of the HRC, supra* note 71 at 25 and *Second and Third Examinations, supra* note 33 at 1013, para. 24.

[81] In its second report, under the heading of Article 1, Canada had simply stated that it subscribed to the principles set forth in the article. See *Second Report, supra* note 31 at 1, para. 12. For criticism of the lack of information provided by the Canadian government on the implementation of Article 1, see *Second and Third Examinations, supra* note 33 at 1010, paras. 46, 48, and 65 ; at 1013, paras. 35, 36. In reply to these criticisms, the Canadian representative stated that the issue of the implementation of Article 1 "had been adequately dealt with in Canada's initial report and the supplementary information submitted with it." While agreeing that the government "could have updated the information provided in the early reports," he "nevertheless felt that there were a number of other sources from which the Committee could have obtained the information requested." See *Second and Third Examinations, supra* note 33 at 1010, para. 82.

[82] See, for example, *Second and Third Examinations, supra* note 33 at 1011, paras. 9, 10, 11, 16, 39, and 60; at 1013, paras. 17, 19, 31, and 36. For the Canadian response, see *Second and Third Examinations, supra* note 33 at 1011, paras. 18, 19, 20.

[83] See *ibid.* at 1011, paras. 84, 85; at 1013, paras. 31, 39. For the Canadian position on this question, see *ibid.* at 1011, para. 86.

[84] See, for example, *ibid.* at 1013, paras. 20, 27.

[85] See, for example, *ibid.* at 1010, paras. 53, 67, 69, 92, and 98; at 1013, paras. 13, 17, 33, and 36. For the Canadian response, see *ibid.* at 1011, para. 3.

[86] Committee member Aguilar Urbina stated that "the derogation clause provided in Article 33 of the Canadian Charter of Rights and Freedoms ... went further than what was provided for in Article 4 of the ICCPR (*ibid.* at 1013, para. 13).

along the way, in the end, most committee members commended Canada for its respect of human rights[87] and for taking seriously its responsibilities under the ICCPR.[88] The quality of Canada's written reports was also singled out. In addition, the committee particularly appreciated the fact that the reports went beyond a mere description of the national legislation,[89] and they commented on the sincerity and quality of the discussions that had ensued during the presentation of the reports.[90]

CANADA'S FOURTH PERIODIC REPORT[91]

In its fourth report, under the heading of "Constitutional Developments," Canada informed the committee that efforts for constitutional reform within the country had culminated in a new constitutional accord in 1992.[92] The Charlottetown Accord was particularly relevant within the human rights context since it recognized Québec as a distinct society within Canada and affirmed the inherent right of self-government of Aboriginal peoples of Canada.[93] Although the accord was ultimately set aside, since the public voted against it, the referendum and the public discussions preceding it had to be viewed as positive since they "gave Canadians an opportunity to participate fully in the democratic process, and consider and debate issues of national concern."[94]

As for Mrs. Higgins, she explained that she "shared the opinions expressed by most members of the Committee on the subject of Article 33 ... which provided for a derogation clause that did not appear to be compatible with Article 4 of the ICCPR *(ibid.* at para. 18).

[87] See *ibid.* at 1010, para. 55; at 1013, para. 22.

[88] See, for example, *ibid.* at 1010, para. 41; at 1013, paras. 12, 25.

[89] See, for example, *ibid.* at 1010, paras. 44, 46, 53, 62, 66, and 97.

[90] See *ibid.* at 1013, paras. 14, 23, 28, 29, 31, 33, 34, 35, and 40.

[91] See *Fourth Report, supra* note 34 at 5. Canada's fourth report covers the period from 1990 to 1994. Given the lapse of time since the period covered by the *Fourth Report* and examination of the report by the HRC, Canada provided information to the committee highlighting some recent developments relating to the implementation of the ICCPR. See *Advanced Notes for the Presentation to the United Nations Human Rights Committee,* available at <www.pch.gc.ca//ddp-hrd/english/AdnotesE.htm> [hereinafter *Advanced Notes*].

[92] *Fourth Report, supra* note 34 at 5, para. 4.

[93] *Ibid.*

[94] *Ibid.* at para. 5.

In discussing the measures it had adopted to give effect to the provisions of the ICCPR, the federal government re-articulated that the Charter did not directly incorporate the Covenant into domestic Canadian law. It explained that while there existed differences in both structure and substance between the Charter and the ICCPR, the rights recognized in the ICCPR were protected by a combination of constitutional, legislative, and other measures.[95] It also reiterated the fact that because Canada is a federal state different aspects of human rights fall within the jurisdiction of different levels of government.[96]

Under the heading of "specific concerns of the Human Rights Committee," the federal government sought to address some of the issues and questions raised during the review of its second and third reports. For example, in examining Canadian compliance with Article 2 of the ICCPR, the government dealt with the committee inquiry[97] of whether the Aboriginal peoples of the Yukon and Northwest Territories could appear before the Canadian Human Rights Commission.[98] It also considered the committee's query[99] of whether the protections in section 4(b) of the Emergencies Act,[100] which appeared to be restricted to Canadian citizens and permanent residents, offended Article 4, paragraph 1, of the ICCPR.[101] Information was also provided about what steps had been taken to ensure that immigrants and asylum seekers were accorded their Covenant rights without discrimination.[102] Concerns about the uniformity of protection of rights across Canada — that is, about the relationship of federal and provincial laws in the field of human rights — were also addressed.[103]

Since committee members had previously raised numerous enquiries concerning the rights of Aboriginal peoples, details relating to this issue were included in the report. Information was provided

---

[95] *Ibid.* at para.22.

[96] *Ibid.*

[97] See, for example, *Second and Third Examinations, supra* note 33 at 1010, para. 43; at 1011, para. 7.

[98] *Fourth Report, supra* note 34 at 5, para. 30.

[99] See, for example, *Second and Third Examinations, supra* note 33 at 1010, para. 90.

[100] Emergencies Act, S.C. 1988, c. 29.

[101] *Fourth Report, supra* note 34 at 5, para. 37.

[102] *Ibid.* at para. 275.

[103] *Ibid.* at paras. 276-8.

on successful land claim settlements,[104] on the adoption of the Nunavut Act,[105] and on the governmental initiative of transferring responsibility for correctional services for Aboriginal criminal offenders to the Aboriginal communities themselves.[106] The practice of consulting with Aboriginal peoples before the ratification of international conventions was also discussed.[107]

According to the Canadian authorities, not only did the Constitution Act, 1982 recognize and affirm the "existing aboriginal and treaty rights of the aboriginal peoples of Canada" but the federal government, following the 1993 federal election, had also expressed its intention to act "on the premise that the inherent right of self-government of the aboriginal peoples of Canada is an existing aboriginal and treaty right."[108] Ongoing discussions continued with Aboriginal people on the implementation of the inherent right of self-government.[109]

The report also set out that a Royal Commission on Aboriginal Peoples had been established in 1991 to "investigate the evolution of the relationship among Aboriginal peoples, the Canadian Government and Canadian society as a whole."[110] The commission, which was charged with proposing solutions for developing a new relationship between Canada's Aboriginal and non-Aboriginal peoples, premised on "trust, understanding and mutual respect," came out with its final report in 1996.[111] The federal government pointed out that in 1998 it had responded to the commission's four hundred recommendations with an action plan that included a "statement of reconciliation."[112]

As in the previous reports, very little information was adduced

---

[104] *Ibid.* at paras. 290-3.

[105] *Ibid.* at para. 300. See also *Advanced Notes, supra* note 91 at 13. Nunavut Act, S.C. 1993, c. 28.

[106] *Fourth Report, supra* note 34 at 5, para. 289.

[107] *Ibid.* at para. 288.

[108] *Ibid.* at para. 6. See also paragraph 299 where the government elaborates that a policy framework is being developed for negotiations on implementation of the right of self-government, which may involve treaties and constitutional status. This process is said to replace the community-based self-government process described in previous reports.

[109] *Ibid.*

[110] *Ibid.* at para. 287.

[111] *Ibid.*

[112] *Advanced Notes, supra* note 91 at 12.

in relation to Article 1 of the ICCPR. In one sentence, the federal government simply asserted that "Canada subscribed to the principles set forth in this document."[113] In regard to Section 33 of the Charter, no new arguments were advanced to explain or justify its existence, despite continuous criticism by the committee.[114] The Canadian government simply stated that "given the infrequency with which the provision had been invoked and the resultant absence of jurisprudence, the precise effects of section 33 remain uncertain."[115]

In its "concluding observations," the Human Rights Committee condemned, more than praised, Canadian efforts.[116] On the positive side of the equation, the committee welcomed the Canadian delegation's commitment to take action in order to ensure the effective follow-up in Canada to the committee's concluding observations and to further develop and improve mechanisms for the ongoing review of compliance with the provisions of the ICCPR.[117] The government's assurance that it would inform all Canadians of committee concerns and recommendations was also applauded.[118] Also viewed positively was the federal and provincial governments' determination to work with Aboriginal peoples to address needed reforms[119] as well as the federal initiative in regard to Nunavut.[120] The committee welcomed the implementation of the Employment Equity Act, which established a compliance regime requiring federal departments to ensure that certain groups comprised a fair part of their workforce.[121]

During their discussion of the Canadian report, a number of committee members reprimanded Canada for not addressing sufficiently the subject of self-determination.[122] Not surprisingly, therefore, in the concluding observation section entitled "Principal

---

[113] *Fourth Report, supra* note 34 at 5, para. 20.

[114] *Ibid.* at paras. 33-4.

[115] *Ibid.* at para. 34.

[116] *Concluding Observations, supra* note 34.

[117] *Ibid.* at para 3.

[118] *Ibid.* For discussion of this issue within the Canadian report, see *Fourth Report, supra* note 34 at 5, paras. 17-19.

[119] *Concluding Observations, supra* note 34 at para. 4.

[120] *Ibid.* at para. 5.

[121] *Ibid.* at para. 6. For details of the act, see *Advanced Notes, supra* note 91 at 8-9. Employment Equity Act, R.S.C. 1995, c. 44.

[122] See, for example, the statements of Elizabeth Evatt and Roman Wieruszewski in *Human Rights Committee Begins Consideration of Canada's Fourth Periodic Report,* HR/CT/529 at 8.

Areas of Concern and Recommendations," Canada was "urged" to "report adequately on implementation of article 1 of the Covenant in its next periodic report."[123] The treatment of Aboriginal peoples in Canada also attracted the committee's attention. After expressing "concern" over the fact that the suggestions of the Royal Commission on Aboriginal Peoples had not yet been implemented, the committee recommended that "decisive and urgent action be taken towards the full implementation" of the commission's recommendations on land and resource allocation.[124] It further advocated that, "the practice of extinguishing inherent aboriginal rights be abandoned as incompatible with article 1 of the Covenant."[125]

Being "deeply concerned" by the fact that Canada had not, as of yet, held a "thorough public inquiry" into the death of an Aboriginal activist who had been shot by provincial police during a demonstration regarding land claims in 1995, the committee "strongly" urged that an investigation, which examined the role and responsibility of public officials in the affair, be set up.[126] The committee also recommended that Canadian authorities turn their attention to the ongoing problem of discrimination against Aboriginal women.[127] Other areas of concern included the fact that inadequate remedies existed for violations of Articles 2, 3, and 26 of the ICCPR;[128] that gaps remained between the protection of rights in Canada and the protection required under the ICCPR;[129] that Canadian authorities failed to comply with requests for interim measures of protection emanating from the

---

[123] *Concluding Observations, supra* note 34 at para. 7.

[124] *Ibid.* at para. 8.

[125] *Ibid.*

[126] *Ibid.* at para. 11.

[127] *Ibid.* at para. 19. After noting that the Indian status of women who had lost status because of marriage was reinstated in 1985 following amendments to the *Indian Act,* the HRC affirmed that these amendments seemed insufficient as they affected only women and their children, not subsequent generations. It thus recommended that the issue of denial of membership be further looked into (*ibid.*). For further discussion of this issue, see the HRC decision in *Lovelace,* Comm. no. 24/1977, Sel. Decs. vol. 1 at 83.

[128] *Concluding Observations, supra* note 34. The HRC recommended that human rights legislation be amended in order to guarantee access to a competent tribunal and to an effective remedy in all cases of discrimination (*ibid.*).

[129] *Ibid.* at para. 10. In order to ensure full implementation of ICCPR rights, the HRC recommended that consideration be given to the establishment of a public body responsible for overseeing implementation of the ICCPR and for reporting on any deficiencies (*ibid.*)

committee;[130] that there existed an attitude in Canada that compelling security interests could be invoked to justify the removal of
aliens to countries where they faced a substantial risk of torture or
cruel, inhuman, or degrading treatment;[131] and that the Canadian
policy in relation to the expulsion of long-term alien residents was
questionable.[132] The committee also questioned and expressed
uneasiness towards the "increasingly intrusive measures" affecting
the right to privacy in Canada, such as the practice of fingerprint-
ing and retinal scanning of people relying on social assistance);[133]
the barriers affecting the right of association;[134] the way in which
the National Child Benefit Supplement for low-income families was
implemented in some provinces (since this could result in a denial
of this benefit to some children);[135] the issue of homelessness;[136]
and, finally, the way women were disproportionally affected by
poverty in Canada (a situation that had worsened in recent years
due to program cuts).[137]

[130] *Ibid.* at para. 14. The HRC "urged" Canada to revise its policy of compliance "so
as to ensure that all such requests are heeded" (*ibid.*). The HRC decision of *Nq*,
Comm. no. 469/1991, in *Report of the Human Rights Committee to the General
Assembly*, A/49/40 at 189 provides one example of Canadian non-compliance.
In *Nq*, despite a request for a stay from the committee, the author of the communication was extradited to the United States. Canada was never able to comply with the committee's view that the author's extradition would constitute a
violation of Article 7 of the ICCPR, since extradition had already occurred
when the decision was rendered (*Report of the HRC, supra* note 12 at para. 7).

[131] *Ibid.* at para. 13. After referring to its general comment on Article 7, the HRC
recommended that Canada revise its policy "in order to comply with the
requirements of Article 7 and to meet its obligation never to expel, extradite,
deport or otherwise remove a person to a place where treatment or punishment
that is contrary to Article 7 is a substantial risk" (*ibid.*).

[132] *Ibid.* at para. 15.

[133] *Ibid.* at para. 16. The HRC recommended that all practices intruding on the
right of privacy be eliminated (*ibid.*).

[134] *Ibid.* at para. 17. Reference was made to the Act to Prevent Unionization with
Respect to Community Participation under the Ontario Works Act, 1997, S.O.
1997, c. 25, which was passed by the Ontario legislature. Such legislation was
said to affect implementation of Article 22 of the ICCPR (*ibid.*).

[135] *Ibid.* at para. 18. This could lead to non-compliance with section 24 of the
ICCPR (*ibid.*).

[136] *Ibid.* at para 12. Canada was asked to take whatever positive measures were necessary to address the problem of homelessness, as was required by Article 6 of
the ICCPR (*ibid.*).

[137] *Ibid.* at para. 20. The HRC recommended that Canada assess the impact on
women of recent changes in social programs and that action be undertaken to
redress any discriminatory effects of these changes (*ibid.*).

It is interesting to note that the committee made no reference in its concluding observations to the "notwithstanding clause" of the Charter. This fact is surprising since the committee, in its previous comments, had expressed the opinion that one of the most problematic areas of Canadian compliance with the provisions of the ICCPR concerned Section 33 of the Charter.[138]

CONCLUSION

Canada's record in regard to the fulfilment of its reporting obligation under the ICCPR has been positive so far. As an example of the quantitative, if not the qualitative, aspect of the Canadian reports, the last report submitted by Canada is over one hundred and forty pages long.[139] In their reports to the committee, the Canadian authorities have so far sought to provide, in most areas, a complete and accurate picture of the measures they have adopted that give effect to the rights recognized in the ICCPR. Relevant Canadian case law has been included so as to demonstrate how the relevant rights are applied in practice. The factors affecting, and the difficulties experienced in, the implementation of the ICCPR have also been addressed.[140] Furthermore, the dialogue that ensued following the presentation of Canada's second, third, and fourth reports was characterized as being constructive, not only by Canadian delegations but also by committee members.[141]

In order to ensure the proper reception of its fifth periodic report, which is due in 2004,[142] Canada will need to do three things. First, at the information level, it will have to provide more details in regard to the implementation of Article 1 of the ICCPR. If review of Canada's previous reports is any indication, it would also seem prudent to elaborate on the applicability and scope of Section 33 of the Charter and on its relationship with Article 4 of the ICCPR. Second, at the substantive level, Canada will have to effectuate a

---

[138] See *Supplementary Examination, supra* note 30. See also the HRC's decision in *McIntyre,* Comm. nos. 359/1989 and 385/1989, in *Report of the Human Rights Committee to the General Assembly,* A/48/40, paras. 7.2-7.3 and 10.2-10.3.

[139] See *Fourth Report, supra* note 34 at 5.

[140] See *ibid.* at paras. 29, 65, 69, 81, and 111.

[141] See, for example, the HRC's comments in Information Service, *Human Rights Committee Concludes Consideration of Reports of Canada,* Press Release HR/2664, October 1990, at p. 7.

[142] This date was set by the HRC at the end of its concluding observations. See *Concluding Observations, supra* note 34 at para. 21.

review of its laws and policies in a number of areas. Particular attention needs to be paid to the rights of Aboriginal peoples, to the fair treatment of minorities and aliens, and to the rights of women.[143] If the reporting obligation is to become more than a simple compilation and writing exercise, proper weight needs to be accorded to committee reprimands and concerns. Third, at the discussion level, Canada will need to ensure that its delegates are able to furnish, upon demand, up-to-date answers and information about provincial compliance with the provisions of the ICCPR.[144]

Hopefully, in the years to come, Canada will continue to take its reporting obligations under the ICCPR seriously, and it will demonstrate a willingness to effectuate internal changes based on committee recommendations that follow the examination of its periodic reports. As a leader in the fight for, and respect of, human rights, Canada cannot afford to simply dismiss the criticism that is directed towards its own record.

MARIE-FRANCE MAJOR
Faculty of Law, University of Ottawa

Sommaire

Rapports au Comité des droits de l'homme: l'expérience canadienne

En 1966, l'Assemblé générale de l'ONU adoptait la Convention sur les droits civils et politiques. En devenant signataire de la Convention, le Canada s'engageait à soumettre des rapports périodiques au Comité des droits de l'homme, un organisme autonome composé d'experts, établi par la Convention. Ces rapports ont pour objet de rendre compte des mesures adoptées par chaque état pour assurer la protection des droits de la personne et pour mettre en oeuvre le nouveau traité. On examine ici les quatre rapports qui ont été soumis par le Canada, ainsi que les commentaires des membres du Comité dans l'analyse de ces rapports, afin d'évaluer dans quelle mesure le Canada s'acquitte de ses engagements dans le cadre de la Convention.

---

[143] These areas have been singled out because they have been the subject of numerous HRC criticisms throughout the years.

[144] In its concluding observations, the HRC expressed concern over the fact that the Canadian delegation (despite its large numbers) was unable to furnish the necessary information in regard to compliance with the ICCPR by the provincial authorities. See *Concluding Observations, supra* note 34 at para. 2.

Summary

Reporting to the Human Rights Committee: The Canadian
Experience

*In 1966, the General Assembly of the United Nations adopted the Covenant
on Civil and Political Rights. Once it had acceded to the Covenant, Canada
undertook the obligation to make regular reports to the Human Rights Committee (the independent body of experts established under the Covenant) in
regard to its protection of human rights and its progress in implementing the
new treaty. In the next few pages, the four reports submitted by Canada, as
well as the comments issued by committee members in the course of analysis
of these reports, are examined, so as to get a better sense of whether, and to
what extent, Canada is fulfilling its Covenant commitments.*

Chronique de Droit international économique en 1999 / Digest of International Economic Law in 1999

I Commerce

préparé par
SOPHIE DUFOUR

INTRODUCTION

L e processus d'intégration des économies à l'échelle planétaire s'est poursuivi en 1999 alors que le Canada enregistrait une croissance économique pour une huitième année consécutive.[1] Cette croissance est due notamment aux échanges commerciaux entre le Canada et ses partenaires étrangers qui ont connu un bond remarquable en 1999 dans le secteur des produits et des services: les exportations se sont en effet accrues de 11,3 % tandis que les importations ont augmenté de 7,4 %, atteignant ainsi 412,4 milliards et 384,6 milliards de dollars canadiens respectivement.[2] Si les États-Unis continuent d'être le principal partenaire commercial du Canada et bien que ce dernier se soit efforcé, tout au long de l'année 1999, de préserver et de renforcer ce partenariat, il a

Sophie Dufour, Avocate, Conseillère à la Direction générale, Fédération des producteurs de lait du Québec (LL.B., Université Laval; LL.M., Osgoode Hall School of Law; LL.M., University of Cambridge; LL.D, Université Laval).

[1] Canada, Ministère des Affaires étrangères et du Commerce international, *Le point sur le commerce en l'an 2000*, Ottawa, juin 2000 à la p. 3.

[2] *Ibid.* Voir également Canada, Ministère des Affaires étrangères et du Commerce international, *L'examen de la politique commerciale du Canada en 2000 — Énoncé de la politique du gouvernement du Canada*; en ligne: Ministère des Affaires étrangères et du Commerce international <http://www.dfait-maeci.gc.ca/tna-nac/reviewoo-f.asp> (date d'accès: 10 juillet 2001) (ci-après *L'examen de la politique commerciale du Canada en 2000*).

néanmoins cherché à intensifier sa présence sur les marchés régionaux et internationaux en participant activement aux négociations tenues lors de la cinquième Réunion des ministres du Commerce des trente-quatre États de l'hémisphère américain et lors de la troisième Conférence ministérielle de l'Organisation mondiale du commerce (OMC) (Section I). Le Canada a par ailleurs connu succès et revers dans le cadre de différends soumis devant l'Organe de règlement des différends (ORD) de l'OMC dont certaines étapes importantes ont été franchies au cours de l'année 1999 (Section II).

I   NÉGOCIATIONS COMMERCIALES RÉGIONALES ET MULTILATÉRALES EN 1999

À l'exception de deux ententes commerciales bilatérales conclues entre le Canada et l'Autorité palestinienne d'une part,[3] et la Chine d'autre part,[4] les principales négociations commerciales auxquelles le gouvernement canadien a été partie en 1999 ont été de nature régionale et multilatérale.

Ainsi, les 3 et 4 novembre 1999, le Canada a présidé à Toronto (Canada) la cinquième Réunion des ministres du Commerce des trente-quatre pays participant aux négociations en vue de la création de la Zone de libre-échange des Amériques (ZLÉA) prévue

---

[3] Le 27 février 1999, le gouvernement du Canada et l'Organisation de libération de la Palestine, agissant au nom de l'Autorité palestinienne, ont signé l'*Accord-cadre Canado-palestinien de coopération économique et commerciale* aux termes duquel les Parties se sont notamment engagées à accroître leurs relations économiques (voir *Accord-cadre Canado-Palestinien de coopération économique et commerciale entre le gouvernement du Canada et l'Organisation de la Palestine, agissant au nom de l'Autorité palestinienne,* Ramallah (Jordanie) 27 février 1999; en ligne: Ministère des Affaires étrangères et du Commerce international <http://www.dfait-maeci.gc.ca/tna-nac/framework-f.asp> (date d'accès: 10 juillet 2001).

[4] Le 26 novembre 1999, le Canada et la Chine en sont arrivés à une entente en matière d'accès aux marchés. Cette entente, qui s'inscrit dans le processus d'accession de la Chine à l'OMC, et qui vient consolider les liens commerciaux déjà bien établis entre les deux partenaires — la Chine constitue le quatrième partenaire commercial du Canada — n'entrera en vigueur qu'une fois ce processus complété. Aux termes de cette entente, la Chine s'est notamment engagée à réduire ses tarifs douaniers sur les importations de produits canadiens, notamment industriels et agricoles ainsi qu'à éliminer certaines barrières non tarifaires restreignant l'accès à ses services financiers, à son secteur des télécommunications ainsi qu'à certains produits canadiens de base tels le canola, le blé et l'orge. Voir à cet égard *Le Canada et la Chine signent un accord bilatéral historique dans le cadre de l'OMC,* News Release, 26 novembre 1999; en ligne: Ministère des Affaires étrangères et du Commerce international <http://webapps.dfait-maeci.gc.ca/minpub/mainmenu.asp> (date d'accès: 5 juillet 2001).

pour l'année 2005. C'est au cours de la quatrième Réunion des ministres du Commerce, tenue à San José (Costa Rica) au mois de mars 1998 qu'il avait été décidé que le Canada présiderait les dix-huit premiers mois des négociations de la ZLÉA, lancées officiellement au mois d'avril 1998 à Santiago (Chili) à l'occasion du deuxième Sommet des Amériques.[5]

Trois principaux sujets ont été au cœur des discussions de la rencontre de Toronto: l'intérêt de la société civile — travailleurs, gens d'affaires, environnementalistes, universitaires — à l'endroit du processus de négociations de la ZLÉA; l'adoption de mesures de facilitation du commerce en vue de simplifier les formalités douanières et d'assurer une plus grande transparence entre les pays de la future ZLÉA; ainsi que les subventions à l'exportation des produits agricoles.[6]

Tout en reconnaissant la relation inhérente entre les processus de la ZLÉA et de l'OMC,[7] les trente-quatre ministres du Commerce ont, dans une Déclaration conjointe adoptée le 4 novembre 1999, insisté sur la nature distincte de l'objectif de la ZLÉA, lequel consiste à "... créer une zone de libre-échange conforme aux dispositions ... de l'OMC ..."[8] tout en tenant compte "... des différences dans les niveaux de développement et la taille des économies de [l']hémisphère [américain] afin d'assurer la pleine participation des économies de petite taille et de relever leur niveau de

---

[5] Voir *Réunion des ministres du Commerce de la ZLÉA*, Toronto (Canada) 3-4 novembre 1999; en ligne: AmériquesCanada.org <http://www.americas canada.org/ eventftaa/menu-f.asp> (date d'accès: 10 juillet 2001).

[6] Voir notamment Canada, Ministère des Affaires étrangères et du Commerce international, "Le Ministre Pettigrew annonce le succès de la réunion des ministres du Commerce de la ZLÉA," Toronto (Canada) 4 novembre 1999, *Communiqué* n° 242; en ligne: Ministère des Affaires étrangères et du Commerce international <http://webapps.dfait-maeci.gc.ca/minpub/mainmenu.asp> (date d'accès: 10 juillet 2001); Canada, "Vers la création de la Zone de libre-échange des Amériques," Notes pour une allocution de l'Honorable David Kilgour, Secrétaire d'État (Amérique latine et Afrique), devant le Conseil canadien pour les Amériques, Calgary (Canada) 26 novembre 1999; en ligne: Ministère des Affaires étrangères et du Commerce international <http://198.103.104.118/ minpub/Publication.asp?FileSpec=/Min_Pub_Docs/102906)> (date d'accès: 10 juillet 2001).

[7] Voir Zone de libre-échanges des Amériques, *Déclaration des Ministres*, Cinquième réunion ministérielle, Toronto (Canada) 4 novembre 1999; en ligne: Zone de libre-échanges des Amériques <http://www.ftaa-alca.org/ministerials/minis_ f.asp> (date d'accès: 10 juillet 2001), par. 20.

[8] *Ibid.*

développement."[9] Si cette cinquième Réunion a été, de l'avis de tous les participants, un franc succès, tel n'a pas été le cas en ce qui concerne la troisième Conférence ministérielle de l'OMC qui, un mois plus tard, subissait un échec retentissant.[10]

Présidée par la Représentante des États-Unis pour les questions commerciales internationales, Mme Charlene Barshefsky, la Conférence ministérielle de Seattle, tenue du 30 novembre au 3 décembre 1999, devait être l'occasion pour les Membres de l'OMC de débuter officiellement de nouvelles négociations globales en vue de poursuivre le processus de libéralisation du commerce international des produits et des services et de tenter d'étendre la portée des règles de l'OMC à des domaines jusqu'ici non couverts tels la concurrence et l'environnement. Toutefois, n'ayant pas réussi à s'entendre sur un calendrier de négociations globales, les gouvernements participants ont dû se contenter de procéder au lancement de négociations sectorielles sur le commerce des produits agricoles et des services,[11] conformément aux prescriptions énoncées à cet égard dans *l'Accord sur l'agriculture*[12] et *l'Accord sur le commerce des services*.[13]

II Différends devant l'OMC en 1999 impliquant le Canada

Bien que le Canada ait été impliqué, en 1999, dans des différends commerciaux survenus aussi bien dans le cadre de *l'Accord de*

---

[9] *Ibid.*, par. 5.

[10] La Conférence ministérielle constitue l'organe suprême de l'OMC. Composée des représentants de tous les Membres de l'Organisation, la Conférence ministérielle doit, conformément à l'article IV.1 de *l'Accord de Marrakech instituant l'OMC*, se réunir à tous les deux ans. La première Conférence fut tenue à Singapour au mois de décembre 1996 alors que la deuxième eut lieu au siège même de l'Organisation, à Genève (Suisse) au mois de mai 1998.

[11] Voir notamment "Déclaration du Gouvernement du Canada sur la suspension des pourparlers de l'OMC à Seattle," Seattle (États-Unis) 4 décembre 1999, *Communiqué* n° 264; en ligne: Ministère des Affaires étrangères et du Commerce international   <http://webapps.dfait-maeci.gc.ca/minpub/mainmenu.asp> (date d'accès: 10 juillet 2001); "Déclaration du Directeur général de l'OMC, M. Mike Moore," Genève (Suisse) 7 décembre 1999, *Press/160*; en ligne: Organisation mondiale du commerce <http://www. wto.org/french/thewto_f/minist_ f/min99_f/french/press_f/pres160_f.htm> (date d'accès: 10 juillet 2001).

[12] *Accord sur l'agriculture*, dans *Résultats des négociations commerciales multilatérales du cycle d'Uruguay*, Genève, GATT, 1994 aux pp. 56-57, art. 20.

[13] *Accord sur le commerce des services*, dans *Résultats des négociations commerciales multilatérales du cycle d'Uruguay*, Genève, GATT, 1994 à la p. 363, art. XIX.1.

libre-échange nord-américain (ALÉNA)[14] que dans celui de l'OMC, il ne fait pas de doute que le système de règlement des différends de l'OMC connaît une "popularité" indéniable auprès des Membres de l'Organisation, y compris les États parties à l'ALÉNA. Ces derniers semblent de plus en plus enclins à favoriser le système multilatéral au détriment de celui mis en place sous l'égide du chapitre 20 de l'ALÉNA.[15] Cette popularité s'explique sans doute en grande partie par la nature contraignante et multilatérale du système érigé à l'OMC.[16]

[14] *Accord de libre-échange nord-américain entre le gouvernement du Canada, le gouvernement des États-Unis d'Amérique et le gouvernement des États-Unis du Mexique*, 17 décembre 1992, Ottawa, Approvisionnements et Services Canada, 1993. Pour une description des différends soumis en vertu des chapitres 19 et 20 de l'ALÉNA en 1999, voir *Décisions et rapports de l'ALÉNA*; en ligne: Secrétariat de l'ALÉNA <http://www.nafta-sec-alena.org/french/decisions/nafta/index.htm> (date d'accès: 10 juillet 2001).

[15] Il pourrait cependant en être différent en ce qui concerne la procédure de règlement des différends établie en vertu du chapitre 11 de l'ALÉNA. Ce chapitre — qui garantit aux investisseurs de la zone nord-américaine de libre-échange un traitement équitable et conforme au droit international lorsqu'ils investissent sur le territoire d'un autre État partie à l'ALÉNA — et, en particulier, ses articles 1115 à 1138 relatifs au mécanisme de règlement des différends, ont, jusqu'ici, été invoqués de façon marginale par les investisseurs (voir *ALÉNA — Chapitre 11 — Investissement*, en ligne: Ministère des Affaires étrangères et du Commerce international <http://www.dfait-maeci.gc.ca/tna-nac/Min_S_Inv-f.asp> (date d'accès: 10 juillet 2001). Cela n'a pourtant pas suffi à apaiser les opposants à ce chapitre qui, depuis son entrée en vigueur en 1994, décrient ce droit reconnu aux investisseurs de poursuivre les gouvernements des États parties à l'ALÉNA.

[16] Voir à cet égard les article 2.4 (et, en particulier, sa note 1), 22.1 et 23.2 du *Mémorandum d'accord sur les règles et procédures régissant le règlement des différends*, dans *Résultats des négociations commerciales multilatérales du cycle d'Uruguay*, Genève, GATT, 1994 aux pp. 448-49 (ci-après *Mémorandum d'accord*). L'avocat montréalais Simon Potter a apporté le commentaire suivant qui décrit avec justesse le caractère innovateur du mécanisme de règlement des différends de l'OMC: "[t]he hallmark of the WTO legal regime has been the Dispute Settlement Undestanding ... The old GATT days of diplomacy-cloaked blocking of panel judgments are gone. Dispute Settlement Body judgments are binding unless they are appealed to the Appeal Body, and Appeal Body judgments are binding" (S.V. Potter, *Recent Developments in International Trade Regulation*; en ligne: LEXPERT <http://www.lexpert.ca/areas/inttrade/html> (date d'accès: 10 juillet 2001) référence omise). Voir dans le même sens J. Cameron et S.J. Orava, "GATT/WTO Panels Between Recording and Finding Facts: Issues of Due Process, Evidence, Burden of Proof, and Standard of Review in GATT/WTO Dispute Settlement" dans *Improving WTO Dispute Settlement Procedures: Issues and Lessons from the Practice of Other International Courts & Tribunals*, F. Weiss (dir.), London, Cameron, mai 2000, 195 à la p. 196.

Deux différends impliquant le Canada ont connu des développements significatifs à l'OMC en 1999. L'un, relatif aux aéronefs civils[17] et l'autre, relatif aux exportations de produits laitiers canadiens,[18] ont en effet fait l'objet d'une première décision de la part d'un groupe spécial et de l'Organe d'appel de l'OMC.[19]

---

[17] *Brésil — Programme de financement des exportations pour les aéronefs* (plainte du Canada): Rapport du Groupe spécial, OMC doc. WT/DS46/R (14 avril 1999) (ci-après *Rapport du Groupe spécial DS46*); Rapport de l'Organe d'appel, OMC doc. WT/DS46/AB/R (2 août 1999) (ci-après *Rapport de l'Organe d'appel DS46*); Recours du Canada à l'article 21.5 du Mémorandum d'accord, OMC doc. WT/DS46/RW (9 mai 2000) (ci-après *Recours du Canada à l'article 21.5 (DS46)*). *Canada — Mesures visant l'exportation des aéronefs civils* (plainte du Brésil): Rapport du Groupe spécial, OMC doc. WT/DS70/R (14 avril 1999) (ci-après *Rapport du Groupe spécial DS70*); Rapport de l'Organe d'appel, OMC doc. WT/DS70/AB/R (2 août 1999) (ci-après *Rapport de l'Organe d'appel DS70*); Recours du Brésil à l'article 21.5 du Mémorandum d'accord, OMC doc. WT/DS70/RW (9 mai 2000) (ci-après *Recours du Brésil à l'article 21.5 (DS70)*).

[18] *Canada — Mesures visant l'importation de lait et l'exportation de produits laitiers:* Rapport du Groupe spécial, OMC doc. WT/DS103/R, WT/DS/113/R (17 mai 1999) (ci-après *Rapport du Groupe spécial DS103/113*); Rapport de l'Organe d'appel, OMC doc. WT/DS103/AB/R, WT/DS113/AB/R (13 octobre 1999) (ci-après *Rapport de l'Organe d'appel DS103/113*); Recours des États-Unis et de la Nouvelle-Zélande à l'article 21.5 du Mémorandum d'accord, OMC doc. WT/DS103/RW, WT/DS113/RW (11 juillet 2001) (ci-après *Recours des États-Unis et de la Nouvelle-Zélande à l'article 21.5 (DS103/113)*).

[19] Deux autres différends — l'un concernant les importations australiennes de saumons canadiens et l'autre portant sur les mesures européennes adoptées à l'endroit du boeuf canadien élevé aux hormones de croissance — dans le cadre desquels les groupes spéciaux et l'Organe d'appel avaient, en 1998, donné droit à la plainte soumise par le Canada, ont par ailleurs franchi en 1999 le stade de l'examen de la confomité et de l'imposition des mesures de rétorsion en vertu des articles 21.5 et 22.6 du Mémorandum d'accord (voir *Australie — Mesures visant les importations de saumons,* Recours du Canada à l'article 21.5 du Mémorandum d'accord, Rapport du Groupe spécial, OMC doc. WT/DS18//RW (18 avril 2000); *Communautés européennes — Mesures communautaires concernant les viandes et les produits carnés,* Recours des Communautés européennes à l'arbitrage au titre de l'article 22.6 du Mémorandum d'accord sur le règlement des différends, Décisions des arbitres, OMC doc. WT/DS48/ARB (12 juillet 1999). Nous vous renvoyons, à cet égard, à notre chronique de droit commercial international en 1998, où nous avons fait état des développements survenus en 1999 dans le cadre de ces deux différends (S. Dufour, "Chronique de droit international économique en 1998 / Digest of International Economic Law in 1998" (2000) A.C.D.I. 287 aux pp. 294-97).

A DIFFÉREND CANADA-BRÉSIL RELATIF AUX AÉRONEFS CIVILS

L'affaire des aéronefs civils[20] a, bien avant 1999, retenu l'attention des gouvernements canadien et brésilien. Le Canada, à l'instar du Brésil, figure parmi les pays les plus performants dans le secteur de l'aéronautique. Sensibles à la concurrence internationale prévalant dans ce secteur hautement spécialisé et à grand capital de risques, les gouvernements canadien et brésilien ont rapidement reconnu l'importance d'appuyer leur industrie aérospatiale nationale. Dans le cas du Brésil, cet appui s'est notamment traduit par l'octroi, en vertu du *Programa de Financiamento às Exportaçöes* (PROEX) — un programme fédéral de subventions à l'exportation[21] — de subventions sous forme de péréquation des taux d'intérêt pour les ventes d'aéronefs de la *Empresa Brasileira de Aeronautica S.A.* (EMBRAER), un constructeur brésilien d'aéronefs régionaux, à des acheteurs étrangers. Dans le cas du Canada, cet appui a entre autres consisté en des prêts et des garanties offerts dans le cadre de programmes gouvernementaux tels le Compte Canada et Partenariat technologique Canada (PTC) à des acheteurs étrangers d'aéronefs fabriqués par la société canadienne Bombardier.

La conformité des programmes d'aide à l'industrie aérospatiale canadienne et brésilienne avec les disciplines de l'OMC a suscité de vives discussions entre le Canada et le Brésil de 1996 à 1998. Toutefois, ces discussions n'ont jamais réussi à amener les parties en présence à une solution satisfaisante. C'est pourquoi, au mois de juillet 1998, le Canada et le Brésil ont chacun formellement demandé à l'ORD de l'OMC la constitution d'un groupe spécial chargé d'examiner les pratiques brésiliennes et canadiennes dans le secteur régional de l'aviation.

Dans leur rapport respectif, distribué aux Membres de l'OMC le 14 avril 1999, les deux groupes spéciaux ont établi que le Canada et le Brésil versaient des subventions à l'exportation prohibées en vertu des dispositions de *l'Accord sur les subventions et les mesures compensatoires* (ASMC).[22] Plus spécifiquement, le Groupe spécial

---

[20] *Rapport du Groupe spécial DS46, supra* note 17; *Rapport de l'Organe d'appel DS46, supra* note 18; *Recours du Canada à l'article 21.5 (DS46), supra* note 17; *Rapport du Groupe spécial DS70, supra* note 17; *Rapport de l'Organe d'appel DS70, supra* note 17; *Recours du Brésil à l'article 21.5 (DS70), supra* note 17.

[21] PROEX a été institué par le gouvernement brésilien le 1er juin 1991 en vertu de la Loi n° 8187, remplacée par la Mesure provisoire n° 1629 du 12 février 1998 (voir *Rapport du Groupe spécial DS46, ibid.*, par. 2.1).

[22] *Accord sur les subventions et les mesures compensatoires*, dans *Résultats des négociations commerciales multilatérales du cycle d'Uruguay*, Genève, GATT, 1994 aux pp. 279-332.

responsable de l'examen de la conformité du programme brésilien PROEX,[23] a conclu que les versements PROEX de péréquation des taux d'intérêts constituaient des subventions subordonnées aux exportations selon les articles 1 et 3.1a) de l'ASMC et que ces versements n'étaient pas autorisés aux termes du paragraphe 1 du point k) de la *Liste exemplative de subventions à l'exportation* contenue à l'Annexe I de l'ASMC.[24]

Par ailleurs, dans l'affaire relative à l'exportation des aéronefs civils canadiens,[25] le Groupe spécial appelé à examiner les allégations du Brésil concernant les programmes d'aide canadiens à l'industrie aérospatiale nationale a constaté que, parmi les dix mesures canadiennes invoquées par le Brésil au soutien de sa plainte, deux ne se conformaient pas aux disciplines de l'OMC applicables en cette matière. Selon le Groupe spécial, "le financement sous forme de crédits accordés au titre du Compte du Canada depuis le 1er janvier 1995 pour l'exportation d'avions canadiens de transport régional" de même que "l'aide de PTC à l'industrie canadienne de transport régional" constituaient des subventions à l'exportation prohibées aux termes des articles 3.1a) et 3.2 de l'ASMC.[26]

Le 3 mai 1999, le Brésil et le Canada ont respectivement notifié à l'ORD leur intention d'interjeter appel de certaines questions de droit soulevées dans les rapports des groupes spéciaux.[27] Dans deux décisions rendues publiques le 2 août 1999, l'Organe d'appel est venu confirmer les conclusions émises quelques mois plus tôt par les groupes spéciaux à l'égard des programmes d'aide brésiliens et canadiens à l'exportation des aéronefs régionaux[28] et a recommandé que le Brésil et le Canada retirent les subventions prohibées dans un délai de quatre-vingt-dix jours.[29] Le 20 août 1999, l'ORD adoptait les rapports des groupes spéciaux et de l'Organe d'appel et recommandait au Brésil et au Canada de

---

[23] *Rapport du Groupe spécial DS46, supra* note 17.

[24] *Rapport du Groupe spécial DS46, ibid.*, par. 8.1-8.2, 8.5.

[25] *Rapport du Groupe spécial DS70, supra* note 17.

[26] *Rapport du Groupe spécial DS70, ibid.*, par. 10.1.

[27] *Rapport de l'Organe d'appel DS46, supra* note 17, par. 8; *Rapport de l'Organe d'appel DS70, supra* note 17, par. 3.

[28] *Rapport de l'Organe d'appel DS46, ibid.*, par. 196; *Rapport de l'Organe d'appel DS70, ibid.*, par. 220.

[29] Voir *Rapport de l'Organe d'appel DS46, ibid.*, par. 197; *Rapport de l'Organe d'appel DS70, ibid.*, par. 221.

mettre leurs subventions à l'exportation en conformité avec les obligations contenues dans l'ASMC.[30]

Toutefois, les nouvelles mesures adoptées par le Brésil et le Canada afin de mettre en oeuvre ces recommandations n'ont pas suffi à mettre un terme au différend. Ainsi, le 23 novembre 1999, le gouvernement canadien annonçait son intention de demander que soit examinée la conformité du nouveau programme PROEX suivant les termes de l'article 21.5 du Mémorandum d'accord alors que le gouvernement brésilien soumettait cette même demande à l'égard des lignes directrices modifiées du Compte du Canada et des règles et règlements reformulés du PTC.[31] L'année 1999 s'est ainsi close sur une note discordante dans les relations canado-brésiliennes et avec la crainte que la question des subventions à l'exportation des aéronefs brésiliens et canadiens ne connaisse pas de dénouement à brève échéance. L'avenir aura eu tôt fait de démontrer la justesse de cette crainte.

B   DIFFÉREND NOUVELLE-ZÉLANDE/ÉTATS-UNIS—CANADA RELATIF
    AUX EXPORTATIONS DE PRODUITS LAITIERS CANADIENS

Les États-Unis et la Nouvelle-Zélande sont sortis gagnants de la première étape du différend enclenché au mois d'octobre 1997 contre le Canada devant l'OMC au sujet de la mise en marché du lait canadien destiné à l'exportation. En effet, tant le Groupe spécial, au mois de mai 1999,[32] que l'Organe d'appel de l'OMC, au mois d'octobre de la même année,[33] ont conclu que le Canada avait agi d'une manière incompatible avec ses engagements pris aux termes de l'*Accord sur l'agriculture* et de l'ASMC de l'OMC.

Confirmant les conclusions générales auxquelles en était arrivé quelques mois plus tôt le Groupe spécial,[34] l'Organe d'appel a

---

[30] *Recours du Canada à l'article 21.5 (DS46), supra* note 17, par. 1.1-1.2; *Recours du Brésil à l'article 21.5 (DS70), supra* note 17, par. 1.1-1.2.

[31] *Recours du Canada à l'article 21.5 (DS46), ibid.,* par. 1.5; *Recours du Brésil à l'article 21.5 (DS70), ibid.,* par. 1.6.

[32] *Rapport du Groupe spécial DS103/113, supra* note 18, par. 8.1.

[33] *Rapport de l'Organe d'appel DS103/113, supra* note 18, par. 144.

[34] L'Organe d'appel a toutefois infirmé l'interprétation donnée par le Groupe spécial aux expressions "subventions directes" et "versements en nature" figurant à l'article 9(1)a) de l'*Accord sur l'agriculture*. Sur ce point, il a ainsi renversé la constatation du Groupe spécial suivant laquelle des subventions directes et subordonnées à l'exportation auraient été octroyées par le Canada aux transformateurs travailllant sur le marché de l'exportation du lait, au sens de l'article 9(1)a). Voir à cet égard *Rapport de l'Organe d'appel DS103/113, ibid.,* par. 84-102.

constaté que le Programme des classes spéciales de lait, auxquel sont parties la Commission canadienne du lait et neuf offices provinciaux de producteurs de lait, avait pour effet de conférer aux transformateurs travaillant à l'exportation une subvention à l'exportation au sens de l'article 9(1)c) de l'*Accord sur l'agriculture*. Par le biais de ce Programme, géré par des organismes issus du gouvernement fédéral et des gouvernements des provinces, le lait destiné à l'exportation est fourni aux transformateurs et aux exportateurs à un prix inférieur à celui prévalant sur le marché intérieur. En d'autres termes, un versement est fait aux transformateurs, sous forme de la partie du prix qui n'a pas à être payée par ces derniers et il résulte de l'application du Programme des classes spéciales de lait, lequel constitue une mesure des pouvoirs publics au sens de l'article 9(1)c) de l'*Accord sur l'agriculture*.[35] Or, étant donné que les quantités de lait exporté en vertu de ce Programme dépassent les engagements assumés par le Canada au terme du cycle d'Uruguay en vue de réduire ses subventions à l'exportation, il s'ensuit que le Canada n'a pas respecté ses obligations en vertu de l'*Accord sur l'agriculture*.[36]

Il a ainsi été convenu, en vertu de deux ententes conclues au mois de décembre 1999 entre le Canada, les États-Unis et la Nouvelle-Zélande, d'accorder au Canada un délai raisonnable — à savoir douze mois se terminant le 31 janvier 2001 — pour assurer la conformité de ses pratiques en matière d'exportation de produits laitiers canadiens avec les disciplines de l'OMC en matière agricole.[37]

Dès le mois d'octobre 1999, le Canada a entrepris de modifier son système de mise en marché du lait destiné à l'exportation de manière à le rendre conforme aux règles de l'OMC. À cet égard,

---

[35] *Rapport de l'Organe d'appel DS103/113, ibid.*, par. 103-23.

[36] Voir *Rapport de l'Organe d'appel DS103/113, ibid.*, par. 144b). Le 27 octobre 1999, l'ORD a adopté les rapports du groupe spécial et de l'Organe d'appel. Voir *Canada — Mesures visant l'importation de lait et l'exportation de produits laitiers*, Rapport de situation du Canada, OMC doc. WT/DS/103/12, WT/DS/113/12 (9 juin 2000).

[37] Voir *Canada — Mesures visant l'importation de lait et l'exportation de produits laitiers*, Accord au titre de l'article 21.3b) du Mémorandum d'accord sur le règlement des différends, OMC doc. WT/DS103/10, WT/DS113/10 (7 janvier 2000); *Canada — Mesures visant l'importation de lait et l'exportation de produits laitiers*, Modification de l'Accord conclu au titre de l'article 21.3b) du Mémorandum d'accord sur le règlement des différends, OMC doc. WT/DS103/13, WT/DS113/13 (13 décembre 2000).

le Groupe spécial avait énoncé un certain nombre de facteurs afin de déterminer le niveau d'intervention gouvernementale exercée dans le cadre du système existant.[38] Réitérés par l'Organe d'appel,[39] ces facteurs ont été pris en compte par le gouvernement fédéral canadien, en collaboration étroite avec l'industrie et les gouvernements provinciaux, afin de rendre compatible son système de mise en marché du lait destiné à l'exportation avec les disciplines de l'OMC. L'histoire nous apprendra toutefois que les États-Unis et la Nouvelle-Zélande ne trouveront pas satisfaction dans les nouvelles mesures canadiennes adoptées en remplacement de celles contenues dans le Programme des classes spéciales et relanceront le différend devant l'ORD dès le mois de février 2001.[40]

CONCLUSION

Caractérisé par une économie de plus en plus orientée vers l'exportation et par une politique commerciale indubitablement libre-échangiste,[41] le Canada a tenté, en 1999, dans le cadre de tribunes régionales ou internationales, de promouvoir activement les valeurs de transparence, d'ouverture et de respect des règles sur lesquelles devrait reposer tout système commercial interétatique. Toutefois, et sans doute en réponse à l'échec de Seattle, le gouvernement canadien a reconnu que la libéralisation du commerce international ne pouvait, à elle seule, constituer la panacée à tous les maux. Ainsi qu'il l'a souligné dans sa politique commerciale des années 1999-2000:

[L]es changements qui accompagnent l'incidence de la mondialisation sur la souveraineté, les politiques sociales, l'environnement et les identités nationales préoccupent autant le Canada que les autres pays. Nous savons que l'OMC ne peut pas aborder seule toutes ces préoccupations; bien des enjeux trouveraient une meilleure oreille au sein d'autres forums ... Si nous voulons tirer pleinement profit des occasions que présente le commerce international et gérer son incidence sociale, il faut des structures internationales économiques et sociales efficaces.[42]

---

[38] Voir *Rapport du Groupe spécial DS103/113, supra* note 18, par. 7.103-7.105, 7.108-7.112.

[39] Voir *Rapport de l'Organe d'appel DS103/113, supra* note 18, par. 116.

[40] Voir *Recours des États-Unis et de la Nouvelle-Zélande à l'article 21.5 (DS103/113), supra* note 18, par. 1.4.

[41] Voir à cet égard L'examen de la politique commerciale du Canada en 2000, *supra* note 2.

[42] *Ibid.*, par. 24.

Il ne fait à peu près pas de doute que le protectionnisme à ou-trance qui a prévalu au sein de plusieurs États dans les décennies passées est révolu. Reste à savoir jusqu'où va s'étendre le processus d'intégration des économies à l'échelle mondiale et dans quelle mesure les gouvernements vont accepter de continuer de suivre dans cette direction. Tel que nous l'a démontré l'épisode de Seattle et tel qu'il se dégage également du nombre sans cesse croissant de différends soumis à l'OMC, les gouvernements, dès lors qu'ils sont élus démocratiquement, sont tenus, presque inévitablement, d'aller dans le sens de leur électorat, qu'ils le veuillent ou non.

II   Le Canada et le système financier international en 1999

préparé par
BERNARD COLAS

Outre le lancement réussi de l'euro au début de 1999, cette année a été marquée par la poursuite d'initiatives destinées à prévenir, gérer et résoudre les crises financières internationales. Le ton de ces initiatives a été donné par le Groupe des Sept (G-7) qui s'est réuni à Cologne (Allemagne) du 18 au 20 juin 1999.[1] Les membres du G-7 ont entériné les rapports préparés par leurs ministres des finances sur l'initiative d'allègement de la dette de Cologne[2] et sur le renforcement de l'architecture financière internationale.[3] Ces rapports qui reprennent plusieurs éléments du plan en six points avancé un an plus tôt par M. Paul Martin, Ministre des finances du Canada,[4] ont largement influencé les activités de nombreuses institutions et instances internationales, particulièrement sur l'allègement de la dette des pays pauvres très endettés (I), le renforcement du système financier international (II), et la lutte contre le blanchiment d'argent et autres délits financiers (III).

Bernard Colas, Avocat associé de l'étude Gottlieb et Pearson (Montréal), Docteur en droit, Président de la Société de droit international économique (SDIE).

[1] *Déclaration du G7*, Sommet du G8 de Cologne, 18-20 juin 1999.

[2] *Rapport des ministres des Finances du G-7 sur l'Initiative d'allègement de la dette de Cologne, présenté au Sommet économique de Cologne*, Cologne, 18-20 juin 1999.

[3] *Le renforcement de l'architecture financière internationale. Rapport des ministres des Finances du G7 au Sommet économique de Cologne*, Cologne, 18-20 juin 1999.

[4] B. Colas, "Le Canada et le système financier international en 1998," A.C.D.I., 1999 (ci-après *B. Colas*). *Communiqué 99-020 du Ministère des finances du Canada, Le ministre des Finances se réjouit des progrès réalisés par les pays du G-7 en vue de promouvoir la stabilité du système financier international*, 20 février 1999.

I ALLÈGEMENT DE LA DETTE DES PAYS PAUVRES TRÈS ENDETTÉS

L'initiative visant à réduire la dette des pays pauvres très endettés (PPTE), lancée en 1996 à la suite du Sommet de Halifax de 1995,[5] était destinée à permettre à des pays lourdement endettés[6] de maintenir le niveau de leur dette à un niveau tolérable et de réduire leur pauvreté. Considérée comme insuffisante par les ministres du G-7[7] au Sommet de Cologne, cette initiative PPTE a été modifiée de manière à accorder un allègement plus important et plus rapide aux pays qui pouvaient justifier de l'application de programmes de réforme.[8]

L'Initiative PPTE renforcée assure un allègement à un nombre plus grand de pays. En 2000, trente-sept pays remplissaient les conditions requises pour bénéficier d'une aide dans le cadre de cette Initiative.[9] L'allègement proposé est plus important car plusieurs seuils d'admissibilité ont été abaissés. Dans le secteur extérieur, le ratio dette/exportations retenu comme objectif a été abaissé de 200–250 % à 150 %, et sur le plan budgétaire, le ratio dette/recettes budgétaires a été ramené de 280 à 250 %, le ratio exportations/PIB de 40 à 30 %, et le ratio recettes budgétaires de 20 à 15 %. L'allègement de la dette est plus rapide. En effet, l'Initiative PPTE renforcée prévoit l'application de mesures d'allègement provisoire et la matérialisation de l'aide de tous les groupes de créanciers au moment où le pays met en œuvre une stratégie globale de réduction de la pauvreté, et notamment d'une politique de stabilisation macroéconomique et d'ajustement structurel.[10]

---

[5] B. Colas, "Le Canada et le système financier international en 1996," A.C.D.I., 1997.

[6] Pays qui bénéficient de l'aide de l'Association de développement international (IDA) aux prises avec un niveau d'endettement intolérable après l'application de tous les mécanismes de réduction de la dette.

[7] Sept pays — la Bolivie, la Guyane, le Burkina Faso, la Côte d'Ivoire, le Mali, le Mozambique et l'Ouganda — ont vu leur demande acceptée en vertu du cadre initial de l'Initiative PPTE. Toutefois, seuls l'Ouganda, la Bolivie, la Guyane et le Mozambique ont franchi toutes les étapes de l'Initiative PPTE et ont eu droit à une aide dont la valeur actualisée totalise près de 2,8 milliards de dollars américains, et à une réduction de 5,5 milliards du service de la dette. *Rapport sur les opérations effectuées en vertu de la Loi sur les Accords de Bretton Woods et des accords connexes 1999* à la p. 67 (ci-après *Bretton Woods*).

[8] *Rapport annuel du FMI 2000* aux pp. 52-56 (ci-après *FMI*).

[9] *FMI, op. cit.* note 6 à la p. iii.

[10] R. Powell, "L'allègement de la dette des pays pauvres," *Finances & Développement*, Décembre 2000 aux pp. 42-45.

Par ailleurs, le Fonds monétaire international (FMI) a, cette année, renforcé sensiblement son mécanisme de prêts concessionnels en remplaçant la facilité d'ajustement structurel renforcée (FASR) par la facilité pour la réduction de la pauvreté et la croissance. Cette dernière vise à lutter contre la pauvreté et à favoriser une croissance durable, sans pour autant porter atteinte à l'objectif visant à renforcer la balance des paiements.[11] La contribution du FMI à ces efforts de financement sera financée en majeur partie par le revenu tiré du placement du produit de la vente "hors marché" d'une fraction de ses avoirs en or.[12]

Très favorable aux efforts de réduction de la dette et de la pauvreté des PPTE, le Canada s'est, en outre, engagé en 1999 à effacer la dette d'un certain nombre de ces pays.[13] En décembre 1999, le Canada a effacé la dette du Bangladesh. Le budget de février 2000 a étendu l'effacement de la totalité de la dette à tous les PPTE admissibles qui font de réels efforts en vue d'améliorer le bien-être de leurs citoyens et de réduire la pauvreté.[14] Le renforcement du système financier international fait également l'objet de vives préoccupations du Canada et des autres pays du G-8.

II Renforcement du système financier international

L'architecture financière internationale et sa consolidation est au cœur des travaux de nombreux organismes internationaux. L'objectif déclaré est de prévenir et de mieux gérer les crises financières et de responsabiliser le plus grand nombre d'acteurs publics et privés.[15] En 1999, des progrès ont été accomplis sur plusieurs fronts. Ils portent sur l'accroissement de la transparence et du contrôle du respect des normes et codes internationalement reconnus notamment au sein du FMI et du Forum de stabilité financière. Ils marquent également la création du Groupe des Vingt.

---

[11] *FMI, op. cit.* note 6 aux pp. 8-9.

[12] *FMI, op. cit.* note 6 aux pp. 61-66.

[13] Bangladesh, Honduras, Madagascar, Tanzanie et peut-être la Zambie. *Bretton Woods, op. cit.* note 7 à la p. 69.

[14] *Bretton Woods, op. cit.* note 7 à la p. 69.

[15] Le Canada favorise l'association du secteur privé à la gestion des crises financières. Outre ses interventions dans les forums internationaux dont les résultats en sont encore au stade embryonnaire, le Canada a annoncé qu'il adopterait des clauses d'action collective pour les obligations et les billets de banque libellés en devises qu'il émettra à l'avenir (e.g., le programme d'eurobillets à moyen terme et programme d'obligations du Canada), dans: Finances Canada, *Le Canada adoptera des clauses d'action collective*, Communiqué 2000-029, 13 avril 2000.

A   FONDS MONÉTAIRE INTERNATIONAL

Le FMI, dont le Comité intérimaire est devenu permanent et a été remplacé par le Comité monétaire et financier,[16] a ajouté un nouveau code aux normes facultatives sur les domaines qui relèvent de ses opérations (diffusion des données, transparence des politiques budgétaire, monétaire et financière, et contrôle bancaire). Il s'agit du Code de bonnes pratiques pour la transparence des politiques monétaire et financière[17] que le FMI a adopté le 26 septembre 1999 et qui s'inspire du code adopté un an plus tôt sur les politiques budgétaires.[18] De plus, le FMI a resserré sa norme spéciale de diffusion des données (NSDD) en exigeant la communication de renseignements complémentaires chaque mois sur les réserves de liquidités internationales et en encourageant la communication hebdomadaire des principaux avoirs de réserve.[19] Le Canada a été, en juillet 1999, un des premiers pays à diffuser les données complémentaires exigées par la norme élargie.

Toutefois, l'événement qui a marqué l'année a été le lancement, en mai 1999, à titre expérimental par le FMI et la Banque mondiale, du programme d'évaluation du secteur financier (PESF). Ce programme PESF, dont l'élaboration a été fortement influencée par le Canada, vise à aider les pays à réduire les facteurs de vulnérabilité au sein du secteur financier, à faciliter l'établissement de priorités pour leur développement et à soutenir un dialogue productif avec les autorités nationales. Il comporte un examen par les pairs du système financier du pays visé et notamment du niveau de respect et d'application des principes de base établis par le Comité de Bâle. Le Canada a été le premier grand pays industrialisé à faire l'objet d'une telle évaluation, laquelle a été rendue publique dans le rapport de 2000 sur les consultations relatives à l'article IV.[20] L'évaluation, préparée par un groupe

---

[16] *Bretton Woods, op. cit.* note 7 à la p. 13.

[17] FMI, *Code de bonnes pratiques pour la transparence des politiques monétaire et financière: Déclarations de principes,* adopté par le Comité intérimaire le 26 septembre 1999.

[18] B. Colas, "Le Canada et le système financier international en 1998," A.C.D.I., 1999 (ci-après *B. Colas*).

[19] *Bretton Woods, op. cit.* note 7 à la p. 16.

[20] À noter que le FMI a lancé, en avril 1999, un programme expérimental de diffusion volontaire du texte intégral des rapports pour les consultations au titre de l'article IV qui, largement encouragé par le Canada, a été accepté par plus de 60 pays. Sur la base des rapports PESF, le FMI a également préparé une évaluation

d'experts,[21] a signalé des dérogations mineures aux principes du Comité de Bâle auxquelles les modifications législatives annoncées en juin 1999 et présentées un an plus tard ont donné suite.[22]

B   GROUPE DES VINGT (G-20)

Afin de répondre aux besoins de représentation des marchés émergents, le Canada et autres pays industrialisés réunis au Sommet de Cologne ont souhaité "l'établissement d'un mécanisme informel de dialogue entre les pays importants sur le plan systémique."[23] La création du G-20, composé des ministres des Finances et des gouverneurs des banques centrales des pays du G-7 et leurs homologues de onze pays en développement ainsi que de représentants de l'Union européenne, du FMI et de la Banque mondiale, répond à leurs attentes. Le ministre des Finances du Canada, Paul Martin, est le premier président du G-20 et ce, pour une période de deux ans. À sa réunion inaugurale de Berlin (Allemagne) en décembre 1999, le G-20 a adopté un programme ayant pour objet de réduire la vulnérabilité aux crises financières internationales. Quatre priorités ont été établies:[24]

- l'établissement d'un inventaire complet des progrès accomplis par tous les pays membres en vue de réduire leur vulnérabilité aux crises;
- l'évaluation par ces pays de leur observation des normes et codes internationaux en matière de transparence ou se rapportant aux politiques qui régissent le secteur financier;
- la préparation de rapports sur l'observation des normes et codes (rapport de transparence) et d'évaluation de la stabilité des systèmes financiers par le FMI, en coopération avec la Banque mondiale; et

---

du secteur financier canadien: FMI, *Report on the Observance of Standards and Codes,* www.imf.org/external/np/rosc/can/index.htm.

[21] Ce groupe d'experts était composé d'agents du FMI, de la Banque mondiale et d'experts du Système de la Réserve fédérale des États-Unis, de la Banque centrale du Brésil et de la Bundesbank d'Allemagne, ainsi que de l'Australie et de la Suède.

[22] *Rapport annuel du Surintendant des institutions financières 1999-2000* à la p. 17.

[23] *Déclaration du G7,* Sommet du G8 de Cologne, 18-20 juin 1999 à la p. 3.

[24] *Bretton Woods, op. cit.* note 7 à la p. 13.

- l'examen des différents régimes de change et de leur rôle en vue d'amortir les effets des crises financières internationales.

Le Canada sera le pays hôte de sa seconde réunion annuelle.

C   FORUM DE STABILITÉ FINANCIÈRE

Le Forum de stabilité financière est une autre émanation du G-7 dont le but consiste à renforcer la stabilité financière globale par l'intensification des échanges d'information et de la coopération en matière de contrôle et de surveillance. Rappelons que le Forum, créé en février 1999,[25] regroupe les autorités nationales des grandes places mondiales, les institutions financières internationales, les organismes internationaux de contrôle et de réglementation, dont le Comité de Bâle qui a consacré l'essentiel de 1999 à la révision de l'Accord sur les fonds propres, ainsi que des groupes d'experts des banques centrales.

Cette année, le Forum a identifié un ensemble de douze normes que les pays devraient s'efforcer d'appliquer en priorité, compte tenu de leur situation, afin de renforcer leur système financier.[26] Cet ensemble, reproduit dans le Compendium de normes du Forum, constitue les normes et meilleures pratiques pour chaque secteur (présentées succinctement au Tableau 1).

Parmi les différents groupes de travail du Forum dont les travaux ont eu un certain retentissement cette année, mentionnons le Groupe de travail sur les centres *offshore*. Présidé par M. John Palmer, surintendant des institutions financières du Canada, ce groupe a permis d'évaluer l'incidence de ces centres sur la stabilité financière internationale ainsi que les progrès qu'ils ont accomplis en vue de mettre en application les normes prudentielles internationales et de se conformer aux accords sur les échanges d'information transfrontaliers.[27] Il a conclu qu'une meilleure application des normes internationales par ces centres, le contrôle ainsi que la communication et le partage des informations, contribueraient à résoudre les préoccupations soulevées par ces centres *offshore*.[28]

Constatant la forte hétérogénéité des régimes réglementaires de ces centres *offshore*, le groupe a en outre classé les pays en trois

---

[25] *B. Colas, op. cit.* note 4.

[26] Compendium de normes du Forum de stabilité financière.

[27] *Bretton Woods, op. cit.* note 7 à la p. 13.

[28] *Rapport annuel de la BRI 2000* à la p. 177.

Tableau 1

Compendium de normes du
Forum de stabilité financière (FSF)

Domaine	Norme	Institution
Politique macroéconomique et transparence des données		
Politique monétaire	Code de bonne pratique de politique monétaire	Fonds monétaire international (FMI)
Transparence de la politique budgé- taire et fiscale	Code de bonne pratique de politique budgétaire et fiscale	FMI
Diffusion des données économiques essentielles	Diffusion de données	FMI
Infrastructure institutionnelle et de marché		
Faillite	Principes et orientations applicables au régime de l'insolvabilité	Banque mondiale
Gouvernement d'entreprise	Principes relatifs au gouvernement d'entreprise	Organisation de coopération et de développement économiques (OCDE)
Information financière et comptable	Normes comptables internationales	Comité des normes comptables interna- tionales (IASC)
Audit	Normes internationales	Fédération interna- tionale des comptables (IFAC)
Paiements et règlements	Principes fondamentaux pour les systèmes de paiement d'importance systémique	Comité sur les systèmes de paiement et de règlement (CPSS)
Blanchiment	Les quarante recomman- dations du Groupe d'action financière sur le blanchiment d'argent	Groupe d'action financière sur le blanchiment d'argent (GAFI)
Régulation financière		
Régulation bancaire	Les principes fondamen- taux de la supervision	Comité de Bâle sur le contrôle bancaire
Régulation des marchés financiers	Les objectifs et principes de la régulation financière	Organisation interna- tionale des commis- sions de valeurs (OICV)
Régulation des assurances	Les principes fondamen- taux de l'assurance	Organisation interna- tionale des contrôleurs d'assurance (IAIS)

catégories selon le niveau de permissivité réglementaire et de risques pour la stabilité financière internationale; les pays du Groupe III étant ceux disposant d'un système juridique et institutionnel de supervision financière le plus pauvre. Sur la base de ce classement, une liste initiale de quarante-sept centres *offshore* a été publié le 26 mai 2000[29] (voir le tableau ci-dessous). À la publication de cette liste, ont fait suite, en juin 2000, les publications des listes du Groupe d'action financière (GAFI) et de l'Organisation de coopération et de développement économiques (OCDE) portant respectivement sur le blanchiment d'argent et les pratiques fiscales dommageables.

III   LUTTE CONTRE LE BLANCHIMENT D'ARGENT ET LES PARADIS FISCAUX

Le GAFI, dont le secrétariat est basé à l'OCDE, publiait, pour la première fois le 22 juin 2000, une liste de quinze pays ou territoires dont les règles et pratiques financières présentent des déficiences majeures en matière de lutte contre le blanchiment. Cette liste a été établie sur la base de vingt-cinq critères adoptés par le GAFI le 14 février 2000.[30]

Ces critères permettent d'identifier les règles et pratiques préjudiciables et de définir objectivement les pays ou territoires non coopératifs en matière de lutte contre le blanchiment. Ils peuvent être résumés comme suit:

- lacunes dans les réglementations financières (e.g., absence ou insuffisance de dispositifs de surveillance des institutions financières, inadéquation des règles d'agrément et d'établissement des institutions financières, ainsi que de leurs dirigeants et actionnaires, insuffisance des obligations d'identification des clients, caractère excessif des régimes de secret applicables aux institutions financières, et absence d'un système efficace de déclaration des transactions suspectes);
- inadéquation des règles de droit commercial concernant l'enregistrement des personnes morales et obstacles à l'identification de leurs actionnaires;
- obstacles à la coopération internationale entre autorités administratives et entre autorités judiciaires; et

---

[29] Communiqué du 26 mai 2000, *Grouping of Offshore Financial Centers (OFCs)*.

[30] *Rapport annuel 1999-2000 du GAFI* à la p. 23 (ci-après *GAFI*).

Tableau 2

Listes du Forum de stabilité financière (FSF),
Groupe d'action financière sur le blanchiment d'argent (GAFI),
et Organisation de coopération
et de développement économiques (OCDE)

	Centres offshore FSF	*Blanchiment GAFI*	*Paradis fiscaux OCDE*
Andorre	II		X
Anguilla	III		X
Antigua et Barbuda	III		X
Antilles néerlandaises	III		X
Aruba	III		X
Bahamas	III	X	X
Bahreïn	II		X
Barbade	II		X
Belize	III		X
Bermude	II		
Chypre	III		
Costa Rica	III		
Dominique		X	X
Dublin (Irlande)	I		
Gibraltar	II		X
Grenade			X
Guernesey	I		X
Hong Kong	I		
Israël		X	
Îles Caïman	III	X	
Îles Cook	III	X	X
Île de Man	I		X
Îles Marshall	III	X	X
Île Maurice	III		
Îles Vierge (GB)	III		X
Îles Vierges (US)			X
Jersey	I		X
Labuan (Malaysia)	II		
Liban	III	X	
Libéria			X
Liechtenstein	III	X	X
Luxembourg	I		
Macau	II		
Maldives			X
Malte	II		
Monaco	II		X

(Suite à la page suivante)

Tableau 2 *(continued)*

	Centres offshore FSF	*Blanchiment GAFI*	*Paradis fiscaux OCDE*
Montserrat			X
Nauru	III	X	X
Niue	III	X	X
Panama	III	X	X
Philippines		X	
Russie		X	
Samoa	III		X
Seychelles	III		X
Singapour	I		
St-Kitts et Nevis	III	X	X
Ste Lucie	III		X
St-Vincent et Grenadines	III	X	X
Suisse	I		
Tonga			X
Turks et Caicos	III		X
Vanuatu	III		X

Notes: Classiment des pays selon le niveau de permissivité réglementaire; les pays de Groupe III étant eux disposent d'un système juridique et institutionnel de supervision financière le plus pauvre.

- inadéquation des ressources consacrées à la lutte contre le blanchiment.

Outre la publication de la liste, le GAFI a poursuivi cette année ses efforts pour assurer une diffusion mondiale à sa politique de lutte contre le blanchiment de capitaux. Dans cet esprit, il a mené à bien le processus d'élargissement de sa composition qu'il avait entamé en 1998 et a accueilli comme membre à part entière l'Argentine, le Brésil et le Mexique.

Il a, en outre, souligné le dépôt par le Canada d'un projet de loi sur le recyclage des produits de la criminalité.[31] Ce projet renforce les dispositions législatives existantes sur la conservation des documents et introduit une obligation de déclaration des transactions suspectes, de même que la déclaration obligatoire des transactions prescrites et des mouvements importants d'espèces et d'instruments monétaires aux frontières.[32] Il crée une unité de renseignements

[31] *GAFI, op. cit.* note 30 à la p. 23.

[32] Finances Canada, *Le gouvernement fédéral dépose un projet de Loi pour lutter contre le blanchiment d'argent,* Communiqué 99-109, 15 décembre 1999.

financiers: le Centre d'analyse des opérations et déclarations financières. Ce projet sera complété de règles d'application en cours
d'élaboration.

Quant à l'OCDE, elle a établi, le 16 juin 2000, une liste de trente-
cinq juridictions qui répondent à des critères définis dans son
rapport de 1998 sur la concurrence fiscale dommageable[33] pour
être qualifiées de paradis fiscaux.[34] Parmi les critères retenus, mentionnons l'absence ou la faiblesse des impôts sur les revenus
d'activités financières, le manque de mécanismes d'échange de
renseignements, le manque de transparence, et l'accueil d'entités
sous contrôle étranger sans obligation d'une présence locale sub-
stantielle ou avec interdiction d'avoir un impact commercial sur
l'activité économique locale. La pression exercée par la publication de cette liste, comme celle du Forum de stabilité financière et
du GAFI, a eu pour effet d'amener plusieurs juridictions dont les
législations ou les pratiques posent problèmes à la communauté
internationale à engager des réformes. À titre d'exemple, le 19 juin
2000, la Bermude, les Îles Caïman, Chypre, Malte, l'Île Maurice
et San Marin se sont engagés à mettre fin aux pratiques fiscales
dommageables d'ici la fin de 2005 et à adopter les normes fiscales
internationales en matière de transparence, d'échange de renseignements et de concurrence fiscale loyale.[35]

Ainsi, la crise financière généralisée des dernières années a
abouti, en 1999–2000, à la création du Forum sur la stabilité
financière et du G-20, au renforcement du Comité monétaire et
financier international du FMI ainsi qu'à d'autres initiatives visant
à alléger la dette des pays pauvres très endettés et à améliorer la
transparence et le respect par l'ensembles des juridictions, comprenant les centres financiers extraterritoriaux, de normes et
pratiques internationalement reconnues.

---

[33] OCDE, *Concurrence fiscale dommageable: un problème mondial*, 1998.

[34] OCDE, *Vers une coopération fiscale globale: Rapport pour la réunion du Conseil au niveau des Ministres de 2000 et Recommandations du Comité des affaires fiscales: Progrès dans l'identification et l'élimination des pratiques fiscales dommageables*, 2000.

[35] Vu leur engagement, leur nom ne figure pas à la liste de l'OCDE.

III Investissement

préparé par
CÉLINE LÉVESQUE

INTRODUCTION

En 1999, l'investissement direct étranger en provenance du Canada se chiffrait à 257 milliards de dollars, tandis que celui à destination du Canada représentait 240 milliards de dollars.[1] En dix ans, soit de 1989 à 1999, l'investissement direct étranger au Canada a presque doublé et celui en provenance du Canada vers l'étranger a presque triplé.[2] Cette croissance importante n'est pas unique au Canada, car elle se produit à l'échelle internationale où la valeur globale de l'investissement étranger direct a "plus que sextuplé au cours des deux dernières décennies, passant de 524 milliards à 3,5 billions de dollars américains entre 1980 et 1997."[3]

Céline Lévesque, professeure à la Faculté de droit, Section de droit civil, de l'Université d'Ottawa, LL.L. (U. d'Ottawa), LL.B. (U. Dalhousie), LL.M. (Coll. d'Europe), M.A. (Geo. Wash. U.), membre du Barreau du Québec.

[1] Statistique Canada, *Bilan des investissements internationaux du Canada, 1999* à la p. 9, en ligne: http://dsp-psd.pwgsc.gc.ca/dsp-psd/Pilot/Statcan/67-202-XIB/67-202-XIB-f.html> (date d'accès: 6 février 2001).

[2] *Ibid.* aux pp. 30-31.

[3] Voir Ministère des Affaires étrangères et du Commerce international, *Ouverture sur le monde: Priorités du Canada en matière d'accès aux marchés internationaux 2000*, en ligne: <http://www.dfait-maeci.gc.ca/tna-nac/2000/03-f.asp> (date d'accès: 6 février 2001) (ci-après *Priorités du Canada 2000*). Du point de vue comparé, "[l]es IED [investissements étrangers directs] ont augmenté dans le monde entier à un rythme très rapide, qui a largement dépassé le taux de croissance du commerce international et du PIB." Voir notamment Ministère des Affaires étrangères et du Commerce international, *Ouverture sur le monde: Priorités du Canada en matière d'accès aux marchés internationaux 1999* à la p. 17 (ci-après *Priorités du Canada 1999*).

Dans ce contexte, il n'est pas surprenant que le Canada considère que "[l]es règles sur l'investissement peuvent jouer un rôle primordial en protégeant et en facilitant les activités d'investissement à l'étranger des entreprises canadiennes."[4] L'action du Canada dans l'adoption de nouvelles règles et dans la mise en oeuvre des règles existantes sur l'investissement étranger est déployée aux niveaux multilatéral, régional et bilatéral. Sur la scène multilatérale, l'année 1999 a été caractérisée par les secousses, ressenties jusqu'à l'Organisation mondiale du commerce (OMC), qui ont suivi l'abandon des négociations de l'Accord Multilatéral sur l'Investissement (AMI) en 1998 (I). Au niveau régional, l'Accord de libre-échange nord-américain[5] (ALÉNA) et les négociations de la Zone de libre-échange des Amériques (ZLÉA) ont occupé — et même préoccupé — le Canada en matière d'investissement (II). Finalement, quatre accords bilatéraux d'investissement étranger sont entrés en vigueur au Canada en 1999 (III).

I   Développements multilatéraux: post-AMI et pré-OMC

L'année 1999 en a été une de calme relatif sur la scène multilatérale quant à l'élaboration de règles visant l'investissement étranger. Cette période d'accalmie a suivi l'abandon des négociations de l'AMI[6] sous l'égide de l'Organisation de Coopération et de Développement Économiques (OCDE) en 1998.[7] La négociation de cet accord a provoqué une levée de boucliers sans précédent de la part de nombreuses organisations non gouvernementales

---

[4] *Priorités du Canada 2000, ibid.*

[5] *Accord de libre-échange nord-américain entre le gouvernement du Canada, le gouvernement des États-Unis d'Amérique et le gouvernement des États-Unis du Mexique*, le 17 décembre 1992, reproduit dans (1993) 32:3 I.L.M. 605 (ci-après ALÉNA).

[6] Selon le mandat de négociation de l'AMI donné en 1995, cet Accord:

- établirait un large cadre multilatéral pour l'investissement international, fixerait des normes élevées pour la libéralisation des régimes en matière d'investissement et pour la protection des investissements et avec des procédures efficaces de règlement des différends;
- serait un traité international autonome ouvert à tous les pays Membres de l'OCDE et des Communautés européennes, ainsi qu'à l'adhésion de pays non membres de l'OCDE.

Voir en ligne: <http://www.oecd.org/daf/investment/fdi/mai/mandate.htm> (date d'accès: 12 février 2001).

[7] La documentation officielle sur les négociations de l'AMI est archivée sur le site de l'OCDE en ligne à: < http://www.oecd.org/daf/investment/fdi/reports-fr.htm> (date d'accès: 6 février 2001) (ci-après Archives de l'AMI).

(ONG),[8] en plus de révéler des réticences sérieuses de la part de plusieurs pays membres.[9] Les questions telles celles des droits des travailleurs, de la protection de l'environnement et de la culture, des réserves pour les programmes sociaux et l'éducation, ou encore celle de l'extra-territorialité, ont heurté des sensibilités vives et suscité des oppositions irréductibles.[10]

Un des problèmes que posait l'accord était celui du forum de négociations. Le Canada a fait écho à cette difficulté dans une

---

[8] Au Canada, cette attaque a été menée par le "Council of Canadians." Pour de l'information sur cette campagne, voir en ligne: <http://www.canadians.org/campaigns/campaigns-mai.html> (date d'accès: 3 mars 2001). Le groupe connu sous le nom de "SalAMI" a également joué un rôle dans cette campagne. Voir en ligne: <http://www.alternatives.ca/salami/html_fr/prempageF.html> (date d'accès: 19 juin 2001).

[9] L'opposition de la France à l'AMI a été particulièrement stridente, comme le démontrent les extraits suivants d'une intervention du Premier ministre Jospin à l'Assemblée nationale le 14 octobre 1998, en réponse à une question au sujet des négociations sur l'AMI:

> En 1996, des négociations ont été engagées dans le cadre à l'OCDE, sur un accord multilatéral sur l'investissement, sans véritable transparence à l'époque, et ensuite. En février 1998, quand les enjeux véritables et les risques d'une telle négociation sont apparus, et qu'une émotion s'est emparée effectivement d'une partie de l'opinion dans notre pays, mais aussi dans d'autres pays, le gouvernement français ... a immédiatement posé quatre conditions pour faire la clarté dans cette discussion, en ce qui concernait la poursuite de cette négociation:
>
> • l'exception culturelle qui à nos yeux devait être respectée — les biens culturels ne sont pas des marchandises;
> • le refus d'accepter, à l'intérieur de ce mécanisme, les lois extraterritoriales américaines dont nous récusons l'application sur notre sol, dans d'autres cadres et dans d'autres discussions
> • le respect du processus d'intégration européenne
> • le respect de normes sociales et environnementales
>
> En avril 1998, le gouvernement voyant que les choses ne pouvaient pas être suffisamment clarifiées, a demandé et obtenu la suspension pour six mois de ces négociations, afin de procéder à une consultation de la société civile et d'avoir aussi une évaluation de cette négociation ... Les contestations de ce projet d'accord ... portent sur la conception même de cette négociation, et ils posent en particulier des problèmes fondamentaux à l'égard de la souveraineté des États, sommés de s'engager de façon irréversible ...
>
> Je veux vous annoncer, Mesdames et Messieurs les députés, que la France ne reprendra pas les négociations dans le cadre de l'OCDE, le 20 octobre.

Voir en ligne: <http://www.minefi.gouv.fr/europe/index.htm> (date d'accès: 3 mars 2001).

[10] Voir Archives de l'AMI, *supra* note 7. Voir aussi P. Juillard, "À Propos du décès de l'AMI" (1998) XLIV, A.F.D.I. 595.

déclaration en date du 27 avril 1998: "Pour le Canada, un AMI restreint aux pays de l'OCDE a une valeur limitée. Nous voulons des règles d'investissement véritablement multilatérales qui aideraient à étendre l'investissement étranger responsable à tous les pays, y compris les pays en développement."[11] Du même souffle, le Canada a suggéré que l'instance appropriée pour tout accord multilatéral sur l'investissement est l'OMC.[12]

Cependant, du côté de l'OMC, on constate peu d'empressement à négocier des règles multilatérales sur l'investissement.[13] Le rapport pour l'année 1999 du Groupe de travail chargé d'examiner les liens entre le commerce et l'investissement[14] est révélateur des obstacles à venir quant à la conclusion d'un tel accord.[15] Les

[11] Déclaration du Canada sur l' "Accord multilatéral sur l'investissement" (AMI) par l'Honorable Sergio Marchi, Ministre du commerce international, réunion ministérielle de l'OCDE, Paris, France, le 27 avril 1998 à la p. 4; en ligne: <http://www.dfait-maeci.gc.ca/francais/news/statements/98_state/98_031f. htm> (date d'accès: 2 février 2001).

[12] *Ibid.*

[13] Il faut rappeler que les Accords de l'OMC contiennent déjà certaines règles sur l'investissement. Les deux Accords principaux comportant de telles règles sont l'*Accord sur les mesures concernant les investissements et liées au commerce* (Accord sur les MIC) et l'*Accord général sur le commerce des services* (AGCS). L'Accord sur les MIC vise principalement les prescriptions de résultats imposées aux investisseurs qui constituent des obstacles au commerce des marchandises. Dans l'AGCS, le commerce des services comprend "la présence commerciale" sur le territoire d'un autre membre, ce qui a pour conséquence que certains investissements vont être touchés par les règles de cet Accord. Voir les Accords reproduits dans GATT, *Résultats des négociations commerciales multilatérales du cycle d'Uruguay — Textes juridiques*, Genève, Secrétariat du GATT, 1994.

Toutefois, ces règles ont des répercussions limitées à cause de leurs champs d'application restreints et parce qu'elles offrent peu du point de vue de la protection des investissements. En effet, comme le reconnaît le Canada, "l'activité d'investissement est loin d'être complètement couverte dans ces accords et, en conséquence, de nombreux pays négocient les questions relatives à l'investissement dans le cadre de divers forums régionaux et bilatéraux." Voir *Priorités du Canada 1999, supra* note 3 à la p. 20.

[14] Ce Groupe de travail a été créé lors de la réunion ministérielle de l'OMC tenue à Singapour en 1996. Voir le paragraphe 20 de la Déclaration ministérielle de Singapour à l'annexe 1 du Rapport du Groupe de travail (OMC doc. WT/WGTI/3 en date du 22 octobre 1999), en ligne: <http://docsonline.wto. org/gen_search.asp> (date d'accès:12 février 2001) (ci-après *Rapport OMC 1999*).

[15] Ce rapport présente un aperçu des travaux du Groupe de travail lors de réunions officielles tenues durant l'année; réunions auxquelles participaient des observateurs de la CNUCED, du FMI, de la Banque mondiale, de l'OCDE et de l'ONUDI. *Ibid.*, par. 1-4.

travaux du groupe portent sur les thèmes suivants: "Incidence des liens entre commerce et investissement sur le développement et la croissance économique," "Liens économiques entre commerce et investissement," "Bilan et analyse des instruments et activités internationaux existants concernant le commerce et l'investissement."[16] Le Groupe désire identifier, entre autres choses, les "avantages et les désavantages que présente l'adhésion à des règles bilatérales, régionales et multilatérales concernant l'investissement, y compris du point de vue du développement."[17] À ce sujet, les discussions rapportées révèlent des désaccords quant à la nécessité ou l'opportunité même de règles multilatérales sur l'investissement. Certains Membres remettent aussi en question le rôle de l'OMC dans l'élaboration de ces règles.[18]

Les questions qui ont retenu l'attention des Membres, et qui ont provoqué dans certains cas de vifs débats, concernent les prescriptions de résultats, les transferts de technologie, les incitations fiscales et autres à l'investissement, l'accès aux marchés, la définition de l'investissement dans un accord éventuel (direct/de portefeuille; à court/à long terme), et la responsabilité des investisseurs étrangers.[19] La question plus générale du rôle de l'État, ainsi que celle des besoins particuliers des pays en développement, ont ponctué la plupart de ces débats.

Le document a, pour toile de fond, une préoccupation centrale: celle de maintenir un équilibre entre des règles qui, d'une part, favorisent la stabilité, la prévisibilité et la transparence en matière d'investissement étranger et qui, d'autre part, réservent aux gouvernements la flexibilité nécessaire à l'atteinte d'objectifs économiques, de développement et autres, sans toutefois créer de distorsions

---

[16] *Ibid.* à l'Annexe 2 — Liste de questions proposées pour examen.

[17] *Ibid.*

[18] Voir par exemple, *ibid.*, par. 82.

[19] En ce qui a trait à la responsabilité des investisseurs étrangers, le rapport du Groupe de travail, après avoir signalé l'opinion de certains Membres qui ne croient pas que l'OMC soit le forum approprié pour traiter de cette question, fait référence aux travaux en cours à l'OCDE pour la révision des Principes directeurs à l'intention des entreprises multinationales. *Ibid.*, par. 101-07. La décision de réexaminer ces Principes, élaborés à l'origine en 1976, a été prise en juin 1998 et le travail s'est poursuivi en 1999, pour mener à l'adoption des Principes révisés en juin 2000. Pour information, consulter en ligne: <http://www.oecd.org/daf/investment/guidelines/indexf.htm> (date d'accès: 12 février 2001).

sur les flux d'investissement.[20] L'atteinte de cet équilibre — entre la prévisibilité et la flexibilité — n'est pas un défi nouveau pour le GATT (et maintenant l'OMC), qui y est confronté depuis plus de cinquante ans. Il reste à savoir si, et le cas échéant quand, les Membres de l'OMC choisiront de relever ce défi en négociant des règles multilatérales sur l'investissement étranger.

II   Développements régionaux

Les développements régionaux qui ont attiré le plus d'attention en 1999 se sont déroulés dans les Amériques.[21] Les deux piliers de ces avancées sont l'ALÉNA (A) et la ZLÉA (B).

A   Dans le cadre de l'aléna

L'ALÉNA[22] renferme entre autres objectifs celui d'augmenter substantiellement les possibilités d'investissement dans la zone de libre-échange.[23] Le chapitre 11 de l'ALÉNA sur l'investissement a été conçu afin de favoriser l'atteinte de cet objectif. La section A, en plus de présenter la portée et le champ d'application du chapitre, comporte les droits et obligations des parties en ce qui a trait au traitement des investisseurs étrangers et de leurs investissements sur le territoire des parties.[24] La section B traite du règlement des différends entre une partie et un investisseur d'une autre

---

[20] Voir par exemple, *Rapport OMC 1999, supra* note 14 aux par. 76, 81, 94-98.

[21] Il faut tout de même mentionner que: "Le Canada participe aussi à des discussions régionales sur les investissements avec les pays du bassin du Pacifique, dans le cadre de l'APEC. Par l'intermédiaire d'un programme de plans d'action individuelle à participation facultative s'inspirant de principes non obligatoires en matière d'investissement, les économies de l'APEC s'efforcent de libéraliser leurs régimes d'investissement en éliminant les restrictions à l'accès aux marchés et en renforçant leur législation pour protéger l'investissement étranger." Voir *Priorités du Canada 2000, supra* note 3. Pour plus d'information sur les activités d'APEC en cette matière, voir en ligne: <http://www.apecsec.org.sg/committee/investment.html> (date d'accès: 12 février 2001).

[22] ALÉNA, *supra* note 5.

[23] *Ibid.*, art. 102(1)c).

[24] Ces droits et obligations couvrent par exemple les sujets suivants: traitement national (art. 1102), traitement de la nation la plus favorisée (art. 1103), norme minimale de traitement (art. 1105), prescriptions de résultats (art. 1106), dirigeants et conseils d'administration (art. 1107), réserves et exceptions (art. 1108), transferts (art. 1109), expropriation et nationalisation (art. 1110), mesures environnementales (art. 1114). ALÉNA, *supra* note 5.

partie, communément appelé l'arbitrage "investisseur-État." Enfin, la section C prévoit les définitions applicables au chapitre.

L'année 1999 a été marquée par la première décision rendue sur le fond sous le régime du chapitre 11 de l'ALÉNA dans l'affaire *Azinian*,[25] concernant une dispute entre des investisseurs américains et le gouvernement du Mexique. Mais, avant même que le tribunal arbitral rende sa sentence, le Canada avait déjà fait part à ses partenaires américains et mexicains de certaines préoccupations quant à l'interprétation de ce chapitre. Dans une note qui se voulait confidentielle, mais qui a été publiée le 12 février 1999 dans l'hebdomadaire *Inside U.S. Trade*,[26] le Canada transmet à ses interlocuteurs deux "issues paper," pour discussion dans le cadre d'un examen du fonctionnement du chapitre 11, l'un sur l'expropriation et l'autre sur la transparence.

En ce qui concerne l'expropriation, la note dévoile la volonté du Canada de faire appel à la Commission du libre-échange afin que cette dernière interprète de façon restrictive l'article 1110 de l'ALÉNA.[27] Cet article stipule qu'"[a]ucune des Parties ne pourra, directement ou indirectement, nationaliser ou exproprier un investissement d'un investisseur d'une autre Partie sur son territoire, ni prendre une mesure équivalant à la nationalisation ou l'expropriation d'un tel investissement" si ce n'est qu'en respectant certaines conditions (dont, le versement d'une indemnité).[28] Dans

---

[25] *Robert Azinian, Kenneth Davitian, & Ellen Baca* v. *United Mexican States*, ICSID Case No. ARB(AF)/97/2 (ci-après *Azinian*). Le texte intégral de la sentence arbitrale est disponible en ligne à: <http://www.worldbank.org/icsid/cases/robert_award.pdf> (date d'accès: 12 février 2001); il a aussi été publié dans: ICSID Review — Foreign Invest. L.J., vol. 14, n° 2, automne 1999. Le 24 juin 1998, une sentence sur la compétence du tribunal a été rendue sous le régime du chapitre 11 dans l'affaire *Ethyl Corporation* c. *Gouvernement du Canada*, 38 I.L.M. 708 (1999), mais aucune sentence finale ne l'a été car les parties ont conclu un règlement. Plusieurs instances étaient en cours sous le régime du chapitre 11 en 1999; à ce sujet, voir *infra* note 66.

[26] *Inside U.S. Trade*, vol.17, n° 6 — 12 février 1999, sommaire et pp. 18-23 (ci-après: *Inside U.S. Trade*). Le "Canadian Memo on Investor-State Provisions" en tant que tel est daté du 13 novembre 1998 et son expéditeur est John Gero, Director General, Trade Policy Bureau II, NAFTA Coordinator, Department of Foreign Affairs and International Trade.

[27] Selon l'art. 1131(2) de l'ALÉNA, *supra* note 5, "Une interprétation faite par la Commission d'une disposition du présent accord liera un tribunal établi en vertu de la présente section." En vertu de l'art. 2001(1), la Commission du libre-échange est composée de "représentants des Parties ayant rang ministériel ou de leurs délégataires."

[28] *Ibid.*, art. 1110(1).

la note, le Canada soulève certaines difficultés d'interprétation que présente cette disposition, notamment que le terme expropriation n'est pas défini à l'ALÉNA.[29] Si l'expropriation directe est assez facile à définir, on admet que le sens à donner à l'expropriation indirecte est moins clair. Cette forme d'expropriation, qualifiée de "rampante,"[30] est effectivement insidieuse parce qu'elle peut résulter de toute une gamme de mesures qui à leur face même ne sont pas des mesures d'expropriation mais dont les effets sont équivalents.[31] Notamment, la note souligne que: "It may be argued that examples include confiscatory taxation, incremental measures with a cumulative expropriatory effect or revocation of or failure to renew licenses or approvals necessary for the enterprise to operate."[32]

Pour ce qui est des "mesure[s] équivalant à l'expropriation," le Canada craint qu'on interprète cette expression plus largement encore.[33] Cette crainte est d'autant plus intense lorsqu'on constate qu'il n'existe aucune formule universelle permettant d'établir une distinction entre "compensable takings" (c.-à-d., dans ce contexte, une expropriation qui tombe dans le champ de l'article 1110) et "non-compensable regulation" (c.-à-d. une mesure gouvernementale qui touche les droits des investisseurs sans leur donner droit à une indemnisation).[34] Dans la note, le Canada a reconnu d'emblée que l'élaboration par les parties d'une telle formule (par le biais

---

[29] *Inside U.S. Trade, supra* note 26 à la p. 20.

[30] Dans la note on utilise en anglais: "creeping" expropriation (ou "*de facto*" expropriation), *ibid.*

[31] "'Indirect' expropriation or nationalization should, by definition, also involve the taking of ownership. The expropriation article refers to 'indirect' expropriation to deal with measures, although they are not *de jure* or explicitly expropriative, have the same result ... In spite of numerous decisions of international tribunals, there is no clear definition of the concept of indirect expropriation." *Ibid.*

[32] *Ibid.*

[33] "The third element of the NAFTA formulation, measures 'tantamount to nationalization or expropriation of such an investment ...' may on its face, mean something more than 'indirect' expropriation or it may be considered redundant. Given the possible breadth of 'indirect' expropriation, measures 'tantamount to' expropriation may therefore be interpreted by some as having the potential to catch an even wider range of government measures." *Ibid.*

[34] *Ibid.* En d'autres mots, comment peut-on faire la différence entre une mesure de dépossession entraînant un droit à indemnisation et une mesure de réglementation ne donnant pas ouverture à un tel droit? Voir J.-P. Laviec, *Protection et promotion des investissements — Étude de droit international économique* (1985) à la p. 165.

d'une liste, par exemple, de mesures réglementaires ne donnant pas ouverture au droit à indemnisation) présente des dangers certains. D'un côté, les parties risquent de réduire la protection offerte aux investisseurs par le biais d'exclusions trop rigides.[35] De l'autre, elles risquent d'exclure de façon accidentelle certaines mesures légitimes ne faisant pas partie de "la liste."[36]

En définitive, la phrase qui révèle le plus clairement la préoccupation du Canada au sujet de l'interprétation de l'article 1110 est la suivante: "NAFTA Parties never intended these provisions to limit the legitimate rights of governments to regulate."[37] Malheureusement pour le Canada, à défaut d'un accord entre les parties sur cette question,[38] il reviendra principalement aux arbitres nommés en vertu de la section B du chapitre 11 de déterminer le sens à donner à cet article sur la base — avant tout — du texte même du traité[39] et du droit international en la matière.[40]

Le deuxième "issue paper" soumis par le Canada vise la transparence, en particulier les différentes façons de rendre la procédure de règlement des différends "investisseur-État" à la fois plus ouverte et transparente.[41] Plusieurs pistes de réflexion proposées à cet égard visent à rendre plus facile l'accès du public à certains documents (y compris, notamment, la notification de l'intention de soumettre une plainte à l'arbitrage, la plainte elle-même, les règles et ordonnances de procédures particulières à chaque cas, et les mémoires des parties).[42] Dans la même veine, le Canada propose

---

[35] En effet, "It is conceivable that any or all types of regulatory measures could be used by governments to effect a taking of property." *Inside U.S. Trade, supra* note 26 à la p. 20.

[36] Après avoir soulevé ces difficultés, et suggéré certaines hypothèses tirées du droit international qui pourraient aider à solutionner le problème de définition, le Canada propose certaines pistes de réflexion surtout sur la façon d'exclure les mesures prises en vertu des pouvoirs de régulation "normaux" de l'État du champ d'application de l'article 1110. Cités en exemple sont un renversement du fardeau de preuve et le recours à une liste d'exclusion. *Ibid.* aux pp. 20-21.

[37] *Ibid.* à la p. 20.

[38] Voir *supra* note 27 au sujet de l'art. 1131(2).

[39] Voir art. 31 de la *Convention de Vienne sur le droit des traités*, 23 mai 1969, R.T. Can. 1980 n° 37.

[40] Voir ALÉNA, *supra* note 5, art. 1131(1) qui stipule qu'"[u]n tribunal établi en vertu de la présente section tranchera les points en litige conformément au présent accord et aux règles applicables du droit international."

[41] *Inside U.S. Trade, supra* note 26 à la p. 21.

[42] *Ibid.* aux pp. 22-23.

un rôle accru pour le Secrétariat de l'ALÉNA afin de faciliter l'accès du public aux documents précités et à d'autres informations pertinentes.[43] Pour ce qui est de l'ouverture du processus, le Canada propose de discuter du rôle des *amici* et de la possibilité de permettre à certains groupes qui ont un intérêt de présenter des déclarations écrites au tribunal arbitral.[44]

Les appréhensions du Canada quant à l'interprétation de l'article 1110 (expropriation) de l'ALÉNA n'ont pas été confirmées dans la première décision rendue sur le fond en vertu de ce chapitre. En effet, la sentence arbitrale dans l'affaire *Azinian*[45] a plutôt établi le caractère spécifique des obligations des parties en vertu de ce chapitre, quant aux personnes qui peuvent en invoquer la violation, mais aussi quant à la nature des violations alléguées.[46] Par exemple, selon le tribunal, la simple rupture d'un contrat entre un gouvernement et un investisseur étranger par la partie gouvernementale ne donne pas ouverture à un recours sous le régime du chapitre 11.[47]

Un rappel des faits dans cette affaire s'impose.[48] En mars 1997, trois investisseurs américains, actionnaires de la compagnie mexicaine Desona, ont déposé une plainte contre le Mexique en vertu du chapitre 11 de l'ALÉNA.[49] Dans cette plainte ils alléguaient la violation par le Mexique de ses obligations en vertu des articles 1110 (expropriation) et 1105 (norme minimale de traitement).[50] La plainte était fondée sur l'annulation par les autorités locales mexicaines d'un contrat de concession pour la collecte et le traitement de déchets consenti par la ville de Naucalpan de Juarez à la compagnie Desona; concession qui avait été consentie pour une durée de quinze ans à la compagnie Desona.[51]

---

[43] *Ibid.* à la p. 22.

[44] *Ibid.* à la p. 23.

[45] *Azinian, supra* note 25.

[46] *Ibid.*, par. 82-84.

[47] *Ibid.*, par. 83 et 87.

[48] Pour une étude plus détaillée de cette affaire voir C. Lévesque, "L'affaire Desona: Réflexions sur la première sentence arbitrale rendue sur le fond sous le régime du chapitre 11 (investissement) de l'Accord de libre-échange nord-américain" (1999) 37 A.C.D.I. 257; voir aussi J.C. Thomas, "Investor-State Arbitration under NAFTA Chapter 11" (1999) 37 A.C.D.I. 99 aux pp. 132-36.

[49] *Azinian, supra* note 25, par. 1 et 24.

[50] *Ibid.*, par. 75.

[51] *Ibid.*, par. 7, 9 et 17.

Tôt dans l'exécution du contrat par Desona, les autorités ont eu des doutes quant à la capacité de la compagnie de respecter ses obligations.[52] Des démarches entreprises par le Conseil de ville ont permis d'identifier de nombreuses "irrégularités" liées à l'exécution mais aussi à la conclusion du contrat de concession; irrégularités qui ont finalement mené le Conseil à annuler le contrat le 21 mars 1994.[53] Les autorités ont considéré, en effet, que le contrat était soit nul en raison des fausses représentations, soit résiliable pour cause d'inexécution.[54] C'est l'aspect des fausses représentations qui a dominé cette affaire. En effet, la preuve faite devant les arbitres, truffée de déclarations fausses ou trompeuses, de promesses intenables et de rétention d'informations clés, était accablante.[55] En réaction à l'annulation de son contrat, Desona s'est pourvue devant différents tribunaux administratifs compétents, qui à chaque étape ont confirmé la décision du Conseil de ville.[56] C'est à la suite de ces démarches infructueuses que les investisseurs américains ont porté plainte contre le Mexique en vertu du chapitre 11 de l'ALÉNA.

Comme il s'agissait de la première sentence arbitrale à être rendue sur le fond sous le régime du chapitre 11, les arbitres ont pris la peine d'énoncer certains principes d'interprétation de base. Aussi, les arbitres auront tôt fait de déclarer qu'une simple rupture de contrat ne donne pas ouverture à un recours en vertu du chapitre 11. Selon eux, il faut des circonstances additionnelles: "Indeed, NAFTA cannot possibly be read to create such a regime, which would have elevated a multitude of ordinary transactions with public authorities into potential international disputes. *The Claimants*

---

[52] *Ibid.*, par. 12.

[53] *Ibid.*, par. 13 et 17.

[54] *Ibid.*, par. 35. Il est à noter que pour ce qui est de l'inexécution, le contrat de concession prévoyait une période de 30 jours pendant laquelle Desona pouvait remédier aux défauts allégués d'exécution; or, la Ville n'avait apparemment pas accordé ce délai à Desona avant d'annuler le contrat. Dans son raisonnement, le tribunal a toutefois choisi de traiter de la question de la nullité du contrat (pour cause de fausses représentations), et de laisser en suspens celle de sa résiliation (pour cause de non-exécution). Cette façon de procéder a permis aux arbitres d'éviter certaines questions épineuses, car des fautes contractuelles étaient alléguées des deux côtés quant à l'exécution du contrat.

[55] "The evidence compels the conclusion that the Claimants entered into the Concession Contract on false pretences, and lacked the capacity to perform it." *Ibid.*, par. 33.

[56] *Ibid.*, par. 20-23.

simply could not prevail merely by persuading the Arbitral Tribunal that the 'yuntamiento' of Naucalpan breached the Concession Contract."[57]

Au fait de cette difficulté, les demandeurs ont prétendu que le Conseil de ville n'a pas simplement rompu le contrat, mais bien procédé à l'expropriation directe des droits de Desona en vertu du contrat de concession, ainsi qu'à l'expropriation indirecte de la compagnie elle-même.[58] Sur la base de la preuve au dossier, les arbitres ont rejeté ces arguments.[59]

Le tribunal aurait pu se limiter à cette conclusion. Toutefois, les arbitres ont choisi d'étudier une question complémentaire à savoir, si la Ville n'avait pas procédé à une expropriation, est-ce que les tribunaux mexicains, eux, avaient agi en contravention des obligations du Mexique en vertu du chapitre 11?[60] Selon les arbitres, pour prouver une telle violation, il ne suffit pas que les demandeurs se disent en désaccord avec le résultat ou même le raisonnement des tribunaux.[61] Selon eux, il faut prouver par exemple un déni de justice ou une décision clairement incompatible avec une règle de droit international.[62] Car, prennent-ils la peine de rappeler, le recours devant une instance internationale comme celle prévue par la section B du chapitre 11 n'est pas de la nature d'un appel.[63] En l'espèce, les arbitres n'avaient aucun reproche à faire aux tribunaux mexicains.[64]

---

[57] *Ibid.*, par. 87.

[58] *Ibid.*, par. 88.

[59] Sans répondre à la question de savoir ce qui fait la différence entre une rupture "ordinaire" et "extraordinaire" d'un contrat du point de vue de la responsabilité internationale de l'État, les arbitres rejettent les arguments des investisseurs: "How can it be said that Mexico breached NAFTA when the 'yuntamiento' of Naucalpan purported to declare the invalidity of a Concession Contract which by its terms was subject to Mexican law, and to the jurisdiction of the Mexican courts, and the courts of Mexico then agreed with the yuntamiento's determination?" *Ibid.*, par. 96.

[60] Il est à noter que les demandeurs n'ont pas prétendu que les tribunaux mexicains avaient, en l'espèce, agi de la sorte. Les arbitres ont, par contre, cru bon de poursuivre la démarche entreprise *"ex abundante cautela,"* afin de démontrer que les demandeurs avaient eu raison de ne pas soulever cet argument. *Ibid.*, par. 100-01.

[61] *Ibid.*, par. 99.

[62] *Ibid.*, par. 98 et 102-03.

[63] *Ibid.*, par. 99.

[64] "The Arbitral Tribunal finds nothing in the application of these standards with respect to the issue of invalidity that appears arbitrary or unsustainable in light of the evidentiary record. To the contrary, the evidence positively supports the conclusions of the Mexican courts." *Ibid.*, par. 120.

En définitive, ils ont décidé qu'il n'y avait pas eu ici de violation de l'article 1110 (expropriation) ni de l'article 1105 (norme minimale de traitement) de l'ALÉNA.[65]

Que faut-il retenir de l'affaire *Azinian*? Somme toute, l'apport de cette sentence à l'interprétation du chapitre 11 est relativement limité. Si elle ne contribue pas à éclairer le problème plus général de la définition de l'expropriation à l'article 1110, ou même à donner des indications utiles sur la façon de distinguer entre la rupture ordinaire et extraordinaire d'un contrat, elle a au moins le mérite de confirmer que la compétence des tribunaux arbitraux formés sous le régime du chapitre 11 est limitée. Ainsi, ce ne sont pas toutes les déceptions ou insatisfactions ressenties par les investisseurs qui constituent des motifs valables de recours aux dispositions du chapitre 11. Et ce, que ces déceptions soient causées par le gouvernement ou par les tribunaux internes des pays membres de l'ALÉNA.[66]

---

[65] Les arbitres se sont prononcés sur l'art. 1105, afin d'éviter toute ambiguïté, même s'ils n'ont pas réellement analysé cette question, car ils considéraient que les demandeurs n'avaient présenté, à l'appui de cette allégation, aucun argument distinct de ceux utilisés dans leur argumentation en vertu de l'art. 1110. Voir notamment *ibid.*, par. 92.

[66] Considérant les plaintes dont les différents tribunaux arbitraux ont été saisis durant l'année 1999, cet énoncé est sujet à caution. En effet, plusieurs investisseurs et leurs conseillers tentent de définir largement le champ d'application du chapitre 11. En 1999, selon l'information disponible publiquement, les affaires suivantes étaient en instance:

- *Metalclad Corporation* (provenance: États-Unis) c. *Mexique* — sujet: enfouissement de déchets dangereux
- *The Loewen Group, Inc.* (provenance: Canada) c. *États-Unis* — sujet: services funéraires
- *Waste Management Inc.* (provenance: États-Unis) c. *Mexique* — sujet: traitement de déchets
- *S.D. Myers Inc.* (provenance: États-Unis) c. *Canada* — sujet: exportation de PCB
- *Sunbelt Water Co.* (provenance: États-Unis) c. *Canada* — sujet: exportation d'eau douce
- *Pope & Talbot Inc.* (provenance: États-Unis) c. *Canada* — sujet: quotas d'exportation de bois
- *Marvin Roy Feldman Karpa* (provenance: États-Unis) c. *Mexique* — sujet: exportation de tabac
- *Methanex Corporation* (provenance: Canada) c. *États-Unis* — sujet: contenu de méthanol dans l'essence
- *Mondev International Ltd.* (provenance: Canada) c. *États-Unis* — sujet: projet de développement immobilier

B DANS LE CADRE DES NÉGOCIATIONS DE LA ZLÉA

Les négociations de la ZLÉA ont débuté en 1998.[67] L'objectif fixé dès 1994 au Sommet des Amériques tenu à Miami, et maintenu depuis, est la conclusion d'un Accord entre les trente-quatre pays "démocratiques" de la Zone au plus tard en 2005.[68] Afin d'atteindre cet objectif, neuf groupes de négociations ont été créés, dont un sur les investissements.[69] Le mandat de ce groupe est d'"[é]tablir un cadre juridique juste et transparent qui crée un environnement stable et prévisible qui protège les investisseurs, leurs investissements et les flux respectifs sans créer des obstacles aux investissements extra-hémisphériques."[70]

Le groupe de négociations sur les investissements s'est réuni officiellement trois fois en 1999.[71] L'un des progrès les plus significatifs accomplis par le groupe durant l'année a été l'élaboration d'un "schéma annoté" du chapitre sur les investissements présenté

Sources: Liste des instances pendantes du CIRDI, voir en ligne: <http://www.worldbank.org/icsid/cases/pending.htm> (date d'accès: 18 juin 2001); A. Lemaire, "Le nouveau visage de l'arbitrage entre État et investisseur étranger: le chapitre 11 de l'ALÉNA" (2001) 1 Rev. de l'arbitrage 43; J.A. Soloway, "NAFTA's Chapter 11 — The Challenge of Private Party Participation" (1999) 16:2 J. of Int'l Arb. 1; H. Mann et K. von Moltke, "NAFTA's Chapter 11 and the Environment: Addressing the Impacts of the Investor-State Process on the Environment" (1999), publié en ligne à: <http://iisd.ca/trade/chapter11.htm> (date d'accès: 1er juin 2000). Toutes ces sources offrent des informations plus détaillées au sujet des affaires décrites.

[67] Le lancement des négociations a eu lieu lors du Deuxième Sommet des Amériques, tenu à Santiago, Chili, les 18 et 19 avril 1998. Voir Zone de libre-échange des Amériques, Deuxième Sommet des Amériques, *Déclaration de Santiago (Chili)*, 19 avril 1998, en ligne: <http://www.ftaa-alca.org/ministerials/chile_f.asp> (date d'accès: le 26 février 2001).

[68] Voir Zone de libre-échange des Amériques, Premier Sommet des Amériques, *Déclaration de Principes*, Miami, Floride, décembre 1994; en ligne: <http://www.ftaa-alca.org/ministerials/miami_f.asp> (date d'accès: 26 février 2001).

[69] Pour de l'information sur les Groupes de négociations, voir Zone de libre-échange des Amériques, Quatrième réunion ministérielle, San José, Costa Rica, *Déclaration conjointe*, 19 mars 1998; en ligne: <http://www.ftaa-alca.org/ministerials/costa_f.asp> (date d'accès: 26 février 2001) (ci-après *Déclaration Ministérielle de San José*).

[70] *Ibid.* à l'Annexe II: Objectifs par sujet de négociation.

[71] Les réunions du groupe de négociation sur l'investissement se sont tenus à Miami en Floride, les 16-17 février 1999; 20-22 avril 1999; et 10-11 août 1999. Voir en ligne: <http://www.ftaa-alca.org/ngroups/nginve_f.asp> (date d'accès: 26 février 2001).

aux Ministres responsables du commerce lors de la réunion ministérielle de Toronto en novembre 1999.[72] Compte tenu des travaux achevés, les Ministres ont demandé lors de cette réunion à
tous les groupes de négociations "de préparer un avant-projet de
leurs chapitres respectifs" qui sera présenté lors d'une prochaine
réunion ministérielle.[73]

Les thèmes qui ont fait l'objet des discussions du groupe en 1999
quant à l'élaboration du chapitre sur les investissements comprennent notamment: la définition des termes "investissement" et
"investisseur," le champ d'application du chapitre, le traitement
national, le traitement de la nation la plus favorisée, le traitement
juste et équitable, l'expropriation et l'indemnisation, l'indemnisation pour pertes, le personnel clé, les transfert de fonds, les prescriptions de résultats, les exceptions générales et réserves, et le
règlement des différends.[74]

Compte tenu des préoccupations exprimées par le Canada quant
à l'interprétation du chapitre 11 de l'ALÉNA, on peut penser que
sa position à la table de négociation de la ZLÉA en sera affectée. Il
reste à voir quelle stratégie sera adoptée par le Canada et le succès
remporté dans sa mise en oeuvre.

---

[72] Il est à noter que les négociations de la ZLÉA étaient sous la présidence du
Canada durant l'année 1999, jusqu'à la réunion ministérielle de Toronto, les 3
et 4 novembre 1999. L'Argentine a ensuite assumé la présidence, ce qu'elle fera
jusqu'en avril 2001. Voir *Déclaration Ministérielle de San José*, *supra* note 65.

[73] Zone de libre-échange des Amériques, Cinquième réunion ministérielle,
Toronto, Canada, *Déclaration des Ministres*, 4 novembre 1999; en ligne: <http://
www.ftaa-alca.org/ministerials/minis_f.asp> (date d'accès: 26 février 2001).
Selon la déclaration, ces avant-projet doivent être préparés: "en tenant compte
des progrès réalisés dans la préparation des schémas annotés pour chaque
domaine, et prenant note du fait qu'ils devraient être considérés comme des
cadres de référence destinés à faciliter les travaux des groupes de négociation et
non comme des ébauches définitives ou exclusives d'un éventuel accord. Ces
avant-projets devraient être remis au CNC [Comité des négociations commer-
ciales] au plus tard 12 semaines avant notre prochaine réunion ministérielle,
qui se tiendra en Argentine en avril 2001. Les groupes de négociation auront
pour objectif de préparer un texte qui soit le plus complet possible et qui con-
tiendra les textes qui ont fait l'unanimité et, entre crochets, ceux à l'égard
desquels il n'aura pas été possible de parvenir à un consensus."

[74] J.M. Salazar-Xirinachs, Chief Trade Advisor, OAS Trade Unit, Organization of
American States (OAS), "Progress in the FTAA Negotiations: A Preliminary
Assessment of the First Eighteen Months," Background paper prepared for the
Andean Development Corporation Annual Conference on Trade and Invest-
ment in the Americas, Washington, DC, 8-9 septembre 1999 à la p.6.

III   DÉVELOPPEMENTS BILATÉRAUX: LE CANADA ET LES TRAITÉS BILATÉRAUX D'INVESTISSEMENT ÉTRANGER

En 1999, quatre traités bilatéraux d'investissement étranger (ci-après traités bilatéraux) signés par le Canada sont entrés en vigueur. Ces traités ont été signés avec l'Arménie,[75] le Costa Rica,[76] le Liban,[77] et l'Uruguay.[78] Ces traités bilatéraux, "basés sur le nouveau modèle (ALÉNA)"[79], ont un contenu très similaire et, à l'exception du traité avec l'Arménie, une structure identique.

Dans ces traités, les parties reconnaissent, en des termes similaires, que: "la promotion et la protection des investissements faits par les investisseurs d'une Partie contractante sur le territoire de l'autre sont des facteurs qui stimulent les initiatives en affaires et la coopération économique entre les deux Parties."[80] Les Accords comprennent également des dispositions sur les définitions (notamment des termes entreprise, investisseur et investissement), les

---

[75] *Traité entre le gouvernement du Canada et le gouvernement de la République d'Arménie pour l'encouragement et la protection des investissements (avec Annexe)*, Ottawa, le 8 mai 1997, en vigueur le 29 mars 1999, R.T. Can. 1999/22 (ci-après *Traité avec l'Arménie*).

[76] *Accord entre le gouvernement du Canada et le gouvernement de la République du Costa Rica pour l'encouragement et la protection des investissements (avec Annexes)*, San José, le 18 mars 1998, en vigueur le 29 septembre 1999, R.T. Can. 1999/43 (ci-après *Accord avec le Costa Rica*).

[77] *Accord entre le gouvernement du Canada et le gouvernement de la République libanaise pour l'encouragement et la protection des investissements (avec Annexes)*, Ottawa, le 11 avril 1997, en vigueur le 19 juin 1999, R.T. Can. 1999/15 (ci-après *Accord avec le Liban*).

[78] *Accord entre le gouvernement du Canada et le gouvernement de la République orientale de l'Uruguay pour l'encouragement et la protection des investissements (avec Annexes)*, Ottawa, le 29 octobre 1997, en vigueur le 2 juin 1999, R.T. Can. 1999/31 (ci-après *Accord avec l'Uruguay*).

[79] Voir notamment Ministère des Affaires étrangères et du Commerce international, *Liste des Accords de promotion et de protection de l'investissement étranger (APIE) conclus par le Canada*, 1999, en ligne: <http://www.dfait-maeci.gc.ca/tna-nac/fipa-f.asp> (date d'accès: 6 février 2001) (ci-après *Liste des APIE*). Cette liste indique que les accords bilatéraux signés depuis 1994 ont été basés sur le nouveau modèle, dit "ALÉNA," tandis que les accords signés auparavant étaient basés sur l'ancien modèle, dit "OCDE."

[80] *Accord avec l'Uruguay*, *supra* note 78 à la p. 3. Une disposition identique existe dans *l'Accord avec le Costa Rica*, *supra* note 76 à la p. 3. On remarque toutefois des divergences dans *l'Accord avec le Liban*, *supra* note 77 à la p. 3, où l'on vise plutôt les initiatives "privées," et dans le *Traité avec l'Arménie*, *supra* note 75 à la p. 3, où l'on parle d'initiatives "commerciales."

normes minimales de traitement (notamment le traitement juste
et équitable, et la protection et la sécurité), la non-discrimination
(notamment le traitement national et de la nation la plus favorisée), les dirigeants, administrateurs et le personnel, les prescriptions de résultats, l'indemnisation en cas de conflit armé, urgence
ou catastrophe naturelle, l'expropriation, le transfert de capitaux,
la subrogation (notamment en cas de garantie ou d'assurance), les
mesures fiscales, le règlement des différends entre un investisseur
et une Partie contractante d'accueil, le règlement des différends
entre les Parties contractantes, la transparence et les exceptions et
règles particulières.[81]

Au chapitre du règlement des différends, il est intéressant de
noter que les quatre traités bilatéraux signés par le Canada en
1999 prévoient la possibilité du recours à l'arbitrage "investisseur-
État," un mécanisme qui, par ailleurs, a été l'objet de nombreuses
critiques ces dernières années.[82] La ressemblance entre les dispositions de ces traités et la section B du chapitre 11 de l'ALÉNA
prévoyant l'arbitrage "investisseur-État" est évidente. Il n'y a rien
de surprenant à cela, surtout lorsque l'on sait que l'origine de cette
section de l'ALÉNA peut être tracée aux traités bilatéraux signés
par les États-Unis.[83] De façon globale, les traités bilatéraux, dont

---

[81] Voir le texte des Accords bilatéraux cités aux notes 75 à 78 disponible en ligne à
partir de la *Liste des APIE, supra* note 79.

[82] Voir par exemple la note préparée par les organismes Friends of the Earth et
Public Citizen, intitulée "NAFTA's Corporate lawsuits" (avril 1999) et publiée
en ligne à: <http://www.citizen.org/pctrade/nafta/cases/fancy.pdf> (date
d'accès: 20 juin 2001). Voir également M. Nolan et D. Lippoldt, "Obscure
NAFTA Clause Empowers Private Parties" (1998), The National Law Journal, 6
avril 1998 à la p. B8.

[83] Voir P. Le B. Douglas et T. Ueno, A Practitioner's Guide to Chapter 11 of
NAFTA, dans *L'ALÉNA et l'Avocat d'Affaires*, Service de la formation permanente
du Barreau du Québec (1998) à la p. 144. Voir également D.M. Price, "Chapter
11 — Private Party vs. Government, Investor-State Dispute Settlement: Franken-
stein or Safety Valve?" (2000) 26 Can.-U.S. L.J. aux pp. 107-08, qui explique que
la procédure de règlement des différends prévue au chapitre 11 de l'ALÉNA
n'est pas une nouveauté: "We hear a lot of criticisms of Chapter 11, in particular
the dispute settlement mechanism, suggesting that it is unprecedented. In fact, it
is heavily precedented ... From the U.S. perspective, Chapter 11 grew out of a
long tradition of negotiating first treaties of friendship, commerce, and navigation, or treaties of amity, and later, bilateral investment treaties. This was not a
trend peculiar to the United States. In fact, looking from the vantage point of the
year 2000, there are now more than 1,500 bilateral investment treaties in force.
Most of them have provisions nearly identical to those one finds in NAFTA Chapter 11, including the feature of investor-state dispute settlement."

le nombre à la fin de l'année 1999 dépassait 1 800,[84] contiennent typiquement des clauses permettant à un investisseur d'avoir un recours direct contre un État partie.[85]

Les ressemblances, entre les dispositions sur l'arbitrage "investisseur-État" dans les traités bilatéraux signés par le Canada en 1999 et les dispositions de la section B du chapitre 11 de l'ALÉNA, sont nombreuses. Par exemple, tous ces traités prévoient que les parties doivent d'abord faire un effort de règlement à l'amiable, avant que l'investisseur puisse recourir à l'arbitrage.[86] Aussi, une période de quelques mois est prévue pour le déroulement de ce processus.[87] En vertu de ces traités, l'investisseur a le droit de choisir entre les règles du CIRDI, du mécanisme supplémentaire du CIRDI ou de la CNUDCI.[88] Des conditions équivalentes sont prévues pour le consentement de l'investisseur à l'arbitrage ainsi que sa renonciation à son droit d'engager ou de continuer d'autres procédures de règlement des différends.[89] Pour ce qui est du consentement de l'État, celui-ci est offert à l'avance et,

---

[84] Voir UNCTAD, *Bilateral Investment Treaties, 1959-1999* (2000), Internet Edition Only, à la p. 1. Ce document est disponible à: <http://www.unctad.org/en/pub/poiteiiad2.en.htm> (date d'accès: 19 juin 2001).

[85] Voir R. Dolzer, and M. Stevens, *Bilateral Investment Treaties* (1995) à la p. 129, et la citation de D.M. Price *supra* note 83.

[86] Voir *Traité avec l'Arménie, supra* note 75, art. XIII(1); *Accord avec le Costa Rica, supra* note 76, art. XII(1); *Accord avec le Liban, supra* note 77, art. XII(1); *Accord avec l'Uruguay, supra* note 78, art. XII(1). Dans l'ALÉNA, *supra* note 5, voir l'art. 1118 (Règlement d'une plainte par la consultation et la négociation).

[87] Voir *Traité avec l'Arménie, supra* note 75, art. XIII(2); *Accord avec le Costa Rica, supra* note 76, art. XII(2); *Accord avec le Liban, supra* note 77, art. XII(2); *Accord avec l'Uruguay, supra* note 78, art. XII(2). Dans l'ALÉNA, *supra* note 5, voir l'art. 1120 (Soumission d'une plainte à l'arbitrage).

[88] Voir *Traité avec l'Arménie, supra* note 75, art. XIII(4); *Accord avec le Costa Rica, supra* note 76, art. XII(4) — il est à noter que le recours aux règles de la CNUDCI dans cet Accord est toutefois conditionnel; *Accord avec le Liban, supra* note 77, art. XII(4); *Accord avec l'Uruguay, supra* note 78, art. XII(4). Dans l'ALÉNA, *supra* note 5, voir l'art. 1120 (Soumission d'une plainte à l'arbitrage).

[89] Voir *Traité avec l'Arménie, supra* note 75, art. XIII(3); *Accord avec le Costa Rica, supra* note 76, art. XII(3); *Accord avec le Liban, supra* note 77, art. XII(3); *Accord avec l'Uruguay, supra* note 78, art. XII(3). Dans l'ALÉNA, *supra* note 5, voir l'art. 1121 (Conditions préalables à la soumission d'une plainte à l'arbitrage).

de façon générale, ne peut être retiré.[90] Ces traités confirment tous le caractère définitif et obligatoire de la sentence arbitrale.[91]

Les différences principales entre ces traités tiennent au fait que le chapitre 11 de l'ALÉNA comporte plusieurs règles de procédure qui ont préséance sur les règles d'arbitrage applicables, que ce soit celles du CIRDI ou de la CNUDCI, ce qui n'est pas le cas pour les traités bilatéraux sous étude.[92] Ainsi, l'ALÉNA prévoit par exemple le nombre d'arbitres et leur nomination,[93] la procédure à suivre lorsqu'une Partie néglige de nommer un arbitre ou en cas de désaccord sur la nomination de l'arbitre en chef,[94] et la possibilité de jonction de procédures.[95] D'autres différences sont liées au fait que l'ALÉNA a trois parties, plutôt que deux. Par exemple, il est prévu qu'un État membre puisse présenter au Tribunal des conclusions sur une question d'interprétation de l'ALÉNA dans un cas où il n'est pas la partie défenderesse.[96] Une étude sommaire démontre donc que les ressemblances sont plus importantes que les différences.[97]

Depuis 1989, année où le Canada a signé son premier traité bilatéral, une vingtaine d'accords visant l'encouragement et la protection des investissements étrangers sont entrés en vigueur au Canada.[98] Ces Accords ont été conclus avec des pays en

---

[90] Voir *Traité avec l'Arménie, supra* note 75, art. XIII(5); *Accord avec le Costa Rica, supra* note 76, art. XII(5); *Accord avec le Liban, supra* note 77, art. XII(5); *Accord avec l'Uruguay, supra* note 78, art. XII(5). Dans l'ALÉNA, *supra* note 5, voir l'art. 1122 (Consentement à l'arbitrage).

[91] Voir *Traité avec l'Arménie, supra* note 75, art. XIII(10); *Accord avec le Costa Rica, supra* note 76, art. XII(10); *Accord avec le Liban, supra* note 77, art. XII(10); *Accord avec l'Uruguay, supra* note 78, art. XII(9). Dans l'ALÉNA, *supra* note 5, voir l'art. 1136 (Irrévocabilité et exécution d'une sentence).

[92] Voir ALÉNA, *supra* note 5, art. 1120(2) qui stipule que: "Les règles d'arbitrage applicables régiront l'arbitrage, sauf dans la mesure où elles sont modifiées par la présente section."

[93] *Ibid.*, art. 1123.

[94] *Ibid.*, art. 1124.

[95] *Ibid.*, art. 1126.

[96] *Ibid.*, art. 1128.

[97] Certaines dispositions, par exemple celles sur les mesures provisoires ou sur le droit applicable, n'ont pas été mentionnées dans cet exposé, car leur étude demanderait un traitement plus détaillé, qui dépasse malheureusement le cadre de cette chronique. Pour plus d'information sur les premiers traités bilatéraux signés par le Canada, voir R.K Paterson, "Canadian Investment Promotion and Protection Treaties" (1991) 29 A.C.D.I. 373.

[98] Voir la *Liste des APIE, supra* note 79.

développement ou en transition à une économie de marché. Comparativement aux autres pays du G-7, à l'exception du Japon, le Canada a signé relativement peu de traités bilatéraux. En effet, selon l'inventaire effectué par le CIRDI, entre 1959 et 1996, l'Allemagne a signé 112 traités bilatéraux, le Royaume-Uni 84, la France 65, l'Italie 48, les États-Unis 37 et le Canada 17, suivi du Japon avec 4.[99] Si l'on se fie aux traités bilatéraux signés par le Canada de 1997 à 1999, au nombre de sept, et aux négociations entamées avec plusieurs autres pays dont la Chine, le Brésil, l'Inde et la Colombie, il semble que le Canada essaie de renverser la vapeur.[100] Pour ce qui est du mécanisme de règlement des différends "investisseur-État," on notera que, malgré la controverse, son inclusion dans les traités bilatéraux signés par le Canada ne semble pas être remise en question.[101]

CONCLUSION

En 1999, la participation du Canada dans l'élaboration et l'interprétation des règles internationales sur l'investissement étranger a été marquée par une grande prudence. À l'OMC, les participants aux discussions sur un traité multilatéral éventuel sur l'investissement, dont le Canada, se sont montrés très prudents, dans la foulée de l'AMI, et on peut penser que ce dossier n'évoluera guère avant quelques années.

Pour ce qui est de l'ALÉNA, l'interprétation de certaines dispositions du chapitre 11 de cet accord, dont l'article sur l'expropriation, cause des problèmes sérieux au Canada qui craint en particulier qu'une interprétation large n'ait pour conséquence la réduction des pouvoirs de régulation du gouvernement. Si la sentence arbitrale dans l'affaire *Azinian* a pu soulager quelque peu les craintes du Canada, elle n'est pas garante de l'avenir. En effet,

---

[99] International Centre for Settlement of Investment Disputes, *Bilateral Investment Treaties, 1959-1996 — Chronological and Country Data, Bibliography*, Doc. ICSID/17, 30 mai 1997.

[100] *Priorités du Canada 2000, supra* note 3.

[101] On pourrait pourtant en croire autrement si l'on se fie à l'affirmation faite par le Ministre du Commerce international Pierre Pettigrew en avril 2000: "[J]e peux vous assurer que nous ne cherchons pas à inclure une disposition relative aux différends investisseur-État à l'OMC ou dans toutes autres ententes." Témoignage du Ministre Pierre Pettigrew devant le Comité permanent des Affaires étrangères et du Commerce international, le mercredi 5 avril 2000, dont le texte est disponible en ligne à partir de l'adresse: <http://www.parl.gc.ca/search/> (date d'accès: 19 juin 2001).

comme le chapitre 11 prévoit la formation de tribunaux *ad hoc,* qui ne sont pas liés par les précédents développés en vertu de ce chapitre,[102] il existe un risque non négligeable que la retenue dont ont fait preuve les arbitres dans cette affaire devienne l'exception plutôt que la règle. De plus, il est douteux que les parties à l'Accord soient capables de s'entendre, par exemple, sur une interprétation mutuellement satisfaisante de l'article 1110. À tout le moins, on sait qu'aucun accord n'a été conclu à cet égard en 1999. Ainsi, on peut croire que les craintes du Canada ont influé sur sa position dans le cadre des négociations de la ZLÉA sur l'investissement et qu'elles continueront de le faire.

Enfin, dans la sphère des relations bilatérales, quatre accords additionnels visant la promotion et la protection des investissements sont entrés en vigueur au Canada, pendant que d'autres accords similaires étaient négociés ou signés.

---

[102] Voir art. 1136(1) de l'ALÉNA, *supra* note 5, qui déclare qu'"[u]ne sentence arbitrale rendue par un tribunal n'aura force obligatoire qu'entre les parties contestantes et à l'égard de l'espèce considérée."

Canadian Practice in International Law / La pratique canadienne en matière de droit international public

At the Department of Foreign Affairs in 1999-2000 / Au ministère des Affaires étrangères en 1999-2000

compiled by / préparé par
MICHAEL LEIR

compiled by / préparé par
MICHAEL LEIR

DROITS DE LA PERSONNE

Réforme des organes de surveillance de l'application des traités

Dans un mémorandum en date du 23 février 2000, le Bureau juridique a écrit:

Le système des traités des droits de l'homme des Nations Unies a atteint un point critique. La prolifération d'instruments de droits de l'homme au cours des dernières décennies, la création de nouveaux organes de surveillance de l'application des traités de droits de l'homme (Organes des traités) et la rareté des ressources au sein du système de l'ONU, sans perspective d'amélioration dans un proche avenir, ont créé de nouvelles pressions sur ce système et sur les États. D'une part, les Organes des traités voient leur charge de travail accroître en raison d'une variété de facteurs, dont notamment les taux record de ratifications des traités et le recours croissant aux mécanismes de plaintes. Les Organes des traités sont composés, pour l'heure, de six comités établis pour contrôler la mise en oeuvre des principaux traités internationaux des droits de l'homme: le Comité des droits de l'homme, le Comité des droits économiques, sociaux et culturels, le Comité contre la torture, le Comité pour l'élimination de la discrimination raciale, le Comité pour l'élimination de la discrimination à l'égard des femmes et le Comité pour les droits de l'enfant. D'autre part, les États s'efforcent de respecter leurs obligations de rapporter qui se multiplient et se chevauchent. Une réforme du système entier s'avère cruciale pour la propre survie de ce dernier et pour assurer l'implantation efficace des normes de droits de l'homme, d'autant plus que les problèmes identi-fiés comme étant urgents en 1989, dans le rapport de l'expert indépen-dant à l'Assemblée générale, demeurent encore à être résolus.

C'est dans ce contexte que le 28 août 1998, le gouvernement australien a annoncé qu'il entreprendrait des actions et continuerait à travailler en étroite collaboration avec les États parties afin de promouvoir une réforme des Organes des traités, dont probablement la tenue d'une con-férence de haut niveau qui permettrait de développer des propositions ainsi qu'une stratégie de réforme. Au mois d'avril 1999, le Canada, l'Aus-tralie et la Nouvelle-Zélande ont produit devant la Commission des droits de l'homme des Nations Unies une déclaration commune sur la nécessité d'améliorer le système des Organes des traités. Au mois de février 2000, le Canada a participé à une rencontre informelle sur l'amélioration du fonctionnement des Organes des traités des droits de l'homme organisée par la Mission permanente de l'Australie aux Nations Unies à Genève. En tant que co-auteur d'une résolution sur le fonctionnement efficace des Organes des traités, le Canada souhaite trouver des solutions positives et s'est engagé à continuer des discussions avec le sous-groupe régional initié par l'Australie en février dernier.

Le Ministère des Affaires étrangères et du Commerce international travaille activement à trouver des solutions pour remédier à la situation critique actuelle. Le Canada partage plusieurs des préoccupations de l'Australie eu égard au fonctionnement des Organes des traités. Ceci dit, il ne croit pas que limiter la coopération avec les Organes des traités puisse s'avérer une stratégie utile aux fins d'améliorer le système, croyant que ce faisant, de telles actions encourageront les autres États parties à faire fi de leurs engagements en vertu des traités. Le Canada demeure totalement engagé aux principes du système des Nations unies et au rôle central joué par les Organes des traités dans leur interprétation et dans leur surveil-lance des normes de droits de l'homme. Le défi consiste à identifier des façons pratiques et financièrement viables pour surmonter les contraintes du système dans son état actuel.

Protocol to Prevent, Suppress, and Punish Trafficking in Persons, Especially Women and Children

On May 30, 2000, the Legal Bureau wrote:

The term "servitude" appears in international law in the *Universal Declara-tion on Human Rights*, article 4 (UDHR); the *International Covenant on Civil and Political Rights*, article 8 (ICCPR); the *European Convention for the Protec-tion of Human Rights and Fundamental Freedom*s, article 4 (ECHR) and the *American Convention on Human Rights*, article 6. However, the term does not enjoy explicit definition in treaty law and there is scant international judi-cial consideration of the term with the European Commission.

There are a number of similar terms that are used in international law and practice that are sometimes used interchangeably. For example, besides servitude, "slave-like practices" or "slavery-like practices," "a per-son of servile status" and "contemporary forms of slavery" are used. These terms exist likely because the classic definition of slavery emerging from the *1926 Slavery Convention* refers strictly to the formal or *de facto* legal status of the person due to the legal right of ownership exercised over the person. Article 1 of the *1926 Slavery Convention* provides:

Article 1
For the purpose of the present Convention, the following definitions are agreed upon:
(1) Slavery is the status or condition of a person over whom any or all of the powers attaching to the right of ownership are exercised.

The international community recognized that there were other forms of restrictions of an individual's freedom and listed some of them in the *1956 Supplementary Convention on the Abolition of Slavery, the Slave Trade and Institutions and Practices Similar to Slavery* (1956 Supplementary Convention) under article 1, para. (a) through (d). These practices include: debt bondage, serfdom, marriage arrangements that force a person to marry upon payment of a reward, and payment arrangements where a child is delivered to another person in order to exploit that child's labour. To describe or classify these practices, commentators and scholars have used the term *"slave(ry)-like practices."* This term lingered on even though it does not have a formal legal definition in international law. Other commentators have used the word "servitude" to describe these practices. Servitude seems in some instances to be interchangeable with "slavery-like" practices. However, this point is still debated by leading academics. Whatever the difference between "slave(ry)-like practices and "servitude," the consensus seems to be that these terms refer to modern forms of slavery even though the person is not "owned" by virtue of his or her loss of legal status. The effects on the person are such that it amounts to slavery in its classic form resulting in a serious and far-reaching deprivation of fundamental civil rights coupled with economic exploitation.

The term *"contemporary forms of slavery"* appears regularly in the documents produced by the Working Group on Contemporary Forms of Slavery which was created by the Sub-Commission on Prevention of Discrimination and Protection of Minorities as a permanent mechanism to advise States how to eliminate slavery as well as suppress the traffic in persons. The Working Group on Contemporary Forms of Slavery continues to report on recent developments on slavery and slave-like practices at the annual session of the Sub-Commission on Prevention of Discrimination and Protection of Minorities. A review of these annual reports reveals that in 1993 the Working Group on Contemporary Slavery broadened its definition of "contemporary forms of slavery" to include sex tourism, the use of child soldiers, the exploitation of migrant workers, and the sexual exploitation of women during wartime. In 1996, they included, illegal adoptions, traffic in human organs and tissues, violence against women, early marriages, incest and detained juveniles. The 1998 Annual Report adds consideration of the illegal activities of certain religious and other sects.

The term *"servile status"* originates from the *1956 Supplementary Convention on the Abolition of Slavery* under Article 7 (b) providing the definition of "a person of servile status." During the December 1999 ICC PrepCom negotiations on the Elements of Crimes, a footnote was adopted explaining that "deprivation of liberty" under the crime against humanity of enslavement is understood as including, in some circumstances, "exacting forced labour or otherwise reducing a person to a servile status." During the March 2000 ICC PrepCom, the same footnote was considered in the discussion on the war crimes of "sexual slavery." However, the Holy See and United Arab Emirates (for the Arab group) defeated the reference to servile status and forced labour. From this experience Canada might expect that the reference to servitude or servile status will be opposed by these States.

The UN High Commissioner endorsed the inclusion of references to forced labour and/or bonded labour and/or servitude in the definition of trafficking and observed that "*servitude*" is consistent with existing international law. The High Commissioner proposed the use of "servitude" in hopes of avoiding the divisiveness among States and the NGO community over the meaning of "sexual exploitation" in the Trafficking in Persons Protocol. (*See* the Ad Hoc Committee on the Elaboration of a Convention against Transnational Organized Crime, Informal Note of June 1, 1999)

The NGO community favours the inclusion of the definition of *servitude* if it includes "slave-like practices" to which newer contemporary forms may be added in the future. For example, there is talk of abusive practices connected to trafficking such as "reproductive exploitation." (The abduction of a woman in order to impose pregnancy on her.) In their view, this practice does not fall within the definition of forced labour, debt bondage, or slavery. In particular, the China shadow report for CEDAW identifies this practice.

A proposed definition of servitude as follows would include the elements of the crimes of extortion and intimidation in conformity with the Criminal Code of Canada. For example: "Servitude" shall mean the condition of a person who is unjustifiably compelled or coerced by another to render any service to the same person or to others and who reasonably believes he or she has no alternative but to perform the service.

ENVIRONMENTAL LAW

Climate Change

In response to a question concerning the prompt start of the clean development mechanism immediately after the sixth Conference of the Parties (CoP 6), the Legal Bureau wrote on July 31, 2000:

Three provisions must be considered in order to answer your question: Article 12 of the Kyoto Protocol (the "Protocol"), Article 7.2 of the Framework Convention on Climate Change (the "Convention") and Article 25 of the Vienna Convention on the Law of Treaties (the "Vienna Convention"). Subject to constitutional law requirements, Article 25 of the Vienna Convention may provide a solution.

... Article 12.5 of the Protocol provides that a decision of the Conference of the Parties serving as the meeting of the Parties (the "CoP/moP") is necessary to "designate" the operational entities that will certify emission reductions. Accordingly, and on the basis of that provision alone, a decision of the Conference of the Parties (the "CoP") is not sufficient to allow an early start up at CoP 6. More generally, we have said in the past that a decision of the CoP with respect to issues that are explicitly within the mandate of the CoP/moP amounts to no more than a recommendation to the CoP/moP to adopt that decision.

While Article 12 should allow for emission reductions to be certified retroactively, I understand that the mechanisms negotiators are not looking for retroactivity but for immediate (after CoP 6) and irreversible certification. We also understand that during a recent mechanisms meeting, most negotiators agreed that the decisions required under Article 12 of the Protocol could be made by the CoP under Article 7.2 of the Convention ... The relevant part of the introductory paragraph of Article 7.2 states as follows:

> The Conference of the Parties, as the supreme body of this Convention, shall keep under regular review the implementation of the Convention and any related legal instruments that the Conference of the Parties may adopt, and shall make, within its mandate, the decisions necessary to promote the effective implementation of the Convention.

Pursuant to this provision, the CoP shall

(a) keep under regular review the implementation of the Convention and any related legal instrument adopted by the CoP
(b) make, within its mandate, the decisions necessary to promote the effective implementation of the Convention.

While the Kyoto Protocol clearly is a related legal instrument adopted by the CoP, according to Article 7.2, the CoP can only keep its implementation under regular review. CoP decisions must be

(a) within the CoP's mandate; and
(b) necessary to promote the effective implementation of the Convention.

Decisions required under Article 12 of the Protocol are explicitly within the mandate of the CoP/moP, not the CoP. Moreover, the drafters did not refer to "related legal instruments" as they have in the first part of Article 7.2.

Subject to constitutional law requirements, Article 25 of the Vienna Convention may provide an adequate solution. Article 25.1 provides as follows:

A treaty or part of a treaty is applied provisionally pending its entry into force if:

(a) the treaty itself so provides; or
(b) the negotiating States have in some other manner so agreed.

We believe that according to Article 25.1 (b), the negotiating States of the Protocol, i.e. the CoP, could, by means of an agreement reflected in a decision ("in some other manner"), apply provisionally Articles 12 and 13 of the Protocol. Article 13 establishes the CoP/moP which, once established, could take the necessary decisions under Article 12. Since these decisions would be taken by the CoP/moP, they would meet the requirements of Article 12 ... The decision would explicitly provide that Articles 12 and 13 apply provisionally immediately upon adoption. Please note that, like all decisions of the CoP, this decision would require consensus.

According to a statement made by a member of the International Law Commission found in the 1965 Yearbook of the International Law Commission (the "Yearbook"), provisional application can serve a useful purpose "... where the subject matter was urgent [or] the immediate implementation of the treaty was of great political significance..." Given the fact that under Article 12.10 of the Protocol, Parties may obtain certified emission reductions from the year 2000, this may be a specific case where the subject matter is sufficiently urgent.

Provisional application must not allow for delayed entry into force of the treaty. The following commentary is found in volume II of the 1962 Yearbook: "It seems evident that if the necessary ratifications ... are unreasonably delayed so that the provisional period is unduly prolonged, there must come a time when States are entitled to say that the provisional application must come to an end."

According to commentators, the Decision/Agreement should provide for a time-limit which could be renewed or not depending on the will of negotiating States. In that regard, we also noted the following commentary made in 1965 by the Chairman of the International Law Commission: "... even if the treaty subsequently lapsed owing to lack of ratification, that dissolution of the treaty would not be retroactive and did not prevent the treaty from having been in force during a certain time." In other words, rights accrued during provisional application may be maintained.

Last but not least, in some States, constitutional law requirements may have to be met before States can agree to be bound by an international instrument. In Canada, an order in council would be required to authorize Canadian officials to agree to a decision that would enter into force upon adoption ...

INTERNATIONAL HUMANITARIAN LAW

*Prosecuting "Leaders," including Non-State "Leaders,"
under the International Criminal Court Statute*

In a memorandum dated January 21, 2000, the Legal Bureau wrote:

The ICC will be able to prosecute leaders, whether military, paramilitary or civilian, for genocide, crimes against humanity or war crimes committed by their subordinates in two ways. First, under article 25, on "individual criminal responsibility," leaders can be prosecuted for ordering, soliciting or inducing the commission of a crime, aiding and abetting or otherwise assisting in the commission of a crime, or intentionally contributing to the commission of a crime under the Statute. Second, under article 28, "responsibility of commanders or other superiors," leaders can be held responsible for failing to prevent, repress or punish genocide, crimes against humanity or war crimes committed by their subordinates. Articles 25 and 28 codify international customary law with respect to criminal responsibility. Therefore, they will prove to be extremely valuable in assigning individual criminal responsibility to non-state leaders.

Under the ICC Statute, non-state leaders can be held liable for crimes against humanity or genocide committed in any context. These crimes apply at all times, whether in peacetime, war, or in situations of unrest such as internal disturbances and tensions. In internal armed conflicts, a non-state leader could also be convicted of war crimes, if the prosecutor proved that the leader was part of an "organized armed group."

L'état des Protocoles additionnels aux Conventions de Genève de 1949 relatifs à la protection des victimes des conflits armés.

En réponse à la demande du Secrétaire général de l'Organisation des Nations Unies, en date du 29 février 2000, le Bureau juridique a soumis le rapport suivant:

I. Les *Protocoles additionnels*

Le Canada est partie aux quatre *Conventions de Genève* de 1949 et aux *Protocoles additionnels* de 1977. Il a déposé son instrument de ratification des *Protocoles additionnels* le 20 novembre 1990 et ceux-ci sont entrés en vigueur pour le Canada le 20 mai 1990. Le Canada a mis en oeuvre ces Protocoles au moyen de *la Loi sur les Conventions de Genève*, L.R.C. 1985, c. G-3, telle qu'elle a été modifiée par la *Loi modifiant la Loi sur les Conventions de Genève*, la *Loi sur la défense nationale* et la *Loi sur les marques de commerce*, L.C. 1990, c. 14.

II. Mesures prises en vue de renforcer les règles en vigueur constituant le droit international humanitaire

A. La Commission nationale canadienne sur le droit humanitaire

La *Commission nationale canadienne sur le droit humanitaire* (la Commission) a été fondée le 18 mars 1998 suite à une recommandation de la 26ᵉ Conférence internationale de la Croix-Rouge et du Croissant-Rouge.

La Commission est composée de membres permanents qui représentent le ministère des Affaires étrangères et du Commerce international, le ministère de la Défense nationale, le ministère de la Justice, l'Agence canadienne de développement international, le Solliciteur général du Canada (représenté par la Gendarmerie royale du Canada (GRC)) et la Société canadienne de la Croix-Rouge. D'autres membres peuvent être sélectionnés pour une période intérimaire par les membres permanents tel que requis par des projets particuliers. Il peut s'agir de représentants d'autres ministères du gouvernement fédéral, notamment Patrimoine canadien, le Bureau du Conseil privé, Élections Canada, Citoyenneté et Immigration Canada, de représentants des ministères provinciaux de l'Éducation, ou bien des universitaires spécialisés en Droit international humanitaire (DIH).

La Commission a pour mandat de faciliter la mise en oeuvre du DIH au Canada, notamment des *Conventions de Genève* et des *Protocoles additionnels*. Ses fonctions principales consistent à:

(a) considérer et, s'il y a lieu, recommander la ratification d'instruments juridiques de DIH;

(b) coordonner la mise en oeuvre des obligations concernant le DIH;

(c) donner des conseils quant à la diffusion du DIH et à la formation relative au DIH au Canada;

(d) coordonner et encourager les actions des différents ministères et autres organismes pertinents pour renforcer le respect du DIH et en encourager la diffusion;

(e) examiner et, s'il y a lieu, recommander des mesures pour promouvoir la mise en oeuvre, en droit interne, du DIH dans d'autres pays compte tenu des ressources et de l'expertise disponibles au Canada;

(f) garder à jour une liste d'experts en DIH et échanger de l'information sur le DIH avec d'autres commissions nationales ainsi qu'avec le Comité international de la Croix-Rouge.

B. Intégration du DIH aux lois et règlements

La *Loi sur les crimes contre l'humanité*

Le Canada a été le premier pays à déposer une loi intégrant les dispositions du *Statut de Rome de la Cour pénale internationale (CPI)* au droit interne. Cette loi, la *Loi concernant le génocide, les crimes contre l'humanité et les crimes de guerre,* a obtenu la sanction royale le 29 juin 2000.

Le *Statut de Rome de la Cour pénale internationale*

Le 7 juillet 2000, le Canada a ratifié le *Statut de Rome de la CPI,* qui aura juridiction sur les crimes les plus graves que l'humanité connaisse — le génocide, les crimes contre l'humanité et les crimes de guerre.

La *Loi sur la défense nationale*

Le Canada a modifié sa *Loi sur la défense nationale* de façon à y intégrer la politique des Forces canadiennes interdisant le déploiement dans les zones de conflits des personnes de moins de 18 ans. Cette modification est entrée en vigueur le 29 juin 2000.

Le *Protocole facultatif à la Convention relative aux droits de l'enfant concernant la participation des enfants aux conflits armés* (le Protocole facultatif)

Le 7 juillet 2000, le Canada a ratifié le Protocole facultatif qui établit de nouvelles normes relativement à la participation d'enfants aux conflits armés. Le Protocole facultatif exige des États qu'ils adoptent des mesures concrètes pour s'assurer que les membres de leurs forces armées âgés de moins de 18 ans ne prennent pas directement part aux hostilités. Le Protocole facultatif aborde également les questions du recrutement, de la conformité, de la mise en œuvre ainsi que de la coopération et de l'aide internationale. Le Canada a été non seulement le premier État à signer ce protocole, mais aussi le premier à le ratifier.

La *Loi de mise en oeuvre de la Convention sur les mines antipersonnel*

La loi mettant en oeuvre la *Convention sur l'interdiction de l'emploi, du stockage, de la production et du transfert des mines antipersonnel et sur leur destruction,* soit la *Loi de mise en oeuvre de la Convention sur les mines antipersonnel,* a reçu la sanction royale le 27 novembre 1997. Cette loi interdit la mise au point, la production, l'acquisition, la possession, le transfert, le stockage et l'emploi de mines antipersonnel et requiert que le Gouvernement du

Canada détruise les mines antipersonnel stockées par le Canada (la destruction des stocks avait toutefois été achevée avant même que la loi ne soit approuvée par le Parlement).

La *Convention sur l'interdiction de l'emploi, du stockage, de la production et du transfert des mines antipersonnel et sur leur destruction*

Le Canada a été le premier pays à ratifier la *Convention sur l'interdiction de l'emploi, du stockage, de la production et du transfert des mines antipersonnel et sur leur destruction*, le 3 décembre 1997, soit le jour même où il l'a signée.

Le *Protocole sur l'interdiction ou la limitation de l'emploi des mines, pièges et autres dispositifs, tel que modifié, à la Convention des Nations Unies sur l'interdiction ou la limitation de l'emploi de certaines armes classiques qui peuvent être considérées comme produisant des effets traumatiques excessifs ou comme frappant sans discrimination*

Le 5 janvier 1998, le Canada a adhéré au *Protocole sur l'interdiction ou la limitation de l'emploi des mines, pièges et autres dispositifs, tel que modifié, à la Convention des Nations Unies sur l'interdiction ou la limitation de l'emploi de certaines armes classiques qui peuvent être considérées comme produisant des effets traumatiques excessifs ou comme frappant sans discrimination* après s'être assuré que sa législation était conforme aux principes énoncés dans la Convention.

La *Convention pour la protection des biens culturels en cas de conflit armé*

Le 11 décembre 1998, le Canada a adhéré à la *Convention pour la protection des biens culturels en cas de conflit armé* après s'être assuré que sa législation était conforme aux principes énoncés dans la Convention.

La *Loi sur l'extradition*

Le 17 juin 1999, des modifications à la *Loi sur l'extradition* ont reçu la sanction royale. Ces modifications aident le Canada à lutter contre l'impunité en lui permettant d'extrader des personnes vers des États de même qu'aux tribunaux pénaux internationaux, notamment ceux pour l'ex-Yougoslavie et le Rwanda, ainsi que la CPI, dès sa création.

Le *Règlement sur le Tribunal pénal international pour l'ex-Yougoslavie* (TPIY)

En juillet 1999, suite au mandat d'arrestation lancé contre Milosevic et consorts, le Canada a promulgué le *Règlement sur le Tribunal pénal international pour l'ex-Yougoslavie* (TPIY), aux termes de la *Loi sur les Nations Unies*, afin de geler tout actif canadien du président Milosevic et des quatre fonctionnaires du gouvernement de la République fédérale de Yougoslavie également mis en accusation.

C. La coopération canadienne avec les tribunaux internationaux chargés de poursuivre ceux qui ont commis de graves violations du DIH

Le Canada a été à l'avant-scène des efforts déployés à l'échelle internationale pour la création de la CPI, et il continue d'agir en vue de favoriser la ratification et la mise en oeuvre du *Statut de Rome de la CPI*. Grâce à un apport financier du Programme de la consolidation de la paix et du développement humain du ministère des Affaires étrangères et du Commerce international, le Centre international des droits de la personne et du développement démocratique et le "International Center for Criminal Law Reform and Criminal Justice Policy" ont récemment lancé un guide sur la mise en oeuvre du *Statut de Rome de la CPI.* Le guide vise à aider les États, particulièrement les pays en développement, à ratifier et mettre en oeuvre le *Statut de Rome de la CPI.* Le projet comporte, comme deuxième phase, des séminaires de mise en oeuvre pour l'Afrique et les Caraïbes.

Le Canada collabore de diverses manières avec le Tribunal pénal international pour l'ex-Yougoslavie (TPIY) et le Tribunal pénal international pour le Rwanda (TPIR).

TPIY

Jusqu'à présent, le Canada a versé des contributions volontaires au TPIY notamment pour des enquêtes médico-légales, l'exhumation de charniers et la mise en oeuvre du programme "Règles de route," qui assure que les arrestations de présumés criminels de guerre par les autorités locales sont conformes aux règles du droit international.

Le Canada a également prêté son soutien juridique au TPIY et l'a aidé à mener des enquêtes. Il a notamment, en 1997, présenté un mémoire d'*amicus curiae* pour appuyer la compétence du Tribunal et, en 1998, y a détaché deux analystes des scènes de crime venant de la GRC. En mars 1999, le Canada a soutenu les efforts pour élargir le mandat de la Mission de vérification au Kosovo, mise sur pied par l'OSCE, afin qu'il comprenne la collecte auprès des réfugiés kosovars d'informations sur les violations des droits de la personne commises par les troupes de la République Fédérale de la Yougoslavie. Six agents de la GRC ont d'ailleurs participé à la cueillette d'éléments de preuve en Albanie. Ces renseignements ont été transmis au TPIY afin qu'il puisse les utiliser aux fins de poursuites ultérieures. De plus, en mai 2000, le Canada a donné son accord pour l'envoi de six équipes d'agents de la GRC, totalisant vingt-quatre experts, afin d'appuyer les enquêtes actuellement menées au Kosovo par le Bureau du Procureur du TPIY.

En juin 1999, le Parlement a adopté des modifications à la *Loi sur l'extradition* et à d'autres lois afin de les rendre entièrement conformes aux obligations du Canada à l'égard du TPIY. Le même mois, en réponse aux demandes du TPIY, le ministre des Affaires étrangères a annoncé le désir du Canada de fournir au Tribunal un service de soutien du renseignement et de l'information. Le Canada a également envoyé au Kosovo une équipe d'experts en questions médico-légales chargés d'effectuer des analyses de scènes de crime au Kosovo afin d'appuyer les efforts du TPIY. Le Canada a envoyé une deuxième équipe lorsque le mandat de la première est arrivé à expiration.

Les Forces canadiennes fournissent également des renseignements et des témoins à ce tribunal aux termes d'accords conclus par le ministère de la Justice aux niveaux bilatéral et multilatéral.

TPIR

Le Canada a versé des contributions volontaires aux TPIR. Le Canada a également offert une aide variée; il a notamment fait don au Tribunal d'une collection spéciale d'articles juridiques et de publications traitant du droit relatif au génocide. En juin 1999, l'adoption de modifications à la *Loi sur l'extradition* et à plusieurs autres lois permet l'extradition d'inculpés directement au Tribunal. Les Forces canadiennes fournissent également des renseignements et des témoins à ce tribunal aux termes d'accords conclus par le ministère de la Justice aux niveaux bilatéral et multilatéral.

D. Efforts déployés par le Canada pour la protection des enfants touchés par la guerre

Le Canada accorde la priorité aux enfants au sein du programme de sécurité humaine, et ainsi il sera l'hôte de la Conférence internationale sur les enfants touchés par la guerre, qui se tiendra à Winnipeg en septembre 2000. Les participants à la conférence dresseront un plan d'action international visant à régler le problème grandissant des enfants touchés par les conflits armés. Les organismes de l'ONU, les gouvernements, la société civile ainsi que des jeunes de toutes les régions du monde seront invités à y participer. Cet événement s'inspirera de la Conférence sur les enfants touchés par la guerre en Afrique de l'Ouest, organisée par le Canada et le Ghana en avril dernier, à Accra.

E. Mesures prises par le Canada pour contrer le fléau mondial des mines antipersonnel

De concert avec plusieurs États et organismes non gouvernementaux, le Canada a été un chef de file dans l'élaboration de la *Convention sur l'interdiction de l'emploi, du stockage, de la production et du transfert des mines antipersonnel et sur leur destruction* de même que dans les efforts pour assurer sa rapide mise en vigueur. Le Canada considère la Convention comme le cadre le plus approprié pour s'attaquer au fléau mondial des mines antipersonnel et pour obtenir l'élimination définitive de cette arme frappant sans discrimination.

En 1998, le Canada a mis en place un fonds quinquennal de soutien à des programmes conformes aux objectifs visés par la Convention. À ce jour, le Canada a versé des millions de dollars de ce fonds pour favoriser le déminage ainsi que des activités d'examen connexes, aider les victimes et soutenir des programmes de sensibilisation aux dangers des mines dans toutes les régions touchées dans le monde. Le Canada a, en outre, versé de l'argent à des organisations non gouvernementales internationales au soutien d'activités menant à l'universalisation des nouvelles normes suggérées dans la Convention.

F. Le DIH et les Forces canadiennes

Manuels à l'intention des Forces canadiennes

Les Forces canadiennes ont récemment mis à jour certaines de leurs publications (en français et en anglais) qui servent d'outils pédagogiques et de référence en matière de DIH, notamment:

• *Le droit des conflits armés au niveau opérationnel et tactique*, Bureau du Juge-avocat général, 1999
• *Code de conduite du personnel des Forces canadiennes*, Bureau du Juge-avocat général, 1999

Les Forces canadiennes travaillent présentement à la préparation de deux publications intitulées:

- *Collection de documents sur le droit des conflits armés (ébauche)*, Bureau du Juge-avocat général, 2000
- Forces canadiennes — Manuel sur le droit des conflits armés (ébauche)

Formation

Le personnel des Forces canadiennes reçoit une formation élémentaire en DIH lors de l'entraînement de base de même qu'une formation intermédiaire en droit des conflits armés et une formation avancée en DIH selon son grade et ses responsabilités. Cette formation plus poussée en DIH peut également avoir lieu avant des déploiements particuliers.

Il est en outre enjoint aux commandants, dans les Directives du chef d'état-major de la Défense aux commandants (1999), d'intégrer le DIH à tous les aspects des opérations, y compris la formation et les exercices.

Experts et conseillers en DIH

Les experts et conseillers en DIH des Forces canadiennes, au Bureau du Juge-avocat général, donnent aux commandants et aux officiers d'état-major des conseils aux niveaux stratégique, opérationnel et tactique. Ils offrent également une formation plus poussée en DIH aux officiers des Forces canadiennes ainsi qu'au personnel non-officier, conformément à l'article 82 du *Protocole additionnel I*. Les Forces canadiennes procèdent à l'examen de tous leurs plans opérationnels afin de s'assurer qu'ils sont conformes au DIH.

INTERNATIONAL INSTITUTIONAL LAW

Procedure to Establish an Intergovernmental Negotiating Committee with the Authority to Negotiate a Legally Binding Instrument on Forests

In an opinion dated October 19, 1999, the Legal Bureau wrote:

The IFF (Intergovernmental Forum on Forests) was established pursuant to a Resolution of the UN General Assembly adopting a Programme for the Further Implementation of Agenda 21 annexed to the resolution (UNGA Resolution S-19/2, para. 40) (Appendix 1, Part B) and to a follow-up resolution of the Economic and Social Council (ECOSOC) (Appendix 1, Part A). The annexed programme called for the creation of the *ad hoc* open-ended Intergovernmental Forum on Forests (IFF) under the aegis of the Commission on Sustainable Development (CSD) with a focussed and time-limited mandate.

The IFF was charged with, *inter alia*: identifying the possible elements of, and working towards consensus on, international arrangements and mechanisms, for example, a legally binding instrument. The IFF was asked to report to the Eighth Session of the CSD in 2000.

The follow-up resolution of ECOSOC is in identical terms and provides that IFF's responsibilities include the following:

Also taking into account the decision of the General Assembly at its nineteenth special session that the Forum should identify the possible elements of and work towards consensus on international arrangements and mechanisms, for example, a legally binding instrument, and should report on its work to the Commission on Sustainable Development in 1999; *based on that report, and depending on the decision of the Commission at its eighth session, the Forum should engage in further action on establishing an intergovernmental negotiation process on new arrangements and mechanisms or a legally binding instrument on all types of forests;* the Forum should convene as soon as possible ...

In sum, the IFF was established by resolution of the General Assembly confirmed by resolution of ECOSOC. It is not specifically authorized to create an intergovernmental negotiating committee although it might be authorized by the CSD to assist with this process, perhaps in a secretariat role.

The CSD itself was created by Economic and Social Council (ECOSOC 1993/207) (Appendix 3) upon the request of the General Assembly (UNGA 47/191) (Appendix 4). These resolutions do not themselves accord to the CSD the authority to launch global negotiations for a legally binding instruments on forests. Instead, the mandate proposed by the General Assembly and accepted by ECOSOC contemplated that recommendations for new arrangements would be made by CSD to ECOSOC and through that body to the General Assembly.

The Commission [should]:

(b) Promote the incorporation of the Non-legally Binding Authoritative Statement of Principles for a Global Consensus on the Management, Conservation and Sustainable Development of All Types of Forests in the implementation of Agenda 21, in particular in the context of the review of the implementation of chapter 11 thereof;

(c) Keep under review the implementation of Agenda 21, recognizing that it is a dynamic programme that could evolve over time, taking into account the agreement to review Agenda 21 in 1997, and make recommendations, as appropriate, on the need for new cooperative arrangements related to sustainable development to the Economic and Social Council and, through it, to the General Assembly.

We conclude that the CSD itself probably does not have the authority to launch an intergovernmental negotiating committee.

ECOSOC itself does have the jurisdiction to authorize negotiations without going back to the General Assembly for an additional resolution. This follows from Article 62 of the Charter of the United Nations which provides in part:

3. It (ECOSOC) may prepare draft conventions for submission to the General Assembly, with respect to matters falling within its competence.
4. It may call, in accordance with the rules prescribed by the United Nations, international conferences on matters falling within its competence.

In light of the above, the procedure to be followed from here would therefore seem to be as follows:

The Role of IFF

In accordance with its mandate, IFF will need to make an appropriate recommendation to CSD at its fourth session in New York, 31 January to 11 February 2000. The IFF has divided its work into three categories with the third category dealing with international arrangements. In its report on its third session, the IFF presented the Co-chairs' compilation text and asked the Secretariat to submit a report to IFF 4 addressing a number of options and inviting submissions on these matters from countries by September 15, 1999. The list of options was as follows:

1. A mechanism for improved coordination of existing arrangements.
2. Ongoing ad hoc intergovernmental dialogue.
3. A new permanent forum for intergovernmental dialogue.
4. Improvement of non-legally binding instruments.
5. A lead role for an existing institution.
6. Use of existing legally binding instruments.
7. Regional mechanisms.
8. A framework convention allowing for regional mechanisms.
9. A new global legal instrument . . .

The Role of the CSD

Based on the mandate of the CSD quoted above it is not clear that the CSD itself can launch negotiations for a legally binding instrument. Our initial research has not indicated any examples of the CSD authorizing negotiations.

It is clear that the CSD is explicitly authorized to make such a recommendation to the General Assembly through ECOSOC and presumably might advise as to the parameters of those negotiations.

The Role of ECOSOC and the UN General Assembly

It is clear that the General Assembly has the jurisdiction to authorize the commencement of negotiations for a multilateral instrument on forests and in this case it seems clear that the General Assembly intended that ECOSOC should not itself commence these negotiations but should act as a conduit for any recommendation originating with the CSD. Nevertheless, as we have seen, as a matter of law, there is little doubt but that ECOSOC could authorize negotiations.

The Content of a Resolution Authorizing a Mandate

Negotiating mandates typically contain the following elements:

1. Authorizes a party (e.g. the Secretary General or perhaps the CSD) to prepare for and convene an intergovernmental negotiating committee.
2. Establishes the membership of the INC (usually open-ended).
3. Establishes the start date of the INC and may establish a timetable consisting of a number of negotiating sessions and a projected completion date.
4. Identifies the body to perform secretariat functions for the negotiations (this might be the IFF in the present case).
5. May establish the terms of reference.

6. Requests a party (e.g. the Secretary General) to convene a diplomatic conference to conclude the negotiations.
7. Calls upon states to provide the requisite financing for the negotiations.

Interpretation of the Antarctic Treaty

In a memorandum date December 24, 1999, the Legal Bureau wrote:

Article 9 of the (Antarctic) Treaty envisages what has been called a double unanimity rule for the adoption and entry into force of a measure. First, "Measures" take the form of recommendations designed to "further the principles and objectives of the Treaty" and which are adopted at a meeting of the Contracting Parties. These meetings are known as Consultative Party meetings. Not all Contracting Parties can attend as voting members but only the original Contracting Parties along with those Parties who accede to the Treaty, and even then only, as Article 9(2) states, "during such time as that Contracting Party demonstrates its interest in Antarctica by conducting substantial scientific research activity there, such as the establishment of a scientific station or the despatch of a scientific expedition." Canada has never "demonstrated its interest" in this way, is therefore not a Consultative Party, and is therefore not entitled to participate in Consultative Party meetings save as an observer.

The second element of the unanimity rule is that a measure adopted under Article 9(1) shall only (Article 9(4)) "become effective when approved by all the Contracting Parties participating in the meetings held to consider those measures." Read together, these paragraphs one and four of Article 9 make it clear that a measure is merely a recommendation and has no further status until "approved" by all participating Contracting Parties.

Article 9 measures are not in any sense amendments to the Treaty and thus a party that accedes to the Treaty after a measure becomes effective cannot be taken by that act alone to have become a party to the measures.

This Interpretation Is Confirmed and Not Denied by the Practice of the Parties and the Depositary

The practice of the Parties as revealed in official reports of meetings of the consultative parties and in recommendations or measures adopted by the parties justifies the following conclusions.

- "Approval" of a measure or recommendation must take the form of an appropriate notice to all other Consultative Parties or at the very least an appropriate notice to the depositary.
- Frequent exhortations to Consultative and non-Consultative Parties serve only to confirm the interpretation that measures do not bind acceding parties to the Treaty even when those measures are already "effective" as of the date of accession for the new Party.
- Notwithstanding the express wording of Article 9(4) of the Treaty (referred to above), the actual practice suggests that Contracting Parties may agree to accept and be bound by existing measures even though they were not at the relevant time entitled to participate in the meeting held to consider those measures.

• Reports prepared and presented by the depositary to all Consultative Party meetings contain an update as to the status of Article 9 measures. Canada has never been listed as having adopted the Agreed Measures.

The Conclusion Is Not Displaced by Article 10 of the Treaty

Article 9 measures are measures designed to further the principles and objectives of the Treaty. Article 10 of the Treaty requires all Contracting Parties to exert appropriate efforts to ensure that no one shall engage in any activity in Antarctica contrary to the principles or purposes of the Treaty. Some have argued, notwithstanding the absence of symmetry between "measures in furtherance of the principles and objectives of the Treaty" and the "principles or purposes" language of Article 10, that measures adopted under Article 9 to further the principles and objectives of the Treaty are also included within the ambit of Article 10 and to that extent binding.

Whatever merit this bootstrap argument may have, it runs up against the formidable objection that Article 9 itself speaks to the means by which a measure becomes binding upon a Party. It would therefore be unreasonable to interpret Article 10 as either requiring that states approve Article 9 measures or as obliging them to treat Article 9 measures as binding even though they had yet to adopt them. In sum, Article 10 does not provide a back-door means to make the Agreed Measures binding upon Canada ...

Adoption of New Protocols under the Biodiversity Convention

In a memorandum dated September 3, 1999, the Legal Bureau wrote:

The Convention (on Biodiversity) specifically deals with two limited situations in which the Conference of the Parties (COP) will be permitted to adopt a new instrument or to amend an existing instrument by vote rather than consensus. These situations are as follows:

The first case is an amendment to the Convention or to an existing protocol. The rule specified in Article 29 is that such an amendment shall be adopted by a meeting of the Conference of the Parties. The Parties shall proceed by way of consensus but may adopt the amendment by a two-third majority vote if all efforts at consensus have been exhausted. Article 29 does not apply to the adoption of a new Protocol.

Second, a new annex may be proposed for adoption or an amendment may be proposed to an existing annex. In both of these cases Article 30 specifies that COP may proceed in accordance with the Article 29 procedure (*supra*) of consensus or voting as a last resort. Article 30 does not apply to the adoption of a new Protocol.

Article 28 of the Convention deals with the Adoption of Protocols. It provides in its entirety as follows:

1. The Contracting Parties shall cooperate in the formulation and adoption of protocols to this Convention.
2. Protocols shall be adopted at a meeting of the Conference of the Parties.

3. The text of any proposed protocol shall be communicated to the Contracting Parties by the Secretariat at least six months before such a meeting.

Unlike Article 30, Article 28 does not cross reference the adoption procedure specified in Article 29.

In the absence of a specific provision in Article 28 dealing with the procedure for adoption of a protocol how does a meeting of the Conference of the Parties "adopt" a Protocol? The general rules for meetings of the Conference of the Parties are specified in Article 23 which has two relevant provisions. First, Article 23(3) indicates that "the Conference of the Parties shall by consensus agree upon and adopt rules of procedure for itself." Second, Article 23(4) provides that

4. The Conference of the Parties shall keep under review the implementation of this Convention, and, for this purpose, shall:

. . .

(c) consider and adopt, as required, protocols in accordance with Article 28.

In fulfilling its obligations under Article 23(4), the COP must act in accordance with its rules of procedure.

The Rules distinguish between matters of procedure and matters of substance. Draft Rule 40(1) was proposed to deal with matters of substance. We agree ... that Rule 40(1) of the Rules of Procedure has never been adopted by the COP and thus, while we have a rule dealing with how to make decisions on "matters of procedure" (i.e. Rule 40(2), a simple majority rule), we have no rule prescribing how to make decisions on matters of substance. We further agree ... that although the printed version of the Rules of Procedure (as printed from the Secretariat's web page) square brackets only part of Rule 40(1), it is quite clear that the COP decision was to the effect that the entirety of Article 40(1) was not to enter into force, not just the square-bracketed portion. Decision 3/1 reinforces this point.

In the absence of a specific Rule of Procedure dealing with matters of substance, or a specific rule in the Convention dealing with adoption of new protocols, we must fall back on the Convention's general rule, prescribed in Article 23(2) (*supra*). This tells us that a decision to adopt a Rule governing decisions on matters of substance must be made by consensus. The Parties by consensus might agree to adopt a voting procedure for such matters but they have not done so yet. Hence, the default position must be that a decision on a matter of substance must still be made by consensus.

You have also asked us to consider whether there any other relevant UN Rules. While we shall continue to review this matter, our preliminary view is that there can be no other relevant rules given the language of Article 23 of the Convention. This Article is specific and must implicitly oust any more general rules of the UN should such a more general rule be potentially relevant. Thus, it is our view that the Convention itself prescribes that the fall back position is the consensus requirement of Article 23(3) and that therefore we do not fall back to any more general UN Rule that might prescribe voting. The Convention occupies the field.

INTERNATIONAL RIVERS

On March 7, 2000, the Legal Bureau wrote:

The right of freedom of navigation on international watercourses is a right long recognized by international law. In North America, the United States and Great Britain historically entered into a series of treaties governing the boundaries between Canada and the United States and their respective rights concerning international or boundary waters. In these treaties the primacy of the principle of navigation has been constantly highlighted. Indeed the history of diplomatic relations and in particular, treaty relations as concerns boundary waters, show the prominence in which "navigation" was held. Article VII of the *Webster-Ashburton Treaty* reiterated the principle of free and equal access for vessels of both sides, explicitly mentioning the Detroit and St. Clair Rivers (both lying within the definition of "waters of the state" in the present Michigan bill):

> It is further agreed, that the channels in the river St. Lawrence, on both sides of the Long Sault Islands and of Barnhart Island; the channels in the river Detroit, on both sides of the Island Bois Blanc, and between that Island and both the American and Canadian shores; and all the several channels and passages between the various Islands lying near the junction of the river St. Clair with the lake of that name, shall be equally free and open to the ships, vessels, and boats of both Parties.

The latest affirmation of the right of free navigation in the Great Lakes for vessels of both Canada and the United States is Article I of the *Boundary Waters Treaty*, 1909:

> The High Contracting Parties agree that the navigation of all navigable boundary waters shall forever continue free and open *for the purposes of commerce* to the inhabitants and to the ships, vessels, and boats of both countries equally, subject, however, to any laws and regulations of either country, within its own territory, not inconsistent with such privilege of free navigation and applying equally and without discrimination to the inhabitants, ships, vessels, and boats of both countries.

The factual test of what is inconsistent with the principle of free navigation requires an understanding of what is contained in the principle. Nowhere in the treaties is there to be found a definition of the principle or its corollary, the interference with the freedom of navigation. It would be safe to say that the construction of a physical barrier that prevented the movement by shipping along a boundary water would interfere with the freedom of navigation. However, it is harder to gauge whether the effects of laws and regulations on the economic viability of merchant shipping, for example, would interfere with freedom of navigation. *Black's Law Dictionary*, 7th ed. (1999), defines "navigable" as: "... capable of allowing vessels or vehicles to pass, and thereby usable for travel or commerce." Courts have traditionally noted that the question of whether a body of water was navigable or not is a question of fact. Article I of the BWT contains a further level of analysis. The Parties shall ensure navigation of navigable boundary waters for the purposes of commerce. At the time of the drafting of the Treaty the right of free navigation for the purposes of commerce was of the utmost importance, navigation by water being the main medium of communication at the time. This would envisage the carriage of goods and passengers by boat ...

In Europe, the law of international river navigation is well-established and has consistently protected the freedom of navigation from unreasonable interference by riparian states:

> All these and similar provisions express the same idea: to preclude the possibility of barring, on the plea of application of municipal laws and regulations, the implementation of the principles of free navigation established in the Treaty of Vienna. As Van Eysinga rightly states, some of the measures and actions of the riparian State may be perfectly lawful in themselves, "but would become unlawful if applied in the such a way as to cause impediments to free navigation."

Although there are differences between the European and North American experiences, one can draw parallels between the two. The history of the often multilateral European international river regime and the bilateral US-Canadian experience with the Great Lakes, while having some differences, share many similarities and common themes. Both place the freedom of navigation in a position of preeminence above other interests. Both state that municipal laws and regulations cannot interfere with the freedom of navigation. Finally, both link the freedom of navigation with the freedom of commerce and extend the freedom of navigation beyond mere passage. Bela Vitanyi, a leading commentator on the law of international river navigation, analyses leading commentators' definitions of the freedom of navigation and its essential elements :

> Consequently, freedom of navigation seems to include the following elements:
>
> (a) Freedom of traffic, which means free movement of vessels as well as freedom to carry goods and passengers. This freedom includes freedom of transit. It also implies freedom to enter ports and use their equipment;
> (b) Free exercise of the shipping trade, which includes freedom to engage in the usual commercial activities of shipping companies ...
> (c) Freedom of freight;

The Helsinki Rules on the Uses of International Rivers, International Law Association, 1966, are also extremely helpful in fleshing out the meaning and scope of the freedom of navigation as well as the degree to which municipal law can affect it. Although the title of these Rules suggests that they apply only to international rivers, Article I widens the scope of the Rules to include 'water basins,' a concept that would include the Great Lakes as is clear from Articles XIV and XV ... which specifically mentions navigation of both lakes and rivers:

> Article I - The general rules of international law as set forth in these chapters are applicable to the use of the waters of an international drainage basin except as may be provided otherwise by convention, agreement or binding custom among the basin States.

Article XIV of the Rules defines the freedom of navigation for the purposes of the Rules:

> Article XIV - "Free navigation," as the term is used in this Chapter, includes the following freedom for vessels of a riparian State on a basis of equality:
>
> (a) freedom of movement on the entire navigable course of the river or lake;
> (b) freedom to enter ports and to make use of plants and docks; and
> (c) freedom to transport goods and passengers, either directly or through trans-shipment, between the territory of another riparian State and between the territory of a riparian State and the open sea.

Article XV then sets out the rule regarding the applicability of municipal law to the freedom as set out in articles ("rights of police" in this context is a broad term encompassing all "policing" of the waterway concerned and would include laws and regulation pertaining to safety, health etc.):

> Article XV - A riparian State may exercise rights of police, including but not limited to the protection of public safety and health, over that portion of the river or lake subject to its jurisdiction, provided the exercise of such rights does not unreasonably interfere with the enjoyment of the rights of free navigation defined in Articles XIII and XIV.
>
> Comment: The right of free navigation is subject to the right of the State to enact and enforce within its territory reasonable measures which are necessary to police effectively its territory. Similarly, customs, public health and precautions against diseases fall within this area of regulation. Such measures must be applied to all the co-riparian States on a basis of absolute equality and must not unreasonably impede freedom of navigation.

... the Rules for the present analysis serve as an important interpretive tool for explaining Article I of the Boundary Waters Treaty which contains provisions protecting the freedom of navigation from interference by riparian States' laws and regulations.

It is clear from the above discussion that interference with the freedom of navigation is not limited solely to physical obstructions or other impediments to maritime traffic. The emphasis on the freedom of commerce within the idea of freedom of navigation, Article I of the BWT's statement regarding laws and regulations, and academic commentary all clearly show that the freedom of navigation also provides for freedom from municipal laws and regulations, even those normally valid and with good purpose, if they interfere unreasonably with the freedom of navigation.

PRIVILEGES AND IMMUNITIES

In a memorandum dated June 28, 2000, the Legal Bureau wrote:

International law has been unsettled in relation to the amenability of visiting naval and military personnel to the exercise of receiving state criminal jurisdiction. A US Supreme Court decision influenced the early US position which upheld the concept of foreign territorial immunity or the principle of the "law of the flag." In *Schooner Exchange* v. *M'Faddon*, 11 U.S. (7 Cranch) 116 (1812), the court held that armed vessels of a friendly foreign nation were not within the jurisdiction of US federal courts. The well known decision of Chief Justice Marshall in Schooner Exchange, prompted American commentators to draw the inference that visiting forces should be considered immune from the exercise of receiving state jurisdiction unless by treaty the sending state waived that immunity.

In *Reference re Exemption of United States Forces from Canadian Criminal Law*, [1943] S.C.R. 483, the Supreme Court of Canada considered whether US forces enjoyed immunity from Canadian criminal courts. Duff C.J.C and Hudson J. held that Canadian criminal courts have full jurisdiction in respect of offenses committed on Canadian soil by US forces except in respect to acts committed within their lines or on board their warships, or of offences against discipline committed by one crew member against another crew member of the same force in which the act or offence does not affect the person or property of a Canadian subject.

Post WWII Canadian law adopted the principle of concurrent jurisdiction. The principle that every sovereign has jurisdiction over criminal acts committed within its territory is embodied in the NATO Status of Forces Agreement of 1951. Article VII of the NATO SOFA envisions three categories of offenses to which sovereign immunity attaches to either the sending State or the receiving State. In the first category, the sending State has the right to exclusive jurisdiction over persons subject to its military law when (a) a security offense — treason, espionage, sabotage — is involved; or (b) when the offense is punishable in the sending State but is not a crime in the receiving State. [Article 7, section 2(a)] In the second category, the receiving State has right to exclusive jurisdiction because the offence — including security offences — is punishable in that State, but not by the sending State. [Article 7, section 2(b)]

In the third category, the two States have concurrent jurisdiction. [Article 7, section 3(b)] Within the concurrent jurisdiction category, the sending State has the primary right to exercise jurisdiction over their force's personnel if the offense was committed against their own members or if the offence was committed while in the course of official duties. Otherwise, the receiving State shall have primary jurisdiction. Even when the primary jurisdiction is held by the sending State, the host state does not lose jurisdiction. A State may waive its primary right and shall notify the other State of its waiver as soon as practicable.

Canada's *Visiting Forces Act* of 1967 implementing the NATO SOFA provides for the extension of concurrent jurisdiction to a list of designated countries including both NATO and non-NATO countries.

The prevailing interpretation of international customary law is that members of foreign warships who happen to be on board are shielded, even where Canada has primary jurisdiction over the matter under the *Visiting Forces Act*. Therefore, Canadian local police cannot enter another country's warship without the permission of the commanding officer, even where there is evidence to believe that the visiting force member committed an offence against a local inhabitant while the visiting force member was not on official duty. The Judge Advocate General Office comments that this immunity is the subject of reciprocal understanding. Our military/naval practice preserves this same practice where Canadian warships are harboured at foreign ports.

LAW OF THE SEA

Vessel Traffic Management

In an amicus curiae brief filed with the United States Supreme Court on October 29, 1999, the Legal Bureau wrote:

Canada and the United States are parties to the bilateral treaty proposed by Canada and accepted by the United States on December 19, 1979, and entitled Agreement for a Cooperative Vessel Traffic Management System for the Juan de Fuca Region (CVTMS Agreement), Dec. 19, 1979, U.S.-Can., 32 U.S.T. 377 (entered into force Dec. 19, 1979). The geography of the Strait of Juan de Fuca region makes the CVTMS Agreement vital to the ability of both countries' ship traffic to operate safely in that region. Canada and the United States are also parties to several multilateral conventions governing international shipping, collectively referred to as the International Maritime Treaties. Canada has participated in good faith negotiating and implementing these treaties with the United States.

Because the State of Washington's Best Available Protection (BAP) regulations, Wash. Admin. Code § 317-21-010 et seq., undermine internationally-agreed standards adopted through these treaties, those regulations threaten the orderly operation of maritime traffic in the region. Moreover, if the State of Washington is permitted to dictate the conditions of operation of this international maritime traffic, the door will be open for other local jurisdictions of the United States to erect their own, varying regulations, thereby creating a regulatory patchwork along North America's sea coasts and inland shores and endangering the uniform system adopted by treaty ...

To promote safe and orderly passage through the Strait of Juan de Fuca, Canada and the United States agreed in the CVTMS Agreement to devise a cooperative system of vessel traffic management. Under this system, all inbound traffic in the strait, regardless of destination, is routed through United States waters, while all outbound traffic is directed through Canadian waters. The International Maritime Organization endorses this vessel traffic separation scheme.

In agreeing to this vessel traffic separation scheme, Canada relied on the United States' undertaking in the CVTMS Agreement that vessels bound for Canadian ports that complied with Canadian regulations regarding "vessel design, construction, manning and equipment" would be deemed in "material compliance" with the United States' own requirements. CVTMS Agreement, art. 204.2 (A-12). Canada has expressed its difficulties with the BAP regulations to United States authorities over many years, as well as through diplomatic representations, the most recent of which was a diplomatic note dated 7 May 1997 ...

The United States Is Required to Honour Its Treaty Obligations in Respect of its Entire Territory

The treaties between the United States and Canada require the United States to honour its treaty obligations in respect of its entire territory. The BAP regulations enacted by Washington State are incompatible with the reciprocity provisions of both the CVTMS Agreement and the International Maritime Treaties ...

Customary international law is binding on the United States. The *Paquete Habana*, 175 U.S. 677, 700 (1900); *Chisholm* v. *Georgia*, 2 U.S. (2 Dall.) 419, 474 (1793). *Pacta sunt servanda* is a well-established principle of international law, which provides that every treaty in force is binding upon the parties to it and must be performed by them in good faith. See 1 *Oppenheim's International Law*, Part 4, § 584, at 1206 (Robert Jennings & Arthur Watts, eds., 9th ed. 1992); *Vienna Convention on the Law of Treaties*, May 22, 1969, arts. 26, 27, U.N. Doc. A/CONF.39/27, 1155 U.N.T.S. 331 (1969) ("Treaty Convention"). It is equally well-established that a party to a treaty may not invoke provisions of its internal law as justification for failing to honour its treaty obligations, and that, unless a different intention is set forth in the treaty in question, a treaty is binding upon each party in respect of its entire territory. Treaty Convention, art. 29; *Estate of Pellat* v. *Mexico*, 5 Reports of Int'l Arbitral Awards 534, 536 (Fr.-Mex. 1929); Ian Brownlie, *State Responsibility in 1 System of the Law of Nations* 1, 141-42 (Fr.-Mex. 1983). When a state party is internally constituted as a federal system, that state party may not justify a failure to comply on the grounds that the noncompliance is the act of a constituent state. The *Montijo* (*U.S.* v. *Colom.* 1875), reprinted in 2 John Basset Moore, *History and Digest of the International Arbitrations to Which the United States Has Been a Party* 1421, 1440 (1898); Ivan Bernier, *International Legal Aspects of Federalism* 83 (1973).

Having undertaken solemn treaty obligations to Canada under the CVTMS Agreement, and to Canada and other parties to the International Maritime Treaties, the United States is not free to allow its constituent states to impose regulations or conditions on maritime traffic within United States waters that conflict with these treaty obligations to Canada.

If Enforced, the BAP Regulations Would Violate the United States' Obligations to Canada Under the CVTMS Agreement

The key to the functioning of the CVTMS system is the parties' joint recognition of each other's regulatory regimes insofar as these affect vessels operating in the Strait of Juan de Fuca region. *See supra* pp. 4-5. This system based on mutual recognition was established in 1979 with the signing of the Agreement; in 1994, it was further strengthened by the Marine Safety and Marine Environmental Protection Comparability Analysis ("1994 Study"), which was conducted jointly by the United States and Canadian Coast Guards.

The 1994 Study was prompted by new legislative and regulatory changes introduced in both countries, in particular the United States Oil Pollution Act of 1990, Pub. L. No. 101-380, 104 Stat. 484 (codified as amended in various portions of Titles 33 & 46 of the United States Code) and the amendments to the Canada Shipping Act, S.C. 1993, ch. 36

(Can.). The Canadian and United States Coast Guards reviewed their respective regulations in the areas of vessel design and construction, shipboard equipment, personnel qualifications and manning, shipboard operations, and pollution response, and determined that "broad overall comparability exists between the United States' and Canada's marine safety and marine environmental protection regimes."

Of special relevance in this case is the provision of the CVTMS Agreement mandating reciprocal recognition of "vessel design, construction, manning and equipment requirements, and the measures for enforcement of these requirements" for ships incidentally transiting the waters of the other party in the Juan de Fuca region. CVTMS Agreement, art. 204.2 (A-12). As a result of these provisions, ships bound for Canada, which are required by the CVTMS Agreement to transit United States waters, are deemed to be in material compliance with United States regulations so long as they comply with Canadian regulations. Similarly, ships outbound from the United States, which are required by the CVTMS Agreement to transit Canadian waters, are deemed to be in material compliance with Canadian regulations so long as they comply with United States regulations.

This reciprocity in according deference to the regulatory regime of each state party is vital to the functioning of the CVTMS Agreement and to the safe operation of ship traffic in the Juan de Fuca region. In the twenty years that the Agreement has been in effect, this system based on mutuality of recognition has worked well; indeed, the CVTMS Agreement has served as a model for the international community.

The BAP regulations repudiate the very basis of the Agreement — the reciprocal recognition of, and acquiescence in, each state party's regulatory regime — for they purport to override Canada's standard-setting by imposing additional requirements on ships bound for Canadian ports. Not only is this result legally offensive, but, on a practical level, the BAP regulations undermine the viability of a traffic management system that was put in place to promote safe passage through a busy shipping corridor and to minimize the occurrence of environmental damage. Ships may seek to avoid the additional Washington State regulations by remaining in Canadian waters, either approaching Canada via the hazardous Johnstone Strait or transiting inbound and outbound in Canadian waters in the Strait of Juan de Fuca. Either way, the chance of an accident causing environmental damage is increased.

The BAP regulations thus threaten the integrity of the system, as well as the ability of the United States and Canada to achieve the goals of the CVTMS Agreement.

If Enforced, the BAP Regulations Would Violate the United States' Obligations to Canada under the International Maritime Treaties

Canada, the United States, and other countries have worked for many years in international fora such as the International Maritime Organization to establish treaties governing international shipping. Under the International Maritime Treaties, the United States owes a number of obligations to Canada that are in addition to those obligations established in the CVTMS Agreement. These obligations include, for example, the acceptance of Canada's certification that Canadian flagged vessels meet the criteria set out in the treaties, unless there are clear grounds for believing otherwise. Canada is similarly bound under these treaties to accept the United States' certification of United States-flagged ships.

Washington's BAP regulations cover subjects squarely dealt with under the International Maritime Treaties, notably the SOLAS Convention and the STCW Convention, in a manner inconsistent with the obligations created by those treaties. For example, BAP creates fleet-wide standards for bridge resource management, Wash. Admin. Code § 317-21-200(2), that are mandatory even for vessels never entering Washington waters. Bridge resource management is a nonmandatory item under the STCW Convention and is treated as such under Canadian regulations. In essence, if compliance with the BAP regulations affecting vessel operations, equipment, and manning were required, the United States effectively would be refusing to recognize as valid Canada's certification that its own ships meet the standards required under the treaties.

If upheld by this Court, the decision below would place the United States in the position of violating its treaty obligations to Canada. Canada therefore urges this Court to set aside the offending BAP regulations and to enforce the United States' obligations under the relevant international agreements.

Access to Ports

In a memorandum dated April 23, 2000, the Legal Bureau wrote:

... A port is part of the internal waters of a State. As the editors of *Oppenheim* state at 572: "Internal waters are legally equivalent to a state's land, and are entirely subject to its territorial sovereignty." As a result, one would expect that a coastal state has a clear right to exclude vessels from its ports absent an agreement to the contrary. This view is supported by one group of writers, including Churchill and Lowe, and O'Connell. A second group of writers, including Colombos, favours the view that, generally, States have an obligation to provide access to their international ports ...

As stated above, Churchill and Lowe favour the view that a State has a right to exclude vessels from its ports subject to some exceptions. They put the point this way:

The existence of sovereignty over internal waters and the absence of any general right of innocent passage through them logically implies the absence of any right in customary international law for foreign ships to enter a State's ports or other internal waters.

These authors note that, as a matter of practice, the international ports of States are presumed to be open to international merchant traffic but conclude that this presumption has not acquired the status of a right in customary law. Even if it had such a status, the right would be subject to at least three types of restrictions. First, a coastal State is entitled to nominate those of its ports that are open to international traffic. Second, a State may close a port to protect its vital interests without thereby violating customary international law. Third, a State may prescribe conditions for access to its ports and may limit access by particular types of vessels, e.g. tankers, nuclear powered vessels and fishing vessels.

The overall conclusion that there is no general right of access to a port of a coastal State is also confirmed by O'Connell who notes that the learned arbitrator in *Saudi Arabia* v. *Aramco* misstated the rule and proposes instead that the proper rule is that if a State permits access to its ports by foreign ships, then it must accord that access on a non-discriminatory basis. O'Connell bases this rule on the 1923 Geneva Convention on the International Regime of Maritime Ports but argues that the Convention may also establish a customary standard and therefore be applicable more generally. Churchill and Lowe are less sanguine and note (at 63) that the Convention has not been widely ratified. Canada has not acceded to this Convention and neither has the United States.

The second group of authors argues for a more general right of access to ports. For example, Colombos states as follows:

> 181 General principles applicable to ports. - The right of sovereignty recognized to a State should not, in fact, be construed as conferring upon it an unlimited power to prohibit the use of its ports and harbours to foreign nationals. This would imply a neglect of its duties for the promotion of international intercourse, navigation and trade which customary international law imposes upon it. It is submitted that the general principles applicable to ports ... are ... as follows: (i) in time of peace, commercial ports must be left open to international traffic. The liberty of access to ports granted to foreign vessels implies their right to load and unload their cargoes ...

The *Third Restatement of the Foreign Relations Law* of the United States is strong authority to the same effect.

Previous advice rendered by this Department is consistent with the views expressed by the first group of writers ... The opinion went on to note that in those cases where access was denied, that denial had been made explicit and made known to the international community. It concluded by noting that, at least as a matter of comity, vessels of a particular State should not be denied access in the absence of advance notification. The opinion cautioned that there was some possibility that denial of access might give rise to a claim in damages ...

To complete the analysis we need to consider whether there is an applicable agreement pursuant to which the vessel in question might claim a right of access. In addition to the 1923 Geneva Convention that accords for its Parties a right of entry to ports on a reciprocal and non-discriminatory basis, Churchill and Lowe draw attention to Article V of the GATT. However, this article only accords a non-discriminatory right of access to ports for the purposes of transit and then only via the most convenient routes ...

In sum, we conclude that the law applicable to the right of a coastal state to exclude particular vessels on a case-by-case basis from its ports is not completely clear. The authorities do support the following propositions. First, subject to specific treaty obligations and entry in cases of distress, a coastal state may close its ports to all international commercial traffic. Second, a coastal state may decide to exclude certain classes of vessels on a non-discriminatory basis. For example, subject to existing treaty commitments and trade obligations, Canada might exclude from its ports all vessels containing wastes or hazardous wastes. Canada might also require more extensive prior notification of imports of wastes than are currently provided for under CEPA [*see prescribed non-hazardous waste reference in s.185 CEPA 1999*]. Finally, the balance of opinion amongst the learned authors is that a State has an even more extensive right to exclude vessels from its ports. This view is based upon the coastal State's full sovereignty over its ports and the conclusion that the 1923 Geneva Convention does not represent a general rule of international law. This general position is of course subject to the terms of any applicable bilateral or multilateral treaty.

LAW OF TREATIES

Reservations, Objections, and the Vienna Convention on the Law of Treaties

In a letter dated May 3, 2000, the Legal Bureau wrote:

... Article 21 deals with reservations that are permissible under Article 19 of the VCLT (Vienna Convention on the Law of Treaties), and provides as follows:

> Article 21 Legal effects of reservations and of objections to reservations
>
> 1. A reservation established with regard to another party in accordance with articles 19, 20 and 23:
>   (a) modifies for the reserving State in its relations with that other party the provisions of the treaty to which the reservation relates to the extent of the reservation; and
>   (b) modifies those provisions to the same extent for that other party in its relations with the reserving State.
> 2. The reservation does not modify the provisions of the treaty for the other parties to the treaty inter se.
> 3. When a State objecting to a reservation has not opposed the entry into force of the treaty between itself and the reserving State, the provisions to which the reservation relates do not apply as between the two States to the extent of the reservation.

Paragraph 3 of Article 21 presents some difficult problems of interpretation primarily because it does not track the language of paragraph 1. Paragraph 1 applies to the situation in which another Party has expressly or impliedly *accepted* a reservation. It is readily understandable and provides for the mutual *modification* of the treaty by the text of the reservation ... On the face of it, paragraph 3 seems designed to establish a different set of rules for the situation in which another state has *objected* to a reservation. In such a case, the text suggests that the provisions of the treaty are not simply modified but "*do not apply*" to the extent of the reservation. While the text continues with the phrase "to the extent of the reservation" (i.e. the same qualifying phrase as is used in paragraph 1), there is clearly a difference between the two main verbs: "modification" in the case of acceptance, and "non-application" in the case of objections.

There are, we believe, two possible interpretations of paragraph 3, neither of which is completely satisfactory. The first possible interpretation is simply that the provisions of the treaty to which the reservation relates do not apply at all as between the reserving and objecting state. This is not completely satisfactory because it fails to do justice to the words "to the extent of the reservation." The interpretation has the merit that it gives full effect to the different verbs used in paragraphs 1 and 3. To that extent it honours the interpretive principle that asserts that by choosing different words the drafters intended a different meaning.

The second possible interpretation is that, notwithstanding the difference in the language between paragraphs 1 and 3, there is no difference between the two in terms of their legal meaning. This interpretation gives fulls weight to the qualifying words "to the extent of the reservation." Sinclair, *The Vienna Convention on the Law of Treaties,* (2nd ed, 1984, at 76-77) canvasses both interpretations before concluding that the majority of commentators prefer the second interpretation. This interpretation also finds some support in the *Anglo-French Arbitration on the Delimitation of the Continental Shelf* (1977), 54 ILR 6 at paragraphs 56-61 but there is no detailed assessment of the issue in that case.

In light of this discussion ... although there remains some doubt about the matter, the majority view is that the combined effect of the Canadian reservation and (an) ... objection is simply to modify provisions of the Convention to the extent of the reservation. In sum, Canada has the same legal relationship with both countries that accept and countries that object to Canada's reservation. Thus, each provision of the Convention that is affected by the reservation must be taken to have been modified so that Canada's obligations under the Convention are limited ... Third, there is a minority (but still credible) view to the effect that any provision of the Convention to which the reservation relates will not apply as between (the objecting country) and Canada as a result of the ... objection. This result would eviscerate the substantive obligations contained within the Convention ... Fourth, in light of this interpretive difficulty, Canada should conduct itself in its relations ... in accordance with the majority view.

Severability of Reservations

In a memorandum dated September 2, 1999, the Legal Bureau wrote:

... The VCT (Vienna Convention on the Law of Treaties) implicitly contemplates two types of objections to a reservation. The first type of objection goes to the *admissibility* of the reservation and must therefore rest on one of the grounds stipulated in Article 19 of the VCT. The second type of objection is an objection on any other ground. In the present case, all four objections are Article 19 objections. This is creative of some legal uncertainty, since, while the VCT implicitly makes this distinction between admissible and inadmissible reservations (and this distinction is certainly supported by the writers), and while the VCT provides relatively precise rules for determining the legal effect of non-Article 19 reservations, it provides very little guidance as to the effect of an objection to a reservation made on Article 19 grounds.

Article 19 creates three exceptions to the general rule that reservations are permissible. The three exceptions are: (a) where the treaty prohibits reservations, (b) where the treaty permits a specified class of reservations and the instant reservation falls outside that class, and (c) where the reservation is incompatible with the object and purpose of the treaty...

An objection to a reservation on an Article 19 ground is a justiciable matter and it is evident that there will be much room for argument about an objection based upon incompatibility with object and purpose. However, if a reservation is authoritatively determined to be incompatible with a treaty's object and purpose, there are two possible interpretations of the legal consequences of such finding. One possibility is that the reserving state is a party to the treaty without the benefit of its modifying reservation. The second possibility is that the reserving state is not a party at all.

Since a treaty can only bind a state that consents to be bound, the relevant question must always be this: did the reserving state intend that its reservation was an unseverable part of its acceptance of the treaty obligation? If the answer to that question is in the affirmative then the result of finding a reservation to be inadmissible must be that the treaty does not bind the reserving state at all. If the answer is in the negative, then the state will be bound by the unmodified treaty.

It is important to emphasise that an objecting state cannot, at one and the same time, object to a reservation on the object and purpose ground of Article 19 and yet still insist upon treaty relations on the basis of the treaty as modified by the reservation (Article 21(1)) or insist upon treaty relations minus any provision of the treaty to which the reservation relates (Article 21(3)). To put the point another way, an objection on object and purposes grounds must always be treated (as stated above) either as precluding entry into force of the treaty as between the objecting and reserving states, or as an offer of treaty relations without the benefit of the reservation. There is no half-way house. This conclusion is supported by the commentators.

Derek Bowett puts the point this way. Following a lengthy quotation from Waldock (as rapporteur and dealing with this issue before the International Law Commission and in which Waldock stated that no state could accept a reservation that fell within what is now paragraph (a) or (b) of Article 19) Bowett continues:

> It will be recalled that paragraphs (a) and (b) covered both expressly and impliedly prohibited reservations. The impossibility of accepting a reservation which is incompatible with the purpose and object of a treaty, that is the category covered by paragraph (c) [the present case] is an a fortiori case. The contradiction in the conduct of a Party which accepts a treaty and then "accepts" a reservation which it acknowledges to be contrary to the object and purpose of that same treaty is self-evident. Thus the conclusion ought to be that impermissible reservations cannot be accepted.

...

Returning to the simple proposition that an impermissible reservation cannot be accepted, the question then arises, what is the treaty relationship between the "reserving" State and the other Parties, if any? As indicated earlier, this does not depend upon the reaction of the other Parties, and the better view is that when the impermissibility arises from the fundamental inconsistency of the reservation with the object and purpose of the treaty, the reservation and the whole acceptance of the treaty by the reserving state are nullities. Conversely, when the reservation is not of this kind, though permissible on other grounds, the reservation alone is a nullity and if severable can be struck out. As to purported "acceptance" of an impermissible reservation, this, too should be regarded as a nullity.

It follows from this discussion that the result of an Article 19 objection to a reservation will always be some legal uncertainty as to the precise regime governing the relations of the parties. The uncertainty is of two kinds. First, in the absence of an authoritative interpretation as to admissibility by a third party, there will inevitably be some room to argue as to whether or not a particular reservation is contrary to the object and purpose of the Convention. Further clarity on this point can only be attained by invoking the dispute settlement procedures of the treaty in order to have the matter resolved.

Second, there may be uncertainty as to whether or not a reserving state regards a reservation as severable or non-severable. Since, as stated above, this is a matter of the intent of the reserving state, it is open to the reserving state to clarify its position on this point by stipulating that its reservation is intended to be an integral and non-severable part of its ratification. While I am not aware of authority on point, it is presumably possible for a state to clarify its intent after the event in response to an objection to its reservation. Prior to that one might argue that the point is moot and therefore clarification prior to that time unnecessary. It is perhaps important to emphasise that any such clarification should be seen as simply that, a clarification, and not an impermissible attempt to modify or amend the text of the reservation.

To revert to our initial distinction as to the two types of reservations and objections . . . , we are now in a position to complete that analysis. The second type of objection to a reservation is an objection under Article 20 to an *admissible* reservation. Such an objection is non-justiciable in the sense that the objecting state need not have anything other than policy grounds for the objection. Article 20 objections give rise to questions of *opposability* and not questions of *admissibility*. Where a state fails to object to a reservation, the treaty, as modified by the admissible reservation, will bind that party and the reserving party (Article 21(1)).

Where a state objects to a reservation but fails to stipulate that the treaty shall not enter into force as between them, the treaty shall enter into force except (Article 21(3)) that "the provisions to which the reservation relates do not apply as between the two States to the extent of the reservation." An objecting state may also object to the treaty entering into force as between it and the reserving state. Article 20(4)(b) creates the presumption that an objection to a reservation will not preclude the treaty entering into force as between the objecting and reserving state, "unless a contrary intention is definitely expressed by the objecting State."

TRADE LAW

In a March 13, 2000 submission to the WTO Appellate Body, Canada wrote:

Canada does not contest the Appellate Body's observation in *EC — Bananas* that certain measures that affect trade in goods may also affect trade in services. That is, the GATT 1994 and the GATS are not mutually exclusive even though there may be measures that fall within one agreement but not the other.

In *EC — Bananas*, the Appellate Body identified three categories of measures: those that could fall exclusively within the scope of the GATT 1994, those that could fall exclusively within the scope of the GATS, and those that could fall within the scope of both the GATT 1994 and the GATS. Measures that could fall within the scope of both the GATT 1994 and the GATS are those measures that involve a service relating to a particular good or a service supplied in conjunction with a particular good.

The Appellate Body made clear, however, that merely because a measure involves a service relating to a particular good that affects the supply of the service, that measure is not necessarily scrutinized under the GATS. As the Appellate Body found:

Whether a certain measure affecting the supply of a service related to a particular good is scrutinized under the GATT 1994 or the GATS, or both, is a matter that can only be determined on a case-by-case basis.

In this case, the import duty exemption does not affect the supply of distribution services within the meaning of Article I:1 of the GATS and does not affect wholesale distribution service suppliers in their capacity as service suppliers. The duty exemption may affect the cost of the goods. However, any effect this may have on the supply of distribution services is so tenuous that the measures in question must fall within the first category of measures identified by the Appellate Body in *EC — Bananas*, namely those that should be scrutinized exclusively under the GATT 1994.

All goods in trade must be distributed and sold. Any measure affecting trade in goods will therefore relate in some way to their distribution and sale. Distributing goods is a service. Thus, virtually all measures affecting trade in goods will relate indirectly to their distribution. If any such relationship were sufficient to "affect" trade in services for the purpose of satisfying the scope requirement in Article I of the GATS, any and all measures affecting trade in goods would be deemed also to affect trade in services.

The relevant test for whether a measure even affects trade in services is that which the Appellate Body implicitly adopted in *EC — Bananas*: "does the measure affect a service supplier in its capacity as a service supplier and in its supply of services?."

As Canada argued before the Panel, the Appellate Body's test is borne out by the definitions in Article XXVIII(c) of the GATS. Article XXVIII(c) defines "measures by Members affecting trade in services" to include measures respecting such activities as the purchase, payment or use of a service, access to services and the presence of persons to supply a service. While the definition in Article XXVIII(c) may be illustrative, every example clearly is directed at the supply of a service itself. None of the examples extends to measures affecting goods, including the purchase.

Parliamentary Declarations in 1999-2000 / Déclarations parlementaires en 1999-2000

Compiled by / préparé par
MICHAEL VECK

Mr. Bill Blaikie (Winnipeg-Transcona):

My question is for the Parliamentary Secretary to the Minister of Trade ... What is the government's position going into negotiations in Seattle? Everyone knows that Canada has now had its ability to legislate in the area of environment challenged by chapter 11 of the NAFTA. We have worries on the water front and on a number of other fronts.

Why does the government persist on going into these negotiations without asking, that whatever agreements it is a part of that there be no more chapter 11 investor state dispute mechanisms and, on top of that, that it seek to get rid of that in the NAFTA?

Mr. Bob Speller (Parliamentary Secretary to Minister for International Trade):

... as the honorary member knows, as he was also part of the standing committee report, the Government of Canada, his caucus, our caucus and the House of Commons went across the country asking for Canadians' views on Seattle.

We are taking forward the views of exactly what we heard from Canadians across the country who told us that the most important thing for them was to make sure we had a rules based system, that for a country the size of Canada, and with the importance of international trade to our economy, that we had a system in place that was negotiated with the bigger countries in the world but that Canada could ...

(House of Commons Debates, October 29, 1999, p. 878)
(Débats de la Chambre des Communes, le 29 octobre 1999, p. 878)

Ms. Sarmite Bulte (Parkdale-High Park):

... my question is for the Parliamentary Secretary to the Minister for International Trade.

The number of lawsuits being initiated by corporations against Canada under the provisions of NAFTA appears to be on the rise. Could the parliamentary secretary tell us what efforts are being made to amend chapter 11 of NAFTA to protect Canada against frivolous claims?

Mr. Bob Speller (Parliamentary Secretary to Minister for International Trade):

... I want to assure the hon. member that Canada takes very seriously the concerns expressed on all sides of the issue about chapter 11. We have consulted widely with the provinces and stakeholders to make sure that the process is more open and fair.

We have met at the deputy minister level with the Mexicans and Americans, and continue to do so, to make sure that the investor-state mechanism reflects what the original parties to the agreement agreed on.

(House of Commons Debates, May 29, 2000, p. 7146)
(Débats de la Chambre des Communes, le 29 mai 2000, p. 7146)

Mr. Bill Blaikie (Winnipeg-Transcona):

... my question is for the Minister for International Trade. One day while the minister was away on his travels, his parliamentary secretary indicated to the House that the government was seeking to redefine and reinterpret the chapter 11 investor state dispute mechanism in NAFTA.

Given that the minister has already indicated in committee that he does not intend to seek this kind of investor state dispute mechanism in any other free trade agreement that the government may be contemplating entering into, why does he not seek to get rid of chapter 11 altogether instead of simply redefining or reinterpreting it?

Hon. Pierre S. Pettigrew (Minister for International Trade):

... as the member knows, chapter 11 is part of the NAFTA that we signed with two trade partners, Mexico and the United States. We are confident that it has helped the Canadian economy a great deal. The NAFTA is a very solid agreement that has helped to promote Canadian exports a great deal in North America.

Chapter 11 is part of the whole treaty. We cannot isolate it completely. I tasked my deputy minister at the last meeting he had with his counterpart in the United States and Mexico to clarify certain aspects of chapter 11 with which we have some difficulties of interpretation.

(House of Commons Debates, June 12, 2000, p. 7822)
(Débats de la Chambre des Communes, le 12 juin 2000, p. 7822)

(b) Santé et éducation / Health and Education

M. Gilles Duceppe (Laurier-Sainte-Marie):

... hier, en dévoilant la position du gouvernement quant aux négociations de l'OMC, le ministre du Commerce international a soutenu trois positions qui paraissent pour le moins inconciliables. Il a d'abord dit que rien n'était exclu. Il a ensuite affirmé qu'il conservait sa pleine capacité de réglementer les secteurs de la santé et de l'éducation. Il a enfin ajouté qu'il ne réclamait aucune exemption. Est-ce que le ministre pourrait maintenant nous donner la véritable position du gouvernement dans ces négociations?

L'hon. Pierre S. Pettigrew (ministre du Commerce international):

... la position de notre gouvernement est absolument claire par rapport aux services de santé ou d'éducation ... Il n'est pas question de négocier les services de santé publique au Canada ou les services d'éducation. Ce n'est pas sur la table. Mais si d'autres pays souhaitent, pour leur part, en discuter à l'intérieur de l'Accord général sur le commerce des services, chaque pays est libre, sur une base volontaire, de s'engager dans un certain nombre de disciplines. Pour sa part, le Canada ne s'y engagera pas.

M. Gilles Duceppe (Laurier-Sainte-Marie):

... j'aimerais donc savoir pourquoi le ministre ne demande pas une exemption si l'ensemble des pays se décidaient à négocier sur cette question, ce qui serait par ailleurs très surprenant. Est-ce que le ministre va exiger une exemption sur cette question, sur tout ce qui est de nature publique quant à des dossiers comme la santé et l'éducation?

L'hon. Pierre S. Pettigrew (ministre du Commerce international):

... l'Accord général sur le commerce des services est un accord avec une liste ascendante, c'est-à-dire que ce n'est pas au Canada à déterminer que certains autres pays ne voudront pas en parler si, dans leur intérêt à eux, ils souhaitent faire du commerce international dans ces services. Ce que je dis, c'est que comme c'est une adhésion sur une base volontaire, nous ne voulons pas empêcher les autres pays d'en parler. Mais comme il s'agira d'une adhésion volontaire de la part du Canada, nous n'avons aucune intention de nous engager dans le service public de la santé ou dans le service de l'éducation.

M. Richard Marceau (Charlesbourg):

... questionné hier, le ministre du Commerce international a été très confus, surtout très vague, sur la position du gouvernement à l'OMC en ce qui a trait à la santé et à l'éducation. Ce n'est pas une surprise, cela n'est même pas du ressort du gouvernement fédéral. Comment le ministre peut-il prétendre bien représenter les intérêts des Canadiens dans les domaines de la santé et de l'éducation, par exemple pour le GATS, alors que ce n'est pas le fédéral qui a l'expertise et la compétence dans ces domaines, ce sont les provinces?

L'hon. Pierre S. Pettigrew (ministre du Commerce international):

... c'est précisément la raison pour laquelle le 7 octobre dernier, avec tous les ministres provinciaux du Commerce, j'ai tenu une réunion de travail extrêmement intéressante. C'est la raison pour laquelle nous avons toutes les semaines, au niveau des fonctionnaires, des rencontres avec les gouvernements des provinces pour être absolument certains que la position canadienne reflète bien les besoins et les intérêts de chacune des provinces de notre pays. Je peux vous assurer que pour le moment, nous sommes absolument confiants d'arriver ensemble avec une voix forte à Seattle pour bien protéger et promouvoir les intérêts de tous les Canadiens.

M. Richard Marceau (Charlesbourg):

... cela n'a pas empêché les premiers ministres provinciaux de demander unanimement, lors des dernières conférences des premiers ministres provinciaux, de pouvoir présenter leurs points de vue à la table de l'OMC. Le gouvernement, encore, dit vouloir négocier dans les domaines qui ne sont pas de son ressort. Est-ce que le ministre s'engage à ne prendre aucun engagement dans les domaines de la santé et de l'éducation sans l'accord des provinces, parce que c'est leur responsabilité et pas la sienne?

L'hon. Pierre S. Pettigrew (ministre du Commerce international):

... permettez-moi d'être très clair: le gouvernement du Canada n'a pas l'intention de prendre aucun engagement sans consulter les provinces. C'est la raison pour laquelle nous travaillons très étroitement avec les provinces. J'ai dit aux ministres provinciaux au cours des dernières semaines que nous travaillerons très étroitement ensemble, et c'est absolument important. Je voudrais faire remarquer au député de Charlesbourg que Bruxelles parle, à la table de négociations, au nom de l'Union européenne, y compris dans ce qui relève des gouvernements nationaux membres de l'Union européenne.

(House of Commons Debates, November 16, 1999, p. 1327)
(Débats de la Chambre des Communes, le 16 novembre 1999, p. 1327)

Ms. Libby Davies (Vancouver East):

... global corporations are itching to profit from Canada's schools and hospitals. The federal government is poised for the first time ever to put health and education on the WTO table. Canadians do not buy that the trade minister can make it easier for wealthy investors to profiteer from health care and education without sacrificing our schools and hospitals.
... Will he change his position and push for a complete carve out of health and education so that all countries can keep private corporations out of their schools and hospitals?

Hon. Pierre S. Pettigrew (Minister for International Trade):

... In the WTO, under the GATS, our universal health care and public education are not subject to any international trade rules unless Canada accepts those rules. We did not accept them in the Uruguay round and we will not accept them in the next round ...

(House of Commons Debates, November 16, 1999, p. 1331)
(Débats de la Chambre des Communes, le 16 novembre 1999, p. 1331)

Mr. Svend J. Robinson (Burnaby-Douglas):

... the Minister knows that if Canadian corporations are going to profit in health care and education in other countries, we are going to have to sacrifice our public health care and education system in Canada.

Last month the heritage minister said "What we are seeking in the Seattle round is an explicit reference in the WTO that culture is not to be negotiated at the WTO "period," not a separate instrument but a carve out in the WTO. Is this the position that the trade minister will be taking in Seattle?

Hon. Pierre S. Pettigrew (Minister for International Trade):

... the position I will be taking is the 50 years experience we have and the recent experience we have on GATS, which is absolutely clear. A country may make a concession to us in a certain field without us having to volunteer a concession in the same field. That is what international trade is all about. A country chooses the sectors in which it makes its concessions. Canada will not make concessions on health and public education.

(House of Commons Debates, November 16, 1999, p. 1332)
(Débats de la Chambre des Communes, le 16 novembre 1999, p. 1332)

Mr. Bill Blaikie (Winnipeg-Transcona):

... my question is for the Deputy Prime Minister or the Minister of Foreign Affairs. It has to do with the WTO meetings in Seattle next week. The Minister for International Trade will be going there representing the government. Can the government tell us whether the Minister for International Trade, at the meetings in Seattle, will be making it absolutely clear that Canada rejects the American position with respect to how health and education services should be dealt with at the WTO?

Hon. Lloyd Axworthy (Minister of Foreign Affairs):

... it is my understanding that the Minister for International Trade has been asked this question several times in the House and has made it very clear that we consider that health is part of the basic protected services and will not be part of those negotiations.

Mr. Bill Blaikie (Winnipeg-Transcona):

... that is not the view that Ms. Barshefsky takes. I wish the government would make it explicit, that it rejects her point of view. The Minister of Canadian Heritage said she desires a carve out of culture in which culture is not "WTO-able" at all, to use her words.

Can the government tell us if that is the position the trade minister will be taking to Seattle, that culture under no conditions will be "WTO-able"? Right now it is, and we would like to know how she plans to change it.

Hon. Lloyd Axworthy (Minister of Foreign Affairs):

... health is not a negotiable item and neither is culture. Canada has taken the lead internationally through the efforts of the Minister of Canadian Heritage and the Minister for International Trade to establish a new multilateral instrument that would promote the diversity of culture around the world. Canada is taking the lead on that matter ...

(House of Commons Debates, November 25, 1999, p. 1754)
(Débats de la Chambre des Communes, le 25 novembre 1999, p. 1754)

(c) Culture

Ms. Colleen Beaumier (Brampton West-Mississauga):

... last spring the trade subcommittee travelled across the country listening to the concerns of Canadians pertaining to the protection of our culture. In the upcoming WTO negotiations in Seattle what action is the Canadian government taking to ensure our independence to determine and maintain our own cultural policy?

M. Mauril Bélanger (secrétaire parlementaire de la ministre du Patrimoine canadien):

... je remercie ma collègue de son importante question, surtout à la veille de cette ronde de négociations de l'Organisation mondiale du commerce. Le Canada a pris une position de leadership dans le dossier. La ministre du Patrimoine est à Paris présentement où elle copréside, sous l'égide de l'UNESCO, avec son homologue française, une table ronde sur la diversité culturelle. De plus, nous sommes très fiers d'être associés avec le gouvernement de la province de Québec au lancement de la Coalition pour la diversité culturelle, laquelle sera présidée par Robert Pilon, à qui nous souhaitons beaucoup de courage et surtout beaucoup de succès.

(House of Commons Debates, November 3, 1999, p. 1052)
(Débats de la Chambre des Communes, le 3 novembre 1999, p. 1052)

Ms. Wendy Lill (Dartmouth):

... yesterday in Toronto the Prime Minister committed himself to making an independent trade agreement for culture a reality. But Canadians remember that last spring this government retreated on magazines because of our present trade agreements. Under the NAFTA we are allowed to protect culture as long as we remain obliged to be punished for doing so. Under the WTO culture is seen as a good like any other.

Is the Prime Minister now saying that Canada will push for an international cultural trade agreement that is not subject to the WTO and the NAFTA?

Mr. Mauril Bélanger (Parliamentary Secretary to Minister of Canadian Heritage):

... as the hon. member knows, the government has accepted the recommendation from SAGIT that we seek a different instrument through the WTO for culture. The minister is in Paris this week meeting with the UNESCO ministers, as well as co-chairing a roundtable with her counterparts from France to advance this cause. The latest announcement, of course, was when we, with the province of Quebec, were delighted to announce our support for the cultural diversity coalition that is being built across the country to ensure that cultural diversity remains.

Ms. Wendy Lill (Dartmouth):

... In light of the fact that we have the premier performers of the country in the House today, can the Prime Minister guarantee them that the Canada Council and the CBC, the pillars of our cultural foundations, are not in danger of being swept away and squeezed out by the straitjacket trade agreements that we are presently party to?

Mr. Mauril Bélanger (Parliamentary Secretary to Minister of Canadian Heritage):

... it has always been the intention of this government to protect, promote and develop our Canadian culture and the instruments by which that culture manifests itself. That remains our commitment.

(House of Commons Debates, November 4, 1999, p. 1130)
(Débats de la Chambre des Communes, le 4 novembre 1999, p. 1130)

Mr. Janko Peric (Cambridge):

... my question is for the Minister of Canadian Heritage. As Canada enters the third millennium, our national culture will be increasingly exposed to the forces of globalization. What action is the minister taking to preserve and to protect Canadian culture?

Hon. Sheila Copps (Minister of Canadian Heritage):

... I want to first underscore that the approach we are taking has been embraced both by the Standing Committee on Canadian Heritage and the Standing Committee on Foreign Affairs and International Trade. We are leading the world in seeking a new cultural instrument to ensure that culture is not captured in the aegis of the WTO. The reason Canada has taken this position and the reason we have worked very hard to bring together like-minded countries from around the world is precisely because we are a country that believes that respect for cultural diversity is part of our constitutional heritage.

(House of Commons Debates, November 22, 1999, p. 1561)
(Débats de la Chambre des Communes, le 22 novembre 1999, p. 1561)

Mr. Bill Blaikie (Winnipeg-Transcona):

... my question is for the Minister for International Trade ... I want to ask him why it was, in respect of the text that was being developed on services "of course, there was no final text" but in the text that was being developed before the meeting, we now have proof that Canada was asking for shorter and less precise language and wanting to suppress certain language because of the sensitivities of cultural industries at home. Why was Canada, given the rhetoric on transparency, conspiring to hide its position?

Hon. Pierre S. Pettigrew (Minister for International Trade):

... As for the question on services, Canada did exactly what it said it would do, it did not take up on health and education.

Mr. Bill Blaikie (Winnipeg-Transcona):

... I have a memo from David Hartridge, the director of WTO services, in which he refers to the fact that Canada along with the EU asked for the suppression of certain language and for shorter and less precise language in order to respond to cultural sensitivities at home. Perhaps the minister could explain what these cultural sensitivities were. Why, given all the rhetoric about transparency, was Canada attempting to suppress the reality of what was being agreed to in this text?

Hon. Pierre S. Pettigrew (Minister for International Trade):

... I do not know what memo the member is referring to. I can say that Canada stands for transparency. We believe in transparency. Of the 135 delegations in Seattle, the one that most engaged in a dialogue with the NGOs was the Canadian one. We engaged in a dialogue with the provincial ministers. On services we will fight for a bottom up approach as we said. The services we do not want to take we will not take up. That is what

Canada did. I am extremely proud of Canada's engagement in Seattle last week.

(House of Commons Debates, December 6, 1999, p. 2172)
(Débats de la Chambre des Communes, le 6 décembre 1999, p. 2172)

(d) Trade and Developing Countries / Commerce et pays en voie de développement

Ms. Sarmite Bulte (Parkdale-High Park):

... my question is for the Minister for International Trade. Will the minister tell the House to what extent will the lesser developed countries be considered in the launch of the Seattle round of the World Trade Organization negotiations?

Hon. Pierre S. Pettigrew (Minister for International Trade):

... trade does lead to development and that is what history is teaching us. Canada and the world know that development will be at the heart of the next round of negotiations. We will work to fight the exclusion and promote development of those countries through trade. With my colleague the Minister for International Co-operation, we will work at capacity building so that developing countries can indeed participate fully in a rules based international trade system. Canada will also promote at Seattle better coherence between the WTO and the other international organizations in favour of developing countries.

(House of Commons Debates, November 17, 1999, p. 1378)
(Débats de la Chambre des Communes, le 17 novembre 1999, p. 1378)

(e) Bulk Water Exports / Exportation de l'eau en vrac

Mr. Nelson Riis (Kamloops, Thompson and Highland Valley):

... we all remember the fiasco of having to pay the Ethyl corporation $19 million. We learned today from Santa Barbara, California, that Sun Belt Water is suing the Canadian government for up to $15 billion under chapter 11 of NAFTA. My question is for the Minister of the Environment. Would he now admit that Canada's water export policy will not be decided by the Parliament of Canada, Canadian laws or the courts of Canada, but that it will essentially be decided by three faceless trade lawyers operating in secret on the basis of NAFTA trade rules?

Hon. David Anderson (Minister of the Environment):

... We do not believe that bulk water is an item of trade. We do not think it should go to NAFTA panels. We think that is covered entirely within Canada by the decision of Canadians ...

Mr. Nelson Riis (Kamloops, Thompson, and Highland Valleys):

... the Minister of the Environment can stand and yell in the House all he wants that this is not a trade deal. The issue of Canada's future water exports is going to a NAFTA trade panel. The suit for $15 billion is being launched now as we sit here in the House of Commons. One reason this is happening is that the government and the minister have been dithering on water policy. Back in 1993 the Prime Minister said that there would be no water exports. We have been calling for legislation. Will he now introduce legislation and initiate talks to remove ourselves from chapter 11 under NAFTA?

Hon. David Anderson (Minister of the Environment):

Mr. Speaker, the hon. member and his party keep insisting that somehow water is an item of trade which can be handled by NAFTA. We say no. We say this is a decision for Canadians, not for people elsewhere. We are saying no to water diversions from any of the major watersheds in Canada.

(House of Commons Debates, Friday, October 22, 1999, p. 556)
(Débats de la Chambre des Communes, le 22 octobre 1999, p. 556)

Mr. Deepak Obhrai (Calgary East):

... in the 1993 version of the red book the Liberal government promised to renegotiate the NAFTA agreement to specifically exempt bulk water exports. Unfortunately, this is one of the promises the government has failed to keep. Exempting water from our international trade agreement is the best way for Canada to protect its waters. Why has the government abandoned seeking exemptions for our water in international agreements?

Hon. David Anderson (Minister of the Environment):

The way to protect water exports is to make sure that there are not inter-water basin transfers of water. If we try simply to protect water exports at the border, we wind up with the problem of this becoming an item of trade and, therefore, the decision on it will be made by an international panel of trade experts, not by Canadians. I believe, and the government believes, that decisions on Canadian water should be made by Canadians and not by foreigners.

(House of Commons Debates, November 26, 1999, p. 1807)
(Débats de la Chambre des Communes, le 26 novembre 1999, p. 1807)

(f) Human Rights / Droits de la personne

Ms. Alexa McDonough (Halifax):

As the WTO huddles in Seattle, a growing worldwide movement of citizens is calling for fundamental change in our approach to trade. They are calling for trade to be about improving the human condition and improving human lives. On Friday in Toronto the Chinese trade representative stated "This is the WTO. This is a trade agreement. It will have nothing to do with human rights." Does Canada stand with China, or does Canada stand with citizens who insist that trade agreements must be about human rights?

Right Hon. Jean Chrétien (Prime Minister):

... they are very serious negotiations. All the countries of the world are there. It is very important that we defend the interests of Canadian products and Canadian programs and make sure that there is more trade around the world. If there is more trade around the world, there is more wealth around the world which will help more people to have a decent way of living. It is the objective of the WTO to stop protectionism and make sure that the industrialized countries for example buy goods and services from the poorest countries of the world.

Ms. Alexa McDonough (Halifax):

... we agree that trade agreements can be beneficial, but it depends on what we put in them. For example, on Friday Canada signed a new deal with China. It gives Canadian banks access to Chinese markets but it ignores child labour. The government had an opportunity to put a human face, a child's face on trade, but it chose not to. Why will the government not stand up to those who would put profits ahead of the interests of people?

Mr. Bob Speller (Parliamentary Secretary to Minister for International Trade):

... our agenda for the world trade talks is to get access to those markets and at the same time to make sure that our social programs are protected. At the same time, the hon. member knows there are other avenues in which Canada takes a leading role in making sure that human rights are protected. In fact, the Prime Minister, the Minister for International Trade, and the Minister of Foreign Affairs on many occasions have stood up internationally to make sure that child labour and human rights issues are at the forefront of the agenda.

(House of Commons Debates, November 29, 1999, p. 1868)
(Débats de la Chambre des Communes, le 29 novembre 1999, p. 1868)

(g) Worker's Rights and Environmental Standards / Droits des ouvriers et normes environnementales

Ms. Alexa McDonough (Halifax):

... yesterday the Prime Minister told the House that increasing trade, without regard to the human cost, is the best way to serve the citizens of the world. Canadians want their government to take a more balanced approach. Canadians recognize, for example, the importance of worker safety and environmental protection. Why then does the Prime Minister ignore workers' rights and ignore environmental standards when he speaks of trade and the WTO?

Right Hon. Jean Chrétien (Prime Minister):

Mr. Speaker, the hon. leader of the fourth party should know that when we formed the government we worked very hard to improve the NAFTA deal. What were the considerations at that time? We said that we had to improve the deal for the protection of workers' rights, for the protection of the environment, and for the protection of water because there was a problem between Canada and the United States. We made these improvements to satisfy exactly the point that the hon. member is making . . .

Ms. Alexa McDonough (Halifax):

. . . that is a sham. No wonder the Prime Minister does not want to talk about the WTO. The Prime Minister knows that the enforcement mechanisms of the WTO are much stronger. When it comes to defending Canadian product abroad, and that is very important, the government goes to the WTO. Why? Because it has teeth. When it comes to people needing health and safety protection, and environmental protection, the government shunts them off to some subcommittee of a subcommittee of a working group because it knows that nothing will happen. Why is Canada's position at Seattle so lacking in balance?

Right Hon. Jean Chrétien (Prime Minister):

. . . the hon. leader of the New Democratic Party should know that we refer problems on labour to the ILO . . . She just made a great concession to us. She said that we should use the WTO to make sure we sell our products abroad. Well I know the workers are the ones who benefit the most when we sell Canadian products abroad and these workers are in unions that give money to the hon. member's party.

(House of Commons Debates, November 30, 1999, p. 1946)
(Débats de la Chambre des Communes, le 30 novembre 1999, p. 1946)

Ms. Alexa McDonough (Halifax):

. . . based on the NAFTA experience it is no wonder Canadians are uneasy about the government actually getting enforceable labour and environmental commitments at the WTO. Enforcement provisions of NAFTA do not apply to labour standards or to the environment, and the Prime Minister knows that. In fact labour and the environment are not even in the agreement. They are relegated to side deals that have no teeth. Why should

Canadians expect that the government would seek at the WTO what it has abandoned in NAFTA?

Mr. Bob Speller (Parliamentary Secretary to Minister for International Trade):

... the standing committee wanted the federal government to make sure there was more co-operation between the WTO and the International Labour Organization and, in terms of the environment, to make sure that environmental standards were high on our list. The Government of Canada has certainly done that. It has brought forward these issues and has supported the idea at the WTO that there be a working group on labour so that we can talk about these issues and make them a priority in the WTO.

Ms. Alexa McDonough (Halifax):

Yesterday the Prime Minister told the House that they insisted before they agreed to NAFTA that labour and environment conditions be in the agreement ... There are no labour and environmental standards in NAFTA, even to this day. It is the difference between enforcement and no enforcement, the difference between teeth and no teeth ...

Right Hon. Jean Chrétien (Prime Minister):

We are very preoccupied with the environment, labour conditions and so on. It is a wide negotiation ... Yesterday she took eight days to have a position on the big question on the referendum. Yesterday she made a big statement, not in the House, in which she claimed that all New Democratic Party governments were on her side in that regard. Perhaps she should call Manitoba and Saskatchewan before getting up next time.

(House of Commons Debates, December 2, 1999, p. 2064)
(Débats de la Chambre des Communes, le 2 décembre 1999, p. 2064)

(h) Labour Standards / Normes du travail

Ms. Alexa McDonough (Halifax):

... yesterday the Prime Minister stated that labour standards do not belong in trade agreements, send them to the ILO. By contrast, President Clinton stated yesterday that core labour standards should be part of every trade agreement and we ought not to buy from countries that oppress workers with poor labour conditions and lack of a living income. Does the Prime Minister stand by his statement that labour standards do not belong in trade agreements or does he agree with President Clinton?

Right Hon. Jean Chrétien (Prime Minister):

... the hon. member should know that we insisted before we agreed to NAFTA that the labour conditions be in the agreement. They were not before we formed the government and we insisted on having them there. I just want to report at this moment that the Minister for International Trade has been named today to be the head of the WTO working group on trade in developing countries, just to show the House of Commons the reputation of Canada with other countries.

Ms. Alexa McDonough (Halifax):

Listen to what else President Clinton said yesterday: "They're going to have to open up the WTO process so that the voices of labour and the environment can be heard." Yet for our Prime Minister, labour issues belong at the ILO and environmental issues just are not on the table. Will the Prime Minister finally admit that trade and labour, that trade and environment are inextricably linked?

Right Hon. Jean Chrétien (Prime Minister):

That is what we demanded before we signed the NAFTA agreement. We were opposed to the previous NAFTA agreement because they were not talking about the environment, because they were not talking about labour conditions and because they were not talking about water.

(House of Commons Debates, December 1, 1999, p. 1990)
(Débats de la Chambre des Communes, le 1er décembre 1999, p. 1990)

Ms. Bev Desjarlais (Churchill):

U.S. President Clinton is pushing for enforceable core labour standards at the World Trade Organization. Core labour standards are the most basic rights: the right of workers to organize, no slave labour, no child labour. The Americans support core labour standards in trade agreements but Canada opposes them. The trade minister even said that the American move calls for damage control. Why has the trade minister become the new poster boy for sweatshop labour?

Mr. Bob Speller (Parliamentary Secretary to Minister for International Trade):

... the hon. member likes to quote President Clinton. Let me also quote him. He said "We know that countries which have opened their economies to the world have also opened the doors to opportunity and hope for their own people. Where barriers have fallen, by and large, living standards have risen and democratic institutions have become stronger." The hon. member should know that the Canadian government supports core labour standards. The Canadian government at every opportunity at the ILO stands very forcibly on this issue. The fair rules of the WTO are good for Canadian jobs, good for Canadian labour and are certainly good for the Canadian economy.

Ms. Bev Desjarlais (Churchill):

... nobody contests that trade with different countries is good, but we also know that labour standards are good as well and they have to be enforceable ... I ask the Minister of Foreign Affairs, why is Canada's trade minister choosing to fight for sweatshop owners instead of fighting for children and adults who are trying to survive in the global economy?

Hon. Lloyd Axworthy (Minister of Foreign Affairs):

The fact of the matter is that Canada has taken the lead at the ILO to implement a protocol to protect against abusive labour and to protect child labour. We have taken to trade forums the need to bring the ILO and the WTO together in a co-operative way to share those issues. Canada was taking a leadership position long before President Clinton ever thought about it.

(House of Commons Debates, December 3, 1999, p. 2114)
(Débats de la Chambre des Communes, le 3 décembre 1999, p. 2114)

(i) Auto Pact / Pacte de l'automobile

Mr. Bill Blaikie (Winnipeg-Transcona):

... my question is for the Deputy Prime Minister who is one of the few members of parliament who was here when the auto pact came into being. He was probably here as well when parliament and Canadians were assured that the auto pact would not be endangered by the WTO.

Given the number of jobs that are threatened by the WTO decision, many in his home city of Windsor, what does the government plan to do to safeguard the auto pact and the tens of thousands of jobs that are associated with that managed trade?

Hon. Herb Gray (Deputy Prime Minister):

I assure the hon. member that we are looking very carefully at the interim ruling which has been received in confidence. We will be making our representations to the WTO with respect to what should be in any final ruling and we will act in our responsibilities as we always have to protect the interests of Canadian workers ...

(House of Commons Debates, October 15, 1999, p. 208)
(Débats de la Chambre des Communes, le 15 octobre 1999, p. 208)

Ms. Sarmite Bulte (Parkdale-High Park):

... my question is for the Minister for International Trade. On Friday the World Trade Organization released its decision regarding Canada's auto pact claiming that it gives favourable treatment to U.S. manufacturers while discriminating against other manufacturers. Can the minister tell the House on what basis does he plan to appeal the decision?

Hon. Pierre S. Pettigrew (Minister for International Trade):

... on Friday my colleague the Minister of Industry and I announced that Canada will appeal the panel's decision. We believe there are compelling legal grounds to certain elements of the panel's ruling. We essentially want to seek clarification on the reasoning and the scope of the panel's decision and report. The government will continue to consult closely with the provinces and key industry stakeholders throughout the appeal process.

(House of Commons Debates, February 14, 2000, p. 3492)
(Débats de la Chambre des Communes, le 14 février 2000, p. 3492)

(j) Duty on Processed Cheese Products / Droits de douane imposés sur des produits de fromage fondu

Mr. Bill Casey (Cumberland-Colchester):

... the Minister for International Trade is aware that a company in my riding, Oxford Frozen Foods, has been for some months seeking relief from a duty that was imposed on February 28 on processed cheese products. This duty is charged even though the binding tariff decision in 1994 said there would be no duty and even though an American product comes to Canada with no duty.

Has the minister resolved this situation, or could he give us an update on it?

Hon. Pierre S. Pettigrew (Minister for International Trade):

I have already asked my department to look into it very carefully. It is a technical difficulty around a classification problem. I will get back to him next week for sure because this is very important for us. My department is already looking into the case of this classification difficulty that Oxford Frozen Foods is encountering.

Mr. Bill Casey (Cumberland-Colchester):

I want to emphasize how important this is because the company has already lost a contract that would have meant 50 full time jobs in my riding and it prevents the company from an expansion which might develop 150 full time jobs.

I would ask the minister to commit the full force of his department to this issue to get it resolved.

Hon. Pierre S. Pettigrew (Minister for International Trade):

I can assure the member that we are very sensitive on this side of the House to job creation. It is very important for us to make sure that Canadians have access to export markets as well, because we have good products and competitive products. One of our objectives is to have a good, solid, rules based system by which everyone would abide.

I can tell the House that this government will commit everything it can to help in this particular situation.

(House of Commons Debates, March 31, 2000, p. 5527)
(Débats de la Chambre des Communes, le 31 mars 2000, p. 5527)

(k) Avantages du libre-échange pour le Canada / The
     Benefits of Free Trade for Canada

M. Marcel Proulx (Hull-Aylmer):

... ma question s'adresse au ministre du Commerce international. Avec l'augmentation accrue des activités internationales de nos PME, le ministre peut-il nous informer si le Canada bénéficie vraiment de l'ouverture des marchés sur la scène mondiale?

L'hon. Pierre S. Pettigrew (ministre du Commerce international):

... je veux aujourd'hui attirer l'attention de cette Chambre pour lui faire savoir comment la libéralisation des marchés est un avantage pour tous, et certainement pour le Canada. Par exemple, l'an dernier, nos exportations ont augmenté de près de 12 p. 100 et nos importations de 7,7 p. 100. Le gouvernement canadien travaille sans relâche pour que le système international soit basé sur des règles claires pour que nous puissions avoir un meilleur accès aux marchés pour nos PME, des PME qui créent des emplois durables et de qualité. Encore plus, cela permet d'améliorer la qualité de vie des Canadiens et des Canadiennes. Chapeau aux petites et moyennes entreprises du Canada ...

(House of Commons Debates, February 25, 2000, p. 4037)
(Débats de la Chambre des Communes, le 25 février 2000, p. 4037)

(l) *Canada-Brazil* Decision by the World Trade Organization /
     Décision de l'Organisation mondiale du commerce dans
     l'affaire *Canada-Brézil*

Ms. Eleni Bakopanos (Ahuntsic):

... my question is for the Minister for International Trade. Since yesterday, we have been hearing all sorts of stories and figures about Canada and the actions of the WTO to clarify the decision by Brazil.

Could the minister tell us about the latest developments in the Canada-Brazil matter?

Hon. Pierre S. Pettigrew (Minister for International Trade):

... last week, my colleague for industry and I announced that Canada would comply with the WTO's decision. We released the specific details of our decision.

Canada is now trying to find out how Brazil will implement the decision. We therefore asked the WTO to advise us. Canada remains open to negotiation.

I would like to remind the House that we are not taking reprisals against Brazil at the moment.

(House of Commons Debates, November 24, 1999, p. 1682)
(Débats de la Chambre des Communes, le 24 novembre 1999, p. 1682)

(m) Wine Exports / Exportations des vins

Mr. Walt Lastewka (St. Catharines):

... my question is for the Minister for International Trade. I raised the issue of trade inequities in international wine markets on previous occasions. In 1996 Canada imported more than $330 million worth of wine from the European Union while Canadian exports to the EU were limited to only $1 million. In 1999 the gap grew.

Why is there this huge imbalance? When will the minister correct the problem?

Hon. Pierre S. Pettigrew (Minister for International Trade):

I can assure the member that Canada will continue to seek improved access for our wines, including the Ontario ice wine which is having major difficulty in Europe. We are working hard on that file.

We have discussed a limited aegis on bilateral wine and spirit issues with the EU, including market access, protection for geographic indications and mutual recognition of winemaking practices. We had an exchange of views between Canadian and EU officials at the end of March. Significant differences remain but we will make further progress.

(House of Commons Debates, April 4, 2000, p. 5665)
(Débats de la Chambre des Communes, le 4 avril 2000, p. 5665)

(n) Obstacles au commerce international / Barriers to
    International Trade

M. Claude Drouin (Beauce):

... ma question s'adresse au ministre du Commerce international. Les États-Unis ont publié dernièrement le document Foreign Trade Barriers, soit leur liste d'obstacles au commerce international pour les entreprises américaines. J'aimerais savoir si le ministre entend nous offrir la même liste pour le Canada et s'il rendra publics certains détails sur l'accès de nos entreprises aux marchés internationaux.

L'hon. Pierre S. Pettigrew (ministre du Commerce international):

J'ai rendu public ce matin le rapport annuel du gouvernement sur les priorités du Canada en l'an 2000 visant à améliorer l'accès aux marchés étrangers. Notre gouvernement veut accroître la performance de nos exportations et éliminer les obstacles au commerce pour les entreprises canadiennes.

Les Canadiens peuvent être très fiers. En 1999, nos exportations ont atteint un nouveau record, à la hauteur de 410 milliards de dollars.

(House of Commons Debates, April 5, 2000, p. 5713)
(Débats de la Chambre des Communes, le 5 avril 2000, p. 5713)

(o) Organisations non-gouvernementales / Non-Governmental Organizations

M. Richard Marceau (Charlesbourg):

... alors que le Canada, par l'entremise du ministre du Commerce international, veut se faire le champion de la participation de la société civile aux négociations de la Zone de libre-échange des Amériques, on constate, à la fin de la rencontre de Toronto, que les ONG n'ont eu droit qu'à 90 minutes pour présenter leurs points de vue, alors que le secteur des affaires, lui, a eu droit à deux jours. Pourquoi le Canada, qui présidait cette rencontre, n'a-t-il pas jugé bon de faire plus de place aux ONG et à la société civile?

Mr. Bob Speller (Parliamentary Secretary to Minister for International Trade):

... the hon. member should know that Canada was the first country in these meetings to push hard for civil society to be involved. In fact, the Standing Committee on Foreign Affairs and International Trade, which held hearings across the country over the past couple of years, met with civil society and made strong representations to the Government of Canada, which listened.

(House of Commons Debates, November 5, 1999, p. 1185)
(Débats de la Chambre des Communes, le 5 novembre 1999, p. 1185)

(p) Mondialisation / Globalization

M. Stéphan Tremblay (Lac-Saint-Jean):

... j'ai déposé une motion à la Chambre demandant la création d'un comité spécial pour étudier les effets de la mondialisation sur la cohésion sociale. Ma question, touchant plusieurs ministères, sera donc orientée vers le premier ministre. Le premier ministre ne croit-il pas qu'il devrait donner l'exemple et créer ce comité parlementaire dans les meilleurs délais?

L'hon. Don Boudria (leader du gouvernement à la Chambre des communes):

... comme le député le sait, l'étude des affaires émanant des députés à la Chambre des communes est décidée par un vote libre de cette Chambre. C'est une position qu'a adoptée notre gouvernement en 1993.

M. Stéphan Tremblay (Lac-Saint-Jean):

... tant que le Parlement ne jouera pas son rôle démocratique, de plus en plus de gens chercheront à débattre de la question par tous les moyens, y compris dans la rue. Qu'attend le premier ministre pour prendre le leadership, interpeller les parlementaires et établir un dialogue avec la société civile afin que nous puissions débattre des impacts sociaux de la mondialisation?

L'hon. Pierre S. Pettigrew (ministre du Commerce international):

... je remercie le député de Lac-Saint-Jean pour la préoccupation importante qu'il manifeste à l'endroit du dossier de la mondialisation et des impacts sur la cohésion sociale. Je peux lui dire que nous sommes très sensibles à ces préoccupations, et que le Canada, la semaine dernière, à Seattle, a appuyé fortement un concept de la cohérence pour que les politiques commerciales tiennent compte des normes du travail et des questions environnementales et qu'il y ait de meilleures relations entre elles. Je peux lui dire que du côté du Canada, nous allons continuer de travailler de très près avec les ONG et avec les milieux d'affaires pour nous assurer d'être capables d'humaniser la mondialisation. Nous allons continuer également d'appuyer la diversité culturelle, qui est très importante.

(House of Commons Debates, December 6, 1999, p. 2173)
(Débats de la Chambre des Communes, le 6 décembre 1999, p. 2173)

2 *Environment / Environnement*

(a) Kyoto

Mr. Rahim Jaffer (Edmonton-Strathcona):

... we are only a week away from the sixth conference on the Kyoto agreement, and Canadians still do not know how the government plans to meet the UN imposed emission targets ... Does the minister plan to break the promise made by the Prime Minister that there will be no new taxes to meet his Kyoto targets?

Hon. David Anderson (Minister of the Environment):

The fact is that we now have in place committees of 450 people from the private sector, the provincial governments and the federal government who are working together to work out a strategy. The position taken by the Canadian government is virtually identical to that announced yesterday by Chancellor Schroeder of Germany. We are on track to achieve our Kyoto targets.

Mr. Rahim Jaffer (Edmonton-Strathcona):

... we still have not heard from the minister on the government's position on the UN imposed emission targets. All we have heard is that the minister will either throw Canadians out of their cars with a gas tax or out of their jobs with a carbon tax. Will the minister end the mystery today and table the government's proposal to meet the Kyoto emission targets?

Hon. David Anderson (Minister of the Environment):

... contrary to what the hon. member said, the agreement in Kyoto was arrived at by 160 countries. It was not imposed by the United Nations. Further to what he said with respect the issue of taxation, all members of the government have made perfectly clear that we do not believe a broad based carbon tax would be an appropriate way to go. There are however many other measures, including incentives whereby we can work together to achieve the Kyoto targets. These targets are very important for us to achieve.

(House of Commons Debates, October 26, 1999, p. 700)
(Débats de la Chambre des Communes, le 26 octobre 1999, p. 700)

Ms. Aileen Carroll (Barrie-Simcoe-Bradford):

I understand the Minister of the Environment has recently returned from Bonn and the council of parties negotiations on council change. Could the minister please update the House on what progress is being made internationally on this very important issue?

Hon. David Anderson (Minister of the Environment):

... indeed, there was progress in Bonn. There was substantial progress on the mechanisms whereby developed and developing countries can collaborate to achieve some of the Kyoto agreements. There was substantial progress with respect to the enhancement of the capacity of developing countries to achieve Kyoto. There was a clear indication from the developed countries that they are taking serious measures to achieve Kyoto which only illustrates the importance of the Prime Minister's decision that Canada also takes this matter very seriously.

(House of Commons Debates, November 23, 1999, p. 1636)
(Débats de la Chambre des Communes, le 23 novembre 1999, p. 1636)

Mr. Dennis Gruending (Saskatoon-Rosetown-Biggar):

... the study by the Pembina Institute shows that the governments greenhouse gas emissions policy is a complete failure. The government is relying on a voluntary program to have major polluters reduce emissions, but those emissions have actually increased by 7% since 1990. We have to move quickly to put in place programs to encourage the move toward the use of renewable resources. When will the government do something real about supporting a move toward renewable resource use?

Ms. Paddy Torsney (Parliamentary Secretary to Minister of the Environment):

... actually the government has been working with governments at the provincial and territorial levels and with experts across the country to put in place an action plan that will see us meet our Kyoto target. On Monday and Tuesday the Minister of Natural Resources and the Minister of the Environment will be meeting with their provincial and territorial colleagues to get that agreement battened down and to make sure that we are getting things in place, because we have a huge responsibility to Canadians and to people across the world. Voluntary action is important. It is not the only thing. We have to do other things, but it is a critical component.

(House of Commons Debates, Mars 24, 2000, p. 5200)
(Débats de la Chambre des Communes, le 24 mars, 2000, p. 5200)

Mr. Dennis Gruending (Saskatoon-Rosetown-Biggar):

... the government has been promising for years to reduce our polluting emission of greenhouse gases but all we have seen so far is foot dragging and delay.

Last week industrial nations met in Japan to get on with setting a specific date for ratifying the 1997 Kyoto protocol but Canada and the United States torpedoed the talks.

When will the government finally ratify the Kyoto accord? By what percentage will the environment minister commit to reducing our emission of harmful greenhouse gases?

Hon. David Anderson (Minister of the Environment):

... contrary to what the member has just said, the meeting in Japan over the last few days was very successful. It is true that there are difficulties with respect to ratification related to American constitutional differences between the senate and the administration, of which the member should be aware. However, we fully intend to put in place our plans to implement the Kyoto agreement. We will be working with the provinces in order to get that in place as soon as possible.

The important thing is not ratification. The important thing is making sure we have plans in place to reduce greenhouse gases.

(House of Commons Debates, April 10, 2000, p. 5891)
(Débats de la Chambre des Communes, le 10 avril 2000, p. 5891)

(b) Northwest Territories / Les Territoires du Nord-Est

Ms. Louise Hardy (Yukon):

... the throne speech noted the particular vulnerability of the environment in the north and that the proposed diamond mine in Northwest Territories would drain a lake at the headwaters of the Coppermine River. The Mackenzie Valley Environmental Impact Review Board, along with aboriginal groups and environmental organizations, have asked that this be put to a thorough environmental assessment panel. Will the minister act in the long term interests of the community and the environment and submit this to a panel for assessment?

Ms. Paddy Torsney (Parliamentary Secretary to Minister of the Environment):

... I can confirm that the minister has received comments from concerned individuals and has received the comprehensive study report. He is going to make a decision shortly and we will all be informed of that.

(House of Commons Debates, November 2, 1999, p. 1003)
(Débats de la Chambre des Communes, le 2 novembre 1999, p. 1003)

(c) "Candu" Nuclear Technology / Technologie nucléaire "Candu"

Mr. Peter Mancini (Sydney-Victoria):

Two years ago in Kyoto, Canada agreed to greenhouse gas emission reduction targets. This week, Canada is behind closed doors in Bonn promoting instead unlimited emissions trading, particularly exchanging Candu nuclear technology for credits with developing countries. My question is for the Prime Minister. Why is the Canadian government ...

Hon. Ralph E. Goodale (Minister of Natural Resources):

... Canada has engaged the active assistance of provinces, environmental organizations and the private sector all across the country in developing a Kyoto implementation plan. That work is going forward with a great deal of vigour. We are working on areas like energy conservation, energy efficiency, diversity among our energy sources, CO_2 sequestrations, carbon sinks, new science and technology and international mechanisms like trading, the clean development mechanism and joint implementation projects. Canada will be a responsible environmental citizen.

(House of Commons Debates, November 2, 1999, p. 1004)
(Débats de la Chambre des Communes, le 2 novembre 1999, 1004)

(d) Ozone Annex to the Canada-US Air Quality Agreement /
    Annexe relative à l'ozone pour l'Accord Canada-États-Unis
    sur la qualité de l'air

Ms. Susan Whelan (Essex):

... air pollution contributes to the untimely death of more than 5,000
Canadians and sends thousands more to hospital each year. The city of
Windsor and the county of Essex have some of the worst air pollution in
Canada. This is a serious matter that requires immediate attention. This
week Canada and the United States begin negotiations for an ozone annex
to the Canada-U.S. air quality agreement. How will this help all Canadians
including those from Windsor and Essex county?

Hon. David Anderson (Minister of the Environment):

... sadly the hon. member's number of 5,000 is likely on the low side. However, I point out that these are largely preventable deaths due to air pollution and we fully intend over the next decade to cut that number in half.
The negotiations with the United States are to establish a protocol with the
United States to reduce smog thus improving the quality of air in Canada
and in the United States with substantial improvements in the life expec-
tancies particularly of young children and older people who are specifically affected to a greater degree by air pollution problems.

(House of Commons Debates, February 14, 2000, p. 3493)
(Débats de la Chambre des Communes, le 14 février 2000, p. 3493)

(e) Commission for Environmental Cooperation /
    Commission de coopération environnementale

Mr. Dennis Gruending (Saskatoon-Rosetown-Biggar):

... when the free trade agreement was being negotiated with the United
States and Mexico, Canadians worried that we were on the way to weaker
environmental laws and lax enforcement. Senior American officials now
confirm that the Canadian government is trying to undermine guidelines
that allow whistleblowing citizens to take complaints to the centre for environmental co-operation.
    The minister's officials will meet with the other two countries this week
and he will meet with his counterparts in June. Will the minister promise
that he does not support and will not allow changes to guidelines governing citizen's submissions to the centre for environmental co-operation?

Hon. David Anderson (Minister of the Environment):

... unfortunately the hon. member's preamble to his question is sheer rubbish. The fact is we have a good system in place. There will be opportunities of course to improve it. It is a new system, virtually unique in the world, where there is such a commission in effect between three countries above what they can do domestically in terms of appeal. Undoubtedly there will be improvements and changes in the approaches that are taken and the mechanisms in the future ...

(House of Commons Debates, May 15, 2000, p. 6821)
(Débats de la Chambre des Communes, le 15 mai 2000, 6821)

Mr. Bill Blaikie (Winnipeg-Transcona):

... my question is for the Minister of the Environment. We now know that the Minister of the Environment, along with Mexico, vetoed a recommendation by the NAFTA environment commission to investigate the enforcement of Canada's environmental laws.

Could the Minister rise in the House and tell us why he did that? While he is on his feet, could he tell us what his response is to the charge by Robert Kennedy, Jr., that Canada is deliberately trying to undermine the NAFTA environmental commission?

He dismissed the claims made by the NDP environment critic on Monday to the same effect as rubbish. Is he prepared to say to Robert Kennedy, Jr., that his claims are also rubbish?

Hon. David Anderson (Minister of the Environment):

... I never thought I would rise in the House to tell members of an opposition party that by their own admission they believe an American political figure with little contact with Canada knows more about what we do in the environment than they do as a group ... Members of the NDP ... are relying upon someone from outside the country as an authority on what happens here.

With respect to the first part of the question, if I may, and with respect to the Quebec livestock case, the Quebec government and the auditor general of Quebec, there has been an investigation. The process has been changed. Any continuation of this investigation would be strictly historical.

(House of Commons Debates, May 18, 2000, p. 7042)
(Débats de la Chambre des Communes, le 18 may 2000, p. 7042)

(f) Biological Diversity / Diversité biologique

Hon. Charles Caccia (Davenport):

... Canada takes great pride in being the first country to have signed the Convention on Biological Diversity at the Rio conference in 1992. As of

May this year, the protocol on biosafety under this convention will be open for signature.

Can the Minister of the Environment indicate whether Canada will be one of the first signatories?

Ms. Paddy Torsney (Parliamentary Secretary to Minister of the Environment):

... the Cartagena protocol set the new global framework for the protection of biodiversity from any potential adverse effects of transboundary movement of living modified organisms resulting from modern biotechnology.

The protocol is very complex and is a demanding instrument. We need to consult with the provinces, with the territories, with Canadians and with industry. We will not waste time but we will do the necessary work to make sure we understand the full implications of the protocol before we sign it.

(House of Commons Debates, May 11, 2000, p. 6712)
(Débats de la Chambre des Communes, le 11 mai 2000, p. 6712)

(g) Gaz à effet de serre / Greenhouse Gas Emissions

M. Guy St-Julien (Abitibi-Baie-James-Nunavik):

... ma question s'adresse au ministre des Ressources naturelles. Le réchauffement planétaire constitue une menace réelle pour les Canadiennes et les Canadiens, ainsi que pour leur mode de vie. À Kyoto, en 1997, le Canada ... s'est engagé à réduire de 6 p. 100 ses émissions de gaz à effet de serre sous les niveaux de 1990 d'ici l'horizon 2008-2012.

Est-ce que le ministre des Ressources naturelles pourrait nous dire quelles mesures les industries canadiennes ont prises pour réduire leurs émissions de gaz à effet de serre?

Hon. Ralph E. Goodale (Minister of Natural Resources):

... I am very happy to have this question on the eve of what will be next week National Mining Week in Canada.

The Canadian mining industry is today releasing a document entitled "Global Climate Change-Taking Action." It recognizes climate change as not just a challenge but also an opportunity. It partners with environmental organizations like the Pembina Institute and Stratos in constructive action. It shows that the Canadian mining industry this year will be more than 4% below its 1990 levels in terms of greenhouse gas emissions, and it promises to do more.

(House of Commons Debates, May 11, 2000, p. 6709)
(Débats de la Chambre des Communes, le 11 mai 2000, p. 6709)

3 *Agriculture*

(a) Foreign Agriculture Subsidies / Subventions agricoles étrangères

Mr. Deepak Obhrai (Calgary East):

WTO negotiations begin next month and the government has no final position on the table. In the meantime our farmers are left to wonder if the government will have their best interests at heart when at the negotiating table. A recent study by the George Morris Centre indicated that Canadian farmers will benefit greatly if this WTO round eliminates all tariff and non-tariff barriers to international trade. Will the government make the elimination of trade distorting agricultural policy the number one priority in Seattle?

Mr. Bob Speller (Parliamentary Secretary to Minister for International Trade):

... I know the hon. member is new to his position as trade critic, but had he been following the subject over the last couple of years, he would know that the standing committee of the House went across the country and consulted with Canadians. The Minister for International Trade consulted with the provinces. They came together with a very strong position for Seattle. I would invite the hon. member, as he is referring to the area of agriculture, to talk to the Canadian Federation of Agriculture and to the different agricultural groups. They strongly support the position of the Government of Canada.

(House of Commons Debates, Friday, October 29, 1999, p. 875)
(Débats de la Chambre des Communes, le 29 octobre 1999, p. 875)

Mr. Ian Murray (Lanark-Carleton):

... my question is for the minister responsible for the Canadian Wheat Board. Yesterday many of us met with a high level delegation from Saskatchewan and Manitoba. It laid the blame for the current farm income crisis on the subsidies and trade distorting export policies of the European Union and the United States of America. What action has the minister taken to address this ongoing, unfair and devastating situation?

Hon. Ralph E. Goodale (Minister of Natural Resources):

... for me this is a never ending crusade in concert with the Prime Minister, the Minister for International Trade, the Minister of Foreign and the Minister of Agriculture and Agri-Food. I pushed for our Canadian trade arguments in personal meetings with Secretary Glickman of the United States and Commissioner Fischler of the European Union. I have done the same with the Australians, the Argentinians, the Brazilians, the Chinese and at the OECD in Paris. I met with the U.S. wheat associates organization and with the trade representatives of 13 U.S. wheat producing states. Just last weekend I carried the same message when I met with the North American millers association in the United States. On this file we hammer on all fronts all the time.

(House of Commons Debates, October 29, 1999, p. 876)

(Débats de la Chambre des Communes, le 29 octobre 1999, p. 876)

M. Odina Desrochers (Lotbinière):

... les négociations à l'OMC débuteront à Seattle le 30 novembre prochain. Dans le secteur agricole, le Canada a respecté les engagements qu'il avait pris dans le cadre des ententes du GATT. Cependant, les autres partenaires commerciaux importants ne respectent pas encore leurs engagements, notamment au chapitre des subventions d'exportation et des règles d'accès aux marchés. Ma question s'adresse au ministre de l'Agriculture. Avant de négocier, ne devrait-il pas exiger que les autres pays respectent d'abord leurs engagements au lieu de placer l'industrie agricole canadienne dans une situation vulnérable?

L'hon. Pierre S. Pettigrew (ministre du Commerce international):

... C'est une question extrêmement pertinente pour la position du Canada au moment où nous nous dirigeons vers l'Organisation mondiale du commerce. Il s'agit en effet d'une constatation que nous faisons. Du côté canadien, nous avons respecté les accords de Marrakech. Nous avons même été un peu en avance. Cela place le Canada dans une position très forte pour exiger à Seattle l'élimination des subventions dans le domaine de l'agriculture et les subventions d'exportation parce que, de notre côté, nous avons respecté ce que nous avions offert par rapport à la gestion de l'offre. Alors cela va améliorer la position du Canada pour obtenir de nouvelles concessions de la part de ses partenaires.

(House of Commons Debates, November 19, 1999, p. 1495)

(Débats de la Chambre des Communes, le 19 novembre 1999, p. 1495)

Mr. Deepak Obhrai (Calgary East):

... reports coming from the WTO in Geneva indicate that a draft agenda for the Seattle negotiations has reached a stalemate. As it stands now the elimination of the export and domestic production subsidies in the agricultural sector could be sidelined as it will be up to various delegations in Seattle's free for all to come up with an agenda. With 11 days remaining before Seattle, why will the minister not guarantee Canadian farmers that the elimination of agricultural subsidies will be his number one priority?

Hon. Pierre S. Pettigrew (Minister for International Trade):

... This is at the top of our list of priorities for the WTO negotiations. I am extremely pleased to tell the House that in early November we developed under Canada's chairmanship a consensus of the 34 democratic countries of this hemisphere, the Americas, to support our position to work very hard on the elimination of export subsidies in the field of agriculture.

(House of Commons Debates, November 19, 1999, p. 1498)
(Débats de la Chambre des Communes, le 19 novembre 1999, p. 1498)

Mr. Howard Hilstrom (Selkirk-Interlake):

... the government has stated that reductions in agriculture subsidies will be a priority in the WTO millennium round of trade negotiations. However, these talks will take up to five years to complete. Farmers cannot wait for five years for these talks to be successful. Foreign subsidies are driving them into bankruptcy today. Why is the Prime Minister refusing to launch a team Canada mission to Europe and Washington aimed at reducing agriculture subsidies immediately?

Mr. Joe McGuire (Parliamentary Secretary to Minister of Agriculture and Agri-Food):

... our government is on record as saying that one of our first priorities is to reduce international trade subsidies and domestic subsidies. That is what we are doing in Seattle today and what we will continue to do.

Mr. Howard Hilstrom (Selkirk-Interlake):

... The Prime Minister has had since 1993 to negotiate reductions in foreign farm subsidies. He has not even tried. Why is the Prime Minister willing to sacrifice thousands of farmers by waiting another five to ten years hoping for subsidy reductions?

Hon. Ralph E. Goodale (Minister of Natural Resources and Minister Responsible for the Canadian Wheat Board):

... in my capacity as Minister responsible for the Canadian Wheat Board, what the hon. gentleman should know is that the Minister of Agriculture and Agri-Food, the Minister for International Trade, the Minister of Foreign Affairs and myself have raised this issue with the Europeans repeatedly, including commissioner Fischler, and with the United States, including the trade representative Charlene Barshefsky and secretary Glickman. We have also raised it with the Argentinians, the Brazilians and the Australians at the OECD.

Mr. Dennis Gruending (Saskatoon-Rosetown-Biggar):

... the government's efforts to get the European and American governments to reduce their agricultural subsidies so far have failed.

On the eve of the Seattle meeting of the WTO, it has become clear that European governments are in no mood to take any action on subsidies. My question is for the Minister responsible for the Canadian Wheat Board. Will the government let farmers pay the price by themselves during a waiting game on European subsidies, or will the government provide the real support Canadian farmers need now to get through the winter?

Hon. Ralph E. Goodale (Minister of Natural Resources and Minister Responsible for the Canadian Wheat Board):

... let me confirm that the government has a multifaceted approach to this problem. It is a serious problem that all of us should treat seriously. In part the answer lies in the aggressive fight that we are fighting and have fought previously in the world trade circles to ensure that the trade-distorting subsidies of other countries are brought down as rapidly as possible. In the meantime we need to keep working on strengthening our farm income safety nets. We have put in a long term way, $1 billion into those safety nets. Another $1 billion ...

Mr. Dennis Gruending (Saskatoon-Rosetown-Biggar):

... The facts remain that the government has slashed agriculture supports more deeply than required under past trade agreements. In fact it cut 40% more deeply than it had to. Now we see that the Europeans will not budge from their position of keeping subsidies in place. The government has a clear responsibility to give our farmers a level of support that is perfectly legal under trade rules and absolutely necessary to save thousands of Canadian family farms. Will the government take up its responsibilities to Canadian farming communities with a meaningful package of emergency assistance, or will it continue to let farmers hang out to dry in the chill wind of the trade fight over agricultural subsidies?

Hon. Ralph E. Goodale (Minister of Natural Resources and Minister Responsible for the Canadian Wheat Board):

... first, we have put together a safety net package with the provinces that totals $1 billion a year ongoing. On top of that, in 1998 and 1999 we have added more than $1 billion more to strengthen that safety net program. In addition, in provinces like Saskatchewan we have topped up the NISA program by $75 million. We have triggered available payments of about $435 million. If the emergency program is fully participated in by the provincial government, $585 million more will be made available to Saskatchewan farmers.

(House of Commons Debates, November 29, 1999, p. 1872)
(Débats de la Chambre des Communes, le 29 novembre 1999, p. 1872)

Mr. Rick Casson (Lethbridge):

... instead of going to bat for our beleaguered Canadian farmers, the international trade minister, to the applause of the Prime Minister, is now spending his time chairing the working group on developing countries. Other countries have made it crystal clear that the reduction of agricultural subsidies is their primary goal and are insisting that they be on the table. Instead of the trade minister spending his time promoting his personal agenda, why is the Prime Minister not insisting that he show some intestinal fortitude and fight for our farmers?

Mr. Bob Speller (Parliamentary Secretary to Minister for International Trade):

... it is somewhat surprising that the hon. member's question is inconsistent with his party's position. How can he on the one hand say that the Government of Canada should be giving more aid to western Canadian farmers when on the other hand his party is asking us to let go of all the barriers that protect some of the farmers in eastern Canada? ...

Mr. Rick Casson (Lethbridge):

... that party's aid package to western Canadian farmers is working so well that its agriculture minister said he would have 100% of the money to Canadian farmers by Christmas, but only 17% of that money has been delivered ... Other countries have made it crystal clear that they are going to stand for their farmers. Why is our trade minister not doing it for our guys?

Mr. Bob Speller (Parliamentary Secretary to Minister for International Trade):

... the Canadian government and the Minister for International Trade are in the forefront on this issue in trying to get the Europeans and the Americans to get rid of their export subsidies. It is those export subsidies which are hurting Canadian farmers. Why is it that his party is the only party not supporting the united front of all farmers across this country which supports the position of the Canadian government at the WTO? ...

(House of Commons Debates, December 2, 1999, p. 2066)
(Débats de la Chambre des Communes, le 2 décembre 1999, p. 2066)

Mr. Rick Casson (Lethbridge):

... Despite the fact that Canada has taken agriculture subsidies away from our farmers, the government has failed to get any commitment from our trading partners to eliminate their trade distorting policies. Canadian farmers from every region of the country are under constant threat of illegal trade actions by our closest trading partners. Our producers need quick action by the government to resolve these disputes. Why does the government not use the same ruthless determination it used when slashing support for our farmers when it is dealing with our trading partners?

Mr. Bob Speller (Parliamentary Secretary to Minister for International Trade):

... that is somewhat funny, coming from the Reform Party which is the only party in the House that did not support the united position of all farm groups across the country on a strong united front for Canada to stand up to the European Union and for Canada to stand up to the United States in terms of export subsidies.

In Seattle today the Minister for International Trade and the Minister of Agriculture and Agri-Food are in very important meetings doing exactly that.

(House of Commons Debates, December 3, 1999, p. 2119)
(Débats de la Chambre des Communes, le 3 décembre 1999, p. 2119)

Mr. Howard Hilstrom (Selkirk-Interlake):

... Canadian farmers' worst fears were realized at the WTO talks in Seattle. The Minister of Agriculture and Agri-Food failed to get any movement on foreign subsidies. Even the Minister for International Trade has been quoted as saying that there was a lack of leadership at those talks. Now that the minister has failed at the WTO, what is he going to do to help farmers suffering from foreign subsidies?

Hon. Lyle Vanclief (Minister of Agriculture and Agri-Food):

... I am sure the hon. member has seen the text and if not, it is available to him, where it was frozen when the talks were suspended. There was a clear reference in that to the elimination of export subsidies. Unfortunately some of the countries could not agree to that and we did not get it. But it certainly was not because Canada was not pushing for it.

Mr. Howard Hilstrom (Selkirk-Interlake):

Given the failure in Seattle, Canada must pursue bilateral agreements on agriculture and provide urgently needed short term assistance. Will the Prime Minister immediately enter into negotiations with the members of the Cairns group and the U.S. to create a trading zone free of agriculture subsidies?

Hon. Lyle Vanclief (Minister of Agriculture and Agri-Food):

... It was very clear last week that the Cairns group, of which Canada is a very important and key member, and the United States stood firm and stood together in the six hour marathon negotiations on agriculture. Unfortunately the European Union could not agree after it went back to consult with its member states. It was not because we caved in. It was because they could not and refused to come our way.

(House of Commons Debates, December 6, 1999, 2173)
(Débats de la Chambre des Communes, le 6 décembre 1999, p. 2173)

Ms. Alexa McDonough (Halifax):

... western farm families are being driven off their land by the deep pockets of European and American treasuries. It is now clearer than ever that European and American agriculture support will not be disappearing any time soon. Will the finance minister at least recognize the real choice that we face and either provide bridge financing now or literally drive thousands of farm families off their land?

Hon. Lyle Vanclief (Minister of Agriculture and Agri-Food):

... the trade minister and I both expressed our disappointment yesterday that the talks in Seattle did not get off to a better start. However we do know that the last round, the Uruguay round, mandated negotiations in agriculture and services. They will start not at the speed unfortunately that we would like them, but in the meantime we continue to work with the provinces and with the industries. I will be meeting with my provincial counterparts later this week in order to continue those discussions and on how collectively we can support those farmers who are badly in need of that support.

(House of Commons Debates, December 7, 1999, p. 2283)
(Débats de la Chambre des Communes, le 7 décembre 1999, p. 2283)

Mr. Dick Proctor (Palliser):

... the agriculture minister is begging other nations to reduce their trade distorting subsidies which he said last week are the root cause of the devastating drop in the incomes of Canadian grain farmers. Whether they are the culprits or not, the minister knows that reducing subsidies are years if not light years away. By adopting such a paws up supine position, is the minister suggesting that Canada is so impoverished that it cannot afford to invest in our grain farmers to the same extent that other nations are investing in theirs?

Hon. Lyle Vanclief (Minister of Agriculture and Agri-Food):

... we have the support of our farmers across Canada in addressing the unfortunate circumstances they are in due to a number of issues, whether it be the weather, international market prices, or an unfair and unlevel playing field as far as subsidies are concerned. Probably our pockets in Canada are not as deep as those in some other countries. We recognize that. We as the federal government are there. I would encourage the hon. member to return to his home province to be there too with the federal government.

(House of Commons Debates, February 17, 2000, p. 3677)
(Débats de la Chambre des Communes, le 17 février 2000, p. 3677)

Mrs. Rose-Marie Ur (Lambton-Kent-Middlesex):

... the Minister of Agriculture and Agri-Food has just returned from a trade mission to China and the Philippines. Could the minister inform the House as to the trade benefits for Canadian farmers resulting from this mission?

Hon. Lyle Vanclief (Minister of Agriculture and Agri-Food):

... the delegation was very successful on two accounts.

I had the opportunity to meet with Vice Premier Weng Giabao in China and the president of the Philippines and their respective ministers of agriculture to stress the importance of all of us working together to eliminate domestic and export subsidies around the world.

In China I was able to sign a protocol that will allow the Canadian pork industry to now ship pork into China, and also another protocol that will allow Canada to be the first and only country at this time to sell seed potatoes into that market.

(House of Commons Debates, May 1, 2000, p. 6210)
(Débats de la Chambre des Communes, le 1er mai 2000, p. 6210)

(b) Barriers to International Trade / Obstacles au commerce international

Mr. Darrel Stinson (Okanagan-Shuswap):

... it was a very simple question. Will you put trade barriers at the top of your priority in Seattle in order for our farmers and all of our trade people in Canada to benefit? The answer is either yes or no. It is simple.

Mr. Bob Speller (Parliamentary Secretary to Minister for International Trade):

... I know the member was involved in some of those consultations and he would know that the answer certainly is yes. The Government of Canada feels that these export subsidies that are being brought on by both the Americans and the Europeans are bad for the Canadian economy and are hurting Canadian farmers. We have put that at the top of our priority to get rid of.

(House of Commons Debates, October 29, 1999, p. 875)
(Débats de la Chambre des Communes, le 29 octobre 1999, p. 875)

(c) Canadian Farmers / Agriculteurs canadiens

Mr. Rick Casson (Lethbridge):

... despite being vindicated by the U.S. International Trade Commission several weeks ago, Canadian farmers are facing further trade challenges from the United States. North Dakota is looking to enforce country of origin labelling and is preparing to challenge Canadian durum exports. Our farmers have suffered enough under the government's weak trade position. It is past time to get tough at the trade table. Will the trade minister guarantee our beleaguered producers that there will be no further border closures? We need positive action and we need it now.

Hon. Harbance Singh Dhaliwal (Minister of Fisheries and Oceans):

... the Minister for International Trade will be in Seattle. This morning, in fact, the minister announced that Canada and China have reached agreement on a wide range of market access issues relating to China's entry into the World Trade Organization. This means that Canadian products will have better access to markets in China. That is good news for Canadians, it is good news for farmers and it is good news for our export business ...

(House of Commons Debates, November 26, 1999, p. 1808)
(Débats de la Chambre des Communes, le 26 novembre 1999, p. 1808)

Mr. Larry McCormick (Hastings-Frontenac-Lennox and Addington):

... this week in Seattle, Washington ministers of the 135 member nations of the World Trade Organization will launch the next round of trade talks on agriculture. WTO critics complain that the WTO favours big business interests and undermines the survival of the family farm which is very important to all of us. What are these talks going to do for the Canadian family farm?

Mr. Joe McGuire (Parliamentary Secretary to Minister of Agriculture and Agri-Food):

... Canada's agricultural industry, especially western Canada's agricultural industry, depends on international trade rules that all countries abide by. Canada is in Seattle to put those agreements in place so our farmers will be competing against farmers, not against foreign treasuries.

(House of Commons Debates, November 29, 1999, p. 1873)
(Débats de la Chambre des Communes, le 29 novembre 1999, p. 1873)

(d) Western Cattle Producers / Éleveurs de bétail de l'Ouest

Mr. Ken Epp (Elk Island):

... Western cattle producers, facing a 6% tariff from the Americans, spent their own money to travel to the U.S. to hammer out proposals to end the dispute. But the trade and agriculture ministers refuse to listen and do nothing to defend the farmers.

Will the minister act immediately to implement the ranchers' solutions which they hammered out to end this discrimination tariff?

Mr. Bob Speller (Parliamentary Secretary to Minister for International Trade):

... the hon. member should know that when the decision came down it was a win for Canada. We won a lot of this decision ...

Before we sat down and before we put forward the Canadian position on this, we talked to the groups, the industry and the provinces to make sure the position being put forward by the Government of Canada was best reflective of their views. We will continue to do that.

(House of Commons Debates, October 15, 1999, p. 206)
(Débats de la Chambre des Communes, le 15 octobre 1999, p. 206)

(e) Canadian Cattle Exports / Exportations de bétail canadien

Mr. Rick Casson (Lethbridge):

... Canadian beef producers recently dodged a bullet when the USITC ruled that Canadian cattle exports do not cause injury to the U.S. cattle industry.

In order to avoid further challenges of this type the international definition of dumping must be changed to reflect predatory pricing and selling below home market prices rather than the current definition. Will the trade minister assure producers that he will immediately renegotiate this definition, or will he continue to leave our producers exposed to the threat of million dollar legal battles?

Hon. Pierre S. Pettigrew (Minister for International Trade):

... we are going into important trade negotiations and indeed a number of topics will be raised. We are well aware of the cattle situation raised by the opposition member. I can tell him that we are giving our full attention to the cattle situation in our country and their export to the United States in particular.

Mr. Rick Casson (Lethbridge):

... the cattle industry in Canada spent nearly $5 million in legal fees fighting these complaints by protectionist American producers, money that did not have to be spent if the government had implemented the changes requested by Canadian producers. It could have spent that money on research and promotion.

Why will the agriculture minister not implement the changes recommended by industry, or is he content to do nothing and leave Canadian producers again exposed to these multimillion dollar battles?

Hon. Lyle Vanclief (Minister of Agriculture and Agri-Food):

Mr. Speaker, the hon. member knows full well that it is not a situation of our doing nothing. We were supporting the Canadian Cattlemen's Association in that challenge. The government was there. I congratulate Canadian cattlemen for the work they did. It was truly a team Canada effort. There are different views on the way dumping or anti-dumping is treated. Some of our sectors are import sensitive and some are export sensitive. The horticultural industry has a different view than the cattle industry. I had a meeting with the cattle industry this week in that regard and it understands that too.

As my colleague the trade minister said, we will be working on this matter as we go into the important start of the WTO.

(House of Commons Debates, November 19, 1999, p. 1496)
(Débats de la Chambre des Communes, le 19 novembre 1999, p. 1496)

(f) Grain

Mr. John Harvard (Charleswood St. James-Assiniboia):

... Well over 70% of the grain produced in western Canada is exported out of the country. Therefore the next round of WTO negotiations beginning in Seattle next month raises several critical issues ranging from those damaging export subsidies to support for the Canadian Wheat Board. What is the minister doing to ensure that farmers will gain maximum benefits from the international marketplace?

Hon. Ralph E. Goodale (Minister of Natural Resources and Minister Responsible for the Canadian Wheat Board):

... I have met with the U.S. wheat associates organization and with the representatives of 13 American wheat producing states. This weekend I will be meeting with most of the major U.S. grain milling companies. The message is always consistent. We are each other's best customers. We have a huge amount in common. Let us not batter away at each other. Instead, let us make common cause against the subsidies, the distortions and the unfair market access rules of the European Union which are the most pernicious source of damage to both Canadian and American farmers and the world's grain trade.

(House of Commons Debates, October 19, 1999, p. 503)
(Débats de la Chambre des Communes, le 19 octobre 1999, p. 503)

4 Human Rights / Droits de la personne

(a) Child Labour / Travail des enfants

Mrs. Sue Barnes (London West):

... my question is for the Minister of Labour. In June of this year, the general conference of the International Labour Organization unanimously adopted the Convention on the Worst Forms of Child Labour. This was to protect vulnerable children. Given Canada's human security agenda, I ask the minister today if Canada is planning to ratify this agreement. What are we going to do?

Hon. Claudette Bradshaw (Minister of Labour):

... in the Speech from the Throne, the Government of Canada underlined Canada's commitment to champion efforts to eliminate exploitation of children and to reach international agreements to protect the rights of children. We have already started working with the provinces and territories as well as our social partners toward Canadian ratification of the new ILO convention.

(House of Commons Debates, November 25, 1999, p. 1759)
(Débats de la Chambre des Communes, le 25 novembre 1999, p. 1759)

5 Foreign Affairs / Affaires étrangères

(a) Defence / Défense

Mr. Gordon Earle (Halifax West):

... Canada is the 51st state of the U.S., according to a top U.S. defence official. The U.S. is preparing to deploy a national missile defence system, violating the anti-ballistic missile treaty and angering and provoking other powers, and it expects this government to play ball. Will the government say no to another arms build-up, no to supporting the U.S. missile defence system and insist that this entire matter be brought before the United Nations? Or, is the government indeed comfortable with being called the 51st state?

Mr. Denis Paradis (Parliamentary Secretary to Minister of Foreign Affairs):

... the United States has not taken a decision yet to deploy a national missile defence system and Canada has not been formally asked to participate in an NMD system by the U.S. Consequently, it is a completely hypothetical question. We cannot yet take a position. There are still too many unknowns. I have to add that the U.S. has confirmed that the deployment of a national missile defence system would require a change to the existing anti-ballistic missile treaty of 1972. The U.S. is pursuing discussions with Russia on this matter.

(House of Commons Debates, March 16, 2000, p. 4773)
(Débats de la Chambre des Communes, le 16 mars 2000, p. 4773)

(b) Antipersonnel Mines / Mines anti-personnelles

Mr. René Laurin (Joliette):

... Canada has assumed the lead role internationally in opposing the use of antipersonnel mines. It signed the UN international treaty on this. It passed Bill C-22 banning these mines and with great pomp and circumstance made the announcement in November 1997 that it had destroyed the last one, boasting about this every chance it got. How can the minister explain that Canadian soldiers are using Claymore mines in East Timor, since these are as deadly as other antipersonnel mines?

Hon. Arthur C. Eggleton (Minister of National Defence):

Claymores are not land mines. Claymores are used as any other weapon would be used in a defensive fashion. They create a shotgun approach. If the troops that are on the defensive are outnumbered by those on the offence, they would only be used under those kind of circumstances, and with somebody actually pulling a trigger. They are not like a land mine that is put in the ground and which somebody trips over to set it off. They are not in the same category. Canada fully complies with the anti-personnel land mines treaty.

(House of Commons Debates, February 17, 2000, p. 3678)
(Débats de la Chambre des Communes, le 17 février 1999, p. 3678)

(c) Nuclear Disarmament / Désarmement nucléaire

Mr. Ted McWhinney (Vancouver Quadra):

... my question is for the Minister of Foreign Affairs.
   Will the minister tell the House what are the implications of the U.S. proposal for a national missile defence system on the international law of nuclear disarmament, in particular the anti-ballistic missiles treaty and interim agreement on protocol of 1972, but also the non-proliferation treaty negotiations that resume in late April?

Hon. Lloyd Axworthy (Minister of Foreign Affairs):

... beginning this coming month the nations of the world will come together to talk about the reinforcement of the non-proliferation treaty.
   The position we take in Canada is that we have to do everything possible to encourage the nuclear states to live up to the commitment to continue to disarm.

Anything that would interfere with that, which would suggest that there is a retreat from that kind of commitment, I think would have a very serious impact on our security as a country and on the security of other countries, because one of the most scary threats that we still face is the threat of nuclear proliferation.

(House of Commons Debates, March 31, 2000, p. 5528)
(Débats de la Chambre des Communes, le 31 mars 2000, p. 5528)

Treaty Action Taken by Canada in 1999 / Mesures prises par le Canada en matière de traités en 1999

compiled by / préparé par
ANDRÉ BERGERON

I BILATERAL

Algeria
Convention between the Government of Canada and the Government of the People's Democratic Republic of Algeria for the Avoidance of Double Taxation and the Prevention of Fiscal Evasion with Respect to Taxes on Income (with Protocol). Algiers, February 28, 1999.

Antigua and Barbuda
Agreement between the Government of Canada and the Government of Antigua and Barbuda Regarding the Sharing of Forfeited or Confiscated Assets and Equivalent Fund. St. John's, October 14, 1999. *Entered into force* October 14, 1999. CTS 1999/36.

Argentina
Exchange of Notes between the Government of Canada and the Government of the Republic of Argentina constituting an Agreement for the Establishment of a Quebec Office in the Argentine Republic. Buenos Aires, October 13 and October 29, 1999. *Entered into force* October 29, 1999. CTS 1999/50.

Armenia
Agreement between the Government of Canada and the Government of the Republic of Armenia on Trade and Commerce. Ottawa, May 8, 1997. *Entered into force* April 1, 1999. CTS 1999/12.

Agreement between the Government of Canada and the Government of the Republic of Armenia for the Promotion and Protection of Investments (with Annex). Ottawa, May 8, 1997. *Entered into force* March 29, 1999. CTS 1999/22.

Austria
Audio-Visual Co-production Agreement between the Government of Canada and the Government of the Republic of Austria (with Annex). Vienna, June 11, 1999.

Protocol to Amend the Convention between the Government of Canada and the Government of the Republic of Austria for the Avoidance of Double Taxation and the Prevention of Fiscal Evasion with Respect to Taxes on Income, done at Vienna on December 19, 1976. Vienna, June 15, 1999.

Bahamas
Agreement on Rum between the Government of Canada and the Government of the Commonwealth of the Bahamas. Ottawa, February 12, 1999. *Entered into force* February 12, 1999. CTS 1999/8.

Bulgaria
Convention between the Government of Canada and the Government of the Republic of Bulgaria for the Avoidance of Double Taxation and the Prevention of Fiscal Evasion with Respect to Taxes

on Income (with Protocol). Ottawa, March 3, 1999.

Brazil
Audio-Visual Co-production Agreement between the Government of Canada and the Government of the Federative Republic of Brazil. Brasilia, January 27, 1995. *Entered into force* January 5, 1999. CTS 1999/53.

Chile
Convention between the Government of Canada and the Government of the Republic of Chile for the Avoidance of Double Taxation and the Prevention of Fiscal Evasion with Respect to Taxes on Income and on Capital (with Protocol). Santiago, January 21, 1998. *Entered into force* October 28, 1999. CTS 1999/37.

Agreement between the Government of Canada and the Government of the Republic of Chile for the Avoidance of Double Taxation of Income from the Operation of Ships and Aircraft. Santiago, July 30, 1992. *Entered into force* January 1, 1996. CTS 1996/5. *Terminated* October 28 1999 upon entry into force of new agreement.

First Additional Protocol to the Free Trade Agreement between the Government of Canada and the Government of the Republic of Chile, done in Santiago on December 4, 1996 (with Annex). Toronto, November 4,1999.

China
Consular Agreement between the Government of Canada and the Government of the People's Republic of China. Ottawa, November 28, 1997. *Entered into force* March 11, 1999. CTS 1999/9.

Costa Rica
Agreement between the Government of Canada and the Government of the Republic of Costa Rica for the Promotion and Protection of Investments (with Annex). San José, March 18, 1998. *Entered into force* September 29, 1999. CTS 1999/43.

Croatia
Agreement on Social Security between the Government of Canada and the Government of the Republic of Croatia (with Administrative Arrangement). Zagreb, April 22, 1998. *Entered into force* May 1, 1999. CTS 1999/5.

Agreement between the Government of Canada and the Government of the Republic of Croatia for the Avoidance of Double Taxation and the Prevention of Fiscal Evasion with Respect to Taxes on Income and on Capital (with Protocol). Ottawa, December 9, 1997. *Entered into force* November 23, 1999, with effect from January 1, 2000. CTS 1999/46.

Cuba
Audio-Visual Co-production Agreement between the Government of Canada and the Government of the Republic of Cuba (with Annex). Havana, April 27, 1998. *Entered into force* September 1, 1999. CTS 1999/26.

Treaty between the Government of Canada and the Government of the Republic of Cuba on the Serving of Penal Sentences. Havana, January 7, 1999. *Entered into force* August 10, 1999. CTS 1999/24.

Egypt
Agreement between the Government of Canada and the Government of the Arab Republic of Egypt regarding Cooperation on Consular Elements of Family Matters. Cairo, November 10, 1997. *Entered into force* October 1, 1999. CTS 1999/27.

El Salvador
Agreement between the Government of Canada and the Government of the Republic of El Salvador for the Promotion and Protection of Investments (with Annexes). San Salvador, May 31, 1999.

European Atomic Energy Community
Agreement between the Government of Canada and the European Atomic Energy Community for Cooperation in the area of Nuclear Research. Ottawa,

December 17, 1998. *Entered into force* January 29, 1999.

European Community
Agreement between the Government of Canada and the European Communities Regarding the Application of Their Competition Laws. Bonn, June 17, 1999. *Entered into force* June 17, 1999. CTS 1999/2.

Agreement Amending the Agreement for Scientific and Technological Cooperation between the Government of Canada and the European Community, done at Halifax on June 17, 1995. Ottawa, December 17, 1998. *Entered into force* April 30, 1999. CTS 1999/17.

Finland
Exchange of Notes Amending the Agreement between the Government of Canada and the Government of Finland for Air Services between and beyond Their Respective Territories, done at Helsinki on May 28, 1990 (with Annexes). Helsinki, September 1, 1999. *Entered into force* October 1, 1999.

Audio-Visual Co-production Agreement between the Government of Canada and the Government of the Republic of Finland (with Annex). Stockholm, March 31, 1998. *Entered into force* April 1, 1999. CTS 1999/11.

Greece
Extradition Treaty between the Government of Canada and the Government of the Hellenic Republic. Ottawa, November 3, 1999.

Grenada
Agreement on Social Security between the Government of Canada and the Government of Grenada. St-George's, January 8, 1998. *Entered into force* February 1, 1999. CTS 1999/51.

Hungary
Air Transport Agreement between the Government of Canada and the Government of the Republic of Hungary (with Annex). Budapest, December 7, 1998. *Entered into force* June 10, 1999. CTS 1999/30.

International Civil Aviation Organization
Amendment to the Supplementary Agreement between the Government of Canada and the International Civil Aviation Organization regarding the headquarters of the International Civil Aviation Organization, done at Montreal on September 16, 1980 (with Annexes). Montreal, May 28, 1999. *Entered into force* May 28, 1999. *Remains in force* for 20 years, from November 1, 1996 to November 30, 2016. This agreement supersedes the Supplementary Agreement signed on September 16, 1980. CTS 1999/20.

Israel
Treaty between the Government of Canada and the Government of the State of Israël on Mutual Assistance in Criminal Matters. Ottawa, October 25, 1999.

Italy
Exchange of Notes Constituting an Agreement between the Government of Canada and the Government of the Italian Republic Providing for Military Exercises of the Italian Armed Forces in Canada (Goose Bay). Rome, September 3, 1999. *Entered into force* September 3, 1999. CTS 1999/49.

Jamaica
Treaty between the Government of Canada and the Government of Jamaica on Mutual Legal Assistance in Criminal Matters. Ottawa, June 3, 1999.

Agreement between the Government of Canada and the Government of Jamaica Regarding the Sharing of the Proceeds of the Disposition of Forfeited Assets and Equivalent Funds. Ottawa, June 3, 1999. *Entered into force* June 3, 1999. CTS 1999/19.

Japan
Protocol Amending the Convention between the Government of Canada and the Government of Japan for the Avoidance of Double Taxation and the Prevention of Fiscal Evasion with Respect to Taxes on Income, done at

Tokyo on May 7, 1986. Ottawa, February 19, 1999.

Jordan

Convention between the Government of Canada and the Hashemite Kingdom of Jordan for the Avoidance of Double Taxation and the Prevention of Fiscal Evasion with Respect to Taxes on Income (with Protocol). Amman, September 6, 1999.

Korea

Agreement between the Government of Canada and the Government of the Republic of Korea on the Exchange and Protection of Classified Military Information. Ottawa, July 5, 1999. *Entered into force* August 11, 1999. CTS 1999/28.

Agreement on Social Security between the Government of Canada and the Government of the Republic of Korea (with Protocol). Seoul, January 10, 1997. *Entered into force* May 1, 1999. CTS 1999/6.

Agreement between the Government of Canada and the Government of the Republic of Korea on Telecommunications Equipment Procurement. Ottawa, July 5, 1999.

Lebanon

Agreement between the Government of Canada and the Government of the Lebanese Republic for the Promotion and Protection of Investment (with Annexes). Ottawa, April 11, 1997. *Entered into force* June 19, 1999. CTS 1999/15.

Luxembourg

Convention between the Government of Canada and the Government of the Grand Duchy of Luxembourg for the Avoidance of Double Taxation and the Prevention of Fiscal Evasion with Respect to Taxes on Income and on Capital. Brussels, September 10, 1999.

Mexico

Exchange of Notes Amending the Air Transport Agreement between the Government of Canada and the Government of the United Mexican States,

done at Mexico on December 21, 1961. Mexico, April 9, 1999.

Agreement between the Government of Canada and the Government of the United Mexican States Concerning the Provision of Satellite Services. Mexico, April 9, 1999.

Netherlands

Protocol Amending the Convention between the Government of Canada and the Government of the Kingdom of the Netherlands for the Avoidance of Double Taxation and the Prevention of Fiscal Evasion with Respect to Taxes on Income, done at The Hague on May 27, 1986, as amended (with Protocol). The Hague, August 25, 1997. *Entered into force* January 15, 1999. CTS 1999/3.

Nigeria

Agreement between the Government of Canada and the Government of the Federal Republic of Nigeria for the Avoidance of Double Taxation and the Prevention of Fiscal Evasion with Respect to Taxes on Income and Capital Gains (with Protocol). Abuja, August 4, 1992. *Entered into force* November 16, 1999. CTS 1999/48.

Norway

Audio-Visual Co-production Agreement between the Government of Canada and the Government of the Kingdom of Norway (with Annex). Oslo, April 2, 1998. *Entered into force* August 20, 1999. CTS 1999/25.

Treaty between the Government of Canada and the Government of the Kingdom of Norway on Mutual Assistance in Criminal Matters. Ottawa, September 16, 1998. *Entered into force* January 14, 1999. CTS 1999/2.

Philippines

Audio-Visual Co-production Agreement between the Government of Canada and the Government of the Republic of the Philippines. Manila, October 16, 1998. *Entered into force* September 30, 1999. CTS 1999/35.

Supplementary Agreement to the Agreement on Social Security between the Government of Canada and the Government of the Republic of the Philippines, done at Winnipeg on September 9, 1994. Winnipeg, November 13, 1999.

Poland

Agreement between the Government of Canada and the Government of the Republic of Poland on Film and Television Co-Production (with Annex). Ottawa, May 27, 1996. *Entered into force* September 3, 1999. CTS 1999/44.

Portugal

Convention between the Government of Canada and the Government of the Portuguese Republic for the Avoidance of Double Taxation and the Prevention of Fiscal Evasion with Respect to Taxes on Income (with Protocol). Ottawa, June 14, 1999.

Romania

Treaty between the Government of Canada and the Government of Romania on Mutual Legal Assistance. Ottawa, May 25, 1998. *Entered into force* June 30, 1999. CTS 1999/29.

South Africa

Treaty on Extradition between the Government of Canada and the Government of the Republic of South Africa. Durban, November 12, 1999.

Treaty between the Government of Canada and the Government of the Republic of South Africa on Mutual Legal Assistance in Criminal Matters. Durban, November 12, 1999.

Switzerland

Mutual Recognition Agreement on Conformity Assessment between the Government of Canada and the Government of the Swiss Confederation. Ottawa, December 3, 1998. *Entered into force* May 1, 1999.

Trinidad and Tobago

Agreement on Social Security between the Government of Canada and the Government of the Republic of Trinidad and Tobago. Port of Spain, April 9, 1997. *Entered into force* July 1, 1999. CTS 1999/10.

Turkey

Exchange of Notes Constituting an Agreement between the Government of Canada and the Government of the Republic of Turkey on Property Reciprocity. Ottawa, August 24, 1999.

Exchange of Notes between Canada and Turkey Regarding the Issuance of Multi-Entry Visas to Diplomatic Representatives, Officials and Non-Immigrants. Ankara, August 21, 1956. *Entered into force* September 21, 1956. *Terminated* on December 1, 1999 by Exchange of Notes.

Ukraine

Agreement between the Government of Canada and the Government of Ukraine on Air Transport. Kyiv, January 28, 1999. *Entered into force* April 28, 1999. CTS 1999/32.

Agreement between Canada and Ukraine on Mutual Assistance in Criminal Matters. Ottawa, September 23, 1996. *Entered into force* March 1, 1999. CTS 1999/7.

Agreement between the Government of Canada and the Government of Ukraine for Cooperation in the Peaceful Uses of Nuclear Energy (with Annexes). Ottawa, December 20, 1995. *Entered into force* January 14, 1999. CTS 1999/16.

United States of America

Protocol Amending the Agreement for Cooperation Concerning Civil Uses of Atomic Energy between the Government of Canada and the Government of the United States of America, done at Washington, DC, on June 15, 1955 (as amended). Washington, DC, June 23, 1999. *Entered into force* December 13, 1999. RTC 1999/40.

Exchange of Notes between the Government of Canada and the Government of the United States of America further to a Treaty between the Government of the United States of America Relating to Cooperative Development of the Water Resources of the Columbia

River Basin, permitting the disposal of the Canadian Entitlement in the United States of America, done at Washington, DC, on January 17, 1961. Washington, DC, March 31, 1999. *Entered into force* March 31, 1999. CTS 1999/18.

Exchange of Letters Amending the Softwood Lumber Agreement between the Government of Canada and the Government of the United States of America, done at Washington, DC, on May 29, 1996. Washington DC, August 26, 1999. *Entered into force* August 26, 1999. RTC 1999/33.

Exchange of Notes Constituting an Agreement Concerning the Canadian Periodical Advertising Services Market between the Government of Canada and the Government of the United States. Washington, June 3, 1999. *Entered into force* June 3, 1999. RTC 1999/21.

Agreement between the Government of Canada and the Government of the United States of America for the Establishment of a Binational Educational Exchange Foundation. Washington, November 15, 1999. *Entered into force* November 15, 1999. CTS 1999/39.

Exchange of Notes Constituting an Agreement between the Government of Canada and the Government of the United States of America to Extend for Ten Years the Agreement of June 17, 1986, Providing for the Continued Operation and Maintenance of the Torpedo Test Range in the Strait of Georgia and to Amend the Annex Attached to the Exchange of Notes of January 13 and April 14, 1976. Ottawa, December 17, 1999. *Entered into force* December 17, 1999. CTS 1999/45.

Protocol between the Government of Canada and the Government of the United States of America Amending the 1916 Convention between the United Kingdom and the United States of America for the Protection of Migratory Birds in Canada and the United States. Washington, December 14,

1995. *Entered into force* October 7, 1999. CTS 1999/34.

Exchange of Notes between the Government of Canada and the Government of the United States of America Constituting an Agreement Relating to the Treaty between the Government of Canada and the Government of the United States of America Concerning Pacific Salmon (with Annexes), done at Ottawa on January 28, 1985. Washington, DC, June 30, 1999. *Entered into force* June 30, 1999.

Protocol Amending the Agreement for Cooperation in the Boreal Ecosystem Atmosphere Study (BOREAS) between the Government of Canada and the Government of the United States of America, done at Washington, DC, on April 18, 1994. Washington, November 30, 1999. *Entered into force* November 30, 1999. CTS 1999/47.

Uruguay

Agreement between the Government of Canada and the Government of the Eastern Republic of Uruguay for the Protection and Promotion of Investment (with Annexes). Ottawa, October 29, 1997. *Entered into force* June 2, 1999. CTS 1999/31.

Agreement on Social Security between the Government of Canada and the Government of the Eastern Republic of Uruguay. Ottawa, June 2, 1999.

Uzbekistan

Convention between the Government of Canada and the Government of the Republic of Uzbekistan for the Avoidance of Double Taxation and the Prevention of Fiscal Evasion with Respect to Taxes on Income (with Protocol). Ottawa, June 17, 1999.

II   MULTILATERAL

Air

Ratification to Montreal Protocol No.4 to Amend the Convention for the Unification of Certain Rules Relating to International Carriage by Air, signed at Warsaw on October 12, 1929 as amended by the Protocol, done at The Hague, September 28, 1955, signed in Montreal, September 25, 1975. *Signed* by Canada September 30, 1975. *Entered into force* June 14, 1998. *Ratified* by Canada August 27, 1999. *Entered into force* for Canada November 25, 1999. CTS 1999/42.

Accession to the Convention, Supplementary to the Warsaw Convention for the Unification of Certain Rules Relating to International Carriage by Air Performed by a Person Other than the Contracting Carrier. *Signed* in Guadalajara, September 18, 1961. *Entered into force* May 1, 1964. *Accession* by Canada September 1, 1999. *Entered into force* for Canada November 30, 1999. CTS 1999/41.

Protocol on the Authentic Quadrilingual Text of the Convention on International Civil Aviation (Chicago, 1944). Montreal, September 30, 1977. *Accession* by Canada March 23, 1994. *Entered into force* September 16, 1999. *Entered into force* for Canada September 16, 1999. CTS 1999/54.

Conservation
Amendment to Article XXI of the Convention on International Trade in Endangered Species of Wild Fauna and Flora (CITES), done at Washington, DC, on March 3, 1973, as amended. Gaborone (Botswana), April 30, 1983. *Acceptance* by Canada February 1, 1999.

Agreement on International Humane Trapping Standards between the European Community, Canada and the Russian Federation. Brussels, December 15, 1997. *Ratified* by Canada May 31, 1999. *Provisionally applied* from June 1, 1999.

Criminal — Bribery
Convention on Combatting the Bribery of Foreign Public Officials in International Business Transactions. Paris, December 17, 1997. *Signed* by Canada December 17, 1997. *Ratified* by Canada December 17, 1998. *Entered into force* February 15, 1999. *Entered into force*

for Canada February 15, 1999. CTS 1999/23.

Criminal — Corruption
Inter-American Convention against Corruption. Caracas, March 29, 1996. *Entered into force* March 6, 1997. *Signed* by Canada June 8, 1999. Not yet in force for Canada.

Culture
Convention for the Protection of Cultural Property in the Event of Armed Conflict. *Done* in The Hague May, 14 1954. *Accession* by Canada December 11, 1998. *Entered into force* for Canada March 11, 1999. CTS 1999/52.

Disarmament
Convention on the Prohibition of the Use, Stockpiling, Production and Transfer of Anti-Personnel Mines and on Their Destruction. Oslo, September 18, 1997. *Signed* by Canada December 3, 1997. *Ratified* by Canada December 3, 1997. *Entered into force* for Canada March 1, 1999. CTS 1999/4.

Amendment to the Treaty on Conventional Armed Forces in Europe. Istanbul, November 19, 1999. *Signed* by Canada November 19, 1999.

Environment
Amendment to the Montreal Protocol on Substances That Deplete the Ozone Layer. *Done* at Montreal on 17 September 1997. *Ratified* by Canada March 27, 1998. *Entered into force* November 10, 1999. *Entered into force* for Canada November 10, 1999.

Protocol to the Convention on Long-Range Transboundary Air Pollution to Abate Acidification, Eutrophication and Ground Level Ozone. *Done* at Geneva on November 13, 1979. Gothenburg, November 13, 1999. *Signed* by Canada December 1, 1999.

Law of the Sea
Agreement for the Implementation of the Provisions of the United Nations Convention on the Law of the Sea of 10 December, 1982, Relating to the Conservation and Management of Straddling Fish Stocks and Highly Migratory

Fish Stocks (with Annexes). New York, December 4, 1995. *Signed* by Canada December 4, 1995. *Ratified* by Canada August 3, 1999.

Navigation — Ships/Vessels — Officers/ Crew
1997 Amendment to the International Convention on Standards of Training, Certification and Watchkeeping for Seafarers. *Done* at London July 7, 1978, as amended (Resolution MSC.66(68)). London, June 4, 1997. *Tacit acceptance* by all parties July 1, 1998 (adopted in accordance with Article VIII(b)(vi)(2) (bb) of the International Convention for the Safety of Life at Sea, done at London on November 1, 1974). *Entered into force* January 1, 1999. *Entered into force* for Canada January 1, 1999.

1997 Amendment to the Seafarers' Training, Certification and Watchkeeping Code (Resolution MSC.67(68)). London, June 4, 1997. *Tacit acceptance* by all parties July 1, 1998 (adopted in accordance with Article VIII(b)(vi)(2) (bb) of the International Convention for the Safety of Life at Sea, done at London on November 1, 1974). *Entered into force* January 1, 1999. *Entered into force* for Canada January 1, 1999.

Postal Matters
Acts of the XXII Congress of the Universal Postal Union. Beijing, September 14, 1999. *Signed* by Canada September 14, 1999.

Weapons
Inter-American Convention on Transparency in Conventional Weapons Acquisitions. Washington, March 31, 1999. *Signed* by Canada June 7, 1999. *Ratified* by Canada June 7, 1999.

Trade
Acceptance of the Fifth Protocol to the General Agreement on Trade in Services. *Done* at Marrakech April 15, 1994. Geneva, February 27, 1998. *Acceptance* by Canada January 18, 1999. *Entered into force* March 1, 1999. *Entered into force* for Canada March 1, 1999. CTS 1999/13.

Acceptance of the Amendment to Article XXI of the Convention on International Trade in Endangered Species of Wild Fauna and Flora (CITES), adopted at Gaborone, Botswana, April 30, 1983. Gland, May 17, 1983. *Acceptance* by Canada on February 1, 1999.

Trade — Law
Agreement Establishing the Advisory Centre on WTO Law. Seattle, December 1, 1999. *Signed* by Canada December 1, 1999.

Trade — Wheat
Food Aid Convention 1999 (part of the International Grains Agreement). London, April 13, 1999. *Signed* by Canada June 21, 1999. *Ratified* by Canada June 21, 1999.

Food Aid Convention 1995 (part of the International Grains Agreement). London, December 7, 1994. *Signed* by Canada June 26, 1995. *Ratified* by Canada June 26, 1995. *Entered into force* for Canada July 1, 1995. *Terminated* by the entry into force of the Food Aid Convention 1999.

Transport
Agreement Concerning the Establishing of Global Technical Regulations for Wheeled Vehicles, Equipment and Parts Which Can Be Fitted and/or Be Used on Wheeled Vehicles. *Done* at Geneva, June 25, 1998. *Signed* by Canada June 22, 1999. Signature done without reservation as to ratification, acceptance, or approval.

I   BILATÉRAUX

Afrique du Sud
Traité d'extradition entre le Gouvernement du Canada et le Gouvernement de la République d'Afrique du Sud. Durban, le 12 novembre 1999.

Traité d'entraide judiciaire en matière pénale entre le Gouvernement du Canada et le Gouvernement de la République d'Afrique du Sud. Durban, le 12 novembre 1999.

Algérie
Convention entre le Gouvernement du Canada et le Gouvernement de la République algérienne démocratique et populaire en vue d'éviter les doubles impositions et de prévenir l'évasion fiscale en matière d'impôts sur le revenu (avec Protocole). Alger, le 28 février 1999.

Antigua-et-Barbuda
Accord entre le Gouvernement du Canada et le Gouvernement d'Antigua-et-Barbuda sur le partage des biens confisqués et des sommes d'argent équivalentes. St. John's, le 14 octobre 1999. *En vigueur* le 14 octobre 1999. RTC 1999/36.

Argentine
Échange de Notes entre le Gouvernement du Canada et le Gouvernement de la République d'Argentine constituant un Accord portant sur l'ouverture d'un Bureau du Québec en République argentine. Buenos Aires, les 13 et 19 octobre, 1999. *En vigueur* le 29 octobre 1999. RTC 1999/50.

Arménie
Accord de commerce entre le Gouvernement du Canada et le Gouvernement de la République d'Arménie. Ottawa, le 8 mai 1997. *En vigueur* le 1er avril 1999. RTC 1999/12.

Accord entre le Gouvernement du Canada et le Gouvernement de la République d'Arménie pour l'encouragement et la protection des investissements (avec Annexe). Ottawa, le 8 mai 1997. *En vigueur* le 29 mars 1999. RTC 1999/22.

Autriche
Accord de coproduction audiovisuelle entre le Gouvernement du Canada et le Gouvernement de la République d'Autriche (avec Annexe). Vienne, le 11 juin 1999.

Protocole portant modification de la Convention entre le Gouvernement du Canada et le Gouvernement de la République d'Autriche en vue d'éviter les doubles impositions et de prévenir l'évasion fiscale en matière d'impôts sur le revenu, fait à Vienne le 19 décembre 1976. Vienne, le 15 juin 1999.

Bahamas
Accord sur le Rhum entre le Gouvernement du Canada et le Gouvernement du Commonwealth des Bahamas. Ottawa, le 12 février 1999. *En vigueur* le 12 février 1999. RTC 1999/8.

Bulgarie
Convention entre le Gouvernement du Canada et le Gouvernement de la République de Bulgarie en vue d'éviter les doubles impositions et de prévenir l'évasion fiscale en matière d'impôts sur le revenu (avec Protocole). Ottawa, le 3 mars 1999.

Brésil
Accord de coproduction audiovisuelle entre le gouvernement du Canada et le gouvernement de la République fédérative du Brésil. Brasilia, le 27 janvier 1995. *En vigueur* le 5 janvier 1999. RTC 1999/53.

Chili
Convention entre le Gouvernement du Canada et le Gouvernement de la République du Chili en vue d'éviter les doubles impositions et de prévenir l'évasion fiscale en matière d'impôts sur le revenu et sur la fortune (avec Protocole). Santiago, le 21 janvier 1998. *En vigueur* le 28 octobre 1999. RTC 1999/37.

Accord entre le Gouvernement du Canada et le Gouvernement de la République du Chili tendant à éviter la double imposition sur les revenus provenant de l'exploitation des transport maritime et aérien. Santiago, le 30 juillet 1992. *En vigueur* le 1er janvier 1996. RTC 1996/5. *Terminé* le 28 octobre 1999 à l'entrée en vigueur du nouvel Accord.

Premier Protocole supplémentaire de l'Accord de libre échange entre le Gouvernement du Canada et le Gouvernement de la République du Chili, fait à Santiago le 4 décembre 1996 (avec Annexe). Toronto, le 4 novembre 1999.

Chine

Accord consulaire entre le Gouvernement du Canada et le Gouvernement de la République populaire de Chine. Ottawa, le 28 novembre 1997. *En vigueur* le 11 mars 1999. RTC 1999/9.

Communauté Européenne

Accord entre le Gouvernement du Canada et les Communautés européennes concernant l'application de leurs lois sur la concurrence. Bonn, le 17 juin 1999. *En vigueur* le 17 juin 1999. RTC 1999/2.

Accord modifiant l'Accord de coopération scientifique et technologique entre le Gouvernement du Canada et la Communauté européenne, fait à Halifax le 17 juin 1995. Ottawa, le 17 décembre 1998. *En vigueur* le 30 avril 1999. RTC 1999/17.

Communauté européenne de l'Énergie atomique

Accord de coopération entre le Gouvernement du Canada et la Communauté européenne de l'Énergie atomique dans le domaine de la recherche nucléaire. Ottawa, le 17 décembre 1998. *En vigueur* le 29 janvier 1999.

Corée

Accord entre le Gouvernement du Canada et le Gouvernement de la République de Corée sur l'échange et la protection de renseignements militaires secrets. Ottawa, le 5 juillet 1999. *En vigueur* le 11 août 1999. RTC 1999/28.

Accord de sécurité sociale entre le Gouvernement du Canada et le Gouvernement de la République de Corée (avec Protocole). Séoul, le 10 janvier 1997. *En vigueur* le 1er mai 1999. RTC 1999/6.

Accord entre le Gouvernement du Canada et le Gouvernement de la République de Corée concernant les marchés publics pour la fourniture d'équipements de télécommunications. Ottawa, le 5 juillet 1999.

Costa Rica

Accord entre le Gouvernement du Canada et le Gouvernement de la République du Costa Rica pour l'encouragement et la protection des investissements (avec Annexe). San José, le 18 mars 1998. *En vigueur* le 29 septembre 1999. RTC 1999/43.

Croatie

Accord de sécurité sociale entre le Gouvernement du Canada et le Gouvernement de la République de Croatie (avec Arrangement administratif). Zagreb, le 22 avril 1998. *En vigueur* le 1er mai 1999. RTC 1999/5.

Accord entre le Gouvernement du Canada et le Gouvernement de la République de Croatie en vue d'éviter les doubles impositions et de prévenir l'évasion fiscale en matière d'impôts sur le revenu et sur la fortune (avec Protocole). Ottawa, le 9 décembre 1997. *En vigueur* le 23 novembre 1999 *avec effet* le 1er janvier 2000. RTC 1999/46.

Cuba

Accord de coproduction audiovisuelle entre le Gouvernement du Canada et le Gouvernement de la République de Cuba (avec Annexe). La Havane, le 27 avril 1998. *En vigueur* le 1er septembre 1999. RTC 1999/26.

Traité entre le Gouvernement du Canada et le Gouvernement de la République de Cuba concernant l'exécution des peines. La Havane, le 7 janvier 1999. *En vigueur* le 10 août 1999. RTC 1999/24.

Égypte

Accord entre le Gouvernement du Canada et le Gouvernement de la République arabe d'Égypte concernant la coopération relative aux aspects consulaires des affaires d'ordre familiale. Le Caire, le 10 novembre 1997. *En vigueur* le 1er octobre 1999. RTC 1999/27.

El Salvador

Accord entre le Gouvernement du Canada et le Gouvernement de la République d'El Salvador sur la promotion et la protection des investissements (avec Annexes). San Salvador, le 31 mai 1999.

États-Unis d'Amérique

Protocole modifiant l'Accord de coopération entre le Gouvernement du Canada et le Gouvernement des États-Unis d'Amérique concernant les emplois civils de l'énergie atomique, fait à Washington le 15 juin 1955 (tel que modifié). Washington, le 23 juin 1999. *En vigueur* le 13 décembre 1999. RTC 1999/40.

Échange de Notes entre le Gouvernement du Canada et le Gouvernement des États-Unis d'Amérique dans le cadre du Traité entre le Gouvernement du Canada et le Gouvernement des États-Unis d'Amérique relatif à la mise en valeur des ressources hydrauliques du bassin du fleuve Columbia, autorisant la cession de la part canadienne aux États-Unis d'Amérique, fait à Washington, DC, le 17 janvier 1961. Washington, DC, le 31 mars 1999. *En vigueur* le 31 mars 1999. RTC 1999/18.

Échange de Lettres entre le Gouvernement du Canada et le Gouvernement des États-Unis d'Amérique modifiant l'Accord sur le bois d'oeuvre résineux entre le Gouvernement du Canada et le Gouvernement des États-Unis d'Amérique, fait à Washington, DC, le 29 mai 1996. Washington, DC, le 26 août 1999. *En vigueur* le 26 août 1999. RTC 1999/33.

Échange de Notes constituant un Accord concernant le marché canadien des services publicitaires dans les périodiques entre le Gouvernement du Canada et le Gouvernement des États-Unis d'Amérique. Washington, le 3 juin 1999. *En vigueur* le 3 juin 1999. RTC 1999/21.

Accord entre le Gouvernement du Canada et le Gouvernement des États-Unis d'Amérique portant sur les échanges binationaux dans le domaine de l'éducation. Washington, le 15 novembre 1999. *En vigueur* le 15 novembre 1999. RTC 1999/39.

Échange de Notes constituant un Accord entre le Gouvernement du Canada et le Gouvernement des

États-Unis d'Amérique en vue de prolonger pour dix ans la validité de l'Accord du 17 juin 1986 prévoyant la poursuite de l'exploitation et de l'entretien de la zone d'essais de torpilles dans le détroit de Georgie et visant à modifier l'Annexe jointe à l'Échange de Notes du 13 janvier et du 14 avril 1976. Ottawa, le 17 décembre 1999. *En vigueur* le 17 décembre 1999. RTC 1999/45.

Protocole entre le Gouvernement du Canada et le Gouvernement des États-Unis d'Amérique visant à modifier la Convention de 1916 conclue entre le Royaume-Uni et les États-Unis d'Amérique pour la protection des oiseaux migrateurs. Washington, le 14 décembre 1995. *En vigueur* le 7 octobre 1999. RTC 1999/34.

Échange de Notes entre le Gouvernement du Canada et le Gouvernement des États-Unis d'Amérique constituant un Accord relatif au Traité entre le Gouvernement du Canada et le Gouvernement des États-Unis d'Amérique concernant le saumon du Pacifique (avec Annexes), fait à Ottawa le 28 janvier 1985. Washington, DC, le 30 juin 1999. *En vigueur* le 30 juin 1999.

Protocole modifiant l'Accord entre le Gouvernement du Canada et le Gouvernement des États-Unis d'Amérique concernant la coopération dans le cadre de l'étude de l'atmosphère et des écosystèmes boréaux (BOREAS), fait à Washington, DC, le 18 avril 1994. Washington, le 30 novembre 1999. *En vigueur* le 30 novembre 1999. RTC 1999/47.

Finlande

Échange de Notes modifiant l'Accord entre le Gouvernement du Canada et le Gouvernement de la Finlande concernant le transport aérien entre leurs territoires respectifs et au-delà, fait à Helsinki le 28 mai 1990 (avec Annexes). *En vigueur* le 1er octobre 1999.

Accord de coproduction audiovisuelle entre le Gouvernement du Canada et le

Gouvernement de la République de Finlande (avec Annexe). Stockholm, le 31 mars 1998. *En vigueur* le 1er avril 1999. RTC 1999/11.

Grèce
Convention d'extradition entre le Gouvernement du Canada et le Gouvernement de la République hellénique. Ottawa, le 3 novembre 1999.

Grenade
Accord sur la sécurité sociale entre le Gouvernement du Canada et le Gouvernement de la Grenade. St-George, le 8 janvier 1998. *En vigueur* le 1er février 1999. RTC 1999/51.

Hongrie
Accord relatif aux transports aériens entre le Gouvernement du Canada et le Gouvernement de la République de Hongrie (avec Annexe). Budapest, le 7 décembre 1998. *En vigueur* le 10 juin 1999. RTC 1999/30.

Israël
Traité d'entraide judiciaire en matière pénale entre le Gouvernement du Canada et le Gouvernement de l'État d'Israël. Ottawa, le 25 octobre 1999.

Italie
Échange de Notes constituant un Accord entre le Gouvernement du Canada et le Gouvernement de la République italienne sur la conduite d'exercices militaires par les Forces armées italiennes au Canada (Goose Bay). Rome, le 3 septembre 1999. *En vigueur* le 3 septembre 1999. RTC 1999/49.

Jamaïque
Traité d'entraide judiciaire en matière pénale entre le Gouvernement du Canada et le Gouvernement de la Jamaïque. Ottawa, le 3 juin 1999.

Accord concernant le partage des produits de la disposition des biens confisqués et des sommes d'argent équivalentes entre le Gouvernement du Canada et le Gouvernement de la Jamaïque. Ottawa, le 3 juin 1999. *En vigueur* le 3 juin 1999. RTC 1999/19.

Japon
Protocole modifiant la Convention entre le Gouvernement du Canada et le Gouvernement du Japon en vue d'éviter les doubles impositions et de prévenir l'évasion fiscale en matière d'impôts sur le revenu, fait à Tokyo le 7 mai 1986. Ottawa, le 19 février 1999.

Jordanie
Convention entre le Gouvernement du Canada et le Royaume hachémite de Jordanie en vue d'éviter les doubles impositions et de prévenir l'évasion fiscale en matière d'impôts sur le revenu (avec Protocole). Amman, le 6 septembre 1999.

Liban
Accord entre le Gouvernement du Canada et le Gouvernement de la République libanaise pour l'encouragement et la protection des investissements (avec Annexes). Ottawa, le 11 avril 1997. *En vigueur* le 19 juin 1999. RTC 1999/15.

Luxembourg
Convention entre le Gouvernement du Canada et le Gouvernement du Grand-Duché de Luxembourg en vue d'éviter les doubles impositions et de prévenir la fraude fiscale en matière d'impôts sur le revenu et sur la fortune. Bruxelles, le 10 septembre 1999.

Mexique
Échange de Notes modifiant l'Accord relatif aux transports aériens entre le Gouvernement du Canada et le Gouvernement des États-Unis du Mexique, fait à Mexico le 21 décembre 1961. Mexico, le 9 avril 1999.

Accord entre le Gouvernement du Canada et le Gouvernement des États-Unis du Mexique concernant la fourniture de services par satellite. Mexico, le 9 avril 1999.

Nigéria
Accord entre le Gouvernement du Canada et le Gouvernement de la République fédérale du Nigéria en vue d'éviter les doubles impositions et de prévenir l'évasion fiscale en matière

d'impôts sur le revenu et sur les gains en capital (avec Protocole). Abuja, le 4 août 1992. *En vigueur* le 16 novembre 1999. RTC 1999/48.

Norvège
Accord de coproduction audiovisuelle entre le Gouvernement du Canada et le Gouvernement du Royaume de Norvège. Oslo, le 2 avril 1998. *En vigueur* le 20 août 1999. RTC 1999/25.

Traité d'entraide judiciaire en matière pénale entre le Gouvernement du Canada et le Gouvernement du Royaume de Norvège. Ottawa, le 16 septembre 1998. *En vigueur* le 14 janvier 1999. RTC 1999/2.

Organisation de l'Aviation Civile Internationale
Modification à l'Accord supplémentaire entre le Gouvernement du Canada et l'Organisation de l'aviation civile internationale concernant le siège de l'Organisation de l'aviation civile internationale, fait à Montréal le 16 septembre 1980 (avec Annexes). Montréal, le 28 mai 1999. *En vigueur* le 28 mai 1999. *Restera en vigueur* pour 20 ans, du 1ᵉʳ novembre 1996 au 30 novembre 2016. Remplace l'Accord supplémentaire du 16 septembre 1980. RTC 1999/20.

Ouzbékistan
Convention entre le Gouvernement du Canada et le Gouvernement de la République d'Ouzbékistan en vue d'éviter les doubles impositions et de prévenir l'évasion fiscale en matière d'impôts sur le revenu (avec Protocole). Ottawa, le 17 juin 1999.

Pays-Bas
Protocole modifiant la Convention entre le Canada et le Royaume des Pays-Bas en vue d'éviter les doubles impositions et de prévenir l'évasion fiscale en matière d'impôts sur le revenu, fait à La Haye le 27 mai 1986, tel que modifié (avec Protocole). Ottawa, le 25 août 1997. *En vigueur* le 15 janvier 1999. RTC 1999/3.

Philippines
Accord de coproduction audiovisuelle entre le Gouvernement du Canada et le Gouvernement de la République des Philippines. Manile, le 16 octobre 1998. *En vigueur* le 30 septembre 1999. RTC 1999/35.

Accord supplémentaire à l'Accord sur la sécurité sociale entre le Gouvernement du Canada et le Gouvernement de la République des Philippines, fait à Winnipeg le 9 septembre 1994. Winnipeg, le 13 novembre 1999.

Pologne
Accord entre le Gouvernement du Canada et le Gouvernement de la République de Pologne sur la coproduction cinématographique et télévisuelle (avec Annexe). Ottawa, le 27 mai 1996. *En vigueur* le 3 septembre 1999. RTC 1999/44.

Portugal
Convention entre le Gouvernement du Canada et le Gouvernement de la République portugaise en vue d'éviter les doubles impositions et de prévenir l'évasion fiscale en matière d'impôts sur le revenu (avec Protocole). Ottawa, le 14 juin 1999.

Roumanie
Traité d'entraide judiciaire entre le Gouvernement du Canada et le Gouvernement de la Roumanie. Ottawa, le 25 mai 1998. *En vigueur* le 30 juin 1999. RTC 1999/29.

Suisse
Accord de reconnaissance mutuelle sur la conformité entre le Gouvernement du Canada et le Gouvernement de la Confédération suisse. Ottawa, le 3 décembre 1998. *En vigueur* le 1ᵉʳ mai 1999.

Trinité-et-Tobago
Accord sur le sécurité sociale entre le Gouvernement du Canada et le Gouvernement de la République de Trinité-et-Tobago. Port of Spain, le 9 avril 1997. *En vigueur* le 1ᵉʳ juillet 1999. RTC 1999/10.

Turquie

Échange de Notes constituant un Accord entre le Gouvernement du Canada et le Gouvernement de la République turque sur la réciprocité de propriété. Ottawa, le 24 août 1999.

Échange de Notes entre le Canada et la Turquie concernant la délivrance aux représentants diplomatiques, aux fonctionnaires et aux non-immigrants de visas utilisables plusieurs fois. Ankara, le 21 août 1956. *En vigueur* le 21 septembre 1956. *Terminé* le 1er décembre 1999 par échange de Notes.

Ukraine

Accord entre le Gouvernement du Canada et le Gouvernement de l'Ukraine relatif au transport aérien. Kyiv, le 28 janvier 1999. *En vigueur* le 28 avril 1999. RTC 1999/32.

Accord d'entraide judiciaire en matière pénale entre le Canada et l'Ukraine. Ottawa, le 23 septembre 1996. *En vigueur* le 1er mars 1999. RTC 1999/7.

Accord de coopération entre le Gouvernement du Canada et le Gouvernement d'Ukraine concernant les utilisations pacifiques de l'énergie nucléaire (avec Annexes). Ottawa, le 20 décembre 1995. *En vigueur* le 14 janvier 1999. RTC 1999/16.

Uruguay

Accord entre le Gouvernement du Canada et le Gouvernement de la République orientale de l'Uruguay pour l'encouragement et la protection des investissements (avec Annexe). Ottawa, le 29 octobre 1997. *En vigueur* le 2 juin 1999. RTC 1999/31.

Accord de sécurité sociale entre le Gouvernement du Canada et le Gouvernement de la République orientale de l'Uruguay. Ottawa, le 2 juin 1999.

II   MULTILATÉRAUX

Air

Ratification du Protocole de Montréal Nº 4, portant modification de la Convention pour l'unification de certaines règles relatives au transport aérien international, signé à Varsovie le 12 octobre 1929, amendé par le Protocole fait à La Haye le 28 septembre 1955, signé à Montréal le 25 septembre 1975. *Signé* par le Canada le 30 septembre 1975. *En vigueur* le 14 juin 1998. *Ratifié* par le Canada le 27 août 1999. *En vigueur* pour le Canada le 25 novembre 1999. RTC 1999/42.

Adhésion à la Convention complémentaire à la Convention de Varsovie, pour l'unification de certaines règles relatives au transport aérien international effectué par une personne autre que le transporteur contractuel. *Signée* à Guadalajara, le 18 septembre 1961. *En vigueur* le 1er mai 1964. *Adhésion* du Canada le 1er septembre 1999. *En vigueur* pour le Canada le 30 novembre 1999. RTC 1999/41.

Protocole concernant le texte authentique quadrilingue de la Convention relative à l'aviation civile internationale (Chicago, 1944). Montréal, le 30 septembre 1977. *Adhésion* du Canada le 23 mars 1994. *En vigueur* le 16 septembre 1999. *En vigueur* pour le Canada le 16 septembre 1999. RTC 1999/54.

Armes

Convention interaméricaine sur la transparence des acquisitions d'armes conventionnelles. Washington, le 31 mars 1999. *Signée* par le Canada le 7 juin 1999. *Ratifiée* par le Canada le 7 juin 1999.

Conservation

Amendement à l'article XXI de la Convention sur le commerce des espèces de faune et de flore sauvages menacées d'extinction (CITES), faite à Washington le 3 mars 1973, telle que modifiée. Gaborone (Bostwwana), le 30 avril 1983. *Acceptation* par le Canada le 1er février 1999.

Accord sur des normes internationales de piégeage sans cruauté entre la Communauté européenne, le Canada et la Fédération de Russie. Bruxelles, le 15 décembre 1997. *Ratifié* par le Canada le 31 mai 1999. *Appliqué provisoirement* depuis le 1er juin 1999.

Commerce
Acceptation du cinquième Protocole de l'Accord général sur le commerce des services, fait à Marrakech le 15 avril 1994. Genève, le 27 février 1998. *Acceptation* par le Canada le 18 janvier 1999. *En vigueur* le 1ᵉʳ mars 1999. *En vigueur* pour le Canada le 1ᵉʳ mars 1999. RTC 1999/13.

Acceptation de l'amendement à l'Article XXI de la Convention sur le commerce international des espèces de faune et de flore sauvages menacées d'extinction (CITES), adopté à Gaborone (Botswana) le 30 avril 1983. Gland, le 17 mai 1983. *Accepté* par le Canada le 1ᵉʳ février 1999.

Commerce — Blé
Convention relative à l'aide alimentaire 1999 (partie de l'Accord international sur le blé). Londres, le 13 avril, 1999. *Signée* par le Canada le 21 juin 1999. *Ratifiée* par le Canada le 21 juin 1999.

Convention relative à l'aide alimentaire 1995 (partie de l'Accord international sur le blé). Londres, le 7 décembre, 1994. *Signée* par le Canada le 26 juin 1995. *Ratifiée* par le Canada le 26 juin 1995. *En vigueur* pour le Canada le 1ᵉʳ juillet 1995. *Terminée* par l'entrée en vigueur de la Convention relative à l'aide alimentaire 1999.

Commerce — Droit
Accord instituant le Centre consultatif sur la législation de l'OMC. Seattle, le 1ᵉʳ décembre 1999. *Signée* par le Canada le 1ᵉʳ décembre 1999.

Criminel — Corruption
Convention sur la lutte contre la corruption d'agents publics étrangers dans les transactions commerciales internationales. Paris, le 17 décembre 1997. *Signée* par le Canada le 17 décembre 1997. *Ratifiée* par le Canada le 17 décembre 1998. *En vigueur* le 15 février 1999. *En vigueur* pour le Canada le 15 février 1999. RTC 1999/23.

Convention interaméricaine contre la corruption. Caracas, le 29 mars 1996.

En vigueur le 6 mars 1997. *Signée* par le Canada le 8 juin 1999. Pas encore en vigueur pour le Canada.

Culture
Convention pour la protection des biens culturels en cas de conflit armé. Faite à La Haye le 14 mai 1954. *Adhésion* du Canada le 11 décembre 1998. *En vigueur* pour le Canada le 11 mars 1999. RTC 1999/52.

Désarmement
Convention sur l'interdiction de l'emploi, du stockage, de la production et du transfert des mines antipersonnel et sur leur destruction. Oslo, le 18 septembre 1997. *Signée* par le Canada le 3 décembre 1997. *Ratification* par le Canada le 3 décembre 1997. *En vigueur* pour le Canada le 1ᵉʳ mars 1999. RTC 1999/4.

Modification au traité sur les forces armées conventionnelles en Europe. Istanbul, le 19 novembre 1999. *Signée* par le Canada le 19 novembre 1999.

Droit de la mer
Accord aux fins de l'application des dispositions de la Convention des Nations Unies sur le droit de la mer du 10 décembre 1982 concernant la conservation et la gestion des stocks de poissons dont les déplacements s'effectuent tant à l'intérieur qu'au delà de zones économiques exclusives (stocks chevauchants) et des stocks de poissons grands migrateurs (avec Annexes). New York, le 4 décembre 1995. *Signé* par le Canada le 4 décembre 1995. *Ratifié* par le Canada le 3 août 1999.

Environnement
Amendement au Protocole de Montréal relatif à des substances qui appauvrissent la couche d'ozone. *Fait* à Montréal le 17 septembre 1997. *Ratifié* par le Canada le 27 mars 1998. *En vigueur* le 10 novembre 1999. *En vigueur* pour le Canada le 10 novembre 1999.

Protocole à la Convention sur la pollution atmosphérique transfrontière à longue distance relatif à la réduction de l'acidification, de l'eutrophisation et de l'ozone troposphérique. *Fait à* Genève le 13 novembre 1979. Gothenburg, le 13 novembre 1999. *Signé* par le Canada le 1er décembre 1999.

Navigation — Bateaux/Vaisseaux — Officiers/Équipage
Amendement de 1997 à la Convention internationale de 1978 sur les normes de formation des gens de mer, de délivrance de brevets et de veille. *Fait* à Londres le 7 juillet 1978, tel que modifié (Résolution MSC.66(68)). Londres, le 4 juin 1997. *Acceptation tacite* des Parties le 1er juillet 1998 (adopté conformément aux dispositions de l'article VIIIb)(vi)(2)(bb) de la Convention internationale de 1974 pour la sauvegarde de la vie humaine en mer, fait à Londres le 1er novembre 1974). *En vigueur* le 1er janvier 1999. *En vigueur* pour le Canada le 1er janvier 1999.

Amendement de 1997 au Code de formation des gens de mer, de délivrance des brevets et de veille (code STCW), fait à Londres le 7 juillet 1978, tel que modifié (Résolution MSC.67(68)).

Londres, le 4 juin 1997. *Acceptation tacite* des Parties le 1er juillet 1998 (adopté conformément aux dispositions de l'article VIIIb)(vi)(2)(bb) de la Convention internationale de 1974 pour la sauvegarede de la vie humaine en mer, fait à Londres le 1er novembre 1974). *En vigueur* le 1er janvier 1999. *En vigueur* pour le Canada le 1er janvier 1999.

Postes
Actes du XXIIe Congrès de l'Union postale universelle. Beijing, le 14 septembre 1999. *Signés* par le Canada le 14 septembre 1999.

Transport
Accord concernant l'établissement de règlements techniques mondiaux applicables aux véhicules à roues, ainsi qu'aux équipements et pièces qui peuvent être montés et/ou utilisés sur les véhicules à roues. *Fait* à Genève le 25 juin 1998. *Signé* par le Canada le 22 juin 1999. Signature faite sans réserve quant à la ratification, acceptation ou approbation.

Cases / La Jurisprudence

Canadian Cases in
Public International Law in 1999-2000 /
La jurisprudence canadienne en matière
de droit international public en 1999-2000

compiled by / préparé par
KARIN MICKELSON

Sovereign immunity

United States of America v. *Friedland* (1999), 182 D.L.R. (4th) 614. Ontario Court of Appeal.

The United States, through the Environmental Protection Agency (EPA), commenced an action against Friedland in Colorado. The action alleged that he was personally liable for environmental cleanup costs, then estimated to be US $152 million, under the Comprehensive Environmental Response Compensation and Liability Act. The United States obtained an *ex parte* garnishment order against Friedland in Colorado for that amount. Relying on the US order, the United States obtained an *ex parte* Mareva injunctions in Ontario, from Borins J. The injunction prevented Friedland from dissipating or disposing of certain share certificates pending disposition of the CERCLA claim. In support, the United States relied upon certain affidavits, one of which contained a statement that "[t]he United States will undertake at the hearing on the motion herein through counsel to pay any damages assessed by this Court that Friedland may suffer should an injunction turn out to have been wrongly given or if the United States does not prevail on the merits." The order of Borins J. granting a Mareva injunction contained the undertaking of the

---

Karin Mickelson is at the Faculty of Law at the University of British Columbia.

plaintiff, by its counsel to abide by any order "this Court may make as to damages in case this Court should hereafter determine that the Defendant has sustained damages by reason of this Order which the Plaintiff ought to pay."

The Mareva injunction was subsequently dissolved. Rather than seeking an inquiry on the undertaking, Friedland filed a statement of defence and counterclaim seeking damages against the United States and the individual defendants, all of whom were lawyers in the employ of the US Department of Justice or the EPA, pursuant to both the undertaking and the common law. The United States and the individual defendants moved to dismiss the counterclaim on the basis of state immunity pursuant to the State Immunity Act (SIA), R.S.C. 1985 c. S-18. Lederman J. dismissed that motion [reported at (1998), 40 O.R. (3d) 747]. The United States and individual defendants now appeal from that decision.

Section 4(2)(a) of the Act creates an exception to the general principle of sovereign immunity where a foreign state explicitly submits to the jurisdiction of the court. Lederman J. held that the statement in the affidavit constituted an explicit waiver of immunity that was not limited to the possibly narrow scope that a court, on an inquiry, may give to an undertaking as to damages and that did not contain words of limitation that excluded tort claims. As such, Friedland could properly assert by way of counterclaim reasonable and viable claims extending from the natural meaning of the undertaking.

On its plain language, the statement in the affidavit is a statement of intention to provide an undertaking in the future. The actual undertaking provided by the U.S. was that given pursuant to the Mareva injunction granted by Borins J. The language of the undertaking in the order of Borins J. clearly constitutes an explicit submission to the jurisdiction of the courts. But any waiver of immunity must be clear and unequivocal; it cannot be presumed. Nothing in the language of the undertaking indicates that the scope of that submission extended to tort claims. By its wording, the submission is limited to the extent undertaken — that is, a submission to the jurisdiction of the court to inquire under the undertaking — and goes no further. The undertaking does not constitute an explicit waiver for the purposes of Friedland's counterclaim within the meaning of section 4(2)(a) of the SIA.

Section 4(4) creates an exception to the general principle of sovereign immunity where a foreign state initiates or intervenes in any proceedings before a court "in respect of any third party proceedings that arise, or counter-claim that arises, out of the subject-matter of the proceedings initiated by the state or in which the state has so intervened or taken a step." Lederman J. held that the U.S. had waived its immunity within the meaning of section 4(4) when it initiated *ex parte* proceedings seeking a Mareva injunction. He found that section 4(4) was not simply a codification of the common law and that there was no requirement that a counterclaim against a foreign state be merely "defensive" in nature.

The requirement in section 4(4) that a counterclaim against a foreign sovereign arise "out of the subject-matter of the proceeding initiated by the state" indicates an intention to exclude counterclaims that are independent of the state's claim. At common law, the "subject-matter" requirement was understood as precluding counterclaims that were not merely defensive in nature. Thus, a defendant could raise any counterclaim that allowed him or her to answer the claim brought by the state, but could not raise any counterclaim that was outside or independent of the state's claim.

Counsel for Friedland argued that section 4(4) contains no words of limitation apart from the "subject-matter" requirement. He contrasted section 4(4) with the equivalent provisions in the US and UK acts providing for sovereign immunity, which expressly limit the amount and kind of relief which may be sought, and noted that Parliament could have similarly limited section 4(4) if it had wished to do so. This argument was unpersuasive. The Act was enacted in the context of common law principles governing sovereign immunity. One such principle was the subject matter requirement for counterclaims against a foreign sovereign. Nothing in section 4(4) indicates Parliament's intention to alter this common law "subject matter" requirement. While the Act contains no limitation respecting the amount and kind of relief that may be sought by way of counterclaim, the requirement that a counterclaim be defensive in nature is distinct from a limitation respecting the amount and kind of relief sought by way of counterclaim. As such, section 4(4) must be understood as allowing a counterclaim against a foreign sovereign only to the extent that it allows the defendant to answer the claim initiated by the state. Here, Friedland sought damages for conspiracy, abuse of process, libel, breach of disclosure duties, loss of business opportunity, and damage to reputation. The counterclaim does not merely answer the claim brought by the United States; it asserts tort claims that are independent of the proceeding initiated by the United States. The counterclaim cannot be said to arise out of the subject matter of the proceeding brought by the United States within the meaning of section 4(4) of the SIA.

Finally, the Court deals with the argument relating to section 6 of the Act, which provides for an exception to immunity in proceedings that relate to any death or personal injury, or any damage to, or loss of, property that occurs in Canada. This issue had not been dealt with by Lederman J. Counsel for Friedland submitted that the torts committed by the United States and the individual defendants caused him injury, loss, and damage, including the loss of use of his shares, damage to his business reputation, the loss of economic opportunities, and emotional upset and personal embarrassment. Addressing section 6(a), counsel for Friedland argued that "personal injury" includes mental distress and emotional upset, and relied upon this court's decision in *Walker* v. *Bank of New York* (1994), 16 O.R. (3d) 504, and, in particular, upon the *obiter* statement of McKinlay J.A. that the scope of personal injury covered by section 6 could include mental distress, emotional upset, and restriction of liberty.

The statement does not mean that section 6 extends to mental distress or emotional upset in all cases. Otherwise, a party could invoke section 6(a) merely by claiming damages for alleged mental distress or emotional upset, an interpretation that would expand the exception far beyond its intended scope and render the doctrine of sovereign immunity ineffective. The "personal injury" exception refers primarily to physical injury. Section 6(a) extends to mental distress and emotional upset only insofar as such harm arises from, or is linked to, a physical injury. This interpretation is consistent with the generally accepted international understanding of the "personal injury" exception to sovereign immunity.

Addressing section 6(b), counsel for Friedland argued that "damage to or loss of property" encompasses any pecuniary loss, including that resulting from damage to business reputation. However, on its face, "damage to or loss of property" refers to physical harm to or loss or destruction of property. The application of section 6(b) depends upon the nature of the harm suffered rather than the nature of the relief claimed. The interpretation urged by counsel for Friedland would allow a party to invoke section 6(b) whenever the damages suffered are capable of monetary quantification, an interpretation that is unduly broad and unsupported by the plain language of the section. The conventional international understanding of the "loss of property" exception is that the exception applies only to physical harm to, or destruction of, property and does not extend to pure economic loss. The court cannot accept that Parliament intended to give the words "damage to or loss of property" a meaning substantially different from the conventional international understanding.

Lederman J. had found that the immunity enjoyed by employees of a foreign state is derivative, rather than independent, of the immunity enjoyed by the sovereign. He therefore concluded that the waiver of immunity by the United States extended to the individual defendants. In light of the conclusion that the United States has not waived its immunity with respect to the claims asserted in Friedland's counterclaim, it is not necessary to determine whether the immunity enjoyed by functionaries of the sovereign is independent of, or derives from, that enjoyed by the sovereign itself. Even if the immunity enjoyed by the individual defendants is merely derivative, they are protected from the claims asserted in Friedland's counterclaim by virtue of the immunity enjoyed by the United States.

Schreiber v. *Attorney General of Canada et al.* (2000), 187 D.L.R. (4th) 146. Ontario Superior Court of Justice.

The Federal Republic of Germany sought the extradition of the plaintiff. The plaintiff then commenced an action claiming, *inter alia,* that Germany was recklessly indifferent or willfully blind to the fact that the arrest and detention of the plaintiff was beyond the scope of the Treaty Concerning Extradition between Canada and Federal Republic of Germany and that the plaintiff would suffer personal injury, including mental distress, denial, and restriction of liberty and damage to reputation as a consequence. Germany brought a motion seeking an order to dismiss the action on the ground that Germany does not have the capacity to be sued because it enjoys sovereign immunity, as codified by the State Immunity Act, R.S.C. 1985, c. S-18. The plaintiff sought to rely on certain exceptions to immunity contained in the Act.

In granting the motion to dismissing the action against Germany, Nordheimer J. deals first with an argument under section 4 of the Act, which provides an exception to immunity in circumstances in which the foreign state has submitted to the jurisdiction of the court. Here Germany had not taken any step in this proceeding other than that necessary to assert its immunity, which by virtue of section 4(3) is expressly deemed not to be a submission to the court's jurisdiction. Nordheimer J. then turns to the argument under section 6(a) of the Act, which provides an exception to immunity in any proceedings relating to personal injury. Germany relied on the *Friedland* decision (noted earlier) for the view that section 6(a) refers primarily to physical injury. The plaintiff argued, *inter alia,* that it is possible that the arrest itself could be a physical injury and that the arrest would then provide the necessary linkage to the claims for mental distress and emotional upset. This aspect of the plaintiff's claim is so novel that it cannot stand against the otherwise clear entitlement to immunity that Germany has. It is difficult to accept the contention that the mere fact of arrest, without any evidence of injuries of the type that would normally be considered physical, could fairly and reasonably be held to constitute physical injury.

Treaties — domestic application

Clarkson v. *Government of the Kingdom of the Netherlands,* 146 C.C.C. (3d) 482. British Columbia Court of Appeal.

The Netherlands sought the extradition of the plaintiff. The Extradition Treaty between the Government of Canada and Government of the Kingdom of the Netherlands required that evidence be admitted in extradition proceedings without having to be taken under oath or affirmation. The extradition judge admitted this type of evidence. The fugitive argued that this violated section 7 of the Canadian Charter of Rights and Freedoms on the basis that there is a common law requirement that evidence be taken under oath or on affirmation. The extradition judge dismissed an application to declare inoperative the relevant provisions of the treaty.

Writing for the Court, Ryan J.A. notes that provisions of an extradition treaty are made part of the law of Canada by virtue of section 3 of the Extradition Act, R.S.C. 1985, c. E-23, which provides that the Act shall be read and construed as to provide for the execution of an extradition arrangement with a foreign state. The evidence offered by the Netherlands was therefore admissible *per se* in the extradition hearing. The question was whether the use of such evidence violates the appellant's section 7 Charter right not to be deprived of his liberty except in accordance with the principles of fundamental justice. In the circumstances of this case, there had been no violation of the principles of fundamental justice, nor was there a breach of section 7.

United States of America v. Stuckey et al. (2000), 181 D.L.R. (4th) 144. British Columbia Supreme Court.

A number of individuals were charged with fraud, money-laundering, and related offences in the United States. The US government made a request for Canadian assistance in gathering evidence of these alleged crimes, pursuant to Article IV.1 of the Treaty between Canada and the United States on Mutual Legal Assistance in Criminal Matters. In accordance with the Mutual Legal Assistance in Criminal Matters Act, S.C. 1988, c. 37, section 7, the minister of justice of Canada approved the request. Under section 17(1) of the Act, the minister of justice provided the Competent Authority in this case, namely the attorney general of the province of British Columbia, with the documents and information necessary to proceed. Pursuant to section 17(2) of the Act, the Competent Authority obtained two section 18(1) evidence-gathering orders. Three of the applicants, all corporations, had banking records seized pursuant to these orders. Similarly, the fourth applicant, the individual owner of a fourth corporation, was compelled to obtain and produce certain business records. They allege that these actions violated their respective rights under sections 7 and 8 of the Canadian Charter of Rights and Freedoms. On the other hand, the Competent Authority has sought a further order pursuant to sections 19 and 20 of the Act to send the information to the United States.

Among the issues dealt with by Owen-Flood J. were whether the Treaty is enforceable as part of the law of Canada; if so, whether the Act and/or the Treaty mandate dual criminality as a condition precedent to the issuance of an evidence gathering order (and whether there is dual criminality at bar); and, if dual criminality is not required as part of the legislative implementation of the Treaty, whether section 8 of the *Charter* is infringed in a manner that cannot be justified under section 1.

In regard to the first issue of whether the treaty was enforceable as part of the domestic law of Canada, Owen-Flood J. notes that while there is no legal requirement that Parliament give its approval to either the signing or the ratification of a treaty, Parliamentary legislation to implement a treaty is required when the treaty necessitates a change in the law of Canada in order for Canada to be able to fulfil any new international obligations incurred under the treaty. Thus, the practice of submitting more important treaties to Parliament for approval has arisen where a treaty requires a change in domestic law. In 1985, under the "foreign affairs power" the Governor in Council negotiated and signed the Canada-United States Treaty. Following political practice, the Treaty was submitted to Parliament for approval by resolution. The fact that the resolution was never approved is of no legal consequence. The normal practice regarding treaties requiring a change in the law is for the government to withhold ratification of the treaty until implementing legislation is passed. That is what was done in this case. In 1988, two years prior to ratification of the Treaty, Parliament passed the Mutual Legal Assistance Act. It is this Act of Parliament that provides the legislative framework for the domestic implementation of the Treaty, as well as any similar treaties with foreign states. The Act enabled Canada to meet its international obligations to be incurred under certain treaties that may come into force internationally in the future. Hence, upon ratification of the Treaty on January 24, 1990, Canada could meet its new obligation under Article II.1 of the Treaty to provide legal assistance to the United States in certain matters. On that date, the Treaty came into force internationally as between Canada and the United States, and the Treaty immediately received legislative implementation as a treaty under the aegis of the Mutual Legal Assistance Act.

Owen-Flood J. rejected a number of arguments made by the applicants regarding the way in which the Act operates to usurp Parliament's role in the implementation of treaty obligations. The Act does not contain any provision enabling the federal executive to bring a treaty into force in Canada. Rather, relevant treaties entered into by the Governor in Council become domestically enforceable by falling within the aegis of the Act and being referentially incorporated into it. Parliament has passed legislation that referentially incorporates the definition of certain terms from treaties it anticipates that the federal executive will enter into regarding international criminal matters. The Treaty does not require further changes in the domestic law of Canada. It is enforceable in Canada.

Owen-Flood J. then turns to the issue of interpretation of the Act and Treaty, specifically, whether they mandate dual criminality as a condition precedent to the issuance of an evidence gathering order. In assessing this question, Owen-Flood J. relies on the distinction implicit in the section 2(1) definition of "treaty" between agreements with the primary purpose of providing for mutual legal assistance in criminal matters ("primary purpose" treaties) and those in which the provision of mutual legal assistance in criminal matters is simply an important part ("important part" treaties). Part of the definition of an "important part" treaty, as set out in section 2(2), is that it contains provisions respecting a number of matters including the restriction of mutual legal assistance to acts that, if committed in Canada, would be indictable offences. (Owen-Flood J. notes both the section 2(1) definition of "treaty" and section 2(2) were recently repealed: 1999, c. 18, section 97. The defined term "agreement" has been added to section 2(1) in their place. However, this repeal and replacement does not operate retroactively and, therefore, is not relevant to this proceeding.)

The Mutual Legal Assistance Act, while stipulating "dual criminality" as an essential prerequisite for "important part" treaties, makes no express stipulation in regard to "primary purpose" treaties. Given that the Canada-United States Treaty is a "primary purpose" treaty, the Act does not expressly make dual criminality a pre-requisite for the Treaty coming under the aegis of the Act. The Governor in Council, in the making of treaties, has a wide power to determine the scope of the treaties purported to be implemented under the Act. In negotiating the Canada-United States Treaty it has exercised this power.

However, Parliament has installed a check on this broad power of the federal executive in the Act itself. It is a condition precedent to the Minister of Justice of Canada implementing a request that the relevant treaty provide for mutual legal assistance with respect to the subject matter of the request. This means that when Canada receives a request under the Treaty from the United States, Canada must have, under the terms of the Treaty, a reciprocal right to make a request to the United States on the same subject matter. In other words, the subject matter on which the request is founded must come within the definitions given in the Treaty as to the meaning of the term "offence" both in Canada and in the United States. There must be a particular reciprocity in that any offence in the request must also be, in substance, an offence within the Requested State. A purpose of the reciprocity requirement is to avoid the "the social conscience of a State" being "embarrassed" by the provision of legal assistance upon certain foreign requests. It does so by ensuring that a State is not required to provide assistance in situations for which it, in return, would never have occasion to make demand.

Owen-Flood J. then turns to a consideration of whether Article II of the Treaty, which provides that assistance shall be provided without regard to whether the conduct under investigation or prosecution in the Requesting State constitutes an offence or may be prosecuted by the Requested State, is in conflict with the enactment in section 8 of the Act mandating, as a condition precedent to giving effect to a request, that the Treaty allow for reciprocity. While at first sight, there may appear to be a conflict between Article II.3 of the Treaty and section 8 of the Act, there is in reality no conflict. Article II.3 must be interpreted in light of the Act and the plain wording of the Treaty. Article V.1 (b) of the Treaty provides that the minister of justice may deny the request if its execution is contrary to its public interest. This is in harmony with section 8 of the Act. Through section 8, Parliament has effectively legislated that if the requested legal assistance regarding a subject matter cannot be reciprocated, then it is not in the public interest of Canada to grant the request. In other words, for requests where the foreign offence is not, in substance, an offence in Canada, Parliament has compelled the minister to exercise his discretion to deny assistance under Article V.1 (b) of the treaty.

Article II.3, by contrast, is not directed at the minister. Rather, it is primarily directed at the courts of the Requested State. Under Article VII.1 of the Treaty and sections 12 and 18 of the Act, Canadian courts may be faced with applications for a search and seizure or evidence gathering order, the latter being the case at bar. Article II.3 amounts to a prohibition on treating these hearings as extradition hearings, in which there is the requirement that the conduct of the accused actually constitutes a parallel offence in Canada. Article II.3 prescribes that this level of scrutiny should not be undertaken in the context of orders sought under the Mutual Legal Assistance Act.

Thus, in essence, the Treaty prohibits an assessment of dual criminality. Assistance cannot be denied on the grounds that the conduct would not constitute an offence in Canada. However, the Treaty allows for, and the Act demands, an assessment of reciprocity. Assistance must be denied if the offences that are the subject matter of the request are not, in substance, offences in Canada. Here, the United States seeks an evidence gathering order, via the Competent Authority in Canada, because of offences that have in each instance their substantive counterparts in Canada. The relevant Treaty does provide for mutual legal assistance with respect to the subject matter of the request. This is so because the definition of offence section in the Treaty is sufficiently wide so as to cover all those offences in both countries.

Owen-Flood J. then turns to a consideration of whether the lack of a dual criminality requirement infringes section 8 of the *Charter*, which guarantees a right against unreasonable search and seizure. Owen-Flood first deals with the question of whether this should be subject to a ruling. Assuming that section 8 of the Charter does require dual criminality, it is not clear that the appropriate remedy would be to sever Article II.3 from the Treaty, as it has been implemented as part of the Mutual Legal Assistance Act, and thereafter as a dual criminality requirement that is read into the Act (as was argued by the Competent Authority). The Treaty is a part of the Act. Thus, part of the legislation remaining after severance would be the Treaty itself, minus Article II.3. Yet the Treaty is the product of negotiations between Canada and the United States. It cannot be fairly assumed that the parties, had they negotiated in light of a dual criminality requirement in the Charter, would have agreed to the Treaty save for Article II.3. At a minimum, procedures for addressing a dual criminality requirement presumably would have been negotiated. Furthermore, severance of Article II.3 of the Treaty from the Mutual Legal Assistance Act would not render the legislation consistent with a dual criminality requirement under the Charter. The Act could not survive the severance independently. The dual criminality requirement would also have to be read into it.

Given all this, as well as the fact that no precedent involving severance of treaties had been provided, if dual criminality is stipulated by section 8 of the Charter and a remedy is in order, a remedy other than severance would be chosen. The Act would be declared or else there would be no force or effect insofar as it implemented the Canada-United States Treaty. In addition, the Act's invalidity would be temporarily suspended for six months so as to give time for the parties to renegotiate the Treaty.

Such a measure is not required, however, as section 8 of the Charter does not mandate an assessment of dual criminality in the context of foreign requests for legal assistance by way of seizures of documentary evidence supporting foreign offences. The principle of dual criminality functions to protect the core liberty interest of individuals subject to extradition requests. Thus, dual criminality is an inappropriate procedural safeguard in the context of gathering evidence of foreign offences. Further, the privacy expectations of individuals in Canada regarding documentary evidence are not unreasonably intruded upon in the absence of a dual criminality requirement being imposed on the state in its pursuit of better law enforcement. The omission of dual criminality from the Mutual Legal Assistance Act is not unreasonable.

However, search and seizure in Canada at the request of a foreign state may be unreasonable where the foreign offence, in substance, does not have a counterpart offence in Canada. A reasonable expectation of privacy could include the expectation that one will not be subject to search and seizure by Canadian authorities in their gathering of evidence of foreign offences that are not considered to be fair, right, or just by Canadians.

This approach to foreign requests involving search and seizure succeeds in balancing the individual and state interests at play. The individual's reasonable expectation of not having his or her privacy intruded upon so as to enforce a foreign law that is unreasonable by Canadian standards of conscience is taken seriously and protected. On the other hand, the state's interest in ensuring better law enforcement through international cooperation is apparently not frustrated or undermined. Legal assistance is still maintained for all foreign requests made pursuant to an implemented treaty save for those that involve foreign offences that are not, in substance, offences in Canada. Such requests will undoubtedly be few and far between. Furthermore, the application of this approach does not threaten to make Canada a safe-haven for international criminals who seek to hide the evidence of their crimes behind onerous foreign laws on search and seizure.

The Act requires reciprocity as a condition precedent to the making of a search and/or seizure order. Section 8 of the Act compels the minister of justice to deny legal assistance where reciprocity is absent. The Treaty both allows for reciprocity as a statutory condition precedent and has received legislative implementation by the Act. Thus, the Act does not infringe the reciprocity requirement of section 8 of the Charter.

However, if the Mutual Legal Assistance Act violates section 8 of the Charter by not requiring reciprocity and cannot be justified under section 1 of the Charter, the Act itself would still be constitutionally valid. The gravamen of the applicants' complaint is that in certain situations, seizure of evidence under the Mutual Legal Assistance Act could violate someone's constitutional rights under section 8 of the Charter. This does not justify striking down the Act in its entirety. If the Act does not require reciprocity, the proper remedial approach is to read the Charter section 8 reciprocity requirement into sections 12 and 18 of the Act which provide the conditions precedent to the issuance of search and/or seizure orders. The Act would thereby be rendered consistent with section 8 of the Charter. Using the remedy of reading in the reciprocity stipulation would respect the rights of individuals without interfering any more than is necessary with the legislation in its facilitation of better law enforcement through international comity

Reciprocity exists on the facts of this case. The offences of fraud, conspiracy, and money laundering, as they are the subject matter of the US request being considering here, are also offences in Canada. Hence, reciprocity existed as a condition precedent to the issuance of the evidence gathering orders.

Re Russian Federation and Pokidyshev et al., 138 C.C.C. (3d) 321. Ontario Court of Appeal.

This was an appeal from two orders made under the Mutual Legal Assistance in Criminal Matters Act, R.S.C. 1985, c.30 (4th Supp.). On January 19, 1996, the Russian ambassador to Canada wrote to the minister of foreign affairs requesting Canada's assistance in respect of an ongoing investigation by the Russian authorities in conjunction with the Royal Canadian Mounted Police (RCMP). The investigation was said to relate to the offences of bribery, the payment and acceptance of secret commissions, and the theft of stable nuclear isotopes from the Russian Federation for sale in Canada. The details of that investigation were set out in letters rogatory, which were incorporated by reference in the ambassador's letter and attached to that letter. The letters rogatory requested information concerning certain bank accounts and also asked that certain persons be questioned by the Canadian authorities. The ambassador's request included the proposal that it, together with the Canadian reply, constitute an administrative arrangement providing for legal assistance, which would enter into effect on the date of receipt of the reply and would remain in effect for six months from that date. Section 6(1) of the Act, which provides that the minister of foreign affairs may, where there is no treaty between Canada and another state, enter into an administrative arrangement with that other state providing for legal assistance with respect to an investigation specified therein. In a letter dated February 7, 1996, the minister of foreign affairs for Canada agreed to the ambassador's request, thus establishing an administrative arrangement under section 6 of the Act that would remain in effect for six months.

On April 5, 1996, the Russian authorities made a formal request for assistance under section 17 of the Act. That request set out the offences being investigated by the Russian authorities (bribery, theft, misuse of official position), detailed the facts which had been revealed by the Russian and RCMP investigations to that point and sought orders requiring production to the Russian authorities of copies of documents seized from the appellant's place of business and from various financial institutions. The administrative arrangement was renewed as of August 7, 1996.

On September 17, 1996, the Canadian authorities, pursuant to section 17 of the Act, formally approved the Russian request dated April 5, 1996. That approval specifically referred to providing copies of documents seized by Canadian law enforcement agencies. The attorney general of Ontario, a "competent authority" under the Act, applied for the two orders that are the subject of this appeal.

Among the issues raised by the appellant is whether the administrative arrangement between Canada and the Russian Federation was ineffective by virtue of its failure to specify the type of legal assistance requested. The appellant argued that the exchange of letters between the Russian ambassador and the minister of foreign affairs did not specify the type of legal assistance requested by the Russian Federation and could not, therefore, constitute an administrative arrangement, within the meaning of section 6 of the Act. As there was no proper administrative arrangement, the court had no jurisdiction to make any order under the Act.

The administrative arrangement does not trigger any application under the Act or necessarily result in any judicial proceeding. It creates the necessary diplomatic channels for a subsequent request by a foreign state for assistance. If a request is made and if the minister of justice approves it, an application for assistance will be made to the court by a "competent authority." The judicial phase of the process contemplated by the Act begins with the application triggered by the foreign state's request and the minister's approval under section 17.

It is doubtful that a judge acting under section 18 or section 20 of the Act can review the terms of an administrative arrangement to determine whether these terms conform to the Act. Nothing in either section suggests that a judge should look behind the application and the request to satisfy herself that the Canadian and foreign authorities have properly established the necessary diplomatic channels for the making of the request.

In any event, in the circumstances of this case the letters

exchanged between the ambassador and the secretary of state considered along with the appended documents made the nature of the requested assistance clear. The letter from the Russian ambassador referred to letters rogatory, which set out the nature of the investigation in some detail. Section 6 does not require more specificity in the description of the type of legal assistance to be provided under an administrative arrangement. The minister of justice could require more specificity, but that is a matter for the minister.

Note. The other issues on appeal dealt with the nature of the documents that could be turned over to the Russian authorities. Throughout its analysis of these issues, the Court appears to emphasize the importance of interpreting the Act in a manner consistent with its original rationale. For example, the appellant had argued that the sending order could not be made because it had been conceded that an unspecified number of documents were not relevant to the Canadian investigation. Doherty J.A. notes that the judge making the order was entitled to approach the question of relevance on a broad basis. Relevance in this context means helpful to the authorities in discovering, understanding, and proving the complex events underlying the allegations, which were the subject matter of the Russian investigation. It would be inconsistent with the spirit of international cooperation underlying the Act to foreclose access to all of the documents, many of which have undoubted relevance to the Russian investigation, simply because an officer had conceded that some were not relevant to the domestic investigation.

Treaties — interpretation; potential conflict between treaty obligations

Suresh v. *Canada (Minister of Citizenship and Immigration)*, [2000] 2 F.C. 592. Federal Court of Appeal.

The appellant is a Tamil and citizen of Sri Lanka who entered Canada in 1990 and was recognized as a Convention refugee in 1991. Later that year, he applied for landing in Canada. His application was not finalized because of a certificate issued jointly by the solicitor general and the minister of citizenship and immigration alleging that he is inadmissible to Canada on security grounds, under section 19 of the Immigration Act, R.S.C. 1985, c. I-2 (as am. By S.C. 1992, c. 49, s. 11), because of his membership in the "Liberation Tigers of Tamil Eelam," an organization alleged to engage in terrorism within the Indian subcontinent. Based on that certificate, the minister issued an opinion letter saying that the appellant poses a danger to the security of Canada. This was an appeal from the judgment of the Trial Division dismissing an application for judicial review with respect to the opinion letter.

Among the issues on appeal was whether under international law there is a non-derogable right against *refoulement* to a country where the person being returned will be at risk of torture and, if there is such a non-derogable right, whether this has become a peremptory norm of *jus cogens* and therefore binding on Canada notwithstanding the provisions of the *Immigration Act*.

The appellant's argument begins with the premise that deportation to a country where a risk of torture exists contravenes Canada's obligations pursuant to Articles 4 and 7 of the International Covenant on Civil and Political Rights. Article 7 contains a right not to be subjected to torture, while Article 4 outlines the circumstances in which derogation from the obligations contained in the Covenant is possible, and specifically lists Article 7 as one of the provisions from which no derogation can be made. Robertson J.A. acknowledges that the Covenant sets out a non-derogable obligation on a state to refrain from subjecting persons to torture. However, this prohibition is restricted to conduct over which a state has control. The Covenant does not address the possibility of torture arising from *refoulement*. The fact that the United Nations Human Rights Committee has indicated that States parties must not expose individuals to the danger of torture or cruel, inhuman or degrading treatment or punishment upon return to another country by way of their extradition, expulsion, or refoulement does not detract from the clear wording of Articles 4 and 7 when read contextually.

Robertson J.A. then considers the Convention against Torture and Other Cruel, Inhuman or Degrading Treatment or Punishment. Article 3, paragraph 1 contains the prohibition against *refoulement*, which exposes a person to a risk of torture. It is clear that the prohibition against torture extends to the act of *refoulement* to a country in circumstances where there are "substantial grounds" for believing that the deportee would be at risk of torture. However, it does not follow from that Article that there is an express non-derogable right against *refoulement* even in cases where the "substantial grounds" test can be satisfied. Certainly, Article 2 cannot be invoked as providing for such an express right. Article 2, paragraph 1, provides that a state shall take appropriate measures to prevent acts of torture "in any territory under its jurisdiction." Article 2, paragraph 2, goes on to provide for no derogation even in times of national emergency such as a civil war. What is significant is that this non-derogable right does not extend to Article 3, which deals with the possibility of *refoulement* to face torture. Furthermore, Article 16, paragraph 2, contradicts the belief that there may be no derogation from the prohibition against *refoulement* if it would lead to the risk of torture. That Article provides that the provisions of the Convention "are without prejudice to the provisions of any other international instrument ... which relates to extradition or expulsion." This qualification is extremely significant once it is recognized that there is another international Convention that expressly authorizes *refoulement* of convention refugees for reasons of national security. This authorization is set out in Articles 32 and 33 of the 1951 United Nations Convention Relating to the Status of Refugees, which Canada has also ratified.

Robertson J.A. is of the view that there is no conflict between the three international conventions that Canada has ratified, namely the Convention Relating to the Status of Refugees, the Convention against Torture, and the Covenant. With respect to the latter two documents, the principle of non-derogation applies only to acts of torture that might be carried out in any territory within a state's jurisdiction. There is no express principle of non-derogation in respect of the prohibition against *refoulement* to a country that exposes a person to a risk of torture, but rather a recognition under the Convention against Torture that the prohibition is without prejudice to the provisions of any other international instrument that relates to extradition or expulsion. Thus, the Convention against Torture neither contradicts nor overtakes the earlier convention. As would be expected, these three conventions complement one another. Accepting that the Convention Relating to the Status of Refugees expressly permits derogation from the prohibition against *refoulement,* it is permissible for a state to rid itself of those who pose a security risk without being in breach of its international obligations.

Even if this interpretation of the Convention against Torture were found to be in error, such that it does provide for a non-derogable right against *refoulement,* the appellant's argument must fail for another reason. The appellant maintains that customary international law can become part of domestic law by absorption into the common law and that the prohibition against torture is part of customary international law. The appellant also argues that the non-derogable nature of these conventions has achieved the status of *jus cogens* under customary international law. Robertson J.A. defines a norm of *jus cogens* as a peremptory norm that is considered to be necessary for the continued existence and operation of the international legal system. Before a customary norm of international law can become a peremptory norm there must be a further recognition by the international community, as a whole, that this is a norm from which no derogation is permitted.

If this argument were accepted then it follows that even if a person were considered a danger to the security of Canada, the minister is necessarily restrained from *"refouling"* that person to a country in circumstances where there are substantial grounds for believing that *refoulement* would expose that person to the risk of torture. However, there is no merit to the appellant's submission. While principles of customary international law may be recognized and applied in Canadian courts as part of the domestic law, this is true only in so far as those principles do not conflict with domestic law. As it happens, the alleged peremptory norm conflicts with Canada's domestic law as evidenced by paragraph 53(1)(b) of the Immigration Act, which itself is a replication of Article 33 of the Convention Relating to the Status of Refugees. In the circumstances, the domestic legislation prevails.

Note. The Court went on to deal with various Charter issues before concluding that the appeal should be dismissed. Leave to appeal to the Supreme Court of Canada was granted on May 25, 2000.

Treaties — interpretation of "Convention refugee," according to the United Nations Convention Relating to the Status of Refugees

Klinko v. *Canada (Minister of Citizenship and Immigration)*, [2000] 3 F.C. 327. Federal Court of Appeal.

This was an appeal from the dismissal of an application for judicial review of the Immigration and Refugee Board's denial of the appellants' claims for Convention refugee status on the ground that the Motions Judge erred in holding that the state must sanction, condone, or support a matter on which the applicant expresses an opinion in order for that opinion to be political.

The appellants were citizens of the Ukraine. In 1995, the husband and father, Alexander Klinko, along with a number of other businessmen, filed with the regional governing authority a formal

complaint about widespread corruption among government officials. They did not have a group name and met only four times.
The complaint was signed by each of them individually. In the end,
the group's complaint was denied by the regional authority. After
filing the complaint, Mr. Klinko suffered retaliation and each of
the Klinkos suffered harassment of various forms. On the basis of
these events the family claimed refuge in Canada. Mr. and Mrs.
Klinko claimed Convention refugee status based on political opinion or imputed political opinion and membership in a particular
social group (that is, the group of businessmen), and Mrs. Klinko
and her son claimed Convention refugee status based on membership in a particular social group (that is, their family).

The Board accepted the testimony of the appellants as credible.
It recognized that Mr. Klinko had a fear of persecution, but it did
not qualify as fear of persecution for reasons of "political opinion."
In determining the meaning of the term "political opinion," the
Board had recourse to two cases: the leading case of *Canada (Attorney General)* v. *Ward*, [1993] 2 S.C.R. 689, which provides a definition of political opinion as any opinion on any matter in which the
machinery of state, government, and policy may be engaged, and
the decision of the Federal Court Trial Division in *Femenia* v.
Canada (Minister of Citizenship and Immigration), [1995] F.C.J. No.
1455, which specified that for a matter to be "engaged" in by the
machinery of state, it must be sanctioned by, condoned by, or
supported by the state. Given these definitions, it ruled that the
complaint against corruption did not amount to political opinion
as the state of Ukraine, far from condoning the corruption of its
officials, was taking active steps to eliminate it. The Board rejected
each of the grounds on which refugee status was claimed.

The Motions Judge dismissed the application for judicial review.
He found no reviewable error in any of the aspects of the decision
of the Board. He accepted the *Femenia* interpretation of *Ward*. The
Board had evidence before it that the Ukraine government did not
sanction, condone, or support corruption by its officials. Based on
this evidence, he concluded that it was reasonable for the Board
to find that the state was therefore not "engaged" in the criminal
conduct of corrupt officials. From this, he believed that the Board
correctly found that Mr. Klinko's complaint could not be said to be
a political opinion within the Convention refugee definition.

The judge certified the question: Does the making of a public
complaint about widespread corrupt conduct by customs and
police officials to a regional governing authority, and, thereafter,

the complainant suffering persecution on this account, when the corrupt conduct is not officially sanctioned, condoned, or supported by the state, constitute an expression of political opinion as that term is understood in the definition of Convention refugee in section 2(1) of the Immigration Act?

After concluding that the appropriate standard of review of the decision of the Board and that of the Motions Judge is that of correctness, Létourneau J.A. turned to a consideration of the certified question. For a proper understanding and analysis of this question, it is helpful to recall the context in which the notion of "political opinion" was first defined and then subsequently evolved into the restriction at issue in this appeal: that a public complaint about corruption of government officials is not an expression of political opinion within the terms of the definition of "Convention refugee" where the corrupt conduct is not officially sanctioned, condoned or supported by the state. The notion of "political opinion" was first considered by the Supreme Court of Canada in the *Ward* case. Clearly in that case, the Court rejected a narrow definition of "political opinion" whereby in order to be political, an opinion would have to hold views contrary to, or be critical of, the policies of the government. The need for a broad definition of the concept was justified by the fact that persecution for having expressed a political opinion may originate from a third party without complicity of the state.

In *Femenia*, the refugee claimant complained of persecution by corrupt policemen as a result of denouncing crimes and corruption among state officials. The Motions Judge accepted the very fact of persecution, but proceeded to define the word "engaged" used by the Supreme Court of Canada in *Ward*. Basically, the learned Judge concluded that even though state officials may be *de facto* carrying out certain activities of corruption, the state is not, for the purpose of determining whether the claimant expressed a political opinion within the terms of the Convention, truly "engaged" in these activities if it officially disapproves of those acts: "engaged" means sanctioned by, condoned by, or supported by.

A careful analysis of the meaning given to the word "engaged" in the *Femenia* case shows that such meaning is inconsistent with the law as set forth in *Ward*. The Supreme Court in the *Ward* case accepted that an opinion could be "political" for the purposes of subsection 2(1) of the Act, whether that opinion accorded or not with the official government position. In other words, the definition chosen by the Supreme Court and given to the words "political opinion" was broad enough to cover all instances where the political opinion expressed or imputed attracted persecution, including those where the government officially agreed with that opinion.

The application of the test articulated in the *Femenia* case also creates an inconsistency among the grounds for persecution recognized in the United Nations Convention Relating to the Status of Refugees. It is common ground that an act of persecution does not require that it be committed by the government and, therefore, that the government be the persecuting agent. It is also common ground that persons who are persecuted without government approval and who are unable to obtain the protection of their government can qualify for refugee status provided that their persecution is based on one of the enumerated grounds, that is, race, religion, nationality, membership in a particular social group, and political opinion. These statements normally hold true for all the grounds recognized by the Convention. However, this would no longer be true for political opinion under the *Femenia* test since the political opinions expressed by the victims of persecution at the hands of third parties who disobey an official government policy would be discarded for Convention purposes. Thus a victim of persecution on the ground of race could still qualify as refugee, subject to the issue of state protection and internal flight alternative, in situations where the government does not condone racism and opposes his or her persecutors, but is not a political opinion claimant. The inconsistency results from a confusion between two concepts related to the issue of persecution: that of the nature of political opinion and that of the state's willingness or ability to protect a victim of persecution. A political opinion does not cease to be political because the government agrees with it.

The certified question should be answered in the affirmative. The Motions Judge erred when he applied the *Femenia* definition or restriction to the opinion expressed by Mr. Klinko. The nature of the claimant's opinion should have been assessed by the test enunciated in *Ward*. This test does not require that the state or machinery of state be actually engaged in the subject matter of the opinion. It is sufficient in order to meet the test that the state or machinery of state "may be engaged." The opinion expressed by Mr. Klinko took the form of a denunciation of state officials' corruption. This denunciation of infractions committed by state officials led to reprisals against him. There is no doubt that the widespread government corruption raised by the claimant's opinion is a "matter in which the machinery of state, government, and policy may be engaged." Indeed, the record contains ample evidence that the machinery of government in the Ukraine was actually "engaged" in the subject matter of Mr. Klinko's complaint. Where, as in this case, the corrupt elements so permeate the government as to be part of its very fabric, a denunciation of the existing corruption is an expression of "political opinion." Mr. Klinko's persecution should have been found to be on account of his "political opinion."

The Board in this case refrained from assessing the issue of state protection and the possibility of an internal flight alternative. It did mention and acknowledge the fact that the Ukraine government had undertaken various measures in its fight against corruption. This evidence of state action is obviously a factor to be considered in assessing the state's willingness and ability to provide Mr. Klinko with protection against persecution, but it is not conclusive evidence of that capacity or willingness. In these circumstances, the matter must be sent back to the Board for a determination of the state's ability and willingness to protect the claimant against persecution as well as a determination of the possibility of an internal flight alternative.

Zhuravlvev v. *Canada (Minister of Citizenship and Immigration),* [2000] 4 F.C. 3. Federal Court Trial Division.

The female applicant was an ethnic Tatar who married an ethnic Russian and converted to Christianity. They lived in the Russian province of Bashkir, north of Chechnya. Because of the war in Chechnya, Chechens fled north to Bashkir. Muslim influence spread and imposed its laws. In their village, a number of individuals who were converts to Christianity or who had married Christians had been harassed and killed. The applicants had been subjected to threats, beatings, harassment, and vandalism of their home. Their adult children had also been threatened and harassed. They had repeatedly sought the assistance of the police, without success. The applicants themselves felt that this was the result of the police sympathizing with the perpetrators of these acts. The couple decided to leave and claim refugee status. The Convention on Refugee Determination Division (CRDD) accepted that the applicants were truthful but decided that they were not refugees because they had not established that they could not obtain state protection. This was an application for judicial review of that decision.

The main issue is the question of the availability of state protection. Counsel for the applicants says that the only conclusion to be drawn from the evidence is that the police refused to assist the applicants and that, in such a case, the question of the inability of the state to protect the applicants does not arise. Counsel for the respondent argues that the CRDD did not find that there was a refusal to assist but rather that the facts were such that there was nothing the police could do.

Pelletier J. considers a number of cases dealing with the issue of state protection and then proceeds to offer some conclusions that can be drawn. The first is that when the agent of persecution is not the state, the lack of state protection has to be assessed as a matter of state capacity to provide protection rather than from the perspective of whether the local apparatus provided protection in a given circumstance. Local failures to provide effective policing do not amount to a lack of state protection. However, where the evidence, including the documentary evidence situates the individual claimant's experience as part of a broader pattern of state inability or refusal to extend protection, then the absence of state protection is made out. The question of refusal to provide protection should be addressed on the same basis as the inability to provide protection. A local refusal to provide protection is not a state refusal in the absence of evidence of a broader state policy to not extend state protection to the target group. Once again, the documentary evidence may be relevant to this issue. There is an additional element in the question of refusal, which holds that refusal may not be overt; the state organs may justify their failure to act by reference to various factors which, in their view, would make any state action ineffective. It is for the CRDD to assess the *bona fides* of these assertions in the light of all the evidence.

Finally, one must consider the issue of internal flight alternative in relation to state inability or refusal to provide protection. A reasonable response to local failure to provide protection is internal migration to an area where state protection is available. However, in states where internal movement is restricted, a failure to remedy local conditions may amount to state failure to provide protection. Whether this is considered from the point of view of state refusal to deal with local conditions from which the state permits no escape or whether one considers it as a state policy that effectively refuses access to state protection elsewhere on its territory makes no difference to the result. If state policy restricts a claimant's access to the whole of the state's territory, then the state's failure to provide local protection can be seen to be as state failure to provide protection and not mere local failure. Once again, this is a matter for the CRDD to weigh in assessing the claim of absence of state protection.

In this case, the CRDD's analysis was perfunctory. It went directly to an assertion that the police had no basis on which to proceed with any investigation and therefore there was no foundation for a claim of refusal to provide state protection. This analysis was insufficient. In response to questions from the panel about leaving the area, the claimants pointed out that there were restrictions on their ability to move. It may be true that the police did not have a great deal to work with, just as it is true that not all police intervention is effective, but a persistent failure to take action, while not necessarily justifying a finding of lack of state protection, does require a close examination of the reasonableness and *bona fides* of the police action, particularly where a citizen's right to internal movement is limited.

The CRDD's cursory analysis amounted to a failure to consider relevant factors and justifies setting the decision aside and sending the matter back for determination by a differently constituted panel.

Treaties — interpretation of Article 1F(b) of United Nations Convention Relating to the Status of Refugees

Chan v. Canada (Minister of Citizenship and Immigration), [2000] 4 F.C. 390. Federal Court of Appeal.

The appellant was arrested in the United States following a "sting" operation in which a substantial quantity of heroin was sold to undercover agents. Pursuant to a plea bargain, the appellant pleaded guilty and was convicted in 1992 of the offence of illegal use of a communication device, an offence defined in connection with offences related to drug trafficking. Under the terms of the plea bargain, the appellant was sentenced to fourteen months imprisonment, with credit for time served, and a probationary period of three years. The appellant also agreed to deportation to his country of origin, China, following his release. In 1996, he arrived in Canada and claimed refugee status. The CRDD of the Immigration and Refugee Board found the appellant not to be a Convention refugee by virtue of Article 1F(b) of the United Nations Convention Relating to the Status of Refugees, part of domestic law under section 2 of the Immigration Act, R.S.C., 1985,

c. I-2 (as am. by R.S.C., 1985 (4th Supp.), c. 28, section 1), which excludes from the definition of refugee a person who "has committed a serious non-political crime outside the country of refuge." The Board's decision was upheld by the Motions Judge. This is an appeal from that decision.

Assuming without deciding that the appellant's conviction qualifies as a serious non-political crime, it is clear that Article 1F(b) cannot be invoked in cases where a refugee claimant has been convicted of a crime and served his or her sentence outside Canada prior to his or her arrival in this country. The broad interpretation that the minister wishes to place on Article 1F(b) is in conflict with the purposes of that provision as discussed in *Pushpanathan* v. *Canada (Minister of Employment and Immigration),* [1998] 1 S.C.R. 982, and as confirmed by academic commentators: that common criminals not be allowed to avoid extradition and prosecution by claiming refugee status. That interpretation fails to recognize that the Act has already in place a statutory scheme for dealing with persons who have been convicted of serious crimes committed outside Canada. Persons such as the appellant are entitled to have their refugee claim heard unless the minister declares them to be a danger to the Canadian public. The broad interpretation that the minister seeks to place on Article 1F(b) has the effect of removing the safeguards built into the Act that are premised on the reality that a person may have a valid refugee claim even though they have garnered a criminal record in another jurisdiction. If one were to accept the minister's interpretation of Article 1F(b), a prior conviction for a serious non-political offence would operate to automatically deny that person's right to a refugee hearing, regardless of the person's attempts at rehabilitation and whether or not they constitute a danger to the Canadian public. The interpretation being advanced by the minister has the effect of virtually abrogating portions of the Act. As a matter of statutory interpretation, the only way in which the apparent conflict can be resolved is to construe Article 1F(b) in a manner consistent with its known purpose. The appeal is allowed, and the matter sent back to the Board for reconsideration on the basis that Article 1F(b) is not applicable to refugee claimants who have been convicted of a crime committed outside Canada and who have served their sentence prior to coming to Canada.

Canadian Cases in
Private International Law in 1999-2000 /
La jurisprudence canadienne en matière de
droit international privé en 1999-2000

compiled by / préparé par
JOOST BLOM

A *Jurisdiction / Compétence des tribunaux*

1 Common Law and Federal

(a) Jurisdiction *in personam*

Constitutionally valid jurisdiction (jurisdiction simpliciter*) — real and substantial connection*

Jordan v. *Schatz* (2000), 189 D.L.R. (4th) 62, [2000] 7 W.W.R. 442

The plaintiff, a resident of British Columbia, was injured when, in Alberta, her car was rear-ended by a car owned and driven by the defendant, a resident of Saskatchewan. The defendant's car was insured with a Saskatchewan government insurance corporation. The plaintiff's lawyer commenced an action against the defendant in British Columbia. The writ did not provide for service outside British Columbia, but it was served on the defendant's lawyer in Saskatchewan. After the writ had expired under the British Columbia Rules of Court, the plaintiff's lawyer realized his mistake of not applying for leave to serve *ex juris*. None of the categories of claim in Rule 13(1), in which service *ex juris* is permitted without leave, applied to the plaintiff's action. The plaintiff applied for an order renewing the writ and granting leave for service *ex juris*. The defendant and his insurer argued that the British Columbia court lacked jurisdiction or should decline jurisdiction on the ground of *forum non conveniens*. The chambers judge granted the plaintiff her order on the ground that an action in Alberta or Saskatchewan was by

Joost Blom is at the Faculty of Law at the University of British Columbia.

this time statute-barred, and the only way the plaintiff's action could survive was by renewal of the writ.

The Court of Appeal held that there was no jurisdiction *simpliciter* because there was no real and substantial connection between British Columbia and the defendant or the cause of action. The bare residency of the plaintiff in the province did not amount to such a connection. The defendant had not attorned by accepting service through his lawyer. Mere acceptance of service *ex juris* was not submission to the jurisdiction of the court, and there was no duty on a defendant who accepted service to advise the plaintiff that he was not submitting to the jurisdiction. The present application for leave to renew the writ and to serve *ex juris* was inconsistent with an argument that the defendant had submitted to the jurisdiction. Nor was the defendant's challenge to the British Columbia court's jurisdiction a submission to it. Since the court lacked jurisdiction *simpliciter*, the issue of whether it should decline jurisdiction on the basis of *forum non conveniens* did not arise. Only if that stage had been reached would it have become relevant that the limitation period in the other provinces had expired and there might therefore be no alternative forum for the plaintiff's action.

Note. Another case on this point, *AG Armeno Mines & Minerals Inc.* v. *PT Pukuafu Indah* (1999), 174 D.L.R. (4th) 748, 32 C.P.C. (4th) 167 (B.C.S.C.) (noted in 37 Can. Y.B. Int'l L. 425), was affirmed on appeal, (2000), 190 D.L.R. (4th) 173 (B.C.C.A.). A British Columbia firm wished to bring an action against a defendant in the United States, claiming that the latter had induced an Indonesian company to break its contract with the plaintiff relating to a mining venture in Indonesia. The Court of Appeal agreed with the chambers judge that the BC court lacked jurisdiction *simpliciter* because the evidence before the court did not support a good arguable case that the defendant had, as the plaintiff pleaded, committed a tort in British Columbia. There was therefore no real and substantial connection between the court and either the defendant or the subject matter of the litigation. In relation to the use of evidence to support an assertion that the court has jurisdiction, see the note below.

Service ex juris — *grounds* — *means of establishing*

Note. By way of contrast with the case noted above, *Furlan* v. *Shell Oil Co.*, [2000] 7 W.W.R. 433, 77 B.C.L.R. (3d) 35 (C.A.), was one in which the court said evidence was not required to support a plaintiff's right to serve *ex juris*. Where service *ex juris* is permitted by the rules of court without leave, and the defendant challenges the plaintiff's right to effect such service, the plaintiff can show compliance with the rules by relying simply on the pleadings. Evidence needs to be adduced only if the claim that is said to entitle the plaintiff to serve *ex juris* is an extremely tenuous one. The pleadings in this case showed that residents of British Columbia were suing the defendants, American firms, for defective plumbing and heating systems in their homes. It was clear from the pleadings that the cause of action was a tort committed in British Columbia (Rule 13(1)(h) of the BC Rules of Court) and no evidence was needed to support a finding of jurisdiction *simpliciter* on that ground.

Service ex juris — *grounds* — *real and substantial connection*

Note. In *WIC Premium Television Ltd.* v. *General Instrument Corp.* (2000), [2001] W.W.R. 431, 266 A.R. 142 (C.A.), the chambers judge had granted leave for service *ex juris* against American corporate defendants who were sued by the holder of a Canadian satellite television broadcasting licence. The defendants were said to have conspired to injure the plaintiff by permitting Canadians to acquire decoders so as to receive their satellite transmissions, which were primarily aimed at the United States and not licensed to be broadcast in Canada. Rule 31 of the Alberta Rules of Court permits service *ex juris* with leave in certain types of case. The arguments revolved around whether there was a real and substantial connection between Alberta and the litigation. The chambers judge held that the pleaded facts and the supporting affidavit evidence showed that there was. The Court of Appeal affirmed the chambers judge's decision, saying that the plaintiff had shown a good arguable case, at this stage of the proceedings, that the defendants had caused it to lose revenues through erosion of its customer base in its allocated territory, and that this was sufficient to establish a real and substantial connection to Alberta. The defendants might be able to show that they had done everything they could to prevent the unauthorized reception of their signals in the plaintiff's territory, but that was a matter for trial.

Service ex juris — *grounds* — *contract and tort*

Note. *Overland Custom Coach Inc.* v. *Thor Industries Inc.* (1999), 46 O.R. (3d) 788 (S.C.J.), involved an action arising out of an agreement by which a Canadian firm licensed an American firm to manufacture buses using the plaintiff's unique design. Service *ex juris* on various defendants in the United States was upheld on a number of grounds contained in Ontario Civil Procedure Rule 17.02, and Ontario was held to be the *forum conveniens.* See also *Tang* v. *Fleming and Berkley Attorneys-At-Law* (1999), 180 Sask. R. 117 (C.A.) (affirming the decision noted in (1999) 37 Can Y.B. Int'l L. 426-27), in which service *ex juris* was held unavailable in an action by a United States citizen against a California law firm for negligence, and California was in any event the *forum conveniens.*

Declining jurisdiction — exclusive choice of forum clause

Morrison v. *Society of Lloyd's* (2000), 224 N.B.R. (2d) 1, leave to appeal refused, 5 Oct. 2000 (S.C.C.). New Brunswick Court of Appeal.

Two Lloyd's "Names" brought separate actions against Lloyd's in the New Brunswick Court of Queen's Bench, apparently effecting service *ex juris.* Both plaintiffs alleged that their contracts with Lloyd's had been procured by fraud, in that Lloyd's concealed information as to the risks of their investments. The contracts included a choice of law clause in favour of English law and an exclusive choice of a judicial forum in England. Lloyd's sought to have the New Brunswick proceedings stayed. The motions judge (whose decision is noted in (1999) 37 Can Y.B. Int'l L. 428) granted the stays. The Court of Appeal affirmed that decision. Allegations of fraud do not render a contract void *ab initio* but only voidable. Hence, the choice of forum clause was binding until a final judgment of a court. Nor could the clause be circumvented by pleading the claim as one in tort rather than for contractual relief; the clause applied in either case. Since courts have encouraged the use of these clauses, as representing the reasonable expectation of the parties and generally aiding in eliminating disputes as to jurisdiction, plaintiffs have a heavy burden if they seek to override the effect of the clause. Strong cause had to be shown why New Brunswick was a more appropriate forum than England. There was no reason to interfere with the motions judge's conclusion that this burden had not been satisfied. The fact that the plaintiffs were alleging breaches of New Brunswick securities law by Lloyd's did not alter the conclusion. They were entitled to have that defence considered and, in other proceedings, the English courts did consider it judiciously, albeit that they held it did not apply. The plaintiffs were not entitled to a guarantee that the defence would be successful.

Note. A very similar case is *Crockett* v. *Society of Lloyd's* (2000), 189 Nfld. & P.E.I. R. 129 (S.C.). The action was stayed, as in *Morrison,* but with extensive consideration of the distinction between a *forum non conveniens* test and the test for displacing an exclusive choice of forum, which requires that circumstances "massively" or "heavily" favour doing so.

Often a choice of forum clause is challenged on the ground that it did not form part of the contract. *Rudder* v. *Microsoft Corp.* (1999), 40 C.P.C. (4th) 394, 47 C.C.L.T. (2d) 168 (Ont. S.C.J.), seems to be the first Canadian case that discusses this issue in relation to software licences. A class action for breach of contract against MSN online service was stayed on the basis of an exclusive choice of forum clause, in favour of the courts of the state of Washington, contained in the licence agreements included with the software supplied to the customers. The argument that a licence agreement provided in electronic form gave inadequate notice of the fact that the clause was rejected. The sign-up procedure required members to accept the terms of the agreement each time they appeared on the computer screen, and was not materially different from a written document where a reader must turn pages. The position of the two representative plaintiffs on this issue was particularly indefensible since they were both law school graduates. The plaintiffs could not show strong cause why the choice of forum clause should not be determinative. Most of the activities in issue took place in Washington, the evidence was there, Microsoft had real connections there, and the plaintiffs purported to represent a Canada-wide class whose connections to Ontario were not readily apparent on the evidence before the court.

Owing to the complexity of some contracts of carriage, standard clauses in bills of lading have been particularly vulnerable to attack on the ground that they were not part of the contract. In *Town Shoes Ltd.* v. *Panalpina Inc.* (1999), 169 F.T.R. 267 (F.C.T.D.), an exclusive choice of forum and choice of law clause in favour of a German court and German law, contained in the bill of lading, was not enforced when the cargo owner sued the carrier for the loss by theft of a cargo of shoes that were shipped to Canada from Italy. The clause was held to be contradicted by the clause paramount in the same bill, by which it was made subject to the Canadian Carriage of Goods by Water Act, with the result that the contract was ambiguous and the ambiguity ought to be resolved in the plaintiff's favour. Moreover, a trial in Germany would, under the circumstances, be severely prejudicial to the plaintiff whereas a trial in Canada would not be prejudicial to the carrier, which had little connection to Germany and had no real desire to have the trial take place there. Along the same lines is *Texserv Inc.* v. *Incon Container USA Ltd.* (2000), 48 O.R. (3d) 427 (S.C.J.), in which a choice of forum clause in a bill of lading, requiring action to be brought in Florida, was not enforced because there were doubts as to whether the terms of the bill formed part of the contract of carriage, and because Ontario was the more appropriate forum. In *Pompey (Z.I.) Industrie* v. *Ecu-Line N.V.* (1999), 179 F.T.R. 254 (F.C.T.D. (Prothonotary)), the terms of the bill, including the choice of forum, were held to have lapsed as a result of the carrier's having made an unreasonable deviation from the contract. The carrier had not shipped the cargo port-to-port from Antwerp, Belgium, to Seattle, Washington, as agreed but shipped it to Montreal and onwards by rail. The damage took place after the transshipment by rail, and was caused by it, because the cargo was delicate equipment that was vulnerable to jolts and vibration.

Even if the clause is valid, courts have the discretion to allow an action to proceed in disregard of it. In *Pre Print Inc.* v. *Maritime Telegraph & Telepone Co.* (1999), 254 A.R. 336 (Q.B.), the plaintiff, an Alberta company that designed software for the production of telephone directories had agreed to customize and licence software to the defendant, based in Nova Scotia. The defendant terminated the agreement and sued the plaintiff in Nova Scotia for damages, and the plaintiff commenced an action in Alberta for damages and a declaration that it was entitled to the return of the source code for the software. The Alberta court ordered a stay of the Alberta proceeding, despite the attornment clause, because Nova Scotia was clearly the more appropriate forum for the resolution of the parties' dispute. The order was conditional upon the defendant's allowing the plaintiff to file a counterclaim in the Nova Scotia proceedings.

In shipping cases, the chosen forum is sometimes rejected because it has relatively little connection with the litigation. This was the case in *Anraj Fish Products Industries Ltd.* v. *Hyundai Merchant Marine Co.* (1999), 176 F.T.R. 221 (F.C.T.D.). In a bill of lading for the shipment of a cargo of frozen fish from Bangladesh to New York, the "notify party" on the bill of lading was an Ontario corporation, which surrendered the bill of lading to the defendant carrier's Toronto office in order to obtain delivery of the cargo in New York. The Ontario firm, together with the shipper in Bangladesh, brought an action against the carrier in the Federal Court of Canada for damages arising out of the contamination of the cargo when it thawed. The carrier's application for a stay of proceedings, on the ground of an exclusive choice of forum clause in favour of a court in Korea, failed. The main factors for disregarding the clause was that the evidence was much more readily available in Canada, the Ontario plaintiff could not afford to make its claim in a Korean court, and the law governing the claim was not Korean law but probably the law of the United States. See also *Itochu Canada Ltd.* v. *Ship Fu Ning Hai* (1999), 173 F.T.R. 203 (F.C.T.C. (Prothonotary)).

Declining jurisdiction — forum non conveniens

Note. Reported cases on *forum non conveniens* are legion. As suggested in a note in (1999) 37 Can Y.B. Int'l L. 430-31, the courts now seldom attach much significance, in applying the *forum non conveniens* doctrine, to whether the defendant was served in or outside the jurisdiction. The only broad distinctions that have any usefulness in this area are those between different classes of litigation.

In commercial cases, the geographical pattern of the transactions in question is the most obvious element the courts refer to, with the law governing the claim also being given weight in some cases. In *Barclay's Bank plc* v. *Inc. Inc.* [*sic*] (1999), [2000] 6 W.W.R. 511, 78 Alta. L.R. (3d) 101 (Q.B.), the plaintiff, a foreign bank, was claiming the return of funds that it had credited in error to a corporation's bank account in the Cayman Islands. The Alberta court stayed the action because the only connection with Alberta was that one of the signing officers of the corporation lived there. The corporation did all its business in the Cayman Islands, and the judge held that the individual's residence in Alberta was fortuitous. Moreover, the bank's unjust enrichment claim was governed by the law of the Cayman Islands, because the contractual relationship that gave rise to the claim was governed by that law or, alternatively, because the enrichment had taken place in that jurisdiction. *Toronto Dominion Bank* v. *Hudye Soil Services Inc.,* [2000] 9 W.W.R. 272 (Man. Q.B.), was an action against companies doing business in Saskatchewan who were said to be liable in respect of farm crop sale proceeds that they allegedly converted or in respect of which they committed breaches of trust. The bank also claimed an interest in certain crops and the proceeds from them. The Manitoba court held that the litigation had a real and substantial connection with Manitoba. The laws of both provinces would apply in the case, but a Manitoba court could interpret and apply the Saskatchewan statutes in question. Saskatchewan had not been shown to be the more appropriate forum. See also *Sundquist* v. *Nehra* (2000), 191 Sask. R. 134 (Q.B.), in which Manitoba was held the *forum conveniens* for litigation concerning a lease of cattle to a Manitoba resident; all the facts were connected with that province.

Matters were evenly divided in *Central Biotec Inc.* v. *eMerge Interactive Inc.*, [2000] 11 W.W.R. 527 (Sask. Q.B.). A Saskatchewan firm assembled *E. Coli* detection kits using technology developed by a California corporation. When the latter firm terminated the arrangement, the Saskatchewan firm sued the California firm and a Delaware company in connection with breach of contract and inducing breach of contract, as well as breach of confidence and breach of fiduciary obligations. Service *ex juris* was proper as against each defendant. The court was not satisfied that the action could be tried more conveniently in California or Delaware. Even if certain claims did not qualify for service *ex juris* without leave, the court could give leave *nunc pro tunc* to ensure that all the claims could be dealt with in one proceeding. Another case where the defendant failed to show the other forum was more appropriate was *Crossley Carpet Mills* v. *Guarantee Co. of N. America* (2000), 181 N.S.R. (2d) 197 (C.A.), an action by a Nova Scotia carpet supplier against a surety on a labour bond and materials bond issued to the plaintiff's buyer, a contractor who was installing the carpet in a golf club in Quebec.

CRS Forestal v. *Boise Cascade Corp.* (1999), 36 C.P.C. (4th) 283 (B.C.S.C.), involved two actions arising out of the contractual arrangements for the development of a strand board plant in Chile using expertise owned by a British Columbia partnership. The project was a joint venture between the partnership and an Idaho corporation, and also involved two Chilean corporations. The court held that British Columbia was the *forum conveniens* for one of the actions but that it lacked jurisdiction in the other because there was no real and substantial connection with British Columbia. The first action, brought by the partnership against the others involved in the project, had many connections with British Columbia, which was also a more appropriate forum than Idaho or Chile. The second action was brought by a British Columbia securities dealer alleging that the defendants, who were the same as in the first action, had conspired or acted so as to interfere with its agreement with the partnership and thus caused it loss. The judge held that there was no arguable case shown, on the affidavit evidence, that any conspiracy or wrongful acts had taken place that had a substantial relationship to British Columbia.

Sometimes it is not the geographical pattern of the past events that determines the issue of *forum non conveniens*. In *Klein* v. *Manfrey Capital Corp.* (1999), 190 Sask. R. 319, 23 C.C.P.B. 35 (Sask. Q.B.), neither the plaintiff, nor the corporation he was suing for breach of its obligation to pay his pension, nor the directors of the corporation whom he was also suing, had any presence in Saskatchewan at the time of the action, although the plaintiff and the corporation were both Saskatchewan residents at the time the obligation was undertaken. The plaintiff now lived in Arizona and the corporation had been continued in British Columbia. Service *ex juris* on the individual defendants, resident in British Columbia, was refused, and jurisdiction was declined on the basis of *forum non conveniens*.

Tort actions tend to be localized in the place where the accident happens, so there is a strong tendency to favour that jurisdiction over others less closely connected. The *Berg* case, noted below, is an example, albeit reinforced by a "juridical advantage" argument. In *Napa* v. *Abta Shipping Co.* (1998), 173 F.T.R. 54 (F.C.T.D. (Prothonotary)), Canada was held to be the *forum conveniens* for actions by crew members, and the dependants of deceased crew members, against the owner of a Cyprus-registered ship that had sunk in Canadian waters. A further instance of the tendency to favour the place of the accident is *Smith & Nephew Inc.* v. *Marriott's Castle Harbour* (2000), 42 C.P.C. (4th) 336 (Ont. S.C.J. (Master)), an action for alleged water poisoning at a hotel in Bermuda. On the other hand, in *Lemmex* v. *Bernard* (2000), 49 O.R. (3d) 598 (Ont. S.C.J.), the court held that Ontario was the *forum conveniens* for third party claims made against a local bus company and driver in Grenada by tour operators and a cruise line, both of whom were being sued by an Ontario resident for injuries suffered on the bus. This seems to place little weight on the convenience of the Grenadan company and driver, and leave to appeal was given partly on this ground ((2000), 51 O.R. (3d) 164 (S.C.J.)).

Forum conveniens is of the essence of many decisions in family law, especially those relating to the custody of children. See below under (e) Infants and Children.

Berg (Litigation Guardian of) v. *Farm Bureau Mut. Ins. Co.* (2000), 5 M.V.R. (4th) 44, leave to appeal refused, 15 March 2001 (S.C.C.). Ontario Court of Appeal.

The court refused to decline jurisdiction in an action brought by a Minnesota resident against the Iowa-based insurer of the Minnesota-registered automobile in which she was injured as a consequence of an accident in Ontario. The insurer had filed a power of attorney with the Ontario Registrar of Motor Vehicles to accept service and appear on its behalf in any action in any Canadian province or territory, arising out of an accident in any Canadian province or territory. The filing was required by Ontario law for any insurer of an out-of-province vehicle that is to drive in Ontario. The court held that the power of attorney applied to actions by the out-of-province insured as well as by third party victims. There was a discretion to decline jurisdiction on the ground of *forum non conveniens,* and the fact that the parties resided in Minnesota and evidence was more readily available there militated in favour of doing so. However, the insured's right to statutory accident benefits was clear in Ontario, since the mandatory filing with the registrar included an undertaking not to raise any defence that would not have been available if the insurance contract had been entered into in the province or territory where the action was brought. The availability of the statutory benefits would be a live issue in Minnesota. The potential loss of that juridical advantage to the insured constituted good reason to enforce the power of attorney.

ECS Educational Consulting Services Canada Ltd. v. *United Arab Emirates (Armed Forces)* (2000), 44 C.P.C. (4th) 111. Ontario Superior Court of Justice.

A Canadian firm, via affiliated companies, had entered into several contracts with the Armed Forces of the United Arab Emirates (UAE) to supply technical instruction facilities and educational services in the UAE. It sued the UAE in Ontario, claiming breaches of the contracts. The UAE applied for a stay of the proceedings on the basis that Ontario was *forum non conveniens.* Nordheimer J. granted the stay. There was no real and substantial connection between Ontario and the subject matter of the action. Alternatively, the court should exercise its discretion to decline jurisdiction. On that point, the plaintiff argued that it could not receive a fair hearing in the UAE and so Ontario was the only viable forum. The judge found that the evidence put forward to support this assertion was thin. The alleged difficulties were ones that the plaintiff had made no real effort to address. It was also important that the contracts included an express acceptance of the jurisdiction of the courts of the UAE. Business people agreeing to such a clause presumably assessed the judicial system in question or they were prepared to take the risk of binding themselves to it. In either event, it would send entirely the wrong message if Canadian courts were to permit Canadian businesses, after the fact when problems arise in order to try to resile from those agreements by permitting them, essentially, to retreat to the courts of this country.

Note. The previous two cases both deal with assertions that the plaintiff should be permitted to maintain a local action because of a legitimate juridical advantage enjoyed there. This is a matter on which the Supreme Court of Canada urged caution in *Amchem Products Inc.* v. *British Columbia (Workers' Compensation Board),* [1993] 1 S.C.R. 897 at 932-33, 102 D.L.R. (4th) 96 at 119-20 (an anti-suit injunction case). The plaintiff's entitlement to the advantage must be scrutinized to see whether, among other things, the plaintiff had a reasonable expectation that the advantage would be available to it. Juridical advantages played a decisive role in *Association of Architects (Ontario)* v. *Deskin* (2000), 19 C.C.L.I. (3d) 275 (Ont. S.C.J.). An Ontario architect, whose professional liability insurance was issued by the Association of Architects in Ontario, was sued in Québec for negligence in connection with work he had done on a project located there. The association brought an application in Ontario to determine its obligation to indemnify the architect. The plaintiffs in the Québec proceedings brought a motion to stay the application on the ground that legal proceedings were pending in Québec and the issue of obligation to indemnify should be determined in the Québec court. The Ontario court denied a stay. The issue of obligation to indemnify, between an Ontario insurer and an Ontario-resident insured, pursuant to a contract probably governed by Ontario law, was more closely connected with Ontario than with Québec. If the association were denied the right to litigate in Ontario, it would be deprived of the immunity from direct action by the injured parties that it enjoyed under Ontario law, but not under Québec law. In *Gotch* v. *Ramirez* (2000), 48 O.R. (3d) 515 (Ont. S.C.J.), the plaintiff, a Pennsylvania resident, had been injured in an accident in Pennsylvania involving a vehicle owned by the defendant, a resident of Ontario. The plaintiff sued in Ontario and the defendant's motion for a stay was dismissed. The limitation period in Pennsylvania had expired, and the loss of juridical advantage to the plaintiff arising from that issue was enough to outweigh all the other considerations, the majority of which favoured Pennsylvania as the appropriate forum.

In *Cortese (Next Friend of)* v. *Nowsco Well Service Ltd.* (2000), 80 Alta. L.R. (3d) 3, 44 C.P.C. (4th) 23 (C.A.), the court affirmed the decision noted in (1999) 37 Can. Y.B. Int'l L. 432. The chambers judge had declined jurisdiction in an action by a driver who was severely injured in an Italian automobile accident, and the driver's wife, against his former Italian employer, an Italian subsidiary of a Canadian corporation, for misrepresenting his insurance coverage. The plaintiffs had argued that they should be allowed to sue in Canada because of a legitimate juridical advantage there, namely, that they would not be exposed to the risk of a criminal prosecution in Italy for the man's driving, which the Italian police believed had caused the accident and killed the man's passenger. The Court of Appeal found this assertion unsupported by the facts. In any event, escaping a foreign prosecution fairly brought by a country with a fair system of courts and law was an illegitimate juridical advantage at best. Nor was it a sound argument that the limitation period for an action had expired in Italy. There was no question of the defendants' having lain in the weeds until that happened. The plaintiffs were aware from an early stage that the defendants wanted the proceedings to be in Italy, and the plaintiffs had not taken any steps to commence an action there to protect their position. Finally, the judge had been right to give weight to the fact that a great deal of Italian law would have to be referred to and a large number of Italian witnesses would be necessary.

Declining jurisdiction — lis alibi pendens

Note. See *Pre Print Inc.* v. *Maritime Telegraph & Telephone Co.*, noted above under the heading Declining jurisdiction — exclusive choice of forum clause. See also *North American Steel Equipment Co.* v. *G.N. Johnston Equipment Co./Equipment G.N. Johnston Ltée* (1999), 34 C.P.C. (4th) 324 (Ont. Gen. Div.). An Ontario corporation that was sued both in Alberta and in Ontario in respect of the same subject matter was successful in having the Ontario action stayed on the ground of *forum non conveniens*. Public policy would be offended if proceedings duplicated each other, and the Ontario court had no juridiction in respect of one issue, which involved a builder's lien on Alberta property.

(b)   Class proceedings

Class including non-residents

Harrington v. *Dow Corning Corp.* (2000), 193 D.L.R. (4th) 67, [2000] 11 W.W.R. 201. British Columbia Court of Appeal.

The plaintiffs, women who had been implanted with silicone breast implants that were alleged to have been unfit for the purpose for which they were marketed, sought certification of certain issues in their claims against the defendant manufacturers and distributors as a class proceeding under the Class Proceedings Act, R.S.B.C. 1996, c. 50. The case management judge had granted the certification on the common issue of whether the implants were reasonably fit for their intended purpose. The judge held that the risk assessment central to the issue could fairly and efficiently be undertaken in a single proceeding at the first stage of a multi-stage proceeding. The Court of Appeal affirmed the case management judge's decision. The policy goals underlying the act were efficiency, access to the courts, and the modification of the behaviour of wrongdoers, all of which would be served by the preliminary determination of whether breast implants carried inherent danger and what the risks were.

One of the issues argued on appeal was whether the British Columbia court had jurisdiction to include in the class action the claims of women who were non-resident in British Columbia or who, although resident, had suffered their alleged injuries outside the province. The claimants had been grouped into "resident" and "non-resident" subclasses, with the latter subclass being included only if they opted in. Counsel for the representative plaintiff acknowledged that many of the non-resident members and some of the resident members could not establish jurisdiction *simpliciter* under a strict application of the real and substantial connection test.

One question was the bearing on the jurisdictional issue that section 16(2) of the act might have. The subsection stipulates that a non-resident of British Columbia "may ... opt into that class proceeding if the person would be, but for not being a resident of British Columbia, a member of the class involved in the class proceeding." The legislation was based on the Uniform Class Proceedings Act promulgated by the Uniform Law Conference of Canada. Some legislatures had chosen to adopt an "opting in" mechanism, with non-residents included in the class only if they signified their consent to be included, and thus would be preluded by *res judicata* from later suing or benefitting from a suit in another jurisdiction. The Ontario statute did not mention residency, but the Ontario courts had approved the creation of "national" classes of claimants purporting to bind both resident and non-resident members who had not opted out: *Nantais* v. *Telectronics Proprietary (Canada) Ltd.* (1995), 127 D.L.R. (4th) 552 (Ont. Gen. Div.), leave to appeal denied (1995), 129 D.L.R. (4th) 110 (Ont. Gen. Div.), and (1996), 7 C.P.C. (4th) 206 (Ont. C.A.).

In the case of alleged defective manufacture or failure to warn, it is assumed that a manufacturer knows the product may find itself anywhere in Canada if it is capable of being moved. By the action of sale, the manufacturer exposes itself to the risk of an action in any province (*Moran* v. *Pyle National (Canada) Ltd.* (1973), [1975] 1 S.C.R. 393, 43 D.L.R. (3d) 239). This rule justified the inclusion in the "resident" class of all women resident in the province who alleged that they were suffering harm from the use of implants manufactured and put into the flow of commerce negligently by a defendant. Section 16(2) could not, however, be read as allowing women resident anywhere, who had suffered as a result of the implantation of the product, to be included in the class. The section did not seek to extend the jurisdiction of British Columbia courts beyond constitutionally recognized limits. The section might preclude the court from certifying a national class on an opting-out basis, as was done in *Nantais*. However, it accorded with the requirements of comity and with the policy underlying the enactment of legislation enabling class actions to determine the liability of defendants for mass injury in one forum to the extent for which claimants might wish and that fairness to the defendants might permit. Jurisdiction *simpliciter* was not a rigid concept. The justification for claiming or refusing jurisdiction rested upon the principles of order and fairness that were sometimes called comity. Comity, especially inter-provincial comity, called for the meshing of the principles of *res judicata*, the rules for the recognition and enforcement of orders, the rules for the issuance of anti-suit injunctions, and the rules for the assumption of jurisdiction. In Canada, this meshing requires a provincial court to place reasonable restrictions on its assertion of jurisdiction. A real and substantial connection is the test of that limit.

The case management judge was right to find that jurisdiction *simpliciter* was established for non-resident claimants who chose to opt into the class. The defendants acknowledged the jurisdiction of the British Columbia courts to determine the claims of at least those resident and non-resident class members implanted in British Columbia. The defendants were defending the class action. It was true that presence in the jurisdiction for the purpose of the defence of one claim did not create presence for the purpose of the prosecution of another independent claim. However, the Court of Appeal did not accept that rule as precluding a court from taking account of that presence for the purpose of determining whether the existence of a certified class action with a common issue provided a real and substantial connection between the province and the subject matter of the claim that a non-resident sought to have resolved in the same class proceeding. The defendants put their products into the stream of commerce and must anticipate the possibility of being haled into any Canadian court. They were defending the claims of all purchasers resident in British Columbia. The Supreme Court had certified an issue common to all purchasers for resolution in a class proceeding. Those were compelling reasons for British Columbia courts to accept jurisdiction. British Columbia had more than a little interest in accommodating a national resolution of the dispute.

To permit, in this way, what the defendants called "piggy-backing" in a class proceeding was not to gut the foundation of conflict of laws principles. Rather, it was to accommodate the values underlying those principles. To exlude non-resident claimants because they had not used the product in British Columbia would contradict the principles of order and fairness that underlie the jurisdictional rules. By opting-in, the non-resident class members were accepting that their claims were essentially the same as those of the resident class members. To the extent that the defendants could establish that they were not, the claimants could be excluded by order of the case management or trial judge upon application. So could a class that was certified in another province.

(c)   Actions Relating to Property

Immovables — disputes as to title to foreign immovables

Montagne Laramee Developments Inc. v. *Creit Properties Inc.* (2000), 47 O.R. (3d) 729, 45 C.P.C. (4th) 345. Ontario Superior Court of Justice.

The plaintiff, based in Ontario, sued the defendants, also based in that province, in the Ontario Superior Court of Justice for breach of an agreement made in Ontario for the purchase of real property in Québec. The relief claim included a declaration that the property was held by the defendants on trust for the plaintiff, and an interlocutory and permanent injunction restraining the defendants from enforcing any rights pursuant to a loan agreement and a deed of hypothec, the latter being a form of property security unique to Québec. The loan agreement, which involved two properties in Ontario as well as the one in Québec, stipulated that it was to be governed by the law of Ontario "except in so far as the laws in effect in the Province of Quebec require otherwise." The defendants moved for an order permanently staying the action against them on the basis that Ontario was *forum non conveniens* and on the basis that the Ontario court had no jurisdiction to adjudicate an action involving an issue of title to a foreign immovable.

Pitt J. granted the stay. It was clear from *Catania* v. *Giannattasio* (1999), 174 D.L.R. (4th) 170 (Ont. C.A.) (noted in (1999) 37 Can. Y.B. Int'l L.441) that the general rule in Canada was still that Canadian courts had no jurisdiction to determine title to, or an interest in, foreign land. The provinces were still separate legal jurisdictions, notwithstanding the suggestions in *Morguard Investments Ltd.* v. *De Savoye*, [1990] 3 S.C.R. 1077, that Canadian conflict rules ought to reflect the intention of the constitution to create a "single country." *Catania* recognized that there was an exception to the rule so as to allow a court to take *in personam* jurisdiction, notwithstanding that foreign immovables were involved, if the claim was for the enforcement merely of personal obligations. However, the exception did not apply if, *inter alia*, the claim was not based on a personal obligation running between the parties or if the local court could not supervise the execution of the judgment. Here the claim was not for specific performance, which would be an *in personam* remedy, but a claim that almost inevitably would require the assistance of the Québec courts. The ownership of the property was not merely incidental to the subject matter of the dispute. The connection between Ontario and the Québec property was too tenuous to satisfy the real and substantal connection test in *Morguard* for founding jurisdiction.

Matrimonial property

Note. In *Pasareno* v. *Pasareno* (2000), 188 Sask. R. 314 (Q.B.), a wife's matrimonial property action in Saskatchewan was not stayed, although the husband was resident either in Alberta or in

British Columbia and had commenced similar proceedings in Alberta. There were assets in both provinces and other relevant records were located in both provinces and in Manitoba. This was a case where there was no single appropriate forum. The wife had chosen Saskatchewan to commence her proceeding; the court could exercise *in personam* jurisdiction over the husband, albeit that part of the property was in other provinces; and Alberta was not clearly a more appropriate forum. See also *Jenkins* v. *Jenkins,* noted below under (d) Matrimonial proceedings — divorce and corollary relief.

Bankruptcy and insolvency

Note. The Quebec Superior Court, sitting in bankruptcy and assisting in the enforcement of the powers of a Belgian trustee in bankruptcy, was held to have no power to make orders that in effect reversed the orders of the Federal Court, Trial Division, enforcing a maritime lien against a ship: *Re Antwerp Bulkcarriers N.V.* (2000), 187 D.L.R. (4th) 106, leave to appeal granted, 31 Aug. 2000 (S.C.C.).

(d)   Matrimonial proceedings

Divorce and corollary relief

Jenkins v. *Jenkins* (2000), 8 R.F.L. (5th) 96. Ontario Superior Court of Justice.

A couple and their two children, all born in, as well as being citizens of, the United Kingdom, relocated to Canada on a temporary work visa based on the husband's secondment to the Canadian subsidiary of a United Kingdom company. The couple separated three years later. The husband returned to the United Kingdom. The wife and the children obtained student visas to remain in Canada and intended to remain there permanently if they could. After negotiations to settle their affairs had broken down, the wife in an e-mail message invited the husband to begin legal proceedings in the United Kingdom. The husband issued a divorce application in England on December 9, 1999. Six days later the wife applied to the Ontario Superior Court of Justice, seeking a divorce, a division of matrimonial property, and an order for custody. She also filed a one-page answer in the English proceeding, contesting some of the grounds of the husband's application and raising the issue of the English court's jurisdiction. The husband now disputed the Ontario court's jurisdiction to proceed with the wife's action.

Perkins J. held that the Ontario court had jurisdiction in respect of all the wife's claims. Jurisdiction to grant a divorce under the Divorce Act, R.S.C. 1985, c. 3 (2nd Supp.), section 3(1), depends upon either party having been "ordinarily resident in the province for at least one year immediately preceding the commencement of the proceeding." Although they had not had the status of permanent residents of Canada, the parties and the children were legally in Canada throughout the three-and-a-half-year period of their residence, and no one had taken any steps to terminate the mother's or the children's residence in Canada at the time of the motion in the present case. Absent any action by the mother to leave or by the government to remove her and the children from Canada, the mother's and the children's residence did not lose the quality of ordinariness. The wife had made claims for custody both as corollary relief under the Divorce Act and under the provincial legislation (Children's Law Reform Act, R.S.O. 1990, c. C.12). Jurisdiction under the Divorce Act existed. The jurisdictional test under the provincial legislation was the habitual residence of the child. Under the definition in section 22(2) of the act, the children were habitually resident in Ontario since they either resided there with both parents or resided there with the mother by consent or acquiescence.

The issue then was whether the Ontario court should decline jurisdiction on the ground that England was the more appropriate forum. The most important issues were the living arrangements for the two sons. The vast majority of the evidence as to the best interests of the children was to be found in Ontario. The mother intended, if she could, to remain there with the sons, and the father seemed content to have her retain custody of them although he would clearly prefer the mother and the children to return to England so he would be closer to the children. For custody and access issues, the balance of convenience overwhelmingly favoured Ontario. On the issues of child and spousal support, the evidence was largely documentary, and so neither forum had the advantage on this score. However, the husband had all the financial resources and the wife could probably not afford to litigate in England, which favoured Ontario as the forum.

As for the matrimonial property, section 15 of the Family Law Act, R.S.O. 1990, c. F.3, contained a statutory choice of law rule in favour of the internal law of the place where the couple had their last common habitual residence. The law of Ontario therefore would have to be applied. Although the majority of the assets in question were in the United Kingdom, there was no immovable property involved. The Ontario court was in the best position to apply Ontario law and it would be cheaper for the parties to do that rather than to prove Ontario law in an English court. And there was the possibility that the English court would want to apply some law other than Ontario law, which the Ontario legislature had declared by the enactment of section 15 to be contrary to public policy. The balance of convenience on this issue favoured the wife because of the Ontario law issue and the economic positions of the parties.

It was immaterial whether the English court would or might proceed to grant a divorce. The English divorce would be recognized in Canada, but the wife's claims, being made under provincial law as well as federal law, did not depend for their existence on a pending divorce case in Ontario. If the English court chose to retain jurisdiction and proceeded to grant a divorce, the wife's other claims could all continue independently of the divorce. It was true that the wife had more or less invited the husband to commence proceedings in England and had participated to a degree in those proceedings. However, her participation did not amount to a submission to the English court's jurisdiction. She objected to the English court's jurisdiction from the outset. Her one-page answer merely denied some of the grounds for the husband's application and contained no pleading on the merits of custody, access, support, or property.

Note. Although it was probably immaterial to the result, the judge's reliance on public policy, in dealing with the scenario that an English court might not apply Ontario law to the matrimonial property issues, seems misplaced. Section 15 of the Family Law Act does not declare other choice of law rules to be against public policy in the sense of violating the fundamental moral and social principles on which the forum's legal system rests. It merely opts for a choice of law rule that, in the view of the legislature, achieves on the whole a fairer result than any alternative rule. The fact that English private international law may take a different view can hardly be described as contrary to public policy "in the international sense."

Support obligations

Note. Jurisdiction to vary support orders made by courts elsewhere was in issue in two cases. In *Harron* v. *Russworm* (1999), [2000] 2 W.W.R. 250 (Sask. Q.B.), the Saskatchewan court held it had jurisdiction under the Reciprocal Enforcement of Maintenance Orders Act, 1996, S.S. 1996, c. R-4.2, to make a provisional order varying a child support order made by the Ontario Provincial Court. It was true that the only reference in the act to variation spoke of "registered orders," but to insist on registration of the Ontario order as a prerequisite of variation of it in Saskatchewan would be inconsistent with the purpose of the act, which was in part to provide parties with an expeditious and cost-effective method for having their ongoing support rights and obligations determined. *Rothgiesser* v. *Rothgiesser* (2000), 183 D.L.R. (4th) 310, 2 R.F.L. (5th) 267 (Ont. C.A.), held that the variation powers under the Divorce Act, R.S.C. 1985, c. 3 (2nd Supp.), with respect to corollary orders was limited to orders made under the act. They could not be used to vary orders made by a foreign court (in this case, South Africa), which was a matter for provincial, not federal, law.

(e) Infants and children

Custody — existence of jurisdiction

Note. Jurisdiction in custody is governed by different rules. Many provinces have adopted uniform legislation that uses the habitual residence of the child as the basic criterion. It is usually assumed that if the case does not satisfy the jurisdictional criteria in the relevant act, the court cannot take jurisdiction, but *Creamer* v. *Creamer* (2000), 8 R.F.L. (5th) 241 (Nfld. S.C.), held that even in such a case it is open to the court to take jurisdiction on the basis of its inherent *parens patriae* powers. In this case, the child had been taken by the mother from Ontario. Since the child was living with her in Newfoundland without the father's consent, the child was not habitually resident in Newfoundland under section 28(1) of the Children's Law Act, S.N. 1988, c. 61. Nor did the exceptional circumstances, in which a court may take jurisdiction over a child habitually resident elsewhere, apply, and nor did the "serious harm" exception in section 29 apply. Yet the *parens patriae* jurisdiction continued to exist because it had not been specifically excluded by the act. Whatever the validity, as a matter of Newfoundland law, the court's conclusion that the Children's Law Act did not exhaustively define its jurisdiction in custody, makes it doubtful that any order made by it would be enforceable in Ontario, should that ever be a relevant issue. Under section 41(1)(e) of the Children's Law Reform Act, R.S.O. 1990, c. C.12, an Ontario court need not enforce an extra-provincial custody order if the extra-provincial tribunal would not, in accordance with section 22 of the act, have jurisdiction if it were a court in Ontario. Section 22 uses the same jurisdictional tests as the Newfoundland statute, and the Newfoundland judge held expressly that these were not satisfied.

Where uniform legislation does not apply, jurisdiction in custody depends on the child being either resident or ordinarily resident in the province, and on whether the court is the *forum conveniens* in the sense that it is best placed to make the decision in the best interests of the child. See *Lariviere* v. *Lariviere* (1999), 184 N.S.R. (2d) 384 (S.C. Fam. Div.), where jurisdiction was declined in favour of Alberta, and *K.J.S.* v. *M.T.* (1999), 182 N.S.R. (2d) 391 (S.C. Fam. Div.), where it was taken. A further case is *B.P.* v. *M.B.* (1999), 241 A.R. 395 (Q.B.), where jurisdiction was also taken although the eighteen-month-old child now lived in Ontario. The application by the Alberta-resident father was for a declaration of paternity and for custody, and most of the child's short life had been lived in Alberta or Saskatchewan.

Jurisdiction in custody under the Divorce Act, R.S.C. 1985, c. 3 (2nd Supp.), exists as part of the jurisdiction to grant a divorce (section 3), or, if the parents are already divorced under the act, it exists if either former spouse is ordinarily resident in the province or both former spouses consent (section 4). There is a power to transfer corollary proceedings to another Canadian court in certain circumstances. In *Brooks* v. *Brooks* (1999), 141 Man. R. (2d) 25 (C.A.), the parties disputed the enforcement of a consent variation order, made in Manitoba corollary to a decree of divorce, that provided for joint custody under a shared parenting arrangement. One of the terms of the order was that each party agreed to relocate to a certain region of Ontario. The father had done so, but the mother still lived elsewhere in Ontario, as she had done since the couple's separation. The Manitoba court refused the mother's application to transfer to Ontario the proceeding brought on by the husband for a further variation of the consent custody order. Section 5(1)(b) of the Divorce Act gives the court jurisdiction in a variation proceeding if both spouses accept jurisdiction, which they had done by the terms of the consent order itself. Although the two children were now most substantially connected with Ontario, their best interests would not be served by a transfer of the proceedings to Ontario (section 6(3)(ii)). The Manitoba court was the court before which the agreement was reached. Given the history of the matter, which extended over three years of legal wrangling in Manitoba and Ontario courts, there was a need to ensure that the issues between the parties were resolved in a timely way, and that could best be done by the court's enforcement of the arrangements to which the parents had agreed, albeit varied in some respects in the light of changed circumstances.

In *Hamel-Smith* v. *Gonsalves* (2000), 185 D.L.R. (4th) 713, 5 R.F.L. (5th) 368 (Alta. Q.B.), the mother had come to Canada with the children from Trinidad and obtained refugee status on the basis that she had a reasonable fear of violence from the father if she returned to Trinidad. It was possible that her removal of the children had been wrongful within the meaning of the Hague Convention on the Civil Aspects of Child Abduction, as implemented by the International Abduction Act, S.A. 1986, c. I-6.5, but the father's application was more than a year after the removal and the children were now settled into their new environment (Article 12), so the court was not obliged to order their return. The children's links to Alberta were so strong that the court had jurisdiction to decide the custody issue even if the children were still technically resident in Trinidad and even if it might later appear that the mother had not been ordinarily resident for the year required to found jurisdiction in divorce. Alberta was the most convenient forum and jurisdiction should therefore be exercised. It was also relevant that the father had probably attorned to the jurisdiction of the Alberta court.

Custody — declining jurisdiction

See *Jenkins* v. *Jenkins,* noted above under (d) Matrimonial proceedings — divorce and corollary relief.

Custody — enforcement of extraprovincial custody order

Wilson v. *Perry* (2000), 184 Nfld. & P.E.I. R. 1, 4 R.F.L. (5th) 154. Newfoundland Court of Appeal.

The parties had a child during a two-year relationship when they lived in British Columbia. The child was about one year old when they separated. The British Columbia Supreme Court made a consent order for joint custody with the child to be primarily resident with the mother. Some months later this order was varied to make the child's residence with the father until resolution of the matter of the apprehension of the mother's other children by British Columbia Child Services. The father, in breach of a term of the amended order, took the child with him to Newfoundland. He said he feared for the child's safety. Two years later, the mother's other children having been returned to her, the mother applied to the British Columbia court for sole custody. She applied for custody to the Newfoundland Supreme Court. The British Columbia court ordered the father to return the child to British Columbia for the custody proceeding there.

The Newfoundland Court of Appeal upheld the decision of the judge of the Unified Family Court to take jurisdiction. The judge applied section 50(1) of the Children's Law Act, R.S.N. 1990, c. C-13, which provides that a court may supersede an extra-provincial order in respect of custody and access where the court is satisfied that there has been a material change in circumstances that affects or is likely to affect the best interests of the child and certain other conditions are met. One of the combinations of factors is that there has been a material change in circumstances and the child is habitually resident in Newfoundland at the start of the application for the order. Under section 28(3) of the act, the fact that the father had removed the child surreptitiously from British Columbia did not preclude a finding that the child had become habitually resident in Newfoundland, if there had been acquiesence or undue delay by the mother in starting judicial proceedings. The failure to take action for custody for a period of two years when that amounted to nearly half a lifetime for the child must be considered to be undue delay. The Court of Appeal therefore upheld the judge's decision that the child was habitually resident in Newfoundland at the relevant time.

Note. This case was decided under the uniform custody jurisdiction and enforcement of custody orders legislation that many provinces have adopted. A case where an otherwise enforceable order was not enforced, because the applicant had abducted the children from that jurisdiction as well as Ontario, was *Miller* v. *Miller* (1999), 1 R.F.L. (5th) 391 (Ont. C.A.). The father's application should be refused until the children were returned.

Child abduction — Hague Convention

Note. Cases involving the Hague Convention on the Civil Aspects of Child Abduction were *Blanchard* v. *Wuest* (2000), 6 R.F.L. (5th)

66 (B.C.S.C.), where the child's habitual residence was found to be California at the time of removal by the mother, but the matter needed to go to trial on whether the father had custody rights at that time; *Mahler* v. *Mahler* (1999), 3 R.F.L. (5th) 428 (Man. Q.B.), where removal by the mother from New York was wrongful as being in violation of the father's custody rights there; *Rechsteiner* v. *Kendell* (1999), 1 R.F.L. (5th) 101 (Ont. C.A.), where the mother's removal of the child from Switzerland was held to have been wrongful because it was in violation of rights of custody being exercised by the Swiss Guardianship Department; and *Finzio* v. *Scoppio-Finzio* (1999), 1 R.F.L. (5th) 222 (Ont. C.A.), where again the removal from Italy had been in violation of the father's custody rights there. In *Mahler* and *Finzio*, arguments that the return of the child should not be ordered, on the ground of a risk of physical or psychological harm to the child (Article 13 of the convention) were rejected. In *Rechsteiner*, the risk of harm was found to exist if the child were suddenly separated from the mother, and the court's order provided for the mother's retaining interim custody and traveling with the child to Switzerland.

2   Québec

(a) Action personnelle

Article 3148 C.C.Q. — fait dommageable se produit au Québec

American Mobile Satellite Corp. c. *Spar Aerospace Ltd.*, [2000] R.J.Q. 1405, autorisation de pourvoi accordée, 19 avril 2001 (C.S.C.). Cour d'appel du Québec.

Dans le cadre de la construction d'un satellite par Hughes Aircraft Co., de Californie, pour le compte de l'appelante AMS, exerçant ses activités en Virginie et n'ayant pas d'établissement au Québec, la première de ces entités a conclu un sous-contrat avec l'intimée Spar, dont le siège social est en Ontario et qui exploite une usine au Québec, où les travaux ont été entièrement exécutés. À la suite de sa mise en orbite et de sa prise de possession par AMS, des dommages importants ont été causés au satellite par des tests de communications menés à partir d'une base aux États-Unis. En conséquence, Hughes a refusé de verser à Spar les primes de rendement prévues par le sous-contrat. Spar a alors intenté au Québec une action à AMS et à trois autres défenderesses, dont aucune n'est domiciliée au Québec. Elle les tient solidairement responsables de la perte de ses primes de rendement (819 657 $), d'une privation de profits futurs en raison de l'atteinte à sa réputation (50 000 $) et des débours engagés pour enquêter sur les dommages au satellite (50 000 $). AMS et les autres défenderesses ont, par exception déclinatoire, demandé le rejet de l'action ou, subsidiairement l'application de l'article 3135 C.C.Q. La juge de première instance a conclu à la compétence des autorités québécoises et a refusé d'appliquer la doctrine du *forum non conveniens* en l'absence d'indices clairs que l'autorité d'un autre État serait plus à même de trancher le litige. En appel, les parties appelantes ont uniquement allégué qu'aucun préjudice n'avait été subi au Québec.

La Cour d'appel a rejeté l'appel. L'article 3148 paragraphe 3 C.C.Q. fait référence à deux concepts différents: la faute et le fait dommageable. Dans le premier cas, il y a manquement à une obligation, alors que cette notion est absente dans la deuxième expression. Spar allègue, parmi ses chefs de réclamation, avoir subi une atteinte à la réputation. Cette attaque est un fait dommageable qui, comme il s'est produit au Québec, donne ouverture à réparation si la faute est prouvée. Bien que l'article 3148 ne caractérise pas l'expression "fait dommageable," la réclamation qui en résulte, lorsque le fait dommageable n'est qu'une assise de revendication parmi d'autres, doit être notable. On ne peut utiliser un fait qui produit des dommages négligeables pour écarter la compétence d'autorités étrangères. À cet égard, le législateur a prévu un facteur de rattachement important à l'autorité étrangère, soit le fait que le litige se rattache d'une façon importante à l'État dont l'autorité a été saisie. La même exigence devrait être remplie lorsque seulement une partie des dommages réclamés découle d'un fait qui s'est produit au Québec, ce qui est le cas en l'espèce.

Article 3135 C.C.Q. — forum non conveniens

Kingsway General Insurance Co. c. *Komatsu Canada Ltée*, [1999] R.J.Q. 2715. Cour supérieure du Québec.

L'assurée de Kingsway, une compagnie ayant son siège social au Québec, a acheté une abatteuse de marque Komatsu d'une compagnie ayant son siège social en Ontario. Le contrat est intervenu en Ontario et la livraison s'est faite sur un chantier situé en Ontario. Lors de travaux d'abattage sur le chantier en Ontario, l'appareil a pris feu. Kingsway a indemnisé son assurée et elle a intenté un recours en dommages-intérêts contre le vendeur, l'importateur et le fabricant. L'importateur a sa place d'affaires en Ontario et le fabricant en a une au Québec. L'abatteuse a été fabriquée aux États-Unis. Les témoins de Kingsway résident au Québec alors que les témoins de l'importateur sont des résidents ontariens. La compétence des tribunaux québécois est reconnue par les parties. L'importateur invoque la règle du *forum non conveniens,* invitant les tribunaux québécois à décliner compétence en faveur des tribunaux ontariens (art. 3135 C.C.Q.). Il allègue que le lieu du sinistre et le lieu de formation du contrat sont en Ontario et que la loi applicable est la loi ontarienne.

L'exception déclinatoire est accueillie. D'une part, Kingsway, l'importateur, le vendeur et ses employés, les employés du client pour lequel l'assurée effectuait l'abattage d'arbres, les témoins et experts de l'importateur et les personnes ayant procédé aux inspections de l'appareil résident en Ontario. Le lieu de formation et d'exécution du contrat est l'Ontario et la loi applicable est ontarienne. L'appareil se trouve présentement en Ontario. Si Kingsway a gain de cause contre l'une des défenderesses étrangères, il faudra qu'elle fasse exemplifier son jugement. D'autre part, les employés de l'assurée, son président et son expert résident au Québec. Compte tenu de tous ces éléments, il serait plus approprié que les tribunaux ontariens tranchent le litige.

Gordon Capital Corp. c. *La Garantie, Compagnie d'assurances de l'Amérique du Nord* (1999), [2000] R.J.Q. 267. Cour supérieure du Québec.

En 1991, Gordon, qui a son siège social en Ontario, a avisé ses assureurs qu'elle avait subi une perte d'environ 40 000 000 $ à la suite d'une fraude d'un de ses employés. En 1993, Gordon a intenté une action au Québec contre les assureurs qui ont leur siège social au Québec. Les défenderesses ont alors intenté une action en Ontario recherchant une déclaration voulant que la police en faveur de Gordon soit nulle et que les recours de Gordon soient prescrits. Ils ont déposé également une requête en irrecevabilité à l'encontre de l'action de Gordon intentée au Québec, alléguant litispendance. La Cour d'appel du Québec a conclu qu'il n'y avait pas de litispendance mais a suspendu l'action jusqu'à ce que les procédures ontariennes soient réglées par un jugement final. Le tribunal ontarien a déclaré prescrite la réclamation de Gordon en raison de son omission d'intenter des procédures judiciaires dans les vingt-quatre mois suivant la découverte de la perte, comme prévoyait la police. La décision du tribunal de première instance est confirmée par la Cour suprême du Canada. Gordon insiste pour que ce soit le tribunal québécois qui statue sur le différend puisque le jugement ontarien ne concerne qu'un jugement déclaratoire et que, par conséquent, le fond n'a jamais été plaidé en Ontario, ce qu'elle pourrait faire ici au Québec, compte tenu du fait que la prescription est de trois ans. Les assureurs demandent le rejet de l'action intentée au Québec en vertu de la règle du *forum non conveniens.*

La Cour supérieure a accueilli les requêtes des assureurs. Lorsque les tribunaux de deux provinces sont tous les deux compétents, il faut étudier d'une façon plus pragmatique et fonctionnelle le lien réel et important entre la réclamation et le tribunal. Pour résoudre l'impasse créée par la compétence des deux tribunaux, il y a lieu d'appliquer la doctrine du *forum non conveniens,* vu que l'article 3135 C.C.Q. n'était pas en vigueur au moment de l'institution de l'action. En l'espèce, le seul facteur de rattachement est que les trois assureurs sont domiciliés au Québec. La Cour d'appel, par son jugement suspendant les procédures de la présente action, a reconnu que la cause d'action avait pris naissance en Ontario et que les débats devaient avoir lieu à cet endroit. Le tribunal ontarien est donc le tribunal le plus approprié. Les tribunaux québécois, en appliquant la doctrine du *forum non conveniens,* doivent reconnaître la décision du tribunal ontarien. Le juge du fond sera saisi du même problème que celui que la Cour doit décider dans les présentes procédures. Il devra statuer que la loi du for est celle de l'Ontario. Il devra lui aussi reconnaître la décision de la cour de cette province et sera incapable de mettre de côté la décision de la Cour suprême du Canada. Il serait contraire à l'intérêt de la justice de laisser continuer des procédures en sachant qu'elles n'ont aucune chance de réussir.

Amiel Distributions Ltd. c. *Amana Co. L.P.,* [2000] A.J.Q. N° 1700. Cour supérieure du Québec.

Amana, ayant son siège social aux États-Unis, a mis fin unilatéralement à une entente de distribution de marchandises en vertu de laquelle Amiel vend et distribue les marchandises de Amana dans tout l'est du Canada. Amana a intenté une action aux États-Unis réclamant le paiement d'un solde pour marchandises vendues et livrées. Amiel a intenté au Québec une action réclamant des dommages-intérêts pour résiliation abusive. Amana demande au tribunaux québécois de décliner compétence en faveur des tribunaux américains, alléguant qu'elle est domiciliée aux États-Unis, que la loi applicable au présent litige est celle des États-Unis, qu'un litige entre les mêmes parties et fondé sur le mêmes faits est pendant devant les tribunaux américains, qui ont récemment rejeté une exception déclinatoire présentée par Amiel en vertu de la règle du *forum non conveniens,* et que le jugement que rendra la cour américaine pourra être reconnu au Québec.

La Cour supérieure a acceuilli l'exception déclinatoire. Le débat litigieux aux États-Unis ne sera pas restreint uniquement à la question du solde dû. La contestation d'Amiel déposée dans le dossier américain prétend à une compensation pour des dommages résultant de la résiliation. Il n'est pas logique qu'il y ait deux procès, et ce cas apparaît exceptionnel au sens de l'article 3135 C.C.Q. Les autorités américaines sont plus à même de trancher le litige.

(b)   Famille

Pension alimentaire — enfant

Note. Veuillez voir *Droit de la famille — 3148,* [2000] R.J.Q. 2339 (C.S.).

Enfants — garde d'enfant — décliner competence

Note. Veuillez voir *Droit de la famille — 3459,* [1999] R.J.Q. 2971 (C.S.).

B   *Procedure / Procédure*

1   Common Law and Federal

(a)   Remedies

Damages — foreign currency — conversion

Note. In *Stevenson Estate v. Siewert* (2000), 191 D.L.R. (4th) 151 (Alta. C.A.), the tort was governed by domestic law, but it was the conversion in Canada of a US dollar bank draft. The court held that damages should be assessed on the basis of the Canadian dollar value of the draft at the time of the conversion. To go by the current exchange rate, ten years later, would give the plaintiff a windfall gain of sorts through appreciation of the US currency. Any loss to the plaintiff's estate could be recognized by an award of prejudgment interest.

(b)   Evidence obtained locally for use in foreign legal proceedings

Letters rogatory — enforcement

   Note. In *GST Telecommunications Inc.* v. *Provenzano* (2000), 73 B.C.L.R. (3d) 133 (S.C.), the court enforced letters rogatory issued by a United States Federal Court in New York, compelling a lawyer in British Columbia to produce documents and give a deposition in connection with a lawsuit by a United States corporation against its American lawyers, arising out of an international business transaction in which the British Columbia lawyer had also acted. Both section 53 of the Evidence Act, R.S.B.C. 1996, c. 124, and section 46 of the Evidence Act, R.S.C. 1985, c. C-5, leave enforcement of letters rogatory to the discretion of the court, but the authorities made it clear that letters rogatory should be given full force and effect unless to do so would be contrary to public policy or prejudicial to Canadian sovereignty. It was also clear that the principle extended to letters rogatory requiring pre-trial discovery. The court, however, could and did limit the enforcement of the letters rogatory by excluding certain aspects that were judged to be unduly burdensome and prejudicial to the witness.

C   Foreign Judgments / Jugements étrangers

Common Law and Federal

(a)   Conditions applicable to enforcement by action or registration

Jurisdiction of original court — presence or residence in the original jurisdiction — corporation

   Note. The Foreign Judgments Act, R.S.S. 1978, c. F-18, s. 4(b), treats carrying on business in the foreign jurisdiction as the criterion for a corporation's presence in that jurisdiction. See *Acura Data Systems Inc.* v. *Compulogic Management Information Systems Inc.* (1999), [2000] 4 W.W.R. 707, 41 C.P.C. (4th) 152 (Sask. Q.B.), and *Brower* v. *Sunview Solariums Ltd.* (1999), 44 C.P.C. (4th) 83 (Sask. Q.B.), in both of which the test was held not to be met despite, especially in the latter case, a degree of commercial activity in the other jurisdiction. The "real and substantial connection" test for enforcement of the judgment is not available in such a case because the act excludes that development in the common law.

Jurisdiction of original court — attornment to the jurisdiction

Note. See *Jenkins* v. *Jenkins,* noted above under A. Jurisdiction, 1. Common Law and Federal, (d) Matrimonial proceedings — divorce and corollary relief, in which a degree of participation in the foreign proceeding was held not to be attornment to the jurisdiction (but no foreign judgment was in issue).

Jurisdiction of original court — agreement to submit to the jurisdiction

Note. In *Dent Wizard Int'1 Corp.* v. *Sears* (1999), 45 O.R. (3d) 237, 37 C.P.C. (4th) 267 (S.C.J.), a Missouri judgment against an Ontario resident, a former employee of its Canadian subsidiary, was held enforceable on the ground of the defendant's having agreed, in the contract that was the subject matter of the action, to the exclusive jurisdiction of the Missouri courts. The defendant's position was all the more untenable because he had previously obtained a stay of an Ontario proceeding against him on the basis of the same clause.

(b)   Defences applicable to enforcement by action or registration

Public policy

Society of Lloyd's v. *Saunders* (2000), 44 C.P.C. (4th) 246. Ontario Superior Court of Justice.

After a group of Canadian "Names" had failed in their efforts to get an Ontario court to hear their claims for fraud and contravention of the Ontario securities legislation (*Ash* v. *Corp. of Lloyd's* (1992), 9 O.R. (3d) 755 (Ont. C.A.), leave to appeal refused, 8 Oct. 1992 (S.C.C.)), Lloyd's proceeded against them in the English courts and obtained judgments against them for moneys owing to Lloyd's under their contracts with it. These contracts were entered into in England and were expressly governed by English law. The English court rejected the Names' defence of fraud on the part of Lloyd's, on the basis that the remedy of rescission was now impossible and no claim for damages could be set off against Lloyd's claims for the sums in question. It also rejected the arguments based on Lloyd's having failed to comply with Ontario securities laws, on the ground that this breach, assuming that it had taken place, was not a defence in an action in England. Lloyd's now applied to register the judgments in Ontario under the Reciprocal

Enforcement of Judgments (U.K.) Act, R.S.O 1990, c. R.6, incorporating the Canada-United Kingdom Convention for the Reciprocal Recognition and Enforcement of Judgments in Civil and Commercial Matters. The judgment debtors relied on, *inter alia,* the defences of natural justice and public policy.

Swinton J. held that the judgments were registrable. The Ontario Court of Appeal had already determined that England was a proper forum for resolving the disputes between Lloyd's and the Names concerning fraud and the effect of Ontario securities legislation on the enforceability of their contracts. They had been fully represented in the English proceedings. It was true that their fraud claim had not been decided on the merits, but there was no bar to their proceeding, in England, with such a claim. As to public policy, there was no doubt that the securities legislation expressed important public policy in Ontario, but there was a competing and important public policy in issue, namely, respect for the decisions of a foreign judicial system in the interests of international comity. Enforcement would not be contrary to public policy as understood in this context in Canada. The Names entered into their contracts in England and knowing that their relationship with Lloyd's would be governed by English law. This was not a case where enforcement of the contract raised serious issues of morality. The fact that important third party interests would be affected if the judgment debtors were not bound by their contracts with Lloyd's militated against the view that the alleged violations of the securities laws of Ontario gave rise to a public policy defence against enforcement of the judgments.

Note. Another decision in which public policy was invoked was *Kidron v. Grean* (1996), 48 O.R. (3d) 775 (Gen. Div.) (reported only in 2000). The Ontario court refused summary judgment in an action on a California judgment that arose out of a dispute relating to the right to participate in the production of a television series. The court held that the inclusion in the judgment of a jury award of US $15 million for emotional distress might, at a trial, be held contrary to public policy if the Canadian judicial policy of strictly limiting non-pecuniary damages in tort were held to prevail over the policy in favour of recognizing foreign judgments. There was also a triable issue on whether the imposition of such damages was contrary to natural justice on the ground that the jury had no opportunity to make an objective assessment upon substantive evidence as to the condition of the plaintiff. The action on the California judgment was stayed pending the outcome of appeal proceedings in California.

Natural justice

Note. See *Kidron* v. *Grean,* noted immediately above, and *Oyj* v. *Reinikka* (2000), 133 O.A.C. 1 (C.A.). In the latter case, an action in Ontario on a Finnish default judgment against an Ontario-resident judgment debtor was defended on the basis of a failure of natural justice, in that the defendant had not been personally served and the Finnish court had proceeded on the basis of sub-stituted service upon inadequate grounds. The Court of Appeal affirmed the motions judge's enforcement of the judgment. The irregularity in question was resolved when the defendant was served with the default judgment and notified that he had the automatic right to a trial on the merits of the claim.

(c)   Registration under uniform reciprocal enforcement of judgments legislation or an international convention

Registration procedure

Note. In *Society of Lloyd's* v. *Van Snick* (2000), 185 N.S.R. (2d) 344, 44 C.P.C. (4th) 365 (C.A.), the issue was whether judgments obtained in England could be registered *ex parte* under the Canada and United Kingdom Reciprocal Recognition and Enforcement of Judgments Act, R.S.N.S. 1989, c. 52, implementing the Canada-UK Convention. The answer was no, since no regulations had been made to that effect. The *ex parte* recognition procedure under the general reciprocal enforcement of judgments legislation was not to be imported. The legislature had given no indication that the usual requirement of notice could be dispensed with when registering under the Canada-United Kingdom statute.

Defences unique to registration statutes

Note. See *Berg* v. *McNorgan* (1999), 36 C.P.C. (4th) 115 (Man. Q.B.). The plaintiffs were Ontario residents who sued a Manitoba resident for breach of a contract to purchase their house, a contract that he had entered into while living briefly in Ontario. The default judgment was held not registrable in Manitoba under the Recipro-cal Enforcement of Judgments Act, R.S.M. 1987, c. J20, C.C.S.M., c. J20, because the defendant had long since ceased to be ordinarily resident in Ontario (section 3(6)(b) of the act) when the action was commenced. It was irrelevant whether he was ordinarily resi-dent there at the time the cause of action arose.

(d)   Registration under uniform reciprocal enforcement of
maintenance orders legislation

*Confirmation of provisional order — foreign variation order of Canadian
order*

Note. *Darel* v. *Darel* (1999), 181 D.L.R. (4th) 360, 75 Alta. L.R.
(3d) 333 (Q.B.), was an attempt to give effect, through the Reciprocal Enforcement of Maintenance Orders Act, R.S.A. 1980,
c. R-7.1 (Supp.), to a New York court's reduction of the former
husband's support obligation as ordered under the Divorce Act,
R.S.C. 1985, c. 3 (2nd Supp.). The attempt was unsuccessful. The
provincial legislation could not be used to validate the variation by
a foreign court of orders made under the federal statute. Only a
Canadian court, exercising jurisdiction under the Divorce Act,
could vary orders made under the act.

*Confirmation of provisional order — proceedings independently brought in
confirming jurisdiction*

Note. *Selmes* v. *Selmes* (2000), 9 R.F.L. (5th) 198 (Ont. S.C.J.),
involved both parties applying, in different provinces, to vary the
child support provisions of a separation agreement. The husband
brought variation proceedings in New Brunswick, and the wife,
without knowledge of the New Brunswick proceedings, applied to
the court in Ontario to enforce the relevant terms of the agreement. Although the husband had attorned to the Ontario court's
jurisdiction by appearing through his solicitor in the proceedings
brought by the wife, the court held it could decide the issues
between the parties by way of a confirmation hearing under section
5 of the Reciprocal Enforcement of Support Orders Act, R.S.O.
1990, c. R.7. The New Brunswick order was confirmed with some
variation.

2   Québec

(a)   Exemplification du jugement étranger

Prescription — loi étrangère

Ginsbow Inc. c. *Pipe and Piling Supplies Ltd.,* [2000] A.J.Q. N° 1707.
Cour supérieure du Québec.

La demanderesse a intenté en 1998 un recours en exemplification au Québec d'un jugement qu'elle a obtenu dans l'État de

Washington en 1988. Le droit de cet état précise qu'un jugement ne peut être exécuté que dans un délai de dix ans après son prononcé. Le recours en exemplification est intenté quelques jours avant l'expiration de la période de dix ans, mais le droit de Washington prévoit qu'aucune exécution d'un jugement n'est possible après cette limite, même celle qui aurait été commencée avant. Le droit de cet État précise qu'il n'existe plus, une fois les dix ans expirés, de lien de droit entre les parties. La demanderesse a invoqué l'article 2892 C.C.Q., qui prévoit l'interruption de la prescription par le dépôt d'une demande en justice. La Cour supérieure a rejeté l'action en exemplification. L'article 2892 C.C.Q. ne change rien au fait qu'il doit exister un jugement à exécuter au moment où l'exemplification est prononcée, comme l'énonce l'article 3155 C.C.Q. Une procédure d'exemplification ne peut avoir pour effet d'allonger la période de validité du jugement que l'on veut faire exemplifier. Le jugement en exemplification ne constitue pas en lui-même un nouveau jugement. Le jugement, une fois exemplifié, ne peut être exécuté au-delà de ce que permet le jugement original. Au surplus, la prescription, comme le prévoit l'article 3131 C.C.Q., est régie par la loi qui s'applique au fond du litige, soit celle du jugement étranger. Le tribunal québécois doit respecter la période de validité du jugement étranger afin d'éviter le forum shopping.

D   Choice of Law (Including Status of Persons) / Conflits de lois
     (y compris statut personnel)

1   Common Law and Federal

(a)   Characterization

Substance and procedure

Note. See *Salminen (Litigation Guardian of)* v. *Emerald Taxi Ltd.* (1999), 50 C.C.L.T. (2d) 180 (Ont. S.C.J.). In an action by an Ontario resident and his family for injuries suffered while he was riding in the defendants' taxi in British Columbia, the defendants sought an order that the plaintiff's claim was governed by the Insurance Act, R.S.O. 1990, c. I.8, as it stood at the time the accident took place. As of that time, Ontario law provided for no-fault benefits and a deduction of $10,000 of any claim for pain and suffering. The defendants argued that the deduction applied. The court disagreed, holding that it was a substantive rule with respect to damages and did not apply, since the *lex loci delicti* was the law of British Columbia.

(b)   Contracts

Formation — capacity to contract

Note. In *Stevenson Estate* v. *Siewert* (2000), 191 D.L.R. (4th) 151 (Alta. C.A.), the court applied section 159(1) and 160 of the Bills of Exchange Act, R.S.C. 1985, c. B-4, to hold that Alberta law, as the place where the contract was made, governed the question of the capacity of a ninety-nine-year-old woman to endorse a US dollar draft. The issue was decided by the fact that she had previously been declared incapable of managing her affairs by an Alberta court.

(c)   Torts

Applicable law

Hogan v. *Doiron* (1999), 221 N.B.R. (2d) 326. New Brunswick Queen's Bench.

The plaintiffs, Ontario residents, sued the defendants, New Brunswick residents, for injuries suffered in a two-car collision in New Brunswick. The defendants moved to determine the effect on the plaintiffs' claims of section 266(2) of the Motor Vehicle Act, R.S.N.B. 1973, c. M-17. It provides that a non-resident of the province has no greater right of recovery than that person would have in the jurisdiction in which he ordinarily resides, and in no event any greater right of recovery than a person resident in this province would have in such other jurisdiction. The defendants said that under the Insurance Act, R.S.O. 1990, c. I-8, the plaintiffs would be barred in Ontario from claiming any damages other than non-pecuniary loss and that this restriction was imported into the New Brunswick action by section 266(2). Garnett J. held, following New Brunswick Court of Appeal authority, that the reference in section 266 to a "right of recovery," as distinct from a right of action, implied only a quantitative restriction. The Ontario plaintiffs would be restricted to recovering damages in the same amount as the benefits they would receive under the Ontario insurance scheme, provided that the defendants established what the benefits were by expert evidence on Ontario law.

Class actions — resolution of common issues in a single proceeding when more than one jurisdiction is involved

Note. See *Harrington* v. *Dow Corning Corp.*, noted above under A. Jurisdiction, 1. Common Law and Federal, (b) Class proceedings — class including non-residents.

(d)   Restitution

Unjust enrichment claim — proper law

Christopher v. *Zimmerman,* [2000] 10 W.W.R. 437, 80 B.C.L.R. (3d)
229. British Columbia Court of Appeal.

An American man and a Canadian woman met in Hawaii in
1988 and lived there together until 1993. The degree to which they
cohabited there in a spousal relationship was disputed. In 1993,
they moved to the mainland United States, residing in three different states until June 1997, when they moved from Florida to British
Columbia. They lived in British Columbia until their separation in
October 1998. The man had movable assets of some value. The
woman brought the present action in British Columbia, seeking a
declaration of constructive trust as a remedy for unjust enrichment
that she alleged the man had received from her. The evidence to
this stage suggested that her opportunity to obtain such relief was
weaker in Hawaii than in British Columbia. The man applied for
an order dismissing the action. The chambers judge characterized
the woman's claim as one of matrimonial property. The judge held
that the law governing her property rights was the law of Hawaii, as
the law of the man's domicile, the woman not having shown that he
had obtained a domicile of choice in British Columbia. The action
should therefore proceed on the basis that the law of Hawaii applied.

The Court of Appeal set aside the chambers judge's order that
the law of Hawaii applied to the claim and remitted the issue to
be tried on the basis that the proper law was to be decided on the
rules relating to unjust enrichment. The claim was not one relating
to matrimonial property, since the parties were not married. On a
claim in equity, the substantive law concerned the principles of
equity and was not dependent upon the nature of the parties' relationship. Scholarly opinion was cited to the effect that a claim to
restore the benefit of an enrichment was the law of the country
where the enrichment occurs, as being legal unit with which, in the
absence of a contract between the parties, the obligation to make
restitution has its closest and most real connection. The matter had
to be remitted because the chambers judge had not made findings
of fact necessary to determine the proper law on the basis that the
claim was in unjust enrichment.

See also *Barclay's Bank plc* v. *Inc. Inc.,* noted above under A. Jurisdiction, 1. Common Law and Federal, (a) Jurisdiction *in personam*
— declining jurisdiction — *forum non conveniens.*

(e)   Property

Movables — tangible — transfer inter vivos

Note. Re Tunney (2000), 15 P.P.S.A.C. (2d) 279 (B.C.S.C. (Master)), involved the claim of an assignee of the security interest of the lessor of a jeep, the lease having been entered into in Ontario but the lessee having later taken the jeep to British Columbia. The issue of priority was held not to be governed by the law governing the lease, but by the law of the situs of the property. The Personal Property Security Act, now R.S.B.C. 1996, c. 359, therefore applied. The security interest, not having been perfected by registration in British Columbia, was invalid as against the trustee.

Admiralty — maritime lien

Note. In *Imperial Oil Ltd.* v. *Petromar Inc.,* [2000] 4 F.C. D-63 (F.C.T.D.), a United States supplier of maritime lubricants to the defendant Canadian vessel was held entitled to a maritime lien in a Canadian court. The proper law of the agreement for the supply of necessaries was the law of the United States, with which the agreement had its closest, most substantial connection. The creation of a maritime lien was a matter of substantive rights that arose out of that agreement. It was therefore United States law that governed the issue of the existence of the lien.

2   Québec

(a)   Statut personnel

Adoption — loi applicable

Droit de la famille — 3403, [2000] R.J.Q. 2252. Cour d'appel du Québec.

Entre 1989 et 1996, les appelants se sont vu confier quatre enfants par les autorités marocaines et ont entrepris par la suite des procédures en vue de leur adoption au Québec. Le directeur de la protection de la jeunesse s'est opposé à cette démarche au motif qu'elle contrevenait à des dispositions d'ordre public concernant l'adoption d'enfants étrangers. Le premier juge lui a donné raison, concluant que la loi marocaine ne permettait pas l'adoption telle que les lois québécoises la conçoivent. Il a également rejeté la prétention des appelants voulant que les enfants soient maintenant domiciliés au Québec, ce qui aurait permis de laisser de côté les règles applicables à l'adoption d'enfants domiciliés à l'étranger. Selon eux, les autorités marocaines avaient consenti au changement de domicile en leur confiant les enfants. De plus, les appelants avaient invoqué l'article 80 C.C.Q., qui prévoit que des enfants mineurs ont leur domicile chez leur tuteur. Or, l'appelant avait été nommé tuteur aux enfants et avait même consenti à leur adoption. Le premier juge a estimé qu'une telle interprétation était contraire à l'esprit de la législation, qui a choisi de tenir compte de la compétence des autorités étrangères. Il a de plus précisé que le changement de domicile n'avait pas d'effet en matière d'adoption et que le domicile des enfants demeurait celui de leur pays d'origine.

La Cour d'appel a accueilli le pourvoi et rejeté la requête en irrecevabilité du directeur. La Cour a retourné le dossier en première instance pour que l'ordonnance de placement soit prononcée et que le dossier d'adoption suive son cours.

Les enfants sont domiciliés au Québec. En effet, ils y vivent en permanence et deux d'entre eux détiennent la citoyenneté canadienne. Cependant, on ne peut invoquer le domicile actuel des enfants pour prétendre que l'adoption doive se faire en laissant de côté les règles relatives à l'adoption internationale. L'évolution législative consacre la volonté du législateur québécois d'agir à l'intérieur de balises acceptées par la communauté internationale. Le Québec s'est en effet déclaré lié à la Convention sur les droits de l'enfant adoptée en 1989 et, s'il n'a pas encore adhéré à la Convention de La Haye sur la protection des enfants et la coopération en matière d'adoption internationale du 29 mai 1993, il poursuit des objectifs similaires et impose des conditions de même nature (*Loi sur la protection de la jeunesse*, L.R.Q., c. P-34.1, art. 72.1.1 et s., et art. 563 à 565 et 302 C.C.Q.). On ne peut donc faire échec aux règles mises en place pour la protection des enfants en invoquant l'écoulement du temps ou la nomination d'un tuteur.

En l'espèce, on n'a pas prouvé le droit marocain. L'article 2809 C.C.Q. prévoit qu'il peut en être pris connaissance d'office pourvu qu'il ait été allégué. Or, aucune des parties n'a invoqué le droit étranger. Le juge de première instance s'est appuyé sur le témoignage dans un tout autre dossier, et sur les opinions d'un professor de droit et un avocat que ne sauraient constituer une preuve valable, car la qualité d'expert en droit marocain de ces derniers n'a pas été établie. Dans de telles circonstances, il était surprenant que les avocats, dans leur mémoire, tiennent pour acquis que l'adoption ne puisse être prononcée par un tribunal marocain pour des motifs religieux. Un jugement d'adoption peut être rendu selon le droit marocain mais les effets d'un tel jugement diffèrent de ceux prévus par le droit québécois puisque le lien de filiation d'origine n'est pas rompu. Le juge saisi d'une demande de placement en vue de l'adoption devait s'assurer que les règles concernant le consentement et l'admissibilité à l'adoption avaient été respectées, ces règles étant celles du droit interne marocain. Il n'avait pas à se préoccuper des effets marocains de la décision d'adoption.

Book Reviews / Recensions de livres

Droit International Public. Par Joe Verhoeven. Précis de la Faculté de Droit de l'Université Catholique de Louvain, Éditions Larcier, Bruxelles, 2000, 831 pp. ISBN 2-8044-0630-X.

L'ouvrage du professeur Joe Verhoeven est structuré en cinq parties traitant successivement des sujets de droit international, des sources, du régime juridique des espaces, de la réparation et des sanctions, et enfin du règlement des différends et de la sécurité collective. La Partie I de cet ouvrage traite des sujets de droit international, à travers ce que le professeur Verhoven appelle les "certitudes," c'est-à-dire l'État et l'Organisation internationale et les "vraisemblances," à savoir les entités confessionnelles, les dégradés étatiques, le peuple et les individus. La Partie II aborde la question des sources de droit international. Elle comprend, d'une part, les sources d'un droit général que sont la coutume, les principes généraux de droit international, et les résolutions "légiférantes" et d'autre part les sources d'un droit international particulier que sont le traité, l'acte unilatéral, et les rapports qu'entretient le droit international avec le droit interne en général et de façon plus particulière avec le droit belge. La Partie III étudie le régime juridique des espaces terrestre, maritime, aérien et polaire, alors que les Parties IV et V de l'ouvrage traitent respectivement des réparations et sanctions des actes internationalement illicites, du règlement des différends et de la sécurité collective.

S'agissant du régime juridique des espaces, l'auteur procède en premier lieu à l'analyse de l'espace terrestre dans ses modes d'acquisition et de délimitation, se penche ensuite sur les problèmes relatifs aux espaces maritimes à travers une classification bien simple. La mer est juridiquement appréhendée sous ces trois caractéristiques principales que sont: la mer "souveraine" (la souveraineté), la mer "exclusive" (l'exclusivité) et la mer "commune" (la communauté). Si les deux premières militent, tout au moins sur une distance de 200 milles des côtes, en faveur la nationalisation des espaces maritimes, nationalisme dont il relativise la portée sur certains points, la dernière défend, au-delà de cette limite, l'internationalisation de la mer dans son usage comme voie de communications internationales et dans l'exploitation de ses ressources biologiques et minérales. La mer n'est pas la terre et les réalités de la première ne sont pas celles de la seconde. Professeur Voerhoven semble bien indiquer cela dans le subtil usage des attributs qu'il donne à la mer, tout en les assortissant de points guillemets ("souveraine," "exclusive," "commune").

C'est là une façon pour l'auteur, et nous le croyons, de dire ou de nous rappeler qu'il faut relativiser les choses quand on aborde l'étude de la mer, cette "mer toujours recommencée" et du droit qui l'encadre. Est enfin examiné, toujours dans la Partie III, le régime juridique de l'espace aérien atmosphérique relativement à son étendue et sa délimitation d'une part, à la souveraineté et aux "libertés de l'air" qui s'y exercent, d'autre part. Quant à l'espace extra-atmosphérique, l'auteur rappelle que son régime juridique reste tout entier dominé par le principe de non-appropriation et son corollaire celui de la liberté de son utilisation par tous, sous réserve que l'exercice de cette liberté soit conforme aux règles du droit international. De fait, l'espace extra-atmosphérique doit être utilisé à des fins pacifiques, dans l'intérêt et pour le bénéfice de tous, car perçu comme étant le patrimoine commun de l'humanité. Le régime juridique des engins ou des objets qui permettent l'utilisation de l'espace extra-atmosphérique (p. ex.: les satellites) et qui rendent possible la navigation spatiale est décrit. Sont en outre précisés le régime de protection des astronautes et celui de la responsabilité de l'État de lancement, en ce qui a trait plus précisément à l'imputation et à la réparation des faits dommageables.

Après cette lecture, un constat vient à l'esprit: l'auteur est sorti des sentiers battus en ne saisissant pas exclusivement l'État dans ou sous sa description classique, à savoir son apparition, ses conditions d'existence, son organisation, ses attributs, ses compétences et ses mutations. En effet, est étudié un sujet à l'ordre du jour et que les manuels de droit international n'abordent pas toujours ou très souvent: il s'agit du "bon gouvernement" ou de la bonne gouvernance, qui consiste à faire en sorte que plus d'espaces de libertés soient reconnus aux peuples et aux citoyens et garantis par les textes fondamentaux de droit interne ou international.

Aussi, les libertés d'expression, de presse, d'association, l'organisation des élections libres et transparentes sont données comme des principes de base de la démocratie que tout État moderne et démocratique doit observer s'il veut éviter la marginalisation au sein des nations libres et soucieuses de la préservation du bien-être de l'homme.

Fort des exigences démocratiques, le droit international devient plus regardant de l'éthique ou de la moralisation dans les relations interétatiques dans la mesure où les graves violations des droits de l'homme, les tortures et autres atrocités inhumaines, les crimes d'État sous quelque forme qu'ils soient, ne sont plus tolérés. Ceux-ci sont désormais dénoncés, condamnés par la communauté internationale et systématiquement réprimés par des juridictions pénales internationales. Ainsi, les tribunaux *ad hoc* internationaux pour l'ex-Yougoslavie et pour le Rwanda, et la future juridiction criminelle permanente qu'est la Cour pénale internationale sont là pour rappeler, aussi bien aux organes officiels d'un État qu'aux simples individus, que les crimes par eux commis, les génocides, les exterminations d'une partie de la population civile par une autre ne seront plus tolérées et que leurs sanctions ne sauraient plus relever de la seule compétence des tribunaux de droit national. Comme l'affirme si bien le professeur Verhoven "on conçoit difficilement sans peine qu'il soit difficile de s'en remettre exclusivement aux tribunaux de l'État intéressé lorsqu'est en cause le respect par ses autorités des droits fondamentaux de la personne humaine. Les négociateurs des traités consacrant ceux-ci se sont dès lors efforcés habituellement d'organiser en la matière un contrôle extérieur pour en accroître l'impartialité." C'est là un signe évident de la bonne perception, sinon de la bonne réception par la communauté internationale du respect dû aux droits de l'homme et dont la protection justifie les ingérences humanitaires ou les interventions d'humanité. Personne d'ailleurs aujourd'hui ne semble contester les fondements, les raisons d'être, morale ou éthique, mais aussi juridiques de telles interventions, puisqu'on reconnaît le droit d'ingérence humanitaire ou d'humanité.

Le droit international moderne se préoccupe par ailleurs des questions reliées à la sécurité collective qui transcende la sphère nationale et dépasse dans certaines circonstances le concept d'État jaloux de sa souveraineté, pour être l'objet d'une attention particulière de la part de la communauté internationale. Aussi, la recherche de la paix est une mission dévolue au Conseil de sécurité de l'ONU qui est en charge du maintien de la paix et de la sécurité

internationale. Et, en vertu du Chapitre VII de la Charte des
Nations Unies, le Conseil de sécurité dispose de la compétence
d'imposer, au besoin par la force, la paix, son maintien et sa consolidation. De sorte que les actions étatiques qui mettent à mal
ou risquent de compromettre la sécurité collective, c'est-à-dire la
paix entre les Nations sont soumises à un système de règlement des
différends, dont l'auteur décrit les principes, notamment ceux
interdisant les recours à la force et les multiples dérogations qui
leur sont apportées, à savoir la légitime défense individuelle et
collective, celle-ci étant, bien entendu, assortie des conditions de
nécessité et de proportionnalité. Ce système de règlement des
différends peut être de nature diplomatique ou politique. Dans ce
cas, il privilégie les négociations, les enquêtes, les bons offices, la
médiation et la conciliation. Il peut être de nature juridictionnelle
et dans cette hypothèse, il est loisible aux parties au différend de
saisir un tiers impartial, soit un juge ou un arbitre qui rend à leur
égard une décision obligatoire et définitive.

Bel ouvrage s'il en est dans la forme et dans le fond, celui de
Verhaeren se présente par ailleurs comme un livre-bilan du droit
international public qui fait le point sur le droit en question, tout
en faisant une mise à jour des récents développements en ce
domaine. Il situe les défis et les enjeux pour le droit international
à l'aube du troisième millénaire où les grandes mutations économiques, sociales, technologiques et géopolitiques du monde
appellent à de nécessaires adaptions de ce droit. On sait que dans
un passé encore récent le droit international était perçu comme
mélange de droit et de politique, avec une prévalence de ce dernier
selon les plus sceptiques quand à sa portée. En effet, et de plus
en plus, ce qui faisait défaut à ce droit, c'est-à-dire la sanction ou
l'exécution forcée, devient une réalité bien tangible. Le ton est
désormais donné et les preuves sont faites en droit pénal international ou en droit humanitaire à la suite des sanctions de crime de
guerre, de crimes contre l'humanité, de génocides ou autres exactions contre leurs principaux auteurs ou complices. L'extradition
du Président Slobodan Milosevic devant le Tribunal pénal international de La Haye et du Général Pinochet devant les juridictions de
son pays d'origine, se veulent, à notre avis, des signaux forts à tous
ceux qui doutent encore de la crédibilité du droit international.

Une autre monographie en droit international public, en cette
fin de millénaire et d'une telle qualité n'est certainement pas une
de trop. Elle vient assurément à point nommé et sera d'une utilité
certaine pour tous ceux qui, praticiens et théoriciens, voudront

clarifier des points du droit international restés pour eux plus ou moins obscurs, ou qui voudront simplement mettre à jour leurs connaissances sur certaines questions.

Il s'agit d'un précis de droit international. C'est le qualificatif donné à l'ouvrage par l'auteur, qui a la modestie de le qualifier ainsi. Il reste de toute évidence que ce qualificatif tranche radicalement avec sa densité et sa force de persuasion. Enfin, le mot précis ne diminue en rien la qualité de l'ouvrage. Bien au contraire. Sauf qu'il nous apparaît s'accomoder d'un qualificatif qui ne lui sied pas. Peut-être que ce faisant, l'auteur a voulu dès le départ annoncer aux lecteurs la simplicité qu'il entendait donner à son œuvre. L'objectif est de tout même atteint, car la simplicité que nous supposons ici recherchée n'a pas sacrifié la profondeur des analyses et les utiles précisions.

CISSÉ YACOUBA
Faculté de droit, Université d'Ottawa

Le principe de l'universalité en droit pénal international, Droit et obligation pour les États de poursuivre et juger selon le principe de l'universalité. Par Marc Henzelin. Genève/Bruxelles: Helbing & Lichtenhahn/Bruylant, 2000. Pp. xxvii, 527. ISBN 2-8027-1455-4.

Les cas de poursuite pour crimes internationaux par les juridictions nationales selon le principe de l'universalité, c'est-à-dire indépendamment de tout lien territorial, personnel ou autres, entre l'État poursuivant et le crime, se sont multipliés ces dix dernières années. En fait, auparavant, ils étaient limités à de rares affaires liées aux crimes commis par les Nazis. Mais, plus récemment, certains crimes commis en ex-Yougoslavie ont été poursuivis dans différents pays d'Europe et certains participants au génocide rwandais ont été condamnés en Belgique et en Suisse. Puisqu'il s'agit de conflits pour lesquels des tribunaux pénaux internationaux *ad hoc* ont également été constitués, ces cas d'application du principe de l'universalité n'ont pas fait l'objet de critique. En revanche, cette année même, des poursuites ont été intentées contre le Premier ministre israélien en Belgique et il a été question de poursuites au Danemark contre un nouvel ambassadeur d'Israël accusé d'actes de torture. À cette occasion, les premières critiques à l'égard de telles poursuites se fondant sur le principe de l'universalité sont apparues.

La thèse de doctorat de Marc Henzelin consacrée au principe de l'universalité est donc sans contredit d'actualité. En fait, selon nous, il s'agit de la première monographie sur ce principe de l'universalité des poursuites en droit pénal international. Elle fait un tour très complet de la question. Henzelin est chargé de cours au département de droit pénal de l'université de Genève. Cet ouvrage démontre sa maîtrise du droit pénal, des théories pénalistes et internationalistes ainsi que de la philosophie pénale. L'auteur est également et à double titre un praticien du droit international humanitaire en tant qu'ancien délégué du Comité international de la Croix-Rouge (CICR) et du droit pénal en tant qu'avocat. Cette dernière fonction l'a d'ailleurs amené, à plusieurs reprises, à rappeler les impératifs de la prévisibilité et des droits de la défense, parfois négligés par les internationalistes dans leur enthousiasme pour la criminalisation des violations du droit international. C'est certainement également parce qu'il est pénaliste que l'auteur épouse une théorie très traditionnelle, positiviste et volontariste (par rapport au droit pénal international, Henzelin utilise les termes "souveranéiste" et "contractualiste") du droit international. Vu cette conception, il nous apparaît logique qu'Henzelin soit critique face à ce qu'il appelle, lui-même, "la doctrine de l'universalité absolue" selon laquelle la compétence de l'État poursuivant n'est pas déléguée par un autre État ayant un lien avec le crime, mais par la communauté internationale. Les internationalistes répliqueront à la position d'Henzelin que beaucoup de phénomènes contemporains, tels que celui du *"ius cogens,"* ne peuvent s'expliquer en partant d'une approche aussi "contractualiste." Monsieur Henzelin réplique que la doctrine de l'universalité absolue "à force de nier et de négliger l'État en tant que législateur," voit celui-ci lui rendre "ce mépris en refusant d'appliquer le principe de l'universalité" dans la pratique (p. 448).

L'auteur se livre dans une première partie à un tour d'horizon très complet des principes de compétence juridictionnelle et de leurs fondements historiques et conceptuels. Les vues sur ce sujet de l'Ancien Testament, du Coran, de la Grèce antique, de Rome, de la France de l'absolutisme y sont tout aussi finement analysées que celles de Vitoria, Grotius, Kant et Kelsen. On devine que le pénaliste Henzelin est particulièrement proche de Beccaria qui rejette toute idée de droit naturel universel et de "répression universelle du péché."

La deuxième partie de l'ouvrage présente les limites que le droit international a graduellement érigées vis-à-vis d'un exercice, par

un État, d'une compétence extraterritoriale en matière de poursuites pénales. Henzelin qualifie une telle extension unilatérale
extraterritoriale de la compétence pénale d'"application unilatérale du principe de l'universalité." Conceptuellement, une telle
application est toutefois la négation du principe de l'universalité.
Ce principe place, en effet, les intérêts de la communauté internationale au-dessus de ceux de chaque État pris individuellement.

Une troisième partie est consacrée à une étude exhaustive et très
fouillée des conventions internationales permettant une application du principe de l'universalité. Cette partie sera d'une grande
utilité pour les praticiens confrontés aux dispositions des traités
du droit international pénal prévoyant une compétence ou une
obligation de poursuivre certains crimes. Henzelin qualifie le
principe de l'universalité se fondant sur de telles dispositions conventionnelles de "déléguée." L'auteur y voit, en effet, de simples cas
de cession et de délégation de compétence par les États compétents
selon des principes de juridiction généralement admis à des États
tiers. Cette construction est logiquement inattaquable lorsqu'on se
place, comme Henzelin, dans une vision "souveranéiste" et "contractualiste" du droit international. N'est-ce toutefois pas artificiel
de considérer, par exemple, comme normes de "délégation" les dispositions des Conventions de Genève de 1949 sur la protection des
victimes de la guerre qui prescrivent la poursuite des criminels de
guerre en vertu du principe de l'universalité? Selon la théorie
d'Henzelin, l'État territorial ou national compétent pour poursuivre ces crimes déléguerait, par de telles dispositions, la tâche de
poursuivre ses propres militaires qui commettraient des crimes de
guerre contre l'ennemi dans un conflit futur, à ses futurs ennemis
et aux États non belligérants. La conception qui nous paraît beaucoup plus proche de la réalité est celle de voir dans ces dispositions
une reconnaissance que les crimes de guerre violent non seulement
les intérêts de l'État dont les victimes sont ressortissantes mais aussi
ceux de toute l'humanité et, par conséquent, tous les États se
doivent de les poursuivre. Que les États aient accepté de telles dispositions ne constitue à notre avis pas une délégation de leur part,
mais un exercice de leur fonction de législateur. Suite à sa revue de
la pratique conventionnelle, l'auteur arrive à la conclusion qu'on
ne peut pas en déduire que "les principes de l'universalité et de *aut
dedere aut prosequi*" soient devenus en soi et en général des principes
de droit coutumier" (p. 376). Il est, en effet, incontestable — et
à notre connaissance incontesté — que le principe de l'universalité ne s'applique qu'à certains crimes. En revanche, la véritable

question est celle de savoir si le principe peut être coutumier pour certains crimes même là où aucune convention ne le prévoit — comme en cas de génocide — ou pour des États non-parties aux conventions prévoyant l'universalité "déléguée." À notre avis, la réponse est affirmative. En fait, même Henzelin l'admet pour le cas des infractions graves aux Conventions de Genève de 1949 du fait de l'acceptation universelle de ces conventions.

La quatrième partie de l'ouvrage est celle où Henzelin défend sa véritable thèse. Elle prête donc plus facilement flanc aux critiques. Elle est consacrée à ce qu'Henzelin appelle le principe de "l'universalité absolue" permettant aux États de poursuivre et de juger, en tant qu'agents de la communauté internationale, certaines infractions du droit international, selon le principe du dédoublement fonctionnel. Henzelin estime que cette vision n'est pas acceptée dans les faits par les États et qu'elle est politiquement indésirable. Dans cette démonstration, il manifeste, premièrement, un positivisme "contractualiste" extrême. Il nie l'existence d'une "communauté internationale," notion pourtant acceptée par les États par le biais de l'article 53 de la *Convention de Vienne sur le droit des traités*. Il remarque, deuxièmement que la préoccupation sous-jacente aux crimes qualifiés de contraires aux intérêts de la communauté internationale serait souvent celle d'un État en particulier ou d'un groupe d'États voulant et pouvant s'approprier le rôle de porte-parole mondial. La troisième critique vis-à-vis du principe de l'universalité absolue part d'une constatation exacte. Les États sont souvent réticents à accepter des compétences pénales selon le principe de l'universalité, et ce même à l'égard d'actes dont ils n'ignorent pas qu'ils violent un principe de "*ius cogens*" et conséquemment, les intérêts de la communauté internationale. À notre avis, ceci n'exclut toutefois pas que le principe de l'universalité soit coutumier pour certains crimes que les États estiment être suffisamment bien définis et attribuables à des individus.

Quant à sa forme, le livre est rédigé dans un français très soigné. Il est étayé d'innombrables références à la pratique et à la doctrine historiques et contemporaines en langue française, anglaise et allemande, ce qui démontre une vaste culture générale et juridique. Il est remarquable que la doctrine et la jurisprudence des pays de la *common law* soient tout autant prises en considération que celles de tradition romano-germanique. En discutant les conceptions de compétence en matière pénale de ces deux systèmes, l'auteur montre d'ailleurs qu'il maîtrise autant l'un que l'autre, ce qui est plutôt rare. Un index facilite la consultation, ce qui en fait un livre de référence.

En conclusion, même la majorité des internationalistes qui ne partageront probablement pas la vision d'Henzelin liront son livre avec beaucoup d'intérêt et en tireront certainement des bénéfices. Dans sa préface, Georges Abi-Saab, qui ne peut certainement pas être accusé d'être un positiviste pur et dur, qualifie l'ouvrage à juste titre de "somme qui constitue désormais la référence en la matière." Nous y voyons en particulier trois mérites. Premièrement, les pénalistes qui s'aventurent dans le droit international sont beaucoup trop rares, ce qui fait souvent perdre à la doctrine en droit international pénal le contact avec la réalité. Henzelin nous ramène à la réalité là même où elle dérange notre engagement pour un monde meilleur. En passant, il remarque, par exemple et à juste titre, que les procès contre des criminels de guerre ex-yougoslaves et rwandais devant des juridictions nationales ne sont apparus qu'après "l'autorisation 'officielle' donnée par les statuts" des tribunaux pénaux internationaux "*ad hoc*" (p. 442). En effet, à l'exception des cas concernant Israël mentionnés en introduction, qui ont provoqué beaucoup de scepticisme, on n'a pas entendu parler de poursuites dirigées contre des présumés responsables de crimes de guerre palestiniens, russes, tchétchènes, afghans, cinghalais, tamouls, congolais, turcs ou kurdes. Or, personne ne prétendra qu'aucun crime international n'a été commis dans ces contextes. Deuxièmement — et c'est un grand mérite — Henzelin ne permet pas à sa vision de départ très tranchée et à la catégorisation qu'il propose d'influencer son analyse de la pratique. Il ne manipule ni les faits ni le lecteur pour les gagner à sa vision. Tout au contraire, son analyse est très nuancée, dès qu'elle aborde la pratique et les détails. C'est ainsi que l'auteur admet que les statuts de la Cour pénale internationale et des tribunaux pénaux internationaux "*ad hoc*" ainsi que la mise en oeuvre de ces derniers renforcent l'idée du principe de l'universalité absolue et incitent les États à y adhérer, ne serait-ce — aimerions-nous ajouter — sous la pression de leur propre rhétorique. Troisièmement, la pratique réelle des États suit malheureusement — contrairement à leurs discours — la vision d'Henzelin. D'ailleurs, même leurs discours deviennent moins universalistes du moment qu'il existe le moindre risque qu'une règle ou un précédent ne puisse s'appliquer également à leurs ressortissants et dirigeants — et non seulement à des ex-yougoslaves et des rwandais. Une règle ne peut pourtant appartenir au droit que si elle est la même pour tous. Enfin, même ceux et celles qui ont une vue du droit international moins centrée sur l'État souverain que celle d'Henzelin doivent admettre ce que Thomas Baty (*The canons of international law,* London, 1930, p. 1) rappela, avec son humour britannique, il y a soixante-dix ans: "Despite all modern theories, international law has still something to do with States."

MARCO SASSOLI
Faculté des sciences juridiques,
Université de Québec à Montreal

Analytical Index / Index analytique

THE CANADIAN YEARBOOK OF INTERNATIONAL LAW

2 0 0 0

ANNUAIRE CANADIEN DE DROIT INTERNATIONAL

(A) Article; (NC) Notes and Comments; (Ch) Chronique;
(P) Practice; (C) Cases; (BR) Book Review
(A) Article; (NC) Notes et commentaires; (Ch) Chronique;
(P) Pratique; (C) La jurisprudence; (BR) Recension de livre

Index of Cases /
Index de la jurisprudence

114957 Canada Ltée (Spraytech, Société d'arrosage v. Hudson (Town)), 47, 59 n. 162

472900 BC Ltd v. Thrifty Canada (1998), 161 n. 15, 183-84

A. and S.N. v. Norway, 262 n. 7

Abdullah Sayid Rajab Al-Rifai & Sons v. McDonnell Douglas Foreign Sales Corp, 163 n. 19

Acura Data Systems Inc. v. Compulogic Management Information Systems Inc. (2000), 472

Aegean Sea Continental Shelf case, 198 n. 23

Aerlinte Eireann Teoranta v. Canada (1987), 19, 20 n. 41, 29, 29 n. 92

AG Armeno Mines & Minerals Inc. v. PT Pukuafu Indah (1999), 445

A.G. Can. Higbie, 203 n. 26

Ahmad v. ILEA, 28, 40, 41

Airbus Industrie GIE v. Patel, 155 n. 1

Akai Pty Ltd v. People's Insurance Co. Ltd, 173 n. 43

Allendale Mutual Ins. Co. v. Bull Data Sys., 164 n. 24, 164 n. 25

Amchem Products Inc. v. British Columbia (Workers' Compensation Board), 185, 454

American Cyanimid Co. v. Picaso-Anstalt, 163 n. 20

American Mobile Satellite Corp. c. Spar Aerospace Ltd, 467-68

Amiel Distributions Ltd c. Amana Co. L.P., 470-71

Amoco International Finance Corp. v. Iran, 96 n. 33

Anraj Fish Products Industries Ltd v. Hyundai Merchant Marine Co. (1999), 449-50

Archbishop of York and Sedgwick (1612), 14

Arrow River & Tributaries Slide & Bloom Co. Ltd v. Pigeon Timber Co. Ltd (1932), 12 n. 18, 12 n. 19, 18 n. 35, 37

Ash v. Corp. of Lloyd's (1992), 473

Ashby v. Minister of Immigration, 50, 52

Association of Architects (Ontario) v. Deskin (2000), 454

Attorney-General for Canada v. Attorney-General for Ontario, [1936], 65

Attorney General for Canada v. Attorney General for Ontario (Labour Conventions), 16, 17 n. 31, 20, 63-79

Attorney-General for Ontario v. Canada Temperance Foundation, 71, 72, 75, 78, 79

Attorney General for Ontario v. Scott, 26 n. 77

Australia v. France, 198 n. 23

Avenue Properties Ltd v. First City Development Corp. (1986), 183 n. 71

Azinian, l'affaire, 322

Baker v. Canada (Minister of Citizenship and Immigration), 3, 21, 29 n. 92, 40, 41, 46-61

Bankinvest AG v. Seabrook (1988), 179 n. 59

Barcelona Traction, Light and Power Co. (Belgium v. Spain), 243 n. 19

Barclay's Bank plc v. Inc.Inc. (1999), 450, 479

Baron de Bode v. The Queen (1848), 19 n. 38

Bell v. Source Data Control Ltd (1988), 243 n. 21

Benin v. Whimster, 20 n. 45

Berg (Litigation Guardian of) v. Farm Bureau Mut. Ins. Co. (2000), 452, 453

Berg v. McNorgan (1999), 475

Bhadauria v. Seneca College (1980), 84